Legislatures in Developmental Perspective

Legislatures in Developmental Perspective

Allan Kornberg   Lloyd D. Musolf   Bernard Crick
Roger H. Davidson   L. M. Singhvi   Weston Harris Agor
Ralph E. Crow   Newell M. Stultz   Robert B. Stauffer
James A. Robinson   Samuel C. Patterson   John G. Grumm
Malcolm E. Jewell   Fred W. Riggs   Robert A. Packenham

Edited by Allan Kornberg and Lloyd D. Musolf

Published in cooperation with the Comparative Administration
Group of the American Society for Public Administration
Duke University Press, Durham, North Carolina   1970

Printed in the United States of America
by the Kingsport Press, Inc., Kingsport, Tennessee

Contributors

Allan Kornberg, born in Winnipeg, Canada, in 1931, received his doctorate in political science from the University of Michigan in 1964. In 1964–65 he was a member of the Department of Political Science at Hiram College. In 1965 he became a member of the faculty of Duke University where he is professor of political science. Currently, he is engaged in an extensive cross-national study of political socialization and political recruitment that is funded by the National Science Foundation and the Canada Council. He is the author of *Canadian Legislative Behavior: A Study of the 25th Parliament* (1967) and has contributed articles to professional journals such as the *American Political Science Review, Journal of Politics, Western Political Quarterly, Australian Journal of Politics and History, The Canadian Journal of Political Science, The Canadian Review of Sociology and Anthropology, Political Science, Parliamentary Affairs,* and *Journal of Constitutional and Parliamentary Studies.*

Lloyd D. Musolf, born in Yale, South Dakota, in 1919, received his doctorate from Johns Hopkins University in 1950. He was a member of the faculty of Vassar College from 1949 to 1959, chief of party of the Michigan State University Advisory Group in Vietnam from 1959 to 1961, and professor of political science at Michigan State University from 1961 to 1963. Since 1963 he has been at the University of California at Davis where he serves as director of the Institute of Governmental Affairs and professor of political science. He has attended several international conferences relating to administrative and legislative problems and was chairman of the Advisory Committee of the Legislative Services Project sponsored by AID-Comparative Administrative Group in 1968. He is presently on the Council and Council Executive Committee of the American Society for Public Administration and is a member of its Comparative Administration Group. In addition to numerous articles, his publications include *Federal Examiners and the*

Conflict of Law and Administration (1953), *Public Ownership and Accountability: the Canadian Experience* (1959), and *Promoting the General Welfare: Government and the Economy* (1965). He is co-editor of *The Politics of Regulation* (1964).

Bernard Crick, born in London, England, in 1929, received his Ph.D. from the University of London in 1956. He was a lecturer at the London School of Economics from 1956 to 1964, and since 1964 he has been at Sheffield University where he is professor of political theory and institutions. He has served as visiting professor at McGill University, Tel Aviv University, and the University of Ghana. He is a member of the executive committee of the Political Studies Association and of the Study of Parliament Group, honorary director of the Acton Society's "Morrell Studies in Toleration," and co-editor of *Political Quarterly.* His publications include *The American Science of Politics* (1959), *In Defence of Politics* (1962), and *The Reform of Parliament* (1964); he is editor of *Essays on Reform 1967* (1967).

Roger H. Davidson was born in Washington, D.C., in 1936 and received his doctorate in political science from Columbia University in 1963. He was assistant professor of government at Dartmouth College from 1962 to 1968 and is currently associate professor of political science at the University of California, Santa Barbara. In 1960 he served as a graduate research assistant for the Brookings Institution's study of federal political executives. He has also served as a research consultant to the George Washington University and the W. E. Upjohn Institute for Employment Research, in connection with studies of manpower policies. From 1963 through 1966, he served as codirector of a study, sponsored by the Dartmouth Public Affairs Center, designed to examine congressional attitudes toward organization and procedure in the U.S. House of Representatives. In 1968–1969 he received a grant from the Social Science Research Council to study public attitudes toward the roles of congressmen. He is the author of two monographs, *Congress and the Executive: The Race for Representation* (1965), and *Coalition-Building for Depressed Areas Bills 1955–1965* (1967). He is the author of *The Role of the Congressman* (1969) and co-author (with David M. Kovenock and Michael K. O'Leary) of *Congress in Crisis: Politics and Congressional Reform* (1966), and (with John F. Bibby) *On Capitol Hill: Studies in the Legislative Process* (1967).

Laxmi Mall Singhvi was born in Jodhpur, India, in 1931. He received a Doctor of the Science of Law degree from Cornell Law School in 1955. In 1956 he was a delegate from India to the UNESCO Conference on International Legal Science at Barcelona. In the same year he took part in the organization of the Indian Law Institute. He was the Institute's first organizing secretary and served as a member of its Governing Council for three years. In 1962 he was elected to the Indian Parliament as an Independent, and in 1964 he served as the Indian delegate to the Commonwealth Parliamentary Conference held in Jamaica. In 1965 he founded the Institute of Constitutional and Parliamentary Studies, and in 1967 he visited and lectured in West Germany at various universities and research institutions. Currently, he is executive chairman of the Institute of Constitutional and Parliamentary Studies, chairman of the editorial committee of the *Journal of Constitutional and Parliamentary Studies,* a member of the executive committee of the Indian Council of World Affairs, convener of the Indian Parliamentary Group of the World Association of World Federalists, a member of the Indian Commission of Jurists, a member of the Indian Bar Association, a life-member of India International Centre, and an Advocate of the Supreme Court of India.

Weston Harris Agor was born in Salamanca, New York, in 1939. He received his doctorate in political science at the University of Wisconsin in 1969. His graduate work and field research in Chile were supported by a Fulbright Grant (1962–63), a Midwest Universities Consortium Fellowship (1967–68), and a grant from the Land Tenure Center of the University of Wisconsin. He has also been employed as a research associate by the Land Tenure Center on Latin American land tenure problems and is currently assistant professor of political science at Wisconsin State University.

Ralph E. Crow was born in Cincinnati, Ohio, in 1924 and received his doctorate in political science from the University of Michigan in 1964. Since 1950 he has been a member of the faculty of the American University of Beirut, Beirut, Lebanon, where he serves in the Department of Political Studies and Public Administration. On leave for two years (1962–64), he taught in the Department of Government at Indiana University and was executive secretary of the Comparative Administration Group of the American Society for Public Administration. During 1965–66 he was a lecturer at the Law Faculty of the Syrian University in Damascus. His writings include articles published in the

Journal of Politics, International Review of Administrative Sciences,
and a chapter in the volume edited by Leonard Binder, *Politics in Lebanon* (1966).

Newell M. Stultz was born in Boston, Massachusetts, in 1933 and received his Ph.D. from Boston University in 1965. He taught at Northwestern University before going to Brown University in 1965 where he
is now associate professor of political science. A onetime Fulbright
Fellow and later Ford Foundation Fellow in South Africa, he is a specialist on that country. He is co-author of *South Africa's Transkei*
(1967).

Robert B. Stauffer, born in Philipsburg, Pennsylvania, in 1920, received his Ph.D. from the University of Minnesota in 1954. He was an
assistant professor at the University of Hawaii from 1953 to 1958, an
associate professor from 1958 to 1963, and since 1963 he has been professor of political science. In addition, he served as a visiting associate
professor at the University of Oregon in 1959 and at the University of
Colorado in 1961 and as a Fulbright visiting professor at the University
of the Philippines in 1963–64. He was director of the University of
Hawaii Asian Studies Field Tour in 1962, a participant in the University of Hawaii Peace Corps Training Program in 1962–63 and 1965,
lecturer for the University of Hawaii AID Training Program in 1966,
and a research associate of the Social Science Research Institute in
1966–67. Currently, he is a member of the Southeast Asia Advisory
Group, a consultant to the Institute of Advanced Projects (East-West
Center), and a member of the boards of editors of *Human Organization* and *Western Political Quarterly.* He is the author of *The Development of an Interest Group: The Philippine Medical Association* (1966)
and has contributed articles and reviews to a number of journals, such
as the *American Political Science Review, Journal of Politics, Journal of
Social Psychology, Orbis, Journal of Asian Studies, Philippine Journal
of Public Administration, The Education Quarterly,* and *Educational
Leadership.*

James A. Robinson was born in Blackwell, Oklahoma, in 1932. He
received the Ph.D. from Northwestern University in 1957. He has been
a Congressional Fellow of the American Political Science Association,
and a member of the Political Science Department and of the International Relations Program at Northwestern. He is now Mershon Pro-

fessor of Political Science and Director of the Mershon Center for Education in National Security at the Ohio State University. His books include *Congress and Foreign Policy-Making* (1962; rev. ed., 1967), *The House Rules Committee* (1963), and *The Case for Lyndon Johnson* (1968). He edits *Handbooks for Research in Political Behavior, Political Science Annual: An International Review,* and is an associate editor of the *Journal of Conflict Resolution.* Among his contributions to symposia are essays in Lynton K. Caldwell (ed.) *Politics and Public Affairs* (1962), Herbert Jacob and Kenneth Vines (eds.) *Politics in the American States* (1965), Herbert Kelman (ed.) *International Behavior* (1965), Alfred de Grazia (ed.) *Congress: The First Branch of Government* (1966), and Peter Rossi and Bruce Biddle (eds.) *The New Media and Education* (1966).

Samuel C. Patterson was born in Omaha, Nebraska, in 1931 and received his Ph.D. from the University of Wisconsin in 1959. He is professor of political science at the University of Iowa. Co-author (with Malcolm E. Jewell) of *The Legislative Process in the United States* (1966), he is also editor of two collections of papers on American legislative behavior—*American Legislative Behavior* (1968) and *Midwest Legislative Politics* (1968). He has published extensively in such journals as *Public Opinion Quarterly, Journal of Politics, Midwest Journal of Political Science, Western Political Quarterly,* and *Social Forces.*

John G. Grumm, born in San Diego, California, in 1922, received his Ph.D. from the University of California at Berkeley in 1957. During World War II he served in the United States Navy in the Pacific. He is presently professor of political science at the University of Kansas, where he has taught since 1956. At the University of Kansas he has also been Assistant Dean of Faculties for Research and research associate of the Governmental Research Center. He also has taught at the University of California at Berkeley. He served as special legislative assistant to Governor Edmund G. Brown of California in 1964–65 and has been research director and a consultant for the Citizens Conference on State Legislatures. During 1967–68 he served as staff director for the Federal Advisory Committee on Higher Education and as a consultant to the U.S. Department of Health, Education, and Welfare. He is also chairman of the State Political Data Committee for the Inter-University Consortium for Political Research. He is author of *A State Agency for Local Affairs* (1961), *Metropolitan Area Government* (1959), and has contributed articles in the field of state and local government and politics to various learned journals and various symposium volumes.

Malcolm E. Jewell was born in Woonsocket, Rhode Island, in 1928. He received his doctor's degree in political science from Pennsylvania State University in 1958. He is a professor at the University of Kentucky, where he has been on the faculty since 1958. He was a visiting associate professor at Duke University in 1963–64, and has taught at the University of Colorado. He has been editor of the *Midwest Journal of Political Science* since 1966. He is the author of *Senatorial Politics and Foreign Policy* (1962), *The State Legislature* (1962), and *Legislative Representation in the Contemporary South* (1967); co-author of *The Legislative Process in the United States* (1966), *The States and the Metropolis* (1968), and *Kentucky Politics* (1968); and editor of *The Politics of Reapportionment* (1962). He has contributed to Paul Tillett (ed.) *Inside Politics: The National Conventions, 1960* (1962), Alexander Heard (ed.) *State Legislatures in American Politics* (1966), Howard D. Hamilton (ed.) *Reapportioning Legislatures* (1966), and to such journals as *American Political Science Review, Journal of Politics,* and *Western Political Quarterly.*

Fred W. Riggs, born in Kuling, China, in 1917, received his doctorate in political science from Columbia University in 1948. He served as a research associate of the Foreign Policy Association from 1948 to 1951, as assistant to the director of the Public Administration Clearing House in New York from 1951 to 1955, and as a member of the Department of Government at Indiana University, where he held the Arthur F. Bentley chair, from 1956 through 1967. Since 1967 he has been professor of political science at the University of Hawaii and a member of its Social Science Research Institute. During 1957–58 he held a fellowship from the Committee on Comparative Politics of the Social Science Research Council for research in Thailand. He has been a visiting professor or lecturer at Yale University during 1955–56; at the National Officials Training Institute in Korea in 1956; at the University of the Philippines in 1958–59; and at the Massachusetts Institute of Technology, 1965–66. He has also been a senior specialist at the East-West Center, University of Hawaii, 1962–63, and a Fellow of the Center for Advanced Study in the Behavioral Science, Stanford, 1966–67. Professor Riggs has been chairman of the Comparative Administration Group of the American Society for Public Administration since 1960 and is a member of the Southeast Asia Development Advisory Group. He is on the editorial board of *Comparative Political Studies* and *Comparative Politics*. He is the author of *Pressures on Congress* (1950); *Formosa Under Chinese Nationalist Rule* (1952); *The Ecology of Public Administration* (1962); *Administration in Developing Countries* (1964); *Thailand, the Modernization of a Bureaucratic Polity* (1966); and is co-author and editor of *Frontiers in Development Administration* (1969). He is also the author of many articles on international relations and comparative administration, including essays in William J. Siffin (ed.) *Toward the Comparative Study of Public Administration* (1957); Klaus Knorr and Sidney Verba (eds.) *The International System: Theoretical Essays* (1961); Joseph LaPalombara (ed.) *Bureaucracy and Political Development* (1963); John Montgomery and William J. Siffin (eds.) *Approaches to Development: Politics, Administration and Change* (1966); James C. Charlesworth (ed.) *Contemporary Political Analysis* (1967); and William J. Crotty (ed.) *Approaches to the Study of Party Organization* (1967).

Robert A. Packenham was born in Watertown, South Dakota, in 1937. He received his Ph.D. in political science from Yale University in 1964. During the academic year 1963–64 he held a postdoctoral fellowship from the Foreign Area Fellowship Program for study in the Institute of Latin American Studies of Columbia University. He continued the fellowship the following year while he did research on the Brazilian federal Congress in Brasília. He has published articles on political development theory and the United States foreign aid program, and is completing a book on foreign aid and political development. He has been a research fellow at the Brookings Institution in Washington, D.C. From 1966 through 1967 he was a consultant to the Ford Foundation for its grant to the Department of Political Science at the Federal University of Minas Gerais in Brazil. He worked briefly for the International Cooperation Administration in 1961, and since 1965 has been assistant professor of political science and faculty associate, Institute of Political Studies, at Stanford University.

Contents

Tables

Chapter 1. On Legislatures in Developmental Perspective

Chapter 3. Parliament in Canadian Society

Chapter 7. Parliament in the Lebanese Political System

Chapter 11. Congressional Committee Professional Staffing: Capabilities and Constraints

Chapter 12. Structural Determinants of Legislative Output

**Chapter 13. Attitudinal Determinants of Legislative Behavior:
The Utility of Role Analysis**

Figures

Legislatures in Developmental Perspective

Chapter 1

On Legislatures in Developmental Perspective

Allan Kornberg and Lloyd D. Musolf

It is only within the last decade that writers on comparative politics have given systematic attention to the phenomenon of political development. Even so, it seems fair to say that at present a notable lacuna involves the place of legislative assemblies in the development of political systems.

So lacking is information and wisdom on this topic that it would be pretentious to contend that the present volume even begins to fill the need. It does, we suggest later, mark an important beginning in weaving elected assemblies into the political pattern. Before describing the aims of the book, a word on its origins is in order.

The oddity of sponsorship of a legislative volume by a group whose central concern is the comparative study of administration may be remarked. In 1966, Fred W. Riggs, Chairman of the Comparative Administration Group (CAG), informally proposed to the Agency for International Development (AID) some ideas for improving the administrative resources of legislatures. His premise concerning the need to strengthen legislatures interested AID which was receptive to ways of implementing a new amendment to the Foreign Assistance Act of 1961. Title IX, adopted in 1966, states: "In carrying out programs authorized in this chapter, emphasis shall be placed on assuring maximum participation in the task of economic development on the part of the people of the developing countries, through the encouragement of democratic private and local governmental institutions."

As a result of the Riggs contact, AID contracted with the American Society for Public Administration, CAG's parent group, for a year-long study. An advisory committee composed of legislative students and practitioners, an advisory panel of scholars, and a principal investigator (initially Larry Margolis, later Lloyd D. Musolf, who also continued as chairman of the advisory committee) was appointed.

At the outset, CAG insisted, and AID concurred, that because relatively little was known of legislatures in the context of political development, a study of the subject would be crucial to the contract. With this in mind, a planning conference was scheduled for Planting Fields, New York, December 8–10, 1967.

The conference brought together four groups of participants. First, a number of scholars whose research interests are legislative institutions and processes in either relatively developed or less developed states were asked to present papers on the role(s) legislatures play in their respective settings. These individuals were encouraged to go beyond a consideration of the tasks traditionally ascribed to legislative bodies and, whenever possible, to structure their analyses at a level of generality relevant for other than a single system. Second, a number of scholars who were primarily "Americanists"—students of either state legislatures or the Congress, with a particular interest in the technical and research facilities available in American legislatures—were asked to prepare papers in their specialties. A third group of individuals with personal experience in legislatures, either as "practitioners" or as staff, were invited to attend and take part in the discussions that followed the presentation of papers. Finally, a fourth group of scholars whose research interest, broadly defined, is political development, were requested to contribute to the conference their expert knowledge of developing areas.

A number of papers presented were revised in light of the internal criticism and discussions at the conference and are included in the present volume. The remaining selections were expressly commissioned by the editors. Certain considerations governed the inclusion of both the conference and the invited papers. The first was our desire to include papers on legislatures in countries in various stages of economic development (*economic* because, arbitrary as such classifications may be, political development groupings would undoubtedly be more so). A second was to obtain a fairly balanced geographic distribution. A third consideration was to include studies of legislatures modeled on the British parliamentary system, on the American congressional system, and on, what might loosely be termed, hybrids of the two. The following table suggests the attention given to these three factors in terms of the papers in this volume.

Legislative Systems

Institutional model	Level of economic development	
	Developed	Less developed
British parliamentary system	Great Britain, Canada	India
Hybrid	—	Lebanon, Kenya, Chile
American congressional system	United States	Brazil, Philippines

Two other considerations should be noted. As we were particularly interested in the role that legislatures play, or can play, in the new nations, and in the relationship of legislative institutions to economic and social development, we have included papers analyzing both the impact environmental (structural and attitudinal) variables have on policy output and general problems associated with staffing legislatures in less developed states. Finally, although we did not assume that the experiences of Western countries with legislative institutions need necessarily serve as models for developing countries, we did feel that at least some of them might be relevant. Thus, a paper is included on the factors associated with staffing a highly complex legislature, the American Congress. Another paper outlines a program for training and research in legislative institutions and processes that could be made available both to Americans and to other nationals at American universities and counterpart institutions overseas. A final paper provides a general overview of the functions that legislatures perform in both developed and developing political systems and evaluates the potential consequences legislative institutions are likely to have on the process of political development.

The choice of countries at least implicitly evidences an interest in democratic development. We feel that countries with developed or potential democratic forms provide the most fruitful sites for exploration of the functions performed by legislatures. It should be made clear, however, that neither we nor the other contributors to this volume regard political development as a process that is necessarily synonymous with democratic development; the various papers primarily analyze legislative functions as they find them rather than in terms of how well they contribute to democratic development. Indeed, the papers' principal value is in delineating the great range and variety of legislative functions when viewed against the political system at large.

In this context, political development can be regarded as an increased capacity of a political system to accommodate the essential demands upon it. This definition approximates the recent thinking of several leading scholars of political development.[1] The views of one of these, Samuel Huntington, are worth noting because he favors an institution-oriented definition, and this volume concentrates on an important political institution. Huntington defines political development as "the institutionalization of political organizations and procedures."[2] Institutions, he notes, are "stable, valued, recurring patterns of behavior," and institutionalization is "the process by which organizations and procedures acquire value and stability."[3] This approach enables Huntington to judge the level of institutionalization of any political system "by the adaptability, complexity, autonomy, and coherence of its organizations and procedures." It also avoids confusing entanglement with such characteristics of "modernization" as rationalization, integration, democratization, mobilization, and participation. Finally, it avoids the notion of inevitable progress and allows for reversibility in the process of political development.

1. See the works of scholars such as S. N. Eisenstadt, Alfred Diamont, Joseph La Palombara, Samuel P. Huntington, and Gabriel Almond.
2. Samuel P. Huntington, "Political Development and Political Decay," *World Politics*, XVII (April, 1965), 386–430, quotation at 393.
3. *Ibid*, p. 394.

There are some problems with this approach, however. Although political development may be defined in such relatively value-free terms as capacity and institutionalization, a specific political system inevitably develops according to certain values and norms. Thus, for a single system, one is entitled to ask, "capacity to accomplish what?" or "institutionalization for what ends?" Huntington's statement that "a strong Presidency is in the American public interest"[4] appears to illustrate the inevitable admixture of values when a seemingly value-free definition is applied to a specific system. Parenthetically (and somewhat ironically), it may be noted that institutionalization per se obviously is more descriptive of processes in well established, relatively stable systems than in young, rapidly changing nations. To sum up, we are skeptical whether a completely value-free definition of political development is either feasible or desirable, but we think that a definition stressing institutional capacity may be the best available.

Legislative Functions

Although some American students of legislative behavior might question the assertion that "of all political institutions, none is more vital to the process of linking governors and governed in relationships of authority, responsibility, and legitimacy, than the modern legislature,"[5] very few would strenuously object to the contention of Musolf and Riggs, *infra,* that Western countries that have successfully achieved industrialization and economic growth while safeguarding other democratic institutions also have had energetic and influential legislatures. Nor would they object to the assertion that it is "principally through the enactment of statutes that the modern [Western] legislature has derived its saliency."[6] Despite this apparent agreement, one con-

4. *Ibid,* p. 414.
5. John C. Wahlke and Heinz Eulau, eds., *Legislative Behavior: A Reader in Theory and Research* (Glencoe, Ill., 1959), p. 3.
6. Norman Meller, "The Identification and Classification of Legislatures," *Philippine Journal of Public Administration,* X (October, 1966), 308.

tributor to this volume, Robert A. Packenham, both questions whether legislatures in new nations will facilitate economic and /or political development and whether their principal function is now, or will be in the future, one of enacting legislation. Indeed, he seriously doubts whether the principal function of Western legislatures is to enact legislation. "Most of them do not allocate values or at least, do not have this as their principal function. Other functions . . . seem to be more important." But, as he also points out, even in Western societies, there is little consensus on the functions that legislatures perform, probably because "there are no functional delimitations to the activity of a legislature. . . . Rather, in any political system the legislature performs functions appropriate to that system." There is still less agreement or systematic knowledge of the consequences of legislative activity for other institutions in the political system. Because of the dearth of such systematic research, it was felt that this volume might make a contribution to comparative politics in general, and comparative legislative studies in particular, if the majority of contributors undertook the tasks of delineating the activities performed by the legislatures they were studying and evaluating the consequences of these activities for other political and social institutions within the respective systems.

If success in carrying out this mandate can be quantitatively measured, then, certainly, Packenham has been singularly successful. Using the Brazilian Congress as his empirical referent, he identifies fully twelve functions—latent and manifest legitimization, tension release, recruitment, socialization, training, lawmaking, "exiting," interest-articulation, administrative oversight, patronage, and errand-running—and the consequences these have for Brazilian politics. One may ask whether a function that is visible to Professor Packenham and the Brazilian military elite really can be considered latent, whether the "exit" function is not simply one dimension of conflict resolution, whether a legislature's control of finance constitutes "patronage," and whether interest-articulation and errand-running cannot be subsumed under representation. In fairness to Packenham, he holds no special brief for the uniqueness or, indeed, the correctness of the set of functions he has delineated. Further, he offers persuasive arguments in support of his hypothesis that the Brazilian Congress's activities, such as the legitimization of decisions made elsewhere and the recruitment and training of individuals for other political roles, are far more important, in functional terms, than its task as a public policy initiator and evaluator.

In contrast, Weston H. Agor, in his study of the Chilean Senate, contends that that particular institution *does* play an important role in the policy process. In fact, he estimates that policy-making is probably the single most important task the Senate performs. The Senate also exercises considerable control over budgetary matters despite a constitutional provision that gives the president exclusive jurisdiction in this area. Agor rejects the notion that presidential "urgency powers" give the executive an important advantage over the Senate in the policy-initiation and policy-evaluation process. Not only is the Senate able to delay or reject a presidential measure labeled "urgent," in fact, it also has used this presidential power for its own advantage; it initiates and attaches numerous new bills to the "coat-tails" of an urgency measure. The president is frequently forced to accept these riders if he desires the passage of his own legislation.

The Senate exercises considerable control over the administrative bureaucracy as well, and more than adequately represents the dominant socio-economic interests in the country. The Senate's rather extraordinary power vis-à-vis other political institutions rests in part upon the prestige ascribed to that institution. This prestige is in turn a function of institutional performance; factors such as long experience, informal behavioral norms that encourage expertise, and relatively elaborate supporting services permit the individual senator to perform his tasks in a manner that cumulatively makes the Senate a power within Chilean society. The functions performed by the Chilean Senate and its importance in the total configuration of Chilean political activity are particularly impressive when one realizes that the political system rests on a rather narrow economic base.

The Philippines, although probably less culturally developed than Chile, also exhibit the syndrome associated with being more developed politically than economically. Robert B. Stauffer's description of the activities of the Philippine Congress reveals that not only is it capable (assisted by a large and adequately trained staff of experts) of overseeing the bureaucracy and initiating and evaluating legislation, but also that it has played a crucial role in developing and sustaining democratic institutions and practices. According to Stauffer, at the height of the Philippine revolution against Spain, Philippine political leaders were faced with the problem of whether to organize their political institutions under the old Spanish community-consensus values or whether to accept conflict as "natural," and thus to create organizations through which conflict could be channeled and ultimately resolved. A conscious decision was made in favor of the latter. Specifically, a representative assembly—the Malolos Congress— was called which was forced almost immediately to make crucial political decisions. In every instance, "the choices were unequivocally made by Congress that favored a system openly favoring conflict. The Republic of the Philippines thus began its life with an assembly that from the first sitting made clear that the proper function of the legislature is not to be a quiet, unobtrusive, and pliant advisory body, but rather to play an active role in helping to resolve important differences of opinion and interest that came before it."

For nearly three decades Congress enjoyed a virtual monopoly on political roles. Accordingly, it became a very important, if not the most important, politicizing agent within Philippine society. Although since independence the task of socializing the electorate to politics has been shared with an elected president, the Congress, as a body, largely defines the dimensions of both elite and mass political behavior. It also is intimately linked to the electorate through elaborate alliances with networks of local leaders whose power in turn depends on their willingness to articulate constituent demands. Thus, the adequate performance of the representative function also is ensured. As is the case in Chile, the ability to perform adequately in great part explains the legitimacy popularly ascribed to Congress and its "central role in keeping democratic politics alive."

Lebanon and the Philippines have been independent for approximately the same period of time. However, the position of the Lebanese Parliament with respect to the role it plays vis-à-vis other political and social institutions is almost the diametric opposite of the Philippine situation described previously. In the Philippines, a conscious decision was made to develop political institutions capable of channeling and resolving overt conflict, but in Lebanon, the decision was made to submerge overt conflict lest it destroy existing political institutions.

Ralph E. Crow has described the Lebanese political system as one that operates in a social environment in which there is no consensus on even the most basic political values "including the legitimacy of the state itself." In consequence, the Lebanese Chamber of Deputies rarely, if ever, is able to consider or to make potentially divisive public policy decisions. Although in theory it possesses formidable constitutional powers, in actual practice it tends to be a weak and fragmented organization that is dominated by a strong president and his administrative bureaucracy. Further, the "real" power within Lebanese society tends to be exercised in other than political institutions, as for example, in the financial and religious communities. The result is that although Parliament may be said to play an important role within the political system in providing an institutional setting in which important actors may perform, in providing sustained collective support for the actions of the executive, and in ratifying or, rather, legitimating decisions made by nonpolitical elites, its overt performance tends to be so desultory that little status is ascribed to it as an organization.

In contrast, considerable prestige is ascribed to Parliament in the Indian political system, although apparently not as much as the public (especially its informed segment) accords the judiciary. According to L. M. Singhvi, in most of the conflicts that have ensued between Parliament and the courts, the latter appear, at least temporarily, to have emerged the victor. Competition between the two institutions generally has resulted from the particular way in which they have viewed their respective roles. The judiciary has perceived itself as the custodian of individual rights and the rule of law, whereas Parliament, in its desire to ameliorate the socio-economic conditions of the individual, has tended to attach diminishing importance to his rights and to stress, instead, the necessity for collective action to achieve his social uplift. Not only has the judiciary tried to share the representational function with Parliament, but also state legislatures and state governments generally have vied for this function with their national counterparts.

The extent to which state political institutions can successfully compete with the national institutions is as yet uncertain because the Indian federal system is still evolving. In fact, this is true, to an extent, of all Indian political institutions which until now have not always been sharply differentiated from the social system of which they are a part. For example, in terms of mere numbers, one could argue that Indian political parties were well-established institutions; there were approximately twenty-four official parties competing at either the state or national level in the election of 1967. Despite this plethora of parties, however, Singhvi argues that variables such as caste, ethnicity, language, religion, and region are superimposed upon, and (when some are congruent) frequently submerge, inter-party conflict. Electors often vote for candidates, and only in a very subsidiary sense, for parties—a fact that helps account for the relatively large number of independents that have been elected to each of India's four Parliaments.

By far the most successful party has been the Indian National Congress. Despite the losses suffered in the last election, it continues to dominate a Parliament which Singhvi terms the "symbolic battleground on which the principal interests engage in and resolve their conflicts." In the sense that Parliament provides a running commentary and a continuous critique of public policies while serving as a public forum and sounding board for public opinion, it may be said to be performing what Bagehot termed the "expressive, teaching, and informing functions." Parliament is, however, neither actively involved in the policy process, nor does it effectively oversee the bureaucracy, which is the principal architect of public policy (". . . parliamentary scrutiny of the bureaucracy is a patchwork with sporadic and piecemeal forays into the executive territory").

Parliament's difficulties are increased by the fact that the legislators suffer from an almost total lack of information; library, research, and staff assistance are virtually non-existent. Thus, the usual disadvantages the individual M.P. in a British model parliamentary system faces vis-à-vis the Cabinet and the administrative bureaucracy are multiplied many times over. The situation is further exacerbated by the low salaries paid M.P.'s, many of whom are forced to supplement their parliamentary income with other work to make financial ends meet. Therefore, for a substantial proportion of Indian parliamentarians, their official position, although a highly visible and prestigious one, is also a part-time and (because of the high turnover rate) temporary interlude in their careers.

Kenya, by far the youngest of the new nations considered in this volume, is a particularly interesting research site because, in a sense, it presents a quasi-experimental situation. Since independence, the government has been transformed from a constitutional monarchy of the Westminster model to a republic of the presidential form, whereas the party system has included first two, then one, and, again, two parties.

Newell M. Stultz finds that the current national legislature has both parliamentary and presidential characteristics. For example, the president, although popularly elected, is dependent upon the support of a majority of the National Assembly, a fact which makes it possible for M.P.'s simultaneously to profess complete loyalty to him and to oppose strenuously particular policies of his Government.

An interesting, albeit not unexpected, consequence of the change from a two-party to a one-party system was that it did not eliminate opposition to the Government, but rather internalized it. The Kenya African National Union (KANU) parliamentary party actually was less cohesive after the union with Kenya African Democratic Union (KADU) than before, with the old members not exhibiting appreciably more unity than their new colleagues. Stultz attributes this lack of party cohesion largely to backbench frustration over their virtual exclusion from the policy-making process. As they have not been involved in making policy, they are not overly inclined to mobilize public support for it in their constituencies. In fact, to the extent that they are active in their constituencies (and many are not, apparently being more concerned with representing their personal rather than constituent interests) their activity is limited to attacking the government. The basis of this opposition, it should be noted, is disagreement over their status rather than public policy. According to Stultz, "legislative support for the policies of the Kenya government has appeared dependent less upon the perceived merit of these policies than upon the respect accorded the dignity and function of ordinary M.P.'s by the executive in the process of decision-making." In their concern over the status ascribed them, Kenyan legislators are certainly not different from their counterparts in more developed systems. American congressmen and members of the British and Canadian Parliaments, for example, have jealously guarded their personal and institutional prerogatives. In a very real sense, they have been far more successful in the former than in the latter endeavor; that parliaments of the British model in particular have progressively lost their initiative to the executive is now accepted as a truism by legislative scholars.

In Canada, parliamentary procedure, like the institution itself, was transplanted almost *in toto* from Great Britain via the legislatures of the four provinces that formed the original federation in 1867. A century later, Allan Kornberg notes, there is seemingly widespread and relatively deep disaffection with Parliament as an institution and with the individuals who populate it. Underlying this disaffection are a number of cogent and well-articulated criticisms. It is claimed, for example, that the demand-inputs that flow into Parliament, or rather those to which Parliament is attentive, come disproportionately from a very small and narrow segment of the population. Related to this, the policy decisions that Parliament makes disproportionately reflect the interests of this small elite. Further, the proponents of policies from outside of Parliament and those who ratify and legitimate these proposals within Parliament frequently are the same people, even though their roles may be analytically distinct. In addition, a structural device, federalism, has been employed as a convenient excuse for not making certain kinds of policy decisions; the fact that Parliament has not initiated constitutional changes that would enable it to legislate in certain areas reflects a conscious, deliberate choice on the part of those who have controlled the national government to maintain the existing patterns of power. Finally, it is claimed the two parties that historically have alternated in power at the national level have basically the same values in that both are oriented toward business, both perform broker-mediator-conciliator functions, and, when in office, tend to be political caretakers rather than innovators. Because of this, Parliament never engages in dialogues that are meaningful to a majority of the public, but instead it functions as a convenient screen behind which the elites who exercise real power are able to operate.

With regard to the tasks traditionally ascribed to Parliament, those of legislating, representing the several interests, and overseeing the bureaucracy, Kornberg finds that only the representative function appears to be performed in a creditable manner. Insofar as policy-initiation and policy-evaluation and the control of the bureaucracy are concerned, procedural devices, an ineffective committee system, and a paucity of information largely limit M.P.'s to intermittently attacking or defending policies that have been determined by party leaders—to either offering sycophantic praise or heaping personal invective. Admittedly, such activities can have a cathartic effect on the "backbencher" and also may facilitate his management by party leaders. However, they are unlikely to earn for Parliament the respect and approval of the public.

The problem in Great Britain, on the other hand, is not one of lack of respect for Parliament; according to Bernard Crick, the mass media (if these can be seen as reflecting public opinion) are astonishingly respectful toward Parliament. And recent British governments, in neglecting the machinery of Parliament, also have neglected their principal method of communicating directly with the public—as opposed to simply negotiating with those who claim to represent organized groups in the public. The failure to utilize Parliament as a vehicle of communication is especially serious because a really basic problem in Great Britain is that despite the stability, efficiency, and self-confidence of the machinery of government, it has been ineffective under both the Labour and Conservative parties alike, not only in solving postwar economic problems but also in changing public attitudes toward work.

A second basic problem faced by both Labour and Conservative governments (but particularly Labour) is that the backbench members of their parliamentary parties have become restive, bored, and frustrated with the traditional role ascribed to the backbench M.P. They are eager, Crick says, to do something beyond waiting for an infrequent turn to speak on the floor or to ask a question. They are almost unanimous in thinking that Parliament should create a comprehensive system of specialized committees that would not formulate policy but rather would be capable of scrutinizing, investigating, and criticizing the working of the administration. And, despite its undoubted talents, the administration requires such attention. Many of its policies are formulated on the basis of exhaustive prior consultations between a particular ministry and the bureaucracy of the interest group that will be affected by legislation. In these interactions the compromises made by ministers and civil servants can be excessive. Further, they are made on the basis of information fed to them by leaders whose attitudes may or may not represent the opinions of their followers, let alone the vast unorganized part of the public.

Although much of the current agitation among M.P.'s for specialized committees is related to their suspicion of the excessive influence that pressure groups exert (and, perhaps, their pique at being largely ignored by these groups), it also stems from the fact that M.P.'s are beginning to understand what they are, in fact, doing. The House is beginning to get away from its fixation of spending so much time on legislation that it cannot in any real sense control, to get away from pretending to be primarily a legislature, and to interest itself more in the formulation of policy at the prelegislative stage and the scrutiny of policy at the postlegislative stage. In other words, they are beginning, says Crick, "to take a wider view of legislation."

Historically, the American Congress has always taken such a view. Constitutionally, the American Congress was designed to be the primary resolver of which goals ought to be given priority in the polity. But to attain its goals, to carry out its tasks, Congress had to work in concert with the executive and judicial structures. The founding fathers, Roger H. Davidson feels, "envisioned a polity not of separate structures performing separate tasks, but of separate structures sharing tasks." In so doing, they laid the foundation for the institutional struggle which persists to this day.

He feels, as does James A. Robinson, that in this struggle the executive has made considerable gains at the expense of Congress (although in absolute terms the scope of Congress's authority has increased tremendously because of the historical tendency to shift conflicts from private to public arenas for their resolution). Tasks normally labeled *legislative* have become executive in locus because the framing of the agenda of issues increasingly has been relegated to the president and his staff. Still, Davidson claims, Congress continues to deliberate and to draft the specific content of certain policy outputs; that is, it continues to perform a rule-making function. It also continues to perform the other two functions Davidson ascribes to "active" legislative bodies, those of representation and consensus building. This is not to say that it does not perform what Davidson calls "ancillary functions" as well—the clarification of policy, oversight of the administration, service to constituents, and the ratification or legitimation of the decisions that are made elsewhere in the system. It would appear, therefore, that if rule-making, representation, and consensus building can be considered the hallmark of strong legislatures and such ancillary functions as constituent service can be seen as characteristic of "truncated" legislatures, then the modern Congress fits neither model. Thus, for example, in domestic areas such as agriculture, public works, and immigration, Congress continues to play a central and creative role. In foreign affairs and national security matters, however, traditional legislative prerogatives have been assumed by executive agencies.

In describing Congress's functional place in the political system, Davidson, of necessity, is concerned both with internal processes within Congress and the public's perception of, and support for, the outcomes Congress produces. Thus, he delineates the purposive and representational role cognitions of congressmen and compares these with the public's expectations. Although not unexpectedly, there is considerable disparity between the public's and Congress's perceptions of the congressman's function, there is also generalized support for, and favorable attitudes toward, Congress as an institution.

There is also astonishing ignorance in cross sections of population concerning the actual operations of Congress. Interestingly, those elements in the public that are attentive to Congress and are aware of what it does or does not do also tend to be a more critical audience. Thus, in a sense, the generalized support that the average citizen affords Congress, together with his relative ignorance of what his particular congressman does or the functions that congressmen collectively perform, constitutes what Davidson terms a "facilitating input" for the operation and continued viability of the congressional system of government. In part, these circumstances also explain why Congress, although increasingly forced to perform such subsidiary legislative functions as policy clarification and constituent service remains, in comparison with virtually all the other legislatures considered in this volume, the model for an "active" legislature.

Variables Affecting Legislative Functions

In a recent review of legislative behavioral research in the United States, Heinz Eulau and Katherine Hinckley[7] point out that there are really two basic models of legislative behavior, the

7. Heinz Eulau and Katherine Hinckley, "Legislative Institutions and Processes," *Political Science Annual, 1966,* ed. James A. Robinson (New York, 1966), pp. 85–190.

"inside" and the "outside." The former is structured in terms of the variables operating upon the individual within the legislative system; the latter focuses on environmental conditions outside of the system that affect behavior within it. James A. Robinson's paper "Staffing the Legislature" is concerned with the former. Robinson's paper considers first the role of legislatures in modern political systems with respect to gathering intelligence, formulating and promoting alternatives, selecting from among alternatives, implementing and executing selected alternatives, appraising the effectiveness of the policies adopted, and terminating, renewing, or revising past policy. Second, he focuses on the performance of these functions within the legislature itself.

Robinson, in part, attributes the loss of legislative initiative to the executive (even in the United States) to the "information revolution" and the fact that the executive adjusted to this revolution much faster and more appropriately than did the legislature. That is, "the executive branch specialized, bureaucratized, and mechanized," whereas it occurred to "few theorists or practitioners that legislatures also might augment their information capabilities by bureaucratizing." Although Congress created the modern American Civil Service by passing the Pendleton Act in 1881, it did nothing comparable for itself until the Legislative Reorganization Act of 1946. In consequence, a substantial alteration in the roles and influence of Congress and the presidency occurred within a generation; legislative predominance was replaced by presidential initiative. And what is true of Congress also applies in even greater measure to American state legislatures, which are handicapped far more than Congress by lack of space, staff, time, and other pertinent resources. Robinson estimates that the shift of initiative and influence from the British House of Commons to the cabinet antedated the American alteration in legislative-executive relations by a considerable margin. In emerging nations, it seems clear that parliaments are almost uniformly dependent on the executive branch or on the single mass party that typically dominates new nations.

If information or the lack of it has altered the institutional arrangements in the principal stages of national policy-making, it also has had an impact on policy-making within the legislature. The main effects, according to Robinson, have been to involve executive officials more intimately in the internal procedures of legislatures, in providing intelligence, in setting the agenda, in determining the form that legislative proposals will take, and in defining for legislative leaders the minimum response they consider acceptable.

Since much of the executive's primacy, as has been indicated, is a function of its superior information sources, Robinson considers the forms of countervailing intelligence that legislatures might acquire. He does not accept the propositions "the more information, the better" and "the more alternatives, the better." Rather, he postulates that suitable practices for obtaining and processing information vary with the developmental status of particular legislatures. He feels, for example, that political systems that can not afford a two-party system because they lack the talent to man an opposition party can be forgiven if they regard large parliamentary staffs as a luxury that can be postponed.

Just as legislatures vary in their information needs, legislators differ in the character of their demands for information. In well-developed legislatures, individual members may have to select from several mechanisms those they find most congenial, whereas the legislator in a developing system, since he normally plays a less prominent part qua individual in the system, is less in need of alternative information sources.

Robinson also feels that information systems ought to be designed to complement or supplement rather than to duplicate the skills that legislators themselves bring to their positions. Recruitment patterns in most democratic societies bring to legislative assemblies an abundant supply of lawyers and businessmen but relatively few individuals acquainted with social problems, military strategy, or the relevance of science. Specialties such as law and commerce may be increasingly irrelevant to the substantive problems with which modern legislatures are concerned. Although it may be congenial for legislators to hire as staff assistants individuals with occupational experiences and skills that duplicate their own, it may not be particularly functional for the legislature as a problem-solving system. In effect, many legislators would be better served by hiring social scientists and technicians rather than lawyers and journalists for their staff.

Again, however, political systems that lack the talent and experience to maintain an opposition party are unlikely to be overrun with either journalists or technicians, let alone social scientists with the expertise to advise and appraise their actions. Robinson suggests that it may be feasible and appropriate for developed countries with reputations for parliamentary stability to contribute through an international organization both money and rotating personnel to encourage and perfect the development of legislative practices in less developed countries. A variation of this suggestion is considered by Musolf and Riggs in their paper to be reviewed shortly.

For the present, it may be noted that Samuel C. Patterson also is concerned with staffing, in this instance the staffing of American congressional committees. Patterson finds that despite the fact that the number of standing committees in Congress was reduced in 1946, the number of subcommittees has doubled in the interim since then. These subcommittees have made considerable use of professional committee staffs so that both the number of professional staff members and the size of the appropriations to support them have increased dramatically in the last two decades. Professional staffs are also utilized by lobbyists and by officials in the executive agencies. The relationship between professionals on congressional staffs and executive agencies has become especially important. Patterson writes that agency officials maintain very close contacts with committee staff personnel and much of the network of legislative-executive relations is filled with daily interactions between committee and agency staffs. The work of committee staffs is both hard and demanding. To this work they bring certain actual or potential capabilities. Patterson lists these as intelligence (i.e., information gathering), integration, innovation, and influence.

Clearly, the most visible capability of committee staffs involves the intelligence function. Staff men are "facts-and-figures" men, and a great deal of their working day is spent in securing, processing, and supplying information to committee members. Committee staffs also contribute to the integration of committees and subcommittees, to inter-cameral integration, and as has been indicated, to integration between the legislative and executive branches. Since they select and feed information to congressmen, committee staffs obviously have both innovative and influence capabilities. Some committee staffs are naturally more innovative than others. Generally, the more specialized and bureaucratized the staff, the more innovative it tends to be. Similarly, the more informed the staff, the more influence it is likely to exert—although always upon its conformity to certain informal but well understood rules of the game. These informal rules include personal loyalty to the committee and subcommittee chairmen, a willingness to remain anonymous, and behavior that generally encourages trust and confidence on the part of the committee.

A variety of biases or constraints that in a sense are the inverse of the capabilities previously described also affect the behavior of committee professional staffs. Patterson focuses on the constraints associated with group norms, committee leadership, staff organization, non-partisanship, isolation, and specialization. One important group norm is that of limited advocacy: the shared understanding that the staff member will never press his own policy positions too far, and that he will be sensitive to the limitations on the presentation of his own proposals. The norm of chairman loyalty is a crucial one; the sanction invoked for failure to be loyal is likely to be immediate termination. Closely related are the norms of deference and anonymity. The latter norm is probably the most difficult for staff members to live with since staff men who come to have considerable expertise quite naturally desire public recognition. When this is not forthcoming, frustrations and a decline in morale may ensue.

Two other structural biases are specialization and limited partisanship. Since the confidence which the committee members have in the staff is in great part a function of their demonstrated expertness, of necessity committee staff members must confine themselves to a rather limited substantive area. And although clearly some committees are more partisan than others in the manner in which decisions are made, a wide range of committee activity is non-partisan. Hence, the most widely respected staff men are also the most non-partisan ones.

Staff organization varies widely, but there are three general patterns to be found in congressional committees. First, the staff can be hierarchically organized and coordinated under a staff director who in turn takes his orders directly from the committee chairman. A second organizational form involves both staff director and staff members dealing directly with the committee chairman. Third, the chairman may deal only with a staff director who organizes and directs the members of the professional staff, while at the same time he gives orders to a chief clerk who organizes and directs members of a clerical staff.

Patterson notes that the latter type of staff arrangement seems excessively prone to tension between the two staff leaders, particularly when the staff director is a professional and the chief clerk is a political appointee. When this situation occurs, staff performance is likely to suffer. Committees which have difficulty developing nonpartisan professional staffs, such as those which deal with education, labor, and welfare legislation, also are likely to have their performance deleteriously affected. On the other hand, the isolation of staff members of one committee from those of others in the same and in the other House does not appear to have a systematically adverse effect upon staff performance. Staff isolation tends to produce duplication and ignorance in the intelligence effort and works against House and Senate integration, but it also tends to facilitate committee integration and probably increases staff influence and expertise.

Although John G. Grumm's analysis focuses on environmental factors (what Eulau and Hinckley term an "outside" model), he is concerned as well with the impact that structural variables, such as the professionalization of a legislative body, have upon policy outputs. Grumm postulates a model of the policy process in which the "inputs" are environmental factors such as the level of urbanization, industrialization, and education. These affect both the characteristics of a political system including the legislative subsystem and the system's "outputs"—public policies that take the form of appropriations or substantive legislation. Public policy outputs also may be affected directly by environmental factors and the structural characteristics of the political system.

Grumm employs a factor analysis to develop five categories of output variables; welfare liberalism, governmental size, financial centralization, progressive taxation, and governmental expansion. His input, or ecological, variables are: economic affluence, population expansion, degree of urbanization, and degree of federal support. Finally, as an example of a structural variable, he constructs a professionalism index that encompasses factors such as the rate of compensation of legislators and the length of sessions during a particular biennium.

Not only is he able to rank the several states in terms of the level of professionalism of their legislatures, and in terms of the various dimensions of their environmental inputs and policy outputs, but also with the use of a Simon-Blalock causal model, he is able to assess the degree of correlation among environmental inputs, structural factors, and policy output. He finds that legislative professionalism has an independent effect on welfare policy output—the more professional the legislature, the more liberal the policy. The explanation Grumm offers is that professionalism tends to facilitate a legislature's response to the demands generated by urbanization and the conditions provided by an advanced level of economic development. Professionalism itself is strongly affected by the level of urbanization. However, the influence of urbanism on policy output is not direct; it is only made effective through legislative professionalism. He suggests, therefore, that "professional" legislatures are more responsive than others, although the evidence is far from complete.

A particularly interesting finding, in view of its relevance for legislatures of developing countries, is that his model indicates that economic affluence per se has no effect on legislative professionalism. Apparently a state, at least in this country, does not have to be rich to provide adequate support for its legislature. Extrapolating from his evidence of legislative professionalism in American states to the international arena, Grumm suggests that altering the legislature to give it a more professional posture might prove generally effective in liberalizing welfare provisions in the economically well-developed and moderately developed countries. It is unlikely, however, to be effective in the nations that are clearly economically underdeveloped.

Malcolm E. Jewell, in his paper "Attitudinal Determinants of Legislative Behavior: The Utility of Role Analysis," points out that the level of political development of a system probably affects the role perceptions of legislators therein. In less developed and less sharply differentiated legislative systems, he suggests, the characteristics which a legislator brings to the legislative position are more likely to determine his role perceptions than would be the case in a developed system. In the latter, institutional constraints are more likely to mitigate and, in fact, to submerge individual predispositions for certain roles. Looked at another way, highly visible political-cultural norms and the strong institutional pressures which (several studies have shown) help structure the roles taken by legislators in the United States and Canada are less likely to be operative and hence to impinge upon legislators' role orientations in underdeveloped systems.

More important perhaps is that role appears to be a concept that can be used to study legislatures cross-nationally. Role, as Jewell makes clear, is important not for its predictive power, but for its analytic utility. The question he poses is: Does a knowledge of legislators' role orientations and the correlates of these roles permit us to know and to explain more about legislative behavior (regardless of the particular institution in which the behavior occurs) than would be the case if we did not have this information? His answer, based on an analysis of a number of studies of legislative behavior that have utilized the role concept, is that it *does* provide invaluable contextual information that permits us to understand better both legislative behavior and the legislative institution itself. Indeed, despite the very real difficulties involved in utilizing the concept in cross-national legislative research (e.g., in order for a question to be equally meaningful or similarly understood by legislators in countries as different as, perhaps, Great Britain and the Philippines, it may be necessary to change the wording of the question, which in turn makes precise comparison of responses difficult), it may be through role that we can begin to accumulate a corpus of truly comparative legislative data.

Elected Assemblies and Political Development

The reciprocal character of the relationship between elected assemblies (as legislatures may be called in order to emphasize their many functions other than decision-making, as well as its absence from some "legislatures") and political development can scarcely be overstressed. Elected assemblies cannot be considered in isolation. It would be shortsighted to strengthen them without heeding the consequences for the rest of the political system. Undoubtedly, there is a strong nexus among elected assemblies, political parties, and electoral laws. As we have noted, the existence of this nexus should not lead to the inference that political development must result in democracy or the appearance of institutions that are mirror images of those in Western democratic countries.

If political development means an increased capacity for problem-solving, as we have suggested, then it is realistic to expect that such change occurs across the spectrum of the political system, but not that a preordained result is inevitable, nor that a particular institution within the system will automatically adopt an exogenous pattern. (For democratic development, however, politically powerful legislatures appear to be critical.) Presumably the two-way flow of influence suggested above means that, in a given situation, elected assemblies either can be dependent or independent variables in political development. Our expectation would be that they would most often be the former because power in political systems just beginning their development tends most often to reside outside elected assemblies.

Some commentators see the possibility of strengthened legislatures as a phenomenon ordinarily not to be welcomed. "In societies that need and want change," writes Robert A. Packenham in the present volume, "and where political development may be defined as the will and capacity to cope with and to generate continuing transformation, it may not make much sense to strengthen the decision-making function of an institution that is likely to resist change." Certainly one can agree with Packenham that improving the legislative staff services of an assembly in an effort to strengthen it is a political action which should be considered carefully in the context of the entire political system. One can also agree that the effects of improving staff services must be taken into account for other functions of assemblies than decision-making.

The same reasoning, nevertheless, that suggests considering the functions of elected assemblies as a bundle, and emphasizes the interdependence of elected assemblies and political development, suggests avoiding an easy readiness to assign a blocking role to elected assemblies in national development, whether economic or political. This volume, as Packenham concedes, outlines a broad variety of roles for legislatures in developing countries. Also, caution must be exercised in equating delay in decision-making with lack of progress in a country eager for modernization. In point of fact, economic planning in a number of developing countries has suffered, the economists tell us, from the lack of adequate machinery for relating plans to political realities. Even where the locus of power is in the executive branch, it is conceivable that an elected assembly can provide soundings or questions that would aid the quality of decision-making. In a broader sense, it is risky to assign rigid roles in political development. David Apter has reminded us that in the development process there is a constant tendency for political systems to become their opposite, for mobilization systems to veer toward becoming reconciliation systems, and vice versa.[8] And John R. Sisson has suggested that legislative institutions may be important simply " . . . by virtue of their being there. They were created, they have been 'staffed,' they have been maintained."[9]

We have suggested above that legislatures might better be

8. David E. Apter, *The Politics of Modernization*, First Phoenix ed. (Chicago, 1967), pp. 425–430, 461–462.
9. John R. Sisson, "Legislatures in Developing Political Systems" (mimeographed, 1968).

termed *elected assemblies*, particularly in developing areas. We now suggest that even if they are elected by a relatively minute proportion of the population, or are picked under conditions that hardly are in keeping with the best practices of the League of Women Voters or, indeed, even if they are partially elected and partially appointed, they can still become relatively important within the total political process. Thus, for example, the Pakistani Parliament is a considerably more vigorous institution than Ayub originally envisaged it would be; the recently elected Assembly and Senate of South Vietnam appear to be making some changes in the general-as-free-agent model of executive leadership; and the Singhalese Parliament has played and continues to play a central role in that country's politics.

One could argue that the latter type of mixed recruitment—executive appointment and popular election—may become the prevailing pattern in many of the new states in Asia and Africa since it at once permits an individual executive, a ruling cadre, or a military elite to establish a synaptic link with its population, to obtain necessary information, to provide a catharsis for societal grievances, and to generate support if not enthusiasm for its policies. In this respect, it may be observed that even when legislative bodies have been abolished by revolutionary uprisings or military coups, they have shown a remarkable resilience; after a time they tend to be re-established, although admittedly with a different set of tasks and a different range of powers (if not in a different structural form) than was previously the case—witness the Soviet Union, Spain, and, more recently, Brazil, Thailand, and Indonesia (and, probably, Greece).

The reason why legislative institutions exhibit such regenerative powers, in our view, is that they are perceived by those who aspire to power or already have tasted it as a legitimizing force, as a necessary condition for maintaining not only themselves but also a given political order, regardless of its form or objectives. Inherent in the term *development* are the notions of change and dynamism rather than homeostasis. Thus, embryonic legislative structures, or "elected assemblies," that simply are facades behind which a ruling individual, oligarchy, or mass party can operate to structure the political game and to control both the players and outcomes may develop into something quite different in the future. Similarly, the fact that most Western legislatures currently perform ancillary functions rather than legislate does not preclude them from again becoming essentially rule-making bodies, from taking on tasks currently performed by other political institutions, or from performing new functions in response to yet inarticulated societal demands. According to Sisson, legislative institutions ". . . having existed, having been publicized, having become part of the public consciousness, may absorb new functions more easily than institutions created with immediacy, either in anticipation of, or as a reaction to, a particular crisis or functional need."[10] If such speculations are grounded in empirical reality, then the continued study of legislative institutions, their processes and outputs, their roles and functions vis à vis other institutions in the political system, and their responsiveness to, and support from, general and specific publics remain important tasks for legislative scholars and "practitioners" alike.

In their paper, Lloyd Musolf and Fred Riggs set out detailed recommendations for the creation of Comparative Legislative Study Centers that would help meet the need for such continuous systematic study. Specifically, they propose that Comparative Legislative Study Centers be established at five carefully selected American universities, that such centers have as their goals the testing of hypotheses and the generation of new knowledge with respect to legislatures and legislative development, that the centers also be concerned with developing teaching and training programs for members of legislative bodies and individuals servicing such institutions, and that these goals be undertaken in the context of an international exchange of resources and knowledge. They recognize that any program of teaching and training must rest on a solid research base, preferably through intensive field studies in this and other countries. The centers could also be employed to deposit and disseminate data, they could serve as a base for visiting scholars, and they could be the site for national and international research conferences and seminars.

10. *Ibid.*

The assumption underlying the establishment of such a program is that, at least in the West, legislatures have promoted political development by channeling inter-group conflict, by giving representation to the several social groups in a society, by enhancing the rule of law, by ratifying and legitimizing public policies, by strengthening the responsive administration of governmental programs, and by helping to promote national integration and the development of a national identity. Parenthetically, it may be noted that their claims that "In those countries which have successfully achieved industrialization and economic growth while safeguarding free democratic institutions, one finds energetic and influential legislatures, parliaments, chambers of deputies, or other types of 'elected assemblies'" and "a vigorous legislature is the best insurance that citizens can find an outlet for their legitimate grievances" illustrate both how difficult it is to generate a value-free theory of political development and why Americans and their assistance, technical and otherwise, are not always greeted with unmixed enthusiasm in foreign countries. The authors themselves are cognizant of this possibility; they fully appreciate that the study of legislatures is a subject of unusual sensitivity and complexity and that basic decisions about the role which elected assemblies will play in political systems must be made by the political leaders of these systems without external interference. They also insist that in any studies outside the United States, foreign scholars must be full and equal participants. But they make a strong and reasonable plea that such research be undertaken, despite the obvious difficulties, at the earliest instance at which supporting funds can be secured.

In concluding, it is appropriate to re-emphasize the tentative nature of this volume. Scholars have long sought to chart the political winds that push nations in one political direction or another. Difficult as this is to do for one country or a group of them with similar cultures, such as the Western community, the advent of the new states vastly complicated the process even while it exacerbated the challenge. The present collection of essays can only hint at the bewildering variety of national experiences at a time when older notions about mature countries have disappeared under an avalanche of unfamiliar place-names and semi-inchoate geographical areas clamoring for recognition by the United Nations.

The focus in this volume upon elected assemblies in somewhat democratically inclined countries may provide no more than a handhold for an assault upon the mountain of political development, but if the present volume contributes to the study of political development to this extent it can be accounted worth publishing. We believe that it modestly advances this study by providing basic but hitherto little-known information on elected assemblies. More importantly, it evaluates the functions legislatures perform in their respective political systems and investigates variables affecting legislative functions. In so doing, the book brings to the forefront of discussion an institution whose ubiquity is itself testimony to its involvement in political development. Conceivably, the present collection of essays can also serve to refine a basic question affecting elected assemblies: whether, in specific cases, they should be strengthened and, if so, when and by what means.

There is another kind of benefit which this book, hopefully, may produce, and that is, to serve as a bridge to future studies of legislatures and political development that are more nearly comparative than was possible in the present study. Students of American legislatures have been prolific in developing or applying concepts such as political socialization, political recruitment, professionalism, role, reference group, institutionalization, generalized and specific support, and responsiveness. Yet, relatively little consideration has been given to the question of the extent to which, or more appropriately, the conditions under which, these concepts are relevant or meaningful in studies outside of the United States, especially in developing countries. Even less time has been allocated to developing the methodological tools necessary to operationalize concepts such as the above so that they can be employed in really comparable legislative research. For example, even if one assumes that recruitment (a concept that to date at least has been structured in great part in terms of parties and elections) is relevant for the study of legislative institutions in non-Western cultures, the problem of developing various measures of this phenomenon that at one and the same time can be employed in studying recruitment in, perhaps, both the American Congress and the Kenyan Parliament, remains. In fact, even when the concepts and methods employed by American legislative scholars have been exported to societies which are essentially similar, such as Canada and the United States, but which have different structural arrangements, the question of salience and relevance may arise. Thus, although the concept of role may be fruitfully employed to study both congressmen and members of Parliament, the utility of scaling roll-call votes (a methodological tool that generally has been extremely useful for analyzing congressional behavior) in the Canadian Parliament is questionable.

The present volume has not really dealt with such problems nor has it been overly systematic or successful in linking legislatures with political development. And, such a link is urgently needed; the overlap between legislative scholars and those studying comparative political development has been small indeed. We have, as we indicated, made a modest start in this direction. In the post-war period, American public administration learned the hard way the necessity of going beyond the application of essentially American or Western concepts and methods in both the study and the granting of technical assistance to developing nations. At the risk, therefore, of restating the obvious, it is important to emphasize that those engaged in comparative legislative research must do the same. To be truly comparative, the concepts used in legislative studies must be cumulatively built from as intimate a knowledge of foreign countries as present scholars have of their own. A not so incidental benefit is that in the process scholars are likely to find a heightened perception of the value premises under which their own countries operate.

Chapter 2

Parliament in the British Political System

Bernard Crick

For a conceptual framework there is little need to go beyond
Walter Bagehot.[1] In *The English Constitution* of 1867 he stated
clearly and analyzed thoughtfully (if impressionistically) five
basic functions of Parliament. "The main function of the House of
Commons is . . . as an electoral chamber; it is the assembly
which chooses our President."[2] (So old, incidentally, is the "Presidential thesis" of Cabinet Government, recently discovered by
Mr. Richard Crossman, M.P., and by Professor J. P. Mackintosh
before he left his Chair for the backbenches.)[3] Factors of popularity in the country may influence greatly the selection of our
British "President," but the field is narrowed by one process
alone, a career in the House of Commons.

"The second function of the House of Commons," continued
Bagehot, "is what I may call an expressive function. It is its office
to express the mind of the British people on all matters which
come before it. Whether it does so well or ill I shall discuss. . . ."
He then spoke of a "teaching function. A great and open council
of considerable men cannot be placed in the middle of a society
without altering the society. It ought to alter it for the better. It
ought to teach it what it does not know. . . ." And, penulti-
mately, there was "the informing function . . . that to some

1. I have taken some sentences and adapted some paragraphs of this essay, by
permission of the publishers, from my *The Reform of Parliament*, 2nd ed.
(London, 1968).
2. This and the following quotations from Bagehot are from *The English
Constitution*, ed. R. H. S. Crossman, Fontana Library ed. (London, 1963), pp.
150–153.
3. *Ibid.*, and J. P. Mackintosh, *The British Cabinet* (London, 1962).

extent it makes us hear what otherwise we should not." Perhaps we would now roll all these together, and purge the slightly moralistic Victorian tone, calling these expressive, teaching, and informing nerves of government the "communications function."

"Lastly," Bagehot concluded, "there is the function of legislation, of which, of course, it would be preposterous to deny the great importance, and which I can only deny to be *as* important as the executive management of the whole state, or the political education given by Parliament to the whole nation."

Bagehot puts the matter well. He does not claim too much. We may question how well Parliament fulfils these functions, particularly considering the very few new strengths that Parliament has gained since his day, and the very many the executive has gained; but that it fulfils some of them is beyond question. The tendency is more and more for governments to deal directly with the electorate, but Parliament is still the essential intermediary with considerable power to determine the issues on which elections will be fought. The whole life of Parliament adds up to this much at least. I will now consider Bagehot's five points, reducing them in modern terms to three: the prime minister as chief executive; the communications function; and the legislative function.

The Prime Minister as Chief Executive

It is now clear that neither Sir Ivor Jennings' description of the British system as "Cabinet Government" nor Lord Morley's famous description of the position of the Prime Minister: *primus inter pares*—perhaps best translated as "top dog among champions"—is adequate. He is now a creature different in kind, not merely status, from the other party chieftains in the cabinet. For the prime minister, as well as being leader of the government as a collective body, is now undisputed leader of the majority party. The heart of the matter is that after 1867 the prime minister has become more and more the choice of the electorate; no party can afford to recognize a leader, however able an administrator or parliamentarian, who does not appear to be the best man to lead the party at a general election. And he is the man who controls the nominations to all other offices including the honorific patronage: if the Queen is still the Fount of Honour, he is the tap who controls and directs the flow. It becomes ever more apparent that patronage is the key to his day-to-day power over his followers, and not his famous right to obtain a dissolution when he requires it. For dissolution as a weapon for disciplining his own followers could never in fact have been any less clumsy than a boomerang with its risks of striking down the whole party. Thus Morley's description is too weak, and so is his phrase "the Prime Minister is the keystone of the Cabinet arch." He is not merely the keystone, but the foundation stone and cement for all the other stones as well. He appoints his colleagues, he holds them together, and his reputation must carry the cabinet and the party forward to victory at the next election. And he controls the party machine as well; even careers in the party organization depend ultimately on his positive blessing.

For as long as the prime minister carries with him the conviction of the party that he will get them victory again, his power remains almost absolute. He may have difficult colleagues with such a following in the country that they cannot be excluded from the ministry, even from the cabinet; but inclusion can be a device for muzzling a rival, and far more effective than exclusion. The rival thoroughbred is chained by the doctrine and practice of collective responsibility and is likely, if he does resign, to earn some general detestation for "rocking the boat" or for being a *prima donna* when there is plainly only room for one. For the prime minister alone decides who takes what posts, and some posts are clearly more helpful than others in furthering—or not —a colleague's public reputation. He need not even be faced with continued dissent within the privacy of the cabinet room. For he controls the agenda. Nothing is raised which is not on the agenda and nothing finds its way on to the agenda which has not been raised with the prime minister beforehand and premeditated by him. He may even forbid papers or policy memoranda to be circulated by cabinet ministers among each other if they appear to grind some axe contrary or unwelcome to his purposes —as Chamberlain did on several occasions.[4]

The former Lord Home, then Foreign Secretary, put the matter fairly clearly:

Every Cabinet Minister is in a sense the Prime Minister's agent—his assistant. There's no question about that. It is the Prime Minister's Cabinet, and he is the one person directly responsible to the Queen for what the Cabinet does.

If the Cabinet discusses anything it is the Prime Minister who decides what the collective view of the Cabinet is. A Minister's job is to save the Prime Minister all the work he can. But no Minister could make a really important move without consulting the Prime Minister, and if the Prime Minister wants to take a certain step the Cabinet Minister concerned would either have to agree, argue it out in Cabinet, or resign.[5]

But "argue it out" may make even this half-truth another understatement. The modern cabinet does not normally settle down happily to long discussions of alternative policies, let alone of "first principles"—as is the received picture of Asquith's stimulating, turbulent, but collectively ineffective cabinets. It normally registers decisions which are practically settled and coordinates their implementation (and the members resign themselves to the fact that many of the most important decisions of foreign policy, defense, security, and budgetary matters will have been made in their name by the prime minister without the least thought of prior and collective consultation). This change of the cabinet from a political decision-making body to an instrument of administrative coordination has been made possible and accelerated by the great and continued development both of standing committees of the cabinet (such as Defense, Home Affairs, Economic Policy, Future Legislation, Foreign Policy, and Atomic Energy) and of *ad hoc* committees which are constantly being set up to report on particular problems. Needless to say, the prime minister appoints and selects these committees, they consult with him before anything goes up to cabinet, and he either takes the chair himself at their meetings or sees to it that they are guided by one

4. See Mackintosh, *op. cit.*, p. 395.
5. See the *Observer*, September 16, 1962.

of his most trusted colleagues: there exists informally, at every stage, an "inner cabinet."

The evidence is great that the cabinet no longer makes policy and that, in any case, little reliance is to be put on the old concept that the cabinet represented a kind of coalition of the diverse forces in a great party and was, therefore, in itself an effective check on the powers of the executive. As Mr. J. P. Mackintosh, M.P., puts it:

> . . . a successful, strong and opinionated Prime Minister can put his impress on a whole government. . . . The Cabinet falls into place as a forum for informing his colleagues of decisions that have been taken. In these circumstances it is very hard for a Minister who begins to have doubts to intervene with effect. He has insufficient knowledge, he is always too late, and is contending with the Prime Minister and the men whom the latter has elevated to a position of trust. And when decisions have been taken, there is little that can be done, except protest in the secrecy of the Cabinet, or resign.[6]

Examples of resignations since 1945 do not suggest that the power of a prime minister is shaken even when such rare events as the resignation of a Bevan or a Thorneycroft take place. Certainly, cabinet ministers can take part in the final stages of a revolt to replace a leader who has already lost the confidence of a clear majority of the parliamentary party that he can lead them to victory come the elections. But his authority must already have been diminished by failure before this is likely to take place. There are several examples of the Conservative Party's being able to get rid of a leader in this century, but in none of them is it likely that the revolt began in the cabinet.[7] Revolt is possible, as the events of October, 1963, showed, but even there the power of the retiring prime minister to influence the choice of his successor appears to have been unexpectedly great. For a revolt to be fully successful, there must be already a widely accepted heir-apparent.

The system of prime minister leading a party and administering through a cabinet (which is not a group of colleagues as

6. Mackintosh, *op. cit.*, p. 420.
7. See Robert McKenzie, *British Political Parties,* 2nd ed. (London, 1963), esp. chaps. ii, iii, x, xi.

much as the focus of the network of committees that he controls) is not necessarily a bad system. It has obvious advantages over many other systems of government in strength, stability, and flexibility. It is far from beyond all control even at the moment, even on the bleakest reading of the decline in Parliament's influence. The need for the prime minister to carry his party with him is a very real restraint when all have to work the ship together in foul, as well as fair, weather. When Mr. Macmillan was struggling to keep control of his party, Mr. T. E. Utley reminded his fellow Tories that: "A Conservative M.P. should at all times have an almost overwhelming pre-disposition in favour of supporting his Parliamentary leader," but that "this extraordinary measure of trust is rendered tolerable only by the Leader's acceptance of his Parliamentary supporters"; and since "loyalty" is itself one of those "convictions" (not mere *opinions,* note), it is "a thing to be honoured not exploited."[8]

But all restraints from within the governing party suffer from at least three obvious and inherent defects as substitutes for parliamentary control. Firstly, they work in private, amid secrecy and rumor far from the public eye; events may be important, so reports will appear in the press, but rarely can anyone feel confidence in their accuracy and relevance—thus public understanding even of *how* we are governed suffers. Secondly, they are so informal as well as secret that they place an extraordinary need for honesty on politicians, both to deal openly with each other and to report accurately the findings from "soundings"—the way the Conservatives chose a new leader, before they were forced into holding proper elections (in 1965), is only the most obvious case. And thirdly, they may work against the public interest and may even prove corrupt now that the economy can be so easily managed in the short run—for a party collectively is likely to think what no one member of it would think individually: that nothing is more important than re-election.

From the very virtues of British government we must return to our point that if the basic check on any British government is the

8. See T. E. Utley, "The Tory Tradition: Leader's Duty Towards His Followers," a long letter in the *Daily Telegraph,* July 25, 1963.

general election, then that election must be seen as a continuous campaign, beginning on the first day of each new Parliament, in which the factors most relevant to its conduct are the procedures and practices of Parliament—the permanent hustings.

The Communications Function

The shaping of public policy and the relationship between Parliament and the electorate is essentially a problem of communications and influence—not of constitutional law and power, as the older books used to have it, nor of more (or possibly less) direct public participation, as many politicians and journalists in Great Britain now begin to argue.[9] Only in the last few years have we begun to see this in Britain, both as a subject for research and as the basic conceptualization of public policy. The owl of Minerva, the Goddess of Wisdom, it is well known (as Hegel said) "only flies at dusk." Economic and social self-doubt now create the conditions for thought. What President Lowell of Harvard once called "a certain condescension in the English" is now less apparent in what was once our pre-eminent ability, politics. No longer is it so easy to take for granted that tradition somehow will always, as even Bagehot thought, spontaneously adapt old institutions to new circumstances. To be specific: it is hard for even the most conservative to believe that in this century the institutions, conventions, and behavior of Parliament have adapted themselves spontaneously and subtly to match both the obvious and vast growth in the power and size of the Government and the administration and the habits of mind that go with it.

Even our justified pride in the stability of British government, its continuity and strength compared over a period of time with any other system, is mixed with more than a little surprise that it has not, for all its efficiency, been more effective in dealing with Britain's economic problems. We know what the system of gov-

9. See my "'Them and Us': Public Impotence and Government Power," *Public Law*, Spring, 1968, pp. 8–27, and also the editorial article, "Participation, Priorities and Planning," *Political Quarterly*, October–December, 1968, pp. 357–365.

ernment can do. As Samuel Beer reminds us, we waged a total war, when it came to war, and the Nazis did not.[10] The "decadent parliamentary system" was in fact capable of mobilizing and planning the resources of its economy and the energy of its people for the purposes of war to a degree unmatched by even the professedly totalitarian powers. But in peacetime it seems in danger of failing either to mobilize that same energy or to make the hard and unpopular, but rather obvious, decisions necessary to deal with the relatively small, but grimly recurrent, "balance of payments problem": to reallocate national resources between consumption and investment, import and export.

The two great problems must, in fact, be seen as one, not as two: Parliamentary control of the executive—historically conceived—has never been the enemy of effective and strong government in Britain, but its primary condition. Only in recent years has Parliament been neglected by the government as a device, in Beer's telling phrase, for "mobilizing consent." We in Britain have been misled by our very pride in Parliament and by an unrealistic theoretical language into a quite unpolitical and unhistorical view of the Constitution as a balance between Parliament and the executive as rivals. Any long view of British history shows that the Parliament arose, not just in opposition to the powers of the crown—the Whig or modern Liberal theory—but as the instrument through which the ancient powers of the crown (now that of the "prime minister in cabinet") could become even more effective and strong in a commercial and industrial civilization in which real power became more and more dependent on the willing and active consent of more and more people. In Britain we need to make pregnant again the oldest platitudes of our constitutional history: that we have never had government *by* Parliament, except possibly for a brief and exceptional period between about 1850 and 1867, but always government *through* Parliament.

The system, quite simply, needs to be seen as a system: things

10. In his essay "The British Legislature and the Problem of Mobilizing Consent," *Lawmakers in a Changing World*, ed. Elke Frank (Englewood Cliffs, N.J., 1966).

are as we see them. Parliament has to be seen as part of a practical, working system of government. To abstract "the glories of Parliament" or "the problem of parliamentary control of the executive" from the carrying on of government is false and unrealistic. Neither can be changed, spontaneously or deliberately, without involving consequences, often unexpected and unwanted, in the other. As Professor A. H. Birch has suggested, in his recent book *Responsible and Representative Government,* there is a theory and language of "Westminster" which talks in terms of *representation, control,* and *democracy;* and there is a theory and language of "Whitehall" which talks in terms of *responsibility, power,* and *administration;* but either, taken alone, is false and misleading. Rationalization will follow when this conceptual schizophrenia is overcome, not before.

The British system of government has been uniquely stable because it has been able to combine strong government and strong opposition—effective parliamentary and public criticism. The government legislates and the two Houses criticize and publicize. There is no point in trying to go back, as a few "romantic reactionaries" (in all three British parties, let it be said) have urged, to the almost mythical mid-Victorian days of "the rights of the private member" (a period, in fact, of about ten years of governmental instability in the 1850's). But neither is there any point in schemes to strengthen the efficiency of the British executive (in the managerial function and reforms of composition and training in the civil service—all of which are underway) which ignore the role that Parliament must play, as the feedback between the executive and public opinion. Governments must govern, but they govern better if subject to a kind of scrutiny and criticism which is in fact performed at the moment by Parliament, but only in an excessively piecemeal, random, and unsystematic manner. For a long time "parliamentary control," realistically conceived, has meant not the threat of overthrowing the government in the House, but the process of informing the electorate; of influencing the government by inquiry, debate, and scrutinizing the administration; and the indirect—but powerful—effect all this has on the electorate. Fundamentally, Parliaments are to be seen not as governments, nor as rivals to governments, but as political communication systems linking governments and electorates. (And this—may it be implied?—makes some aspects of British government more interesting to countries plagued with governmental instability than does the perhaps too obstructive or democratic United States Congress.)

Mr. Crossman put the matter with great candor in the Debate on Reform of Procedure of December, 1966:

Procedurally we still behave as though we were a sovereign body which really shared with the government in the initiation of legislation. The House of Commons has largely lost the three functions for which its procedures were evolved, and to which they are relevant. The making of Ministries, the initiation of legislation shared with the Cabinet, and the watch-dog control of finance and administration. It is no good trying to reform ourselves by harking back to ancient days. An effective reform must be an adaptation of obsolete procedures to modern conditions and to the functions we should fulfil in a modern highly-industrialised community. Today, for example, it must be the electorate, not the Commons, who normally make and unmake governments. It must be the Cabinet that runs the Executive and initiates and controls legislation. And it must be the Party machines that manage most of our business, as well as organising what was once a congeries of independent back-benchers into two disciplined political armies. Since this is the structure of modern political power, the task of the reformer is to adapt our institutions and procedures to make them efficient.[11]

Let me come down to institutional earth: in Britain at the moment there is more theoretical disagreement—and doubt—about the true function of Parliament than there is practical disagreement about the kind of changes needed if Parliament is to adjust its procedures, largely unchanged in essentials since the 1900's, to these vast changes in the power and size of the executive.

It seems that four types of change or adjustment are now slowly underway: (1) a decrease in the amount of time the House of Commons spends in consideration of legislation (which

11. House of Commons, *Debates*, December 14, 1966, cols. 479–480.

is going to be introduced and passed anyway, by virtue of parties with programs winning majorities in general elections) and an increase in both the amount of time it spends examining and publicizing the broad outlines of future legislation and policy, and the amount of time it can spend (particularly by select-committee procedure) examining the efficiency and effectiveness of the day-to-day administration of the country;[12] (2) the creation of facilities to enable individual M.P.'s to participate in these processes more fully and be more fully informed, most important of which is the rapid expansion of the Research Division and the graduate staff of the House of Commons Library into something recognizably like an American State Legislative Reference Service;[13] (3) the turning of the House of Lords into a genuine upper house of scrutiny for and to the Commons, that is, to do those things which the busy Commons leaves undone, rather than to presume to censure those things which it ought not to have done —a functional division of powers, more than an historically comic one;[14] and (4) the increase in the experience, adaptability, and flexibility of the higher civil service by the stepping up of the amount of horizontal mobility between it and other professions. Most people say that they are concerned with entrance qualifications and internal training in the civil service, but these considerations are derived from an unstated preconception—that bureaucracy means the settled expectation of being in the same job for forty years.[15]

The nineteenth-century reforms of the franchise were relatively simple: social crises took on, at least superficially, the almost purely and narrowly constitutional shape of franchise reform as in 1832 and 1867. But Britain is now, as nearly everyone

12. See my "Slow New Deal With an Old Pack," *Reform of Parliament,* chap. ix, which contains references to the recent reports of the Select Committee on Procedure.

13. See David Menhennet, "The Library of the House of Commons," *Political Quarterly,* July–September 1965.

14. See "Possible Changes in Functions and Procedure," Appendix II of the White Paper, *House of Lords Reform,* Her Majesty's Stationery Office, November, 1968, Cmnd. 3799.

15. See generally the report of the Fulton Committee, *The Civil Service,* Vol. I, Her Majesty's Stationery Office, June, 1968, Cmnd. 3638, esp. chap. iv, "Mobility, Pensions and a Career Service," and chap. viii, "The Civil Service and the Community."

admits,[16] in the middle of another kind of crisis—one quite as great but much less clearly formulated and quite impervious to any great legislative stroke: a seeming loss of energy in business and commerce; a widespread acceptance of economic planning, but confused and fragmentary application; and deep worries about the availability and use of knowledge. Many of these problems appear to be ultimately related to the class structure and more immediately to the educational system, which we are then oddly reluctant to involve in politics (as if it had ever been independent of politics). These problems are quite as real as anything in the decades before the two great Reform Bills: the polity could founder on them, or certainly run down to an intolerable level of bicker, inflation, and emigration.

The problem is the social problem of making existing knowledge available and preparing people for their involvement in new economic policies; it is not a problem of lack of the right kinds of knowledge. The British system does find difficulty in bringing together experts in the professions and occupations in the political processes of administration. It is profoundly important to see that distinctions between pure and applied knowledge, between politics and administration, and between expert, political, and public opinion are all ultimately relative, not absolute. The British assumption is that any small group of people of different skills and backgrounds involved in a common problem and meeting together is worth a multitude of experts in administration demarcating functions on paper. Parliamentary changes thus become a way of incorporating scientists, and specialists of all kinds in the processes that go to make political decisions. But another British instinct has all too often been to try to keep these things "out of politics"—which only means frustrating the things themselves and narrowing politics to the kind of unfocused, general debates in which the House of Commons far too often indulges

16. There is now a "Matter of Britain" literature almost as large and sometimes as embarrassing as the "Whither America?" literature. See, especially, Max Nicholson's *The System: The MisGovernment of Modern Britain*, London, 1967); the collection of essays edited by myself, *Essays on Reform* (London, 1967); and references to other such books in the opening paragraphs of William A. Robson's "The Fulton Report on the Civil Service," *Political Quarterly*, October–December, 1968.

itself. And some Tories still believe that communication takes place spontaneously—or would if all these experts and people happened to be gentlemen and still joined the old clubs—whereas some radicals have mistrusted formal meetings and too much gregariousness as the way in which rational plans get watered down and compromised. Even among the soberest Labour left-wingers, there is a germ of that disease which has become virulent among the new student socialist leaders—a raging distrust of all institutionalization as such.

But this is to anticipate. "The executive mind" on both sides of the House has little patience with even the existing opportunities of parliamentary participation in the process of government. One thinks (to take worthy examples) of the procedural reforms of Attlee's 1945–1950 administration, all being aimed simply to put through government business more quickly, and of his later counsel to M.P.'s in a Fabian Society journal not to waste much time on work for individual constituents, for "Government Departments deal, I think, with cases on their merits, and intervention by an M.P. is often quite unnecessary." The mind boggles at an American president even wanting to say such a thing.

But to some extent this kind of thing is endemic to government. A little pride in their own ability and a little indifference to control and criticism is part of the confidence needed to govern at all firmly a complicated and individualistic country. But this proper pride of office has grown toward extreme limits in Britain owing to the conjunction of four circumstances: first, the very success, stability, and continuity of British parliamentary government since at least the Glorious Revolution; secondly, the mutual aid between the new public schools and the reformers of the civil service in the 1860's to create a professional but gentlemanly administrative *elite*—not so much non-political as above politics; thirdly, the growing habit of the civil service to consult directly with, and to attempt to compromise with, all major pressure groups affected before ever legislation comes before Parliament; and fourthly, the great effect of the two world wars on British administration, strengthening their prestige, increasing their size, and seemingly validating even their disputable characteristics:

secrecy, discretion, high-handedness, and freedom from detailed parliamentary control.

These attitudes usually combine a great public-spiritedness with a considerable distrust of the actual public and, above all, a dislike of publicity. (The public only appears to them in the rather misleading form of the representatives of organized interests—whether of business or of trade unions.) Hence, such different things as the concentration of the administrative class in Whitehall, rather than its dispersal over provincial towns; the strong taboo on identifying policy-makers by name in the press; and the lack of realistic studies of administration by either political scientists (denied access) or civil servants (who do not see the need).

All this constitutes heavy interference along the communication waves between Parliament, the public, and expert opinion, which otherwise is the probable direction of both administrative and parliamentary change. Another powerful interference is the habit of "keeping things out of politics." In this century it has meant, for instance, the replacement of the late nineteenth-century parliamentary select committee, as an instrument of advice and investigation on current social problems by either departmental committees of civil servants or by the many types of advisory committees with independent chairmen, hybrids of civil servants, and our strange race of private "public servants"—the Lords and the Knights of academia, the professions, commerce, and industry.

Great issues are inevitably political. Even if both parties decide to try to keep an issue out of politics, it is unlikely that this will produce more realistic advice and more information than the traditional select committee procedure. For there witnesses appear, make their report, but are examined searchingly by a committee aware of political factors (that is, whether people are likely to tolerate particular solutions) and the committee can then, if necessary, produce a minority report as well. It is impossible to divorce political considerations from planning, so the best way to include political considerations is to include the experts and specialists at politics—who are politicians; just as the best way to include scientific considerations is to include scientists rather than to read popular science magazines.

But institutional change, let it be remembered, rarely follows from conversion to "bright ideas," but from changing political needs. Within the Labour Party two such political factors are currently emerging. The first concerns the parliamentary party: the restiveness, even boredom and discontent, of many of the government's own supporters in Parliament at the traditional role of the backbench M.P. Partly as a spontaneous product of social change, partly as Wilson's deliberate remaking of the image of the Labour Party, the last two elections have brought into the House far fewer retired trade-union officials, happy just to be an M.P., and far more young professional men, teachers, technologists, businessmen, doctors, and even nine previous university teachers. And, what is more, they have friends, acquaintances, and contacts in specialized fields; they know where to go for expert advice. These new men cannot all be absorbed into government jobs. They are eager to do something beyond waiting for an infrequent turn to speak on the floor or to ask a question. They are a source of trouble within the government party when their sense of public service and importance is frustrated. They are almost unanimous in thinking that Parliament should create a comprehensive system of specialized committees, like many other legislatures, though not to formulate policy, but to scrutinize, investigate, and criticize the working of the administration. They are unlikely to be satisfied with token gestures.[17]

The second political factor concerns Labour as a government and is far more profound and important. It is nothing less than this strange disparity between the stability, efficiency, and self-confidence of the machinery of government and its ineffectiveness, under Conservative and Labour alike, in solving Britain's economic problems and in changing popular attitudes to work. With no fear of political defeat in Parliament, with a superbly talented civil service, and with a highly centralized administra-

17. See "Three Dozen Parliamentary Reforms by One Dozen Socialists," the special supplement to *Socialist Commentary* (a very middle-of-the-road to right-wing Labour monthly), July, 1964, and a volume of essays by newly elected Labour backbenchers, *A Radical Future*, ed. Ben Whitaker, M.P. (London, 1967).

tion, successive British governments have seemed incapable either of formulating new economic policies to deal with the balance of payments crisis or of influencing popular behavior.

Why is this? It is possible to believe in an excess of a virtue, and the virtue is that of consultation and conciliation. It is now a long-established practice (I would say a convention of the Constitution) for the civil servants in the ministries to consult at the very earliest stages of the formulation of policy or the drawing-up of new legislation with all organized interests who might be affected; they do this regularly and thoroughly. In some respects the political results are excellent; governments are not caught by surprise at unexpected opposition from industry or the unions; and very often essentially political compromises can be made before ever the bill becomes public and debated in Parliament. Businessmen like this system, so do the union leaders; they like being consulted and feel that they are able to drive a more realistic bargain with the government directly than if they had to rely on advocacy by M.P.'s in public debates or even on committees.

This is, of course, a form of representation—as Samuel Beer (whom I here follow) has argued: informal, functional representation appears to arise alongside the formal, geographical representation of the constituencies. But two doubts arise: first, the compromises may be excessive, and ministers and civil servants, in always dealing privately with the representatives of organized interests, may have become unduly pessimistic about their own room for maneuver in relation both to the interests and to the people the business or union leaders claim to represent. (It is quite clear that these leaders are often far from representative on every issue that comes up, but that, even so, it is convenient to deal with them because the ministries have no other way of discovering what might happen if they do this or that.) And, secondly, this kind of informal, functional representation tends to be accepted by the political leaders as a fixed datum; it helps them to lose whatever confidence they have left that they can influence events by influencing popular opinion. They are loath to speak above the heads of the leaders of pressure groups to the members of the groups and also to the still vast working public who are not represented nor even misrepresented in this way.

If this diagnosis is even partly correct, the remedy that Parliament could offer is obvious: select committee procedure applied to many of these problems would, with its examination of witnesses and publication of their testimony, be a way of establishing how representative the spokesmen of pressure groups in fact are and how much importance their ordinary members actually attach to *being* members. Much of the agitation for specialized committees among M.P.'s at the moment is on account of the suspicion that pressure groups have an improper influence upon Whitehall and can usually, in the British system, afford to ignore Westminster. But the future will lie not in attacking pressure groups as such, but in the rather obvious discovery that M.P.'s are more likely than civil servants to identify which pressure groups are politically useful and which not, to sort out, with their greater political experience, the representative from the unrepresentative.

Parliament, however, does more than that; it is a device for preparing and influencing public opinion as well as for representing it. Historically this could be shown—the great, innovating prime ministers of the nineteenth century used Parliament as a way of being heard by the nation. Even today, amid the great and often quite independent importance of radio, television, and the mass-press, these media treat Parliament at least as the focus of political news; they are astonishingly respectful toward it. In recent years governments, by neglecting the machinery of Parliament, have in fact neglected their own main means of communicating directly with the public, not just negotiating with those who claim to represent organized groups among the public.

Perhaps, indeed, it is a general truth that all legislatures are primarily devices to mobilize and organize consent and are communication centers between governments and populations, far more than they are devices to choose and destroy governments. To give one concrete example: the attempt to have a national wages and incomes policy in Britain in 1965 was agreed to by leaders of industry and the unions. They assumed, and the gov-

ernment assumed, that they could carry their members with them
—no such thing. It is now said that there should have been more
"preparation of public opinion." Some of us thought at the time
that we were being realistic, not naive, in arguing that that was
just what Parliament was there for. One cannot, to amend Bagehot, make men work by Act of Parliament—but only by persuasion and example.

There is a political, a theoretical, and a sociological conclusion.
The first is that political events will force (indeed are forcing)
some "reforms" on the government and may force them to make
these reforms politically palatable: to increase the speed with
which legislation is considered, but to increase occasions and
facilities for scrutiny, investigation, and publication. Second is
the fact that the more M.P.'s come to see that all these problems
are related, the more informal changes are likely to follow. A
change in the way M.P.'s understand what they are in fact doing,
however inadequately, is more important than whole cargoes of
evidence on procedural gimmickry. Thirdly, more specialists and
experts need to be involved with M.P.'s (the experts on conciliation), together informing themselves and (however indirectly)
the public through the press.

Perhaps it is this third conclusion that takes us closest to the
very heart of the changing British scene. All of us in Britain know
how to spell out the details of the conclusion: more research
assistance for select committees, more time for the press to read
and review parliamentary papers before they are published, an
expanded Westminster "counter-bureaucracy"—or rather complementary bureaucracy—to Whitehall, and so forth. All this is
very obvious, dull, and intricate in detail. But, basically, "informed circles" arise and widen themselves through rubbing
shoulders with people in other vital but almost fantastically distinct vocations and occupations, not just through reading books,
reports, and abstracts. William Sampson concluded in his (John
Gunther-like) *Anatomy of Britain* that we do not have "a power
elite," but several rather different and mutually exclusive elites.
So the sociological prophecy is not that Parliament will involve

more V.I.P.'s and I.B.P.'s (Impossibly Busy People) as consultants in advisory committees, but that the profession of government (I mean the civil service) and the profession of politics will begin to follow what is beginning to happen in other professions: an increase in "horizontal mobility."

Knowledge is disseminated by the contact and circulation of informed people more than by the writing of books—to this extent the old English Tory theory of government, with the Tory stress on men rather than measures, was right. But the theory comprehended the wrong people, and the Tories' prestige corrupted the few of the right people who ever came their way. It was easier for a "new man" to become a "gentleman" than for a gentleman to become a new man.[18] Their reputation for ability and wisdom depended largely on their ability to maintain silence —unflappable because ineffable. What may now be slowly emerging is a circulating and highly mobile elite that is a product of a common educational system, and all of whose knowledge, all of whose concerns, at some stage passes through or before Parliament and is broadcast by Parliament. This is the safest, the most efficient, and effective context in which the government of a democratic and political mass industrial society can be carried on.

The Legislative Function

It should be plain from the above, and from Bagehot's order of priorities, that Parliament's legislative function, in the strict sense of conceiving, shaping, amending, rejecting, and accepting bills, is far less important than that of the United States Congress. And, what may seem more surprising, is that there is no serious body of political opinion in Britain which thinks that it should be radically otherwise. All important legislation is government legislation and, with very few exceptions, goes through without sub-

18. As the novels and the career of Lord Snow so well illustrate; contrast his Grammar School snobs in Cambridge as social ideals with G. B. Shaw's "new man," Mr. Henry Striker, from the "Poly" in *Man and Superman*.

stantial amendment—outright defeat is politically inconceivable
and withdrawal phenomenally rare.[19]

Over a century ago, Palmerston complained that "we cannot go
on filling up the statute book for ever." He has been proved
wrong. Even from 1900 to 1965 the pages of new statutes have
increased, despite the great use of delegated legislation, from 202
to 1,187 pages. But amendments and government defeats have
grown steadily less (they were few even then), and private
members' bills have declined in numbers drastically. Even so, the
House spends about half its time considering public bills, a figure
remarkably constant throughout the century. The suspicion is not
that backbench M.P.'s want more time to deal with important
legislation, but that the government is happy to keep them at
it—in conditions where party discipline is at its height—but
dislikes more time being given to general debates, particularly
emergency debates, where damaging things can be said which
may filter down (particularly intra-party dissension) to public
opinion.

The House is beginning, however, to get away from its fixation
with spending so much time on important legislation, which it
cannot in fact control, to get away from pretending to be prominently a legislature, to interesting itself more in the formulation
of policy at the pre-legislative stage and in the scrutiny of legislation at the post-legislative stage. Or, to put the matter more
subtly, they are beginning to take a wider view of legislation.
When a bill comes to the floor it is already cut and dried to be an
act; but what factors influence whether or not a bill ever emerges
from Whitehall and Downing Street? And what do the administrators and the courts make of it afterwards?

It is at this point that the tendency, not to be exaggerated, but
nonetheless the tendency, of procedural reforms of the last few

19. Ronald Butt, the chief political correspondent of the *Sunday Times* has
recently argued, *inter alia,* in an otherwise brilliant and scholarly book, that
backbench pressures within the government party have, of recent years, achieved
some notable and major amendments—but all his examples are drawn from the
closing years of the Macmillan administration, when the government was plainly
in decline, and they would, anyway, seem small beer compared to the routine of
Congress. Ronald Butt, *The Power of Parliament: An Evolutionary Study of the
Functions of the House of Commons in British Politics* (London, 1967).

years become important. The House is equipping itself better to study the processes of administration from which the need for legislation emerges, and also to follow through the consequences of legislation which, after all, usually result in subsequent amendment or in new legislation as conditions change. The legislative process, in its broadest sense, is nearly the whole of modern politics; it is surprising that the opposition and the government backbenchers at Westminster have been content for so long to limit their major commitment of time to the formal stages of the passing of fully drafted bills into fully predictable acts. Broadly speaking, the "Crossman reforms" of the last session have traded a swifter passage of legislation and a greater predictability by the government of the timetable of the House for more occasions for general debate on the floor and for the establishment (although on other grounds too) of more specialized committees.[20] And the committees thrive and gradually increase their powers, even though none directly considers legislation. But their influence on future legislation and on the whole character of administration, though again the changes must not be overstated, increases.[21]

Recently, the Select Committee on Procedure devoted a whole report to public bill procedure.[22] It recommended many minor changes, the most important of which were to take much minor legislation off the floor and put it to committee, to urge that some bills should be taken by select committees (which can examine witnesses, not simply debate like the standing committees on bills), and to argue that the government should put more state-

20. The new ones since 1964 are Science and Technology, Agriculture, and Education (even though a cloud at the moment hangs over Agriculture); a previous Scrutiny Committee now is given much greater powers to look at the whole field of delegated or subordinate legislation, and a Race Relations Committee is being established. The great fields of Foreign Affairs, Defense, Economic Affairs, and the Home Office are still protected, but the feeling is that slowly but surely a comprehensive system will emerge.

21. See Nevil Johnson, *Parliament and the Administration: The Estimates Committee, 1945–65* (London, 1966); David Coombes, *The Member of Parliament and the Administration: The Case of the Select Committee on Nationalized Industries* (London, 1966); "Ministerial Control of the Nationalized Industries," *First Report from the Select Committee on Nationalized Industries, 1967–68,* 3 vols., H.C. 371: and generally, Harry Hanson, "The Purpose of Parliament," *Parliamentary Affairs,* Summer, 1964; *Parliament and the Executive* ed. H. Victor Wiseman (London, 1966), his introductory essay; and D. N. Chester, "The British Parliament—1939–66," *Parliamentary Affairs,* Autumn, 1966.

22. *Sixth Report from the Select Committee on Procedure,* H.C. 539, 1967.

ments of legislative intent ("Green Papers") before the House prior to actual bills. But it did not add up to anything like a consistent theory of Parliamentary influence in the processes of public legislation. A recent book, the only book for many years, on the legislative process of Parliament concludes:

However, when and if the complex question of Parliamentary reform reaches an outcome, the position will never be regained—nor should it —when Parliament can be termed in any but the broadest sense a legislature. The legislative process in Britain is first and foremost an executive process, and this it will, and should, remain. Parliament has many virtues and many capacities, particularly those associated with a wide and varied membership, an ability to reflect electoral fears and wishes, and to represent to a government the "state of the nation." Its capacity for detailed work of a specialist kind, is, however, necessarily limited by the capacity and experience of its members; it is far greater than most Ministers and civil servants would credit it with, and rather less than some Parliamentary reformers wish to believe. But policy needs to be developed and legitimized by the activity of an informed and representative assembly. To advocate changes that would ensure this is not to advocate Parliamentary dominance of what is and should be an executive function. It is, however, to attempt to add a realistic and powerful political dimension to the work of government. That is what Parliament exists for; that is what it often finds difficult to do at present.[23]

23. S. A. Walkland, *The Legislative Process in Great Britain* (London, 1968), pp. 103–104.

Chapter 3

Parliament in Canadian Society*

Allan Kornberg

The Problem

In a recent paper, John C. Wahlke suggested that the continued vitality of democratic institutions and processes largely is dependent on the maintenance within a society of a certain level of psychological satisfaction with the existing political mechanisms.[1] Data derived from recent public opinion polls suggest that Canadians are neither particularly enchanted with their existing national political mechanisms nor with the individuals who operate them. For example, in 1964, 45 per cent of a national sample of the population expressed the opinion that Parliament was doing a "poor job" in dealing with problems facing the country, whereas only 16 per cent said that Parliament was doing a "good job."[2] Two years later, another query indicated that 70 per cent felt that "political favoritism and corruption" in Ottawa "are increasing" or "about the same," whereas only 10 per cent

* This is a revised version of a paper presented at the Legislative Services Planning Conference, Planting Fields, New York, December 8–10, 1967. I am grateful to Mr. Erik Spicer, the Parliamentary Librarian, Canadian House of Commons, and to Mr. J. P. Joseph Maingot, Law Branch, Canadian House of Commons, for their kindness in providing me with data on the disposition of public bills in the Canadian House of Commons. I am also indebted to Professor Roman March and to Professor John Meisel and his associates, Professors P. E. Converse, M. Pinard, P. Regenstreif, and M. S. Schwartz, for making data which result from studies that have not yet been published available to me. Although I am grateful for their invaluable assistance in the preparation of this paper, I naturally absolve them of any responsibility for the manner in which their data are used here. Any errors of fact or interpretation are my own.

1. John C. Wahlke, "Public Policy and Representative Government: The Role of the Represented," a paper prepared for the Seventh World Congress of the International Political Science Association, Brussels, September 20–31, 1967.
2. Canadian Institute of Public Opinion Survey, December 17, 1964.

said these were "decreasing."[3] Although, as will be indicated, high status individuals generally have been members of the Canadian House of Commons, the public ascribes little status to the position of M.P. Thus, 75 per cent of a national sample polled in 1956 said they would not run for Parliament if they were nominated by a party; the proportion unwilling to run for Parliament increased to 81 per cent a decade later.[4] Nor does the public ascribe status to politics as a profession. For example, when asked whether they would like to see their son make politics a career, only 13 per cent of a national sample in 1953 said "yes"; this proportion rose to 15 per cent in 1961 and to 25 per cent in 1965. But, at no time, did less than 60 per cent say they would prefer a profession *other than politics* for their sons.[5]

However, the mere fact that the public may not like what a particular government is doing, or that they may not ascribe prestige to the legislative position, does not, in itself, imply that they are dissatisfied with the existing political institutions and processes per se. For, as Wahlke also says, "Citizens are apparently able to dislike something or other about the actions of government and at the same time support its continuation institutionally unchanged."[6] He points out, for example, that 41 per cent of a sample in a Midwestern city said, in 1961, there were things Congress had done they did not like. Only 20 per cent, however, thought any proposals for changing Congress should be given serious attention.[7] If Wahlke is correct in his view, it would seem (at least on the surface) that Canadians not only dislike certain

3. Canadian Institute of Public Opinion Survey, April 16, 1966.
4. Canadian Institute of Public Opinion Survey, November 20, 1965. On the other hand, a 1965 national sample of Canadians who ranked 204 occupations in terms of their prestige, ascribed considerable status to members of Parliament. In fact they receive a score of 84.8 and members of the Senate receive a score of 86.1. These scores compare very favorably with those given other high status professions such as lawyers (82.3), physicians (87.2), and university professors (84.6). Thus Pineo and Porter were led to remark "We may question, therefore, the view that what has been described as a decline of political skill in Canada can be attributed to a 'relative loss in the attractiveness and prestige of politics as compared to other vocations.'" See Peter C. Pineo and John Porter, "Occupational Prestige in Canada," *Canadian Review of Sociology and Anthropology*, IV (1967), 29. The position that politics is not as attractive or prestigeful as other occupations is taken by John Meisel, "The Stalled Omnibus: Canadian Parties in the 1960's," *Social Research*, XXX (1963), 386.
5. Data supplied by the Canadian Institute of Public Opinion.
6. Wahlke, *op. cit.*, p. 39.　　　　　　　　7. *Ibid.*, p. 40.

actions of their government but also are deeply dissatisfied with their political institutions; a majority (52 per cent) of a national population sample recently indicated they wanted a government to remain in office for a fixed period of time, even if it lost the "confidence" of the House of Commons. This would entail a major constitutional change in the Canadian parliamentary system. A fixed term of office for the executive is a characteristic one normally associates with American presidential government. A few months earlier, 53 per cent said that two, rather than the current four parties, would be better for Canada.[8] During the previous year, the majority of another national sample (54 per cent) had indicated that minority governments in a parliamentary system were bad for the country.[9]

Given Canada's respected status in the community of nations and the fact that the national government neither has involved them in disastrous and nationally debilitating foreign entanglements nor failed to meet at least the basic social and economic needs of significant domestic groups, the question arises as to why Canadians should express such profound dissatisfaction with their parliamentary system.[10] In this paper, I shall try to suggest

8. Canadian Institute of Public Opinion, April 2, 1966, and July, 1966.
9. Canadian Institute of Public Opinion, October 23, 1965.
10. In a paper delivered at the thirty-ninth annual meeting of the Canadian Political Science Association, Ottawa, June 9, 1967, titled, "The Political Outlook of Canadian Voters in the November 1965 Election," Mildred Schwartz has written,

> The severest indictment of the federal government is delivered for its differential treatment of voters. About three-quarters of our sample think that at least some of those in the highest level of government pay more attention to big interests rather than to the ordinary voter. For these questions we have comparable data from a Survey Research Center survey in the United States. Unfortunately, the wording of this particular question was not identical in the two countries. Yet it is still noteworthy that only over one-quarter of a national sample of Americans, interviewed after the 1964 election, responded in terms of the government being run for a few big interests. Over half the Canadian sample feel that quite a few of the people running the government do not know what they are doing. This compares with about one-quarter in the United States, again indicating the extent of disillusionment in Canada.

(Other data from the study to which Professor Schwartz refers are cited later in this study.)

However, another Canadian scholar, David Hoffman, has questioned whether Canadians *really are* deeply disaffected and disillusioned with their parliamentary institutions. Rather, the evidence from a study of the social and political attitudes of Ontario adults carried out by Professor Frederick Schindeler and him seems to be mixed. Thus, although a majority (53 per cent) of the respondents disagreed

at least a partial answer by evaluating the manner in which the Canadian Parliament performs its basic tasks. These are subsumed under the rubrics "representation," "legislation," and "control." I assume that what it does and how it does it are not unrelated to public attitudes toward Parliament. I also assume that, unlike the British Empire of the nineteenth century, political institutions do not stand in splendid isolation from the social systems of which they are a part. Thus, I also will delineate certain salient social-political characteristics that both affect, and are affected by, Parliament. Specifically, these are population patterns, elite groups, federalism, the electoral system, the party system, and the ubiquitous presence of the United States. Finally, I shall try to suggest how some specific problems of the Canadian Parliament may be conceptualized as a more general problem of political development.

Canadian Society—Population Trends

Like the United States, the current population of Canada is derived from a polyglot of ethnic groups, the largest of which is the Anglo-Scotch-Irish. Unlike the United States, a substantial proportion of her approximately 21,000,000 people are of French descent. The cleavage between French-speaking and English-speaking Canadians, according to one student of comparative politics, is the most important characteristic of Canadian society and "bulks larger than any division south of the border."[11]

Since the majority of French-speaking Canadians always have lived in Quebec, the cleavage (although it has been manifest in other regions as well) generally has been between that province and the rest of Canada. It has its roots in the British conquest of

---

with the statement that "once they are elected members of Parliament continue to pay attention to those who have elected them," only 27 per cent agreed (as opposed to 69 per cent who disagreed) that "most of the time you cannot trust the government to do what is right." Further, another 49 per cent tended to agree with the statement that "public officials care what people like me think"; 45 per cent tended to disagree. (Private communication from David Hoffman, January 14, 1969.)

11. Leon D. Epstein, "A Comparative Study of Canadian Parties," *American Political Science Review*, LVIII (1964), 46–59.

Quebec in 1760. Although, in the years following, an English-speaking elite largely displaced and/or excluded their French-Canadian counterpart in commerce, the military, and public life; French culture, rather than being extinguished, survived and flourished because the British colonial authorities permitted the French to control their educational system; to retain their language, civil laws, and customs, and not only permitted them to worship freely, but also re-established the statutory authority of the Catholic church to tithe.[12] The legitimacy of the French culture, thus, was immediately established and through the socialization opportunities inherent in the educational process, it was passed on to succeeding generations.

Also of importance in *la survivance* was an almost phenomenally high French-Canadian birth rate. According to one demog-

Table 1. *Distribution of the Canadian Population by Major Ethnic Groups, 1871–1961*

	Time periods		
Ethnic background	1871–1901	1902–1931	1932–1961
Anglo-Scotch-Irish	58.8%	54.0%	47.1%
French	30.6	28.2	30.5
Other	10.6	17.8	22.4

Source: 1961 Census of Canada, Population: Ethnic Groups.

rapher, world population during the last 200 years has multiplied by three; European by four; and French-Canadian by eighty.[13] Thus, despite the fact that immigration from France virtually ceased after 1760, the proportion of the population that is French-Canadian has remained relatively constant since the establishment of the Dominion of Canada in 1867. (See Table 1.)

With respect to other major European ethnic groups in the

12. See Richard Coupland, *The Quebec Act: A Study in Statesmanship* (Oxford, 1925); A. L. Burt, *Guy Carleton, Lord Dorchester, 1724–1808, Revised Version* (Ottawa, 1960); and O. D. Skelton, *Life and Letters of Sir Wilfred Laurier* (New York, 1922), Vol. I.

13. Jacque Henripin, "From Acceptance of Nature to Control: The Demography of the French-Canadian Since the 17th Century," *Canadian Journal of Economics and Political Science*, XXIII (1957), 10–19.

population, the rate at which they have increased has been uneven, varying with periods of heavy immigration. For example, the proportion of Polish- and Ukrainian-Canadians increased almost three-fold (2.96) from 1921 to 1941, but the proportion of Italians increased only by 1.69 during the same interval. Conversely, the size of the latter group quadrupled during the period from

Table 2. *Distribution of Major Ethnic Groups by Region, 1961*

Major European groups	Proportion of total population	Proportions distributed by region			
		Eastern[a]	Quebec	Ontario	Western[b]
Anglo-Scotch-Irish	43.8%	72.1%	10.8%	59.5%	48.6%
French	30.4	18.7	80.6	10.4	6.1
Eastern Europe (Yugoslav, Polish, Ukrainian, Russian)	5.4	.4	1.3	5.6	11.6
Central Europe (German, Austrian)	6.3	2.9	.9	7.0	12.8
Northern Europe (Danish, Swedish, Norwegian, Icelandic)	2.1	.6	.2	1.0	6.2
Southern Europe (Italian, Greek)	2.8	.3	2.4	4.8	1.4
Holland	2.4	1.8	.2	3.1	4.0
Jewish[c]	1.0	.1	1.4	1.0	.6
Others	5.8	3.0	2.7	7.6	8.7
Total number	18,238,247	1,897,425	5,259,211	6,236,092	4,808,075

a. Eastern region includes the provinces of Newfoundland, Prince Edward Island, New Brunswick, and Nova Scotia.

b. Western region includes Manitoba, Saskatchewan, Alberta, and British Columbia.

c. It is, of course, a matter of some dispute whether Jews are an ethnic group. In the present analysis, it is assumed that they do constitute a distinct ethnic group.

Source: 1961 Census of Canada, *Population: Ethnic Groups*, Table 35.

1942 to 1961, whereas the Polish-Ukrainian population increased only 1.68 times during that interim.[14]

As is indicated in Table 2, the members and descendents of the

14. 1961 Census of Population, *Population: Ethnic Groups*, Table 34. The proportion of Italian immigrants continued to rise during the period 1961–1965. In fact, they constituted fully 19.4 per cent of the immigrants entering Canada during that time. For the period 1946–1965 they made up 14.8 per cent of the 2,504,020 immigrant arrivals, second only to the 33.2 per cent coming from the British Isles during that time. For an intensive analysis of post-war Canadian immigration patterns see Anthony H. Richmond, *Post-War Immigrants in Canada* (Toronto, 1967). Source for above data is Table I.1, p. 5.

major ethnic groups also are disproportionately distributed geographically; they are almost entirely absent in the four Easternmost provinces and are overly concentrated in Western Canada and/or the major urban centers of Ontario. More important than the geographic, is their distribution within the several categories of education, income, and occupation. Available data[15] reveal that (other than the Jews[16]) they generally tend to be overrepresented in the lower educational, income, and occupational strata of the population. The French, unlike their fellow charter group members, the Anglo-Scotch-Irish, also tend to occupy the lower rungs of the educational, income, and occupational ladders.[17] In Quebec an archaic "classical" educational system, geared to the needs of a traditional doctor-lawyer-clerical trinity, until recently helped perpetuate both the subordinate position of the masses and the existing pattern of rigid social stratification.

The political consequences of such social-economic arrangements both in and out of Quebec are readily apparent. As numerous empirical studies have established,[18] an individual with low education, income, and occupation is less likely to have a generalized interest in and awareness of politics, or to participate in the

15. John Porter, *The Vertical Mosaic: An Analysis of Social Class and Power in Canada* (Toronto, 1965).

16. Porter also treats Jewish-Canadians as an ethnic rather than as a religious group. He finds they are probably the best educated group in Canadian society, and like the Anglo-Scotch-Irish, they also are disproportionately represented in the high income occupations, particularly, the professions. As Porter points out, however, these acquired characteristics have not provided the Jews, as they have the Anglo-Scotch-Irish, with access to positions of power and influence in Canadian society. Canada is probably unique in the Western world in that Jews are strikingly absent in the higher levels of the intellectual community, including the academic (p. 501).

17. In a recent paper, Anthony Richmond tested Porter's thesis with hitherto unpublished census data for metropolitan Toronto. He found that "generally speaking, the evidence confirms Porter's view of the association between ethnicity and occupational status. The British and Jewish groups are more heavily represented in the higher status occupations. Those of French origins are underrepresented in the professional and managerial categories." With respect to income, he ranked males of all ages by ethnicity and mother tongue and found that Jewish, British, and German males were in the top income categories, whereas French, Ukrainian, and Italian males were in the bottom. See Anthony H. Richmond, "Ethnic Origin, Occupational Status and Income in Metropolitan Toronto," a paper presented at the meeting of the Canadian Association of Sociology and Anthropology, Calgary, June 6–7, 1968.

18. These findings are conveniently summarized in Lester Milbrath, *Political Participation* (Chicago, 1965), pp. 110–128, and Robert E. Lane, *Political Life* (New York, 1959), pp. 220–234.

recruitment, election, and demand-input aspects of the political process. Canadian political elites historically have been able to exploit ethnic cleavages, but rarely have had to play the game of ethnic politics. That is, other than the French, Canadian political leaders have never had to "physically" recognize ethnic groups by allocating substantial numbers of party, public, and other office positions to them; to provide verbal gratification by articulating issues and by taking positions that are of concern to ethnic groups per se; or to make the other kinds of psychic pay-offs their American[19] counterparts have had to make in turn for the disproportionate voting support of particular ethnic groups.

Insofar as the French of Quebec are concerned, public and high party office at both the provincial and national levels until very recently have tended to be virtually monopolized by the aforementioned doctor-lawyer-clerical trinity who, like the Bourbons of the American South,[20] have skillfully manipulated the potential threat to existing social-cultural arrangements posed by the presence of an external group (the English, in this instance) to maintain their favored position in the social structure.[21]

Although both components of population growth, natural increase and net immigration, have been of considerable importance during Canada's one hundred year history, the former has contributed more heavily to growth than the latter, principally, because the United States always has been extremely attractive to newly arrived European immigrants. Even after American immigration laws had become relatively rigid, large numbers of immigrants to Canada remained only a short time before emigrating to the United States. One estimate of population for the period from 1946 to 1956 put immigration at approximately 3,000,000 and emigration to the United States at 300,000.[22] Exam-

19. See, for example, Nathan Glazer and Daniel P. Moynihan, *Beyond the Melting Pot* (Cambridge, 1963). The comparative impact of ethnicity on political life in Canada and the United States is more fully developed by Joel Smith and Allan Kornberg, "Some Considerations Bearing upon Comparative Research in Canada and the United States," *Sociology,* III (1969), 341–357.

20. See V. O. Key, *Southern Politics in State and Nation* (New York, 1965).

21. This point is extensively developed in J. A. A. Lovink, "The Politics of Quebec: Provincial Political Parties, 1897–1936" (unpublished doctoral dissertation, Duke University, 1967).

22. A. H. LeNeveu and Y. Kashara, "Demographic Trends in Canada, 1941–1956, and Some of Their Implications," *Canadian Journal of Economics and Political Science,* XXIV (1958), 10.

ining these population trends, Porter[23] has compared Canada to a kind of giant demographic railway station that receives immigrants on the one hand, and produces emigrants, both native-born and "birds of passage" (i.e., those stopping over in Canada on their way to the United States), on the other.

The Distribution of Power

In his provocative analysis, remarkable for its power and clarity, John Porter has argued that power within Canadian society is exercised in great part by a number of small, easily defined, and frequently overlapping elite groups in the economy (corporate and labor), public bureaucracy, political system (legislature and judiciary), mass media, academic, and religious communities. Of these, both the most powerful and the most important politically, are the corporate, mass media, bureaucratic, and political elites. All (particularly, the corporate elite)[24] have certain characteristics in common: they tend to be disproportionately of Anglo-Scotch-Irish descent; they tend to be members of high-status Protestant churches; they tend to be the sons of upper- and middle-class fathers; and they tend to be graduates of a small number of select private schools and Eastern Canadian universities. They tend, also, to be informally linked, both internally and across groups, by ties of kinship and friendship. More formal linkages are through common membership on commissions, boards, councils, and through career interchange.

With respect to career interchange, Porter found that although there are few members of really wealthy Canadian families who

23. Porter, *op. cit.*, p. 35.
24. The Canadian corporate elite is certainly not unique in this respect. The American corporate elite, for example, shares many of these characteristics and is also linked formally and informally by kinship, friendship, common organizational membership, etc. See, for example, A. A. Berle and Gardiner C. Means, *The Modern Corporation and Private Property* (New York, 1933). See also the series of monographs published by the temporary National Economics Committee, *Concentration of Economic Power* (Washington, 1939–1941); E. Digbee Baltzell, "'Who's Who in America' and 'The Social Register': Elite and Upper Class Indexes in Metropolitan America," in *Class, Status and Power*, ed. R. Bendix and S. M. Lipset (Glencoe, 1953), pp. 172–184, and *The Protestant Establishment: Aristocracy and Caste in America* (New York, 1964); and W. Lloyd Warner and James Abegglen, *Big Business Leaders in America* (New York, 1963).

actually make their way into the political elite,[25] there is close liaison between the two major political parties, the Liberal and Conservative, and the corporate elite. Most frequently, the lawyers in the corporate elite provide the link; they are the most likely members of the corporate elite to have overt political affiliations (equally divided between the Liberal and Conservative parties), to have held elected or appointed public office, and to have held top offices in the provincial and national party organizations.[26]

There has been considerable career interchange between the bureaucratic and political elites, certainly insofar as the movement of bureaucrats into the political arena is concerned. Even if they do not take formal political positions, however, there is ample evidence to suggest that the federal bureaucracy has had an exceedingly important influence on the political elite. Thus, Porter writes: "It is generally accepted by students of Canadian government that the senior public service has had a crucial position in the overall structure of power, particularly after the appointment in 1932 of W. C. Clark, an Economics professor from Queens University" (pp. 425–426).

Of Professor Clark, R. Taylor Cole[27] has said: "Dr. Clark was the center of a small coterie of Deputy Ministers and of permanent and temporary 'civil servants' and officials, mostly economists, who constituted the inner spring of the governmental mechanism in Canada and largely determined its economic policies from 1939–1945."

25. The present leaders of the Liberals and Conservatives, Pierre Elliot Trudeau and Robert Stanfield, respectively, are conspicuous exceptions.

26. Data derived from a 1967 comparative study of the political socialization and recruitment patterns of party leaders in metropolitan Vancouver, Winnipeg, Seattle, and Minneapolis carried out by the author and Joel Smith tend to support Porter. They show substantial differences in the social origins and current life status of officials of the two "major" (Liberal and Progressive Conservative) as opposed to "minor" (NDP and Social Credit) Canadian parties. For example, 42 per cent of the former but only 23 per cent of the latter officials were raised in homes which, by the standard of the time, could be considered "above average" or "very well off"; the fathers of 51 per cent of the Liberals and Conservatives but only 33 per cent of the NDP–Social Creditors were "professionals," "managers," "proprietors," and "officials"; 53 per cent of the major and 29 per cent of the minor party officials were educated beyond the high school level; and 63 per cent of the former and only 37 per cent of the latter reported annual family incomes of over $10,000.

27. See R. Taylor Cole, *The Canadian Bureaucracy* (Durham, N.C., 1949), p. 269.

With respect to the interaction between economists and cabinet members, John Meisel[28] has written that the Liberal party leaders "appeared mesmerized by the cult of the Gross National Product." He went on to show that the 1957 Liberal party election platform was generated not by the party organization in the electorate or by the Liberal parliamentary caucus, but rather, by certain high level bureaucrats.

The potentially undesirable consequences inherent in a situation in which senior positions in a public bureaucracy are systematically employed as vehicles for entry into the political executive and in which the elite in the bureaucracy so identify their own interests with a particular party that the party's policies as well as public policies are both formulated by them (the bureaucratic elite) rather than by party and elected officials has been commented upon by interested scholars[29] and by certain members of the bureaucratic elite as well.[30] That the power of bureaucratic officials extends beyond policy-making to policy-execution is well known and requires no elucidation here.

Although there has been a far smaller incidence of the kind of career interchange among mass media and political elites, the former always have had remarkable access to and influence upon the latter. In great part, as Porter points out, their influence is a function of the generalized role of the mass media as articulators of the official ideology—an ideology that provides the justification for on-going economic and political institutions and processes. In part, it stems from the concentration of ownership in Canada of the daily press, radio, and television (but not the magazines, which tend to be American), and the pattern of generational continuity of that ownership. Successive generations

28. See John Meisel, "The Formulation of Liberal and Conservative Programmes in the 1957 Canadian General Elections," *Canadian Journal of Economics and Political Science*, XXVI (1960), 571.

29. See J. E. Hodgetts, "The Liberal and the Bureaucrat," *Queen's Quarterly*, LXII (1955), 176–83; and "The Civil Service and Policy Formation," *Canadian Journal of Economics and Political Science*, XXIII (1957), 467–479.

30. See John Deutsch, "Parliament and the Civil Service," *Queen's Quarterly*, LXIII (1956), 565–573. For a description of the growth of the national bureaucracy see Jacques M. Des Roches, "Evolution of the Organization of the Federal Government in Canada," *Canadian Public Administration*, V (1962), 408–427. The manner in which the members of this elite perceive their roles is suggested in J. H. Bieler, R. M. Burns, and H. W. Johnson, "The Role of the Deputy-Minister," *Canadian Public Administration*, IV (1961), 352–373.

of great publishing families such as the Siftons and Southams always have supported the two major parties, and the conservative, brokerage, and *status quo* politics to which these parties are (presumably) oriented.[31]

Finally, career interchange among elites is not an asymmetrical process. Although the incidence is smaller, there also is movement from the political to the corporate and bureaucratic worlds. After doing a stint in politics, members of the political elite at times take or return to top positions in the corporate and administrative bureaucracies.

Implicit and frequently explicit in the above criticisms by Porter and other scholars are three basic themes. First, the demand-inputs that flow into Parliament, or rather those to which Parliament is attentive,[32] come disproportionately and, in fact, almost exclusively from a very small and narrow segment of the population. Second, and relatedly, the policy decisions that Parliament makes disproportionately reflect the interests of this small elite. Third, the proponents of policies from outside of Parliament and those who ratify and legitimate (in the form of legislation) these proposals within Parliament frequently are the same individuals even though their roles may be analytically distinct.

Canadian Political System—Federalism

As a consequence, in part, of the American experience with federalism, the framers of the British North America Act of 1867 allocated formidable powers (general, express, and residual) to the national government. The latter also was to exercise concurrent jurisdiction with the provinces in Agriculture and Immigration, the federal power prevailing in the case of conflict. As well,

---

31. See Porter, *op. cit.*, pp. 458–490.

32. A 1965 study of the Canadian electorate by John Meisel and his associates affords some empirical evidence in support of this claim. In response to the question, "Do you think that all people who are high in government give *everyone* a fair break, whether they are big shots or just ordinary people, or do you think some of them pay more attention to what the big interests want?" only 15 per cent of the interviewees said government gives everyone a fair break. The majority (74.5 per cent) said government pays attention only to big shots.

the governor general in council (cabinet) seemingly was given the power to unilaterally define the extent of the national government's jurisdiction through a grant of power to disallow "offensive" provincial legislation.[33]

In contrast to the power allocated the national government, the provinces were given only sixteen express powers "of a merely local or private nature in the Province" (Section 92:16). Despite this unequal distribution, the provincial governments not only have not become mere ciphers, but indeed, they probably exercise more power vis-à-vis the national government than do the states in the American federal system.[34] The expansion of provincial powers usually has been explained by the tendency of the Judicial Committee of the Privy Council to loosely interpret the provincial right to legislate "Property and Civil Rights." The increasingly vociferous claims made by French-Canadian nationalist elements (and the willingness of party leaders to discuss at least the more moderate proposals) that at a minimum Quebec enjoys a kind of special constitutional status, and at the other extreme that there is not one, but, in fact, two Canadas, Quebec and the other nine provinces, also have helped increase the scope of provincial jurisdiction. It is, after all, difficult to deny to nine provinces the revenues from a certain tax field or the power to administer a welfare program and simultaneously to discuss, even in theory, the right of a tenth to negotiate treaties! Further, although no formal constitutional doctrine such as "dual federalism" was ever articulated in Canada, the industrial-financial forces of the late nineteenth and early twentieth centuries tried (as they did in the United States) to circumvent public regulation by pressing upon the judiciary the claim that either the provincial or national governments (depending upon which gov-

33. An interesting collection of essays on Canadian federalism is A. R. M. Lower *et al.*, *Evolving Canadian Federalism* (Durham, N.C., 1958). See also Alexander Brady, "Federalism in Canada," in *Federalism in the Commonwealth*, ed. William S. Livingston (London, 1963), pp. 11–28.

34. A dramatic illustration of the importance of the provinces in the Canadian federal system is provided by data collected by John Meisel *et al.* In response to the question, "As far as you are concerned personally, which government is more important in affecting how you and your family get on? The one in Ottawa or in this province?" 40 per cent of a national sample said their provincial government was more important as compared to 30 per cent who said the federal government was more important. An additional 21 per cent said both were important.

ernment had initiated the legislation) were unconstitutionally
usurping the authority of the other.[35] As it might be expected, the
ultimate result of their efforts was to blur a division of powers
that initially had appeared to be well defined. An increasingly
wide range of public decisions began to be made in political
arenas outside of the national and, as was the case with state
institutions in the United States, once the powers of the provincial governments had been expanded they, quite naturally,
sought both to maintain and to broaden them still more. The
rhetoric of "provincial rights" based upon cultural particularism,
as well as the specter of a monolithic and oppressive national
government periodically were invoked by provincial politicians
and their allies in the corporate and bureaucratic worlds whenever their powers were threatened by the predatory incursions of
the federal government. Thus, not only did the corporate and
bureaucratic elites disproportionately affect policy decisions
made by the national government, they also helped the smaller
and even more permeable provincial governments to acquire
jurisdiction over new substantive areas and to retain their right to
administer fields whose scope and public importance increased
dramatically in a relatively short time.

Among the powers provincial governments have been able to
retain is the right to legislate in the field of education. The result
has been seen as unfortunate for the development of Canadian
education. It has not been democratized in that post-public
school education is still largely a preserve of the wealthy. Further, the system has not been able to disseminate to any significant proportion of the population either the intellectual or the
technical skills required in an advanced industrial society.

For example, a recent analysis by Nathan Keyfitz[36] points out
that, although the extent of schooling has been increasing in both
Canada and the United States, the American increase has been
substantially greater. In fact, the differential between the two
countries is presently such that young Canadians in the 1960's

35. See J. R. Mallory, *Social Credit and the Federal Power in Canada* (Toronto,
1954), *passim*.
36. Nathan Keyfitz, "Human Resources," in *Contemporary Canada*, ed. Richard
Leach (Durham, N.C., 1968), pp. 26–29.

actually are more disadvantaged, in comparison with their American counterparts, than were their countrymen a generation ago. (See Table 3.)

Given the positive association between educational attainment and economic well-being, and their own low socio-economic status, it is not surprising that non-British ethnic groups have suffered the most serious educational loss. Unlike the United States, such ethnic groups have not been able to employ the educational system as a vehicle of social and economic mobility. Thus, a fourth criticism of the political system made by Porter is that the

Table 3. *Educational Attainment of the Male Labor Force by Age Groups, United States, 1960, and Canada, 1961*

Age group	Percentage of labor force with four years high school only		Percentage of labor force having completed university	
	United States	Canada	United States	Canada
Total, 25–34	30.8	8.7	14.7	6.0
35–44	29.5	9.5	11.9	6.3
45–54	20.0	8.5	8.8	5.0
55–64	12.2	7.4	7.0	4.2

Source: Economic Council of Canada, *Second Annual Review: Towards Sustained and Balanced Economic Growth* (Ottawa, 1967), p. 81.

dominant elites through their influence in and on the national government have used federalism as a convenient excuse for not making certain kinds of policy decisions. Parliament, in theory, has the power to initiate and to carry out constitutional changes that would enable it to legislate in areas in which the provinces currently are active. The fact that such innovations rarely have been made is not accidental. It reflects a conscious and deliberate choice to maintain the existing patterns of power in Canadian society. Summarizing the effect of federalism on Canadian politics, Porter has written, "As it has developed, Canadian federalism has imposed a conservative tone on the Canadian political

Allan Kornberg

system and political parties . . . federalism has been for political parties and political elites an important condition for the exercise of their power."[37]

The Electoral System

Until the national election of June, 1968, Canadians, by plurality voting, elected 265 members of Parliament from 263 constitu-

Table 4. *Urban-Rural Distribution of Population[a] and Electoral Polls[b]*

	Population				
	1921[c]	1931	1941	1951[d]	1961
Urban	50%	54%	54%	63%	71%
Rural	50	46	46	37	29
Number	(8,787,949)	(10,376,786)	(11,506,655)	(14,009,429)	(18,238,247)

	Electoral polls				
	1925	1930	1940	1953	1963
Urban	34%	37%	44%	47%	55%
Rural	66	63	56	53	45
Number	(25,143)	(28,124)	(31,983)	(40,742)	(50,386)

a. The census definition of rural-urban population was modified in 1951 to include the whole metropolitan area in the case of larger cities having urbanized or built up areas surrounding the city proper. Only incorporated places had previously been included. In addition, any community of 1,000 persons or more, whether or not incorporated, is included. In 1956 suburban areas of additional major urban centers other than census metropolitan areas also were included.

b. The poll, like the precinct in the United States, is the basic unit of electoral organization. The number within any constituency, of course, varies with the size of the constituency.

c. Based on population living in incorporated areas.

d. Based on 1956 census definition.

encies that apportioned by province, varied in size from tiny (12,000) and completely rural Ile-de-la-Madelaine to sprawling (267,000) and urban York-Scarborough. Although over the years Canadian society has become increasingly urban, a disproportionately large number of constituencies remained rural. Table 4,

37. Porter, *op. cit.*, p. 385.

which indicates that over time the proportion of polling districts that have been classified as rural have greatly exceeded the proportion of population classified as rural, illustrates this tendency. The redistribution of constituencies following the 1966 census corrected many of the gross inequities,[38] but the populations of metropolitan-area constituencies remain, on an average, about 30 per cent larger than the populations of constituencies outside metropolitan regions. Thus, there are still more rural and rurally oriented constituencies than the actual distribution of population warrants. And unlike the situation in most Western countries, Canadian rural constituencies generally have had higher voter turn-out rates and have been more, rather than less, politically competitive than urban areas.[39]

One consequence of this phenomenon is that there is no cadre of rural-based legislators (as there is in the American Congress, for example) with long years of seniority in the Commons. Although M.P.'s representing urban constituencies are blessed with somewhat less vicissitudinous electorates, they also are not likely to acquire much tenure. In fact, Dawson and Ward[40] claim that rarely is the turnover in House membership after a national election less than 40 per cent. Further, they estimate that only 8–10 per cent of any current crop of M.P.'s have had ten or more years of experience in the Commons. March's data tend to support their claim with respect to attrition rates.[41] (See Table 5.) Our own data indicate that in 1962 only 12 per cent of the backbench members had seven or more years of tenure[42] and,

38. For example, Ile-de-la-Madelaine is no longer a constituency and York-Scarborough has been divided so that there are now two constituencies. As well, both two-member constituencies were abolished and the total number of constituencies increased from 263 to 264.

39. See Allan Kornberg, "Some Differences in Role Perceptions among Canadian Legislators" (unpublished doctoral dissertation, University of Michigan, 1964), p. 127. See also Howard A. Scarrow, "Patterns of Voter Turnout in Canada," *Midwest Journal of Political Science*, V (1961), 351–366.

40. R. M. Dawson and N. Ward, *The Government of Canada*, 4th ed. (Toronto, 1963), p. 345.

41. See Roman R. March, "An Empirical Test of M. Ostrogorski's Theory of Political Evolution in a British Parliamentary System" (unpublished doctoral dissertation, Indiana University, 1967). The elections of 1965 and 1968 continued this trend.

42. See Allan Kornberg, "The Social Bases of Leadership in a Canadian House of Commons," *Australian Journal of Politics and History*, XI (1965), 331.

although the equivalent figure for House leaders was 64 per cent,
they (the leaders) were still far less experienced than a group of
congressional leaders of the Eighty-eighth Congress.[43] For example, only 1 per cent of thirty-nine Canadian leaders had nineteen
years or more tenure in the House,[44] whereas fully 72 per cent of

Table 5. *Proportions of New Members by Party, 1872–1963*

Elections	Liberal	Conservative	CCF-NDP	Social Credit
1872–1900	40%	33%		
1904–1930	40	38		(1940–1963)
1935–1963	35	40	38%	34%
Highest Turnover	62 (1896)	62 (1957)	87 (1940)	83 (1962)

an equivalent number of congressional leaders had such experience. Such data suggest that the life of a Canadian member of
Parliament, although it may be happy, is not likely to be a long
one. They may also help explain why the two major parties have
frequently coopted their Parliamentary leaders from the bureaucracy or from the corporate world.

43. With Norman C. Thomas we compared a group of thirty-nine leaders of the
Twenty-fifth Parliament with thirty-nine leaders of the Eighty-eighth Congress.
Our Canadian leadership panel included all national leaders of their parties,
deputy leaders, cabinet ministers, and parliamentary assistants, party whips, and
caucus chairmen who fell within the sample. The American congressional leadership panel included the elective leaders of each congressional party group—majority and minority leaders, whips and caucus or conference chairmen as well as the
speaker of the House—and seniority leaders—chairmen and ranking minority
members of those committees that play a major role in congressional policy-making or that deal with important substantive policy areas and upon which membership is highly desired. We used David B. Truman's criteria for identifying elective
leaders. See *The Congressional Party* (New York, 1959), pp. 94–134, 197–246. In
selecting seniority leaders, we chose those committees which George B. Galloway
classified as *top* and *interest*, omitting the *pork* and *duty* committees. See *The
Legislative Process in Congress* (New York, 1953), pp. 278–279.
　　For a report of this work see Allan Kornberg and Norman C. Thomas, "The
Political Socialization of National Legislative Elites in the United States and
Canada," *Journal of Politics*, XXVII (1965), 761–775.
　　44. A recent study by J. A. Schlesinger tends to support these findings. He
reports that 2 per cent of Canadian cabinet ministers, 1921 to 1957, had twenty or
more years of parliamentary experience and that only 49 per cent had more than
five years of tenure in the House. See Joseph A. Schlesinger, "Political Careers and
Party Leadership," in *Political Leadership in Industrialized Societies,* ed. Lewis
Edinger (New York, 1967), p. 287.

The Parties[45]

The roots of the two major parties are imbedded in the economic and political struggle that took place in the third decade of the nineteenth century.[46] The Conservative party grew out of a United Empire Loyalist (business, professional, established Church) elite which held such a monopoly of the available administrative and judicial offices in the pre-Confederation era that in derision they were termed the *Family Compact* in Upper Canada (Ontario) and the "Chateau Clique" in Lower Canada (Quebec). At Confederation, John A. MacDonald was able to unite these groups with the English economic oligarchy and the ultramontane Catholic hierarchy of Quebec into a Conservative party coalition, which, except for a five year period (1873–1878), was to govern until 1896.

The Liberal party's ancestry goes back to a coalition of anti-Catholic, nonestablished church, and radical reform groups of rural western Ontario, the so-called Clear Grits,[47] with the radical, anti-business, anti-clerical "Party Rouge" of Quebec. Denied victory at the national level, the Liberals concentrated their efforts on the provinces, and by the time they came to power in 1896 they controlled the government of every province but Quebec. In that province, Wilfred Laurier, the future national leader and Prime Minister, broadened the base of Liberal support by transforming the Rouges into a moderate reform party that was palatable to the Catholic Church hierarchy and the traditional doctor-lawyer elites of the small towns.[48]

45. This section draws on my work, *Canadian Legislative Behavior* (New York, 1967).
46. The single best treatment of the origins of Canadian parties probably is Escott M. Reid, "The Rise of National Parties in Canada," *Papers and Proceedings of the Canadian Political Science Association*, IV (1932), 187–200. For excellent bibliographies of the available literature on Canadian parties, see *Party Politics in Canada*, ed. Hugh Thorburn (Toronto, 1963), pp. 168–172, and F. C. Engelmann and Mildred A. Schwartz, *Political Parties and the Canadian Social Structure* (Scarborough, 1967), pp. 255–266.
47. For a biography of a founding father of Canadian Liberalism, see Dale C. Thomson, *Alexander McKenzie: Clear Grit* (Toronto, 1960).
48. An interesting biography of Laurier is provided by Joseph Schull, *Laurier* (Toronto, 1966).

A national convention modeled on the American conventions chose Laurier as the Liberal leader in 1893. A combination of his own political skills, economic prosperity, and the chauvinism generated by the inclusion in the federal union of the new western provinces of Saskatchewan and Alberta kept his Liberal administration in office from 1896 to 1911. His downfall is usually ascribed to the alienation of isolationist elements[49] within his own province (who objected to his proposal to begin building a Canadian Navy) and the loss of important business support in Ontario (because he had championed limited reciprocal free trade with the United States).

The alliance between Quebec nationalism and Ontario anti-Americanism that brought the Conservatives under Robert Borden to power[50] dissolved during the "Conscription Crisis" of 1917. The bitterness of French Canada toward the Conservatives was not dispelled when Borden subsequently retired, and Arthur Meighen, the very symbol of Conscription to many French Canadians, became prime minister in 1920.

In the previous year W. L. Mackenzie King had been elected leader by a national Liberal party convention. The results of the 1921 election suggested that his tenure as party leader and prime minister might be short; the newly formed Progressive party had cut sharply into Liberal prairie strength, electing sixty-five M.P.'s from that area and forcing King to form a minority government. Accordingly, his first years in office largely were given over to resolving the differences between Liberals and Progressives and bringing the Progressives back to the Liberal fold. Apparently such a task was consistent with King's political philosophy. He viewed a party principally as a mechanism for mediating and resolving intergroup conflicts rather than generating policy pro-

49. As a portent of events to come during World Wars I and II, the editorials of the influential *Le Devoir* claimed that Laurier's navy would conscript French-Canadian boys "to maintain at the price of their blood, the supremacy of the British flag in Asia or Africa." Quoted in Bruce Hutchinson, *Mr. Prime Minister: 1867–1964* (Toronto, 1964), p. 139.

50. Certain elements in the Conservative party periodically have manifested the anti-Americanism which was an important pre-condition of Canadian existence. In the elections of 1930, 1957, and 1963 the Canadian-American relationship was an important issue that was successfully exploited by many Conservative candidates.

posals. Thus, R. M. Dawson[51] wrote of him, "He considered that the parties in Canada had two major functions: the propagation and carrying out of ideas and policies, and the bringing together of diverse and even conflicting groups and interests so as to secure a working agreement and a measure of common action. The second function was in his eyes even more important than the first."

Despite his supposed preference for the honest broker role and his reluctance to initiate policy proposals that might generate conflict, the foundation of much of Canada's welfare program was laid during his tenure of office. This program, together with proposals intended to broaden the industrial base of the Canadian economy, were pursued by King's successors during the years from 1948 to 1957. In one respect, it was the insistence of the Liberals (particularly, C. D. Howe) on pursuing what was, in their view, an essential if unpopular industrial policy that led to the famous "Pipeline Debate" and their subsequent defeat in the election of June, 1957.

In that year, John Diefenbaker,[52] a small-town Saskatchewan lawyer, who only had been recently (1956) chosen leader of his party, led the Conservatives to a close victory, and from his colleagues formed a minority government. The next year, largely as a result of his personal charisma, the Conservatives won the greatest electoral victory in Canadian history.

Although the Conservatives suffered so sharp a reversal in fortunes in 1962 that they were again reduced to forming a minority government, they, nevertheless, have generated some important changes in the nature of party representation in Parliament. First, their party that was for so many years dependent on

51. R. MacGregor Dawson, *William Lyon Mackenzie King: A Political Biography* (Toronto, 1958), p. 319. J. M. Beck and D. J. Dooley perceived King only in the role of "broker." According to them, "In King's view a Canadian political leader could not be doctrinaire; he had to balance one pressure group against another, and he had to prevent issues becoming so clearly defined that they caused deep divisions," J. M. Beck and D. J. Dooley, "Party Images in Canada," *Queen's Quarterly*, LXVII (1967), 437.

52. For an interesting, albeit biased, description of Mr. Diefenbaker's tenure as prime minister, see Peter C. Newman, *Renegade in Power: The Diefenbaker Years* (Toronto, 1963).

urban Ontario for its electoral support[53] and that was an anathema to prairie and maritimes voters, now draws its sustenance principally from the latter regions and fares poorly in the former.[54] Second, the Liberals, who for years and with justification claimed to be Canada's only "national" party, can no longer make that claim, since they were virtually annihilated by the Conservatives in the four Western Provinces,[55] and had their parliamentary strength sharply reduced in the maritimes during the period from 1957 to 1965. Although they made substantial gains in the West (particularly in British Columbia) in 1968, the party continued to be weak in the maritimes, winning only seven of thirty-two possible seats.[56] Third, the undisputed hegemony which the Liberals enjoyed in Quebec national politics was disrupted by the Conservatives in 1958. Although the fortune of the Conservatives again has declined in Quebec, a substantial other-than-Liberal vote has persisted from which the Creditistes[57] principally have benefited.

As for the two minor parties, both rose out of the short-lived Progressive party.[58] The first, the Social Credit, under the leadership of William Aberhart, was able to parlay strong support from former Progressives and from members of the United Farmers of Alberta into victory in the Alberta provincial election of 1935. By the end of the depression the party was so well entrenched in that province as to be virtually unopposed in the legislature. Since 1952 it also has formed the government in British Colum-

53. See Lionel H. Laing, "The Patterns of Canadian Politics: The Election of 1945," *American Political Science Review*, XL (1946), 760–765. Laing showed that in both the 1940 and 1945 elections approximately two-thirds of the Conservative M.P.'s were able to win election in constituencies within a radius of eighty-seven miles from Toronto, Ontario.

54. In 1968 the party failed to win even one of the twenty seats in metropolitan Toronto.

55. From 1957 to 1962, when the Conservatives were in office, the Liberals won less than 7 per cent of the parliamentary seats in the four Western provinces. The proportion rose to 12 per cent in the 1963–1965 elections and to 38 per cent in the election of 1968.

56. The Liberals were victorious in 34 per cent of the electoral contests in the maritimes in the 1957, 1958, and 1962 elections. Their proportion of victories rose to 48 per cent during the 1965 elections, but, as indicated above, dropped to 22 per cent in the last election. In contrast, during the years 1926 to 1953 they captured 64 per cent of the seats in these provinces.

57. For example, they were able to win nine seats in 1965 and fourteen seats in the 1968 election.

58. See William Morton, *The Progressive Party in Canada* (Toronto, 1963).

bia. Despite this regional success at the provincial level, the party made virtually no headway nationally until Real Caouette,[59] a small-town car dealer, led twenty-six Quebec "Creditistes" into the House of Commons in 1962. For approximately a year he had appeared weekly on television to reiterate such themes as poverty in the midst of plenty, prosperity through the creation of social credit, the corruption and moral bankruptcy of the two old parties, and the failure of the two old parties to either offer a meaningful choice or to articulate the interests of the people.

This revival of slogans and doctrine which initially had helped make Social Credit successful in the West[60] was somewhat ironic as the Western party leaders had for some time ceased to pay more than periodic lip service to them. Instead, they emphasized the stability and success of their provincial regimes, and at the national level, former Premier Ernest Manning[61] and ex-national party leader Robert Thompson periodically called upon Conservatives to join them in a new and *real conservative coalition*[62] that could successfully oppose the now-socialist Liberal party.

By the same token, although the initial intention of the Co-operative Commonwealth Federation (CCF) was to eradicate the capitalist economic system and to establish a socialist society, this was modified[63] as the party sought to broaden the base of its electoral support and to encourage middle-class participation in organizational activity. Like the Social Credit, the CCF experienced initial success in the West and was able, in fact, to generate sufficient support among rural voters in Saskatchewan[64] to gain control of the provincial government in 1944 and to main-

59. During the next (Twenty-sixth) Parliament, Mr. Caouette and eleven other Social Credit M.P.'s from Quebec split with party leader Robert Thompson and formed a new party, Le Ralliement des Creditistes. During that Parliament, two other Social Creditors left their party and joined the Conservative caucus.
60. See John Irving, *The Social Credit Movement in Alberta* (Toronto, 1959).
61. This position is best articulated in Mr. Manning's recent book, *Political Realignment: A Challenge to Thoughtful Canadians* (Toronto, 1967).
62. Apparently Mr. Thompson grew tired of waiting for Conservatives to join his party, since after the announcement of the 1968 election, he resigned from the Social Credit party, joined the Conservative party, and sought the Conservative nomination for his Red Deer constituency. He not only won the nomination but was victorious in the June, 1968, election.
63. In their 1956 Winnipeg Declaration, the party expressed their willingness to tolerate a "mixed" planned–free enterprise economy.
64. See Seymour M. Lipset, *Agrarian Socialism* (Berkeley, 1950).

tain that control for approximately twenty years. However, they were less successful at the national level, never having elected more than twenty-eight M.P.'s to any House of Commons. In 1961, the close ties between the CCF and organized Canadian labor were formalized, and from this marriage emerged the current New Democratic party (NDP). To date, the only fruit of this union has been the marked increase in support the NDP has received in metropolitan areas. However, they have been able to console themselves with the belief that they pushed a series of reluctant Liberal administrations into passing the bulk of the welfare legislation enjoyed by Canadians.

Despite the fact that Liberal administrations passed these measures, Porter, among others,[65] feels their actions were motivated by opportunism rather than a desire for social progress. In the view of these scholars, Liberal and Conservative party values are basically the same. Both parties are oriented toward business; both perform broker-mediator-conciliator functions; and both, when in office, tend to be political caretakers and administrators rather than innovators. They articulate no clear and/or differentiated goals; they engage in no debates over basic values; they give no meaningful dialogue to which the electorate can attend; and they make no attempt to either educate the electorate or to provide them with the kind of dynamic leadership that could mobilize their creative energy.[66]

In summary, the two major parties in Canada were rooted in the social, economic, and cultural cleavages of the nineteenth century. As Canada grew to include areas not encompassed by the original union of 1867, and became increasingly urbanized and industrialized, a regional protest movement in western Canada evolved into two new parties. The latter two parties have experienced limited success nationally, but have held office for

65. See, for example, Gad Horowitz, "Conservatism, Liberalism, and Socialism in Canada: An Interpretation," in *Party Politics in Canada*, ed. Hugh Thorburn, 2nd ed. (Scarborough, 1967), pp. 55–73. Horowitz writes, "[In the United States] the party of big business is the Republican party. In Canada business is close to both the Conservatives and the Liberals. The business community donates to the campaign funds of both and is represented in the leadership circles of both" (p. 69).

66. Cf. Porter, *op. cit.*, pp. 373–379.

long periods of time in three of the four western provinces. Over time they appear to have changed from parties protesting the established order to *status quo* and/or moderate reform organizations. A kind of political convergence has taken place. On the left, the NDP seemingly has abandoned its goal of establishing a socialist society,[67] whereas the Liberal party, under pressure from the NDP,[68] appears to have moved left on the ideological continuum.[69] On the right, the Western wing of Social Credit has soft-pedaled and largely forgotten the financial panaceas it advocated during the 1930's. Instead, it has become a solidly conservative party that continually "points with pride" to the stability and responsibility of its provincial administrations in Alberta and British Columbia.

If we can extrapolate from Porter's claim that there are few, if any, meaningful differences between the major parties, there would currently seem to be little for the electorate to choose from among the four parties. Despite this, and the periodic spectacular defections of leading Social Creditors, each party has continued to maintain a separate existence. Coupled with the fact that since 1957 neither the Conservatives nor the Liberals have received the massive sustained support from Quebec upon which, historically, their long periods of national dominance were predicated, the result has been a period of minority government. In four of the five national elections between 1957 and 1965, the winning party failed to elect a majority of its candidates to the House of Commons and had to rely on informal coalitions with the minor parties to maintain itself in office.

Such arrangements, as will be indicated in Table 12, are not conducive to passing legislation. Since Parliaments normally have

67. Leo Zakuta, "The CCF-NDP: Membership in a Becalmed Protest Movement," in *Party Politics in Canada,* ed. Hugh Thorburn (Toronto, 1963), pp. 96–108.

68. Horowitz writes: "The Liberals, unlike the liberal Democrats, have not been a party of innovation. As a centre party, they have allowed the CCF-NDP to introduce innovation. They have waited . . . for signs of reassurance against possible electoral reprisals before actually proceeding to implement the innovations" (p. 70).

69. During the Twenty-sixth and Twenty-seventh Parliaments, the struggle within the Liberal cabinet between Messrs. Gordon and Sharp, the respective leaders of the left and right wings of the party, indicated this leftward drift was not being unopposed.

the function of legislating ascribed to them by the public, an inability to legislate may explain why the Canadian public seemingly regards minority government as "bad for the country."[70] In a sense, the inability of Canadian parties to win majorities in four of five elections is a direct consequence of the public's idiosyncratic voting behavior. If Porter's criticism is valid, the fault may lie with the parties themselves, particularly, the major parties and their inability to project sharply different images[71] or to articulate different policies between which the public may choose.

The Influence of the United States

It is not too great an exaggeration to state that the most important dimension of "Canadianism" appears to be "Americanism," pro, anti, and ambivalent.[72] It would be rather extraordinary if politics, the economy, the mass media, the arts, education, indeed, all of Canadian society, were not deeply and continuously affected by the presence of an adjacent society ten times as

70. Meisel *et al.'s* study of the 1965 electorate also revealed the public's concern over minority government. Fully 61 per cent said "it made a great difference" whether or not the party forming the government had a majority of the seats and another 22 per cent said it made "some difference."

71. Empirical data from Meisel and his colleagues' 1965 national election study tend to support this contention. They show, for example, that most electors tend to see both major parties as center parties; approximately 41 per cent saw the Liberals as being at the center of a left-right continuum and 39 per cent saw the Conservatives in the center. Also, virtually similar proportions saw them as being left of center (16 per cent and 13 per cent, respectively) and right of center (33 per cent and 37 per cent, respectively). There also is evidence to support the convergence theory since 34 per cent of the electorate saw both the NDP and the Social Credit as being a center party and, although more people (30 per cent) saw the NDP as left of center, 16 per cent perceived them as a right of center party, a proportion not substantially larger than the 21 per cent who saw the Social Credit party as one to the right of center. Of particular interest is the fact that larger proportions of the electorate perceived both the Liberals and the Conservatives as being more to the right of center than the Social Credit party.

72. See, for example, the continuous focus on the United States in a recent collection of essays on Canadian nationalism in *Nationalism in Canada,* ed. Peter Russel (Toronto, 1966). See also governmental reports such as *Report of the Royal Commission on National Development in the Arts, Letters and Sciences, 1949–51* (Ottawa, 1951); J. Grant Glassco, *Certain Aspects of Taxation Relating to Investment in Canada by Non-Residents,* Royal Commission on Canada's Economic Prospects (Ottawa, 1956), and *Report of the Royal Commission on Publications* (Ottawa, 1961).

large and the premier power in world affairs. With respect to politics, the principal effect has been a slow but continuous trend toward "Americanization." Since 1919, virtually all major party leaders have been chosen by conventions that included not only the parliamentary delegation of the party, but, also, representatives of the party organization outside of Parliament and from the provincial legislatures. The tendency toward American-style national leadership contests was especially pronounced in the vigorous cross-national campaigning, the strenuous fights for delegates, and the complex convention organizations that characterized the selection of Messrs. Stanfield and Trudeau as the new leaders, respectively, of the Conservative and Liberal parties. Interviews with Canadian party officials[73] indicate they are intrigued by what, supposedly, are the most sophisticated American electioneering tactics, as for example, the employment of advertising specialists to conduct campaigns, the extensive allocation of resources to television, the generation of support from para-political "citizens for" groups, the necessity of projecting the "proper" image and of not "peaking" too early in a campaign. Moreover, since history continuously is made in Washington and disseminated at the mass level by *Time, Life,* and *Newsweek,* whereas television daily provides Canadians with vivid impressions of great American power figures, particularly, the President and the major congressional leaders, there is a tendency, a natural one, to compare constantly the operation of the American presidential system of government with the Canadian parliamentary system. Such comparisons invariably flatter the Americans; to the average Canadian the problems with which Canadian parliamentary leaders deal seem petty and their leadership style a pale carbon of the vigor and flamboyance that seemingly characterize top American politicians.[74] It seems reasonable

73. In connection with "A Comparative Study of the Political Socialization and Recruitment of Party Activists in the United States and Canada," supported by National Science Foundation Grant GS-1134.

74. In a series of interviews with young businessmen and professionals in Toronto during 1966, Erwin C. Hargrove found that few could articulate specifically political symbols. Not one mentioned the prime minister, the Queen, or the government. All but two felt the then prime minister, Lester Pearson, was a poor political leader lacking in strength. The majority deplored the fact that Canadian leaders usually lacked color and popular appeal. The late John F. Kennedy had

to assume, although we lack supporting data, that the Canadian dissatisfaction with parliamentary institutions and leaders revealed by public opinion polls is, in part, a function of the invidious comparisons they are forced continuously to make with the American system.

Roles of Parliament

One reason for scholars having devoted so much attention to legislative bodies is that they seemingly are easier to study than the societies of which they are a part; although the subject matter (and hence some "functions") with which they deal changes over time, certain attributes of legislatures, such as communication, structure, and normativeness (the existence of formal and informal rules) are common to all and change very little.

Both the current structure and the formal procedural norms are largely an inheritance from Great Britain and the colonial past. Under the British North America Act, Parliament was to consist of an executive and a bicameral legislature, an appointed Senate and a popularly elected House of Commons. Not unnaturally, the executive was to be the British monarch, whose prerogative powers were to be exercised by the crown's representative, the governor-general. Although even today, in theory, all acts of Parliament are proclaimed and appointments made by the governor-general on behalf of the Queen, in actual practice, executive powers of government have, since 1926, rested in the hands of the prime minister and his cabinet.

As is the custom in a Parliament of the British model, the cabinet formulates and carries out all executive policies, exercises total control over all financial matters, assembles most of the legislative program that Parliament considers, and serves as the political head of the several departments of government. The

influenced them greatly and almost all named him as the modern leader they most admired. See Erwin C. Hargrove, "Popular Leadership in the Anglo-American Democracies," in *Political Leadership in Industrialized Societies,* ed. Lewis J. Edinger (New York, 1967), cf. pp. 201–202.

prime minister, of course, is the head of the cabinet, the leader of the party that was victorious in the last national election, and has his seat, as do all his colleagues but one,[75] in the House of Commons.

The bulk of Canadian parliamentary procedure was transplanted from Great Britain, although, over the years, certain routines have developed that are indigenous to Canada. Procedural norms are functional for maintaining the viability of the legislature as an organization, for regularizing and making predictable the behavior of members, and for enabling the legislature to achieve its goals. Since the Canadian Parliament is of the British model, in effect, its procedures are intended to facilitate the passage of a government's legislative program. We shall deal with this more extensively in analyzing the legislative function of Parliament.

For the present, it should be noted that the Canadian Senate is unique among parliamentary second chambers in that it has retained virtually a full set of legislative muscles, but consistently has refused to make real use of them. That is, the Senate has been extremely reluctant to interfere with the popular will, insofar as that will is expressed by the House of Commons. Although it has done some useful work over the years, two serious handicaps limit its effectiveness. First, the Senate has only a limited amount of serious work at the beginning of a session when legislation has not yet passed the Commons. Then, it is inundated by bills from the House toward the end of a session. Second, most of the work that is undertaken by the Senate is carried out by a small group of no more than fifteen to twenty individuals. Therefore, Senate participation in the Canadian legislative process is sufficiently limited that hereafter we will focus exclusively on the House of Commons and use the terms *Parliament* and *House of Commons* interchangeably.[76]

75. Normally, the leader of the government in the Senate has a place, although not a portfolio, in the cabinet.

76. For an extensive treatment of the Senate, see F. A. Kunz, *The Modern Senate of Canada, 1925–1963: A Re-Appraisal* (Toronto, 1965). See also Henry S. Albinski, "The Canadian Senate: Politics and the Constitution," *American Political Science Review*, LVII (1963), 378–391.

Functions of Parliament

Among the "original" but changed (and changing) basic functions[77] that Sartori[78] ascribes to Parliament, and with which we will now be concerned, are "representation," "legislation," and "control." Under representation we will distinguish, as did Sartori, "representivity" (the social congruence between representatives and their publics) from the "representative relationship" (the interaction between representatives and their publics). The legislative function includes both policy initiation and evaluation, while under control, we subsume both executive and bureaucratic supervision.

Representivity

The question of whether legislators mirror the social characteristics of societies of which they are a part does not become particularly salient until the adults of a particular society begin to participate en masse in the electoral process.[79] In Canada, the universal right to participate in elections is of relatively recent origin. A rather significant proportion of the male population did not vote until 1900, and universal suffrage was not achieved until 1921.[80]

In an intensive analysis of the several Canadian Houses of Commons during the period from 1867 to 1963, Roman R. March found that a significant proportion of the freshmen members of nineteenth-century Parliaments were what he termed "Nota-

77. Malcolm E. Jewell and Samuel C. Patterson have ascribed the following functions to legislatures: conflict management under which is subsumed deliberative, decisional, adjudicative, and cathartic functions; and integration of the polity, which subsumes authorization, legitimation, and representation. See Malcolm E. Jewell and Samuel C. Patterson, *The Legislative Process in the United States* (New York, 1966), pp. 5–25.

78. Giovanni Sartori, "Introductory Report," Round Table Meeting on Parliamentary Government, Bellagio, 1963.

79. *Ibid.*, p. 23.

80. See Norman Ward, *The Canadian House of Commons: Representation* (Toronto, 1950), p. 230.

bles,"[81] and that the proportion of freshmen Notables elected to the several Parliaments has been inversely related to the expansion of the Canadian electorate. Thus, 43 per cent of the freshmen members were Notables during the period from 1867 to 1896 when the electorate was small and property-based. As the proportion of population eligible for enfranchisement rose (1900–1917), the percentage of freshmen Notables elected declined to 21 per cent, and has dropped to 11 per cent since universal suffrage was achieved in 1921.

Although the proportion of Notables may have declined, the Canadian House of Commons now, as then, is an institution whose members are remarkably atypical of a cross section of population, insofar as social status (as measured by principal occupation) is concerned.[82] An analysis of the newly elected members of three nineteenth-century and three twentieth-century Parliaments reveals that a disproportionately large number of Canadian M.P.'s always have been lawyers. Although this proportion is lower than one normally finds in the American Congress,[83] it is considerably higher than in the British House of Commons.[84] Alexander Brady has argued that the number of

81. See Roman R. March, *op. cit.*, pp. 48, 49, 56 (Table II-2). His criteria for classification of members as notables are: (1) the member was the son of a present or a former member of one of the legislatures of the British Empire, or a first degree relative of such a person; (2) the member was a peer or related to a titled ancestor—in the case of a French-Canadian, the member was a seigneur or the son of a seigneur; (3) the member held a commission as an officer in one of the regiments at the grade of lieutenant-colonel or higher; (4) the member was related to a churchman whose rank was at least that of a bishop; (5) the member was related to a justice of one of the superior courts.

82. This is true of virtually all Western national legislative bodies. See, for example, Donald R. Matthews, *United States Senators and Their World* (New York, 1960); Peter G. Richards, *Honourable Members: A Study of the British Backbencher* (London, 1959); Mattei Dogan, "Political Ascent in a Class Society: French Deputies 1870–1958," *Political Decision Makers: Recruitment and Performance*, ed. Dwaine Marvick (Glencoe, Ill., 1961); Henry Valen, "The Recruitment of Parliamentary Nominees in Norway," *Scandinavian Political Studies*, I (1966), 121–166. See also comparative studies such as Harold D. Lasswell, *The Comparative Study of Elites* (Stanford, 1952) and Donald R. Matthews, *The Social Background of Political Decision-Makers* (Garden City, N.Y., 1954).

83. See Matthews, *op. cit.*, p. 26.

84. In their analysis of backbench members of the British House of Commons, 1955–1959, H. E. Berrington and S. E. Finer, "The British House of Commons," *International Social Science Journal*, XIII (1961), 601–605, found that 13 per cent of the 270 backbench Conservative M.P.'s were lawyers. The proportion of Labour M.P.'s who were lawyers apparently is smaller and is contained in the general category "Professional" (31 per cent). Their estimate is supported by Austin

lawyers in any Canadian House of Commons is higher than in the British because Canada, unlike Britain, has never had a governing class with the leisure, interest, or skills required for high public office. Lawyers have served as a surrogate for such a group because they have the requisite skills and because law and politics are apparently congruent professions.[85] Table 6 indicates

Table 6. *Occupations of Freshmen Members of First, Fourth, Eighth, Thirteenth, Twentieth, and Twenty-Sixth Parliaments*

	First Parliament (1867)	Fourth Parliament (1878)	Eighth Parliament (1896)	Thirteenth Parliament (1917)	Twentieth Parliament (1945)	Twenty-Sixth Parliament (1963)
Professional, technical, and kindred workers	44%	51%	49%	48%	48%	56%
Managers, officials, and proprietors except farm	49	41	39	30	25	25
Clerical and kindred workers	3	3	—	—	5	—
Sales workers	a	—	—	2	3	6
Farm owners	4	3	10	15	15	6
Craftsmen, foremen, and kindred workers	—	—	—	2	3	2
Unskilled and service workers	—	—	—	—	—	a
Non-labor force	a	1	2	3	1	4
Lawyers	24	31	22	24	32	29
	(N = 176)	(N = 86)	(N = 106)	(N = 113)	(N = 100)	(N = 48)

a. Less than 1 per cent.
Source: Data supplied by R. March.

other professions also are greatly overrepresented; that the proportion of business executives and proprietors, although still large, has been declining over the years; and that skilled and unskilled workers not only have been grossly underrepresented, but, indeed, have been virtually absent from the several Parliaments.

Ranney, who found that 15 per cent of the Labour and Conservative candidates for the British House of Commons were barristers and solicitors. See Austin Ranney, *Pathways to Parliament* (Madison, Wis., 1965).

85. Although the congruence between politics and law has been cited a number of times to explain the proliferation of lawyers in legislatures, the only extensive and systematic treatment of this empirical phenomenon is that of Heinz Eulau and John Sprague, *Lawyers in Politics: A Study of Professional Convergence* (Indianapolis, 1964).

As might be expected, the same occupational pattern holds for the occupants of formal leadership positions. In a longitudinal analysis of the social backgrounds of Canadian cabinet ministers, 1867 to 1957, Leon D. Epstein[86] found that "of the 275 individuals to occupy Canadian ministerial positions from Confederation in 1867 until the beginning of 1957, no more than six can definitely be categorized as of working-class background." As did March, he found that this distribution held fairly constant over time. "When the data are arranged by ministries, those with working-class, farm, and uncertain backgrounds are represented in roughly the same proportions in each period."[87]

Their educational levels were equally impressive in that 85 per cent of those for whom there are reliable data had university training.[88] Thus, Epstein writes, "It is apparent that only a very few men become Ministers without having had the educational advantage enabling them to secure middle-class status first if they had not been born to such status."[89]

We have no equivalent data with respect to the social origins and the educational levels of all of the nineteenth- and twentieth-century Canadian parliamentarians. Given the intercorrelation of these variables with an individual's occupation, however, and the fact that the education of parliamentary leaders is not significantly higher than that of non-leaders,[90] we may infer that they also have been disproportionately high and unrepresentative of the Canadian population. Support for this inference is obtained by scoring the occupations of candidates for Parliament, 1945–1965, listed in the several *Report of the Chief Electoral Officer* during this period with a scale estimated by Otis D. Duncan.[91] The Duncan scale is a two-digit score ranging from zero to 96 and is a composite of information on occupations, educational attainment, and prestige ascribed to occupations. It pro-

86. Leon D. Epstein, *Political Parties in Western Democracies* (New York, 1967), p. 196.
87. *Ibid.*, p. 197.   88. *Ibid.* See Table 3, p. 198.
89. *Ibid.*, p. 198.
90. Cf. Allan Kornberg, "The Social Bases of Leadership in a Canadian House of Commons," *Australian Journal of Politics and History*, XI (1965), 327.
91. The rationale and method of computing the scores are described in Albert J. Reiss *et al.*, *Occupation and Social Change* (New York, 1961).

vides a convenient and reliable[92] measure of socio-economic status (SES) and permits occupation to be treated as a linear and continuous variable in statistical analysis.[93]

Analysis indicates that the mean SES of a random sample of 4,168 members of the eight Parliaments during the ten year period is a remarkable 60.9.[94] However, the relative status of members varies considerably with the region they represent. In-

Table 7. *Mean Status Scores of Winning and Non-Winning Candidates for House of Commons 1945–1965*

Election years	Quebec		Ontario		Residual area	
	Winners	Non-winners	Winners	Non-winners	Winners	Non-winners
	X̄	X̄	X̄	X̄	X̄	X̄
1945, 1949, 1953	80.0	58.2	66.6	52.7	55.4	51.0
1957, 1958, 1962	73.1	69.3	68.9	59.5	59.0	55.1
1963, 1965	71.5	62.9	73.9	62.1	60.1	58.2
	(N = 407)	(N = 783)	(N = 391)	(N = 904)	(N = 492)	(N = 1,191)

dividuals with the highest status represent constituencies in the province of Quebec, while somewhat less prestigious members represent Ontario and the other provinces (what is termed *residual area* in Table 7). Not only have the actual members representing Quebec been a more prestigious group, but also the losing candidates from that province generally have had higher mean

92. In a report of a study of the prestige ascribed to occupations by popular opinion in the United States, Great Britain, New Zealand, Japan, the Soviet Union, and West Germany, Alexander Inkeles found that despite cultural differences occupations were ranked in a relatively standard hierarchy. See Alexander Inkeles and Peter H. Rossi, "National Comparisons of Occupational Prestige," *American Journal of Sociology,* LXI (1956), 329–339. That the scale is appropriate for scoring Canadian occupations is indicated by Bernard Blishen who, in describing a Canadian occupational class scale he subsequently constructed, said, "Rank correlations were computed between the ratings of occupational prestige in each of these countries (studied by Inkeles and Rossi) and the scale under review. The highest ranked correlation, 0.94, was found between Canada and the U.S." See Bernard Blishen, "The Construction and Use of an Occupational Class Scale," *Canadian Journal of Economics and Political Science,* XXIV (1958), 523.

93. For a multivariate analysis in which the Duncan scale is employed, see Allan Kornberg, "Parties as Recruiters in the Canadian Parliamentary System," a paper delivered in 1966 at the annual meeting of the American Political Science Association held in New York.

94. This figure probably is somewhat conservative because many members of the Parliament elected in 1945 still were in Canada's armed forces. The latter occupation received a low score in the Duncan scale, so the 1945 figures are artificially depressed.

status scores than losing candidates from other provinces. This was the case during the Liberal party's "salad days" in office (1945–1956); during the Conservative era of Mr. Diefenbaker (1957–1962); and during the two Liberal minority governments of 1963 and 1965. (See Table 7.) Thus, these data would seem to support the claim that high public office in Quebec has been virtually monopolized by a small traditional elite.[95]

Although there is little doubt as to their socio-economic unrepresentativeness, Canadian members of Parliament seem to reflect the distribution of ethnic-religious characteristics in the Canadian population more adequately. For example, March found that 30 per cent of 2,050 freshmen members of the first twenty-six Parliaments were Roman Catholic, 57 per cent were affiliated with major Protestant denominations, and somewhat less than 1 per cent were of the Jewish faith.[96] In a study of the Twenty-fifth Parliament,[97] the author found the members even more representative of the ethnic-religious character of Canadian society in 1961 than did March. Further, this was also true of the leadership of the House. Their representativeness with respect to these two characteristics is dramatically illustrated if we compare them with thirty-nine leaders of the Eighty-eighth Congress. (See Table 8.) Moreover, Canadian leadership posts were fairly evenly distributed among members from the several geographic regions, whereas, in contrast, the majority of American leadership positions (given the operation of the seniority system) were held by Southern and Midwestern congressmen.

Finally, in terms of age, the Canadian parliamentary leaders overrepresented the middle-aged portion of the Canadian population over twenty-one, but, again, they were more representative of the age distribution of their society than were congressional leaders of American society. For example, 44 per cent of the Canadian leaders were fifty years of age or less, 49 per cent were

95. The success of Real Caouette's Creditistes has been interpreted as a protest by low status groups against this elite domination. See, for example, Hubert Guindon, "Social Unrest, Social Class and Quebec's Bureaucratic Revolution," *Queen's Quarterly*, LXXI (1964), 150–162.
96. March's data—his source normally is *The Canadian Parliamentary Guide*.
97. See Allan Kornberg, "The Social Bases of Leadership in a Canadian House of Commons," p. 329.

Table 8. *Ethnic-Religious[a] Backgrounds of Canadian Parliamentary and American Congressional Leaders*

	Ethnic	
	Canadian parliamentary leaders	American congressional leaders
Anglo-Scotch-Irish	48%	67%
French	36	—
Northern Europe	5	15
Germany	5	15
Eastern Europe	6	—
Negro	—	3
	Religious	
	Canadian parliamentary leaders	American congressional leaders
Protestant	53%	87%
Catholic	44	13
Jewish	2	—
Other	b	—
	(N = 39)	(N = 39)

a. Interestingly, the substantial proportion of Catholics and French-Canadians in the leadership panel and in the 1962 House of Commons as a whole cannot be attributed simply to the fact that a majority of Catholics and French-Canadians reside in Quebec and thus can make their votes more effective (in terms of the number of legislators they elect) than would be the case if (as in the United States) they were more evenly distributed geographically. For example, although 58 per cent of the Catholic M.P.'s were elected by the 55.6 per cent of the Catholics living in Quebec, the remaining 42 per cent were elected by the 44.6 per cent of Catholics living outside of Quebec. Similarly, 77 per cent of the French M.P.'s represented constituencies in Quebec, the province that in 1961 had 76.6 per cent of all French-Canadians residing within its boundaries. The 23.4 per cent who lived outside of Quebec elected the remaining 23 per cent of the French M.P.'s.

b. Less than 1 per cent.

in the fifty-one to sixty-four age category, and only 7 per cent were sixty-five or more. The American proportions were substantially reversed: 49 per cent were sixty-five years of age or more, 45 per cent between fifty-one and sixty-four years of age, and only 5 per cent were under fifty.

How should these data be interpreted? One interpretation would be that they strongly support Porter's claims concerning the elitist character of Canadian society and the brokerage politics which the elites traditionally have practiced. For example, it is obvious that, although in theory, the parliamentary recruitment channel is open—in that anyone twenty-one years of age or older who can persuade twenty-five voters in a district to sign his nomination papers and is able to raise the necessary deposit ($200) can become a candidate—in practice, the opening is for those with sufficient financial resources to make a substantial contribution to their own campaign costs and, in the event of election, to maintain two residences.[98] Since such resources are most frequently possessed by high income professionals or businessmen, and because the latter occupations generally require at least an undergraduate education, and as the Canadian universities are still largely the preserve of the wealthy, all but a fraction of the public are barred a priori from competing for or holding high public office. When to this barrier one adds the fact that the recruitment of candidates for Parliament is largely in the hands of the several constituency organizations of the parties, with their often private and idiosyncratic recruitment standards, the pathway to Parliament is one that very few can successfully traverse.

The relative congruence between the ethnic, religious, regional, and to a lesser extent, age backgrounds of parliamentary leaders, backbenchers, and the publics they represent, may be conceptualized as illustrative of the tendency of elites to bargain with one another over the distribution of scarce values—such as high public office. The allotment by region of a position such as cabinet minister presumably provides the population of each area with dramatic evidence that their economic interests are being represented in national councils. Whenever regional and ethnic-religious cleavages coincide, as in the case of Quebec, the allocation of leadership positions to certain members from a narrow elite stratum takes on added significance; it not only provides lower status members of the group with empirical proof that they are being taken care of economically, but also offers them psychic gratification in that the worth and legitimacy of their cultural values are being publically "recognized."

98. There is no formal constitutional requirement that M.P.'s reside in the districts they represent. By convention, however, virtually all do.

Certainly, most Canadian scholars are agreed that the sagacity of Prime Ministers MacDonald and King in naming a series of French Canadian "right hand men" was principally responsible for the dominant positions that the Conservative and Liberal parties, respectively, were able to maintain for long periods of time. Evidently the strategy also was employed and, in fact, refined by Mr. Diefenbaker, who during his tenure of office appointed a woman, a Ukrainian, and a Salvation Army member to his cabinet, as well as a full-blooded Indian to the Senate.[99] From one point of view these appointments can be said to exemplify the cynical opportunism characteristic of non-ideological and non-programmatic brokerage politics. From another, however, they illustrate successful political integration—a process with which Canadian political leaders have been constantly and even exclusively concerned.[100] It is, after all, a considerable feat to maintain for a century the national integrity of a vast area without myths to inspire, heroes to emulate, symbols to manipulate, authority figures to politicize, or ideologists to guide.

The Representative Relationship

In a penetrating analysis of Edmund Burke's Bristol speech, Heinz Eulau argued that any empirical treatment of the representative relationship required one to distinguish analytically be-

99. John Meisel writes of Mr. Diefenbaker that he "promulgated his view of Canada as a country composed of unhyphenated citizens—Canadians, plain and simple. In effect this concept of Canada gave a greater place to 'new Canadians' than had formerly been recognized in the Conservative party." John Meisel, "Recent Changes in Canadian Parties," in *Party Politics in Canada*, ed. Hugh G. Thorburn, 2nd ed. (Scarborough, 1967), p. 49. Not all of Mr. Diefenbaker's colleagues shared his desire to recognize ethnic minorities other than the French nor did they approve of his articulation of specifically "ethnic" issues—a practice in which American politicians have long engaged. His attempt to transform the Conservative party from an Eastern, business, and WASP-oriented organization into a champion of the lower income ethnic groups was responsible, in no small part, for the intra-party conflict that characterized his tenure as leader.

100. For example, Hargrove claims that Canadian "national unity has been so fragile that it has had to take precedence over all other issues. Canadian elites would not have found a left-right polarity congenial, but it is also true that such a polarity would be a luxury Canada could not afford. It has been more important for political leaders to build bridges between sections, religions and interests than to seek to divide them." See Hargrove, *op. cit.*, p. 198.

tween the "style" (i.e., the manner in which the legislator carries out his perceived function as representative) and "focus" (i.e., the geographic area to which the legislator's actions are oriented) of representation.

Such an analysis of the representational role styles[101] of members of the Twenty-fifth Parliament indicated that Canadian legislators can be arrayed along a bi-dimensional consultation-service continuum, ranging from those who felt they were required neither to consult with nor perform services for their constituents, through those who tried to combine some consultation and service with a degree of independence from the constituency, to those who sought constantly to consult with, and perform services for, constituents. The first and smallest (15 per cent) group, because of their affinity for Burke's prescriptions, have been termed *trustees*. A larger (36 per cent) group, who were termed *politicos,* tried to span the chasm between independent thinking and behaving and constituency influence and control. The remaining 49 per cent were termed *delegate-servants* since they felt that their position required them to perform services requested from them as well as to consult and seek advice from constituents. Other data suggested that the service dimension probably was more important, at least for members of the Conservative and Social Credit parties, than was consultation with constituents.[102]

Insofar as their foci of representation was concerned,[103] their responses revealed that the largest (47 per cent) group of M.P.'s perceived the nation as the geographic area to which they owed primary responsibility. At the other end of the continuum were the 34 per cent who perceived their constituencies as being of primary importance. The remaining 19 per cent could not or

101. The legislators were asked, "What do you think your representational role entails?" See Allan Kornberg, "The Correlates of Representational Roles," in *Canadain Legislative Behavior,* p. 106. The question is derived from Eulau's earlier study of American state legislators. See Heinz Eulau, "The Legislator as Representative: Representational Roles," in *The Legislative System: Explorations in Legislative Behavior,* ed. John Wahlke *et al.* (New York, 1962), pp. 267–286.

102. See Kornberg, "The Correlates of Representational Roles," p. 118, n. 10.

103. Legislators were asked, "Some M.P.'s feel that their primary responsibility is first to their constituency and then to their province or country as a whole. Others feel quite differently. How do you feel about this?"

would not articulate a preference for any geographic area. We have termed these orientations *national, local,* and *national-local* respectively.

In comparing Canadian M.P.'s with the congressmen studied by Roger Davidson,[104] it was apparent that, insofar as the distribution of role *styles* was concerned, the American congressmen fit Burke's model of the "good legislator" much better than Canadian M.P.'s. Canadian M.P.'s, however, adhered more closely to Burke's prescription concerning the propriety of representing a national constituency.

That members of the Canadian House of Commons, given that institution's responsible parties, should have been more nationally focused and less inclined than their congressional counterparts to take a role style structured in terms of independence from both constituency and party is not surprising. Miller and Stokes have pointed out that both the responsible-party and instructed-delegate models of representation are really two sides of the same coin. Both models share the notion of control, the difference being that the controller in the first theory is conceived as a national constituency and party.[105]

Sartori also has pointed to the increased importance of party in the representational process and has argued that parliamentary representation can no longer be conceptualized as a dyadic relationship of legislator with constituent, as was the case during the eighteenth and much of the nineteenth centuries, but instead must be seen as a triad of electors, parties, and the elected.[106]

March's data tend to support Sartori's assumption concerning the increased salience of modern parties in the legislative process. One reason for their increased importance in Canada, of course, was the rapid growth of electoral machinery at the constituency level.[107] As these constituency organizations developed, the number of members elected to the House by acclamation (their

---

104. See Roger Davidson, "Congress and the Executive: The Race for Representation," in *Congress, the First Branch of Government,* ed. Alfred DeGrazia (Washington, 1966), pp. 377–413, cf. p. 394.

105. Warren E. Miller and Donald E. Stokes, "Constituency Influence in Congress," *American Political Science Review,* LV (1961), 345–357.

106. Sartori, *op. cit.,* p. 26.   107. See March, *op. cit.,* p. 89.

candidacies were uncontested) dropped sharply.[108] Another indication of party organizational growth and the concomitant dependence of candidates upon party machinery for their election is seen in the decline and virtual disappearance from Parliament of Independent members (i.e., Independent-Liberals, Independent-Conservatives, Liberal-Conservatives, and "pure" Independents). Thus, during the twenty year period, 1867–1886, fully seventy-two Independents were elected at general and by-elections, but during the forty year period, 1921–1961, only eighteen were elected. The decline of the Independent member in the Canadian House of Commons is even better illustrated, if, over

Table 9. *The Proportion of Independent Candidates Elected to the Canadian House of Commons, 1887ᵃ–1961*

Period	Total number of independent candidates	Proportion of independent candidates elected (%)
1887–1899	52	67
1900–1920	74	26
1921–1961	459	4

a. No data are available for the total number of independent candidates for the period 1867–1886. See March, op. cit., p. 38.

time, we look at the sharp decrease in the proportion of Independent candidates who actually were elected. (See Table 9.)

Apparently the Independent Liberals and Conservatives of the nineteenth century really were independent of party in more than name. For example, an analysis of the recorded votes of members of the First (1867) and Twenty-sixth (1963) Parliaments indicates that on thirty divisions only 28 per cent of the nineteenth-century body had never voted against their parties. By comparison, fully 78 per cent of the members of the Twenty-sixth Parliament had never voted against their parties—despite the fact that there were approximately four times as many oppor-

108. *Ibid.*, p. 86.

tunities (124 divisions) for them to ignore the party whips. It is estimated that the over-all defection rate of members from their parties in 1867 was approximately 20 per cent, but was only a minuscule 1.2 per cent from 1963 to 1965.[109] Although the latter data do not take abstention—a popular form of backbench dissent—into account, there is little doubt that the members of current Canadian parliamentary parties almost always act in concert with their colleagues.

One reason for their concerted action likely stems from the psychological gratification they derive from the service aspect of their representational roles.[110] The responses of 1962 members of Parliament indicate genuine pleasure over their perceived ability "to guide people through the maze of government," or "to get people a hearing," or "to help people solve their problems if they have to do with government."[111] They also are encouraged to undertake case work by party leaders,[112] the mass media,[113] and, undoubtedly, the grateful recipients of their favors. Yet such labor, rewarding and useful as it may be to the individual citizen and M.P., is unlikely to stir the public's imagination. For one thing, there are physical and time limits on the number of cases even the most willing and hard-working legislator can handle without a staff. Also, some of the requests for assistance he receives cannot be satisfied simply because they are beyond the legal and/or constitutional limits of his authority. Hence, some citizens are bound to be disappointed with his performance. Finally, requests for services to legislators are aspects of more generalized political participation and generally emanate from individuals of relatively high rather than low social status. Thus, the tasks that consume the bulk of the time and energy of a Canadian M.P., and that he normally performs in a very credit-

---

109. *Ibid.*, pp. 98–99.
110. See *Canadian Legislative Behavior*, pp. 146–147.
111. For more extensive comments see Allan Kornberg, "Perception and Constituency Influence on Legislative Behavior," *Western Political Quarterly,* XIX (1966), 285–292.
112. Kornberg, "The Correlates of Representational Roles," pp. 146–147.
113. See Peter Dempson, "A Good Member Earns His Pay," *Telegram,* Toronto, January 28, 1959, in *Politics: Canada,* ed. Paul Fox, 2nd ed. (Toronto, 1966), pp. 274–275.

able fashion, are virtually unknown to and unseen by the majority of the population.[114]

The Legislative Function

One function of current parliamentary procedures, as was previously stated, is to facilitate the passage of a government's legislative proposals. This was not always the case, however. From 1867 to 1906 the House operated under procedural rules that by current standards permitted broad member participation in the policy process. The introduction and discussion of private members' bills consumed a considerable proportion of the House's time. In fact, such bills constituted most of the legislation receiving royal assent. Further, the cabinet made no move to increase their control of the House during this period despite the fact that on at least two occasions the determined obstruction of opposition members compelled the government to accept serious amendments to their legislative proposals.[115]

The first serious steps taken by the cabinet to control the time and the opportunity available for private members to participate in the policy process and to establish its primacy over Parliament were taken during the period from 1906 to 1913. First, the right of any member to sidetrack government business by moving the adjournment of the House was severely restricted. Until the adoption of Standing Order 26 in 1906, any member could move to adjourn the House in order to discuss an issue he considered important. The new rule restricted both the number of times *and the circumstances* (i.e., to discuss a matter of "urgent public importance") under which motions of adjournment could be made. A second rule change prevented a member from interrupt-

114. Meisel *et al.* found that among respondents who *were aware* of the identity of the incumbent M.P., only 15 per cent said they remembered something he [the M.P.] had done for the people of this constituency; 11 per cent said he had done nothing; and 33 per cent were unable to remember anything he had done. In response to the question, "Has he done anything for you or your family personally?" 57 per cent said he had done nothing, while only 2 per cent said he had.

115. W. F. Dawson, *Procedure in the Canadian House of Commons* (Toronto, 1962), p. 27.

ing another member making a speech unless the latter gave his permission. According to Dawson, this tactic had been employed by members wishing to obstruct government business.[116]

A further restriction on the participation of backbenchers was achieved by two rule changes in 1910: one change required "relevancy" in speeches made in Committee of the Whole; a second change permitted both the Speaker and the chairman of the Committee of the Whole considerable latitude in determining which remarks were relevant in the House or in Committee of the Whole. Three years later Standing Orders 17A and 17C limited the number of motions which could be debated in the House and also placed further restrictions on motions that were debatable. In 1927, the time allocated to backbench speeches was curtailed by the introduction of rules that limited such speeches to forty-five minutes and which set an eleven o'clock adjournment time for the House. Changes to the standing orders adopted in 1955 and 1960 further reduced speech time to forty minutes on most occasions when the Speaker is in the chair and to thirty minutes in Committee of the Whole.

During the period from 1927 to 1961, numerous changes were made in the rules pertaining to private members' bills. Not only did such bills lose the pre-eminence they had enjoyed over government bills during the nineteenth century, but opportunities available to introduce such bills also were limited so severely (currently, to eight days during a session) that their utility as a vehicle for ensuring backbench participation in policy-making has effectively ended.

The impact that these changes have had, in terms of limiting the opportunity available to ordinary members to take part in the formal legislative process in the House, is vividly illustrated by data that chronicle the differential participation rates of members of the Twenty-sixth Parliament. (See Table 10.)

Although the ability of the private member to initiate legislative policy was drastically curtailed during this century, there still remained, in theory, substantial opportunity for him to evaluate the legislative proposals of the government in Committee of

116. *Ibid.*, p. 23.

the Whole and in the several standing committees. We shall consider the latter possibilities shortly. For the present, it should be noted that other procedural changes have seriously restricted the participation of the backbencher in the policy-evaluation opportunities afforded by the Throne Speech, budget debates, and on motions for the House to resolve itself into a Committee of Supply. That is, in addition to the aforementioned curtailment of speech time and the requirement of relevancy, the over-all time allocated to the "Address" and to the budget de-

---

Table 10. *Participation Scores*ᵃ *of Canadian M.P.'s in the Legislative Process, 1963–1965, in the House of Commons*

Participation scores	Number of members	Participation scores	Number of members
0–9	16	103–140	23
10–20	23	143–195	21
21–29	18	200–299	30
31–40	14	311–399	20
41–49	11	435–767	19
51–60	14	812–980	8
62–80	14	1,023–1,827	7
83–99	14	2,457–2,668	2

a. The legislator's score is based on all speeches, questions, motions, and amendments he made during the three sessions of the Twenty-sixth Parliament. The speaker and thirteen members who were not present because of illness, etc. during the entire Parliament are not included.

Source: March, Table III-5, p. 101.

---

bates has been cut to eight and six days, respectively. Backbench participation has been circumscribed further by certain informal arrangements such as "pairing" and by agreements reached "behind the speaker's chair" among party whips with respect to the frequency and the order in which members will be heard.[117] A more formal procedure to limit the time available for debate was adopted provisionally by the Twenty-sixth and Twenty-seventh Parliaments. The new rule (Standing Order 15A) provides for

117. *Ibid.*, pp. 103, 104, 169, 176.

the establishment of a Business Committee composed of one representative from each party to allocate debate time. This rule applies to Supply and all bills involving expenditures.[118] Finally, two other procedural devices, "closure" and "putting the previous question," are now available to a government to ensure that debate on any issue ultimately will end.[119]

It might be argued that the lack of backbench participation on the floor of the House is not critical since activity in the House "is only one side of the political firmament. Behind the public display lies most of the operating process of politics—the complex and involved invisible world of discussion, bargaining, policy- and decision-making."[120] According to one veteran M.P., the work of standing committees in the Canadian House of Commons is part of this invisible but important process. "Committee work does not always get the headlines, but this *is* the legislative process. This is Parliament enacting laws, and it is in this process that the country gets the kind of laws it voted for."[121] And, in defending the tasks performed by Canadian parliamentarians, Paul Fox suggests both that the committee stage is an important part of policy-making and that the average M.P. can influence the policy process through his committee activities. "He can be an

118. See Phillip Laundy, "Procedural Reforms in the Canadian House of Commons," *The Table: The Journal of the Society of Clerks-at-the-Table in Commonwealth Parliaments,* XXXIV (1965), 17. See also House of Commons Provisional Reprint of the Standing Orders for the First Session, Twenty-seventh Parliament. According to political scientist and former M.P. Pauline Jewett,

> It was not intended that this procedure, starting with the summoning of the business committee, would supplant the customary informal meetings of party House leaders to work out "gentlemen's agreements" on time allocations. The "usual channels" would be respected. It was expected, however, that the new rule would be invoked if "gentlemen's agreements" could not be reached, or if too many informal agreements were being broken, or if a bill promised difficulties in all its stages. It was hoped, too, that the very existence of the rule would act as a deterrent to unnecessarily prolonged and repetitive debate.

Pauline Jewett, "The Reform of Parliament, *Journal of Canadian Studies,* I (1966), 12.
119. For an explanation of these two devices see Allan Kornberg, *Canadian Legislative Behavior,* p. 38, n. 18.
120. Paul Fox, "Our MP's—Their Roles and Need," *Politics: Canada,* ed. Paul Fox, 2nd ed. (Toronto, 1966), p. 276.
121. Cited by Peter W. Johansen, "An Investigation into the Relative Prestige of the Standing Committees of the House of Commons" (unpublished paper, Department of Political Science, Carleton University, 1967).

assiduous committee man, for example, working quietly but effectively on House committees or on his party's caucus committees, a function that is very important, especially in relation to policy-making, though it is not likely to result in much publicity."[122] However, other evaluations of the function of standing committees in the Canadian House of Commons and of the part played by M.P.'s in these committees are not quite as flattering. For example, Dawson and Ward suggest that not only do most standing committees meet infrequently, but, in fact, in many instances years go by in which they do not meet at all.[123] Although they perceived some changes occurring during the Twenty-fourth Parliament (1958–1962), their opinion of the work of standing committees generally is negative. Their evaluation of the *ad hoc* special committees that are periodically constituted to investigate some aspect of the governmental process also is negative. They point out, however, that such committees do have some utility in that they at least help educate their own members[124]—a rather important contribution in a Parliament in which approximately 40 per cent of the members are freshmen.

A number of empirical studies of Canadian standing committees carried out under the direction of Roman March tend to support the views of Dawson and Ward. Thus, although one study[125] indicated there was consensus among M.P.'s as to which were the most and least prestigious standing committees (i.e., External Affairs and Public Accounts were rated the most prestigious and Veterans' Affairs and Private Bills were rated the least prestigious), analysis indicated that even in the most prestigious committees attendance was extremely poor. For example, the Public Accounts Committee did not meet from March 1, 1966, until May 10 of that year, because there was never a quorum present (thirteen members).[126] The quorum was then reduced to ten members and in the meetings that followed a bare quorum

122. Paul Fox, *op. cit.*, p. 277.
123. R. M. Dawson and Norman Ward, *The Government of Canada*, 4th ed. (Toronto, 1964), pp. 380–381.
124. *Ibid.*, p. 382.   125. Johansen, *op. cit., passim.*
126. Dennis Blais, "Report on the Public Accounts Committee for the 1966–67 Session of the Twenty-Seventh Parliament" (Department of Political Science, Carleton University, 1968).

was attained three times, whereas at five other meetings only eleven members were present. Further, some individuals who were recorded as being present stayed only for a few minutes and left. Attendance at the External (Foreign) Affairs Committee was equally dismal; during the three sessions of the Twenty-sixth Parliament, 14 per cent of committee meetings had less than 10 per cent attendance, 20 per cent had between 11 and 30 per cent attendance, and 15 per cent of the meetings had 31 to 50 per cent of the members present.[127] In other words, in one-half of the meetings of the committee, fewer than half the members were present.[128]

Among members who did attend, participation in committee deliberations varied fairly sharply among individuals and by party. Thus, analysis of the rate of participation of twenty-eight members of the Public Accounts Committee in 1966 showed that five (18 per cent) never spoke at any meeting they attended, another five (18 per cent) spoke an average of one to five sentences per meeting, one (3 per cent) member spoke six to ten sentences, six (21 per cent) members spoke eleven to twenty-five sentences, another six (21 per cent) members spoke twenty-six to forty sentences, three (11 per cent) members spoke forty-one to ninety-nine sentences, and two (7 per cent) members spoke an average of 100 or more sentences per meeting. Insofar as differences in participation by party were concerned, this study found

---

127. William S. Longhurst, "The Standing Committee on External Affairs of the Twenty-Sixth Parliament, 1963–64" (Department of Political Science, Carleton University, 1968).

128. A former M.P. and a frequent commentator on the Canadian Parliament, Douglas M. Fisher, feels such attendance rates, given the conditions under which committees function in the House, are not only acceptable but, in fact, are rather extraordinary.

> Many members, of course, sit on more than one committee. At various times last session I was on six of them. Further, a member only needs to appear for a few minutes to be classed as present. Despite these qualifications, when one considers the fact that most members were on committees which met at the same time, that many sittings took place while the House was working, and that most members visit their constituencies several times during the session, committee attendance was phenomenally good.

D. M. Fisher, "Parliamentary Committees in the Twenty-Fourth Parliament," *Politics: Canada*, ed. Paul Fox, 1st ed. (Toronto, 1963), p. 208.

that the average Conservative member participated twice as much as the average Liberal member.[129]

Another indicator of the relative lack of importance of parliamentary committees in the policy process is suggested by the fact that the "turnover" rates of membership on these two most prestigious committees, External Affairs and Public Accounts, were 40 per cent and 37.5 per cent, respectively. If one assumes that standing committees perform an important task in the Canadian parliamentary process, one also would assume that members would not be likely to give up their seats on such committees. Accordingly, one must conclude both that committees do not play an important role in the legislative process and that the turnover rate is probably far higher on less prestigious committees. A succinct summation of the work of parliamentary standing committees is provided by Douglas M. Fisher, who, in describing a report prepared by his committee said,

The report was a pastiche of the ideas, even whims, of six or seven of the more active members, including myself. It was pieced together in parts in an atmosphere of hurry, "let's have done with it!"; the evidence, a 100 pages in print, was not digested by the committee or even by smaller subcommittees. In sum, it was uneven and amateurish, finished with a rush, and unrelated to the overall policy of the government and its financial position.[130]

Even if they do not take any significant part in discussions on the House floor or in standing committees it may be, as Paul Fox

129. Fisher feels that this is a French-Canadian rather than a Liberal party failing. French-Canadian members, he says, seemingly are more constituency- and less policy-oriented than English-speaking members, and "any genuine development of committee work in the future must take their parliamentary disinterest into account." *Ibid.*, p. 209. However, a second study of the Public Accounts Committee in 1966 by David M. Rayside of Carleton University indicated that both the attendance and the activity of French-Canadian Liberal members on the committee were greater than their English-speaking colleagues. Thus, he questioned Fisher's assumption that French-Canadians are less policy-oriented and proposed instead that the Liberal members of Parliament may be less policy-oriented than their opponents in the other parties. The author's own study of the Twenty-fifth Parliament indicated that M.P.'s with French-Canadian cultural characteristics are not significantly less policy-oriented than legislators who lack such characteristics. See Allan Kornberg, "The Correlates of Representational Roles," p. 89.

130. Fisher, *op. cit.*, p. 213.

has suggested, that backbenchers still are able to exert considerable "behind-the-scenes" influence on legislation through discussions in party caucus.[131] However, the available empirical evidence suggests otherwise. For example, the author found that in 1962 the Liberal and to some extent the New Democratic parties largely used the caucus to discuss strategy and tactics rather than to formulate or criticize policy proposals.[132] Pauline Jewett's description of the actions of Liberal parliamentary leaders during her recent tenure as a member of the Liberal caucus tends to support our findings.

No effort was made to initiate new MP's into the complexities of existing legislation and departmental organization. No executive assistants were provided MP's to enable them to spend a little less time on routine constituency matters and a little more time delving into, and preparing speeches on, proposed legislation. . . . Even with respect to its own backbenchers the government showed little continuing concern about the quality of debate. It did make some effort, in 1963 and 1964, to improve its own backbenchers' knowledge and understanding of proposed legislation, even allowing them on occasion to participate in the policy-making process. For example, Ministers and senior officials occasionally met with caucus groups to explain and discuss proposed policies before they were given first reading in the House. Backbenchers were also encouraged—although not strongly enough or often enough—to specialize in one or two fields of inquiry and, sometimes even, to speak on these matters in the House. But these innovations, and others like them, although encouraged by the Prime Minister and a few other ministers, were never taken up gladly by the majority of ministers and, so far as can be discerned, have been given little nourishment in the past year or two.[133]

Another account, this one by a top-level Liberal leader, indicates that such behavior on the part of Liberal party leaders is not a recent occurrence. According to him, the late and long-time Liberal prime minister, W. L. Mackenzie King, employed the Liberal

131. Dowse and Smith suggest that British M.P.'s, particularly, in the government party, *are*, in fact, able to exert just such an influence on legislation through their positions on caucus subcommittees. See R. Dowse and T. Smith, "Party Discipline in the House of Commons," *Parliamentary Affairs*, XVI (1962–63), pp. 159–164.

132. See Allan Kornberg, "Caucus and Cohesion in Canadian Parliamentary Parties," *American Political Science Review*, LX, No. 1 (1966), 86.

133. Jewett, *op. cit.*, pp. 13–14.

caucus as a kind of cheering section that functioned principally to sanction policies that had already been decided by party leaders. In his words, King explained "the whys and wherefores of Government action and suggested lines on which the Government could be supported most effectively."[134] Finally, Douglas Fisher, a former member of the New Democratic parliamentary party has written (and David Rayside's quantitative study of the activities of members of the Public Accounts Committee supports him) that the members, regardless of party, who participate most often in House debates (generally, the party leaders) also participate the most in the standing committees and in the party caucuses.[135]

The progressive exclusion of the backbencher from the policy-initiation and the policy-evaluation process generally has been rationalized in terms of goal attainment in a modern democracy. Very simply put, the argument is that the procedural rules that governed nineteenth-century Parliaments (and that were taken over almost *in toto* from Great Britain) were appropriate for them because they really had very little to do; the population was small, the economy was underdeveloped, and political participation was limited. Consequently, the demands made upon Parliament were light, and relatedly, the scope of governmental activity was narrow.

The twentieth century witnessed a rapid although uneven increase in population; the addition of two new provinces, Alberta and Saskatchewan; urban-industrial growth; the development of internal communication and trade; and the increased importance of issues such as public welfare, external trade, and foreign relations. Although many of the policy decisions that these changes necessitated may have originated outside of Parliament (as Porter and others have claimed), that institution still was required to consider and to ratify an ever-increasing volume of complex legislation. To meet these legislative demands, twentieth-century parliamentary procedures had to be made more efficient. In Canada, efficiency was achieved by centralizing control over the

---

134. J. W. Pickersgill, *The Mackenzie King Record* (Toronto, 1960), p. 9.
135. Douglas Fisher, "How Good or Bad is Your MP?" *Maclean's*, February 5, 1966.

substance and the ratification of legislation in the hands of the executive.[136] Every procedural change that increased a cabinet's authority over Parliament was justified by the claim that it also increased its (Parliament's) smooth and efficient operation and permitted the cabinet, acting under a mandate from at least a plurality of the electorate, to meet its responsibilities to the public. If these rationalizations are valid, we would expect that the several Canadian Parliaments have worked increasingly longer and, although the proportion of private members' bills may have diminished, that they have considered and passed an ever-expanding number of legislative proposals. We propose to test, albeit crudely, these expectations by examining the public bills (government and private members')[137] introduced and passed by every Canadian Parliament of the past century.

There is some difficulty in constructing adequate measures for, unlike the Congress, the life of a Parliament of the British model is not fixed. Also, the number of days the House actually sits during a particular session may vary considerably. Naturally, both of these factors affect the legislative activities of the House. In Table 11, our measures of relative length of Parliament (column 6), relative success of Parliament (column 7), relative legislative load (column 8), and relative legislative output (column 9) try to take these variables into account. Respectively, the measures are ratios of: the number of sitting days to the number of days of a session; bills passed to bills introduced; bills introduced to sitting days; and bills passed to sitting days.

A cursory examination of the data in Table 11 suggests that modern parliamentarians, in fact do labor notably longer than their predecessors since the length of parliamentary sessions and the number of days members actually sit have increased in the past 100 years. Interestingly, however, the number of bills introduced and passed each day Parliament actually sat was greater in the nineteenth century than in either the years 1900 to 1940 or

136. Even the cabinet itself was hierarchically organized—parliamentary assistants, junior ministers, senior ministers, and the prime minister.

137. Private members' bills do not include divorce bills. Largely because of Catholic Quebec, up to and including the Twenty-third Parliament, divorce "bills" were introduced into the Commons. They normally included up to 95 per cent of the legislation that received royal assent.

Table 11. Legislative Activity in the Canadian House of Commons, 1867–1968

Parliament	Duration	Type of government	Number of days in session	Number of actual sitting days	Number of bills introduced into parliament	Number of bills passed by parliament	Relative length of parliament (ratio of sitting days to days in session)	Relative success of parliament (ratio of bills passed to bills introduced)	Relative legislative load (bills introduced per day)	Relative legislative output (bills passed per day)
1st	Nov., 1867–June, 1872	Majority	446	283	610	422	.63	.69	2.16	1.49
2nd	Mar., 1873–Nov., 1873	Majority	177	70	157	125	.40	.80	2.24	1.79
3rd	Mar., 1874–May, 1878	Majority	362	262	579	421	.72	.73	2.21	1.61
4th	Feb., 1879–May, 1882	Majority	379	259	523	344	.68	.66	2.02	1.33
5th	Feb., 1883–June, 1886	Majority	472	324	613	406	.69	.66	1.89	1.25
6th	Apr., 1887–May, 1890	Majority	375	256	622	447	.68	.72	2.43	1.75
7th	Apr., 1891–Apr., 1896	Majority	695	458	825	575	.66	.70	1.80	1.26
8th	Aug., 1896–July, 1900	Majority	593	402	739	487	.68	.66	1.84	1.21
9th	Dec., 1900–Sept., 1904	Majority	578	394	748	564	.68	.75	1.90	1.43
10th	Dec., 1904–Sept., 1908	Majority	712	460	786	639	.65	.81	1.71	1.39
11th	Dec., 1908–July, 1911	Majority	491	303	596	423	.62	.71	1.97	1.40
12th	Oct., 1911–Oct., 1917	Majority	870	568	895	726	.65	.81	1.58	1.28
13th	Mar., 1918–Oct., 1921	Union (coalition)	515	355	500	406	.69	.81	1.41	.48

Table 11. Continued

Parliament	Duration	Type of government	Number of days in session	Number of actual sitting days	Number of bills introduced into parliament	Number of bills passed by parliament	Relative length of parliament (ratio of sitting days to days in session)	Relative success of parliament (ratio of bills passed to bills introduced)	Relative legislative load (bills introduced per day)	Relative legislative output (bills passed per day)
14th	Mar., 1922–Sept., 1925	Minority	549	366	471	370	.67	.78	1.41	1.14
15th	Jan., 1926–July, 1926	Minority	177	111	110	24	.63	.22	.99	.22
16th	Dec., 1926–May, 1930	Majority	439	292	491	396	.66	.81	1.68	1.36
17th	Sept., 1930–Aug., 1935	Majority	772	507	454	359	.66	.79	.89	.71
18th	Feb., 1936–Jan., 1940	Majority	533	365	340	252	.68	.74	.67	.50
19th	May, 1940–Apr., 1945	Majority	1750	565	282	196	.32	.69	.50	.35
20th	Sept., 1945–Apr., 1949	Majority	748	487	439	366	.65	.90	.90	.75
21st	Sept., 1949–June, 1953	Majority	1154	527	473	389	.46	.82	.90	.74
22nd	Nov., 1953–Apr., 1957	Majority	787	507	388	296	.64	.76	.76	.58
23rd	Oct., 1957–Feb., 1958	Minority	111	78	62	41	.70	.66	.79	.52
24th	May, 1958–Apr., 1962	Majority	919	605	576	331	.66	.57	.95	.55
25th	Sept., 1962–Feb., 1963	Minority	132	72	127	24	.54	.14	1.76	.33
26th	May, 1963–Sept., 1965	Minority	717	418	528	183	.58	.35	1.26	.44
27th	Jan., 1966–Apr., 1968	Minority	718	405	565	170	.56	.30	1.40	.42

from 1940 to the present. Further, the proportion of days in which Parliaments sat, as compared with the number of days they were in session, was higher before World War II than after it. Table 12 neatly summarizes these facts. It is true, of course, that members of Parliament may be in session more hours a day currently than in the past, and in this sense they may also be said to work longer than previous parliamentarians. Pauline Jewett points out that one of the "reforms" adopted during the Twenty-seventh Parliament was to abolish luncheon and dinner adjournments and that this was a major reason for the passage of forty-three items of government business from January to July, 1966. She notes, however, that by November of that year, "the House was adjourning for lunch on Fridays and for dinner on Mondays, Tuesdays and Thursdays, just like old times."[138]

It is also true that the greater number of bills introduced and passed a day during nineteenth-century Parliaments reflects the fact that the bulk of them were private members' rather than government bills.[139] Unfortunately, we do not have data necessary to calculate the proportion of private members' as opposed to government bills that the House considered during the several Parliaments. We do know, however, that private members' bills constituted only 32 per cent of the bills receiving royal assent from the Twentieth through the first session of the Twenty-seventh Parliaments. Thus, we may assume that the proportion of private members' bills was rarely any lower and likely was far higher in the past.

The inverse relationship between time and the volume of legislation considered by Parliament also may reflect bureaucratic growth, and the fact that over time the bureaucracy has shared and even supplanted Parliament as a rule-making body. The data for the Nineteenth Parliament are particularly revealing in this respect; under pressure to successfully prosecute the war, the Liberal government of Mackenzie King virtually dispensed with

138. Jewett, *op. cit.*, p. 13.
139. The relative success of Parliament as measured by the number of bills passed over the number introduced was somewhat less during the first eight Parliaments when party discipline was not stringent and a large number of Independents were elected. It was even smaller during the last nine Parliaments, four of which have had minority governments.

Table 12. A Comparison of Legislative Activity in the Canadian House of Commons during Three Time Periods

Parliament	Average number of days in session	Average number of actual sitting days	Average number of bills introduced into Parliament	Average number of bills passed by Parliament	Average relative length of Parliament (ratio of sitting days to days in session)	Average relative success of Parliament (ratio of bills passed to bills introduced)	Average relative legislative load (bills introduced per day)	Average relative legislative output (bills passed per day)
1st–8th	437.3	289.2	583.5	403.3	.66	.69	2.02	1.39
9th–18th	563.6	372.1	539.1	415.9	.66	.77	1.45	1.12
19th–27th	781.7	407.1	382.2	221.7	.52	.58	.94	.54

Parliament and, together with the top bureaucracy, governed by executive decrees and Orders-in-Council.[140]

Further, there can be little question that the decreased legislative output of this century stems from the fact that the kind of government bills that current Parliaments consider are qualitatively and quantitatively different than those considered by nineteenth-century Parliaments.

Finally, the data also reflect the increased incidence of minority governments since World War II. A comparison of the legislative activities of the five majority and four minority governments since 1940 makes it plain that minority governments work longer but are less successful than majority governments. With regard to productivity, the four minority governments have introduced more bills per day; their difficulty lies in getting legislation passed. (See Table 13.)

Still, given Parliament's adequate size and large pool of highly educated members (who possess a variety of specialized professional and technical skills) and the fact that each increase in centralization of authority supposedly has further streamlined and expedited the legislative process, one might expect that the volume of legislation Parliament currently disposes of would be somewhat larger than actually is the case. The fact that it is not helps account for the almost obsessive interest in procedural reform that was characteristic of the last two Parliaments—an interest that competed successfully for attention with more intrinsically popular and newsworthy events such as the adoption of the new Canadian flag and scandal in high places.

Parliament's seeming failure to pass legislation also may account for the low regard with which it is currently held by the public. Even sympathetic critics tend to be dismayed by its performance. For example, in his discussion of the government's tendency to delegate legislative functions to the bureaucracy during the war, J. R. Mallory noted that there *is* a provision for the laying of delegated legislation before Parliament. The problem, according to Mallory, is that with the exception of a handful

140. See J. R. Mallory, "Delegated Legislation in Canada," *Canadian Journal of Economics and Political Science,* XIX (1953), 462–471.

Table 13. *A Comparison of the Legislative Activity of Majority and Minority Governments, 1940–1968*

Parliament	Average number of days in session	Average number of actual sitting days	Average number of bills introduced in to Parliament	Average number of bills passed by Parliament	Average relative length of Parliament (ratio of sitting days to days in session)	Average relative success of Parliament (ratio of bills passed to bills introduced)	Average relative legislative load (bills introduced per day)	Average relative legislative output (bills passed per day)
Majority (5)	1071.6	538.2	431.6	315.6	.50	.73	.80	.59
Minority (4)	419.5	243.3	320.5	104.5	.58	.33	1.32	.43

of individuals, the average M.P. lacks the ability to evaluate such legislation properly.[141] Mallory's observation was not intended to be a criticism of the intelligence of Canadian M.P.'s, but rather to point out that they simply lack the information necessary to evaluate legislative proposals originating in the government and its bureaucracy.

Traditionally, there are three ways such information has been acquired. First, the legislator can employ a competent staff of assistants to generate and evaluate data relevant to a particular legislative problem. Second, he can employ the research facilities and the personnel of a legislative reference service that normally services the needs of a legislative body. Third, he can use the staff and resources of the various committees on which he is a member to acquire information.

With respect to "staff," the Canadian member of Parliament, except if he is a cabinet minister or an opposition leader, is provided with a single clerk-typist. The leader of the official opposition is provided with a staff of thirteen in which are included two executive assistants and a senior secretary, as well as clerks and messengers. Each of the leaders of the smaller parties is provided with a staff of only three secretaries. However, a cabinet minister is allocated $78,000 each year for staff. These funds are usually divided among three administrative assistants, a secretary, and two or three clerks. Lest it be thought that members of the cabinet are particularly affluent, it should be noted that the average American senator employs a staff of thirteen to fifteen people. Senators from large states may employ up to thirty people. The Canadian M.P.'s counterpart in the House of Representatives has approximately $50,000 per year to spend on a staff of up to ten people. Unlike the Canadian M.P., he also receives fairly generous allowances for renting an office in his district and for enabling his staff to travel.

Insofar as the availability of a reference service is concerned, a research branch of the Library of Parliament, consisting of ten people, was inaugurated in June, 1965.[142] Although it is an ideal

141. *Ibid.*, p. 465.
142. The library also maintains an Index and Reference Branch which locates references in Hansard debates for which there are not printed indexes.

toward which they are striving, rather than an immediately obtainable objective, the parliamentary Library ultimately hopes to provide one research assistant for every ten members of Parliament.[143] In contrast, the Library of Congress is presently staffed by approximately 225 research assistants!

With respect to the use of legislative committee staff to obtain information, Dawson and Ward, Jewett, and Fisher all point out how hampered in their deliberations standing committees are by their acute lack of staff assistance.[144]

The deleterious consequences of lack of staff facilities and of information on the legislative performance of Canadian M.P.'s has been succinctly summed up by the late C. G. Power, a veteran M.P. and former cabinet minister. Although he was addressing himself to a Liberal party convention, his remarks are applicable to the other parties as well.

The most important lack is research facilities. Without adequate personnel and materials, the Cabinet can sledgehammer the caucus into submission by using the tremendous resources of the civil service, which it controls, for its exclusive use. Unless the MP's establish their own machinery for research and publication, the caucus as an effective force can be destroyed by a lack of cohesion coupled with a sense of inadequacy. But with the proper resources at his disposal, a member can have an influence on Cabinet. Only when his potency is restored can he achieve the respect due him as the voice of his electorate.[145]

Control

We have distinguished analytically between representation, legislation, and control, although empirically the three functions

143. Erik J. Spicer, "The Library of Parliament," a paper prepared for a symposium on library services to the legislature, New South Wales (1966), p. 9.

144. Dawson and Ward, cf. pp. 380–381; Jewett, cf. pp. 14, 15; and Fisher, cf. pp. 212–214. Fisher writes, "The staff of the Clerk of Committees is a meagre one of half-a-dozen able but harried men, each of whom serves with several committees. They spend all their time arranging meetings, checking attendance, advising on procedure, checking transcripts, and arranging printing. They cannot be considered as a possible nucleus of the kind of expert guidance which some British Committees and all American Committees have" (p. 212).

145. Quoted by Anthony Pearson, "Toward a New Liberal Party," working paper presented to the Canadian University Liberal Federation, Annual Convention, 1966.

are interrelated. Thus, a particularly important dimension of the representational role of the Canadian M.P. is constituency service —case work. Case work almost invariably involves the M.P. with the bureaucracies of the several ministries. In turn, such interaction may inspire him to introduce his own legislation in the form of a private members' bill; to place a resolution on the order table requesting the House's and particularly, the government's support; or, if he is a member of the governing party, to try to obtain the support of a minister to redress the grievances which concern him.

In addition to the "behind-the-scenes" supervision that is a product of individual member requests for information, assistance, and satisfaction of constituent complaints, there are two institutionalized opportunities to "control" the cabinet and administrative bureaucracy. The first and most frequently used is the daily[146] afternoon question period. Technically, such questions to the administration are asked before the first "order" for any day and are referred to as "questions asked on the Orders of the Day." "Questions" almost always produce heated exchanges between the government and the members of the opposition. Insofar as the public is concerned, the question period is by far the most interesting feature of debate in the House; the packed galleries during question period attest to this.

Questioning of cabinet ministers periodically has brought to light and helped rectify administrative abuses of the public. However, the question period falls short as an effective instrument for eliciting the kind of information that would afford Parliament some measure of control over the government. Largely because of the high rate of turnover of members and a lack of staff assistance, questions frequently tend to be clumsily and inappropriately worded; they tend also to be based on limited or incorrect information. Consequently, a substantial proportion are ruled out of order by the speaker. Many questions also tend to be trivial.[147] Their triviality, again, in part, can be ex-

146. On three occasions in each session when "Notices of Motions" stand first on the day's business, there is no question period.

147. *Montreal Gazette* of February 8, 1957, noted that "if the Opposition backbenchers have not been able to come up with any $64.00 questions, they have apparently decided that sixty-four $1.00 questions will do just as well."

plained by the backbencher's lack of competent staff. Most important, a minister may refuse to answer any question without giving a reason. Generally, rather than refusing outright, they will offer as an excuse the more politically expedient reasons of "security" and the "public interest." In this event, the Speaker will enforce the claim of a minister that he has answered a question despite protestations by the opposition that an adequate answer has not been given. Further, the refusal of a minister to answer a question may not be made the subject of another question or be raised as a matter of privilege.[148] In particular, ministers have refused to answer requests for specific information relating to the conduct of crown (government) corporations on the ground that such questions deal with the internal business of the corporation. Hence, they are outside the scope of the government's knowledge and are not answerable.[149] Ministers have refused even to pass on written questions to a corporation on the ground that such questions can be asked of corporation executives when they testify before an appropriate standing committee.

There are twenty-one such standing committees currently. Their membership is large (from twenty-five to sixty members) and reflects the distribution of party strength in the House. Although theoretically they perform supervisory and investigatory as well as legislative functions, in practice they have done relatively little of any of these things.

Thus, Lloyd Musolf,[150] in his excellent study of parliamentary control of crown corporations, concluded that the standing committees' review of corporate activities left much to be desired. Although a few highly visible corporations came under relatively

148. See W. F. Dawson, *Procedure in the Canadian House of Commons* (Toronto, 1962), p. 153. Under a new rule (S.O. 41A) adopted in the last reform of parliamentary procedure previously referred to, members seeking to raise a matter of privilege on anything but questions of procedure must give the speaker a written statement of the privilege in question at least one hour before it is raised in the House.

149. *Ibid.*, pp. 155–156. Summing up his evaluation of the modern question period in the House, Dawson says, "There is little to be said for a question period which on one side is noteworthy for a virtual absence of rules except the patience of the Speaker and on the other by a growing disinclination on the part of the Ministers to disclose any information no matter how trivial" (p. 158).

150. Lloyd Musolf, *Public Ownership and Accountability: The Canadian Experience* (Cambridge, 1959).

steady scrutiny, opposition members claimed that they lacked information to adequately evaluate corporate performance. Also, they were not permitted to discuss corporate policies, and corporate officials could refuse to answer questions by claiming "managerial discretion." Insofar as the less visible corporations were concerned, Musolf writes, "It is questionable, however, whether the low level of visibility of the remainder of the corporations justifies the committees and Parliament itself in ignoring them almost completely."[151]

He also was critical of the fact that Canadian M.P.'s apparently were reluctant to make use of those devices for control that were available to them, as for example, the Public Accounts Committee. The previously mentioned study by Dennis Blaise tends to support Musolf. Of particular interest is the fact that when the Committee did meet its deliberations tended to be dominated by members of the bureaucracy; in the year 1966–67 the auditor-general himself spoke 27 per cent of the time, other high-level bureaucrats took up an additional 27 per cent of the Committee's time, the Committee chairman spoke 16 per cent of the time, and all other members combined spoke only 30 per cent of the time.

One reason for the ineffectiveness of parliamentary committees as instruments of control, in addition to their high turnover of members during a parliamentary session and their lack of competent staff and adequate information upon which to make decisions, is that contrary to national legislative bodies in other Western democracies, the Canadian House of Commons has, in one sense, resisted the trend toward professionalization. We have already noted that a distinctive feature of Canadian Parliaments is the very large proportion of new members each is likely to contain. A second characteristic is the decreasing proportion of newly elected members who have had some experience as local (mayor, alderman, reeve, school trustee, etc.) office-holders or as members of the several provincial legislatures. (See Table 14.)

Pre-parliamentary office-holding experience is considered desirable for would-be national legislators for essentially the same reason that experience in baseball's minor leagues is considered

151. *Ibid.*, p. 126.

Table 14. *Proportion of Canadian M.P.'s with Pre-Parliamentary Experience in Local or Provincial Office, 1867–1965*

Time period	Provincial legislative office only	Both local and provincial public office
1867–1873	46%	66%
1874–1877	24	55
1878–1895	20	52
1896–1899	24	61
1900–1910	22	51
1911–1929	19	41
1930–1939	16	44
1940–1953	12	39
1954–1958	4	36
1959–1965	7	27a

a. Data derived from studying a random sample of 165 members of the Twenty-fifth Parliament indicate a somewhat larger proportion (46 per cent) had pre-parliamentary public office experience. One reason for the discrepancy between March's and our data (other than the fact that March's data for each time period are for newly elected members only) is that our data were obtained from personal interviews with the members, whereas March's figures were generated from *The Canadian Parliamentary Guide,* a generally reliable but not always complete data source. March also may have defined "public office" more strictly than we did. It should be noted that Schlesinger found that 48 per cent of the Liberal and Conservative M.P.'s in the 1957 House had prior public office experience (p. 279). His data were derived not only from *The Canadian Parliamentary Guide* (1958) but also from *Who's Who in Canada.*

Source: March, *op. cit.,* p. 66. Figures from graph are rounded to the nearest whole number.

desirable for future major league players—they are able to learn the specialized skills they will ultimately require from such an apprenticeship. According to Sigmund Neumann: "The usual apprenticeship of democratic aspirants through institutional channels of Parliament, local government, and party organization is a selective process which tests particular qualifications: the capacity for effective statement, for framing legislation, for mastery in parliamentary debate, for teamwork, co-operation and successful compromise."[152]

In summary, there still are few "permanent" members who can make a career of the parliamentary position in Canada although data gathered by Roman March suggest that over time fewer individuals have left Parliament of their own accord. That is, they tend to be defeated rather than to voluntarily relinquish their position. (See Table 15.)

One inference that can be drawn from the data above, assuming the proportion of patronage appointments available to M.P.'s has

Table 15. *Initial Cause of Retirement from House of Commons, 1867–1962*

	1867–1899	1900–1939	1940–1962
Electoral defeat	57%	59%	81%
Died, Did not stand	14	16	11
Federal patronage (Senate and Judiciary)	14	18	4
Provincial patronage (lieutenant governor)	7	2	2
Other patronage and reasons for not standing	8	5	2
	(N = 526)	(N = 636)	(N = 379)

remained fairly constant, is that the position of member of Parliament is currently more attractive than it was previously. Even if a parliamentary career is more desirable, however, we have seen that few members are able to retain their seats for any considerable period of time. An increasingly smaller number of individuals have had prior public office experience before their election to Parliament and once there, unless they are members of a government, they rarely are able to specialize and become expert in any substantive area.

First, the institutions within a legislature that customarily permit a member to acquire expertise in a particular area (the

152. Sigmund Neumann, "Toward A Comparative Study of Political Parties," in *Comparative Government: A Reader,* ed. Harry Eckstein and David Apter (New York, 1963), pp. 360–361.

committees) either function very poorly or not at all in the Canadian House of Commons. Second, the average backbencher, despite the fact that he generally is a highly educated individual, is unable to exploit any institutionalized opportunities to either legislate or control because he is literally starved for information. He has no staff at his disposal to generate relevant data, make and maintain contact with the bureaucracy, provide him with ideas, or even relieve him of some of the routine clerical work involved in case work. The House provides only rudimentary research assistance and the several committees, when they do meet, operate almost without staff. Nor, as Porter[153] points out, can he turn to "extra-parliamentary" sources for help. The national parties do not employ even minimally adequate research organizations, nor does the academic community involve itself in "politics." Those academicians who do become involved in the political process almost invariably are employed in a research capacity by the administrative bureaucracies of the governing party—the very groups that Parliament is to control.

Consequently, his participation in the legislative and control functions of Parliament is limited to one of intermittently attacking or defending policies that have been generated by party leaders, and either to offering sychophantic praise or heaping personal invective. Such activity may have a cathartic effect on the backbencher, and also may be useful to the party leaders, but it is likely to evoke only contempt and amusement from the portion of the population that normally is attentive to public affairs and monumental indifference from the portion that is not.

153. Porter writes:
> It would probably be difficult to find another modern political system with such a paucity of participation from its scholars. In almost all countries in the western world scholars work close to political parties and even take on important political roles. The absence of any dynamic quality to the Canadian political system could probably in a large measure be attributed to its separation from the world of the higher learning. The association of the intellectuals with the bureaucracy of governments is clear enough. . . . Judged by the internal standards of their function within Canadian social institutions, the universities and their leading teachers can be said to be appropriate to other institutional aspects of Canadian society. Upward social mobility is limited, the British charter group dominates, the political system is depoliticized in a crippling federalism. Over all this ruminate the disengaged fellows of the Royal Society of Canada, section II.

Porter, *op. cit.*, pp. 503–504.

Conclusion

We began this paper by noting that it was rather remarkable that Canadians express such fundamental dissatisfaction with a national government that has neither involved them recently in debilitating foreign entanglements nor failed to provide for at least their basic social needs. During the course of this paper, we have tried to indicate that essentially there are four basic criticisms that have been made of the Canadian Parliament. First, there has been increasing unhappiness over the fact that the policies considered by Parliament and the legislation that Parliament ultimately produces have their origins in, and disproportionately reflect the economic and social interests of, a narrow elite stratum of the population. Second, Parliament has been criticized for its lack of innovation, for its failure to generate ameliorative policies (e.g., legislation that would upgrade and standardize the educational system) that would meet the needs of a majority of Canadians of all social classes. Third, Parliament, and particularly the leaders of Parliament, have been criticized because historically they have been and continue to be a socioeconomic elite who are grossly unrepresentative of a cross section of the population. Fourth, Parliament has been criticized for the manner in which it performs the roles popularly ascribed to it, particularly, those of legislating and of controlling the bureaucracy.

We have tried to delineate the variables that explain these criticisms: the ethnic-religious cleavages within Canadian society; the unstable and irregular population patterns; the overrepresentation of most non-British ethnic groups in the lower educational, income, and occupational strata of the population; the restricted political participation of these groups; the dominant position of power exercised by a small number of homogeneous, easily defined, and frequently overlapping elite groups; their high incidence of career interchange; the disproportionate influence of the provinces in the Canadian federal system; the highly volatile electorate; the overrepresentation and political competitiveness of rural constituencies; the high turnover in House membership each election; the non-ideological orientation of the two major parties; the overwhelming presence of the United States; the allocation of leadership positions by region and ethnic-religious background; the progressive exclusion of the backbencher from the policy-initiation and policy-evaluation process; the recruitment by the major parties of leaders outside the parliamentary system; the paucity of information and resources available to the M.P.; the centralization of authority in the cabinet; and the domination of Parliament by the cabinet and the administrative bureaucracy.

Obviously, many of these phenomena are not unknown to other polities. For example, the tendency of non-socialist parties to blur and to play down group economic differences, the preference of the mass media for conservative party candidates, the lack of ideological distinctiveness among parties, and the power exercised by the corporate elite in, and on, the process of legislative decision-making, all have been experienced, although in varying degrees, by most Western European and Anglo-American democracies. Others are what might be termed *circumstantial* variables, as for example, the adoption of a British-model parliamentary system for what eventually became an extremely heterogeneous society, and the deleterious impact the United States was to exercise on a developing national identity. Still others can be conceptualized as variables associated with political development. Thus, one could argue that the Canadian form of federalism with the disproportionate influence it permits provincial units of government, the allocation of national political leadership positions on an ethnic-religious and regional basis, the restriction of demands made upon the political system, the dampening and avoidance of potentially inflammable class issues, even the imposition of the values and preferences of a small, educated, and socially homogeneous elite on other social groups within society, have been adjustments the political system or, rather, the elites within the system, have had to make to maintain national viability and unity. Certainly, scholars studying developing countries have identified similar (and, frequently, far more drastic) behavior by indigenous elites and have rationalized it as being functional for the maintenance of viability of a particular system.

One can similarly argue that what appear to be structural weaknesses in a parliamentary system peculiar to Canada in reality are manifestations of a more general lack of institutional development. In a perceptive article, Nelson W. Polsby[154] has traced the "institutionalization" of the United States House of Representatives. According to Polsby, one aspect of institutionalization is the differentiation of an organization from its environment. In an undifferentiated organization, entry from outside to positions of leadership is quite common, and persistence of leadership over time is rare. Polsby points out that in the past both practices were characteristic of the United States House of Representatives. For example, in the fifty-one Congresses elected between 1790 and 1892, turnover of House members exceeded 50 per cent in fifteen elections, whereas, in the twentieth century, the incidence of turnover has been but a fraction of this.[155] We may note, then, that the high turnover of members that has been a characteristic of the Canadian House of Commons during the past hundred years also was a feature of the U.S. House of Representatives during the first century of its existence.

Polsby shows that until the twentieth century, members of the House attained positions of leadership at a relatively early age, possessed little or no seniority at the time of their appointment, served for a time in the position, and then left for a career elsewhere.[156] As has been indicated during the analysis, virtually the same pattern of leadership recruitment is to be found in the Canadian House of Commons. Thus, Schlesinger[157] points out that over 35 per cent of Liberal party cabinet ministers, 1921 to 1957, had less than a year's experience in the House of Commons before receiving their appointment; that 48 per cent of both Liberal and Conservative cabinet ministers were less than fifty years of age when they were appointed; and, as Porter and others

154. Nelson W. Polsby, "The Institutionalization of the U.S. House of Representatives," *American Political Science Review*, LXII (1968), 144–168.
155. *Ibid.*, pp. 145–146.   156. *Ibid.*, p. 149.
157. Schlesinger, *op. cit.*, pp. 286–292.

have made abundantly clear, many of these cabinet appointees either went on to, or returned to, careers in the corporate and bureaucratic worlds after a relatively short period of political service.

A second aspect of institutionalization of an organization is the growth of its internal complexity. Three measures of internal complexity suggested by Polsby are (*a*) growth in the autonomy and importance of committees; (*b*) growth of specialized agencies of party leadership; and (*c*) a general increase in the provision of various emoluments and auxiliary aids to members in the form of office space, salaries, allowances, staff, and committee staffs. Polsby reveals that until the early years of the nineteenth century relatively little use was made of standing committees, and that the committee system, as we know it today, only began after the revolt against Cannon's Speakership in 1910–11. With respect to party organization within the House, he shows that the institutionalization of majority and minority leadership positions, of party whips, and of formal procedures for canvassing members, are innovations of the twentieth century. Finally, he points out that the relatively lavish internal resources, measured in terms of personnel, staff facilities, and the money available to the House, also are recent innovations. In fact, as recently as the beginning of the present century, Congress carried out its work almost entirely without expert assistance.

Again, there is an obvious parallel between what occurred in the Congress and what is current practice in the Commons, as, for example, the part played by standing committees. Further, the same lack of internal resources that we currently find in the Canadian Parliament with respect to features such as staff assistance, office space, and a research branch also characterized nineteenth-century Congresses. And, although we would expect a fairly well-developed party leadership organization in the Canadian House of Commons (given the fact that it is a Parliament modeled on the British), leadership positions such as parliamentary assistant are of relatively recent origin.

Polsby finds that over time entry into the Congress became difficult and turnover less frequent, leadership became stabilized, and individuals aspiring to leadership positions first had to serve long periods of apprenticeship. A career in the Congress became an end in itself. There was a marked shift from discretionary toward automatic decision-making in that the seniority system— an automatic, universally applied, non-discretionary method— became the *sine qua non* for promoting individuals from within the system to positions of leadership.

Another indicator of the institutionalization and professionalization of the Congress was that the number of contested elections decreased. Controversies that did arise were settled strictly on their merits. In essence, as the responsibilities of the national government grew, and as a larger proportion of the national economy was affected by decisions taken at the center, the agencies of national government, of which Congress was one, were institutionalized.

Again, a somewhat similar pattern may be discerned in Canada. In the nineteenth century, there was relatively little for Parliament to do; the problems with which it dealt were not overly complex, the scope of its activity was fairly narrow, and it operated under a set of rules which did not completely structure individual and group behavior. During the period a substantial proportion of Members of Parliament retired from Parliament for reasons other than electoral defeat, generally, for a more desirable career than a seat in Parliament afforded. Data gathered by March (not shown) indicate there also was a high incidence of disputed and "stolen" elections during the period.

The twentieth century witnessed a growth in population, in the economy, in the administrative bureaucracy, in the size of Parliament, and in the quality and quantity of demands made upon it. Concomitant with this growth (but in contrast to the Congress which became increasingly decentralized) came an attempt to integrate the functions performed by Parliament by centralizing control over the substance of legislation and the procedures by which legislative decisions were made in the cabinet. Increased use was made of standing and select committees, although by far the most important committee continues to be the Committee of the Whole House.

A modest start also has been made toward institutionalizing the internal resources of the Commons. Members now have individual offices, an embryo staff, a small but growing research branch, and a more substantial salary (from $10,000 to $18,000 since 1963). And, as was the case in the House of Representatives, the number of disputed and "stolen" elections has decreased and an increasing number of individual members seemingly have come to regard service in the national legislative body as a career. Thus, one would be fairly safe in predicting, if the present trend toward institutionalization is extended, and if Parliament continues to pass through the same processes as did the U.S. House of Representatives, that by approximately 2040 Parliament *also* may enjoy the same high status and possess the same powers vis-à-vis other political institutions as does the current Congress. Given its present level of development, however, the questions arise as to whether it is necessary to wait another hundred years for Parliament to become a truly effective and prestigious legislative body and whether, instead, it might not be more desirable for the process of institutionalization to "skip a stage?"

Insofar as variables outside of and acting upon Parliament are concerned, one may speculate that after a hundred years of economic development and political stability, Canadian society is no longer so fragile a flower that its continued good health requires that all socio-economic cleavages be submerged for the sake of national unity. And, by this time, class-based left-right politics and issues no longer are luxuries that cannot be indulged in lest they rend the polity asunder. This is not to suggest that class politics would impart the dynamism or generate the kind of innovations in the system that Porter and others have claimed for them. It is to say that two or more class-based parties articulating reasonably clear and differentiated policies likely would stimulate and refresh the electorate. At worst, they would pose no grave threat to the viability of the political system.[158] Relatedly,

158. Gad Horowitz makes an excellent case for the introduction of left-right class politics in Canada and argues that the contention that Canada can only be held together if class cleavages are avoided is the "exact opposite of the truth." According to him, "the promotion of dissensus on class issues is a way of

one could argue that it is no longer necessary to restrict the demands made upon Parliament to those emanating from a narrow elite segment of the population. The system appears strong enough to bear the weight of the articulated preferences of other social strata without becoming overloaded. Further, there is reason to believe that more sustained concern by Parliament with issues that are salient for members of major economic groups and less attention to abstract symbols[159] might now be appropriate. Certainly, it would make it more difficult for critics to claim that the values of the two major parties are the same; that Parliament never engages in dialogues that are meaningful to a majority of the public; and, in fact, that Parliament is a screen "behind which the controlling interests pull the strings to manipulate the Punch and Judy who engage in mock combat before the public."[160]

Within Parliament itself, rapid progress toward institutionalization might better be made by a decentralization of its procedures (principally, through more extensive and effective employment of standing committees) and by a substantial increase in the internal resources available to the House and to individual members. Decentralization, it can be claimed, would make the backbencher something more than a cipher, would help create a substantial number of new and interesting positions in the House, and would afford individuals who desire it with the opportunity to specialize in substantive policy areas.

Although even the provision of an adequate staff and of greatly expanded research facilities would permit the average M.P. to become an expert in only a relatively narrow policy area, cumulatively, the impact on the quality of House debates and on its general performance probably would be both salutary and highly

mitigating dissensus on many non-class issues." See Gad Horowitz, "Toward the Democratic Class Struggle," *Journal of Canadian Studies*, I (1966), 3–10.

159. For example, the study by Meisel and his associates indicated that the majority of the 1965 electors he studied were concerned with economic issues such as unemployment; 50 per cent said that such issues were "very important" while another 26 per cent said they were "fairly important." Similarly, 39 per cent said social welfare issues were very important and 25 per cent said they were fairly important. In contrast, only 20 per cent felt the new Canadian flag was an important issue, whereas an additional 16 per cent felt it was fairly important.

160. Frank H. Underhill, *In Search of Canadian Liberalism* (Toronto, 1960), p. 168, quoted in Porter, *op. cit.*, p. 376.

visible. As well, such a step would help redress the informational balance that currently is so heavily weighed on the side of the bureaucracy. It would at once permit energetic opposition members to perform more effectively and provide cabinet members with alternative sources of necessary information. Their almost complete reliance on a bureaucracy, however able, for information obviously is not an unmixed blessing.

In the past, the increased and more effective use of standing committees has been resisted on the ground that it would seriously undermine the authority of the cabinet. It is possible that this might be the case, but this is an empirical question! There is some reason to believe that the relative autonomy enjoyed by American congressional committees rests as much on the institutional separation of the executive and the legislative branches and on the loose coalitional nature of the congressional parties—features not duplicated in Canada—as it does on their power over legislation.

It also could be maintained that greatly increasing the internal resources of the House of Commons and the emoluments of individual members would transform the organization from one whose general goal is to generate public policy to one whose primary concern is to maintain organizational perquisites. Again, such a possibility cannot be discounted, but more likely outcomes would appear to increase individual incentive to make the parliamentary position a career; to maximize backbench participation in Parliament's tasks; and to increase the power of the House of Commons within the political system. Most important, in light of the problem posed at the beginning of this paper, it should drastically increase public respect for and confidence in the Member of Parliament as an individual and Parliament as an organization. The performance of a political institution and the legitimacy the public ascribes to it are closely interrelated. In a sense, they are two sides of a single coin.

Chapter 4

Congress in the American Political System

Roger H. Davidson

Of all the parts of the most thoroughly examined political system in history, the Congress of the United States is surely the most closely watched and assiduously worried over. This fact alone is of no little significance. The recent vogue of congressional behavior research among academic students of politics is the product of many factors, some transitory and some not. Perhaps the most compelling reason is the unique susceptibility of Congress to the probing of analytical and empirical tools employed by the growing cadre of American social scientists.[1]

The sheer volume of available information concerning Congress might itself be sufficient to justify its inclusion in a volume of essays on legislatures and political development. But more fundamental reasons compel yet another, albeit brief, examination of Congress. Our assumption is that there is a common core of legislative functions in all political systems—whether or not these functions are performed by institutions labeled *legislatures.* Perhaps if we start from a vantage point where relatively much is known, we will know what to look for in systems which are less thoroughly researched. And if we discover, as certainly we shall, that institutions we call legislatures differ in the manner and degree to which they perform such functions, we will be led to search for the sources of the differences. Moreover, it is of empirical and prescriptive significance to be able to ascertain where,

1. For one attempt to explain the recent attention to Congress as an object of research, see Roger H. Davidson and David M. Kovenock, "The Catfish and the Fisherman: Prescriptive Political Science and Congressional Reform," *American Behavioral Scientist,* X (June, 1967), 23–27.

and with what success, such functions are actually performed in political systems.

There are other persuasive arguments for beginning our survey from the vantage point of Capitol Hill. The political system within which Congress operates has experienced virtually the entire range of forces associated with modernization in the Western world. The aftermath of the Industrial Revolution, the growth of technology and communications, the increased social and economic interdependence—these and other aspects of the phenomenon usually (and relativistically) termed *development* have exerted an impact upon the American system and its national legislature. We need not assume, of course, that patterns of development are identical for all political systems or that non-Western cultures respond to modernizing forces in the same way that Western cultures have. However, the forces at work in the United States since 1789 (and even before) are not unlike those with which developing nations must contend.

The United States Congress has, moreover, been relatively successful in combating obsolescence in the face of the anti-legislative aspects of modernization. It remains questionable whether Congress can long maintain its autonomy in the face of continuing pressures toward executive hegemony; but few would question that it has been uniquely successful thus far. Much of the institution's durability is traceable to the decentralized nature of the American polity; the diffusion of electoral risk, in particular, gives the majority of senators and representatives a local base of power which no executive can trespass. Even so, Congress has deployed its resources so as to minimize executive incursions. Development of committee specialization, relative generosity in providing for staff assistance, and jealous husbandry of procedural traditions—all have helped to maintain the vitality of the national legislature. For strategies of legislative survival, Congress is rich in example.

It is not inappropriate, therefore, to examine a relatively strong legislature in a mature political system as a prelude to considering the role of legislatures in political development. We harbor no illusions about the extent to which Congress may, or may not, serve as a model for legislative institutions elsewhere. What we shall be concerned with, however, is the functional position of Congress in its own developing political system, with the impact of development upon the institution, and with the stratagems it has adopted in retaining its vitality.

Society and Polity in the United States

A political system's primary function is the specification and attainment of the goals of the larger society.[2] This political task actually embraces a dual problem. Within any society of constituent parts operating in an unpredictable environment, a multiplicity of goals is inevitable. Thus, the polity must provide mechanisms for the setting of priorities among competing goals. Secondarily, the polity must seek to mobilize the society's material and psychological resources to realize the goals that have been selected.

Many observers have been impressed by what appeared to have been a low level of conflict over goals in the American political system. Some have seen the absence of a feudal tradition as the basis for a broad consensus on goals.[3] Both the conclusion and the explanation are open to serious question. First of all, the level of political conflict and even violence in the system has always been significant. On one occasion the nation was ripped apart by civil strife; and from Shays' Rebellion to the urban ghetto riots, conflicts have been frequent and intense. Moreover, whatever stability the system has enjoyed has most certainly not been the product of goal consensus, even on procedural matters. As Greenstein has noted, ". . . the findings of public opinion research over the years converge in suggesting that there is re-

2. Talcott Parsons, *The Social System* (Glencoe, Ill., 1951); David Easton, *The Political System* (New York, 1953), pp. 130 ff.; William C. Mitchell, *Sociological Analysis and Politics* (Englewood Cliffs, N.J., 1967).
3. For a compelling statement of this thesis, see Louis Hartz, *The Liberal Tradition in America* (New York, 1955).

markably weak commitment to what seem to be fundamental democratic ground-rules."[4]

What accounts for the stability of American political institutions? The answers to this question are many and go to the very heart of the American experience.[5] Two considerations appear particularly decisive. However diverse and heterogeneous the subpopulations that settled on the North American continent, their differences have normally been crosscutting rather than cumulative. A multitude of fluid, crisscrossing allegiances tend to cancel out one another—a fact which lends sociological substance to the concept of *e pluribus unum.*[6] There have been notable exceptions to this generalization. In each instance—the sectional disputes which resulted in the Civil War, class conflicts at the turn of the twentieth century, the contemporary revolt of black citizens—cumulative differences produced severe strains in the operation of the system.

A second force for stability—perhaps the most important in the long run—has been the system's abundant resources for meeting goal demands. The North American continent possesses immense natural wealth and, for the greater part of its modern history, its immigrant inhabitants have considered this wealth amenable to unlimited exploitation. An "agreement to disagree" could be predicated upon the expectation that many private goals could be realized concurrently with a minimum of governmental intervention. Thus, the level and intensity of goal demands upon political institutions have remained for the most part at manageable levels.

Yet however impressive its resources, no polity—including this one—can hope to resolve more than a portion of the conflicting

---

4. Fred I. Greenstein, *The American Party System and the American People* (Englewood Cliffs, N.J., 1963), p. 9. See also James W. Prothro and Charles M. Grigg, "Fundamental Principles of Democracy: Base of Agreement and Disagreement," *Journal of Politics,* XXII (March, 1960), 276–294.

5. A particularly useful summary of the problem is found in Robin M. Williams, Jr., *American Society: A Sociological Interpretation,* 2nd ed. (New York, 1960), pp. 347 ff.

6. "A society riven by many minor cleavages is in less danger of open mass conflict than a society with only one or a few cleavages." Robin M. Williams, Jr., *The Reduction of Intergroup Tensions,* Bulletin 57, Social Science Research Council (New York, 1947), p. 59.

demands made upon it to pursue various goals. Leonard A. Lecht estimates that the objectives proposed by President Eisenhower's Commission on National Goals would require at least one and a half trillion dollars in the 1970's.[7] Even if there were no doubt that the goals could be obtained (and obviously some goals are beyond human grasp), there is serious question whether consent could be gained to rechannel the necessary resources from diverse private uses. Consequently, some goals are rejected out of hand; others receive only token recognition; and still others are granted varying degrees of support.

If priorities are agreed upon, the polity must perform another task: it must find ways and means of mobilizing the needed resources or facilities to realize the goals that have been selected. Administration and coordination are required at a minimum to implement any collective enterprise. What is more difficult, the numerous goal-oriented segments of the society must be reconciled to the choices which have been made, so that they will make whatever sacrifices may be required. In reconciling various interests, political structures must possess the quality of legitimacy; that is, they must appear to operate in conformity with the society's values. Although the American polity commands impressive loyalty from the large majority of its citizens, the legitimacy ascribed to the system has been hard-won and must be reinforced by socializing new generations of citizens and responding to the expectations of goal-oriented individuals and groupings.

The polity's outputs, in the currency of power, take the form of concrete decisions or policies, which, considered as a whole, define the goal priorities of the society. These priorities are expressed in directives which demand action, or restraint from action, on the part of citizens. In a complex society, such directives are commonly drafted in great detail and appear in a variety of forms—as laws or regulations, judicial decisions, or executive orders of various kinds. However, goal priorities are also manifested in "non-decisions," or the absence of action upon a particular problem or demand.

7. Leonard A. Lecht, *The Dollar Cost of our National Goals* (Washington, 1965).

In resolving the problem of goal-attainment, developed political systems have evolved complex and varied substructures. One of these is the legislature, which contributes to goal-attainment by securing support and integrating conflicts among members of the system. The powers may be extensive (as in the United States) or token (as where the legislature merely ratifies and legitimates decisions made elsewhere in the system). The writers of the federal Constitution clearly intended the national legislature to be the primary arena for setting the society's goal priorities (or at least those priorities which were appropriate for government to set). Moreover, the Founding Fathers wanted Congress to participate in the widest possible range of specific tasks, performing them in concert with executive and judicial structures. They envisioned a polity not of separate structures performing separate tasks, but of separate structures sharing tasks. As James Madison expressed it, the Constitution created a government of blended powers.[8]

The Distribution of Power

The Constitutional charter thus left to the devious workings of history the precise boundaries of institutional power. By creating institutions that were designed to share tasks while possessing rival bases of influence, the compromise document of 1787 laid the groundwork for the institutional struggle which persists to this day. Historical evolution has been far from continuous, but two trends seem to have become dominant and irreversible. First, the federal government's sphere of action has broadened at all levels—local, state, and national. Second, within the federal establishment, executive structures have made relative gains at the expense of Congress.

American political structures were designed by men who deeply distrusted governmental power. This familiar maxim bears repeating in an age when American governments move freely in spheres of initiative formerly forbidden to limited gov-

8. *Federalist,* 48.

ernments. In his probing analysis of the early Washington community, James S. Young has characterized national government in Jeffersonian times as follows: "Almost all of the things that republican governments do which affect the everyday lives and fortunes of their citizens, and therefore engage their interest, were in Jeffersonian times *not* done by the national government."[9]

To describe how a government of limited powers has been transformed into an interventionist state would be to review virtually the entire social and legal history of the nation. Suffice it to say that public expectations of government's role in goal-attainment—in such fields as defense, economic stability, education, and welfare—are quite different in urbanized and industrialized twentieth-century America than in the rural and agrarian society of the late eighteenth century. As Sidney Fine has concluded,

As the mid-point of the twentieth century was reached, Americans would appear to have rejected the admonition that government is best which governs least and to have endorsed the view that in the interests of the general welfare the state should restrain the strong and protect the weak; should provide such services to the people as private enterprise is unable or unwilling to supply, should seek to stabilize the economy and to counteract the cycle of boom and bust, and should provide the citizen with some degree of economic security.[10]

Thus governments at all levels undertake tasks that were performed little or not at all by their predecessors. Although national institutions have received disproportionate attention since New Deal days, local and state structures have grown at least as spectacularly.

Congress has benefited from the over-all tendency to shift controversies from private to public arenas of conflict. Not even its most bitter critics could confuse the contemporary Congress with the chaotic and sporadic institution of the early nineteenth century.[11] The contemporary Congress considers (with what

9. James S. Young, *The Washington Community, 1800–1828* (New York, 1966), p. 31. (Italics in original.)
10. Sidney Fine, *Laissez-Faire and the General Welfare State* (Ann Arbor, Mich., 1956), pp. 399–400.
11. Young, *op. cit.*, pp. 94–97, *et passim*.

must be conceded are impressive expertise and decorum) a host of social and political issues that in earlier days were the province of local or private entities, or of no one at all. As John F. Kennedy was fond of pointing out, the Clays, Calhouns, and Websters could afford the luxury of a generation or more to refine the few overarching problems of the Republic. Modern legislators, in contrast, are inundated with a staggering number and variety of public issues in which Congress assumes a significant role. One telling sign of broadening congressional involvement is the growth within the past decade of the twelve-month session as a normal state of affairs. Legislators understandably deplore this development, but few indeed believe it will ever be reversed. Thus, there has been no absolute decline of congressional influence.

The relative positions of Congress and the executive establishment are quite another matter. On this point, there is virtual consensus that the high-water mark of "congressional government" has subsided. Many tasks normally labeled *legislative* in character have become presidential or executive in locus. The essential function of framing the agenda of issues has been relegated to the president and his staff. Contestants in political struggles, moreover, increasingly tend to press their claims and resolve their differences through executive agencies rather than in the halls of Congress.[12] There is, thus, more than a kernel of realism in the now-common observation that the president is chief legislator.

The causes of Congress's relative decline are rooted in the environment of contemporary governments. Historically, wars and foreign involvements have provided occasions for executive expansion. The reasons—expedient ones which even such advocates of limited government as John Locke understood keenly—are validated in constitutional dicta which recognize the executive as commander-in-chief and "sole organ of the nation in foreign affairs."[13] So long as the United States enjoyed generations of

12. David B. Truman, "The Presidency and Congressional Leadership: Some Notes on Our Changing Constitution," *Proceedings of the American Philosophical Society* (October, 1959), pp. 687–692.

13. *United States* v. *Curtiss-Wright Export Corp.*, 299 U.S. 304 (1936).

innocent isolation from world affairs, executive pre-eminence remained largely uncharted territory; but in an age of prolonged
international semi-crisis, the president and the executive establishment are advantaged.

A related factor in the relative decline of Congress is the
mounting diversity and complexity of goal-specification problems. Informational requirements of decision-making have esca-
lated sharply; and though Congress has struggled valiantly and
with some success to keep abreast, it is hardly a match for the
federal bureaucracy and its army of full-time experts.

Congress engages in many tasks which contribute to the societal function of goal specification and goal implementation. Of
these tasks, at least six are relevant to our present discussion of
the role of Congress in the American polity. First, through deliberation and drafting the specific content of policy outputs, Congress participates in the actual making of rules. Rule-making is
the primary element of the popular conception of "legislation"
—drafting and adopting legislaton. Second, Congress represents
the demands or interests of various geographic, economic, ideological, or professional claimants for goal priorities. The analogy
of the fiduciary agent acting on behalf of his principal, the sovereign electorate, is useful in understanding the traditional notion
of the legislator-as-representative.[14] An institution of fiduciary
agents which plays an active role in rule-making of necessity
performs a third key function, consensus building—the outcome
of the process of bargaining or brokerage through which various
claims are combined (or aggregated) in such a way that no
significant constituency is permanently or severely damaged.

These three broad tasks are the mark of an active legislative
body and comprise a reasonable summary of the legislative theory of the Constitution, which asserts that "all legislative powers
. . . shall be vested in a Congress of the United States" (Article I,
Section 1). According to constitutional theory, political bargains
will be struck primarily within the legislative branch; executive

14. William Riker, *The Theory of Political Coalitions* (New Haven, Conn.,
1962), pp. 24–28. See also Hanna Pitkin, *The Concept of Representation* (Berkeley and Los Angeles, 1967).

agencies ratify these bargains when the president signs them into law and when bureaucrats act to implement them. In functional terms, the traditional Congress is the polity's primary formal instrument for aggregating interests.[15]

If, on the other hand, the legislature is not a primary participant in the formal aggregation of policy demands, its role will be limited to secondary tasks which serve as surrogates for rule-making, representation, and consensus building. These ancillary tasks, which are implicit in the workings of a "strong" legislature, become overriding for a legislature which is denied meaningful participation in the resolution of goal demands. Rather than making rules, such a truncated legislature clarifies policy and provides oversight of policy-administration. Legislative bodies promote policy clarification by serving as a public forum where issues can be identified and communicated. They oversee or review implementation of policy directives by executive agents. Rather than representing its clienteles, a truncated legislature may resort to constituent service tasks—the so-called errand boy role of acting as lobbyist or advocate for clientele problems or demands. And instead of exploring the avenues of consensus, the weak legislature is confined to ratifying, or legitimating, prior bargains that have already been struck elsewhere in the political system.

Each of the tasks we have outlined—both the primary tasks and the ancillary ones—are performed in some measure by all institutions classed as legislatures. It is the particular mixture of tasks, however, that serves to define the character of the legislature's partnership with other political structures in the specification and implementation of societal goals. Any legislature which performs the three central legislative, or rule-making, tasks will perform the ancillary tasks (or most of them) as a matter of course. Such an institution would, by definition, play a central

15. Implicit in this discussion is the notion that political rule-making is actually the aggregation of goal-oriented demands by official instruments of the polity. "Aggregation may be accomplished by means of the formulation of general policies in which interests are combined, accommodated, or otherwise taken account of, or by means of the recruitment of political personnel more or less committed to a particular pattern of policy." Gabriel Almond and James S. Coleman, *The Politics of the Developing Areas* (Princeton, N.J., 1960), p. 39.

role in specifying the nation's goals. By contrast, a legislature that is reduced to emphasizing the ancillary tasks has a smaller "piece of the action": its total role and level of influence is intermittent and interstitial rather than continual and central.

Congress stands somewhere between these two models of functional participation.[16] Thus, the institution's impact upon the political system is mixed and defies simple generalization. Some observers are overly pessimistic: "The only really important law originated, shaped, and passed by Congress since World War II is the Taft-Hartley Act," columnist Stewart Alsop has said, "and there may never be another." Yet the rule-making, representing, and consensus-building legislature—most certainly the legislature of John Locke and the Founding Fathers—remains a fair approximation of how the contemporary Congress functions, at least on some occasions and in some issue areas. Especially in domestic matters, members of Congress—or more frequently, congressional committees—play a central and creative role in aggregating interests. Because recruitment and tenure in Congress are rooted in local constituencies, localized demands are especially well represented on Capitol Hill. Thus, Congress retains an activist view of its prerogatives in such policy areas as agriculture, tax provisions, public works, immigration, and military manpower.

In assessing the role of Congress in policy formation, it is probably beside the point that Congress only rarely initiates policy proposals. Indeed, in a complex society interwoven with communications of all kinds, it is often virtually impossible to identify the real "initiator" of a policy alternative. Analyzing ninety major pieces of legislation during several decades preceding World War II, Lawrence Chamberlain concluded that Congress exerted a preponderant influence in the passage of about 40 per cent of them. The legislative imprint was especially marked in tariff and immigration measures.[17] Unquestionably a similar examination of post-war lawmaking would yield rather different

16. See Roger H. Davidson, David M. Kovenock, and Michael K. O'Leary, *Congress in Crisis: Politics and Congressional Reform* (New York, 1967), esp. chap. i.

17. Lawrence Chamberlain, *The President, Congress and Legislation* (New York, 1946).

conclusions. But even though it works from an agenda supplied primarily by the executive, Congress continues to exert meaningful, if not always consistent, influence. Such an agenda may reflect lobbying on the part of legislators, and it certainly embodies the executive's anticipations of "what the traffic will bear" on Capitol Hill. Moreover, what the executive proposes, Congress can substantially modify—if not right away, then as time passes. A dramatic case in point was the Economic Opportunity Act of 1964, a package of programs drafted exclusively in the office of the president and in the absence of compelling legislative or public demands. On initial passage, Congress added little to the measure. Yet as time passed and legislators gained more experience in the content and impact of the legislation, Congress became a more potent force in shaping both the content and the operation of anti-poverty programs.[18]

In the twentieth century, however, Congress finds itself confronted by a mounting body of decisions which are legislative in nature yet executive in locus. Nowhere is this phenomenon more marked than in the fields of foreign affairs and national security. In such cases, traditional legislative prerogatives—bringing political combatants together to hear their claims, and then resolving these claims into directives—are performed in the first instance within executive agencies. As Huntington has concluded with regard to decision-making for military strategy,

No congressional committee is competent [to select military programs], not because it lacks the technical knowledge, but because it lacks the legal authority and political capability to bring together all these conflicting interests, balance one off against another, and arrive at a compromise or decision. . . . No congressional body gets more than a partial view of the interests involved.[19]

The executive's ability to perform these traditional legislative tasks has profound implications for the future of Congress. As Arthur F. Bentley foresaw in 1908," "[W]hen the adjustment is

18. See Sar A. Levitan, *The Design of Federal Antipoverty Strategy* (Ann Arbor and Detroit, 1967).
19. Samuel Huntington, *The Common Defense* (New York, 1961), pp. 131–132.

not perfected in the legislature, then the executive rises in strength to do the work."[20]

Most commentators agree that the secondary tasks—including policy clarification, administrative oversight, constituency service, and policy legitimation—are increasingly characteristic of the contemporary Congress. Because these tasks are directed more to the articulation and communication of interests than to their resolution, or aggregation, these tasks closely link Congress with other institutions that perform these roles, most notably interest groups and political parties. It is not implied that Congress will cease to be a decisive force in policy-making. It does mean, however, that the national legislature is more claimant than mediator, and that it "revises and extends" rather than frames the agenda.

The overseer role is illustrative. Review of administrative agencies has become a major congressional preoccupation, a concern reinforced by the 1946 Legislation Reorganization Act's admonition that committees exercise "continuous watchfulness" over the agencies and programs within their jurisdictions. Although not all congressional committees have displayed equally zealous watchfulness, Congress has in the past generation explored new methods of post-legislative control—through annual appropriations review, informal committee clearance of policies, and periodic investigations. "For twenty years," Richard Neustadt writes, "entrenchment of the new bureaucracy has given rise to efforts aimed at tightening congressional control over the details of administrative operations."[21] Typically these controls are wielded not by the houses as a whole, but by subgroups within the houses. Such legislative relationships with administrative agencies and relevant clientele groups have frequently blossomed into informal policy-making arenas which Douglass Cater has labeled *subgovernments*.[22]

20. Arthur F. Bentley, *The Process of Government* (Chicago, 1908), p. 359.
21. Richard E. Neustadt, "Politicians and Bureaucrats," in *The Congress and America's Future*, ed. David B. Truman (Englewood Cliffs, N.J., 1965), p. 105.
22. Douglass Cater, *Power in Washington* (New York, 1964), chap. ii. For a detailed study of one of these "subgovernments," see J. Leiper Freeman, *The Political Process: Executive Bureau–Legislative Committee Relations*, rev. ed. (New York, 1965).

Often the oversight task is indistinguishable from constituency service, which is performed not only by relevant committee members but by all representatives and senators. With the proliferation of governmental programs affecting the daily lives of citizens, new devices are required to help citizens deal with administrative agencies. As locally based representatives with a stake in performing such services, legislators have come—sometimes reluctantly—to perform such services. And in doing so, they exercise a "continuous watchfulness" over the way in which programs are handled. The geographic biases of members, of course, lend a certain localism to the resulting adjustments that are made in programs.

The transition of congressional roles has been uneven and incomplete, a fact which engenders a high degree of individual and institutional frustration on Capitol Hill. Congressional activists, supported by political groups with a stake in preserving legislative powers intact, are vocal in denouncing any retrenchment from the constitutional design of legislative power. Executive-oriented critics, supported by liberal interest groups with a stake in presidential activism, counter by advocating the secondary tasks as the only appropriate ones for an age of executive ascendancy. Moreover, contemporary events and decades of executive activism have taken their toll, with legislators themselves ever more frequently forced to retreat to a "second-strike" position which emphasizes the ancillary roles. This conflict over the role of the national legislature produces competing expectations for congressional performance—a prolonged and profound "constitutional crisis" within the political framework.[23]

The Congressional Career

Only three qualifications—age, citizenship, and residency—are specified by the Constitution for service in Congress. With the advent of popular election of senators early in this century, at last it could be said of recruitment to the national legislature that "No

23. See Davidson, Kovenock, and O'Leary, *op. cit.*, pp. 34–37.

qualification of wealth, of birth, of religious faith, or of civil profession is permitted to fetter the judgment or disappoint the inclination of the people."[24] Democratic procedures of choice do not, of course, ensure that legislators will be a cross section of citizens. For while formal rules of entry remain permissive, *de facto* rules are more demanding; and in consequence, members of Congress differ radically from the electorate at large. Although this fact of political life often dismays egalitarians, it presents no surprise to students of politics: it was Aristotle, after all, who first observed that elections are essentially oligarchic affairs.

In this section we shall describe several distinctive social and political attributes of members of Congress. Although our discussion is necessarily selective and fragmentary, it will delimit some of the salient characteristics of congressmen and senators as members of a political elite. These in turn should suggest linkages of this elite with a developing political system.

Occupational Characteristics

Occupational background is a key indicator of socio-economic status. (And while data concerning occupations are not always reliable, they are at least available.)[25] All of our knowledge about senators and representatives confirms the fact that they are drawn overwhelmingly from a relatively small number of high-status occupations. Fairly typical are the occupational backgrounds of eighty-seven members of the House of Representatives in the Eighty-eighth Congress (1963–1964), as presented in Table 1.[26] Slightly more than 60 per cent of the congressmen possessed legal backgrounds. Not all of these actively practiced

24. *Federalist*, 57 (Hamilton or Madison). The Seventeenth Amendment (adopted in 1913) substituted direct election of senators for choice by state legislatures. However, even before that legislatures frequently ratified the popular selections of statewide "canvasses."

25. Two major problems with occupational data are, first, that occupational categories themselves are broad and imprecise, and second, published biographical sources are sometimes incomplete.

26. Data for this table were obtained from questionnaires submitted to each respondent's office as well as from materials in published sources. The eighty-seven Members constituted a random sample of the total membership, stratified by party affiliation and leadership status. That is, the sample had the same ratio of Democrats to Republicans and the same ratio of leaders to non-leaders (within each party grouping) as the House as a whole. For a methodological explanation of the survey, see Davidson, Kovenock, and O'Leary, *op. cit.*, Appendix A.

law, but all had completed their legal training. Nearly a third of the sample were experienced in business or banking, yet these constituted the primary occupation for no more than a quarter of the sample. Agriculture or farming was listed by 14 per cent, though again often in combination with other occupations. (Not infrequently members owned land which was farmed by others and thus listed themselves as "farmers.") Similar proportions (9 per cent) of the sample possessed experience in education (including teaching and school administration) and in other profes-

Table 1. *Occupational Backgrounds of Eighty-seven Members of the Eighty-eighth Congress (1963–1964)*

Occupation	
Law	61%
Business and banking	31
Agriculture	14
Education	9
Other professional	9
Journalism	6
Other non-professional	6
Union official	2
Total	138[a]

a. Totals more than 100 per cent because many respondents listed more than one occupation.

sions—including medicine, clergy, accounting, and engineering. Six per cent of the sample had journalistic experience.

Most of these congressmen, therefore, were recruited from relatively high-status occupations. The exceptions, in all, would embrace no more than a quarter of the members sampled. Agriculture, for example, might be classed as lower status, but in the case of congressmen it usually involved ownership or proprietorship. The non-professional group embraced primarily lower status white-collar jobs, typically sales or clerical work. The two union officials in the sample began their careers as skilled laborers; but even they had spent most of their adult lives in white-collar jobs within their unions.

Senators' careers show, if anything, even less conformity to the "log-cabin-to-Capitol-Hill" myth. In examining senatorial careers (1947–1957), Matthews found that 64 per cent of the senators had been principally engaged in one of the professions (usually law); 29 per cent had been proprietors or officials; and 7 per cent, farmers.[27] The senators began their careers, moreover, with decided advantages. Very few future senators grew up in working-class families, and virtually all boasted high educational attainment. Fully 81 per cent won high-status jobs from the very start of their own careers.[28]

The "professional convergence" of law and politics is especially marked in the American political system, though the phenomenon occurs in varying degrees in other western nations.[29] There are several reasons for this convergence. Lawyers typically enjoy what is termed *job dispensability:* they can move readily in and out of their profession without jeopardizing their careers. In fact, a foray into politics can be an effective means of ethical advertising. For this and other reasons, young people aspiring to a political career often enter law to further their ambitions. The profession also emphasizes personal skills—verbalization, advocacy, and negotiation—which are useful in seeking and holding public office. Finally, the profession monopolizes certain public jobs (in law enforcement, particularly) that are important gateways to electoral office.

Historically, representation of lawyers in Congress has varied considerably. This finding is shown by Figure 1, which presents the distribution of major occupations in the House of Representa-

27. Donald R. Matthews, *U.S. Senators and Their World* (Chapel Hill, N.C., 1960), p. 32. See the same author's *The Social Backgrounds of Political Decision-Makers* (Garden City, N.Y., 1954).

28. Matthews, *U.S. Senators and Their World*, pp. 20, 30–31, *et passim.*

29. The phrase is from Heinz Eulau and John Sprague, *Lawyers in Politics: A Study in Professional Convergence* (Indianapolis, 1964). See also Charles Hyneman, "Who Makes our Laws?" *Political Science Quarterly*, LV (1940), 556–581; Joseph A. Schlesinger, "Lawyers and American Politics: A Clarified View," *Midwest Journal of Political Science*, I (May, 1957), 26–39; David Gold, "Lawyers in Politics," *Pacific Sociological Review*, IV (Fall, 1961), 84–86; and Matthews, *Social Background of Political Decision-Makers*, pp. 30–32.

Figure 1. *Occupations of Members in Ten Selected Congresses*

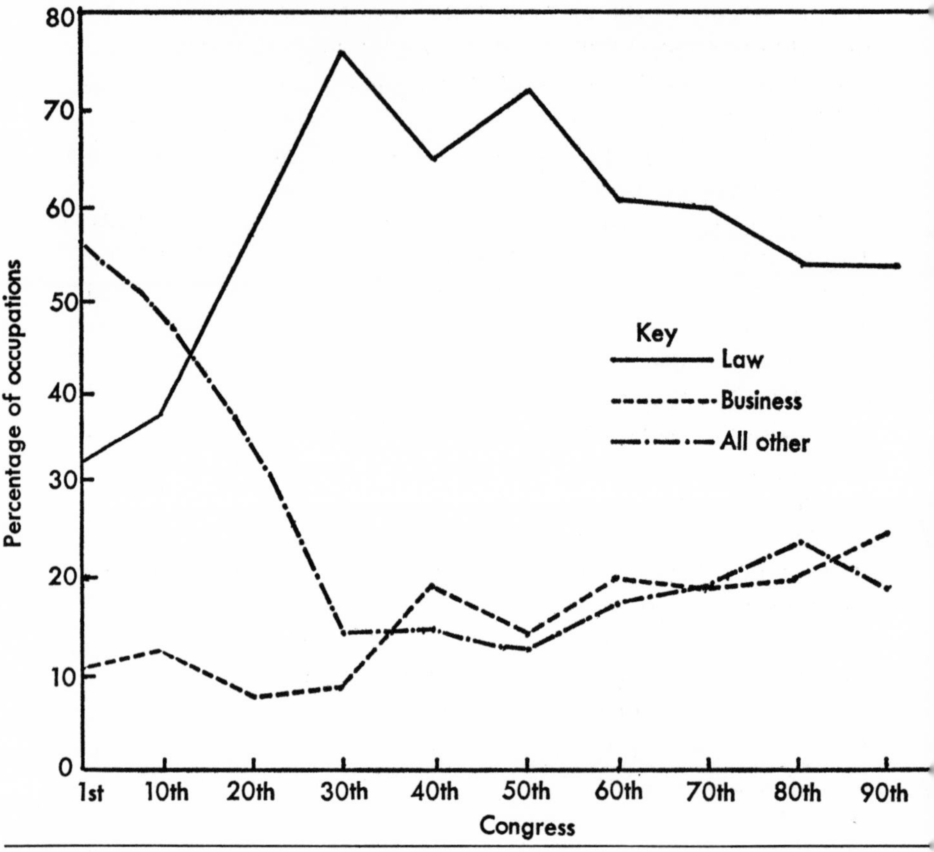

tives for ten selected Congresses.[30] Non-legal callings actually predominated in the First and Tenth Congresses, but legal train-

30. Historical data are drawn from analyses of the membership of the House in the First and Tenth Congresses and every tenth succeeding Congress, ending with the Ninetieth. Primary source of information was the *Biographical Directory of the American Congress, 1774–1961* (Washington, 1961); for recent Congresses this material was supplemented by *Congressional Directories* and by *Who's Who in America*. The figures represent the members' primary occupations before election to office. When a member engaged in more than one occupation, the one at which he was engaged for the longest period of time was chosen. In a few cases where no decision could be reached, more than one occupation was allowed. For purposes of the chart, the categories have been collapsed to three—law, business (including banking), and all others. The author wishes to acknowledge the assistance of Richard C. Neuhoff, who collected and analyzed the data.

ing quickly became the norm in the nineteenth century. During the twentieth century, the proportion of lawyers in the House has actually declined, though their share of the active labor force has remained relatively constant at .3 per cent. In post-World War II Congresses, lawyers have comprised slightly more than half of the total membership. As representation of the legal profession has declined, the proportions of business and other occupations have risen concomitantly.

Underlying the surge and ebb of the legal profession are regional variations which manifest economic and social development. In the East, the predominance of lawyers has been somewhat less marked than in other regions. Businessmen have been heavily represented in eastern delegations (from 23 to 32 per cent since the Civil War), a fact which no doubt reflects the concentration of industrial and financial institutions in that area. Of the four regions, therefore, the East seems to manifest the most stable and balanced occupational mixture. Legal backgrounds have been most over-represented in the newer and less developed regions. Thus, new states in the Midwest and West sent especially large contingents of lawyers to the nation's capital during their early years of representation—a fact which accounts for the growth of legal backgrounds in the mid-nineteenth century. In both regions, the proportions of lawyers subsequently declined—gradually in the Midwest, precipitously in the West. The South, traditionally considered an underdeveloped region, has shown a particularly marked and consistent affinity for legal backgrounds. However, lawyer-congressmen from the South are currently declining in relative strength, a trend which broadly parallels the region's economic coming of age.

In historical perspective, the occupational bases of the two major parties are startlingly similar. (See Figure 2.) Only in the South of recent years has there appeared a widening gap between the occupational mixture of the two parties' delegations (with the Republican party recruiting significantly more businessmen than the Democrats). This variation, in fact, accounts for most of the differences between the parties nationally. However, very real differences in partisan recruitment undoubtedly

Figure 2. *Party and Occupation of Non-Southerners in Ten Se-lected Congresses*

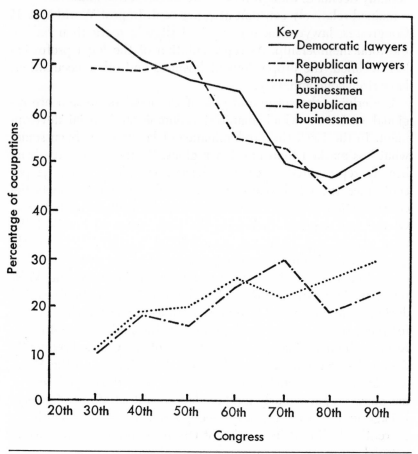

exist within occupational categories. Among senators of the 1947–1957 period, Matthews discovered that the Democratic businessmen were primarily merchants, contractors, oil and gas producers, and insurance or real estate men; Republicans, on the other hand, tended to be publishers and manufacturing execu-tives.[31] Similar differences presumably occur within the legal pro-

31. Matthews, *U.S. Senators and Their World*, pp. 40–42.

fession: there is a vast difference, for example, between the county-seat lawyer (southern Democrat) and the corporate or Wall Street lawyer (northern Republican).

If we may summarize our findings concerning occupational recruitment, it is clear that membership in neither house reflects a cross section of the electorate. Two occupations—law and, to a lesser extent, business—have predominated throughout the history of Congress. By contrast, those occupations which make up the vast majority of the labor force have been represented hardly at all. Yet trends in occupational recruitment suggest a certain widening of the occupational base. The decline of law and the rise of business backgrounds, for example, have been steady tendencies since the late nineteenth century. Other occupations, too, have been appearing somewhat more frequently. Moreover, as less developed regions of the country increase their resemblance to the urbanized, industrialized, and economically diversified East, a further "leveling downward" of the legal fraternity's position in the halls of Congress may well occur.

The Professional Politicians

An equally important feature of the pre-congressional career is the apprenticeship members serve in local and state politics—by holding public office or working for party organizations. Most persons in high public office are veteran political activists. The typical senator, Matthews found,

. . . started his political career shortly after graduating from college by being elected state legislator or becoming a prosecuting attorney or some other law-enforcement officer. By the time he was elected to the Senate he had held three previous offices and had spent about 10 years or half of his adult life in public office.[32]

In the House of Representatives, too, political careerism is an almost inviolable rule. The figures for our sample of eighty-seven members of the Eighty-eighth Congress, presented in Table 2, show strikingly the extensive apprenticeship of House Members. Only six per cent of the respondents had no discernible prior

32. *Ibid.,* p. 66.

political experience. Members in the sample held an average of 2.2. positions prior to their election to Congress.

Political apprenticeship has marked national legislators since the very first Congress.[33] Though uncomfortably incomplete, the data from our ten selected Congresses underscore this fact. If anything, there has been a slight downward trend in prior formal office-holding among members of recent Congresses. Whether

Table 2. *Prior Political Experience of Eighty-seven Members of the House (Eighty-eighth Congress)*

Type of experience	
State or local party position	75%
State legislature	47
City or county law enforcement	26
City or county elective position	12
City or county judicial position	12
State appointive position	9
National party position	9
Other city or local position[a]	8
Other federal position[b]	8
Federal law enforcement position	6
State elective position	1
No previous political experience	6
Total	218[c]

a. Includes appointive boards, commissions, etc.
b. Includes executive, civil service, and legislative staff.
c. Totals more than 100 per cent because members averaged 2.2 positions apiece.

this trend is significant in magnitude can only be guessed at, but it may be related to diminution of what might be called the "Founding Fathers" syndrome. Virtually all (97 per cent) of the members of the First Congress had previous experience in public life. Indeed, the initial Congress was perhaps the most politically professional group ever to convene as our national legislature: most of the men who met in New York in 1789 had participated in the Constitutional Convention, the Continental or Confedera-

33. George B. Galloway, *History of the House of Representatives* (New York, 1961), p. 33; and Charles O. Paullin, "The First Elections under the Constitution," *Iowa Journal of History and Politics*, III (January, 1904), 28.

tion Congresses, or in various local or state councils. This phenomenon was repeated in the two frontier regions, the Midwest and West, during their earliest years of representation on Capitol Hill. In each case, virtually every one of the small number chosen from these new regions had significant prior political experience. In each case, too, the proportion of politically experienced members soon dropped to "normal" levels—just as happened in the original states of the East and South following 1789.

In summary, members of Congress are political professionals. Probably well over 90 per cent of the members of any contemporary Congress have served apprenticeship in some segment of our political system. Important variations in political career patterns no doubt exist between the parties and among the various states and regions.[34] A slight over-all diminution of prior public office-holding seems to have occurred, but there is no evidence that this extends to partisan office-holding. On occasion aspirants can substitute nonpolitical accomplishment—for example, military service or celebrityship of some kind—for the normal route of political apprenticeship. But in general, Congress has been and continues to be limited to those who have proved themselves in other political assignments.

The Norm of Localism

Localism is one of the most rigorous norms of American electoral politics. One of the few constitutional qualifications for members of the national legislature is that they be "inhabitants" of the state from which they are elected. The norm manifested itself in electoral behavior as early as 1789 and remains firmly fixed in the minds of voters.[35] Indeed, *de facto* standards are somewhat more stringent than the letter of the Constitution: although the term *inhabitant* can be interpreted loosely, voter prejudice against "carpetbagger" candidates usually works to restrict office-holding to those with long and intimate association with the locale. Local ties are an important component of the generalized norm of apprenticeship and can be bypassed only

34. Joseph A. Schlesinger, *Ambition and Politics* (Chicago, 1966).
35. See Paullin, *op. cit.*, p. 13.

under unusual circumstances. Although localism comprises a potent independent power base, it has also exposed legislators to the charge of parochialism. Some political scientists have even suggested that some of Congress's conflicts with other institutions are traceable to the narrower geographic backgrounds of its members.[36]

Are congressmen and senators more local in their backgrounds than other groupings in our society? The answer is probably yes, if we are to rely upon available statistics on geographic mobility. From our examination of House members in selected Congresses, it appears that about 75 per cent of the members of recent Congresses were born in the state which they represent. (This number includes many individuals who moved within the borders of a single state, but it excludes those who moved between states early in their lives.) In comparison, about 70 per cent of the general population reside in the state in which they were born.[37] Among other elite groupings, the proportions of "immobile" persons are much lower, a fact which lends strength to the contention that these elites are more "cosmopolitan" than members of Congress.[38] The independent effect of this fact upon legislative behavior is hard to determine, for demographic immobility is intertwined with other kinds of localized political pressures. Moreover, local backgrounds do not necessarily lead members to assume localist roles of behavior—a matter we will elucidate presently.

Geographic mobility of legislators has fluctuated over time. In analyzing the backgrounds of members of our ten selected Congresses, we find that mobility levels have followed a convex curve. Early Congresses closely resembled contemporary Congresses: slightly less than three quarters of those in the First and Tenth Congresses were born in the state which sent them to

36. Andrew Hacker, "The Elected and the Anointed," *American Political Science Review*, XV (September, 1961), 544–545; and Samuel P. Huntington, *op. cit.*, pp. 12–16.

37. U.S. Bureau of the Census, *Historical Statistics of the United States, Colonial Times to 1957: Continuation and Revisions to 1963* (Washington, 1963), p. 8.

38. Huntington, *op. cit.*, p. 13. Percentages of persons in selected groupings experiencing no interstate mobility are: business leaders, 40 per cent; cabinet members, 30 per cent; and subcabinet federal political executives, 14 per cent.

Washington. As the nineteenth century progressed, however, congressmen became increasingly mobile. In the Fortieth Congress (1867–1869), for example, slightly more than half the legislators were born in another state;[39] but by the Fiftieth Congress (1887–1889) the number of geographically mobile legislators was on the downswing. The major factor associated with the mobility of nineteenth-century congressmen was apparently the addition of new states. The frontier regions of the Midwest and West accounted for most of this rise in mobility levels. During the early years of the new states' representation in Congress, virtually all in the delegations were born elsewhere. Native-born aspirants soon appeared, however, and as the region matured they came to dominate its delegations. By the late 1960's, only in the Far West was a large portion (almost half) of the congressmen born elsewhere. In contrast, the East has shown marked consistency over the 180-year period, electing predominantly "localist" members. The South is notable mainly for the "carpetbag" post-Civil War delegations, but throughout the twentieth century it has elected more localist members than any other region.

Available data concerning geographic mobility, then, confirm the common observation that the typical congressional background encompasses a narrow geographic area. The expectations of voters, the recruitment habits of local parties, and the normal patterns of political activism all encourage this attribute. Historically, levels of mobility have varied primarily with the addition of new frontier states. One relatively consistent party difference also appears: Democrats tend to recruit from among less mobile persons, even within the same professions. In comparison with other categories of persons, congressmen are slightly less mobile than the general public and much less so than other elite groupings.

The Washington Career

Working in fragmented and largely uncoordinated fashion, the electoral process yields a collectivity of legislators possessing

39. This included a large number of transplanted "carpetbag" Republicans in the South: twenty-six of the twenty-eight southern Republicans were born out-of-state, compared with two of the twelve Republicans twenty years later.

strikingly similar characteristics. Yet if the collectivity is to function harmoniously, the talents and interests of members must somehow be meshed into an institutional system which can cope with a complex environment and a mounting quantity of business. As Congress has matured, the two houses have evolved distinctive hierarchies of leadership, historic procedures and traditions, and accepted patterns of behavior.[40] Once settled in Washington, new legislators find themselves a part of an ongoing group whose shared experience supplements the parallel experience of prior careers. And every evidence is that this institutional experience is an increasingly pervasive segment of the legislators' environment.

Today's politicians are apt to make a career out of legislative office. In the House, especially, tenure in office has risen steadily. In the First Congress, of course, all members started afresh— though, as noted previously, many had already served in national legislative bodies. In the nineteenth century the average tenure of congressmen ranged between two and two and a half terms. At the turn of the century the average passed three terms, and by the Ninetieth Congress, the average member had served no less than 5.5 terms—or approximately eleven years.[41] In the Senate of the late 1960's the average seniority was slightly more than two terms or 13.25 years.

Extensive tenure in office means that few members of any given Congress are newcomers to Capitol Hill. When the Ninetieth Congress convened in January 1967, for example, only seven senators and sixty representatives were new to their jobs. In the House, the biennial turnover rate is typically between 15 and 20 per cent; in the Senate, only a third of whose members are up for re-election each two years, the figure is somewhat lower. Turnover has not always been so low. In examining the Jeffersonian era, James S. Young found on Capitol Hill not a stable commu-

40. Matthews, *U.S. Senators and Their World,* esp. chap. v; Richard F. Fenno, Jr., "The Internal Distribution of Influence: The House," in *The Congress and America's Future,* ed. David B. Truman (Englewood Cliffs, N.J., 1965); and William S. White's two volumes, *Citadel* (New York, 1956) and *Home Place* (Boston, 1965).

41. Nelson W. Polsby, "The Institutionalization of the House of Representatives" *American Political Science Review,* LXII (March, 1968), 146–147.

nity, but "a society of transients." Young found that average biennial turnover in the House during the first forty years of the nation was 41.5 per cent of the total membership. "While there were a few for whom the Hill was more than a way station in the pursuit of a career," he concluded, "a man's affiliation with the Congressional community tended to be brief."[42]

The rise of the congressional career has been accompanied by several corollaries. The average age of members has risen rather steadily, despite the fact that there has been no long-term increase in the age of newcomers.[43] Moreover, lateral mobility—movement of members to other political or nonpolitical posts—

Table 3. *Proportion of Cabinet Appointees With Congressional Experience, Selected Periods*

Time period	Percentage with congressional experience
1795–1832	67
1861–1896	37
1897–1940	19
1941–1963	15

Source: Data for the period 1795–1832 are from Young, *op. cit.*, p. 176. Other data are from Huntington, *op. cit.*, p. 12.

has declined precipitously. In the nation's early years, large numbers of legislators resigned their posts. Because more than two thirds of those who resigned later held political office elsewhere, Young concludes that "it was not from the political vocation that the Members tended to resign, but rather from the Washington community."[44] Today, even prestigious political opportunities find few aspirants on Capitol Hill. Table 3, for example, shows the decline in the proportion of cabinet members with prior service in Congress. During the early nineteenth century many

42. Young, *op. cit.*, p. 89.
43. T. Richard Witmer, "The Aging of the House," *Political Science Quarterly,* LXXIX (December, 1964), 526–541.
44. Young, *op. cit.*, 57.

cabinet members were recruited directly from Congress, sometimes in reward for supporting a successful presidential con-
tender. Nowadays this practice is rare. The impression persists
that lateral mobility from Congress to other positions has similarly dwindled. The contemporary senator or representative is
likely to view his office as a career in its own right, separate and
distinct from alternative political or nonpolitical career ladders.

Numerous factors have led to the distinctiveness of the congressional career, and we have neither space nor data adequate to
explore them all. Increased life expectancy, of course, is one
condition of lengthened tenure. Another, and a more important
condition, has been the existence of noncompetitive states and
congressional districts where incumbents, once seated, could expect repeated re-election. Studies have repeatedly demonstrated
that the smaller the electoral unit, the more it is likely to deviate
from perfect party competition. Individual states thus tend to be
less competitive than the nation as a whole, and congressional
districts even less competitive. In the case of House districts,
there has been a long-term trend away from competitiveness, and
today perhaps no more than a quarter of the districts are truly
two-party in character.[45] Once seated, incumbents enjoy overwhelming advantage at the polls over non-incumbent challeng-
ers.[46] And though we cannot pinpoint long-range trends with
certainty, it seems likely that the resources of men in office—in
terms of staff, information, and access to media exposure—will
continue to widen the "visibility gap" which separates incumbents from their opponents.

Though promise of physical and political longevity are precon-
ditions, they are insufficient to explain the rise of the congressional career. If rewards of office were absent, incumbents would
have scant incentive to make a career of legislative service. This

45. Charles O. Jones, "Inter-Party Competition for Congressional Seats," *Western Political Quarterly*, XVII (September, 1964), 461–476. See also Milton C.
Cummings, Jr., *Congressmen and the Electorate* (New York, 1966), pp. 186–187;
and Lewis A. Froman, *Congressmen and Their Constituencies* (Chicago, 1963),
pp. 81–82.
46. See H. Douglas Price, "The Electoral Arena," in *The Congress and America's Future*, ed. David B. Truman, pp. 42–45; and *Congressional Quarterly
Weekly Report* (December 7, 1962), pp. 2225–2230.

appears to have been the disposition of early legislators, many of whom declined to run for re-election or resigned to take posts that would today seem less prestigious. Few contemporary legislators leave for such reasons, and few at all leave Congress voluntarily. It is often said of today's legislators that "they never go back to Pocatello." We can only speculate at the reasons behind the attractiveness of the modern Congress: perhaps it is heightened institutional prestige, perhaps increased glamor of national and world politics, perhaps increased physical amenities in the nation's capital, perhaps all of these factors. One important component is probably the proliferation of internal leadership positions to which members may aspire on the basis of long tenure.

Internal career ladders in the House and Senate have in the twentieth century proliferated and formalized. In the House, leadership positions open to members on the basis of seniority were broadened by the separation of party and committee leadership hierarchies—an accomplishment of the Progressive revolt against Speaker Joseph G. Cannon early in the century.[47] The seniority system itself was undoubtedly strengthened in both houses when the Legislative Reorganization Act of 1946 reduced the number of standing committees. Party positions, though not strictly subject to seniority selection, are nonetheless bestowed on experienced legislators. Although Henry Clay could be elected Speaker of the House as a freshman in 1811, no twentieth-century Speaker has had less than fifteen years in the House before his selection.[48] Senate party leadership posts show less rigorous recruitment patterns, but here too, experience and apprenticeship are important prerequisites.

In sum, it is probably true that Congress as an institution exerts increasing influence upon its members. Although the parallel characteristics of pre-congressional careers remain undiminished, the shared experiences in Washington increase in duration and intensity. Contemporary legislators may be localists, but they are

47. Randall B. Ripley, *Party Leaders in the House of Representatives* (Washington, 1967), pp. 51–52.
48. See Polsby, *op. cit.*, pp. 147 ff.; and Garrison Nelson, "Leaders of the U.S. House of Representatives: Patterns of Recruitment and Selection, 1789–1967" (unpublished doctoral dissertation, University of Iowa, 1968).

not transients. And once settled in Washington, they are subject to the professional norms and traditions of the institution—forces that are strengthened by long tenure and year-long sessions.

Homogeneities of backgrounds and career patterns contribute to the stability and cohesion of Congress. Legislative bodies are perpetually in danger of fragmentation, for insofar as members act the part of fiduciary agents, they are by nature each other's competitors. Especially is this the case when (as in the United States Congress) legislators represent individual and discrete electoral units. No two constituencies are exactly alike, but the agents must bargain among themselves to maximize their constituents' interests. This bargaining process is smoothened by homogeneity of the bargainers. Similar socio-economic backgrounds and parallel pre-Washington careers lend to both houses a fraternalism of professional and personal feelings.[49] To these common elements must be added interaction of the legislators on Capitol Hill, which further promotes institutional loyalty and shared norms of behavior. Which is to imply that, whatever their political differences, members of Congress come to hold a distinctive view of the political system and their place in it.

The Roles of Congressmen

All political decision-makers perform certain roles with reference to the larger political system. That is, they assume certain patterned and functional relationships in dealing with other actors, other institutions, and the system in general.[50] We have already observed that those who are called legislators can be identified by functionally requisite roles—in other words, the things they do which assist the system in setting and implementing goal attainment. They may play their roles well or badly, actively or passively. In any case, these roles must be assumed by someone if

49. See Donald R. Matthews, *U.S. Senators and Their World*, chap. v; William S. White, *Citadel*, esp. chaps. vii, ix; Clem Miller, *Member of the House*, ed. John W. Baker (New York, 1962), pp. 80–81.

50. "For most purposes, *the conceptual unit of the social system is the role*. It is the point of contact between the system of action of the individual actor and the social system." *Toward a General Theory of Action*, ed. Talcott Parsons and Edward A. Shils (Cambridge, Mass., 1951), p. 190. (Italics in original.)

the system is to survive; and if not by members of Congress, then by "legislators" located elsewhere in the system.

There are several empirical methods of interpreting the roles of legislators or other political actors. These roles may be derived, for example, by analyzing legislators' behavior (enacted roles), other people's ideas about what they should do (norms), or their own expressed standards of behavior (role cognitions).[51] These aspects of role behavior are closely intertwined: in any social situation, an actor responds to expectations which others associate with incumbents of his position, as well as to his own interpretation of his position. Conflict as well as consensus of roles is inevitable.[52] Two legislators, for example, may hold varying views of what persons in their positions should do. By the same token, a legislator's role cognitions or behaviors may be at variance with the expectations others have for him.

In this section we shall attempt to describe some of the views held by legislators concerning the roles they should assume. In a sense, we are seeking a job description as legislators themselves would write it. Our data pertain primarily to the House of Representatives and are drawn from intensive interviews with a sample of members of the Eighty-eighth Congress (1963–1964).[53] Available research suggests that the role cognitions of senators are not fundamentally different, and wherever possible we shall attempt to draw comparisons. The following section will be devoted to the expectations which the general public seems to hold for congressional performance. Finally, we shall attempt to explore the meaning of these findings in terms of the interaction between the national legislature and the developing political system.

"Rules of the Game"

Legislators, of course, operate within a complex institutional and political environment. Thus they perform not a single legislative role, but a set of roles through which they relate to their tasks

51. The notion of role is treated extensively in sociological writings. Several of the leading items are: John W. Thibaut and Harold H. Kelley, *The Social Psychology of Groups* (New York, 1959); Neal Gross, Ward S. Mason, and Alexander McEachern, *Explorations in Role Analysis* (New York, 1958); and *Role Theory: Concepts and Research,* ed. Bruce J. Biddle and Edwin J. Thomas (New York, 1966).

52. Gross *et al., op. cit.,* chap. 3.   53. See footnote 26 above.

and to relevant "others" in their environment. Our list of key role dimensions, though certainly far from exhaustive, would certainly include those unwritten but informally understood norms—sometimes called "folkways" or "rules of the game"—which govern legislators' relationships with each other. Matthews has identified a number of such norms in the Senate—including (among others) committee specialization, courtesy, reciprocity, seniority, and institutional loyalty.[54] Political demands or personality variables may produce deviations from these norms, but it seems clear that general adherence to such unwritten rules is indispensable for cohesion in a potentially divisive arena of competitive bargaining.

There is every reason to believe that such norms are at least as strong in the larger and more hierarchically structured House of Representatives. If anything, adherence to what Richard F. Fenno, Jr., has termed the "seniority-protegé-apprentice system" is more universal in the House than in the Senate.[55] The norms of courtesy, compromise, and reciprocity are bound up in the late Speaker Sam Rayburn's famous advice to junior colleagues: "If you want to *get* along, *go* along." Sanctions—some subtle, some not—are imposed upon errant members. The 1967 censure of Representative Adam Clayton Powell (D-N.Y.) was not so much a response to his race as to his continued flouting of House norms and threat to its institutional integrity. The following year, a freshman congressman who made disparaging remarks about his colleagues was denied passage of a routine bill he had sponsored, and faced damaging criticisms from his home state for his lack of restraint.[56]

54. Matthews, *U.S. Senators and Their World*, chap. v.

55. Richard F. Fenno, Jr., "The Internal Distribution of Influence: The House," in *The Congress and America's Future*, ed. David B. Truman (Englewood Cliffs, N.J., 1965), pp. 71 ff.

56. The legislator, Representative Sam Stieger (R-Ariz.), opined on a television program that "there are Members of Congress that you would not hire to push a wheelbarrow." Later in the session, the House failed to pass a local bill sponsored by Stieger which would have permitted the city of Glendale, Arizona, to acquire a tract of federal land. Local bills are usually passed routinely as a matter of courtesy to sponsors. An influential senior colleague, Representative John J. Rhodes (R-Ariz.), declared that Stieger's remarks on this and other occasions had not been "helpful to the fortunes of the state or the effectiveness of the delegation." See *Congressional Quarterly Weekly* Report, XXX (July 26, 1968, Sec. I), 1862–1863; and *New York Times*, February 6, 1968, p. 25.

Institutional loyalty, a persuasive and widely shared attitude, leads legislators to take an expansive view of their institution's place in political decision-making. In the House of Representatives, fully two thirds of the members interviewed during the Eighty-eighth Congress evidenced a "Whiggish" view of congressional powers: that is, they agreed to the proposition that Congress should play the major role in the making of public policy. Moreover, large numbers of representatives mentioned some form of executive branch "encroachment" as a complicating factor in their legislative work.[57] Thus representatives, no less than Matthews' senators, are proud of their status and their institution, ambitious for its role in policy-making, and sensitive to the incursions of competing forces.

Purposive Roles

Another key role sector is what has been called the legislator's purposive role—a generalized notion of the ultimate aim of his activities which is "shaped by both historic conceptions of the functions of the legislature and by contemporary circumstances in the governmental power structure."[58] The distribution of purposive role orientations thus provides a rough indication of the importance of various activities in the congressman's scheme of things. The roles, as revealed in our sample of eighty-seven congressmen, are presented in Table 4. For each of the respondents a dominant or "primary" role was determined, although most members also manifested from one to three subsidiary roles. (The eighty-seven congressmen indicated an average of 2.1 role orientations.)

The Tribune role is clearly strongest in the minds of members. This orientation could be taken as the classic definition of the legislator-as-representative: the discoverer, reflector, or advocate of popular needs and wants. As a senior Republican expressed it, "Represent the people . . . that's the first duty . . . do exactly what the name 'Representative' implies."[59] The Tribune concep-

57. See Davidson, Kovenock, and O'Leary, *op. cit.*, pp. 68–71.
58. John Wahlke *et al.*, *The Legislative System* (New York, 1962), pp. 12, 242, 260, *et passim*.
59. Personal interview.

tion is historically rooted in the legislator's function of fighting the people's battles against royal prerogative. In the American colonies, elected representatives were expected to defend the interests of their neighbors and constituents against the interests of the crown and its appointed governors. The Tribune role is articulated in many ways and is often held in conjunction with other purposive roles. It matters not to which constituents the member's ear is attuned, nor even how he comes to ascertain their interests. The only requirement is that he perceive himself as the people's spokesman.

The Ritualist orientation, in contrast, tends to focus the mem-

Table 4. *Purposive Roles of Eighty-seven Members of the House of Representatives*

Role	Primary	Secondary	Percentage of members[a]	Percentage of all roles mentioned
Tribune	47%	33%	82%	40%
Ritualist	41	24	67	33
Inventor	7	23	31	15
Broker	4	13	17	8
Opportunist	1	7	8	4
Totals	100	100		100
	(N = 87)	(N = 91)		(N = 178)

a. Since many members articulated more than one role, the sum of the per cent of members indicating all of the roles considerably exceeds 100 per cent.

ber's sights upon the institution itself. Ritualists emphasize the formal aspects of Capitol Hill duties: legislative work, committee specialization, investigation and oversight, and floor debate. Despite its label, the Ritualist role is rarely narrow or technical; it includes a broad range of activities and conforms with frequently expressed norms of legislative "insiders." As one southern Republican leader described his interests, "I tend to legislative matters —committee work, where the spade work is done; and I remain on deck when fighting is in progress on legislation—to be present and deliberate. For me, work on the floor and in committee is most important. This is where the work is done."[60] As might be

60. Personal interview.

expected, Ritualists are found disproportionately among House influentials (both party and committee leaders) and high-seniority members generally. Nonetheless, newcomers to Congress are quickly exposed to norms associated with the Ritualist conceptions—norms that, incidentally, resemble those of Matthews' "effective senator." And although Ritualists are frequently "insiders," they are not insensitive to external demands: often their concern for substantive expertise or procedural mastery stems from the need to champion their constituents' interests.

Although these two roles seem to be the dominant purposive orientations of House "outsiders" and "insiders," respectively, three additional roles are sufficiently distinct to be considered separate types. Most numerous of these is the Inventor, who emphasizes problem-solving and policy innovation. One Inventor, a midwestern Democrat, expressed this role in the following manner: "The first demand on us is the legislative program, in its national and international aspects. One must, of course, be a legislator. . . . Then, there are the things you crusade for—for example, a Humane Society bill, renewal of servicemen's life insurance (and so forth)."[61] Inventors are found frequently among middle-seniority liberals, but there are also a few conservative Inventors. Interestingly enough, the Inventor is probably the closest contemporary approximation of the Burkean—the nationally minded legislator who is nonetheless responsive to external popular needs and demands.

Brokers exhibit a substantive concern for the classic role of the politician operating in a pluralistic society, balancing and blending diverse geographic, occupational, or ideological interests. As one eastern Republican leader expressed it, "The public has a false impression of Congress, an idea that all we do is talk . . . we should be more like jurors than like attorneys. . . . More judging than talking."[62] To be sure, brokerage pervades legislative activity, underlying many of the "rules of the game" that govern interpersonal relationships on Capitol Hill. For Brokers, however, this represents a substantive interest and not merely a style of resolving competing political claims.

61. Personal interview.   62. Personal interview.

The final role, that of Opportunist, is relatively rare in the House. Opportunists have an overriding interest in campaigning and gaining re-election. At the very least, this orientation conforms to the oft-repeated dictum that, after all, "you can't be a statesman unless you get re-elected." But as a substantive focus this concern is rarely articulated. As one former representative has written, "All Members of Congress have a primary interest in being re-elected. Some Members have no other interest."[63]

Representational Roles

While Congressmen display striking consensus on the importance of representing external constituencies (82 per cent manifested the Tribune role as either primary or secondary focus), they differ widely in their stylistic orientation to this function. Traditional debates over representation have focused on the so-called Burkean conception—the ideal that legislators should serve as trustees for the "general reason of the whole [community]," rather than spokesmen for "local purposes . . . and local prejudices."[64] In reality, two role dimensions are embedded in the distinction between the Burkean Trustee and the Instructed Delegate. One dimension turns upon the legislator's *style* of representation: whether he accepts instructions (Delegate), acts upon his own information or convictions (Trustee), or acts upon some combination of the two (Politico). The second dimension is his *focus* of representation: the particular constituency used as referent, whether the whole nation (Burke's "mystic corpus" of the commonwealth), a geographic constituency, a non-geographic policy constituency, or some combination of these.[65] In actuality, legislators undoubtedly employ several or all of these roles as the situation demands. In democratic electorates, the Burkean ideal is often an unpopular and risky course; yet for

63. Frank E. Smith, *Congressman from Mississippi* (New York, 1964), p. 127.
64. Edmund Burke, speech to the electors of Bristol (November 3, 1774), in *Burke's Politics*, ed. Ross J. S. Hoffman and Paul Levack (New York, 1959), pp. 114–116.
65. See Wahlke *et al.*, chaps. xii, xiii; and Heinz Eulau and LeRoy C. Ferguson, "The Role of the Representative: Some Empirical Observations on the Theory of Edmund Burke," *American Political Science Review*, LIII (September, 1959), 742–756.

a great many issues, citizen ignorance or indifference may confer considerable freedom of action on the legislator. The roles described here may be thought of as members' generalized orientations or predispositions to constituent demands.

The Politico role is clearly the prevalent stylistic orientation to representation in the House. (See Table 5.) Many congressmen who adopt this style reveal sophisticated understanding about the kinds of choices for which they can play the Trustee and those for which the Delegate role would be expected. As a western Democrat observed, the legislator ". . . must remember his district but he must also vote as he personally sees fit on an issue. There is a balance which each Congressman works out between these two factors which defies definition in any succinct man-

Table 5. *Representational Style in the House*

Role	
Trustee	28%
Politico	46
Delegate	23
Undetermined	3
Total	100
	(N = 87)

ner."[66] The Politico role is an inevitable response to the pressures that converge upon legislators. "Both the shifting political demands and the finely balanced equities of choice," Sorauf writes, "force [the legislator] to choose only tentatively and cautiously, one issue at a time."[67] Politicos also fulfil the normative requirements of the fiduciary function. The fiduciary must act independently in his constituent's interests, even when the constituent is unaware or uninformed. At the same time, however, the fiduciary must not normally violate the constituent's expressed wishes.

Perhaps a quarter of the House members can be classed in each of the two "pure" categories, Trustee and Delegate, and the

66. Personal interview.
67. Frank J. Sorauf, *Party and Representation* (New York, 1963), p. 126. On this point, see also Pitkin, *op. cit.*, p. 165.

conflicting norms associated with these roles are widely expressed by legislators. Most members cherish their independent judgment.[68] As one Republican leader declared, "the Founding Fathers intended us to exercise our own judgment, not to weigh mail."[69] At the same time, the democratic idea of popular will runs strongly. Because both norms possess considerable force, legislators typically find it expedient to play off the two roles as the situation dictates. Or they may emphasize one or the other role according to the amount of breathing space their electoral margin gives them. Trustees disproportionately represent electorally safe districts, whereas Delegates tend to come from competitive districts. For most legislators the Trustee-Delegate problem, although recurrent, is not overwhelming. On the one hand, the issues on which the electorate speaks with a clear voice are relatively few. On the other, the legislators' local backgrounds reduce the likelihood that their views will be at odds with those of the constituency.

As we have already pointed out, the most fundamental attribute of congressmen and senators is that they are selected by local constituencies. The localist flavor of campaigns and elections is, as we have also noted, reinforced by recruitment patterns which favor "locals" and discourage "carpetbaggers." It is hardly surprising, therefore, that localism is viewed by many as the dominant orientation of congressmen. As will be seen from Table 6, this conclusion is borne out in the House of Representatives, though with important qualifications. A large plurality of members manifests a predominantly district-oriented focus. But it is noteworthy that slightly more than half (51 per cent) of the interviewees place at least equal weight upon the claims of some larger constituency. This includes members who give equal emphasis to national and district claims, as well as those who clearly express a genuinely national orientation. A few members are attuned primarily to non-geographic clienteles—ethnic or economic groupings, for example. As with representational style, a

68. Sixty-eight per cent of the interviewees *disagreed* with the statement that "a Representative ought to work for what his constituents want, even though this may not always agree with his personal views."
69. Personal interview.

legislator's disposition to focus on a particular constituency seems to be mainly a function of the degree of safety he enjoys at the polls. Nationalists are drawn disproportionately from safe constituencies, Localists from marginal districts.

Unfortunately, we have no comparable information for the upper house. Senators are usually thought to be more detached from particular constituencies, because of larger, more heterogeneous statewide electorates and longer six-year terms. The Founding Fathers held this conception when they devised the system of indirect selection that prevailed until the Seventeenth

Table 6. *Representational Focus in the House*

Role	
Nation dominant	28%
Nation-district equal	23
District dominant	42
Non-geographic	5
Undetermined	3
Total	101
	(N = 87)

Amendment.[70] Although this description still has some intuitive validity, it is appropriate to mention a balancing factor: proportionately more states than congressional districts are politically competitive, a fact which undoubtedly sharpens the salience of constituency demands upon members of the upper house.[71]

Public Support for Congress

The question of public support for political processes and institutions is fundamental, no matter what the values under which

70. *Federalist*, 64 (Jay). For a modern expression of this viewpoint, compare William S. White's hardly restrained praise of the Senate (*Citadel*) and his more cool assessment of the House (*Home Place*). Being something of a Burkean conservative, White naturally admires a "citadel" more than a "home place." On the House of Representatives, see Neil MacNeil, *Forge of Democracy* (New York, 1964).

71. Price, *op. cit.*

the polity operates. In the context of democratic values, however, the question assumes even greater centrality. Classic theories of legislative supremacy, for example, rested upon the assumption that the legislative branch would dominate, if not monopolize, the lifelines of support between governors and governed. The Founding Fathers applied this theory to the House of Representatives which, Madison wrote, "will derive its powers from the people of America."[72] In describing the eclipse of the presidency during the Monroe administration, Justice Joseph Story observed that "the House of Representatives has absorbed all the popular feelings and all the effective power of the country." Although the accuracy of Story's judgment is open to question, his assumption remains undoubted: the strength of political institutions (and of the polity as a whole) rests to a large degree on a generous reservoir of popular support.

Regrettably, the subject of public support has received less attention than its theoretical and practical significance would justify. Most obviously, such inquiry is time-bound: only in the last thirty or so years have techniques of opinion research been developed, and to push our knowledge backward over time would be a frustrating (though not hopeless) objective.[73] This limitation is especially severe in a system which has developed over the space of many decades. Even contemporary opinion linkages have received less than satisfactory treatment, and only today is there serious promise of significant theoretical and empirical breakthrough. For the time being, at least, we must concur with Donald E. Stokes's conclusion that "although the importance of evaluations of government formed by large-scale publics is widely seen, only the most fragmentary information is available on these evaluations in actual political systems."[74]

Though undoubtedly subject to variation over time, citizen support levels in the United States are apparently high. When asked what aspect of their country they admire most, citizens are

72. *Federalist,* 39.
73. See, for example, Lee Benson, "An Approach to the Scientific Study of Past Public Opinion," *Public Opinion Quarterly,* XXXI (Winter, 1967–1968), 522–567.
74. Donald E. Stokes, "Popular Evaluations of Government: An Empirical Assessment," *Ethics and Bigness,* ed. Harlan Cleveland and Harold D. Lasswell (New York, 1962), p. 61.

likely to mention their governmental institutions. In this respect, citizens of the United States may well resemble citizens of newly created states, for whom the recent achievement of independence is more salient than cultural or historical heritage.[75] The common revolutionary experience, reinforced by similar emphasis of civic education, may account for the similarity. In other respects, however, Americans manifest a uniquely keen sense of participation and civic competence. Favorable cognitive and affective orientations toward the system and its values, gained in children's early socialization into their environment, are reinforced by the system's capacity to promote individual and collective achievement of goals.

Contrary to conventional wisdom on the subject, a large majority of the public apparently looks with favor upon politics and politicians. According to the most current survey findings, citizens hold senators and representatives in high esteem and would be proud to have their children pursue such a career. When asked to describe the characteristics of a representative, respondents (whose replies were favorable by a 9 to 1 ratio) stress the qualities of service-orientation, good personal character, capability, good education, and personality.[76] (Interestingly enough, the comments were very similar to the replies of congressmen themselves to the same question.) The legislator's public image seems as positive as that of other types of public servants or those in respected private careers. During the periodic flurries of publicity concerning congressional misbehavior, public attitudes are shaken but nonetheless generally positive. As one student ob-

75. Compare, for example, attitudes in the United States and Mexico as reported in Gabriel Almond and Sidney Verba, *The Civic Culture* (Princeton, N.J., 1963), pp. 102–104. See also David Easton and Robert D. Hess, "The Child's Political World," *Midwest Journal of Political Science*, VI (August, 1962), 229–246.

76. The question was: "If you were to describe your general idea of a U.S. Congressman, what sort of a person would that be?" See the testimony of Franklin P. Kilpatrick in U.S. House of Representatives, Committee on Standards of Official Conduct, *Hearings*, 90th Congress, 1st session, 1967, pp. 19–20; and M. Kent Jennings, Milton C. Cummings, Jr., and Franklin P. Kilpatrick, "Trusted Leaders: Perceptions of Appointed Federal Officials," *Public Opinion Quarterly*, XXX (Fall, 1966), 380–381. These findings are somewhat at variance with the conclusions in William Mitchell, "The Ambivalent Social Status of the American Politician," *Western Political Quarterly*, XII (September, 1959), 695, and cited in Davidson, Kovenock, and O'Leary, *op. cit.*, pp. 48–49.

serves, "the American public shows a great capacity to dissociate Congress as an institution and Congressmen in general from the individual congressman whose propriety or ethics is being questioned."[77]

High public respect for Congress constitutes a facilitating input for the operation of the legislative system. This phenomenon, however, conveys a somewhat misleading picture of the linkages between the public and the legislature; and although our information remains distressingly incomplete, several aspects of these linkages must be tentatively considered.

Low Public Information and Interest

However benign his view of the national legislature, the average citizen displays little understanding or information concerning its operations. In fact, the average citizen views Congress dimly if at all. No doubt the collective nature of congressional decision-making puts the institution at a serious disadvantage in attracting public attention. Greenstein has shown that school children learn about Congress long after they learn about the president; and then frequently they view senators and congressmen as "the President's helpers."[78] This disparity of knowledge persists into adulthood. Although virtually everyone (95 per cent or more) is able to identify an incumbent president, ignorance about legislative institutions is shocking. A 1965 Gallup Survey told the now-familiar story of the extent of public perception of Congress: of the nationwide sample of adults, 57 per cent could not identify the name of their own congressman, 41 per cent did not know his party affiliation, 70 per cent did not know when he next stood for re-election, 81 per cent did not know how he voted on any major legislation during the year, and 86 per cent could not name anything he had accomplished for the district.[79]

77. Kilpatrick, *loc. cit.*, commenting on public attitudes during the 1966 publicity concerning Senator Thomas J. Dodd (D-Conn.). A slightly more critical judgment is reflected in surveys conducted by Louis Harris and Associates, as reported in *Washington Post*, May 8, 1967, A-2.

78. Fred I. Greenstein, *Children and Politics* (New Haven, Conn., 1965), pp. 61–63, 82. See also Hazel Gaudet Erskine, "The Polls: Textbook Knowledge," *Public Opinion Quarterly*, XXVII (Spring, 1963), 133–140.

79. AIPO Survey (November 7, 1965).

Public Assessments of Congress

Considering the lack of specific knowledge about the institution, its personnel, or its performance, it is not surprising that public assessments of Congress (as distinguished from generalized affective orientation) fluctuate widely, even within a relatively short space of time. Nor are such assessments always based on direct perceptions of institutional performance. The average citizen's evaluation of Congress tends to reflect orientations to more familiar objects in his environment—in particular, the "goodness" or "badness" of the times or his estimate of how the president is doing *his* job. Figure 3 shows the rise and fall of public ratings of Congress and the president during a recent five-year period, 1963–1967. The fluctuations represent a reasonably accurate fever-chart of public attitudes toward over-all system performance during that period; and, except during the 1963 period, ratings of other branches of the federal government generally paralleled these figures. The figures reinforce the impression that Congress is not usually evaluated directly, but rather through a prism of attitudes to more familiar political objects.[80]

In examining public assessments in the past half decade, however, the conclusion is inescapable that citizens expect Congress to respond with deliberate haste in dealing with goal-allocations. Legislative activism has invariably yielded public favor, while stalemate has inevitably produced dissatisfaction. During the stalemate which preceded President Kennedy's assassination in 1963, only 35 per cent of the national sample of adults gave Congress a favorable rating. For those expressing a negative judgment (51 per cent of the sample), the chief irritant seemed to be dilatory handling of lawmaking: "not done much," "avoided major bills," "too slow," and "everything stalled" were most frequently mentioned. The aftermath of the assassination, with its long "honeymoon" between President Johnson and Congress, unblocked major legislation in many fields. Public support for Con-

80. For example: "Supporters of the President's party tend to view Congress more favorably than do members of the 'out' party, whether or not the Presidential party also controls one or both houses of Congress." Davidson *et al., op. cit.,* pp. 61–62.

Figure 3. *Public Approval of Congressional and Presidential Performance, 1963–1967*

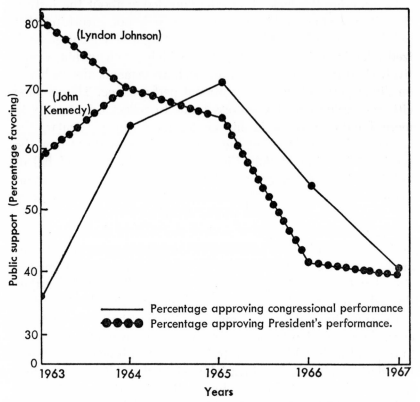

Source: Louis Harris and Associates. The question in each survey was: "How would you rate the job the [Congress/President] has done this past year—excellent, pretty good, only fair, or poor?" The first two response categories (excellent, pretty good) are reflected here as "favorable" responses.

gress soared and late in 1965 support was even higher for it than for the president. Congressional action on legislation drew most of the favorable judgments: "passed a lot of bills," "passed civil rights bill," "made progress," and "supported president" were comments volunteered by citizens. As the crises of Vietnam and civil disorder again gripped the nation, public support fell: in late

1967, only 41 per cent of the sample gave Congress a favorable rating and 59 per cent gave a negative rating.

Individual groupings of citizens sometimes manifest distinctive assessments of Congress. In part these variations stem from system outputs which have a differential impact—favorable or adverse—upon certain categories of people. During periods of falling farm prices, for example, farmers judge Congress more harshly than do members of other economic groups. Again, such judgments are usually leveled against the system as a whole rather than the legislature exclusively.

In addition to these short-term fluctuations, certain persistent attitudes confront Congress with a particularly acute problem of institutional support. Highly educated citizens are a particularly critical audience. One recent survey found that elite segments in the polity (e.g., college teachers, college seniors, business executives, and federal executives) manifest significantly less favorable attitudes toward congressmen than does the public at large.[81] Elite disaffection (if the phenomenon can be so termed) presents an acute problem for a political institution, for such people are more explicit in their expectations, more informed in their judgments, and more likely to translate their opinions into actions, than the mass of citizens.

Expectations of Performance

Less is known about public expectations of political institutions than any other aspect of public support. Given the lack of clarity with which the public views the legislature, it is unlikely that average citizens hold elaborate views of how their elected representatives should perform. Congressmen themselves complain frequently about voters' failures to understand their jobs and their problems—though lack of public concern (here as elsewhere) tends to shield legislators from intense public demands. If all citizens were concerned about all public issues, the congressman's lot would indeed be an unhappy one. Fortunately for political decision-makers, however, the threshold of public awareness and interest—even for educated and involved citizens

81. Jennings *et al., loc. cit.* See also Davidson *et al., op. cit.,* pp. 50–52.

—is relatively low. At the same time, the absence of clear instructions from the electorate brings its own problems for the legislator, because it heightens uncertainty over probable public repercussions.

Generally speaking, the public seems to view elected legislators as servants of the people rather than as policy experts.[82] Thus, citizens apparently expect their representatives to follow instructions rather than exercise independent judgment.[83] In this respect, public expectations may conflict somewhat with the norms of incumbents—the latter giving greater weight to independent judgment (the Trustee role). This conflict normally is not serious, because the range of issues upon which this expectation is operative is, as we have said before, extremely narrow.[84] Again, attentive publics pose a greater problem for legislators than the larger masses of inattentive citizens. Not only are the "attentives" concerned about a broader range of issues, but they are even more likely than others to expect the legislator to be a Delegate.

As for public expectations of purposive role performance, we regrettably know next to nothing. It is safe only to say that the citizen's perceptions of the legislator's role are undoubtedly very sketchy.

Conclusions

Our consideration of the United States Congress has necessarily been selective and cursory. It could hardly be otherwise, in view of the complexity of the subject and the multitude of works written about it. Our objective has, however, been neither an exhaustive review of legal powers nor a catalogue of behavioral patterns. We have sought rather to describe some of the linkages between Congress and the evolving polity. Three broad topics

82. Jennings *et al.*, *loc. cit.*
83. Carl D. McMurray and Malcolm B. Parsons, "Public Attitudes toward the Representational Role of Legislators and Judges," *Midwest Journal of Political Science*, IX (May, 1965), 167–185.
84. Warren E. Miller and Donald E. Stokes, "Constituency Influence in Congress," *American Political Science Review*, LVII (March, 1963), 45–56.

were chosen for this purpose. First, we examined the national legislature's functional place in the political system. We then described certain trends in the recruitment and career patterns of congressional personnel. Finally, we sought to compare the role cognitions of congressional personnel with expectations held by outside publics. In each case, we have endeavored to demonstrate points of convergence between legislative functioning and political development.

We have defined a legislature in generic fashion as an arena of conflict-resolution in which elected agents compete over the society's goal priorities. Thus, the legislature assists the larger political system in the all-important task of goal-attainment. And insofar as it is invested with the legitimacy of democratic representation, a legislative body contributes to building consensus behind the system's goal decisions—an essential task if the society's resources are to be mobilized behind political choices. Constitutionally, the American Congress was designed as the primary resolver (in the federal government) of societal conflict; and insofar as it conforms to its legal prerogatives, it provides a working example of the active legislative body—assuming the tasks of rule-making, representation, and consensus building. In the American experience, these functions have been facilitated by the relative absence of cumulative societal cleavages, the marked abundance of resources for goal-achievement, and the traditional assumption that goal-priority decisions would be resolved largely without recourse to formal instrumentalities of government.

The advent of the general welfare state has placed added burdens upon political institutions, including Congress. At the same time, contemporary issues concerning priorities have produced a functional drift away from legislative arenas of decision-making. Though no absolute decline of legislative participation has taken place, the historical trend of executive aggrandizement has meant a partial transferal of key legislative functions—rule-making, representation, and consensus building—to executive agencies and tribunals. Comparatively speaking, though Congress is still an example (perhaps unique) of an active legislature, it is frequently seen to be taking up a secondary position and emphasizing such subsidiary legislative functions as policy clarification, constituent service, and ratification of policy initiatives.

The evolution of the American society has also had an impact upon legislative personnel and career patterns. Congress is not, nor has it ever been, a mirror of the society at large in any demographic sense. However, the door to congressional office is probably open wider today than in the past. The decline of what we have called the "Founding Fathers syndrome," and the growth of regional economic diversity, have both contributed to broadening the recruitment base. At the same time, observers have noted an institutionalization of the congressional career. Contemporary senators and representatives tend to follow a career which is distinct from other ladders of political advancement; they are apt to make a career out of legislative service; and they are not inclined to move laterally to alternative jobs, political or otherwise. Professionalization is an aspect of systemic development. It has undoubtedly strengthened institutional cohesion; but whether it has also produced institutional insularity and rigidity is a crucial unanswered question.

The group character of Congress is also revealed in the role cognitions of incumbents. We have described four central dimensions, or segments, of role cognitions—folkways, purposive role, representational style, and representational focus. In each case the orientations of congressmen encompass a limited range of relatively explicit categories. Although any composite picture of the legislators' role orientations would be an over-simplification, it can be said that the average representative emphasizes the substantive task of representation (Tribune), and secondarily his internal legislative responsibilities (Ritualist). As a representative, the average member is a Politico and a Localist. It is doubtful whether the legislators' relevant publics harbor any explicit conceptions of purposive roles; but they probably see the elected official as a representative who should (to the extent that issues are salient) follow the district's instructions in making choices. If the average voter expects somewhat greater subservience from legislators than the latter are willing to concede, this discrepancy is usually reconciled by the voters' limited threshold of information or interest concerning the legislators' activites.

Although no historical perspective upon legislative role-taking is likely to have much empirical validity, it is interesting to speculate on the probable trends. What we have discovered concerning the professionalization of legislative office, in particular, suggests that long-term development has been in the direction of internally based roles, such as the Ritualist conception, which revolve about the activities and procedures of the legislative body itself. Most legislators are no longer sojourners on Capitol Hill; they are long-term residents. The greater saliency of institutional roles may serve to emphasize the distinctiveness and even the insularity of legislators as members of an ongoing group. At the same time, the rising educational level and media exposure of the electorate may yield more stringent expectations of legislative performance. As the developing institution pulls the member inward, so rising demands from external clienteles force him to look outward. A creative tension between these forces could enhance the vitality and viability of Congress. An overriding question is whether the legislators are capable of mediating these tensions, which are the by-products of institutional and systemic development.

The uniqueness of legislators as individuals, and the increased cohesion of legislators as a political elite, gives rise to a second area of tension. On the one hand, the achieved and ascribed status of legislators remains impressive, and is imprinted upon the legislators' consciousness by institutional norms embracing a flattering self-image. On the other hand, the influence of the legislative elite—relative to competing elites—is ebbing from the high-water mark of nineteenth-century "congressional government." This disparity between image and reality already produces recurrent frustration among senators and representatives who feel the personal and institutional anguish of functional change. Any widening of the gap may yield a potentially dangerous estrangement of Congress, for internally reinforcing norms may yet cause the members of the institution to turn and fight. As usual, to predict public reactions would be hazardous: while public attitudes remain favorable, they are relatively "shallow" and, moreover, are highly favorable to executive leadership. Thus, the constitutional crisis promises to be severe and prolonged, as an ever-more intransigent legislative elite faces its deteriorating role within the polity.

These two areas of tension are by-products of systemic development. The legislative elite is more distinctive and cohesive than perhaps at any point in the nation's history. These trends— aspects of the institutionalization of Congress—have been conducive to the evolution of a relatively coherent set of self-expectations or norms which serve to define for the legislator his place within the polity. At the same time, functional shifts produced by the activism of rival elites (particularly the executive establishment) and public expectations bode ill for the legislator's historic view of his position. The resulting dissonance, although probably not as severe as in some other polities, places the national legislature on more tenuous ground than at any point in its evolution.

Chapter 5

Parliament in the Indian Political System

L. M. Singhvi

To understand the working of the Indian parliamentary system and to evaluate its role in the functional dynamics of contemporary Indian politics, we must briefly consider the social context in which the system operates. Particularly notable are the demographic and ecological factors; the transforming pressures of socio-economic change; the structure, mobility, and socialization of old and newly emerging elites; and the kaleidoscope of national, regional, and group aspirations. These determinants, among others, have shaped and conditioned the scope of individual freedom, the institutions of federalism, the electoral process, and the party system. In turn, these influence the quality and delineate the form and functions of the Indian parliamentary system. I do not intend to present a comprehensive survey of the social context of the parliamentary system in India. What follows is a bare and minimal description of some of the salient factors.

Population

In 1951, India's total population was 360 million.[1] In 1961, it had risen to 439 million, an increase of 21.5 per cent. In 1966, it was estimated to be about 495 million. Studies based on census data for 1951 and 1961 indicate births at an average rate of 42 per thousand per annum, and deaths at an average rate of 23 per

1. For statistical data and their interpretation, see, generally, *Census of India;* also *India: 1967* (Publications Division, Government of India, December, 1967); and *The Gazetteer of India,* Vol. I, *Country and People,* 1965.

thousand per annum, giving a rate of natural increase of population of 19 per thousand per annum. The infant mortality rate obtained in the National Sample Survey in 1958 (fourteenth round) was 146 per thousand live births. Earlier in this century, the infant mortality rate was at a level of 250 per thousand births. The current increase in the population growth rate, then, can be explained largely by the sharp decline in the death rate since 1961. During 1951–1960, the highest birth rate (43.6) was in northern India (Punjab and Rajasthan) and the lowest (38.5) in southern India (Andhra Pradesh, Madras, Kerala, and Mysore). The highest death rate (24.4) was in north central India (Uttar Pradesh and Madhya Pradesh) and the lowest in northern India. The highest rate of natural increase was in northern India (24.6) and the lowest in southern India (16.2). During the decade 1951–1960, life expectancy of males was 41.9 and that of females 40.6—figures substantially higher than the preceding decades. The highest life expectancy—49.6 for males and 44.6 for females —during the 1951–1960 decade was in northern India, whereas the lowest expectancy—39.8 for males and 38.8 for females—was in central India (Uttar Pradesh and Madhya Pradesh).

The age distribution of India's population indicates that India is a young nation; in 1961, 41 per cent of the total population was below fifteen years of age and 32.1 per cent was between fifteen to thirty-four years. Only 7.9 per cent were fifty-five years or more. Roughly half of India's population is estimated to be below the age of eighteen years. The sex ratio shows that in the year 1961 there were 941 females per 1,000 males.

With regard to the distribution of population, 1961 figures indicate an average density of 138 people per square kilometer. The variance is considerable, ranging from eight in Andaman and Nicobar Islands to 1,792 in Delhi.

Ethnicity and Religion

India constitutes a virtual mosaic of religious and linguistic groups. In 1961, Hindus accounted for 83.5 per cent of the total population and although Muslims made up only 10.7 per cent, they showed the highest percentage increase (25.6 per cent) among all the religious communities in the decennium 1951–1961. Table 1 shows the distribution of major religious communities in

Table 1. *Distribution of Religious Groups, 1951 and 1961*

Religious community	Percentage of total population in 1951[a]	Percentage of total population in 1961[b]	Percentage increase, 1951–1961[c]
Buddhist	.05	.74	1,670.70
Christian	2.30	2.40	27.40
Hindu	85.00	83.50	20.30
Jain	.45	.46	25.20
Muslim	9.90	10.70	25.60
Sikh	1.70	1.80	25.10
Other	.52	.38	−13.01
Total	100.00	100.00	21.50
N[d]	(361,088,090)	(439,234,771)	

a. These statistics exclude Jammu and Kashmir, Pondicherry and NEFA; the total population excludes only NEFA. In calculating the percentage of total population, 268,602 out of the Punjab population have been excluded because of lack of relevant data.

b. Data are unavailable for part of NEFA.

c. Percentage increase in 1951–1961 does not include populations of NEFA and the Tuensang district of Nagaland.

d. Includes Sikkim.

Source: *India, 1967*, p. 13.

1951 and 1961, their percentage of total population, and their rate of increase during the period.

Languages

Some 826 languages, dialects and "mother-tongues" are spoken in India although the Constitution of India recognizes only fifteen languages (including Sindhi, which was recognized only in 1967). These fifteen languages, however, subsume several hundred mother-tongues. About 383.5 million (including a Sindhi speaking population of 1.3 million) or 87.3 per cent of the total 1961 population speak these fifteen constitutionally recognized languages. With the exception of Sanskrit, Sindhi, and Urdu, each one of these languages is an official language of a constituent state of the Indian Union. English is not recognized as one of the national languages of India, although it continues by law to be the associate official language of the Union. In actual practice English is the main official language of the Union. No figures are officially available as to the prevalence of the English language, but it is estimated that about 1 per cent of the total population speak or understand some English. Hindi, which is the official language of the Union and is generally described as the link language, is spoken by 30.3 per cent of the total population. Because of its origin from Sanskrit and its close connection with Urdu, however, it justifiably can be claimed that Hindi is understood by a substantial portion of the total population of India.[2]

Urbanism

There is a slow but steady shift toward urbanization in India. Thus, in 1921, 88.8 per cent of the total population lived in villages and 11.2 per cent in cities and towns; in 1961, about 82 per cent of the population was rural, and the proportion of urban dwellers rose to 18 per cent. According to the 1961 census, there are 2,699 towns and 566,878 villages in India. Fully 107 towns have populations of 100,000 or more; about 657 have populations ranging between 20,000 and 100,000; and approximately 1,935 have populations of less than 20,000. With respect to the villages, approximately 776 villages have populations of 10,000 or more; about 3,421 have populations ranging from 5,000 to 10,000; and the remaining villages, which constitute the bulk of the rural landscape, have populations under 5,000. Table 2 is a distribution of towns and villages according to population in 1961.

2. See *India, 1967*, pp. 13–14.

Table 2. *Distribution of Towns and Villages by Size of Population, 1961*

Towns					
Number of inhabitants	100,000 plus	50,000 to 99,999	20,000 to 49,999	10,000 to 19,999	5,000 to 9,999	Less than 5,000
	4.0%	5.2%	19.2%	30.4%	31.3%	9.9% (N = 2699)

Villages					
	10,000 plus	5,000 to 9,999	2,000 to 4,999	1,000 to 1,999	500 to 999	Less than 500
	.14%	.6%	4.7%	11.5%	21.0%	62.0% (N = 566,878)

Source: *India, 1967*, pp. 15–16.

Literacy

Although literacy programs have not made spectacular strides, 24 per cent of the total population in 1961 was literate, the percentage among males being 34.5 and that among females 13.0.[3] Literacy in India does not always mean the ability to read and write. Often, it may merely signify that a person can affix his signature. Neo-literates constantly relapse into illiteracy. Consequently, literacy programs have difficulty keeping pace with the increasing population and the problem of backlog.

In 1961, about twenty million students were on the rolls of about 75,000 secondary schools. In 1963–1964, the number of students going to secondary schools had risen to a little over twenty-four million, and the number of schools to over 88,000. The total number of educational institutions in the country currently is over 500,000; the number of teachers exceeds two million. The total student population, which is now over seventy million is expected, by 1985, to be of the order of 170 million, or about the total population of Europe.

3. See *Report of the Education Commission,* 1966, p. 1.

In 1966, there were seventy universities in India and several other institutions which also impart higher learning and professional and technological training. Some of these institutions of research and higher learning concentrate on specialized studies, and, for the purposes of receiving assistance from the University Grants Commission (which was set up as an autonomous body under a parliamentary statute in 1956), are accorded the status of "deemed universities." There were also about 1,700 colleges in 1962–1963 affiliated with the universities. The number of undergraduate and postgraduate students was estimated in 1965–1966 to be about 845,245, of which approximately 20 per cent were women.[4]

A study of socio-economic backgrounds of the students in vocational and professional schools was carried out by the Education Commission[5] in 1965. It was concerned with 87,358 students admitted to 341 vocational, technical, and professional institutions and suggested the relative dominance of the urban middle class in the elite pattern of India. For example, the students admitted to the more important of these institutions (such as the Indian Institutes of Technology) came from urban areas, from good schools, and from well-to-do homes. It would appear that the academically bright and the socially well-connected graduates of better educational institutions find good jobs and rewarding career opportunities. The graduates of lesser institutions occupy most of the white-collar positions. Many others, however, are not satisfactorily employed, and the problem of educated but unemployed is an acute one that looms large on the political horizon.

Occupation and Income

The occupational distribution of India's population shows that 72.3 per cent of the population in 1961 were engaged in primary sectors (agriculture, forestry, fishing, etc.). Another 11.7 per cent

4. Appendices, *Report of the Education Commission,* 1966, p. 584.
5. *Ibid.,* pp. 118–120, and Supplementary Vol. I, Part I.

were employed in secondary sectors (transport, storage, communications, etc.), whereas 16 per cent were in tertiary sectors (trade and services). These proportions have not changed significantly over the years.[6]

In 1964–1965, the per capita income at current prices was 421.5 rupees per annum (about $104 U.S. at the rate of exchange prevailing before the 1967 devaluation of the rupee). National income during the same year was about 200 billion rupees at current prices.[7]

Caste

The 1961 Census gives the figure of the Scheduled Castes throughout the country as 64.4 million or 14.7 per cent of the total population. Scheduled Tribes account for 30.1 million or 6.9 per cent of the total population. The Scheduled Castes and Tribes are generally considered to be economically and culturally less advanced than other elements of the population and so are eligible (under a directive of the Constitution) for special treatment by way of reservation of seats in the legislatures, services, and educational institutions. The Scheduled Castes and Tribes tend to be disproportionately located in rural areas. Together they make up slightly less than 10 per cent of India's total urban population.[8]

Elite Structure

The data on Indian elites is extremely limited. Certainly, it is insufficient to permit comprehensive or categorical generalizations. In the opinion of the present writer, caste, as such, is no longer a decisive factor in the composition of elite groups; indeed, caste as a factor has been blurred by the far-reaching pressures of socio-economic changes and political ethos. Sociolo-

6. See *The Gazetteer of India*, I (1965), 340.
7. *Hindustan Year Book*, ed. S. C. Sarker, 1968, p. 368.
8. See *The Gazetteer of India*, p. 347.

gists have shown that there formerly was considerable congruence between the caste hierarchy and the economic hierarchy. Wherever the economic status was high and the "ritual status" in the caste low, the latter tended to move upward. Even in the traditionally hierarchical orientation of Indian society, there was this upward movement and the attendant adoption of the symbols of higher status. In the Indian context this process was called *Sanskritization*.[9] On the one hand, the movement for Sanskritization has become quite widespread; on the other hand, there is increasing secularization, rationalization, and humanization in the upper caste elites. The divisive chasm has not been completely obliterated by any means, but the structural distance between the various castes has narrowed considerably because of the climate of democracy, social reform, the impact of adult franchise, and new economic and ideological factors. As M. N. Srinivas has shown, castes have now undertaken new activities which may be described as reformist and philanthropic, educational, economic, and political.[10] It is true that in politics, intercaste tensions are often employed as weapons of electoral warfare, and caste makes its appearance in many disguises. At the same time, the very fact that caste is a subterranean factor and has to adopt disguises testifies to its diminishing importance as a rallying point. In a negative sense, until the advent of adult franchise those belonging to Scheduled Castes and Tribes did not participate in any notable measure in national or regional elite groups. Since the coming into force of the Constitution in 1950, they have become a strong pressure group. Minorities are generally adequately represented in the political elite groups but are not a distinct or sizable component of the civil service elites. They have, however, generally done well in trade and commerce.

As one would expect, functional elites have a middle- and upper middle-class orientation. The socially most influential and politically most powerful are the political, civil service, and mercantile-industrial elites. Next in importance are the intellectual and mass media elites. The military elite, drawn largely from Western-oriented upper middle-class backgrounds and belonging

9. *Ibid.*, p. 561.   10. *Ibid.*, p. 563.

to regions and communities with established military traditions, generally remains aloof from the political process.

The rise of professional elites in the fields of law, medicine, engineering, civil service, teaching, communications, and arts had its beginnings in the last quarter of the nineteenth century and is related to Western-oriented education and competitive merit. Knowledge of the English language is common among the professional elites. And, as is the case in Western societies such as the United States, education has been conducive to economic and social mobility. Foreign education, for which opportunities have increased in recent years, continues to be a basis for graduation into the elite group. However, its importance, as well as the importance of the so-called public school education, has been diminishing. The cost of higher education is not prohibitive and there exist considerable if not ample opportunities for the truly meritorious who may be without means. Thus, the composition of elites increasingly cuts across caste lines.

To seek to explain the composition of professional elites in terms of the traditional fourfold caste system appears to be an exercise in irrelevance. All that can be said is that the resources and the background of the family may often be a decisive element in the preparation of a candidate for recruitment to the civil service or to the professions. On the other hand, the political elites tend to be partially based on dominant regional and caste affiliations and financial resources. The former ruling princes are, however, a class by themselves, and they continue to exert considerable (though possibly diminishing) influence on the popular vote. This is not because of their wealth, but because of the position they have traditionally enjoyed. On the whole the participation of the princes in the electoral process has been conducive to their political socialization. The politics of universal adult suffrage has had a transforming impact on the composition of political elites. In the rural areas caste is an important factor, whereas in the urban and industrial areas it plays only a subdued role. Reservation of seats in Parliament and state legislatures for Scheduled Castes and Tribes provides sheltered access for members of these communities to the political elite groups, but the influence they wield is by no means commensurate with their numbers. It is only the capital-owning and the economic entrepreneurial elites in trade, commerce, and industry (who belong, preponderantly, to the traditional mercantile communities) who tend to support the party in power and the ideologically moderate parties.

The influential sections of the press in the English language which are controlled by the mercantile-industrial elites are freely critical of the government and generally take watchful, critical, and moderate positions. The so-called language press, with a far higher circulation, however, does not have the same influence with the government and the policy-makers.

There is increasing evidence of career interchange among the elite groups, but this is not yet a sizable phenomenon. One finds only a sprinkling of former (generally retired) civil servants, businessmen, and intellectuals in the legislatures. Civil servants have permanent tenures; with the high premium on security that characterizes the general outlook in India, they have scarcely any incentive to enter the arena of politics. The professionals, particularly lawyers, at one time constituted a significant component of the political elite, but their numbers as well as their influence seem to have been declining steadily.

The bureaucracy at different levels exercises far-reaching influence on the political elite, particularly those in the government, whom they advise and whose thinking is conditioned by such advice in a decisive sense. The bureaucracy, in spite of its conventional political neutrality, makes and unmakes policies at all stages and determines the mode and manner as well as the scope and quality of implementation.

The farmers are fast becoming a force to reckon with, but they do not yet have a powerful elite of their own. The labor unions are sharply divided, but are articulate and have informal affiliations with different political parties, which are led by middle-class elites. There is considerable mobility, interchange, and communication within the political elite and between elites dominant in different sectors such as trade unions, party organization, and legislatures.

The Constitution

Next in importance to the sociological background of India and its people in the understanding of the Indian parliamentary system is the constitutional context. The norms and the aspirations of the Indian polity are expressed in the Constitution of India, which is both a balancing wheel and institutionally a socio-political force. In its Preamble, the Constitution proclaims the resolve of the people of India to constitute India into a Sovereign Democratic Republic and to secure for all its citizens: *Justice,* social, economic, and political; *Liberty* of thought, expression, belief, faith, and worship; *Equality* of status and of opportunity; and to promote among them all *Fraternity* assuring the dignity of the individual and the unity of the Nation.

It is not merely in the evocative words of the Preamble but also in the formal system devised by the Constitution that one finds this commitment to and concern for justice, liberty, and equality.

More particularly, the basic postulates of India's constitutional polity are fourfold: (*a*) protection of the fundamental rights and liberties of the citizen; maintenance of the rule of law and judicial review; (*b*) socio-economic justice; (*c*) quasi-federal framework of government based on the division of legislative powers between the Center and the states; formally, there was an overriding bias for a strong Center; and (*d*) political democracy through free elections based on universal adult suffrage; and representative government based on the parliamentary model of Great Britain.

The Indian Constitution contains an elaborate and self-contained Bill of Rights. Part III of the Constitution not only embodies guarantees of fundamental rights but also lays down corresponding limitations on them. These limitations, which are an integral part of the Bill of Rights, include saving and enabling clauses of permissible exceptions for special provisions for the advancement of any socially and educationally backward classes of citizens or for the Scheduled Castes and Tribes. They also provide for laws imposing "reasonable restrictions" on the exercise of fundamental rights; for preventive detention; for compulsory service for public purposes; for regulation of secular activity associated with religious practice; for social welfare and reform; for acquisition and requisition of private property for public purpose; for restriction and modification of fundamental rights in their application to the members of the Armed Forces; and for restriction of fundamental rights while martial law is in force in any area.

A notable feature of the Indian Constitution is that it also guarantees the remedial right to move the Supreme Court for the enforcement of fundamental rights (Article 32). State high courts have been invested with a somewhat wider original jurisdiction to issue appropriate writs and directions for the enforcement of any of the fundamental rights conferred by Part III and for any other purpose (Article 226). The fundamental rights enshrined in Part III have been variously described by the Supreme Court of India as "basic," "paramount," "inalienable," "inviolable," "sacrosanct," "transcendental," and even "immutable" and "unamendable." Whether or not an analysis of the economic backgrounds of the framers of the Constitution or an economic interpretation of the Indian Constitution (no such attempt having been made so far) would bear out any palpable measure of economic determinism, one is bound to treat the guarantees of fundamental rights in the Constitution as an essential part of a constitutional settlement in a "secular" state, giving tangible safeguards to racial, religious, linguistic, and social minorities on psychological and political grounds. The preponderant rationale for the inclusion of a Bill of Rights in the Indian Constitution, however, appears to have been the liberal philosophy of liberty and freedom which formed the milieu and the ideological climate of the independence movement and which inspired the Western-oriented higher echelons of India's middle-class leadership in the course of India's struggle for "Swaraj."

Article 13 of the Constitution declares all previous laws in force in India as void to the extent of their inconsistency with the fundamental rights contained in Part III. Furthermore, it lays down that "the State shall not make any law which takes away or abridges the rights conferred by Part III and any law which contravenes this injunction shall to that extent be void." Article 13 read with Article 32 and 226 thus arms the judiciary with a far-reaching power to test all legislation on the touchstone of fundamental rights and to give appropriate relief by issuing writs and directions.

The role of the judiciary as the "constituted custodian" of fundamental rights and the rule of law guaranteed in the Constitution has on occasions led to sharp and unresolved confrontations between the judiciary and the legislature. This has accentuated the factor of "role conflict" between the judiciary and the legislature. There is a real cleavage in their respective conceptions. Generally speaking, the judiciary attaches somewhat the same original importance to fundamental rights, including the right of property as adumbrated in the Constitution of 1950, and to its supremacy in the matter of interpretation and enforcement of law. Conversely, with the decline of the land-owning classes, the change in the electorate's composition, the emergence of new and different "rural elites" and the exigencies of the legislative and governmental processes, Parliament, as a collectivity, has come to attach progressively diminishing importance to individual rights and more particularly to property rights, frequently speaking in terms of "the sovereignty of Parliament."

Instances of this cleavage are many and varied. Thus, for example, the legislatures do not acknowledge the power of the courts to intervene in any manner in matters relating to breach of privileges, although in Keshav Singh's case[11] the courts claimed and, in a limited sense, asserted this power. Again in I. C. Golaknath's case,[12] after the Constitution had been amended some twenty-one times and amendments restricting and abridging fundamental rights had been enacted four times, the Supreme Court, albeit by a slender majority of one, reversed its two earlier decisions and declared that the Parliament cannot even by constitu-

11. A.I.R. 1965, S.C. 745.
12. Decided on February 27, 1967 (The case has not yet been reported in S.C.R. or A.I.R.).

tional amendment abridge or take away any of the fundamental rights conferred by Part III of the Constitution. Unprecedented and far-reaching in its implication, the majority judgment in I. C. Golaknath's case postulates an assumption of constituent power by the Court under the authority of interpretation, and a denial of any constituent or amending power to the legislature in respect of fundamental rights. Mr. Justice M. Hidayatullah, a judge of the Supreme Court who subscribed to the majority view, preferred to put it simply: "It is the duty of this Court to find the limits which the Constitution has set on the amendatory power and to enforce those limits."[13]

On the other hand, Parliament is vociferous in claiming the power to amend the Constitution, and a joint select committee of its two houses has recommended restoration of this power by means of constitutional amendment. A bill purporting to declare fundamental rights within the ambit of the amending power contained in Article 368 of the Constitution is at present on the anvil. Any such amendment of Article 368 or any other provisions of the Constitution by the Parliament is, however, inescapably subject to the jurisdiction of the Supreme Court and cannot ultimately evade the test of conformity to, and consistency with, the fundamental rights contained in Part III. It means, in effect, that in so far as Part III is concerned, the Constitution is what the Supreme Court says it is. Article 141 provides that the law declared by the Supreme Court shall be binding on all courts within the territory of India and that these shall act in aid of the Supreme Court. Although there are several express provisions in the Constitution that bar the jurisdiction of the Courts in the matter of infringement of certain private proprietary rights[14] in the enforcement of directive principles of state policy[15] and in the working of political institutions,[16] the extent of jurisdiction which is effectively exercised by the Courts is, nevertheless, considerable. The broad political role of the judiciary in the interpre-

13. *Ibid.*
14. For example, see clauses (2), (4), and (6) of Article 31; also see Article 31A.
15. See Article 37.
16. For example, see Article 74(2), Article 122, and Article 329(a).

tation of the Constitution and in the judicial review of administrative action brings it into competition and conflict with the legislature's representational functions and redress-of-public-grievances role.

As the interpreter and the balancing wheel of the Constitution, the judiciary has an upper hand in these conflicts. What sustains the courts and their verdicts, when in conflict with the executive and the legislature, are factors of decisive significance in the Indian polity. These are: the commitment and the adherence of the various organs of the state to the constitutional system; the strength of legalism and considerations of legitimacy; the restraining power of the opposition, the press, and the intelligentsia; and the highly prestigious, influential, and independent position of the judiciary based upon its reputation for objectivity and impartiality.

Legislatures have not always readily acquiesced to the judicial invalidation of legislative enactments. There are a number of instances in which, after the courts had declared an act or any part thereof to be invalid or void, the legislature proceeded to validate the act or such part thereof as may have been invalidated by a judicial decision. Mostly, such validation is with retrospective effect.

On the other hand, there have been occasions on which impassioned support was extended to the cause of individual liberty and freedom of citizens in the Houses of Parliament. On these occasions, the members of the ruling party have been as enthusiastic as the courts in their advocacy of constitutionally guaranteed freedoms. It would appear, therefore, that at times Parliament is competing with the judiciary for the function of "representing" and safeguarding the civil liberties of the individual. Further, there is an almost continuous confrontation between the legislature and the judiciary over the performance of their allotted functions under the Constitution. It is noteworthy that, on the whole, liberty and freedom have triumphed in the judicial courts rather than in the legislatures.

The relationship of the judiciary and the legislature, their respective role expectations and role conflicts, and the resultant divergent motivation and deviant behavior, are matters of the deepest significance in the constitutional interpretation and the political sociology of the Indian system in its relational ramifications. Their interactions constitute a significant part of the constitutional dynamics of the Indian polity. One more condition arising from the Constitution and touching both the courts and legislatures should be noted. The socio-economic philosophy of the Constitution is set forth in the Directive Principles of State Policy embodied in Part IV of the Constitution. The Directive Principles, though not enforceable by any court, are declared to be fundamental in the governance of the country and it shall be the duty of the state to apply these principles in making laws (Article 37).

The founding fathers of the Indian Constitution were not unaware of the cleavage between fundamental rights and Directive Principles of State Policy. At one stage, B. N. Rau, the constitutional advisor, felt it was necessary to ensure that directive principles intended for the welfare of the state as a whole prevail over individual rights, and actually suggested, though unsuccessfully, the incorporation of a provision that no law, which may be made by the state in the discharge of its duty under the Directive Principles of State Policy, shall be void merely on the ground that it contravened any of the provisions of fundamental rights guaranteed by the Constitution. There are some who wistfully look back upon the failure of B. N. Rau's suggestion as a missed opportunity. Such a provision would have vouchsafed a certain primacy to the Directive Principles, for the Supreme Court opined in the year 1951, that "the Directive Principles of State Policy have to conform to and run subsidiary to the chapter on Fundamental Rights."[17] Emphasis, has, however, shifted in the later opinions of the Supreme Court,[18] and an effort is being made to accord a grudging recognition to the Directive Principles "in determining the scope and ambit of Fundamental Rights"[19] on the basis of the rule of harmonious construction.

17. A.I.R. 1951, Supreme Court 226.
18. See, for example, A.I.R. 1958, Supreme Court 731, and A.I.R. 1958, Supreme Court 956.
19. Ibid.

The Directive Principles illustrate the social purposes of the Indian states. The chapter on Directive Principles represents the answers envisioned by the architects of the organic law to the major contemporary questions at the seedtime of the Indian Republic. These answers are based on aspirations rather than on experience. In their programmatic content, they are largely tentative formulations. To attempt to make the fundamental rights "subserve" the Directive Principles would be tantamount to rewriting the Constitution. But positive social legislation properly and progressively implemented could certainly establish a more vital and harmonious correspondence between the Directive Principles and the State Policy, and could establish the rule of law on an increasingly realistic, democratic, and egalitarian basis —a basis without which the concerns of democracy can scarcely endure or prosper.

The prolific procreative propensity of the Indian legislatures is evidenced by a large mass of social legislation enacted by them, an effort resulting from an exaggerated faith in the creative and constitutive capacity of legislation in reforming the society. Such faith probably is natural in a highly politicized elite-dominated society where law is seemingly the most obvious and the easiest weapon to wield. The Indian statute book has on it laws to prohibit and punish every conceivable civic offense and social misdemeanor ranging from bribery, graft, and adulteration to untouchability, hoarding, and dowry. If these laws have often appeared to be an exercise in futility, it is so because: (1) the society has not been sufficiently educated for the changes in advance, and is not ready for them; (2) the implementation is indifferent; (3) the administrative resources for giving effect to these laws are extremely limited; (4) the legislature does not interest itself in the subsequent developments relating to enactment and, therefore, cannot keep track of the quality of implementation; and (5) there are inherent limitations on the use of legislation as an effective instrument for reform.

There is a need, therefore, to undertake extensive legislative case studies if we are to assess the developmental role of the legislature in a political system such as the Indian.

The Federal Structure

India is a federation, with a difference. Historically, the British Indian provinces received grants of power by administrative devolution under central tutelage, whereas the "native" Indian states enjoyed a restricted measure of autonomy under British authority. With the advent of independence, considerations of the vast size of the country and its pervasive diversity inevitably led to the choice of a federal framework, but the choice was conditioned by an assertion of, and pronounced commitment to, cohesive national unity in the wake of the partition of the country. As K. Santhanam, a member of the Constitution Drafting Committee put it: "The main constitutional result of the partition of India was that the pendulum swung from one extreme to another extreme. From the idea of minimal federation, almost all leaders, and much more than leaders, the followers wanted a maximum federation."[20] Essentially, Indian federalism represents a centripetal system in the midst of decentralizing forces and centrifugal socio-cultural environs.

The overriding bias of the Indian Constitution for a strong Center, which has earned for the system the appellation of "quasi-federal," is reflected in the heavily loaded distribution of legislative powers in favor of the Union (Seventh Schedule), the vesting of residuary powers in the Parliament (Article 248), emergency provisions (Part XVIII) which enable the Union Parliament and the Union executive to function as the sole and exclusive repository of all legislative and executive power throughout the country (thus enabling the conversion of the system into a unitary framework), and several other special provisions conferring fundamental and far-reaching powers on the legislative and the executive organs at the Center.

The existence of the concurrent List in addition to the Union List in the Seventh Schedule of the Constitution gives wide scope and superior authority to the central legislature. Furthermore,

20. See K. Santhanam, *Union-State Relations in India* (Brooklyn, N.Y., 1960).

while a Proclamation of Emergency is in operation, Parliament has power to make laws for the whole or any part of the territory of India with respect to any of the matters enumerated in the State List. Even in normal times, the Council of States can in the national interest empower Parliament by a resolution supported by not less than two-thirds of the members present and voting to make laws with respect to any matter enumerated in the State List specified in the resolution (Article 249). Similarly, if legislatures of two or more states so desire, the Parliament is empowered to enact legislation for such states even in respect of a matter which falls within the exclusive competence of states (Article 252). A far-reaching provision which confers a blanket power on the central government and which cuts across the distribution of powers in the Seventh Schedule is embodied in Article 253, which reads thus:

Legislation for giving effect to international agreements—notwithstanding anything in the foregoing provisions of this Chapter, Parliament has power to make any law for the whole or any part of the territory of India or implementing any treaty, agreement or convention with any other country or countries or any decision made at any international conference, association or other body.

Exigencies of national planning and the processes of fixing priorities and allocating scarce resources have brought about a profound interpenetration between the central and state spheres, with a dominant role for the Center. Particularly notable is the emergence of the Planning Commission as a powerful institution, though an extra-constitutional growth. The Planning Commission, until recently, functioned as a kind of national economic cabinet, but because of the paucity of economic resources the role of the Planning Commission has been recast with an emphasis on its advisory character. The Finance Commission is also an advisory body, but constituted under the mandate of the Constitution (Article 280). The Finance Commission makes recommendations as to the distribution between the Union and the states of the net proceeds of taxes which are to be, or may be, divided between them. It also allocates between the states the respective shares of such proceeds and sets out the principles that govern the grants-

in-aid to the revenues of the states. To a limited extent, the
Finance Commission may seek to rectify imbalances between
allotted functions and allocated resources. The Center, however,
has the final say, and this frequently impinges on the orthodox
federal principles. The freedom of interstate commerce declared
by the Constitution is limited by constitutionally permissible
legislation and has not had, at least so far, a decisive or distinct
impact on developing a common integrated national economy.

It may be noted here that in strict constitutional terms, states
in India are merely creatures of parliamentary statutes. According to Article 2, Parliament may by law admit into the Union or
establish new states on such terms and conditions as it thinks fit.
According to Article 3, "Parliament may by law—(*a*) form a new
State by separation of territory from any State or by uniting two
or more States or parts of States or by uniting any territory to a
part of any State; (*b*) increase the area of any State; (*c*) diminish the area of any State; (*d*) alter the boundaries of any State;
and (*e*) alter the name of any State."

The Constitution goes so far as to lay down under the head of
Administrative Relations in the framework of relations between
the Union and the states, that "The executive power of every
State shall be so exercised as to ensure compliance with the laws
made by Parliament and any existing laws which apply in that
State, and the executive power of the Union shall extend to the
giving of such directions to a State as may appear to the Government of India to be necessary for that purpose" (Article 256).
And, again: "The executive power of every State shall be so
exercised as not to impede or prejudice the exercise of the executive power of the Union, and the executive power of the Union
shall extend to the giving of such directions to a State as may
appear to the Government of India to be necessary for that
purpose" (Article 257 [i]).

Emergency provisions in the Constitution can enlarge the
ambit of union powers to such a degree that the Indian Union can
function as a unitary state. A Proclamation of Emergency is
issued when the president is satisfied that a grave emergency
exists, whereby the security of India or of any part of the territory

thereof is threatened, whether by war, or external aggression, or internal disturbance (Article 352). Under Article 353, while a Proclamation of Emergency is in operation, then—

(*a*) notwithstanding anything in this Constitution, the executive power of the Union shall extend to the giving of directions to any state as to the manner in which the executive power thereof is to be exercised;

(*b*) the power of Parliament to make laws with respect to any matter shall include power to make laws conferring powers and imposing duties, or authorizing the conferring of powers and the imposition of duties, upon the Union or officers and authorities of the Union as respects that matter, notwithstanding that it is one which is not enumerated in the Union List.

Apart from a Proclamation of Emergency under Article 352, the Constitution also permits pervasive interference by the central government in the affairs of the states (Article 356 [1]). The provisions of Article 356 have been pressed into service for promulgating presidential rule on as many as fifteen occasions since the adoption of the Constitution in 1950. The use of these powers has not always been free from the taint of partisan considerations, although there are obvious political limitations on a gross and palpable abuse of such power.

Another extremely potent although so far unused weapon in the constitutional armory of the Center in its relationship with the states is the concept of financial emergency adumbrated in Article 360 under which the president may proclaim a financial emergency in the whole or any part of India.

Other than emergency provisions and the power of subventions, the position of state governors (who are at once appointees of the central government and the incumbents of a constitutional office) is a matter of considerable moment to the federal system of India. In the wake of the results of the fourth general election, the gubernatorial power of naming the majority party leader who is to form a government was variously exercised. The power was put to an acid test in Rajasthan, Punjab, Haryana, Uttar Pradesh, and Madhya Pradesh where lists and counterlists of the members of a state legislative assembly were submitted to the governors.

In the states of West Bengal, Bihar, Uttar Pradesh, Haryana and Punjab, the governor was involved in making critical decisions about the capacity of different parties to carry on government on the basis of majority support in the legislatures. In the states of West Bengal and Punjab, the governors had to decide on the relative powers of speakers and state governments. It was on the basis of the reports of the governors that the president (advised by the central cabinet) dissolved the state legislatures and promulgated presidential rule (which means that the governor is responsible for the administration of the state, and the central government is answerable to Parliament in respect to all state matters) in West Bengal, Uttar Pradesh, Haryana, Bihar, Punjab, and Pondicherry after the general election in 1967. Consequently, demands have been voiced in Parliament and the press that gubernatorial appointments should not be partisan, and that such appointments should be required by means of a constitutional amendment to be ratified by Parliament. So strong has been the reaction to this display of partisanship that in states with non-congressional governments, the concurrence of such governments in gubernatorial appointments (though not conceded as such by the central government) appears to be an operating precondition.

As has been the case in other federal systems, the most important single factor in the federal equation in India is the financial dependence of the states on the center. The constitutional devolution of financial resources from the center to the states is through the grants and loans given by the center to the states on the recommendations of the Planning Commission. As a Study Team on Center-State Relationships[21] recently pointed out, the sense of dependence has been heightened by the fact that plan grants are discretionary in character. Moreover, the indebtedness of the states to the center has assumed alarming proportions. In 1966 the states were indebted to the center to the tune of Rs. 4,094 crores, which was more than the total outlay on the planned expenditure of all the states in the Third Plan period.

21. *Report of the Study Team on Centre-State Relationships* (headed by M. C. Setalvad), Administrative Reforms Commission, 1968.

Structural arrangements and clearly defined norms and procedures embodied in the Constitution have provided the guidelines for India's fledgling federalism, but it is in the operating dynamics of center-state relationship that one sees the true nature of the Indian federal equation. Constitutionally, as has been indicated, Parliament has the power to form new states by adjustment and redistribution of territories, to increase and diminish the area of any state, and to alter the boundaries or the name of any state. In actual practice, the exercise or non-exercise of this power is largely a culminating point in the decision-making process in the background of which state politics and several other extra-parliamentary factors play a decisive part. The central fact is that once a state is established, it has a personality of its own and it functions irrespective of, and without being controlled by, its formal legislative parentage. For a while the union government, and with it the union Parliament, resisted the idea of linguistic reorganization of states, but they finally yielded to it. The new states which were brought into existence as a result of linguistic reorganization of states are, if anything, more conscious of their identity and more ready to assert it against the center than are others.

On the other hand, even such fields as public health, education, and agriculture, which are enumerated in the exclusive State List, are very much subject to central direction and coordination. For fifteen years, the Planning Commission, working under the mandate of the central government, had an unquestioned authority to allocate resources, and to evaluate, implement, and, generally, determine the framework of the economic and industrial activities of the states. Again, vast powers of licensing, which determine the nature, quantum, and location of industrial activity are vested in the central government. The substance of the power to take initiatives and to formulate strategy in the economic field thus falls somewhat outside the purview of states. Handicapped by want of resources and, for the time being, by comparatively inelastic sources of revenues, and held by the leash of proximal subventions flowing from the federal financial entrepot, states must, of necessity, defer to the central government, which is in a position to further augment its resources by receiving foreign aid and by resorting to deficit financing. More often than not, the states are willing victims for they are anxious to secure greater central involvement and participation in their development schemes and to obtain an increased amount of central funds, even at the cost of their autonomy. The alternative of raising resources from within the state is fraught with unpopular political reper-cussions. Central assistance and overdrafts on the Reserve Bank of India provide the line of least political resistance within the states.

It is possible that authority without resources makes for lack of responsibility. It would, however, be wrong to labor under the impression that financial dependence and lack of resources make for helpless and acquiescent states in the Indian federal frame-work. States deploy all kinds of pressures, and here, very often, party considerations are forgotten. State governments and legisla-tures compete effectively with the central government and Parlia-ment in the performance of the representational function. The Parliament itself is a great unifier of the Indian nation, but mem-bers of Parliament also have loyalties to the states from which they hail. Emotionally, people readily respond to and rally around the claims of their home states, be it for a steel plant, for the revision of territorial boundaries, or for water rights. This has been particularly true since the linguistic reorganization of states in India. In addition, the center always has been dependent to a large degree on the states for the actual implementation of major national programs, so that functionally the powers of the center are essentially normative. It is this interdependence and the com-mon idiom and platform of Indian politics which is conducive to the growth of cooperative and mutually interdependent federal-ism in India. As Dr. Paul Appleby[22] discovered in his pioneering survey of Public Administration in India, the center had powers largely of coordination rather than administration, and influence rather than power.

In summary, India's federalism is still in the making. It is not

22. Paul H. Appleby, *Public Administration in India: Report of a Survey* (Delhi, 1953).

easy to evaluate precisely the complex and competing cultural, economic, social, and political emphases involved, but it is clear that the constitutional strategy makes for central hegemony and the socio-political forces predicate greater autonomy and even separatism. There are those in India like the late Mr. M. C. Mahajan, a former Chief Justice of India, who believed that India should have opted for a unitary form of government, and that the adoption of a federal framework was a great mistake. The proponents of the idea of unitary government for India are alarmed by the threat of balkanization posed by the diffuse forces of subnationalism and provincial chauvinism. On the other hand, there are those like the Dravida Munetra Kazagam (the party in power in the state of Madras since the 1967 election) who at one time clamored for secession and are now content to advocate maximum autonomy for the states. Obviously these extremes represent impractical, even utopian ideals. On the whole, the prevailing scheme of Indian federalism provides a viable framework for unity in diversity and leaves considerable room for creative evolution and adjustment.

The Electoral System

India was divided for the Fourth General Elections in 1967 into 520 territorial parliamentary constituencies (an increase of twenty-six from the general elections of 1962) that elected their representatives to the House of the People (Lok Sabha). In 1967, the total number of assembly constituencies for elections to the state assemblies was 3,563; it had stood at 3,196 in 1962, when the average population of a constituency was 873,924. The delimitation of constituencies is governed by constitutional provisions which require that, upon the completion of each decennial census, the allocation of seats in the House of the People to the several states, the total number of seats in the legislative assembly of each state, and the parliamentary and assembly constituencies into which each state is divided, shall be readjusted by such authority and in such manner as may be determined by an act of Parliament. Accordingly, Parliament enacted the Delimitation Commission Act of 1962 which was broadly on the same lines as the Act of 1952. The Delimitation Commission Act of 1962 provided for single-member constituencies; the Act also laid down that every state assembly constituency should be so delimited as to fall completely within one parliamentary constituency. Thus, each national parliamentary constituency was to comprise an integral number of state assembly constituencies. The Act also contained the directive that constituencies in which seats were to be reserved for the Scheduled Castes should be distributed in different parts of the state and located, as far as practicable, in those areas where the proportion of their population to the total was comparatively large.

Under the Act of 1962, the Delimitation Commission consists of three members out of whom the chief election commissioner *ex officio* is one; each of the other two members is a sitting or retired judge of the Supreme Court or of a high court appointed by the central government. The impartiality of the Delimitation Commission's proposals has seldom been challenged. Certain factors underlie the decisions they make. The main principles are that constituencies shall be more or less equal in population; that all constituencies shall be geographically compact areas; and that, in forming them, administrative units shall not be unnecessarily broken. Physical features, facilities of communication, and public convenience are also taken into account. As would be expected, only a handful of constituencies are exclusively urban. The remainder vary with respect to the proportion of population that can be termed urban. The states vary also with respect to the number of constituencies they contain; to cite an extreme example, Uttar Pradesh had 85 parliamentary constituencies in 1967, whereas the entire state of Nagaland comprised a single constituency.

The holding of an election in a nation as populous as India is an enormously complex undertaking. The administrative machinery responsible for the preparation of electoral rolls and for the conduct of elections in each state is drawn essentially from the state governments' apparatus. But, the state government officials who form part of the electoral machinery are supervised by and responsible to the Election Commission in the discharge of their duties. In each state, there is a chief electoral officer assisted by a permanent and full-time deputy; for each assembly constituency there is an electoral registration officer whose duty is to prepare and revise the electoral rolls for the constituency. When elections are held simultaneously with the state legislative assemblies and with the House of the People, the returning officers and assistant returning officers of all the state assembly constituencies within a parliamentary constituency are appointed as assistant returning officers for the parliamentary constituency.

The electoral rolls are revised from time to time in accordance with the parliamentary statute and the rules framed thereunder. The proceedings in respect of electoral registration are quasi-judicial and are reviewable by the highest courts. Every citizen twenty-one years of age on the first day of January of the year in which the electoral roll for a constituency is prepared or revised, and who is ordinarily a resident in the constituency at the time of such preparation or revision, is entitled to be registered in the roll. The total number of electors at the time of the general election in 1967 was about 250.3 million, an increase of 14.7 per cent over 1962. Considering the prevalence of illiteracy, poverty, and the difficulties of communication, voter participation in India tends to be quite high. Thus, in the first general election, held in 1951–1952, roughly 62 per cent of the total of about 173 million eligible voters exercised their franchise. In the second general election in 1957, 48 per cent of 190 million eligible electors actually voted; in 1962, about 55 per cent of the electors went to the polls; and in 1967, the proportion of voters rose to 61 per cent. The steady rise since 1957 in the number and proportion of the voting electorate underscores the increasing involvement of the common citizen with the machinery and the functions of democratic self-government, the growth of political consciousness, and the deepening of the competitive character of political parties.

Although Indian psephology is still in its infancy (and available studies on the composition and the voting behavior of the Indian electorate are scanty and sectional), there is considerable material for a measure of cautious generalization. It is safe to say that the size of the constituencies and the electorate is a significant factor in the conduct of elections, increasing, as it does, the dependence of the candidates on the social and caste elites and the local leadership—both in the local bodies and in the local party organization.

Castes, as well as local and regional factors, play a crucial role in the recruitment of candidates and in the electorate's behavior. They often override considerations of status, prestige, wealth, education, and merit in the choice of candidates. Although they furnish stable loyalty patterns, particularly in rural areas, the political cohesion of caste, tribal, and religious groups is variable, and sharp in-fighting is not unknown. When intra-group conflicts occur, other factors such as the personalities and ideologies of candidates and their workers play a more notable part. In this sense, caste identification may be said to be merging gradually into class awareness.

Voting behavior is greatly influenced by an emerging "elite" of opinion leaders in the rural and urban areas, a consequence of universal adult franchise and new politico-economic institutions and activities. These opinion-making elites are, in keeping with S. F. Nadel's definition, a stratum of the population which, for whatever reason, can claim a position of superiority and, hence, a corresponding measure of influence over the fate of the community. They are, however, essentially transitional and confined to their particular kinship, factional, regional, or occupational group. They provide many of the election workers, agents and managers, and are important variables in the electoral process.

As has already been suggested, electors often vote for candidates, and only in a subsidiary sense for parties. In part, this explains the sizable number of Independents that have been returned. Indians are by habit and temperament not oriented toward parties. Thus, individual campaigns frequently have to concentrate on the merits of candidates rather than expatiate on ideologies and programs. It is true that current events are discussed and, occasionally, certain broad policies are debated. But party programs and manifestos are neither analyzed nor explained in depth. Issues also tend to be obscured because of the large number of candidates who have contested the national and state elections. For example, 2,400 candidates contested the 513 Lok Sabha seats in 1967. As a consequence of these and other factors, party loyalties are not yet intense or particularly widespread.

With the fourth general elections, Indian politics entered a new phase, an era of restlessness and instability. Eric da Costa described the ferment as "a break with the past,"[23] and thought that the twenty-one to thirty-five age group, the lower literates, and the lower income groups in the majority community were shifting their loyalties both to the Right and the Left and away from the Congress.[24] Professor Norman D. Palmer considered it one of the most significant aspects of the Indian political scene, namely, the acceleration of "The Indianization of Indian politics."[25] Another observer explained the debacle of the Congress party in terms of the revolt of the masses, "an angry electoral repudiation of the structure of power built since 1947."[26] Whether this is indeed the case or whether, in the words of another commentator, "Things have changed much less than we think, and they will continue to be the same much more than we think,"[27] is a matter upon which we can only speculate at present.

The Parties

A notable fact about the Indian political system is that it has not lacked political parties. On the eve of the general elections in 1967, there were as many as twenty-four political parties which were recognized by the Election Commission and which had reserved symbols allotted to them in one or more states and union

23. Eric da Costa, "The General Elections," *Economic Times*, January 30, 1967.
24. *Statesman*, March 9, 1967.
25. Norman D. Palmer, "India's Fourth General Election," *Asian Survey*, VIII (May, 1967), 277.
26. Shiv Shastri, "The Indian Cultural Revolution," *Indian Express*, March 1, 1967.
27. Ashok V. Desai, "Small Thoughts on the Elections," *Economic and Political Weekly*, March 4, 1967; quoted in *India Votes* (Bombay, 1968), p. 175.

territories. The relative strength of political parties in the Lok Sabha after the four national elections India has experienced is shown in Table 3. Of these, the Indian National Congress, founded in 1885 by an English civil servant and several urban middle-class Indians, clearly is the most important. The nucleus of the present organizational structure of the Congress was established in 1908. Although the generation of leaders who preceded Mahatma Gandhi had articulated the basic message of nationalism, it was left to Gandhi to impart to the organization its national character, its rural base, its philosophical and practical espousal of non-violence, its constructive approach, and its reformist temperament.

Table 3. *Distribution of Parliamentary Parties after Four National Elections*

| | Proportion of seats won | | | |
Party	1952	1957	1962	1967
Indian National Congress	74.4%	75.1%	72.9%	54.4%
Communist party of India and Communist party of India (Marxist)	3.3	5.4	5.9	8.1
Praja Socialist party and Samyukta Socialist party	2.4	3.8	3.7	6.9
Swatantra	a	a	3.7	8.4
Bharatiya Jana Sangh	.6	.8	2.9	6.7
Republican party of India	a	a	.6	.2
Other parties and independents	19.2	14.8	10.4	15.2

a. Data missing.

During the freedom struggle, the Indian National Congress was an umbrella organization, inclusive and diverse in its composition. Ideologically, also, the Indian National Congress was composed of a miscellaneous entourage. There were in the camp of the Indian National Congress idealists, revivalists, Socialists, Communists, unaffiliated nationalists, followers of Gandhi's philosophy of truth and non-violence, and adherents of his constructive program. The Congress did not exclude individuals on the basis of their ideology, because ideology was not considered to be a criterion for one's commitment to the cause of national freedom and independence.

After the advent of independence, the Congress Socialist party broke loose from the Indian National Congress. So also did many other splinter groups and leading individuals. But, in the years before the first election, the Congress was still a movement rather than a party. Even the central government was then organized on a national and essentially non-partisan basis. However, within the Congress there were at least two distinct groups led by Jawaharlal Nehru and Vallabhbhai Patel, respectively, as well as several other shades of opinion. After the death of Mr. Patel, the charisma of Nehru cast a spell over the party.

Under Nehru's leadership, the Congress party committed itself more consciously to establishing a socialistic pattern of society in India. During this period, the Congress party continued to be both a heterogenous social group and an ideological conglomeration. According to Myron Weiner,[28]

The Congress Party of India is surely one of the most successful political parties to be found anywhere in the developing areas. Its success in recruiting political workers, in dissolving internal conflict, and, above all, in winning four successive national elections, has made it possible for India to sustain a stable and relatively effective government at the local, State, and national levels since independence was achieved in 1947.

Weiner has attributed the success of the Congress party to its organizational vitality, its responsiveness to national, regional, and local needs, its traditions of service, its cadres of party workers, its capacity for settling internal disputes, and above all, its open elite system. There is no denying that there are grave shortcomings in the capacity of the Congress party to maintain an optimum combination of these factors. Nevertheless, it has been a party of mature thinking, national outlook, and extensive organization.

The party's manifesto is comprehensive in its sweep and inclusive in its approach. It proclaims its categorical choice in favor of

28. Myron Weiner, *Party-Building in a New Nation* (Chicago, 1967), p. 2.

an open and democratic society. Although regional parties and local platforms have an edge over the Congress because the national approach does not always have an immediate appeal for locally oriented electors, the other national parties have frequently found their thunder stolen by the Congress. Most of them, therefore, charge the Congress with permitting a yawning gulf between its theories and practice. The parties of the Right accuse the Congress of camouflaged Communist infiltration; those of the Left decry it as a stooge of capitalists.

If major national political parties in India were to be arrayed along an ideological continuum, the Swatantra party and the Bharatiya Jana Sangh could be classified as parties of the Right, the Congress party and the Praja Socialist party as left of the Center moderate parties, and the two Communist parties as parties of the extreme Left. The Samyukta Socialist party is an activist political party which could also be defined as a party of the Left. The Republican party tends to be a sectional party of the Scheduled Castes and the Buddhist converts from those castes. The Indian Muslim Majlis-e-Mushawarat is another example of a sectional and sectarian party. On the other hand, the Dravida Munnetra Kazhagam (D.M.K.) is a regional party confined to the Tamil speaking areas of South India, mainly in the state of Madras. Similarly, there are several regional and sectional parties like Bangla Congress, Shiromani Akali Dal, Janata party, Forward Block, Lok Sewak Dal, and so forth. These sectional and regional parties are creatures of fortuitous circumstances and regional or sectional peculiarities, and it is difficult to plot a precise position for them on any ideological continuum.

The Swatantra party which won forty-eight seats in the Lok Sabha at the fourth general election is the largest opposition group. To be duly recognized as a full-fledged party in Parliament, a party has to have a strength of a minimum of 10 per cent of the total membership of the House. The Swatantra party was conceived as a "clear-cut alternative" to the philosophy and principles of the Congress party both in the domestic and international fields. It is a liberal democratic, non-denominational, and non-sectarian party. Some of its leaders were in the forefront of the struggle for independence. The impression is that the Swatantra party is a party of the intelligentsia, reflecting primarily the interests of business. Its plea is that the Congress is responsible for the ebbing tempo of industrial and commercial activity and for the spiraling prices in the country. It holds that as a result of the Congress party's patronage of class conflicts, the country and the people are so divided that the national unity achieved in 1947 is fast disappearing. In the sphere of international policy, the Swatantra party's views are diametrically opposed to those of the Congress party. In the domestic area, it promises to cut governmental expenditure and taxes, abolish land revenue, check rising prices by increasing production, and help the farmer, trade, and industry. It also promised on the eve of the fourth general election to end all monopolies, restore fair and free competition in the service of the consumer, dissolve the Planning Commission, and scrap the disastrous Fourth Plan.

The Bharatiya Jana Sangh, another party of the Right, is in some ways close to the outlook of the Swatantra party. Unlike the Swatantra party however, the Bharatiya Jana Sangh is a highly disciplined organization with a more militant outlook on national problems. To date, all efforts to effect a coalition between it and the Swatantra party have failed.

The Samyukta Socialist party has been a projection of the late Dr. Ram Manohar Lohia's social philosophy and political program. It won spectacular electoral victories in 1967 and has insisted on the implementation of some of its radical ideas.

The Communist movement in India has been split by the Sino-Soviet schism. The Communist party of India (Right) considers the official Soviet approach to be the most suited to the present conditions. The Marxist Communist party, on the other hand, draws its inspiration from the Chinese communism of Mao, holding the Russians to be guilty of revisionism. The approaches of the Communist factions, however, are remarkably similar and their differences often times appear to be superficial.

The Republican party of India was founded by the late B. R. Ambedkar, a leader of the Scheduled Castes and one of the principal architects of the Indian Constitution. The party is particularly committed to the reconstruction of the rural economy of India by nationalization of land and by encouraging cultivation on a cooperative basis. The Republican party is articulate in its concern for the welfare of the backward classes, particularly the Scheduled Castes, and the Buddhist converts from these classes, in the matter of education, services, and economic well-being.

The D.M.K. is confined as was previously indicated to the Tamil-speaking areas of South India, mainly in the state of Madras (where it was returned to power at the fourth general elections). It represents a social protest of the Tamil masses against the elitist Brahmin hierarchy and has, in recent years, become the political vehicle for organized opposition against alleged north Indian "imperialism."

Personnel and the leadership elites in the political parties in India belong largely to the urban middle class. Even the Communist party of India is manned largely by leaders and workers drawn from the urban middle class rather than from the proletarian masses. Their (party leaders') politics alternate between ideology and opportunity, commitment and career. They also make for a degree of mutual understanding and tolerance that at times has been able to cross party lines. Thus, notwithstanding their loudly proclaimed differences, there have been coalition governments in several states in which opposition parties as divergent as the Jana Sangh and the Communists participated. Consequently, it seems fair to say that the straitjacket of manifestos, labels, and shibboleths do not provide a wholly dependable frame of reference for evaluating the Indian party system.

In brief, parties in Indian politics are in a melting pot. Factors such as interest groups, pressures of public opinion, economic developments, and emergent elite groups may in the course of time cast the party system in a more logical and functional mold. Despite the many shortcomings of the party system, however, political parties in the legislatures of India contribute substantially to the direction and purposiveness of the parliamentary and public debate. They provide the "duelists" and the "wooden swords" in the parliamentary battles; they facilitate an organized "appeal to the people"; they furnish a range of alternative choices to the electorate; and last, but not the least, they aid and assist the process of making, maintaining, and unmaking governments. It is in the context of these functions that the role of Indian legislatures can be properly analyzed and assessed, and not on the basis of any classic models and preconceived notions that bear no relationship to the operating realities.

Parliament

The office of the Speaker is institutionally and functionally the cornerstone of the legislative arch. Although the British parliamentary system was adopted in India, and the Indian speakership resembles the British speakership closely, there is one essential difference—the continued link of several Indian Speakers (both of the House of the People and those of the state legislatures) with their parties. In Great Britain, there has been a convention (though not without exception) that the Speaker's seat will not be contested and that he will be returned unopposed. In India, the office of the Speaker seems to be considered fair political game. As there is no assurance that the Speaker's seat will not be contested, most Speakers at the center and in the states have continued to belong to their parties and to retain their political affiliations even after their election as Speakers.

It appears to the present writer that the independence and the impartiality of the Speaker as the umpire of the legislative process is central to the proper functioning of the legislature. His office is not a mere ceremonial device. He is clothed with enormous powers in regulating the business of the House. He rules on points of order, decides on the admissibility of questions and motions, determines the arrangement and the allocation of time for the business of the House, and guides the committees and the House, generally, in procedural matters and matters of conventions. In the performance of some of these functions he is aided by party whips, party leaders, and the leader of the House, but it is his imprimatur which puts the seal of near-finality on the legislative process.

Social Background of Legislators

The composition of the Parliament and the state legislatures determines the character and contours of legislative politics. The position of legislator is both highly visible and prestigious. As a student of the Indian Parliament puts it: "The social prestige accruing to members of parliament is a strong inducement to the ambitious. Men and women from landholding rural families re-gard the parliament as a royal court, where proximity to the seat of power bestows reflected glory. To others it represents an arena where prestige and power may be won through verbal duels."[29]

Table 4. Age Distributions of Four Lok Sabhas[a]

Ages	First Parliament		Second Parliament		Third Parliamen		Fourth Parliament	
	Number	%	Number	%	Number	%	Number	%
25–34 years	82	18	73	15	45	9	43	9
35-44 years	126	27	162	33	143	30	119	24
45–54 years	164	36	140	29	142	30	177	36
55–64 years	76	16	95	19	116	24	106	21
65 years and over	11	2	16	3	29	6	49	10
Totals	459		486		475		494	

a. Differences in totals reflect missing data.

As is true of virtually every legislative body, the incumbents tend to overrepresent the "over forty" segment of the general population. (See Table 4.) The steady increase in the proportion of members in the two oldest age categories indicates this tend-ency is growing more pronounced. It should be noted, however, that in comparison to most Western parliaments, the Indian is relatively young.

The available information on the occupational backgrounds of members tends to be incomplete, imprecise, and overlapping. Several members indicate more than one occupation. For exam-

29. Surinder S. Suri, "Political Life Cycle of Lok Sabha Members," *Journal of Constitutional and Parliamentary Studies,* I (July–September, 1967), 30.

ple, there are some who are at once lawyers, farmers, journalists, and social workers. Thus, although the data in Table 5 should be viewed with caution, it does appear that there has been a decline in the recruitment and election of individuals from the professions, including education and journalism, and from the business world. Inversely, the proportion of agriculturalists and social and political workers has increased—reflecting, perhaps, their emergence as new elite groups. The turnover rate in the parliaments to date all have exceeded 50 per cent. Although such a large proportion of new members in each parliament may have an adverse

Table 5. *Occupations of Members of the Four Lok Sabhas*

Occupation	First Lok Sabha	Second Lok Sabha	Third Lok Sabha	Fourth Lok Sabha
Lawyers	36.0	30.1	24.1	19.0
Agriculturists	22.1	29.1	27.1	29.0
Traders and industralists	12.1	10.1	10.1	9.0
Civil and military service	4.0	4.1	1.0	a
Medical practitioners	5.0	3.0	3.1	3.0
Teachers and educationists	10.0	11.1	6.0	6.0
Journalists and writers	10.1	10.1	6.0	5.0
Former rulers	1.1	1.1	2.1	2.0
Political and social workers	—	—	19.0	23.0
Engineers and technologists	—	—	a	a
Industrial workers	—	—	a	a
Religious missionaries	—	—	a	a

a. Less than 1 per cent.

effect on the operation of the system in the sense that there is a paucity of experienced individuals available, it is a pattern that apparently is characteristic of the parliaments and congresses of new nations. If India develops as the United States and Canada have, for instance, one would expect that the proportion of new members in each future parliament will slowly decline. Finally, it should be noted that the percentage of members without any previous legislative experience is comparatively low among the Congress M.P.'s, but is considerably higher among the parliamentary members of the other parties.

Functions of Parliament

Modern legislatures in the parliamentary system have a predominantly debating and consultative function; they inform and
legitimize. They correct by influence more than by specific com-
mand. The Indian Parliament is in that sense the grand inquisitor
of the nation. It is a symbolic battleground on which the principal
elements engage in conflict. It provides a running commentary
and a continuous critique of public policies; simultaneously, it
serves as a public forum and a sounding board for public opinion.

Parliamentary debate in India is widely reported in the press
which, in turn, functions as an indispensable complement and
adjunct to Parliament (and in a lesser measure to state legislatures). In the sixteenth session of the Third Lok Sabha, some 259
press correspondents were admitted to the press gallery; the
combined circulation of Indian newspapers represented in the
press gallery was about four million.[30] The All-India Radio regularly broadcasts summaries of parliamentary proceedings. There
is a constant interaction through editorials, articles, and correspondence from readers in the press. A large number of citizens
attend the visitors' galleries; on important occasions the galleries
of the Lok Sabha are packed to capacity. During the sittings of
the Third Lok Sabha, almost 400,000 visitors sat in different
galleries.

Often, debates and controversies travel back and forth between Parliament and the outside elite segments. Important issues are publicly discussed at length by academicians, interest
groups, and citizens in general. Public demands, issues, and viewpoints are brought literally to the doors of Parliament by means
of processions, demonstrations, fasts, flags, and placards on a
spacious lawn just outside the precincts of Parliament House.
Members of Parliament are thus constantly exposed to expressions of public opinion and they have the feeling (some might
call it an illusion) that the discussion in the House counts, and

30. See "Third Lok Sabha: A Souvenir," Part II, *ibid.,* p. 77.

that they are there to play a significant part in the big decisions of the day. The fact that parliamentary debates are free and relatively uninhibited by party considerations, particularly insofar as the participation of Congress party members is concerned, facilitates a certain give-and-take in the proceedings, and enables the opposition groups to impress their demands on "like-minded" sections in the ruling party.

In formal terms, the principal function of the Parliament, as well as the state legislatures, is to pass legislation. But, legislation is only a part of the Parliament's business. A study of the allocation of parliamentary time for different kinds of business gives us an insight into the pattern of Parliament's functional processes. Out of a total of 3,732 hours and 40 minutes for which the Third Lok Sabha was in session, only 748 hours and 24 minutes (19.8 per cent of the total time) was spent on government bills; another 119 hours and 34 minutes (3.2 per cent of the total time) was spent on private member's bills, which, though mostly still-born, provide a springboard for parliamentary debates on important public issues. Besides, such modalities as parliamentary interpellation, private member's resolutions, motions, half-hour discussions, short-duration discussions, and, most of all, the working of parliamentary committees, furnish valuable opportunities for criticizing, questioning, and embarrassing the government, for influencing and even for correcting policies. These modalities and the control of the purse strings are essential aids to the broad supervisory function of Parliament, and the proportion of time they consume is indicated in Table 6.

The Question Hour, though a procedurally limited device, is a daily reminder of the accountability of the executive to the legislature. Akin to its British analogue, the Question Hour in India is, to adopt the words employed by a British parliamentary committee, "perhaps the readiest and the most effective method of Parliamentary control over the actions of the Executive." Besides being a mechanism of parliamentary control and oversight, the question procedure is also a powerful medium for ventilating grievances, for testing ministerial competence, and for keeping the civil service on its toes. It is in the Question Hour that the

Table 6. *Time Taken by Third Lok Sabha on Various Kinds of Business*

Type of business	Time taken on each item		Percentage of total time
	Hours	Minutes	
Adjournment motions	41	25	1.1
Bills			
Government bills	748[a]	24	19.8
Private members' bills	119	34	3.2
Budget			
Railway budget	151	26	4.1
General budget	762	39	20.4
Kerala budget	20	06	0.5
Calling attention notices (Rule 197)	111	00	3.0
Discussions			
Half-an-hour discussions (Rule 55)	53	17	1.4
Short duration discussions (Rule 193)	59	13	1.6
Motions			
Motions (Rules 191 and 342)	378[b]	43	10.2
Motions of no-confidence in the Council of Ministers	102	13	2.8
Motions for modification of statutory rules (Rule 235)	6	28	0.2
Debates on president's addresses	105	01	2.9
Questions	564	41	15.1
Resolutions			
Statutory resolutions	88	59	2.4
Government resolutions	5[c]	45	0.2
Private members' resolutions	122[d]	39	3.3
Statements by ministers (Rule 372)	68	40	1.8
Miscellaneous	222	27	6.0
Total	3,732	40	100.0

a. Certain statutory resolutions were discussed together with government bills during the 10th, 11th, 12th, and 15th Sessions. Time taken has been shown under statutory resolutions.

b. Discussions under rule 193 and motions under rule 191 were discussed together during the 5th Session. Time taken has been shown under discussions under rule 193.

c. Statutory resolutions and government resolutions were discussed together during the 3rd Session. Time taken has been shown under statutory resolutions.

d. Discussion under rule 193 and a private members' resolution were discussed together during the 12th Session. Time taken has been shown under discussions under rule 193.

largest number of members are able to participate, and it is in this hour that reputations are made and lost.

An abnormally large number of questions are notified in the Lok Sabha, most of them being notices of starred questions requiring oral answers. Statistical data on the questions in the Third Lok Sabha shows that notices of starred questions account for 89.7 per cent of all the notified questions received (N = 162,334). Only about 35 per cent of the notified questions were admitted, however, the rest being inadmissible on one or more of the many grounds mentioned in the Rules of Procedure.

A detailed analysis of the subjects of the questions answered by different ministries would be a marathon task, but Table 7 gives at least an indication of the interests of the members and the range of a ministry's functions in terms of public policy. Thus, out of 58,440 admitted questions, each of the following ten ministries shown in the table had to answer more than 2,000 questions.

Table 7. *Frequency of Questions Addressed to Ministries, Third Lok Sabha*

Name of the ministry	Number of questions
Food, Agriculture, Community Development and Cooperation (including erstwhile Ministry of CDPR and Coop. up to 13th Session	6,265
Home Affairs	5,115
Education (including erstwhile Ministry of SR and CA up to 5th Session)	4,849
Railways	4,747
Commerce (including erstwhile Ministry of Commerce and Industry up to 5th Session and International Trade—6th to 8th Sessions)	4,227
Finance	3,564
Defense (including erstwhile Department of Economic and Defense Coordination 4th and 5th Sessions)	3,159
External Affairs	3,031
Irrigation and Power	2,259
Labor, Employment and Rehabilitation (including Department of Rehabilitation 7th to 15th Sessions)	2,048

In addition, the Department of Parliamentary Affairs was responsible for twenty-two answers; and Supply, the Cabinet Secretariat, the Prime Minister's Secretariat, the Department of Social Welfare, and the Ministry of Law for 42, 107, 132, 494, and 602 answers, respectively.

Qualitatively as well as quantitatively, the exertions of members with respect to the Question Hour vary widely. As might be expected in any organization, a large proportion of the members either never ask questions or ask questions only occasionally. Excluding about fifty-nine ministers and parliamentary secretaries who could not ask questions, there were, in the Third Lok Sabha, 274 members who asked more than 700 questions each. The requirements and mechanics of giving advance notice of questions, coupled with the apathy of the average member and the keen competitiveness of a small coterie of them, have led to a situation where the privilege of asking the bulk of the oral questions is confined to about fifty-two members.

The Committees

The Parliament functions through its committees to probe administrative operations in detail. Three committees of Parliament, namely, the Public Accounts Committee, the Committee on Estimates, and the Committee on Public Undertakings, constitute the infra-structure of parliamentary surveillance and correction of the executive branch of government, and whose objective is in the words of Tocqueville, "to prevent the government from abusing its aptitude and strength."

The Public Accounts Committee consists of fifteen members from the Lok Sabha and seven members from Rajya Sabha. The Committee on Public Undertakings consists of ten members from the Lok Sabha and five members from Rajya Sabha; and the Committee on Estimates consists of thirty members of the Lok Sabha but does not have any members of Rajya Sabha on the grounds that it deals with current estimates and the financial working of the government which is vouchsafed exclusively to the Lok Sabha. Elected on the basis of proportional representation by a single transferable vote, the members of these committees represent a cross section of the members of Parliament. By and large, belonging to these committees does not mean for individual members conspicuous public recognition. Consequently, many of the more active and prominent members of the House prefer to perform on the floor of the House rather than behind the doors in the committees. The chairmanships of the committees are coveted positions and until recently were reserved for members of the ruling party. After the fourth general election, the chairmanship of the Public Accounts Committee was entrusted to a prominent member (Mr. M. R. Masani) of the largest single opposition group, namely, the Swatantra party.

These committees do not function along party lines, and as a result of patient and careful inquiries, their reports have at times been extremely critical of the government. One can get some idea of the complexity and the range of work of these committees from the following figures. Thus, for example, the Estimates Committee sat for 210 hours in the year 1964–1965 and for 248 hours in the year 1965–1966. During these two years the Committee had to study 28,144 and 17,964 pages of materials, respectively. Similarly, the Committee on Public Undertakings sat for 159 and 127 hours, respectively, in 1964–1965 and 1965–1966, and studied 13,608 and 19,950 pages of materials. Equally arduous is the work of the Public Accounts Committee. The latter is helped in its work by the comptroller and auditor general of India and his sizable professional organization.

The reports of these committees are regularly "laid on the Table" and are published widely in the press. They supply the most effective ammunition for public and parliamentary criticism of the government. Although most standing committees lack expertise, continuity of membership, and numerically adequate and professionally specialized secretariats, and although the committee system in general requires radical improvements and reorganization, the aforementioned three committees are effective instruments. They represent the high watermark of Parliament's investigatory and "supervisory" functions in operation.

There are twelve other standing committees of the Lok Sabha that perform special functions: (1) Committee on Petitions; (2) Committee on Privileges; (3) Committee on Government Assurances; (4) Committee on Subordinate Legislation; (5) Committee on Absence of Members from the Sittings of the House; (6) Business Advisory Committee; (7) Committee on Private Members' Bills and Resolutions; (8) Rules Committee; (9) Committee on Offices of Profit; (10) House Committee; (11) Library Committee; and (12) the Joint Committee on Salaries and Allowances of Members of Parliament.

Among these standing committees, the roles of the Committee on Government Assurances and the Committee on Subordinate Legislation are particularly noteworthy in the matter of overseeing the administrative leviathan. The Committee on Government Assurances, patient and plodding, is a unique institutional device for securing the implementation of the assurances given by the government. The Committee on Subordinate Legislation, dealing as it does with a highly specialized field, has of late not been able to function as effectively as one would desire, and means should be devised to make it a more effective instrument of parliamentary control. The Committee on Petitions has been passive to a disappointing degree and does little more than process, forward, and circulate petitions received by it instead of being able to provide adequate parliamentary machinery for investigation of complaints and redress of grievances. This committee can conceivably grow into a robust parliamentary arm for the all-important task of dealing with the difficulties and the grievances of the citizen, a task which is at the very root of democratic government. As one who initiated the proposal for the establishment of the ombudsman institution in the Indian Parliament and who has waged a public campaign for it, this writer is of the view that a reorganized Joint Committee on Petitions and Public Complaint aided by the ombudsman institution is likely to prove as valuable (if not more so) as the Public Accounts Committee aided by the comptroller and auditor-general. The bill for the establishment of an ombudsman-type institutional framework (Lokpal-Lokayukta) is already before a Joint Select Committee of the two Houses of Parliament.

Finally, an interesting innovation has been made in India in the form of informal consultative committees attached to the ministries. The innovation has been an unmitigated failure because (1) the informal committees are devoid of specific forms and functions; (2) they have not been properly organized and have not been given a fair trial; (3) they meet fitfully and without inculcating specialized interest; and (4) members as well as ministers are indifferent to these committees. A careful and constructive effort is required to rehabilitate the committees and build them into the scheme of working parliamentary institutions.

Parliament and the Bureaucracy

It has been said often, and with increasing clamor, that close parliamentary surveillance either on the floor of the House or in the committees undermines the initiative and the morale of the civil service. It is also claimed that it slackens the pace of development, which a country like India can ill afford. The underlying contention is that parliamentary supervision is time-consuming, that it interferes in an inordinate measure with the essentially administrative responsibilities of the state, and that such interference strikes terror in the heart of the civil service and in turn leads to a clogging of the decision-making process.

There is no doubt that the exigencies of developing administration require it to be effective, strong, and enterprising, and that legislative oversight should not paralyze the administration or make it weak or indolent. On the other hand, the elected representatives of the people cannot abdicate their responsibility in the discharge of their correctional (cathartic) function. The need for controlling the bureaucracy and preventing abuse of authority is all the greater in a developing country. What is more, a traditional bureaucracy has to be adapted to the needs of modern technology and development. An optimum reconciliation has to be attempted between these competing objectives, that of effective administration and effective parliamentary surveillance. The two are not incompatible polarities. The point is that at present parliamentary scrutiny of the bureaucracy is a patchwork with sporadic and piecemeal forays into the executive territory; parliamentary jurisdiction is visitatorial in operation and essentially involves spot-checking. What is needed is not a reduction in the role of parliamentary supervision, but a more sustained, studied, and systematic performance of the watch-dog functions by par-

liamentary institutions and procedures, tempered by an insight
into administration.

The Indian parliamentary model does not postulate any direct
relationship between Parliament and the civil service. In practice,
every member of Parliament knows that bureaucracy thrives behind the cloak of cabinet government. Therefore, he often uses
his status as legislator to establish a direct channel of communication with civil servants "to get things done." Members of Parliament meet civil servants socially as well as officially (for example,
in informal consultative committees, standing committees, and
the like). There is reason to believe that the professional ethos of
the Indian Civil Service generally has come to terms with the
indigenous favoritism. Civil servants, like politicians, are known
to display, though behind the scene and in subtler ways, a certain
preference and partiality for their home states. Although a code
of conduct has been proposed to regulate and guide the relations
between legislators and public servants, its basic dictates are
honored more in their breach than in observance. There is a rule
against a legislator sponsoring individual cases, but the rule is not
always adhered to. Moreover, it is in individual cases that injustices are usually perpetrated and unless such cases are taken up
with the administration in some way, their neglect does violence
to a basic premise of democracy.

Although ministers have made their peace with the civil service, antipathy and suspicion between legislators and the bureaucracy remain. This antipathy is probably inherent in the way in
which both legislators and bureaucrats define their respective
roles. It also is a legacy of the struggle for "Swaraj," when the
civil service cooperated with the British. The civil service feels
confident of its superior capacity and training and is sure of its
contribution to stability and order. Shielded by cabinet supremacy in Parliament, it tends to think of Parliament as a necessary
albeit incorrigible nuisance. Parliament and state legislatures in
turn reflect the popular notion that civil service signifies labyrin-
thine procedures and endless red tape. Whatever the reasons,
legislative-bureaucratic interactions are far from smooth.

Parliament and the Executive

The working of cabinet government in the parliamentary system of India and its place in the decision-making process is a relatively uncharted and unexplored field. The cabinet, though a committee of Parliament, has an institutional design and momentum of its own. The Indian cabinet, like its British counterpart, is the board of directors for the national corporation. The Indian cabinet is supposed to function on the principle of collective responsibility, but the principle has been considerably weakened by internal dissensions among the members of the cabinet. For sheer heterogeneity, the Indian cabinet is difficult to match.

An important function of Parliament, of course, is to provide leadership to the nation. In the three prime ministerial successions following Nehru's death, the role of Parliament has not been consistent. In the first election, the president of the ruling party more or less ignored Parliament. At the time of the second election, the state chief ministers played the decisive role. By the time of the third prime ministerial election in 1967, Mrs. Gandhi had improved and consolidated her position. As a result of her experience, political bargaining, mediation, negotiation, compromise, and conciliation were used more candidly and with greater deliberation than was previously the case. These actions indicate not only the beginning of institutionalized leadership selection procedures, but also the enhanced political maturity of parliamentary party leaders. If the future of Indian politics is bound up with the restoration and re-establishment of national consensus, and with the emergence and acceptance of coalitions within the party or between parties, then this enhanced maturity and capacity for constructive compromise will undoubtedly help preserve and fortify the processes of self-government.

In the field of legislation proper, the role of Parliament is limited and marginal. Nevertheless, the decennial average of the legislative output of the Lok Sabha for the years 1957–1966 (both years inclusive) was sixty-one bills per annum. The quality of legislation passed has been reasonably good, although from the point of view of preparation, precision, clarity, and elegance, there is considerable scope for improvement. Although the author succeeded in gaining general acceptance of the Select Committee Procedure in principle for the consideration of all legislation (exceptions to be made by the Speaker on stated grounds) in the Third Lok Sabha, the government usually has been in a rush to pass legislation. It has, therefore, resorted increasingly to the houses of Parliament directly for the passage of legislation. This is a distressing tendency, one that is not likely to be curbed except under severe and sustained pressure.

Until now, Parliament has been described largely in institutional terms. It seems appropriate to end this paper with a few words about the individual members. It should be noted that although the position of M.P. or member of a state legislature is both a highly visible and prestigious one, the compensation for members is quite small. Even with subsidized housing and a non-taxable daily allowance, the average member has great difficulty making financial ends meet. Thus, in terms of material compensation, there is little if any incentive for professionals to become legislators. Many of those that do, of necessity, cannot regard the position as a full-time one. The necessity for supplementing one's income frequently leads to large-scale absenteeism; the Lok Sabha at times has had to adjourn for lack of a quorum. Those who do attend cannot always give their complete attention and interest to parliamentary work. Consequently, there is a certain lack of professionalism of outlook and of interest in parliamentary procedures among Indian legislators.

Nor is the level of professionalism enhanced by the supporting services available to Parliament. Research, reference, and secretarial services available to individual legislators at present are entirely insufficient. The holdings of the library of the Indian Parliament amount to approximately 20,000 books. These, however, include gazettes, government and United Nations reports, acts, bills, debates of the legislatures, and are woefully inadequate. The information and reference wings of the Parliamentary

Library are small. For the years 1962–1967, an average of about 382 references were received per annum by the reference wing, in addition to which, approximately 330 spot references were orally answered every year. This indicates the extremely low utilization of an already limited service. Most of the time, members have to search for their own materials. As was indicated above, no research and no secretarial assistance is provided to members. In the state legislatures, these facilities are slender to the point of being non-existent.

The Institute of Constitutional and Parliamentary Studies founded in 1965 in New Delhi is trying to ameliorate these conditions by establishing Orientation Programs for Legislators, by providing legislative reference, research, and information services on a nationwide scale, and also by training personnel to serve as legislative staff members. Its limited resources and restricted training facilities, together with a certain apathy among Indian legislators, make this a difficult task. Although the process may be a long one, it is felt that the provision of adequate supporting services to members of Parliament ultimately will significantly enhance their performance as legislators. A better legislative game is well worth the candle of such sustained effort.

Chapter 6

The Senate in the Chilean Political System*

Weston H. Agor

Introduction

Chile is a highly centralized, unitary, quasi-presidential politi-cal system.[1] The president has a fixed term (six years), and members of the cabinet are chosen by and responsible to him, although Congress has the constitutional right to impeach minis-ters.[2] If the president taps a congressman for a cabinet post

* The author would like to thank the senators and staff members (particularly Pedro Correa Opaso, Jorge Tapia Valdés, Iván Auger Labarca, Rodemil Torres Vásquez, Rafael Eyzaguirre Echeverría, Luis Valencia Avaria, Raúl Charlín Vicuña, members of the Office of Information of the Senate) who gave so freely of their time. I am also grateful to members of the statistics and archives departments of the Superintendencia de Compañías de Seguros, Sociedades Anónimas y Bolsas de Comercio and Bancos for their aid, and to Allan Kornberg, Lloyd Musolf, John Manley, and John Strasma for comments on an earlier draft of this paper. Fellowship support is also acknowledged from the Midwest Universities Consor-tium and the Land Tenure Center of the University of Wisconsin. The responsibil-ity for errors of fact or interpretation are mine alone. In the interest of responsible scholarship, the author actively solicits correction of any errors which may exist.

1. In view of the objective of this study and the limited space available, the introductory background to Chile must be brief. For more details, see the footnotes that follow.
2. Silvert prefers to describe the Chilean political system as *semi-parliamentary* (K. H. Silvert, *Chile: Yesterday and Today*, New York, 1965, p. 93) or *neo-parlia-mentary* (K. H. Silvert, *The Conflict Society: Reaction and Revolution in Latin America*, rev. ed., New York, 1966, p. 27). Federico G. Gil uses the term *restricted parliamentary* in his *Political System of Chile* (Boston, 1966), p. 89. Their contention is that in a fully presidential system, cabinet ministers are the servants *only* of the president. In Chile, Congress may impeach ministers, who are "answerable" for their actions before Congress. It seems more accurate to describe the system as "quasi-presidential" in view of the way the system actually works. First, the president has a fixed six-year term, which can not be cut short by a vote of confidence. Congress has the constitutional prerogative to impeach the president under certain limited circumstances, but it has not been exercised in modern times. Second, although Congress also has the constitutional right to impeach ministers, the Chilean scholar, Carlos Andrade Gewitz, notes that such proceedings have seldom passed both houses. Finally, it is customary for ministers to explain their

(usually a deputy and rarely a senator), he must give up his congressional seat. The Congress is bicameral—the Senate currently numbers 45 members and the Chamber of Deputies, 147.[3] The military has traditionally abstained from active participation in politics, "acting as a veto group only in so far as their own interests are concerned."[4] A proportional representation system is used for congressional elections in an effort to assure faithful representation of all shades of political opinion.

Although it is debatable how "faithful" representation is,[5] the electoral process has enabled Congress (especially the Senate) to serve as an effective opposition site. Robert Dix has characterized Chile (as well as Costa Rica and Uruguay) in this regard as follows, "The opposition role is substantially (though not definitively) legitimized. The presidency has been won two or more times by the opposition during the 25-year period; the opposition wins over a third of the votes of the legislative seats in most elections; there have been no or only very brief (e.g., Costa Rica, 1948–49) periods of non-constitutional rule."[6]

"The result has been one of the most stable multi-party systems in Latin America,"[7] one that "has successfully evolved from an aristocratic oligarchic democracy into one in which the masses

---

actions to Congress, and even participate in debates on key legislation. But, this is not unlike the American system, where cabinet members appear before hearings of well-publicized congressional standing committees.

3. The respective membership will increase from 45 to 50 and 147 to 150 with the 1969 congressional elections.

4. Silvert, *The Conflict Society*, p. 23. Witness the recent comment by General Sergio Castillo Aránguiz, Chief of Staff, at the Conference of American Armed Forces in Rio, "The function of the armed forces should not be political, but rather to take advantage of modern technology to bring the country along the road of development, as occurs in Chile, where the armed forces enjoy much prestige." *El Mercurio*, September 29, 1968, p. 33.

5. The degree to which the system "faithfully" represents all shades of opinion is examined in a now somewhat outdated work, Ricardo Cruz Coke, *Geografía electoral de Chile* (Santiago, 1952). The most recent account which touches on this and other subjects is German Urzua Valenzuela, *Los partidos políticos chilenos: las fuerzas políticas* (Santiago, 1968), pp. 128–129, 148, 165, 175. See also Carlos Andrade Geywitz, *Elementos de derecho constitucional chileno* (Santiago, 1963), pp. 313–324.

6. Robert H. Dix, "Oppositions and Development in Latin America," Paper delivered at the 1967 Annual Meeting of the American Political Science Association, Pick-Congress Hotel, Chicago, September 5–9, 1967 (Copyright, 1967, APSA), p. 24. Note his other comments on Chile, pp. 6–9, 11 (n. 11), 17, 26.

7. Silvert, *The Conflict Society*, p. 27.

play the leading role."[8] Indeed, Flanigan and Fogelman's index of democratization for the period 1900–1950 places Chile fifth behind Canada, England, the United States, and Switzerland. Chile is not only placed ahead of the important European nations of France, Italy, and Germany, but also ahead of the Philippines and Brazil, states with Latin cultural origins whose legislatures are discussed in this volume.[9]

"Chile is the only Latin American country where political forces are clearly and distinctly aligned, as in many European countries, into three great blocs: the Right, the Center, and the Left."[10] In a period of approximately one hundred years during which the multi-party system has functioned in Chile, the number of parties in existence has varied widely, reaching a maximum of thirty-six in 1953. Recently, five major parties have dominated the political field, ranging from Right to Left as follows: National, Radical, Christian-Democrat, Socialist, and Communist. Ideologically, the Chilean political scale leans to the Left, with important factions in the two largest parties (Christian-Democrat and Radical) tending toward detentes with the Socialist and Communist parties.

Chile also appears to be characterized by a Congress whose predominant function is decisional (influence), thus deviating from the mode of world legislatures surveyed to date.[11] For exam-

8. Charles O. Porter and Robert J. Alexander, *The Struggle for Democracy in Latin America* (New York, 1961), p. 6. For a Chilean interpretation of this evolution, see Julio Heise González, *150 Años de evolución institucional* (Santiago, 1960).

9. William Flanigan and Edwin Fogelman, "Patterns of Political Development and Democratization: A Quantitative Analysis," Paper delivered at the 1967 Annual Meeting of the American Political Science Association, Pick-Congress Hotel, Chicago, September 5–9, 1967 (Copyright, 1967, APSA). The index updated to 1968 would not alter this placement. An index of democratization is, of course, normative. The author *does not* wish to imply in its use that political democracy, especially that modeled after the United States, necessarily is equated with political development (i.e., "will and capacity to cope with and to generate continuing transformation toward whichever values seem appropriate in the particular context"). However, it is one means (among others) by which valued goals may be achieved, and it *is* the system that has been adopted with appropriate Chileanization in this country. Therefore, when speaking of Chile, it is correct to make this equation.

10. Gil, *op. cit.*, p. 244.

11. For comparative purposes, the author has adopted Packenham's decisional function outline as discussed in Robert A. Packenham, "Legislatures and Political Development," in this volume.

ple, Robert Scott notes that although the legislatures in most of the countries of Latin America only go through the formal steps of lawmaking, whereas their acts are frequently dictated by presidents, in Chile, "The center of power has virtually been transferred from the president to legislature. . . ."[12] Robert Packenham, in an excellent survey of world legislatures, concludes, "There is little evidence that more than a mere handful of national legislatures in the world have decision-making as their principal functions." However, when examining the Scott article cited above, he singles Chile out as an exception, "Among the larger countries (above eight million population), only in Chile, and possibly Peru and Venezuela, may it be said of the legislature that decision-making is an important function except on rare occasions."[13] Numerous other American, Chilean, and Cuban scholars have presented specific examples of Congress's decisional voice, and selected statements from President Frei's 1968 Message to Congress provide still further evidence.[14]

12. Robert E. Scott, "Legislatures and Legislation," *Government and Politics in Latin America*, ed. Harold E. Davis (New York, 1958), p. 331. For his other comments on Chile, see pp. 298–299, 303–307, 309–312, 321–322, 324–325, 327, 329, 331.

13. It is not clear why Packenham uses "above eight million people" as a definition of large countries, or more importantly, why a cut-off point is used at all. It is interesting to note, however, that by doing so Costa Rica and Uruguay—normally cited as having legislatures which have important influence in the political system—are eliminated. If they along with the three countries Packenham mentions are considered, we find five (25 per cent) of the Latin American countries may fall outside Scott's mode generalization. This suggests the necessity for further research on these legislatures.

14. For examples, see William S. Stokes, "Parliamentary Government in Latin America," *American Political Science Review*, XXXIX, No. 3 (1945), 527; Silvert, *op. cit.*, pp. 93, 191; Gil, *op. cit.*, pp. 117–118; Federico G. Gil and Charles J. Parrish, *The Chilean Presidential Election of September 4, 1964* (Washington, 1965), pp. 3, 5; Martin C. Needler, *Latin American Politics in Perspective* (New York, 1963), p. 156; Albert O. Hirshman, *Journeys Toward Progress: Studies of Economic Policy-Making in Latin America* (Garden City, N.Y., 1963), pp. 260, 268. Frederick M. Nunn, "Chile's Government in Perspective: Political Change or More of the Same?" *Inter-American Economic Affairs*, XX, No. 4 (Spring, 1967), 83–84, 87–88; Charles J. Parrish, Arpad J. vonLazar, and Jorge Tapia Videla, *The Chilean Congressional Election of March 7, 1965: An Analysis* (Washington, 1967), pp. 27–28; Orville G. Cope, "The 1964 Presidential Election in Chile: The Politics of Change and Access," *Inter-American Economic Affairs* (Spring, 1967), p. 17, n. 25; Constantine C. Menges, "Public Policy and Organized Business in Chile: A Preliminary Analysis," *Journal of International Affairs*, XX, No. 2 (1966), 354; Jorge A. Tapia Valdés, *La técnica legislativa* (Santiago, 1960), pp. 40–41, 43; Ada I. Manriquez G., *El senado en Chile* (Santiago, 1965), p. 164; *Cuatro Mensaje del Presidente de la Republica de Chile don Eduardo Frei Montalva al inaugurar el período de sesiones ordinarias del congreso nacional, 21 de mayo de 1968* (Santiago, 1968), pp. 52, 74, 76–78.

Although they would agree that the primary role of Congress and particularly the Senate is decisional, they probably also would contend that vis-à-vis one another, the executive has a more important role insofar as policy-initiation is concerned, than the Congress. They would base this contention on certain executive prerogatives which, on paper, appear similar to those of the Brazilian executive.[15] First, the president may classify certain legislation urgent, thereby setting a time limit in which Congress "must" pass the bill. He also has "exclusive" areas of initiative, for example, in proposing the annual budget, and Congress is "limited" to reducing the requested expenditures of funds. Congress may also grant extraordinary powers to the executive in emergency situations, and he also has wide veto powers. It should be noted, however, that these assertions have not generally been the subject of systematic empirical analysis to probe the degree to which they are true. The evidence which does exist suggests that the President's considerable formal powers may be subject to, at the very least, considerable slippage.

Thus the purpose of this paper is to demonstrate that the Chilean Senate's most important function, as measured by Packenham's "world scale" of functions, is decisional.[16] Specifically, we will try to show that the Senate exercises considerable initiative with respect to the budget; that despite the president's extraordinary urgency powers, the Senate can delay, alter, and defeat legislation generated by the executive; and that it can help shape, initiate, and evaluate a wide range of public policy proposals. We also will consider the Senate's role in overseeing the bureaucracy and in representing the several interests (what Packenham terms the patronage function). Further, we will try to explain the bases of the Senate's rather extraordinary powers. Finally, whenever it is appropriate, we will compare the functions of the Chilean Senate with those of other legislatures treated in this volume. The Chamber and Congress as a whole will also be discussed when the author feels qualified to do so.

The principal data sources on which this paper is based are:

15. For Brazil, see Packenham in this volume.
16. See footnote 13 above.

in-the-field interviews (forty-three [96 per cent] of the forty-five Senate universe, one ex-senator [who was also a former minister of finance], twenty Senate staff members, one Chamber candidate for 1969, four Chamber staff members, and officials in the executive and the political parties); a detailed analysis of documents, committee reports, floor debates, and the work of other scholars; and extensive empirical observation of the operation of the Chilean Congress. In this essay, political parties will be abbreviated in the following manner: National (PN), Radical (PR), Christian-Democrat (PDC), Vanguard of the People (VNP), National Democrat (PADENA), Socialist (PS), Communist (PC), and Independents (I).

Historical Context

The decisional function of the Senate can best be understood by examining the historical development of this institution. Unlike the Brazilian Congress which, "has seldom been a strong legislature," the Senate's influence is rooted in "the long struggle carried on by the Liberal-Federalists in the 1820's, and since the 1850's by opponents of the Conservative-centralist regime founded by Diego Portales in the 1830's.[17] At first (1812), the Senate was little more, in functional terms, than a legitimating body, with its members being selected by the executive (see Table 1). But, by 1818, disagreements began to arise between the two powers when President O'Higgins violated the formal Constitution; in 1822, he decided to dissolve the body. Williamson says of the period, "The body didn't merit such a sad end. . . . It guarded with tenacity the integrity of the institutions and the interests of the nation, reviewing the acts of the Government as far as its powers allowed."[18]

After several subsequent changes, a Senate was set up under the Constitution of 1833 which was to last until 1874. The first

17. Nunn, *op. cit.*, p. 84.
18. Luis E. Williamson Jordan, *La evolución del senado en Chile* (Santiago, 1937), p. 21.

Table 1. *The Evolution of the Chilean Senate, 1812–1969*

Date	Number of members[a]	Term	Age required	How selected
1812	7	3 years	NA	Not elected—named by presidential intervention.
1814	7	2 years	NA	Elect seven from list of twenty-one.
1818	5	4 years	30	
1822–1823[b]	9	6 years	30	Named by president.
1828	16	4 years	30	Two for each of eight existing provinces, provincial assemblies elect.
1834	20	6 years	36	One for every three deputies, provincial assembly election.
1876	37	9 years	36	Direct election by province.
1888[c]				
1892[d]				
1925[e]	45	8 years	35	Direct election by agrupación.
1969[f]	50	8 years	35	Direct election by revised agrupación—five for each of ten.

a. Does not count replacements also elected before 1925.
b. First time bi-cameral system established.
c. Ended system of election replacements to take over if regular senator not in seat (1812 on).
d. Senators could now no longer make contracts with the state.
e. Increased the limitations on personal business activities by senators which might create a conflict of interest. In 1943, however, senators were made advisors (*consejeros*) on key governmental agencies, but this ended in 1961.
f. Constitutional amendment alters districts (*agrupación*) to give greater representation to far southern zone.

Source: Compiled from data in Luis Valencia Avaria, *Anales de la República Tomo II* (Santiago, 1951), and Senate debates establishing the tenth *agrupación*.

seeds of increasing decisional power were planted here, when member selection was "formally" shifted from the president to provincial assemblies, and later, in 1874, to the public. Although the objective of the 1833 Constitution was, "to establish a strong Executive independent of the pressure and tyranny of Parliament,"[19] Manuel Antonio Tocornal returned from European travels in 1848 with a new concept of Congress's role. His ideas

19. "Versión oficial de la conferencia dictada por S. E. el Presidente del la República, Arturo Alessandri Palma, en el Salón de Honor, de la Universidad de Chile, el dia Viernes, 3 de julio, 1925," in *Actas oficiales de las sesiones celebradas por la Comisión y Subcomisiones encargadas del estudio del Proyecto de Nueva Constitución Política de la República* (Santiago, 1925), p. 689.

subsequently led to even greater decisional influence for Congress with a corresponding decrease in the relative importance of its legitimating role. This movement culminated in the "Revolution of 1891" with the establishment of a parliamentary regime which was to last until 1925. "In a word, a strong dictatorial parliamentary regime was established, irresistible and irresponsible. The Executive Power was subordinate to, and submitted to it."[20]

On balance, despite all of the bad effects generally attributed to this period, it should also be recognized that, "It facilitated the development of new social groups: the middle class and the proletariat. Also, it made possible the organization of popular political parties: Workers Socialist and Communist. . . . In this manner, the Parliamentary period was a magnificent civic school for the Chilean people. . . ." Functionally and institutionally, presidential veto power was modified, the need for Senate approval of diplomatic appointments established, and ethical guidelines for member activities outside Congress defined.[21] The evolutionary trend toward greater congressional influence proved difficult to reverse or overcome in 1924, when attempts were made to re-establish presidential pre-eminence. Many of President Alessandri Palma's proposals for stronger executive power (for example, the right to dissolve Congress) were rejected by the Committee (many members of which were congressmen), which helped write the Constitution of 1925.[22] Some congressional members of the Committee (Radical, Conservative, and Communist parties) simultaneously presented to the public an alternative plan, which called for substantially less change than the reform actually adopted.[23] Even after passage of the Constitution, the effective reduction of Congress's decisional role was limited by the number of 1924 congressmen who continued to serve in 1926 and who carried with them parliamentary traditions and habits which reinforced its persistence. As Table 2 indicates,

---

20. *Ibid.*, p. 702.   21. González, *op. cit.*, pp. 81–82.
22. "Sesiones de la subcomisión de reformas constitucionales" *Actas oficiales,* pp. 382–388, and p. 5 for list of members of the first session of La Comisión Consultiva, which also added members later.
23. "Fórmula disidente," *Actas oficiales,* pp. 644–646.

Table 2. *Proportion of 1926 Congressmen Who Also Were Members of 1924 Congress*

Carryover from 1924	Membership of 1926 Congress		
	Chamber	Senate	All Congress
Number of members	37	27ᵃ	64
Percentage	28	60	36
	(N = 132)	(N = 45)	(N = 177)

a. Of the twenty-seven senators, fourteen were deputies in 1924 who moved up to the Senate, and thirteen were senators in 1924 as in 1926.

twenty-seven (60 per cent) of the forty-five senators elected in 1926 were also members of Congress in 1924. This represents a clear linkage to Congress's (particularly the Senate's) influence today,[24] and helps set the stage for a consideration of the Senate's decisional powers.

Decisional Function

Lawmaking—the initiation of policy

Does the Senate initiate legislation? The answer is yes—despite the 1943 constitutional reform of Article 45, Section 3, that supposedly gave the president "exclusive initiative in public expenditures." Congress's ability to legislate in this area is graphically illustrated by President Frei's 1968 message to Congress. According to Frei, it was "absolutely essential to provide for exclusive presidential initiative in projects of law relative to salaries of the public and private sector, and those referring to expenses in and reform of social security. The grave fact is that legislation has been creating irritating discrimination beneficial to the privileged sectors that can apply strong pressure in Congress."[25]

Again, Arnaldo Gorziglia Balbi quotes a Senate standing committee report, "All initiatives that are not determined or specifically referred to in this article [Article 45], such as for example,

24. See José Guillermo Guerra writing in 1929 after the constitutional reform in *La constitución de 1925,* esp. pp. 192–194.
25. *Cuatro mensaje,* p. 77.

public works . . . of progress and local development . . . of incentives and more, continue in the hands of Congress, which conserves the widest liberty and right to pass such laws even when they require expenses of the State."[26] And, Jorge Tapia Valdés points out that 55.2 per cent of the laws passed between 1938 and 1958 were over particular matters such as pensions and retirement benefits (*asuntos de gracia*). "These laws have been converted into a real panacea for the economic problems of those favored by them . . . many times pensions are given to persons . . . that don't need them to escape misery. . . . In fact, many of these laws are justly motivated to correct imperfections of our social security system."[27]

Despite this evidence, scholars frequently argue that Congress's initiative with regard to the national budget is quite restricted.[28] This requires qualification, however, beginning with an examination of the budget itself: what it does and does not include. The annual budget, according to Article 44, Section 4, of the Constitution, may not alter the expenses or resources of general or specific laws (e.g., salary increases).[29] But, one may ask, who is it that initiates or often modifies the general or specific laws that the budget *must* include and not modify? The answer is Congress! For example, in dealing with the Salary Readjustment Bill of 1968, the Senate not only forced the government to considerably modify its original plan, but also introduced several amendments. Simply put, this "restriction" tells Congress that it can not alter by way of the annual budget that which it has already passed.

Congress may also decrease, although it can not increase, variable expenses during the fiscal year. This power, when it chooses to exercise it, permits Congress to bargain with the executive.[30] Similarly, although it is "restricted" from altering the calculation of expenses and source of budget funds, it is able to circumvent

26. Arnaldo Gorziglia Balbi, *Facultades presupuestarias legislativas* (Santiago, 1960), p. 134.
27. Valdés, *op. cit.*, p. 47.
28. For example, see Manuel Matus Benavente, *Desniveles entre presupuestos iniciales y presupuestos realizados* (Santiago, 1957).
29. "Constitución política de la republica de Chile," in *Manual del Senado* (Santiago, 1966), p. 29.
30. *El proceso presupestario fiscal chileno* (Santiago, 1958), p. 40.

this restriction by passing laws during the regular session that entail permanent expenses, and, hence, are necessarily included in either the next annual budget or are provided for in the same budget year through budgetary increases.[31] Finally, Congress is "restricted" from approving any new expenses without, at the same time, indicating the source of financing. It escapes this shackle by indicating that the source of funds is future budgets.[32] It is evident that a more accurate view of Congress's lawmaking initiative as to the annual budget would be gained by examining what is passed during the year which automatically forms a part of the budget, rather than a study of the passage of the budget law itself.

Let us now consider the president's urgency powers. These powers are said to "limit" congressional initiative. "The extreme urgency designation (*extrema urgencia*) obligates the respective chambers to discuss and dispatch the bill in a very brief period of time."[33] In fact, it is not quite that simple. First, Article 138 of the Senate *Reglamento* (internal rules and procedures) prohibits the Senate or a standing committee from considering at the same time two or more urgency bills.[34] This provision obviously enables them to draw out the time period in which they consider executive-inspired urgency legislation. Secondly, the essential significance of the president's prerogative is considerably weakened if he lacks a majority in either chamber, for it then will simply reject the proposed bill in the required time limit. Faced with this alternative, the president will either: (*a*) withdraw and re-submit the bill several times (starting the urgency period over again from the beginning each time); (*b*) attempt to reach a compromise solution with the opposition; or (*c*) simply give Congress more time to consider it. He may even discard the bill altogether.[35]

Two examples of this process are the bill on Public Housing Developments (see Table 3) and the 1968 University Reform Law. The Public Housing Development Bill was sent to the

31. *Ibid.*, p. 41.   32. Balbi, *op. cit.*, p. 124.
33. Gil, *op. cit.*, p. 103.
34. "Reglamento del Senado," in *Manual del senado*, p. 158.
35. Geywitz, *op. cit.*, p. 439.

Senate standing committees of Public Works and Finance on September 7, 1965. After more than three months in committee, the president decided to ask for urgency classification of the bill, thereby requiring passage within thirty days. Two weeks later, it became clear to the president that the committees would report out the Bill within the required time limit, but not in the form he desired. Therefore, on January 12, 1966, the executive retired and immediately presented the same bill again, thereby starting the time limit all over from the beginning. By mid-July, this proce-

Table 3. *Senate Action on Bill on Public Housing Developments*

Date	Session	Senate Action
September 7, 1965	43	Bill sent to Senate Committees of Public Works and Finance.
November 11, 1965	27	Included in list of bills to be considered.
December 22, 1965	46	Presents Executive urgency request. Classified simple urgency.
January 4, 1966	52	Agree to give committees extra week to review bill.
January 12, 1966	57	Executive retires urgency and presents bill again. Classified simple urgency again.
January 25, 1966	67	Executive retires urgency again.
May 31, 1966	1	Executive presents urgency again for third time. Classified simple urgency.
July 7, 1966	3	Time limit of July 15 is given to Committee of Public Works to report out the bill.
July 15, 1966	7	Executive for the fourth time retires urgency.

Source: Senate Office of Information, 1967 File.

dure had been repeated four times, and over ten months had elapsed since original submission to the Senate.

In the case of the University Reform Law, the president arrived at a compromise solution with the Senate opposition which allowed for rapid dispatch of the bill (sixty days), but also provided more time for a committee study than a simple urgency classification would have. Hence, in May, 1968, the representatives of the PC, PDC, PR, and PS (*comités*) issued this public statement:

The representatives declare that the project contains matters of great importance which require study and careful legislation. . . . The periods for a petition of urgency are insufficient to make such a study. . . . In view of this, we have asked the Minister of Education . . . to ask the President to retire the urgency . . . and we indicated that a period of sixty days was a prudent and legitimate period to study the initiative, obtain all of the relevant data, and hear the opinions of the authorities of the universities.[36]

Finally, even if an executive bill clears these hurdles relatively unscathed, Congress has a signficant lever by which it can initiate legislation. Congressmen will simply make numerous amendments which have little relevance to the bill in question (*las leyes misceláneas*), thereby taking advantage of a bill's urgency to initiate numerous bills of their own on its coattails. If the president lacks a sufficient majority in one of the two chambers, which is usually the case, he will be forced to "tolerate" many of them.[37] Two senators and an important staff member observe:

These miscellaneous laws have the advantage of accelerating passage —it is the only way some bills would get passed. There are many bills, perhaps, that shouldn't get passed, but they get tacked on important legislation. The presidents of standing committees have the power to rule unconstitutional or extraneous to the material of the bill such amendments, but they often don't or can't use this power depending on the situation.[38]

The congressman must add on items of importance to him—it is the only way to get them passed, and the executive has to accept some of this. Presidents of standing committees do also—there is a certain amount of tolerance.[39]

This process of amendments is worse than ever before, but it is a way of putting pressure on the president as well as getting your own bills through.[40]

36. *Declaración de los comités comunista, democrata christiano radical y socialista del senado en relacion con el estudio del proyecto que legisla sobre las universidades* (*ND*).
37. Valdés, *op. cit.*, pp. 41, 43–45.
38. Personal interview number 38, June 3, 1968.
39. Personal interview number 44, June 26, 1968.
40. Personal interview number 59, March 4, 1968.

By way of example, there is the 1968 Salary Readjustment Bill which President Frei tagged, "as important as the annual budget."[41] It was retired on January 30, 1968, after the Standing Committee of Interior Government of the Senate reported out in favor of rejection. "Minutes before the Senate began debate on the project . . . the President . . . retired the Bill . . . to avoid a 'sterile clash between the Government and the Senate.' "[42] Four months later, the president was forced to retire the bill again, and accept a Senate proposal for its passage.[43] Before final clearance by the Senate, it was the subject of more than 2,000 attempted amendments (often new bills not related to the law in question), underwent significant modification, and saw two finance ministers come and go.[44]

There is also abundant evidence to indicate that Congress exercises an important influence on the president's legislative program even before it is formally presented to the legislature. This takes two forms. First, there is an anticipated response by the administration of what Congress (especially the Senate opposition) will accept. One means of gauging Congress's expected reaction follows a process similar to that which takes place in Great Britain, Canada, and Australia when cabinet ministers will "try out" their legislative proposals on party congressmen, colleagues in caucus. In Chile, ministers not only try out prospective legislation on party supporters in Congress—to get their reactions to the proposals—but they also solicit their response as to what they sense the opposition will accept. These party and permanent contacts with congressional standing committees help the administration determine how its legislation will fare. One opposition senator states, "If it involves a project of major national impor-

---

41. *Cuatro mensaje*, p. 76.
42. "El ejecutivo retiró proyecto de reajuste de la convocatoria," *El Mercurio*, January 31, 1968, pp. 1, 18.
43. "Retiro de urgencia," *Boletin de información parlamentaria*, No. 389 (Santiago, April 27, 1968), p. 1; "Acuerdos de los comités," *Boletin de información parlamentaria*, No. 392 (Santiago, April 27, 1968).
44. *Indicaciones formuladas al proyecto de ley que reajuste las remuneraciones de los empleados y obreros de los sectores publico y privado, para el año 1968*, *Boletin No. 23.519-Senado* ND; based on standing committee reports, debates, interviews, and observations during this period. For an excellent service, see the photocopies of all newspaper accounts: "Cambios Ministeriales," *Boletin de información general*, No. 37 (OIS), May 9, 1968.

tance, the government knows what they can count on from us without asking beforehand."[45]

The second form is similar to the procedure in the United States, where the president or his cabinet try to generate support from congressional leaders for legislative programs by prior consultation. One government (PDC) senator said of these exchanges, "Sure, a minister may call the presidents of the respective parties (who are often Senators), and have them over for an informal dinner one night. . . ."[46] And, the president himself indicated his frequent communication with Congress when urging constitutional reforms, "I can say that Senators and Deputies of the most distinct political viewpoints, in private conversations, have told me of their conviction that this situation [salary adjustment and unfinanced social security system] can not continue and should be solved soon. . . ."[47]

A tangible example of the interaction between the administration and Congress is provided by the 1968 Salary Readjustment Bill referred to previously. After Sergio Molina, Minister of Finance, resigned over the Senate's opposition to his proposal in January, 1968, Raul Sáez replaced him.[48] Sáez began to explore possible modification with leaders of opposition parties such as Luis Corvalán (PC) and Luis Fernando Luengo (PADENA) who were senators as well as secretary-generals of their respective parties. Victor García, president of the PN, declared after talking with Sáez, "The Minister . . . has pointed out the need to discuss the general aspects of the project before it is sent to Congress. . . . Sáez called us to know our opinion, and not to impose his point of view. . . ."[49] Sáez himself was quoted as saying, "I think that if they have rejected the previous bill, they have proposals to make. I hope to hear them and see what can be done. . . ."[50] Opposition subsequently centered on Article 66 of a

45. Personal interview number 39, July 23, 1968.
46. Personal interview number 37, July 3, 1968.
47. *Cuatro mensaje*, p. 77.
48. "Juro el nuevo gabinete," *El Mercurio*, February 16, 1968, p. 1.
49. "Positivo primer contacto de Sáez con dirigentes políticos," *El Mercurio*, February 23, 1968, p. 1.
50. "Función de la empresa privada destacan dos nuevos ministros," *El Mercurio*, February 24, 1968, p. 1.

new version of the Bill (product of the above discussions) which limited the right to strike. When Sáez refused to modify his proposal, the Senate opposition indicated they would reject the Bill in the Senate.[51] The Government, by-passing its own minister, then withdrew Article 66 in exchange for PC support in the Senate. Sáez subsequently resigned and was replaced by Andres Zaldívar.[52]

Lawmaking—the modification or delay of policy

We have already hinted at Congress's capacity to modify or delay legislation. At first glance, Table 4, which is concerned with

Table 4. Major Bills Considered and Action Taken by Congress, 1961–1968

	1961		1962		1963		1964		1965		1966		1967		1967–1968[a]		1968 Ordinary[a]	
	%	N	%	N	%	N	%	N	%	N	%	N	%	N	%	N	%	N
Approve	81	189	57	219	59	129	94	158	77	100	94	159	61	183	100	23	86	142
Disapprove	1	2	—	—	2	5	1	2	5	7	3	5	6	18	—	—	1	2
Filed	18	44	43	166	39	84	5	8	18	23	3	6	33	101	—	—	13	22
Total	100	235	100	385	100	218	100	168	100	130	100	170	100	302	100	23	100	166

a. 1967–1968 was an extraordinary session, and 1968 was an ordinary session of the total calender year. Note that in addition to modification of bills passed, many are filed; that is, they never leave committee but become dead bills.

Source: Senate Office of Information, 1967 File and 1968 File.

congressional action on legislation, suggests that Congress functions as a kind of rubber stamp which routinely ratifies legislative proposals coming before it. However, the remarks of Senators Palma (PDC) and Aylwin (PDC) suggest that this hardly is the case:

It is affirmed that the Senate has not refused to collaborate . . . this is inevitable, because no one can detain the life of the nation . . . But

51. "Directivas de partidos de oposición rechazan el Proyecto de reajuste," *El Mercurio*, March 13, 1968, p. 1.
52. "Consecuencias políticas ante apoyo comunista al reajuste," *El Mercurio*, March 15, 1968, p. 1; "Andrés Zaldívar juró como ministro interino de hacienda," *El Mercurio*, March 16, 1968, p. 1.

the creations, the transformations, the fundamental things. How much it has cost us to obtain passage![53]

Despite the contradictions between the three parties, they have joined to resist the completion of our program. . . . As to the constitutional reform project, after eighteen months, the Senate has passed only one article—that relating to the right of property. . . . I recall . . . in the last thirty years there have been many constitutional reform projects . . . there are no less than 20 that sleep here . . . that have been approved in one committee, and in one chamber at times, but are detained in the other.[54]

Except by special Senate agreement or executive urgency (and we have seen that the latter is not a particularly effective action), a standing committee does not have a fixed period in which it must report out a bill.[55] Matters pending in Senate standing committees as of May, 1968, filled a sixty-page booklet.[56] Should the originating chamber reject a law, it may not be introduced again for another year.[57] The president's substantial veto powers —item and additive—can be overruled by two-thirds of both Houses. Granted, this is as difficult to achieve for Congress as it is for the president to obtain a majority in both Houses. But, Congress seldom is required to perform this trick. Frequently, a bill can be delayed long enough to force the president to act—either to modify the law itself to obtain passage, or to make informal bargains on how he will exercise his veto power once the bill is passed. Furthermore, on matters of constitutional reform, the president may not additive veto (add totally new pieces of legislation) as he can with an ordinary bill.[58]

An examination of some recent legislative action illustrates this ability to delay and block executive action. Parrish, von Lazar, and Tapia summarize the fate of two of President Frei's most

53. *Diario de sesiones del senado, legislatura extraordinaria*, Sesión 87a, February 23, 1967, p. 4331.
54. *Ibid.*, p. 4263.
55. Valdés, *op. cit.*, p. 28.
56. *Senado-asuntos pendientes en comisiones al 21 de Mayo de 1968* (Santiago, 1968).
57. Adela Ramos Pazos, *La función legislativa* (Concepción, 1965), p. 32.
58. Geywitz, *op. cit.*, p. 650. See also Alejandro Silva Bascuñán, *Tratado de derecho constitutional*, Tomo III (Santiago, 1963), p. 493.

important bills, "The PDC was unable to get the [Chileanization Copper Bill] signed until late 1966. . . . Similarly the Agrarian Reform Bill was not signed until July 1967 after incredible hassles and repeated delays."[59] The "incredible hassles" alluded to involved a reform of Article 10, Section 10, of the Constitution providing deferred payment for non-rural expropriated properties. A conference version of the Bill, which favored a Senate interpretation, was vetoed by the president. The Senate refused to consider the veto, arguing that it was "additive," and, therefore, unconstitutional according to Article 109 of the Constitution. By refusing to consider the veto, the Senate did not reject it, thereby preventing Frei from exercising his prerogative to call a plebiscite.[60]

The president, having consulted the controller general respecting the treatment of the controversial item, finally promulgated the constitutional reform on January 18, 1967, eliminating both the original phrase and the proposed modification, thus making no provision for long-term payment for expropriation of non-rural properties. In the process, PDC President of the Senate, Tomás Reyes, resigned, and was replaced by Frei's 1964 campaign opponent, Salvador Allende. The opposition-chaired Senate proceeded to exercise Article 43, Section 2, of the Constitution, and refused Frei permission to complete a scheduled visit to the United States with President Johnson.[61]

Frei promptly responded, sending still another constitutional reform bill to Congress. This bill would allow the president to dissolve Congress once in his term.[62] After rapid passage in the PDC-dominated Chamber, the bill died on February 23, 1967, in the Senate.[63] The president then attempted to stamp the April, 1967, municipal elections as a "plebiscite" in support of his program, and confidently predicted a plurality of 40 per cent. "A

59. Parrish *et al.*, *op. cit.*, pp. 27–28.
60. "Senado versus Frei: Constitución puesta a prueba," *Ercilla*, December 14, 1966, pp. 4–5.
61. "Un hecho insolito y mesquino," *Ercilla*, January 18, 1967.
62. "Reforma para disolver el congreso," *El Mercurio*, January 29, 1967, p. 31.
63. "Rechazo de reforma," *El Mercurio*, February 26, 1967, p. 17. Also for very useful debates, see *Diario de sesiones del senado, legislatura extraordinaria*, sesión 87a, which is, in effect, a book on Chile.

vote against the party is a vote against the Government" was the slogan.[64]

This proved to be a grave miscalculation. Although the PDC percentage (36.5 per cent) rose from the 1963 municipal election total of 22.8 per cent, it still fell considerably short of the expected 40 per cent. Senator Renán Fuentealba, frequent president of the PDC, began to hedge, "It is evident that the popularity of the President is greater than that of the party."[65] Perhaps a more objective interpretation of the outcome of this total process is that the Chileans desire to change things, but not much.

Table 5. *Time Taken by Senate to Pass Eight Key Administration Bills*

| | Time in Senate | | | | | |
| | In committee | | On floor | | Total | |
Title of bill	%	Days	%	Days	%	Days
Creation of a Committee to Adjust National Defense Pensions	98	85	2	2	100	87
Creation of New Ministry of Housing and Urbanization	97	131	3	4	100	135
1965 Salary Readjustment	84	21	16	4	100	25
Rules to Place Stock on Sale	84	31	16	6	100	37
1966 Salary Readjustment	85	33	15	6	100	39
Exemption of Property from Tax if Valued Less Than E 5,000	86	101	4	17	100	118
Rules to Stimulate Exports	84	84	16	16	100	100
Creation of a Director of National Boundaries & Frontiers	49	97	51	98	100	195

Source: Senate Office of Information, 1967 File.

One PDC senator was quoted as saying, "It seems that in Chile the majority is . . . progressive conservative. And in this strange climate, the steps that are possible should be short, slow, and careful."[66]

Table 5 summarizes the period of time to dispatch eight additional key pieces of legislation during this administration. Note that, unlike the Canadian or Indian parliamentary systems where

64. Alejandro Cabrera Ferrada, "Voz y silencio de las cifras," *Ercilla*, April 5, 1967.
65. "Escuchar la palabra del FRAP," *Ercilla*, April 5, 1967.
66. Cabrera, *op. cit.*

standing committees play a minor role, the standing committees of the Chilean Senate virtually dominate the legislative process. It is in committee and not on the floor that bills are carefully studied and most compromises are made. "Without public tribunes, official versions, and so on, there is more calm; it is much easier to produce a climate which leads to agreement on different points of view. There is less passion, and more give and take when an idea has merit."[67]

Delay should not be considered as necessarily negative or conservative (to the Right) in effect. There is considerable evidence that the Senate improves the laws it modifies or delays, which in turn reflects a serious and professional standing committee analysis comparable to the United States Senate.[68] Those who regard Senate delays or modifications as undue harassment of a government which currently leans to the Left should not forget that the Senate has acted no differently when the president represented the Right. The excerpts from Senate debates make this clear:

[*Altamirano (PS)*] No other President had his initiatives approved in block. . . . The Government says that all of its predecessors were given extraordinary faculties. This is a half truth. . . . During the last administration of Mr. Ibáñez, he was not given faculties to restructure either the Central Bank or the Controller General's Office. And, if I remember correctly, Senator Enríquez, who is also President of the PR, demanded substantial modifications of the faculties asked by former President, Jorge Alessandri. . . .

[*Aguirre Doolan (PR)*] For example, faculties to legislate over social security and the petroleum industry were not given.[69]

Basis of Congressional Influence on Lawmaking

We have already touched on one important variable which gives Congress such a strong voice in lawmaking—the presence of an opposition majority in one of the two chambers. The existence, traditionally, of such a majority is in turn a product of several factors: (1) Congress is elected in a different year than

67. Geywitz, op. cit., p. 446.
68. Valdés, op. cit., p. 31; Guillermo Bruna Contreras, Estatuto de la profesión parlamentaria (Santiago, 1963), p. 8.
69. Diario de sesiones del senado, legislatura extraordinaria, Sesión 87a, p. 4306.

the president; (2) the Senate is only partially renovated, and, in such a way, that it is difficult to win a majority; (3) the president himself rarely wins more than a plurality (Frei is an exception); and (4) even when a president obtains a majority, his "legitimacy" is questioned and tested in the next congressional election.

Public opinion also appears to support Congress's demands for a powerful voice in the policy process. Thus, Eduardo Hamuy conducted a Santiago (capital city) random sample in January, 1965, which was just after Frei's presidential election and before the congressional election in March, 1965, a time when the President's support was probably at its apex. It stated, "Returning to

---

Table 6. *Santiago Survey, January, 1965: A Hypothetical Conflict between President Frei and Congress*

	N	%
Dissolve Congress	205	36.8
Wait until 1969 elections	250	44.9
President renounce	18	3.2
Plebiscite	7	1.3
Unite, combine with other parties	4	0.7
Pressure Congress	—	—
Other, or in error	16	2.9
Do not know, no answer	57	10.2
Total	557	100.0

Source: See footnote 13.

---

the subject of the actual Government, let us suppose that Frei can not govern because Congress obstructs his work. Would you be in favor of dissolving Congress so that the Government could complete its program, or would you be in favor of waiting until the parliamentary elections of 1969 in order to obtain a favorable Congress?" Although 67.1 per cent of the sample recognized that a conflict existed between the president and Congress, and 73 per cent felt the president was correct, Table 6 indicates that only 36.8 per cent favored dissolving Congress, 44.9 per cent preferred to wait until the 1969 congressional elections, and only 1.3 per cent favored a plebiscite. Even when social class is controlled, the variation in attitudes are relatively similar.[70] One may conclude that although the vast majority in the sample supported the president on this hypothetical conflict, at this point in time, the majority were not prepared to undercut Congress's constitutionally guaranteed decision-making role by opting for dissolution or a plebiscite.

The public's reluctance to support dissolution may be due, in

Table 7. *The Occupational Backgrounds of Senators, 1933–1937 and 1965–1969*

Profession/activity	1933–1937 Senate		1965–1969 Senate	
	N	%	N	%
Lawyer	21	46.8	21	46.3
Doctor	2	4.6	2	4.4
Businessman	4	9.0	3	6.8
Civil engineer	—	—	2	4.5
Newspaperman	—	—	1	2.2
Worker	3	6.6	2	4.5
Chemical engineer	—	—	1	2.2
Accountant	—	—	2	4.5
Engineer	2	4.4	—	—
Agronomy engineer	—	—	1	2.2
Professor	—	—	2	4.5
Agriculturalist	6	13.2	2	4.5
Ex-military	2	4.4	—	—
Writer	—	—	1	2.2
Industrialist	1	2.2	3	6.8
Winemaker	2	4.4	—	—
Architect	—	—	1	2.2
Ex-policeman	1	2.2	—	—
No data	1	2.2	1	2.2
Total	45	100.0	45	100.0

Source: Senate Office of Information, 1966 File.

part, to Congress's demonstrated capacity for change. One measure of change is seen in the different career backgrounds of the Senate membership of 1933 and 1965 (see Table 7). In 1933, ten (22 per cent) of the senators were ex-military men or rural representatives. But in 1965, there were only two (4.5 per cent)

70. These data were generously provided by Eduardo Hamuy from his January, 1965, IBM printout sheets, question 6Y, Universidad de Chile, Facultad de Ciencias Económicas—Centro de Estudias Socio-Económicos's study. The author thanks Mr. Hamuy also for his time in reviewing the results of these data.

such individuals. The author interprets the difference as a response to greater urbanization, reduction of corrupt electoral practices, and civilian predominance in political life. Correspondingly, careers other than in law totaled fifteen in 1965 as opposed to eleven in 1933 and represent a wider spectrum, which reflects Chile's economic and political development during the period.

An organizational package of member stability and informal norms that emphasizes Chamber-Senate "apprenticeship" and "hard-work" (comparable to the United States Senate) also contributes to the influence of the Chilean Senate. Table 8 shows that of forty-five present members, thirty-one previously have served in the Chamber (eighteen of twenty-five in 1961, thirteen of

Table 8. *Present Senators Who Were Previously Deputies*

Term	PC	PS	PADENA	PDC	VNP	I	PR	PN	TOT
1961–1969	3	2	—	1	1	1	6	4	18
1965–1973	2	1	—	7	—	—	3	—	13
Total	5	3	—	8	1	1	9	4	31

Source: Compiled from Library of Congress Biographical Data Project Files.

twenty in 1965 or after). Of those originally elected in 1961 and 1965, thirty-five (78 per cent) were previously deputies. Further, in the last thirty-five years only three senators have given up their positions to accept others—specifically, the presidency, the ambassadorships to the United States and Argentina (see Table 9).

Not only do a high percentage of the 1968 senators have previous Chamber experience (see Table 10), but they also frequently represent the same district repeatedly while in the Chamber. Once in the Senate, their Chamber district often forms a part of their *agrupación* (group of provinces), and they generally continue to represent it there. Thus, we again find a pattern similar to that in the United States. Thirty-four of the thirty-five senators who previously served in the Chamber represented the same district throughout their entire tenure. For twenty-six (74 per cent), their Chamber district formed a part of the same *agrupación* they represented once they were in the Senate. The

Table 9. *The Institutionalization of Congress*

Year	Chamber Total %	N	Number of Former Congressmen %	N	Number who Accepted other post %	N	Year	Senate Total %	N	Number of Former Congressmen %	N	Number who Accepted other post %	N
1930–32	100	141	33	47	4	5	1933–37	100	27	41	11	4	1
1933–37	100	145	25	36	3	4a	1933–41	100	27	71	19	7	2
1937–41	100	156	46	71	5	8	1937–45	100	28	71	20	7	2
1941–45	100	150	46	69	2	3	1941–49	100	22	68	15	—	—
1945–49	100	150	60	90	1	1	1945–53	100	29	83	24	3	1b
1949–53	100	152	51	77	1	1a	1949–57	100	23	74	17	4	1b
1953–57	100	147	39	58	1	1	1953–61	100	25	60	15	—	—
1957–61	100	147	54	79	—	—	1957–65	100	21	72	15	5	1b
1961–65	100	148	59	88	—	—	1961–69	100	25	84	21	—	—

a. Become senator in mid-term.
b. Become president of Chile.
Note: Different numbers correspond to change in number of members over time, and to deaths, which cause other y-elections.
Source: Compiled from data in Guillermo Bruna Contreras, *Estatuto de la profesion parlamentaria* (Santiago, 1963, memoria de prueba), pp. 19–25.

most typical Chamber-Senate career (see Table 11) covers a period of nineteen years (nine in the Chamber and ten in the Senate) as compared with an average of seventeen for all of the forty-five senators elected in 1961 and 1965 (see Table 12).

This Chamber apprenticeship and district stability enable the senator to acquire the knowledge, skills, and local contacts necessary for an influential legislative career. But this process goes further. Frequently, a senator will have served on the same standing committee in both the Chamber and the Senate. For example, Senator Bulnes served from 1945 to 1953 on the Committee on Constitution, Legislation, and Justice (one of the three most important committees) while in the Chamber. Elected to the Senate, he served on the same committee from 1953 to 1965. Senator Bossay served on the Finance Committee in the Chamber from 1949 to 1953, and in the Senate from 1965 to 1969. Fernando Alessandri, whose total career has been in the Senate, has worked on Constitution, Legislation, and Justice Committee continuously since 1937. This is one key link to the Senate's lawmaking role in the political system.

In Chile, as in the United States and the Philippines, most real study, work, and modifications are made in the standing committees.[71] Method of selection, stability, and staff support thus become important. There are fourteen standing committees in the Senate, each with five members. Interviews indicate the two most important committees are Finance and Constitution, Legislation, and Justice. An analysis of the membership of these two committees from 1894 to 1965 shows a high level of continuity and stability over time. Table 13 points out that at least two or three of the total membership continue from one congressional period to the next, and at times, four (80 per cent) or the total commit-

Table 10. *Congressional Experience of Members of the Senate, 1968*

Name	Chamber career	Senate career
Aguirre (PR)	1949–53	1953–69
Ahumada (PR)	1945–61	1961–69
Alessandri (PN)	—	1934–69[a]
Allende (PS)	1937–41[b]	1945–69
Altamirano (PS)	1961–65	1965–73
Ampuero (PS)	—	1953–69
Aylwin (PDC)	—	1965–73
Baltra (PR)	—	1967–73[c]
Barros (I)	1956[d]	1961–69
Bossay (PR)	1941–53	1953–69
Bulnes (PN)	1945–53	1953–69
Campusano (PC)	1961–65	1965–73
Carrera (PS)	—	1967–69[e]
Castro (VNP)	1949–57	1961–69
Contreras C. (PC)	1926–41	1941–49
		1961–69
Contreras V. (PC)	1945[f]	1961–69
Corvalán (PC)	—	1961–69
Curti (PN)	1945–53	1953–69
Chadwick (PS)	—	1965–73
Durán (PR)	1945–57	1957–73
Enríquez (PR)	1949–61	1961–69
Ferrando (PDC)	—	1965–73
Foncea (PDC)	1953–65	1965–73
Fuantealba (PDC)	1957–65	1965–73

71. For Chile, see Valdés, *op. cit.*, p. 32; for United States, see Richard F. Fenno, Jr., *The Power of the Purse: Appropriations Politics in Congress* (Boston and Toronto, 1966); for the Philippines, see Robert B. Stauffer's essay in this volume.

tee do so. Also, many senators have served several periods together on the same committee. For example, from 1953 to 1965, Senators F. Alessandri, H. Alvarez, and F. Bulnes served together on the Constitution, Legislation, and Justice Committee. On Finance, Senators E. Frei, Faivovich, and Amunátegui worked together from 1953 to 1961.

More important than the stability is the quality of membership. Interviews indicate that all political parties are guided by norms of expertise and specialization similar to the United States Senate when selecting members for standing committees:

Generally members are selected who have the greatest competence in the material. (PN)[72] I was selected for the Committee on Agriculture

Gomez (PR)	1957–61	1961–69
González (PR)	1941–53	1953–69
Gormaz (PDC)	1957–65	1965–73
Gumucio (PDC)	1957–65	1965–73
Ibáñez (PN)	—	1961–69
Jaramillo (PN)	1953–61	1961–69
Juliet (PR)	1945–65	1965–73
Luengo (DN)	—	1965–73
Mauras (PN)	1949–61	1961–69
Miranda (PR)	1949–65	1965–73
Musalem (PDC)	1953–65	1965–73
Noemi (PDC)	—	1965–73
Pablo (PDC)	1957–61	1961–69
Palma (PDC)	1953–61	1965–73
Prado (PDC)	—	1965–69g
Reyes (PDC)	1949–65	1965–73
Rodríguez (PS)	1949–53	1953–69
Sepúlveda (I)	1949–61	1961–69
Tarud (I)	—	1957–73
Teitelboim (PC)	1961–65	1965–73
Von Mühlenbrock (PN)	1953–61	1961–69

a. Replaced A. Nunez in 1934. b. Accepted ministry in 1939.
c. Won by-election. d. Removed under Law of Defense of Democracy.
e. Won in by-election to replace her husband who died.
f. Accepted a ministry. g. Won election to replace Senator Tomic who became ambassador to the United States.
Source: Compiled from Library of Congress Biographical Data Project File.

72. Personal interview number 4, July 3, 1968.

Table 11. *Most Typical Congressional Career in 1968 Senate, by Party*

Name	Chamber Province	Years	Senate Agrupación	Years	Total years
National party					
Bulnes	10	8	5	16	24
Curti	17	8	7	16	24
Radical party					
Bossay	6	10	3	16	26
Miranda[a]	4	16	2	8	24
Durán	21	12	8	16	28
Juliet	11	20	6	8	28
Enríquez	17	12	7	8	20
Independent					
Sepúlveda	23	12	9	8	20
Von Mühlenbrock	24	8	9	8	16
National Vanguard of the People					
Castro	9	8	5	8	16
Christian-Democrats					
Reyes	7	16	4	8	24
Palma	22	8	2	8	16
Musalem	7	12	4	8	20
Fuentealba[b]	4	8	8	8	16
Gumucio	7	8	4	8	16
Pablo	17	4	7	8	12
Socialist party					
Rodríguez	7	4	9	16	20
Altamirano	22	4	4	8	12
S. Corbalán	17	8	5	6	14
Communist party					
Teitelboim	6	4	4	8	12
Campusano	7	4	2	8	12
Career mode		9		10	19

a. Is also president or secretary-general of his party.
b. Died in 1967 and replaced by wife in off-year election.

because of my interest in that field, and the fact I am an agricultural engineer. (PR)[73] The most important factor is capacity. For example, Alywin is a lawyer and professor, so he is best suited for C, L, and J. Ferrando is a professor and interested in education, so he is best suited for Education. Also important is a Senator's interest, and his *agrupación*'s characteristics. (PDC)[74] The specialization each one has is important. A doctor will go to Health, a former union director to

73. Personal interview number 1, June 11, 1968.
74. Personal interview number 6, June 12, 1968.

Table 12. *Average Length of Congressional Career by Party, Senate, 1953–1965*

Year	PN	PR	MNI	AGL	UNI	I	PDC	PADENA	VNP	PS	PC	Total
1953												
Number	9	4	2	4	1	—	—	1	—	4	—	25
Years	25	15	8	9	8	—	—	13	—	16	—	17
1957												
Number	8	5	—	3	—	—	1	—	—	3	—	20
Years	18	28	—	12	—	—	15	—	—	9	—	19
1961												
Number	6	6	—	—	—	3	2	—	1	4	3	25
Years	22	22	—	—	—	15	14	—	16	20	14	19
1965												
Number	—	3	—	—	—	1	11	1	—	2	2	20
Years	—	24	—	—	—	16	15	8	—	10	12	15

Note: abbreviations not noted elsewhere are: MNI—National Movement for Ibáñez; AGL—Agrarian Labor; UNI—Independent National Union.

Work and Social Security. (PS)[75] Each Senator's knowledge is our prime criterion. (PC)[76]

Dedication and preparation should be the criterion for selection. Over the years, a Senator will indicate an interest in special subjects, and specialize in these. (I)[77]

Certain informal norms also help promote the full use of the Senate's store of expert knowledge. Thus, if a senator has special knowledge or interest in a bill which is under study in the committee of which he is not a member, he may attend the sessions and take part in the debates, or in deference, replace his party's member temporarily while this bill is in committee.

A committee member can be replaced for several reasons. A bill which is of special interest to another Senator is one, if another member has more knowledge on that particular issue, if a member is sick or traveling abroad. But it should be noted that a member is not replaced by just any Senator of his same party. Usually, a Senator with similar training takes over—for example, Bossay and Baltra (PR) on Finance, or Alywin and Fuentealba (PDC) on C, L, and J. This is necessary in order to maintain some kind of rhythm in the work.[78]

75. Personal interview number 5, June 11, 1968.
76. Personal interview number 15, June 11, 1968.
77. Personal interview number 40, June 27, 1968.
78. Personal interview number 40, June 27, 1968.

Table 13. *Stability of Constitution, Legislation, and Justice and Finance Committees in Senate, 1894–1965*

Year	Members of Committee on Constitution, Legislation, and Justice who continue	Members of Committee on Finance who continue
94–97	3	2
97–00	5	2
00–03 March[a]	1	3
00–03 April[a]	3	5
03–06	4	4
06–09	1	3
09–12	2	5
12–15	1	3
15–18	3	5
18–21	3	4
21–24	5	4
24	3	2
26–30	2	2
30–32	4	4
33–37	1	—
37–41	3	5
41–45	4	2
45–49	4	5
49–53	3	4
53–57	3	3
57–61	4	3
61–65	3	1

a. There were two elections in 1900–03; one in March and another in April.

Unlike the Canadian House of Commons, whose norms stress conflict mitigation and play down rules which encourage expertise and hard work, the Chilean Senate's system norms encourage hard work, specialization, bill study, and thorough preparation. When senators are asked what advice they would give a new senator who wishes to be effective in a standing committee and gain the respect of his fellow members, a typical response is "There is a period of observing and acting little. You should study the bill, act with good criteria, and try to work as objectively and as rationally as possible."[79]

The Senate's capacity for a lawmaking role is further enhanced

79. Personal interview number 6, June 12, 1968.

by the support of a highly competent staff (see Table 14), which compares favorably with the Philippines, and even with the staff available to American congressmen. Certainly the staff assistance available to Chilean senators is far more adequate than that available to most parliaments of the British model or to the Lebanese Chamber of Deputies. Senators González Madariaga

Table 14. *Senate Staff Not Including Personal Secretaries of Senators, 1967*

Position	Men	Women	Total
Personnel of secretary of senate	23	—	23
Office of Information	6	3	9
Editing personnel	19	2	21
Treasurer	2	—	2
Edecan	1	—	1
Auxiliary services	1	5	6
Service aids	56	—	56
Dining room	14	—	14
Other positions	2	6	8
Contracted personnel	3	2	5
Building	28	4	32
Chefs	2	—	2
Total	157	23	179
Chamber	166	24	190
Positions vacant	26	1	27
Library of Congress	28	28	56
Health Services	9	6	15

Source: Senate Office of Information, 1967 File.

(PR) and Castro (VNP) give testimony to their reliance on the senate staff:

The Senate knows how much we value the collaboration of all the staff of the Senate, because they are our greatest allies in the legislative action that Congress achieves. Practically nothing can be done without the aid of all the personnel of the Secretary . . . their collaboration through their experience, which has been acquired over a long period of work, at times, leads us to a common solution. . . .[80] We have always maintained that it is the staff of Congress . . . to a great extent that carries on the democratic tradition . . . they are the ones who show the way to those Deputies and Senators who arrive for

80. *Diario de sesiones del senado*, leg. *extro.*, sesión 12a, November 2, 1960, p. 643.

the first time to Congress . . . on their stability and good judgment depends to a great extent the efficiency and capacity to work of Congress.[81]

Except for personal secretaries, the senate staff is filled through competitive public examinations. Advancement is based on demonstrated ability and a long period of apprenticeship (*escalafón*).[82] Two of the most important components of the senate staff are the standing committee secretaries, and the Office of Information (OIS). Standing committee secretaries are an important force in a system where the principal work is done in committees, in that they are the ones who really study the laws and help inform the congressmen of their contents. They generally serve on the same committee for years, thus acquiring a high level of expertise and specialization in their committee's subject matter. One senator asserts, "The secretaries are extremely important. They are highly efficient, and are the product of many years of experience in the Senate . . . they are the tradition of the Senate. I ask my friends—that is how we regard them—for their opinion on a project. That doesn't bother me at all. After all, many were in the same law classes, and we have been friends for years. . . ."[83]

A typical career is that of Jorge A. Tapia Valdés, secretary of the Committee on Constitution, Legislation, and Justice. Graduating in law in 1960, and author of the book, *La técnica legislativa*, Tapia began working in the Senate in 1954. After more than twelve years of apprenticeship, he became the secretary of his committee.[84] Similarly, Rafael Eyzaguirre Echeverría received his law degree in 1947, became a secretary of that committee in 1962, and presently is working on the Special Committee on Constitutional Reform. Eyzaguirre is also a professor of constitutional law at the University of Chile.[85]

81. *Diario de sesiones del senado, leg. extro.*, sesión 22a, December 6, 1961, p. 1009.

82. Valdés, *op. cit.*, pp. 32–33.

83. Personal interview number 43, July 17, 1968.

84. *Diccionario biográfico de Chile-decima tercera ed.* (Santiago, 1967), p. 1533.

85. *Ibid.*, p. 484. "Disposiciones legales y labor que desarrolla la oficina de informaciones del senado," *Boletin de Información general, No. 18* (Santiago, May 31, 1967).

The secretaries and their aids are supplemented by the OIS, created in 1959. Also chosen by competitive examination, OIS is made up of economists, political scientist–public administrators, lawyers, translators, and a newspaperman. In addition to the publication of numerous information bulletins for the public media, OIS carries out valuable in-depth studies for senators and

Table 15. *Senate Office of Information Activities for the Period 1964–1968*

Type of activity	1964	1965	1966	1967	1967–1968a	1968b
Consultations						
Sent out	740	1,017	1,049	967	621	318
Reports received	158	288	356	316	204	126
Communications						
Sent out	116	342	302	307	211	126
Received	165	125	261	244	271	166
Bulletins published						
Press information	29	13	6	—	1	6
Parliamentary information	40	52	45	57	65	40
Translations	34	29	34	65	71	17
Economic reports	10	17	22	28	23	11
General information	2	—	1	20	12	4
Statistical information	3	4	4	3	2	1
Documents loaned	375	525	461	355	252	232
Communications sent	1,885	2,311	1,834	1,572	1,273	974
Communications received	1,983	NA	2,217	1,835	1,040	593
Messages	217	NA	201	270	223	76
From Chamber	1,165	NA	390	731	217	176
From Ministries	433	NA	954	536	414	239
From Comptroller et al.	26	NA	136	113	94	63
Requests of concern	81	NA	74	48	11	18
Other contacts	61	NA	462	137	81	21

a. Extraordinary session.
b. Regular session.
Source: Senate-Office of Information (compiled from annual work reports).

secretaries of standing committees (see Table 15). The OIS religiously conducts these studies for senators of all parties in a confidential manner.

The Senate staff demonstrates a high degree of adaptability to the periodic increase and decrease of demands made on it. As a rule, secretaries and their aids work only on one or two standing committees. But some committees work more than others, and some hardly at all. Therefore, in times of stress, for example, during consideration of the 1968 Salary Readjustment Bill, or in the absence of a secretary, a temporary shift of secretaries or aides will take place to augment the capacity of a committee such as Finance. Work hours follow a similar cycle and increase in response to demands made on the system. Standing committees can and do call on experts for testimony and assessment. Senators also have a personal staff, but it is modest by United States standards although this varies with individual senators. Any lack of staff is overcome in part by calling on party experts to help keep them informed on important bills. The significance of this party aid varies with individual senators and by party.

A senator's personal ties (economic and kinship) and past experience should not be underestimated as yet another source of lawmaking influence. John Porter has established a link between the major political parties and the corporate elite in Canada, and Allan Kornberg in his essay in this volume has called attention to the significance of ties of kinship and friendship in the same country. These linkages may also be significant in Chile.

Although it has been a subject of frequent debate, it is still quite legal for a congressman to be a director of a private company or bank as long as it does not have a contract directly with the state.[86] If a congressman is at the same time a director in an important private company or bank, a potentially powerful linkage between public and private careers is created which may be useful in initiating or modifying proposed legislation. Furthermore, if a congressman through service in the executive branch has acquired knowledge of the ins and outs of a ministry, personal loyalties, or expertise, a similar base is created.

The author's study of the directors and top 10 stockholders of the top 200 *sociedades anónimas,* top 25 insurance companies, and all domestic banks at the end of 1966 makes it clear that

86. See Guerra, *op. cit.,* pp. 188–196, for his views in 1924 and 1929, and Manríquez G., *op. cit.,* p. 176, for a 1965 position. The PDC has as part of their constitutional reform project (passed the Chamber and is still in committee in the Senate) taken a position against the continuation of this linkage. If it passes, some of their own members will have to order their personal affairs.

career overlap does exist. First, it is necessary to make clear the importance of the group we are talking about. For example, the top 10 stockholders of the top 193 *sociedades anónimas* (7 are foreign), or .3 per cent of all *sociedades anónimas* stockholders, own 62.3 per cent of all *sociedades anónimas* value (*valor patrimonial*). Of the total number of directors of the top 193 corporations, 28 per cent are also stockholders in these companies, which represents a personal ownership of 6.4 per cent of the value of all *sociedades anónimas.*[87] If a person is a director or director-stockholder in one of these top 193 companies, he is a potentially influential individual in the economic community. If he is also horizontally linked to the institutions such as the top insurance companies and banks, his potential is still greater. Add to this, at the same time, the position of congressman, and an immense

Table 16. *Corporate Links of Senators by Party, 1966*

	Top group of corporations							Any group						
	PC	PS	PDC	PR	PN	Total	%	PC	PS	PDC	PR	PN	Total	%
Senators	—	1	—	3	5	9	20	—	2	—	5	5	12	27
Deputies	—	—	—	—	1	1	.7	—	—	4	2	1	7	5
Total	—	1	—	3	6	10	6	—	2	4	7	6	19	10

Note: Independent senators are grouped with party that supported them in elections.

potential for influence is created. It is multiplied even further if the congressman also happens to sit regularly on one of the two most important standing committees in either house.

An examination of relevant data (see Table 16) indicates that 20 per cent (nine) of all senators in 1966 were directors or director-stockholders in the top group of companies mentioned above. If we add to this participation in any *sociedades anónimas,* insurance companies, or banks, the number increases to 27 per cent. The respective percentages for the Chamber are .7 and 5 per cent. At least two secretaries of Senate standing committees

87. Forthcoming. Raw data were provided by the Superintendencia de Compañías de Seguros, Sociedades Anónimas y Bolsas de Comercio, and by the Superintendencia del Bancos from their most recent complete files. 1967 should be available within the year ending 1968. The analysis and conclusions are the responsibility of the author.

are also directors or director-stockholders in the "any group"—
one in the same company as a senator. In one case, two senators
of ideologically opposite political parties are directors on the
same company. Also, at least eleven senators have served in the
executive branch prior to their Senate career, usually as a minister.

This author is not fully qualified to say whether this potential is
in fact used for or against the public interest. Some observers
have reached such conclusions, and one Senate staff member
remarked, "On Finance, there is always a fight over seats . . .
Senators of the Right are particularly interested in serving on this
committee."[88]

Administrative Oversight and Patronage

On the world scale, the Chilean Congress, particularly the
Senate, appears to perform an oversight function to a far greater
degree than in Brazil or Canada, falling much closer to the
United States. Kornberg in his essay points out that the opposition in Canada lacks adequate staff or information to perform this
function well, and Packenham notes in Brazil that "ministers
seldom testify before congressional committees . . . ," and on the
floor only under very limiting circumstances. This is not the case
in Chile.

All of the factors that give the Senate an important voice in
lawmaking aid in the oversight function as well. But there is
more. Article 5 of Law 13.609, which created the OIS in 1959,
provides that (for OIS of the Chamber as well), "All services of
the Administration of the State . . . fiscal or semi-fiscal institutions, autonomous agencies, corporations of the State, judicial
persons created by law or corporations in which the State has
representatives or capital, municipalities and Social Security organs . . . must forward to OIS the information or data deemed
necessary to fulfill its function."[89]

Tested and upheld over a period of eight years, this law has

88. Personal interview number 53, May 3, 1968. For possible implications of
these ties, see Ricardo Lagos E., *La concentración del poder económico—su teoría,
realidad chilena ed. 5* (Santiago, 1965), pp. 168, on to end.
89. "Disposiciones legales," p. 1.

given the Senate the power to review energetically the actions of the government, and has, ". . . enabled congressmen to base their interventions on official information of the Public Agencies . . . which should not be kept from Congress."[90] OIS, at the request of any senator, will apply this prerogative whenever necessary. The most recent test was a request for the balances of agriculture *asentamientos* (settlements) of CORA (Agrarian Reform Corporation) in response to urging from opposition Senator Pedro Ibáñez Ojeda (PN). After some resistance on the part of CORA, the comptroller general ruled on July 6, 1968, that, as in the past, the information must be provided. It subsequently was provided.[91]

Since their need for information normally is greater, it is only

Table 17. *Senate Office of Information Consultations by Party, 1967–1968 Ordinary Session*

	PC		PS		PADENA		PDC		I		PR		PN		Total	
	%	N	%	N	%	N	%	N	%	N	%	N	%	N	%	N
1967	38	109	31	89	0.4	1	10	28	5	14	10.5	30	5.1	14	100	285
1968	41	32	24	19	1.0	1	8	6	3	2	22.0	17	1	1	100	78
Total	39.4	141	30	108	0.6	2	9	34	4	16	13.0	47	4	15	100	363

Note: Coverage is to March 1968 and does not include consultations to committee secretaries or other personnel.
Source: Senate Office of Information Consultations.

logical that whoever is in the opposition will call on OIS more frequently than will government senators. Analysis of OIS *consultas* (consultations) for the period 1967–1968 (see Table 17) reveals that OIS is, in effect, an institutionalized guarantee of information for the opposition that enhances its capacity both for review and control. Thus, 329 (91 per cent) of a total of 363 consultations were requests by opposition senators.

The presidency of a standing committee is another source of information and control. Presidents are apportioned on the basis

90. *Ibid.,* p. 6. This document also provides an excellent summary of the staff and services of OIS.
91. For a more detailed account, see the author's, "Senate vs. CORA: An Attempt to Evaluate Chile's Agrarian Reform to Date," *Inter-American Economic Affairs* (Autumn, 1968), and a shorter version in *Newsletter Number 2* (Madison, Wis., March–August, 1968), pp. 1–7.

of Senate party representation or party leader (*Comités*) agreement.[92] They can influence the calendar of a committee, who is cited, the tempo of work and debate, and the number and type of amendments to a bill.[93] In August, 1967, all five of the presidents of the committees that were judged most important were chaired by opposition senators (two of which were Socialists and one Communist).[94] Interviews and extensive personal observation show that ministers regularly attend standing committee sessions on important bills, or at a committee's request, even when they are reluctant to do so. One Senator explains, "A minister or high official is frequently cited by the president of a committee, and they have the obligation to come. Their role is to explain the Government view, and try to avoid amendments. Minister Pacheco will appear on the Education Bill. Discussions are usually cordial."[95]

Although in theory a minister has preference on the floor, in fact the Senate can and does limit his comments or interrupt him repeatedly.

A violent verbal confrontation resulted in the brusk exit from the floor of the Senate by the Minister of Mining, Alejandro Hales . . . Hales . . . suffered a strong demonstration of intransigency by the Senators, especially from the President of the body, Salvador Allende . . . who limited his speaking time to one-half hour:

Hales: I don't know the rules of you gentlemen, but I know that this is not a parliamentary regime in which you can limit the time of a Minister of State. . . .

Allende: . . . If the Minister feels it is desirable to leave, do it as soon as possible, because it would represent an attitude that I, as a Senator, reject categorically and energetically.

Hales: . . . you don't concede interruptions nor give time to speak,

92. In 1965, the PR decided that they did not wish any chairs, in order to avoid pacts with other parties, and thereby create an image of independence and honesty. This was described in interviews and is confirmed in *Actas de Comités* (Santiago, Senado), July 1, 2, 9, 19–20, and September 1, 1965, on file in the Office of the Mayor.

93. Ingrid Ahumada Muñoz, *Las comisiones parlamentarias en Chile y otros países* (Santiago, 1967), pp. 73–75.

94. *Senado—nomina de senadores por agrupaciones provinciales y partidos políticos—comites parlamentarios—periodos para los que fueron elegidos y sus domicilios—miembros de comisiones* (Santiago, August, 1967).

95. Personal interview number 20, June 20, 1968.

and after you claim that you haven't been kept informed by the Minister.[96]

The Chamber can and does start impeachment proceedings of a minister (or of the President, under certain circumstances). If the measure passes the Chamber, the Senate must make the final

Table 18. *Congressional Accusations against Ministers of State, 1926–1966*

Year	Total Number	Chamber approved	Senate approved[a]
1926–1927	1	—	0
1931	9	6	1
1935	2	—	0
1936	2	—	0
1938	2	—	0
1939	2	1	—
1940	3	2	1
1944	1	—	0
1945	1	1	1
1946	1	—	0
1947	1	—	0
1948	1	—	0
1951	1	—	0
1952	3	—	0
1954	1	—	0
1955	3	1	0
1956	1	—	0
1957	3	2	1
1958	1	—	0
1959	1	—	0
1960	4	—	0
1962	1	—	0
1963	2	—	0
1966	2	—	0
Total	49	13 (27%)	4 (8%)

a. Zero is used for the Senate to indicate that it does not need to consider the case if the Chamber itself rejects the charges.
Source: Senate Office of Information, 1967 File.

decision. As Table 18 indicates, as a rule the Senate votes not to impeach, but if sufficiently provoked or justified, it will vote otherwise, as happened on several occasions during the Ibáñez administration (1952–1958). The same is true of local officials, for

96. Personal interview number 39, June 17 and 23, 1968.

example, mayors. Senate approval is also required for military advancements, diplomatic appointments, and presidential travels abroad. In 1967 and 1968, the Senate refused to approve both a presidential trip and a diplomatic appointment.[97]

Three other sources of control deserve mention. Each has the same objectives: to call attention to a problem; to solve a problem; or simply to discredit the government. First, the president of the Senate may call a special session whenever he sees fit.[98] Usually, it is designed to discredit the government by obtaining extensive publicity through colorful debates. A good example of such an attempt is the session on the 1968 saltpeter agreement with foreign companies. A second control is the *hora de incidentes,* similar to the question period in Canada or the privileged hour in the Philippines. During this period, senators can bring up or debate whatever matter they think is in the public interest or compatible with their public responsibilities. A sample of subjects covered recently includes: a rejection of permission to the president to leave the country; the housing problems in Santiago; an analysis of the president's annual message to Congress; a release to the press on the pay of Congress; an accusation against the minister of finance; the foreign monopoly of industry; and government corruption.

Third, the Chamber may and does set up special investigating committees to explore a specific problem. With the present PDC majority in the Chamber, this control is more symbolic than real. However, the situation could change if, as many forecasters predict, the PDC wins a majority in the Senate in the 1969 election and loses it in the Chamber.

We mentioned earlier Congress's indirect initiative relative to the budget, and its patronage function (*asuntos de gracia*). Senators also perform an "errand-boy" role for their *agrupación*. Such activity is even more common in the Chamber of Deputies. Since congressmen, as a rule, represent the same area during their total

97. We discussed earlier Senate refusal to allow Frei to travel to the United States in 1967. It also rejected a diplomatic appointment to Peru in 1968.

98. Article 56 of "Reglamento del Senado," *Manual del Senado,* p. 130. Though rarely used, Article 55 also provides that the Senate may call for extraordinary sessions as well as the president.

career, constituency service becomes an important key to re-election. Reviewing his mail, one senator cited a typical group of solicitations, "Here is a request from a man who wants to be an elevator operator in a hospital. Another here is a wife trying to get a naval pension because her husband died recently."[99]

It appears that important standing committee secretaries are also in a position to perform this role. The author observed one secretary on several occasions "asking favors" of a minister. Another staff member specifically refers to such activity, "Secretary _____ is more than a Senator. I have heard him many times asking Minister _____ for favors for friends of his, including pensions."[100]

An American professor who has spent many years in Chile suggests this is one way the government bargains for Senate votes. "The Minister of Finance can hold up payment on many pet projects of pensions until opposition Senators come around."[101] But, as Chileans are fond of saying, the sword has two edges. A quotation from an interview with a secretary illustrates this fact:

One day I received a call from the Minister of Lands during the Ibáñez administration. He said, 'I understand you have a member in your family who is interested in this piece of land. Now, if we could get some action on _____ in the committee, I think we could do something about that.' I thanked him very much, but told him that I was not prepared to, nor could not alter the *tabla* [order of bills].[102]

Interest Articulation and Conflict Resolution

Congress not only articulates interests, but resolves conflicts, in part by initiating or modifying legislation in response to demands made upon it. This takes place on three levels—particular groups, provincial (*agrupación*), and national.

Pressure groups have a long history in Chile and, unlike Brazil, there is close contact between such groups and Congress. We have already described the linkage on a personal level by which congressmen are at the same time directors or director-stockholders in top companies and banks. Constantine Menges writes:

99. Personal interview number 9a, May 16, 1968.
100. Personal interview number 53, May 31, 1968.
101. Personal interview number 83, March 13, 1968.
102. Personal interview number 63, June 19, 1968.

Chile's business associations have the usual types of formal access to
the legislature. They may testify on bills before appropriate committees, and they submit documentation stating their views on legislation
under discussion. Each of the major peak organizations keeps a close
watch over the legislative calendar and informs potentially interested
members of developments. The peak organizations also very often
serve as middlemen in transmitting the views of member associations
and individual companies to the Congress . . . Following the pattern
of American business group activity, however, it seems that the really
important contact with the legislature involves informal relations with
individual congressmen. . . . In the case of controversial legislation,
business association leaders present their views and perhaps even
coordinate strategy with sympathetic congressmen. . . .[103]

Menges also notes that, as in England, where MacKenzie found
that parliamentary groups of the two major parties effectively
made policy, this may also be true on some or all issues in Chile
(my interviews suggest similar conclusions). If this is the case,
"Contact of business association leaders and prominent individual congressmen would be tantamount to contact with a party
organization rather than a free agent."[104]

But, if the business community has its linkage to Congress, so
does the Left. There are at present six PS and five PC senators of
a total forty-five (not including Independents or small parties
tied to this group). One PC senator was a former director of the
party paper, *El Siglo*, two others were former union directors,
and they view their role as representing the worker and marginal
groups. Just as the Right attempts to chair the standing committees of Finance or Economy and Commerce, the Left shows
interest in Work and Social Security, or Public Health. Coloniza-
tion of the presidencies of different committees and linkages to
individual congressmen ensures access to competing interests,
"permitting a balance of forces, more facts, and resolution with
greater clarity."[105]

Before 1925, senators were elected by provinces. President
Alessandri Palma attempted to make the Senate less provincial

---

103. Menges, *op. cit.*, p. 354.   104. *Ibid.*
105. Valdés, *op. cit.*, p. 41. For a description of the place of this structure in
conflict management, see Malcolm E. Jewell and Samuel C. Patterson, *The
Legislative Process in the United States* (New York, 1966), p. 11.

and more national in outlook, but was forced to accept a compromise solution, whereby senators are now elected from a group of provinces (*agrupación*) directly by the people. As in the United States, senators maintain frequent contact with their *agrupación*, and have on occasion voted against their party in preference to regional interests. "Pork" committees like Public Works and Interior Government are popular among senators, because they control funds for roads and water which directly involve the electoral interests of each congressman.

A typical example of constituency-oriented legislation is a jointly sponsored bill by Senators Prado (PDC) and Von Mühlenbrock (I) creating regional information bureaus for tourists in their respective senate districts. Norms of deference and reciprocity help ensure passage for such a bill. As was previously indicated, the regular member of a committee is expected to step down temporarily if a member of the same party wishes to watch over the passage of a bill of interest to his *agrupación*. This enables him to argue more effectively in its behalf, make amendments, and exercise a vote. Then, he may present himself on his next trip home as a champion of local interests, distributing committee reports and debates to the public and the press. Privately, parties will often exempt a senator from voting against a bill his party opposes if it favors his *agrupación;* he will walk out before a vote or not attend a particular session. Senators also will support local measures across party lines in return for later reciprocal support.

Many senators find regional election and representation of interests highly functional to national integration and system persistence. One senator argues, ". . . in my view, [it] is the escape valve (*valvula de escape*) which preserves our system. With our unitary system which tends toward control from Santiago, and at the same time, regions with such diverse characteristics and needs, direct representation by *agrupación* is necessary."[106] But, many senators do not share this view. They find "errand boy" tasks distasteful, concern for re-election degrading, and prefer to

106. Personal interview number 40, June 27, 1968.

see the Senate representing the "national interest," at times as a brake (*freno*) on the Chamber. They contend that the objective of the partial election of senators is to encourage a national as opposed to a regional view on issues. Certain senators even would favor disallowing re-election for this purpose. Some of this latter group of senators find re-election difficult, and others gravitate to "safe" *agrupaciónes*. But some are re-elected consistently because they so admirably perform this role. Herein lies the importance of the form which the Senate interest articulation and conflict resolution functions take. It is the meshing of each level—group, region, and nation—which aids national integration and political system persistence. One senator sums it up nicely:

On the one hand is the problem of national disintegration. . . . Each region tries to obtain privileges, principally on taxes. . . . This tendency is seen primarily in the frontier zones, and at times, one hears talk of total separation. Some see a national Senator a response to this problem. On the other hand, there is the question of centralism in capital and geographically—a trend considered adverse to our development. If you create a national Senator, this process would be accentuated. The conclusion has always been that the existing system is the best overall solution to both problems.[107]

Exit Function

On rare occasions, Congress performs what Packenham in his essay has termed an "exit" function. It has taken two forms in the past, constitutional and unconstitutional. As to the latter, a revolution headed by various congressional leaders deposed President Balmaceda in 1891, when the political system seemed unable to resolve the question of which way the government should legitimately go. Constitutionally, Article 42, Section 7, requires the Senate to give its opinion whenever consulted by the president.[108] On rare occasions, usually on foreign policy issues, this has been done. Thus, for example, President Rios in 1943 consulted the Senate as to whether or not Chile should break with the Axis powers.

107. Personal interview number 3, July 31, 1968.
108. "Constitución política de la república de Chile," *Manual del senado*, p. 28.

Summary and Conclusions

This paper has attempted to demonstrate that the Chilean Senate's most important function is decisional as measured by Packenham's "world scale" of functions. As evidence, we have indicated that the Senate: (1) exercises considerable initiative with respect to the annual budget by passing or modifying laws during the year which signify permanent expenses, and, therefore, must be included in the budget; (2) passes laws which require increased budget expenditures by indicating future budgets as the source of financing; (3) decreases proposed expenditures by the executive; (4) delays, alters, and defeats executive legislation despite the president's extraordinary urgency powers, by applying Article 138 of the Senate *Reglamento* which limits simultaneous consideration of urgency bills to only two; (5) forces the president to re-submit bills, withdraw them entirely, or reach compromise solutions, since he generally lacks a sufficient majority for passing legislation in both Houses; (6) takes advantage of the urgency designation of bills by initiating "amendments" on their coattails which have little or no relevance to the bills themselves; (7) helps to shape, initiate, and evaluate public policy proposals by indicating directly and indirectly what bills are likely to pass; (8) aggressively reviews administration policies and activities by the application of OIS prerogatives, by reliance on its staff studies, by use of standing committee sources of information and control, by floor debates, and by Chamber committee investigations; (9) performs a patronage function by passing *asuntos de gracia* and completing "errand-boy" tasks for Senate districts; and (10) articulates interests and resolves conflict through member representation or participation in key standing committees, and by meshing of group, regional, and national interests.

We also have suggested that the Senate's decisional role is based on: its long evolutionary historical development which included a period of parliamentary government (1891–1925); the presence of an opposition majority in one of the two congressional chambers (usually the Senate), which in turn is a result of the off-year election of senators and the president and partial renovation; public support for a democratic system which includes a Congress independent of the executive; an organizational package of member stability and informal norms which emphasizes apprenticeship and "hard work" in standing committees; and the personal links (economic and kinship) of congressmen.

The claim was made that public support for the Senate's demands for a powerful voice in the policy process is in part linked to its capacity to change. One example of this ability to change is seen in the different career backgrounds of senate members in 1933 and 1965.

Finally, the Senate staff has become professionalized and enlarged since 1933. The OIS has been added, library services have been improved, and plans for a new congressional building are ready. Few political institutions demonstrate the capacity to incorporate the extreme Left and Right as well as the Chilean Senate, or to distribute power internally to all parties in a real rather than in a symbolic manner. Indeed, one cannot help but admire what must be classified as a highly developed political institution operating as an integral part of a highly developed political system.

Chapter 7

Parliament in the Lebanese Political System[*]

Ralph E. Crow

Introduction

The Lebanese political system is at the same time one of the most fragile and one of the most enduring among Arab governments. It has survived in the face of severe pressures, both internal and external, under a Constitution adopted in 1926, and as an independent country since 1943. Its system of government as set forth in the Constitution is ordinarily described as "parliamentary," and the legislature is envisioned as playing a major role, both as a lawmaker and as the political controller of the executive branch. The proposition set forth in this paper is that the legislature is an essential element in the Lebanese political system, although it makes only a minimum contribution to the policy-formation and rule-making functions and is not effective as a check on the executive and bureaucracy.

The Image of the Legislature

The Lebanese public and press, as well as the "experts," all tend to share a negative image of the Chamber of Deputies. Lebanese newspapers constantly complain about the ineffectiveness of the Chamber and almost daily cite readily available examples of unbecoming, disorganized, and irrelevant behavior of

[*] The author wishes to express his appreciation for the contribution to this essay of Mr. 'Aref Abdul Khalik, Graduate Assistant in the Department of Political Studies and Public Administration of the American University of Beirut, especially for the tabulation of the material appearing in Tables 3 through 8 from the records of the Lebanese Chamber of Deputies.

individual members or officers of the Chamber. The activities of the legislature are reported regularly, often with a tone of ridicule or irony. The "expert" opinion may be less pungent but hardly less damning with such phrases as:

"A close examination of the Chamber in Lebanon reveals some serious shortcomings."[1]
". . . notorious for its hesitation, weakness and avoidance of its responsibilities."[2]
"The Puppet Chamber of 1947 does not merit much discussion."[3]
"Mais cette omnipotence parlementaire quant au contrôle politique du Cabinet n'est que théorique."[4]
In a crisis ". . . the Lebanese Chamber of Deputies is completely crippled."[5]
Lebanese ". . . legislatures that have no definite national policy or program and which are generally willing to do the bidding of the chief executive."[6]
". . . the traditional subservience of the parliament to the executive is notorious. . . ."[7]
"Parliament was managed with consummate skill [by the President] or allowed to languish. . . ."[8]
". . . the limited effectiveness of an assembly which always hesitates about debating delicate questions. . . ."[9]

When ten leading Lebanese politicians, interviewed in 1961, were asked to enumerate what they thought to be the greatest weaknesses of the political system, their replies centered heavily around three issues all connected with the Chamber of Deputies:[10] (1) Lack of political parties as a basis for the organization

1. Adnan Iskander, *Bureaucracy in Lebanon* (Beirut, 1964), p. 45.
2. Muhammad Majthoub, *Malaise of Democracy and Arabism in Lebanon* (Beirut, 1956), pp. 50–51. In Arabic.
3. Nicola Ziadeh, *Syria and Lebanon* (London, 1957), p. 208.
4. Charles Rizk, *Le Régime Politique Libanais* (Paris, 1966), p. 124.
5. Michael W. Suleiman, *Political Parties in Lebanon* (New York, 1967), p. 51.
6. Labib Zuwiyya-Yamak, "Political Parties in the Lebanese Political System," in *Politics in Lebanon*, ed. Leonard Binder (New York, 1966), p. 163.
7. Malcolm Kerr, "Political Decision Making in a Confessional Democracy," in *ibid.*, p. 202.
8. Leonard Binder, "Political Change in Lebanon," in *ibid.*, p. 324.
9. Pierre Rondot, "The Political Institutions of Lebanese Democracy," in *ibid.*, p. 133.
10. Maurice Gemayel (cousin of the leader of the Kata'ib party), Alfred Nakkash (former president of the Republic), Abdullah Yafi (several times prime minister), Raymond Edde (deputy and leader of National Bloc), Camille Chamoun (former president of the Republic), Besharah El-Khoury (former president

of the Chamber; (2) The unrepresentativeness of Parliament due to the electoral system and confessionalism; and (3) The fact that the deputies were subservient to the cabinet and to the president.

This low opinion of Parliament is in stark contrast to the enthusiasm with which membership in it is sought. Seats in Parliament are hotly contested, and the position of deputy is highly valued and respected. The reason for this is best seen by a glance at the structure and, more importantly, at the functioning of the political system.

The Political System

A brief enumeration of the environmental factors, the formal institutions of government, and the informal rules of the game is necessary before we can address ourselves directly to the role of the legislature.

The Political Environment: Three factors must be emphasized from the beginning. First, Lebanon is small, with a population of about 2,000,000. It has often been referred to as a city-state, not entirely a misnomer, since all villages in Lebanon are within a few hours travel time from Beirut, the capital, which is the center of most activities in the country. But for our purposes, the importance of this fact is that Lebanese politics are personal. It is impossible to avoid the personal element in Lebanese politics and administration, which immensely complicates the political process. Second, Lebanon is a collection of minorities. A mountainous region, it has traditionally provided refuge for minority groups throughout history and has often enjoyed a degree of autonomy which emphasized and strengthened the distinctive quality of each community. Third, the fundamental reference group of Lebanese society has been, and still is, largely the religious communities, six of which are large enough to consistently play signif-

---

of the Republic), Adnan Hakim (leader of the Najjadeh party), Fuad Butros (deputy), Ghassan Tweini (former deputy and vice speaker of the Chamber), Abdullah Sa'adeh (leader of the P.P.S. party). Reported in Samia Bikhazi, "The Lebanese Chamber of Deputies" (unpublished master's thesis, American University of Beirut), pp. 95, 96.

icant political roles.[11] Table 1 below lists these communities with their approximate proportion of the total population. Two factors stand out, namely, that no one community has a majority and that the Christian-Moslem ratio is about equal.

The political system operates in an environment in which there is no consensus on even the most basic political values, including the legitimacy of the state itself. There is only a minimum commitment to the Lebanese nation and its established authorities. Added to this fragile structure is the increasing conflict between the traditional and modern sectors of society. As an example, although there are many small political parties, the political proc-

Table 1. *Distribution of Lebanese Religious Communities*

Maronite	30%	Protestants	
Sunni	20	Jews	
Shi'ites	18	Syrian Orthodox	
Greek Orthodox	10	Latin (Roman Catholic)	4%
Greek Catholic	6	Chaldeans	
Druze	4	Syrian Catholic	
Armenian Orthodox	5	Others (Alawi, Baha'i,	
Armenian Catholic	1	Nestorians, etc.)	

Note: Total does not equal 100 per cent because of rounding error.

ess continues to be dominated by the traditional elements. But this traditional sector of society is itself torn by a series of cleavages, namely, the Christian–non-Christian split; an Arab-World orientation vs. a Western orientation; regional differences; and rivalries among leading notables, often within the same communities. Michael Hudson has best summed up the basic characteristics of the Lebanese political environment as follows:[12] "(1) A particularistic 'mosaic' society; (2) An authoritarian and hierar-

11. For a brief and penetrating description of the characteristics of the various religious communities see Kamal S. Salibi, *The Modern History of Lebanon* (London, 1955), pp. xi–xxvii.

12. Michael Hudson, "Pluralism, Power, and Democracy in Lebanon," a revised version (April, 1967) of a paper presented at the annual meeting of the American Political Science Association, Chicago, Illinois, September 12, 1964.

chical family structure; (3) Religious institutions that are politically influential; (4) Power dispersed in religious sects, regional groupings, economic pressure groups, and ideologically oriented political movements; (5) Foreign influence in politics; (6) A distinct entrepreneurial habit which has produced both a small class of 'merchant princes' and a large, stable petty bourgeoisie; and (7) A cult of leadership, historically the result of feudalism, which has produced factions of notables, each with local clientele."

Political Institutions: In briefest form, the legislative authority is vested in the Chamber of Deputies, and the executive authority is vested in the president of the Republic, who exercises it with the aid of "his" ministers. The president is elected by the Chamber of Deputies for six years and may not succeed himself. He appoints the ministers, designates one of them as the president of the Council (the prime minister), and can dismiss them. The president can, with the agreement of the Council of Ministers, implement as valid legislation bills deemed "urgent" upon which the Chamber has not acted within a period of forty days and, under specified circumstances, dissolve the Chamber of Deputies.

The Constitution may be amended by a two-thirds vote of the Chamber of Deputies. A three-fourths majority is required if the Council of Ministers is opposed to the amendment. The electoral system is based on a combination of a single electoral college and a proportional representation of the religious communities. The deputies of the Chamber are elected according to the simple-majority, single-ballot system. All the electors of a constituency vote for all the seats to be filled. The latter are apportioned in advance among the several religious communities. In sum, the system envisions a strong president who is the de facto executive; it also envisions a legislature designed to represent and to reconcile the interests of various communities, on the one hand, and to check the executive, on the other. It is in this dual function that we find the key to legislative impotence.

The Rules of the Game: In this context the overriding principle has become the moderating and containing of conflict and the maintenance of a balance of power.[13] "The Lebanese appear to believe that their institutions are not capable of resolving severe conflicts. . . . Thus instead of utilizing political institutions to resolve conflicts, the problem is to prevent fundamental conflict over ideological issues from destroying Lebanese political institutions."[14]

Manifestation of the policy of balance of power can first be seen in the National Pact established in 1943 by the first president and prime minister which has become a de facto part of the Constitution. It provides that the Christians recognize Lebanon as an Arab state that must coordinate its policies with its sister Arab states. In turn, the Christian population can be assured of the allegiance and support of the Moslem communities within an independent Lebanon. The pact also provides for a balance of authority and the sharing of the highest offices, so that the president is a Maronite Christian and the prime minister, a Sunni Moslem. The speakership of the Chamber of Deputies is reserved for the third largest community, the Shi'ites, the vice-speakership for the Greek Orthodox, and so forth.

An example of institutionalization of the balance of power is the constitutional guarantee that the various communities will be equitably (proportionately) represented in the formation of the Council of Ministers and in the public service. An electoral law that allocates the seats of the Chamber of Deputies before the elections to the various religious communities spells out this constitutional guarantee. In this way the electoral conflicts are contained within a religious community (a Maronite running against a Maronite and a Greek Orthodox against a Greek Orthodox) rather than creating intercommunal competition. Theoretically, this requires that a successful candidate for the Parliament must have the support of at least some members of his constituency in addition to those of his own religious community. The

13. The concept of moderating and containing of conflict as the central theme of the Lebanese political process is developed by Leonard Binder in "Political Change in Lebanon," in his *Politics in Lebanon* (New York, 1966), pp. 283–327. A discussion of the balance of power concept growing out of the Lebanese traditional pluralism is treated in the insightful essay by Michael Hudson, "Pluralism, Power, and Democracy in Lebanon."

14. Binder, *op. cit.*, p. 291.

effect of this is to give an advantage to the moderate candidate and, hopefully, to produce a Parliament composed of more moderate elements—one that can operate harmoniously and avoid outright expression of extremes.

The political process as a whole reveals this concern for limiting conflict and maintaining the balance of power. Malcolm Kerr has described this as follows:[15]

Governments are not made to create public policy, nor to choose between clearcut alternatives entailing the triumph of one set of demands over another, but to reflect faithfully and adjust the competing interests of various groups. Nor is the government expected to transcend the demands of all factions by deliberately reforming society itself and thereby altering the character of the dramatis personae.

One other factor must be emphasized. Lebanese politics, more than most, must constantly take into consideration the political attitudes and policies of its neighbors (the Arab states). Survival of a separate Lebanese entity depends upon avoiding the internecine struggles among competing Arab movements, or at least appearing to be in sympathy with, if not on the side of, those stronger and dominant tendencies throughout the Arab World.

The Structure of the Parliament

Background

The Lebanese Parliament was established in 1926 with the adoption of a Constitution under the French Mandate, and has been in continual operation since that time, except for two periods when the Constitution was suspended (1932–1934 and 1939–1943). Originally established as a bicameral body with a Chamber of Deputies and a Senate, the legislature soon underwent change. The Senate was abolished in 1927, and the appointed members of the Chamber were eliminated with independence in 1943. Since that time the legislature has been

15. Kerr, *op. cit.*, p. 190.

unicameral, with its membership entirely elected, since 1953, by universal male and female suffrage.

Since independence, the size of the Chamber of Deputies has varied greatly from a low of forty-four members to a high of ninety-nine, its present number.[16] As the number of deputies in the Chamber has changed, so has the size of the electoral districts, which naturally has affected electoral patterns, particularly the traditional ability of the notables to carry a list of subordinates to victory with them.[17]

The Authority of Parliament

The formal powers of the legislature can be divided into several categories. The first deals with regular legislation, which is the sole prerogative of Parliament. However, the power to initiate legislation is shared with the executive. Bills submitted to the Chamber take one of three forms: "regular," "urgent," or "double urgent," which will be discussed in more detail later.

The second responsibility of Parliament is financial. The major activity of the legislature in this area concerns the budget. The Council of Ministers is required by the Constitution to introduce the budget in the fall session of Parliament, and if the Chamber has not adopted the budget by the end of the year, a special session must be held in January specifically for that purpose. If, at the end of that month, action has not been taken, the president in consultation with the Council of Ministers may promulgate the budget by decree. In addition, tax legislation and laws governing loans, contracts, and concessions fall within the jurisdiction of Parliament.

The third responsibility of Parliament involves political control over the executive. This takes several forms, one of which is the election of the president for a six-year term. However, in the day-to-day operations of the legislature, the deputies have the opportunity to exercise their influence through questions directed

16. From 1943 to 1951, 55 members; from 1951 to 1953, 77 members; from 1953 to 1957, 44 members; from 1957 to 1960, 66 members; and from 1960 to the present, 99 members.

17. See Table 3, showing the number and size of electoral districts in Lebanon from 1943 to 1960, in Ralph E. Crow, "Religious Sectarianism in the Lebanese Political System," *Journal of Politics*, XXIV (August, 1962), 503.

to the Council of Ministers or to individual ministers, or by a more formal interpellation. The Chamber also has the authority to establish special parliamentary investigatory committees to look into any problem they deem necessary. Last and most important (formally at least) is the vote of confidence or lack of confidence by which the Parliament can support or bring down a government.

Two other responsibilities of the Parliament should be mentioned, namely, its role in amending the Constitution and special judicial powers of the Chamber of Deputies. A supreme council made up of deputies elected by the Chamber sitting along with higher judges constitutes the highest judicial authority in the nation and presides over cases of impeachment of the president and of the ministers. In practice, neither of these functions has been important.

Internal Organization of the Chamber

Various organizational features of the Chamber are determined by constitutional provision, including the location of the Parliament, the authority of the deputies to judge the validity of their elections, the number of regular sessions (two each year, one from March through May, and the second from October through December), the calling of special sessions by the president, the definition of a quorum as a majority of the total membership, the public nature of the proceedings of the Chamber (with provisions for closed sessions when required), and the voting procedure. The more detailed features of the internal organization and procedure, however, are set forth by the Chamber itself. The original internal regulations were promulgated in 1930 and a new set, still in operation, was adopted in 1953.[18] For the most part, these regulations are in keeping with the pattern of conventionally established parliamentary procedure and need not be cited in detail here. However, a few of the salient features which figure in the subsequent discussion must be mentioned.

18. In addition to the internal regulations themselves, see the detailed analysis of Anwar al-Khatib, *Procedures of Parliaments in Lebanon and the Arab Countries* (Beirut, 1961). In Arabic.

The Officers of the Chamber

The Speaker of the Chamber is elected annually at the first meeting of the October session. This office is by custom reserved to the third largest religious community in Lebanon, the Shi'ite Moslems. The Speaker is not only responsible for conducting the meetings of the Chamber but also for organizing the agenda. He also serves as the channel between the Chamber and its committees and between the Chamber and the Council of Ministers and the presidency. Other officers of the Chamber include a vice-speaker (a Greek Orthodox), two secretaries elected from among the deputies, and three other deputies who serve as "members" of the Parliamentary office.

The Secretariat and the Parliamentary Committees

The Parliamentary Secretariat (Diwan) today has about seventy-two employees and its own police force of approximately forty members. The Diwan provides secretarial services for the deputies and is responsible for recording the debates in the Chamber and maintaining the records of the committees.

There are at present eight committees in Parliament, the membership of which is drawn from the deputies and elected annually at the beginning of the March session.[19] The size of the committees varies from five to seventeen members. The committees elect their own chairman. Each committee is permitted to have a representative on the Committee of Budget and Finance who may participate in its debates, but who does not have a vote.

Procedure

Legislation may originate from the president, the Council of Ministers, or from the deputies themselves. Bills presented to Parliament under the regular procedure are read and sent to the appropriate committee. The committee then reports back to the Chamber where the bill is debated, article by article, and finally

19. The eight committees are Budget and Finance, Justice and Administration, Foreign Affairs and Defense, Public Works and P.T.T., Social Affairs and Public Health, National Economy and Agriculture, Education, and Tourism.

voted on as a whole. Two other forms of legislation exist. The first is for bills which the Council of Ministers and the president may designate as "urgent." After introduction, such a bill is sent to committee. It must be reported to the Chamber within one week and acted upon within forty days by the Chamber; if such action is not taken, the president may issue it as a law. The second form is that any deputy or the Council of Ministers may designate a bill as "double urgent," in which case it must be debated and voted on in the Chamber immediately rather than being sent to a committee. If a "double urgent" bill does not receive approval by the Chamber immediately, it will then follow the procedure established for the "urgent" legislation.

In the debates on bills, ministers who attend the sessions of the Chamber have priority over the deputies in discussing proposed legislation. Written and oral questions by the deputies can be directed to any minister or to the Council of Ministers as a whole. Such questions may lead to a formal interpellation and, eventually, to a vote of confidence.

A variety of voting procedures is used, but for the final adoption of laws and for votes of confidence a roll-call vote is required. Elections to committees and for officers of the Parliament are conducted by secret ballot.

Parliament in Action

Political Groupings in Parliament

There are a variety of political organizations in Lebanon. One authority has identified seventeen so-called political parties, plus two political-religious groupings, which he classifies under the following headings: Trans-national parties, Arab and non-Arab; religious and ethnic organizations, including Moslem groups and Armenian parties; and exclusively Lebanese parties, with Moslems, Druze, or Christians as dominant members. Some of these organizations reflect the Western type of political party, with formal programs and individual membership.[20] Others have only

20. Michael W. Suleiman, *Political Parties in Lebanon* (Ithaca, N.Y., 1967).

limited objectives and membership, whereas still others are, in fact, blocs of traditional notables with their unorganized followings. Before 1951, membership in these blocs and parties in the Parliament was so flexible as to be of no significance in legislative proceedings. Since 1951, by contrast, it is possible to delineate roughly the degree of political party representation in the Chamber of Deputies, and this is indicated in Table 2. As can be seen, members of organized political groups have never constituted a majority of the members of Parliament. Other organized political groups have regularly had small representations of one, two, or three members. The largest representation of an organized group

Table 2. *Parliamentary Membership of Parties in Lebanon, 1951–1968*

	1951	1953	1957	1960	1964	1968
Total Number of Deputies	77	44	66	99	99	99
Number of Party Members	10	8–10	12	33–37	27	34
Approximate percentage of parliamentary membership	13	24	18	35	27	34

Source: For 1951–1964, adapted from Table 8 in Michael W. Suleiman, *Political Parties in Lebanon* (Ithaca, N.Y., 1967), p. 265, and for the 1968 figures from *An-Nahar* (April 9, 1968). It should be noted that this definition of political parties is a broad one. It includes stable political blocs which do not have formal party organization or members, but it does not include the more ephemeral parliamentary coalitions.

in Parliament has never exceeded five or six deputies, and these usually come from the loose electoral coalitions of a more traditional bloc. Therefore, the majority of the deputies in Parliament are independents, frequently but temporarily, combined into parliamentary alliances.

The membership of the Chamber of Deputies is often characterized as being conservative, oriented toward keeping the status quo, and traditional. Although this has been true and still is true to some extent, changes are taking place in the membership and occupational background of the deputies. Hudson has noted that there is a tendency for a hard core of perennials to dominate the Parliament (from 1943 to 1964, "Nearly one third of the seats available have been occupied by 14 per cent of all the Deputies elected to these seven parliaments").[21] Nevertheless, whereas in 1943 only 10 per cent of the deputies had been born after 1910, by 1964 65 per cent were post-Ottoman. Although in 1943 the landlords and lawyers (the traditional oligarchy) made up 80 per cent of the Chamber, by 1964 the number had decreased by 50 per cent. Meanwhile, the number of professionals (doctors, teachers, engineers, salaried employees) had trebled during the same period from the 1943 figure of 10 per cent to 32 per cent in 1964:

Between 1943 and 1953, landlords comprised the single largest occupational group among new entrants; in 1957, this predominance shifted to the lawyer group; and in 1960 and 1964 the professionals took the lead. Since 1960, the business and professional groups combined have supplied more than half the number of new entrants.[22]

Forty-five out of ninety-nine members of the 1964–1968 Parliament did not reappear in the new Chamber elected in April, 1968. Thirty-five failed to be elected, eight did not stand for election, and two had died. The forty-five new members in the 1968 Chamber included seventeen who had been in Parliament at one time or another before 1964, all but two of whom could be considered members of the traditionally oriented notable families. The remaining twenty-eight new members (serving in Parliament for the first time) included: ten from the professions (mostly lawyers and medical doctors); ten from wealthy business families; five from traditional notable families; and five who might be labeled "listists" (i.e., candidates with little personal political support but elected on the coattails of a traditional leader on whose list they ran). There is, however, a hidden factor here, in that several cases of change in occupation are simply changes in generation of the long-established notable families which continue to rely on traditional support and to represent traditional interests. Hudson concludes: "while the trend toward broadened recruitment is important, it should not be exagger-

---

21. For these and the following figures see the excellent analysis by Michael Hudson, "The Electoral Process and Political Development in Lebanon," *Middle East Journal*, 1966, pp. 173, 186.

22. *Ibid.*, p. 179.

ated. The Chamber of Deputies remains a most exclusive club. Among those excluded are the petty bourgeoisie, workers, peasants and women."[23]

Facilities Available to the Deputies

A word might be said about the facilities available to the members of the Chamber. Lebanese legislators, like those of most of the world, are not well served. Deputies do not have individual offices or any staff assistance. The Diwan provides minimum services within the Parliament building where phone calls are received and deputies meet their constituents or meet with each other. There are plans to renovate the Parliament building and to provide one office for each five deputies as well as receiving rooms, a restaurant, and a library with an archives collection.[24] More serious than these physical difficulties, however, is the fact that the Diwan of the Parliament falls far short of meeting the needs of the deputies. Beyond the minor services of telephone calls, coffee, and running errands, little is provided to increase the effectiveness of the deputies in handling the complex material in their committees and on the floor of the Chamber. The library and reference room of the Parliament hardly warrant the name, and the present archives almost defy use. Anyone who has attempted to utilize the published verbatim record of the parliamentary debates, which are poorly organized, not always accurate, and lack even tables of contents or indexes, quickly realizes the limitations of this office.

The only assistance available to the deputies for the drafting of legislation is provided by a bureau in the Ministry of Justice, where limited advice can be sought concerning difficult legal questions. This does not, however, provide much assistance. In March, 1967, the Parliamentary Committee on Administration and Justice approved a bill for the creation of a consultative

23. *Loc. cit.*
24. *Le Jour,* November 10, 1967; see November 18, 1967, for an interview with Sheikh Pierre Gemayyel and his plans for building an entirely new Parliament building. One journalist noted, however, that if the present rate of increasing absenteeism continues we will soon find a notice in the newspapers "For rent or sale, one large parliament, modern comfort assured."

commission on legislation to be established in the Ministry of Justice. In November, 1967, the minister of justice accused the Parliamentary Committee on Finance of having buried the project (previously approved by the Committee on Administration and Justice). The chairman of the Finance Committee denied this and maintained that the text of the bill had never been transmitted to the Committee on Finance.[25] This deficiency in parliamentary staff for the drafting of legislation allows the individual ministries and the secretariats of the president and the Council of Ministers to exercise the greater influence by default. Given the limited degree to which the Chamber and its committees alter legislation (see below), this adds considerably to the dominance of the executive over the legislature. Although legisla-

Table 3. *Numbers of Meetings and Sessions of Parliament*

Type	1950	1955	1960	1966	Total
Regular sessions	2	2	2	2	8
Special sessions	2	5	3	4	14
Meetings at regular sessions	20	32	21	21	94
Meetings at special sessions	24	22	20	17	83
Total sessions	4	7	5	6	22
Total meetings	44	54	41	38	177

tive services are no substitute for the desire and ability of Deputies to comprehend and shape legislation and, hence, policy, the limitations of the present Diwan seriously hamper the efforts of the few deputies who now are willing to give the business of Parliament serious and detailed consideration.

Sessions and Meetings

How long does Parliament work? Table 3 shows the number of regular and special sessions and the meetings held in both during four sample years 1950, 1955, 1960, and 1966. These years represent "normal" years (i.e., a minimum of national crises) during

25. *Le Jour*, March 10, 1967, and November 18, 1967. *Le Jour* maintains that this is not the first time that a project has been lost in the labyrinth of Parliament.

the regimes of each of the four Presidents Bishara El-Khoury, Camille Chamoun, Fuad Shihab, and Charles Helou.[26]

On the average during these four years a total of 5.5 sessions and forty-four daily meetings were held each year. This means that an average of approximately eight meetings were held per session. When one takes into account the fact that a number of these forty-four meetings per year are given over to formalities such as the election of officers and the reading of programs of new ministries, plus the fact that a significant portion of an often rather short meeting is taken up with the reading of telegrams and messages from organizations and parliaments abroad, it can be seen that the time during which the Chamber is active in the course of a year is rather limited.

Table 4 gives some indication of the percentage of absences in

Table 4. *Attendance of Deputies and Ministers at the Regular and Special Sessions of Parliament*

	1950	1955	1960	1966	Total
Deputies absent	27.2%	22.3%	19.2%	22.2%	22.2%
Ministers absent	8.9	28.6	38.1	31.0	28.2
Prime minister absent	0.0	20.3	7.3	5.2	10.6

both regular and special sessions on the part of deputies, ministers, and the prime minister during these same four sample years. Although the deputies were absent approximately 22 per cent of the time, the ministers were somewhat less regular in their attendance. However, the prime minister maintained the best record, being absent only approximately 10 per cent of the time. Two important factors are not revealed in this table. The first is the number of times when a quorum was not present, thereby preventing a meeting from being held, and second is the number of times when pressure was exerted to have scheduled meetings

26. The information of this subject and the following discussion of the operation of the committees and of legislative action of the Chamber is derived from the records of the Parliament for the years 1950, 1955, 1960, and 1966. They were chosen as a sample because they represented periods of reasonable stability and absence of major crisis. In one sense these years are not typical because Lebanese history during the last twenty-five years has been characterized by almost continual crisis.

adjourned. The charge is often made that the Council of Ministers (this often implies the president's approval or initiation of the action as well) frequently engineers the lack of a quorum in order to avoid embarrassing criticisms in Parliament or the development of an opposition which might bring down the government. Conversely, opponents of the group in power are often absent themselves and prevent a meeting of the Chamber in order to demonstrate the strength of their opposition to the government and its policy.

The Role of Speaker

The Speaker of the Chamber is a key figure in the political system. His office is described as the second office of the Republic and is recognized as the third most powerful political position. The Speaker, elected from among the deputies, is a man of some political power in his own right. Although he is supposed to play a neutral role in the proceedings of the legislature, he represents one of the major political communities of the nation and has an important personal political following.

The Speaker represents the official contact point between the legislative and executive branches of government. All communications going both ways must pass across his desk. In the day-to-day operation of the Parliament he has a number of ways to influence the direction and outcome of events, including assigning bills to the appropriate committees, the election of members to the various committees, recognizing deputies on the floor of the Chamber, organizing the agenda, and interpreting the propriety of remarks and behavior during the course of the debates. The Speaker holds a weekly meeting with the president and keeps in close touch with the prime minister and the plans of the cabinet. During the formation of a new government, the president relies upon the advice of the Speaker (among others) in assessing the political climate among the deputies. Because the Speaker has influence among the deputies, he also has influence with the various ministers and with the prime minister and the president. Because he can marshal parliamentary support for executive measures, he can also demand favors and cooperation from the ministers for individual deputies. During the twenty-four years of independence, only five deputies have occupied the office of Speaker; and the present incumbent has held the office for a total of fifteen of those years. His long experience and extensive contacts with deputies and ministers reinforce the formal authority of the office. A six-line note in a daily paper describes the Speaker's role as an honest broker very simply: "M. Fouad Bizri, Ministre des Travaux Public, a recu, hier matin, le President de la Chambre, M. Sabri Himade et les deputes. . . . Le ministre a passé en revue avec les parlementaires certain projets interessant leurs regions respectives."[27]

The Committees in Operation

An examination of the operation of the committees gives the impression of great activity. In actual practice, we see that this activity is unevenly divided among the committees and, much of the time, amounts to pure formality. All deputies serve on one or two committees. Naturally there is a significant degree of continuity of committee membership from one session to another. The membership of three of the most important committees in 1966 (Budget and Finance, Justice and Administration, and Public Works) totaled forty-seven, with about one quarter (twelve) serving for the first time. The remaining three quarters of the members were serving repeat terms, with four of them having served since 1960.

The distribution of work among the committees, as previously noted, is very uneven. In four sample years (as shown in Table 5), the Committee on Budget and Finance handled 60 per cent of the total number of bills reported by all committees. This committee and the second most active committee, Justice and Administration, considered and reported out 78 per cent of all bills. The remaining six committees dealt with 22 per cent of the bills. Of these, only the Committees on Foreign Affairs and Defense, and Public Works, acted on any significant number.

The appropriate ministers are permitted to meet with the committees and usually do so. Since an overwhelming number of

27. *Le Jour*, November 4, 1967.

bills presented to Parliament originate with the cabinet, and since the consideration of these measures is discussed in the presence of the minister concerned, one can say that the committees operate in the shadow of the executive. This is reinforced by the fact that the committees have no staffs of their own (beyond a recording secretary) and must rely almost entirely on the minister and his civil servants to supply the information about the current situation and future needs.

It must be added that the committees do not have the authority to "kill" a bill by burying it in committee. A bill must be

Table 5. *Number of Bills Reported by Committees of Parliament, 1950, 1955, 1960, and 1966*

Budget and finance	237
Justice and administration	66
Foreign affairs and defense	37
Public works and P.T.T.	31
Social affairs and public health	12
National economy and agriculture	7
Education	6
Tourism	1
Total number of committee reports	397

reported out in one form or another to the Chamber. Table 6 shows the total number of bills reported by the committees to the Chamber in four sample years, according to the type of legislation and whether or not amendments were made by the committees. Forty per cent of all bills (regular or urgent) were left unchanged by the committees and sent to the Chamber as received (almost all from the cabinet). The majority, about 60 per cent, were amended in some way. The report of a committee must contain an explanation of any changes introduced by the committee and a justification of such action.

Recently, proposals have been made for the reform of the committee system. In 1967 a member of the Committee on Justice and Administration called for an enlargement of the number of committees to sixteen—one for each ministry of the government.[28] With the present concentration of the majority of bills in one or two committees, much more would have to be done than establishing new committees, as little use is now made of half of those which currently exist. The real problem is the limited degree of subject-matter specialization. Instead of recognizing that all government actions involve financial and legal aspects and allowing these to be handled in the context of the issue with which the bill is concerned, the present practice is to handle bills in an undifferentiated fashion, emphasizing the legal and financial aspects. More recently, the same deputy suggested the augmen-

Table 6. *Committee Action on Regular and Urgent Bills, 1950, 1955, 1960, and 1966*

Type of bill	Percentage	Percentage as proportions of total
Regular		
Unchanged	42	33
Amended	58	45
Urgent		
Unchanged	31	7
Amended	69	16
	(N = 344)	

tation of the staff of the committees in order to improve the effectiveness of legislative control over the executive, and the preparation and distribution of the agendas of the committees twenty-four hours before each committee meeting. The newly elected Speaker of the Chamber expressed interest in the project and promised to undertake a reform of the staffing procedures and facilities, which he felt was entirely unsatisfactory upon taking office.[29]

28. *Le Jour*, August 16, 1967, for an account of the proposal of Deputy Anwar al-Khatib.
29. "Les presidents des commissions decident de renforcer le controle sur L'Executif," *Le Jour*, June 8, 1968. The newly elected speaker charged that the majority of the employees on the Chamber's payroll were relatives of the previous speaker and that some only came to collect their salaries. Plans were announced for establishing a systematic and controlled procedure for the recruitment and control of the parliamentary staff.

Activities on the Floor of the Chamber

Securing a quorum for meetings of the Chamber is never assured, and it is seldom achieved without considerable delay.[30]

Opening Preliminaries: It is customary for Parliament to receive petitions from individual citizens and more often from groups. Village councils, syndicates, groups of consumers, or producers may, and often do, express their grievances to Parliament. These are noted in the proceedings but are not formally dealt with on the floor unless some deputy chooses to discuss a particular issue.

More important, however, is the first half hour of every meeting (often extended to an hour, or an hour and one half) during which time the deputies are permitted to make remarks to the Chamber and for the record. This is the opportunity for a deputy to get the spotlight, to pursue the problems of his district, and to express his personal opinions and set forth his views on matters he deems important (often to attack an opponent). Although this process does not visibly advance the legislative process and often generates conflict among the deputies, it undoubtedly has a cathartic effect. An examination of these remarks probably reveals more graphically than anything else—the daily content of the Lebanese political process.

The Conduct of Debate: The level and cogency of debates in the Chamber is not notably higher than that of most legislative bodies. On occasions personal exchanges grow heated, disorder may erupt, and a recess is called. More often vague expressions of opinion sometimes only remotely connected to the issue at hand go on for extended periods. Less often, but more important, the issue may be joined with clear-cut positions and alternatives, but in keeping with the underlying principle of limiting conflict, these are usually avoided or deflected when they manage to appear during the course of the debates.

Adopting Legislation: Table 7 lists the number and percentage

30. A study done of the 150 meetings of the Chamber held during the period August, 1960–April, 1963, showed that on the average the Chamber began one and one-half hours after the scheduled opening time. *An-Nahar,* February 25, 1964.

of the three different types of legislation undertaken by the
Chamber in four sample years. The majority (67 per cent) is
according to the "regular" legislative procedure and accounts for
the bulk of the Chamber's action. The remainder of the bills fall
about equally into the categories of "urgent" and "double urgent"
(15 and 18 per cent, respectively).

A different picture emerged, however, from the unusually active period of August, 1960, to April, 1963, during which time
President Shihab was pushing through a series of reform measures. The pattern was almost the reverse of that shown in Table 7,
with only 26 per cent of the bills passed by the regular procedure,
whereas 41 per cent were treated as urgent, and 33 per cent as

Table 7. *Kinds of Legislation Acted on by the Chamber, 1950, 1955, 1960, and 1966*

Type of bill	%
Regular	67
Urgent	15
Double urgent	18
	(N = 384)

double urgent. As might be expected, the number of bills presented to the Chamber was greater during this period, and a high
percentage of them was passed.[31]

Turning to the action taken by the Chamber on the bills which
came before it (Table 8), one is immediately struck by the fact
that a total of 60 per cent of all legislation in these four sample
years was voted into law unanimously and was unchanged as it
came from the committees. If one adds to this the bills which
passed unchanged by a majority vote, the total is 82 per cent. Of
the 17 per cent of the bills amended by the Chamber, 10 per cent
were adopted without dissent. Perhaps the most striking fact here
is that of the 384 bills acted upon by the Chamber during this
period, none was rejected!

31. *An-Nahar*, February 28, 1964.

Interpellations and Votes of Confidence: The legislature in the Western model of a parliamentary government has as its ultimate sanction the ability to force a change in the executive through interpellations and votes of no confidence. Both of these are formally provided for in the Lebanese Constitution. However, in fact, neither procedure ever operates in this open, direct form. Although deputies frequently do address questions to individual ministers, and on occasion actually call for a vote of confidence, the process always falls short of open and outright defeat for the existing government. No cabinet in the history of independent Lebanon has been voted out of office by Parliament. This is not to say that the deputies have no power, or that the cabinet is not

Table 8. *Action of the Chamber of Deputies on All Bills, 1950, 1955, 1960, and 1966*

Action	Number	%
Adopted unchanged		
Unanimously	238	60.7
Majority	83	21.6
Amended		
Unanimously	39	10.1
Majority	29	7.5
Total	384	100.0

dependent to some degree on their support. But the legislature as a body is not the forum in which a change of government is decided.

Instead, cabinets tend to break up internally, because they are always constituted as a coalition of the various political groups within the country. Consequently, when a serious issue is before the cabinet and a minister senses the discontent of his own community and supporters, he ensures his future by resigning. Once one or two ministers have breached the "wall of unity," it is usually only a matter of days before the whole cabinet is forced to resign (although a new coalition may be formed under the same prime minister). Less often, a cabinet may find itself without the support of the majority of the Chamber, and if it cannot delay matters or, with the help of the President, reconstitute majority support (by techniques well known to and practiced by most professional politicians), then the cabinet will "voluntarily" resign, rather than be subjected to the humiliation (and the jeopardy of their future political careers) of being defeated by Parliament and forced to resign.

The Budgetary Process: Naturally, the Committee on Budget and Finance plays a most important role in the budgetary process. In the Chamber the budget is debated and adopted section-by-section, rather than as a whole document. The Chamber is not empowered to increase the budget, but it may reduce the proposal submitted by the cabinet. The Chamber follows the guidance given by the reports of the Budget and Finance Committee, where the detail work is done in conjunction with officials from the Ministry of Finance, particularly the minister and the director general. The lack of a clear-cut program and set of priorities on the part of the government, and the line-item form of the budget, make it very difficult for an individual deputy to form an independent opinion on budgetary matters. Although a few do make a serious effort to study and to understand the budget proposals, they do not have the basis for determining the desirability or suitability of proposed expenditures. Perhaps the strongest evidence of the "hit or miss" nature of the budgetary process is that an estimated one-third of all legislation which comes before Parliament deals with supplementary appropriations, transfer of funds from one agency to another or one ministry to another, or the carrying over of unspent funds from one budget year to the next.

Grants of Legislative Powers to the Executive: Although the Lebanese Constitution does not explicitly provide for the possibility of Parliament granting legislative powers to the executive (in fact, it designates the Parliament as having sole legislative powers), there have been five major occasions on which this has been done. In 1952, 1954, 1958, and 1965, Parliament voted legislative powers to the cabinet, usually for a period of three or six months (but in 1965 for an undesignated period), to issue decree laws in a series of broad, designated areas. Cabinets so empowered have taken the opportunity to promulgate a large number of measures (sometimes amounting to sixty or seventy) of a fundamental nature, e.g., reorganizing municipal government, the structure of the administration, the judiciary, the press, and the tax structure, and even effecting a purge of the civil service (in which a number of higher officials were retired). In sum, the Council of Ministers has been asked by Parliament to deal with basic organic matters and politically controversial issues which would be very difficult for Parliament to deal with "out in the open." However, the procedure creates its own tensions. In the fall of 1967 when Deputies (and aspirants to seats in the next cabinet) demanded that the cabinet submit to a debate (or possible interpellation) in the Chamber over decree laws promulgated under a grant by the Chamber of emergency powers (but never re-submitted to the Chamber), the prime minister offered to meet "interested" deputies in his office but refused to have the matter debated in Parliament.[32]

Assessment of the Role of Parliament

The validity of the widespread charge that Parliament is ineffective as a lawmaking body and as a legislative check on the executive now seems clear. But two questions remain: Why is Parliament so weak? What, if any, function does Parliament serve?

Causes of Parliamentary Weakness

Many maintain that the Lebanese political system is in fact a presidential system, or at least a quasi-presidential system. There is no doubt that the president is strong, formally by constitutional power and informally by the nature of a system that permits him to "manage" the other institutions of government. The techniques open to the president for the exercise of influence over the legislature include: his ability to affect elections (sometimes directly through the electoral law, districting, etc.); his participation in

32. For a discussion of this issue see *Le Jour*, November 2 and 3, 1967.

arranging the coalitions and the electoral lists of candidates; and his use of the resources of his office to reward and punish those who do or do not cooperate. If the legislature is deadlocked and unable to resolve a conflict over basic issues, thus threatening the system itself, a strong president (Shihab in 1961) and one less strong (Helou in 1968) in the last resort may even resign, leaving the country in a perilous state. In the two instances cited above, this resulted in an outpouring of support from all quarters, permitting the President to resume his office with the assurance that all parties would agree on a solution to the issue at hand.

It was pointed out above that one of the effects of the sectarian features of the electoral system is to favor the moderate candidates and to exclude the extremists who cannot draw support from outside their own religious community. To the degree that this feature succeeds, it creates a Parliament that can more easily work together, but to the same degree, it distorts Parliament in the other direction, i.e., by not providing representatives of the extreme points of view; and it is this unrepresentativeness that is one of the factors which weakens Parliament.

Another weakening factor is that the deputies tend to represent particular interests rather than programmatic, ideological, or doctrinaire interests. The resulting Chamber (without major political parties or groupings as a basis of organization) is fragmented. As each deputy's strength depends in the long run on his ability to satisfy demands of his supporters, and as there is no established basis of internal organization to increase demands on the executive, the deputies find that the most effective way to share in the proceeds of the society is to be in favor with the strongest power, the president and his ministers, who are in direct control of the administration and resources of the government. This makes it possible for the executive to reward support and deny opposition. Consequently, the Chamber of Deputies is seldom a stable opposition to the executive, since its membership can usually be pierced before the opposition has actually been formed, or at least before it has been formed long enough to be effective.

For years political analysts and many political figures have advocated larger, more disciplined political parties (preferably two parties) as the solution to the ineffectiveness of Parliament, as the basis of control over the executive, and as a means for the development and implementation of development policy. It is now with some alarm that observers note what might be termed the prototype of such a pattern. Since 1966, the deputies who formed a majority in the Chamber under former President Shihab and who supported his policies on many domestic and foreign policy issues have drawn together and overcome some of their traditional differences. This group (*al-Nahj*—the Programists) has achieved some degree of unity of action in the Chamber of Deputies. The result was a coalescing of opponents into an alliance of the three major Maronite parties, which exhibited surprising success in the elections of 1968, thereby threatening to dominate the new Parliament. The first issue over which these two groups clashed was the election of the Speaker of the Chamber, eventually decided by a single vote. Then, the inability to form a Cabinet acceptable to both groups resulted in the threatened resignation of the president.

In the abstract, this pairing off into what might become a two-party system seems to promise greater responsibility and "rationality" in the political system. But, in practice, it must not violate the cardinal principle of Lebanese politics, namely that divisions on issues must cut across religious community lines and not coincide with them. If the present tendency were to violate this principle (as there is some reason to believe it might), then the legislature would be rendered impotent, or the group forced into a minority position would probably withdraw and attempt to settle the issues in another arena, possibly the streets.

One of the most fragmenting factors in the Chamber is the practice of choosing the ministers from among the deputies. As this is not done on the basis of political parties, it is a matter of negotiation (within the context of sectarianism). Although some deputies are in a much stronger position than others, there is hope for all, and one does not increase his chances by displeasing the chief of state (or the prospective chiefs of state). As a result an experienced and expert president can "manage" Parliament.

It is an exaggeration to say that the president and his cabinet

are all-powerful. They are not. The deputies and others outside of
the Chamber are also strong, and a successful regime (of a
president) requires constant building and adjusting of support. It
is an endless process of shifting coalitions. Even momentary inat-
tention or miscalculation may tempt some participant or group of
participants to threaten to break down the system by resorting to
violence or to withdraw from the system (rebellion). Parliament
is not the only participant in this process of building of support.
Even deputies do not restrict their activities to the Parliament.
There are a large number of organized interest groups in
Lebanon which are increasingly active and which tend to bring
pressure to bear on the Council of Ministers and the president
directly rather than on Parliament. Individuals and groups not in
Parliament (including heads of religious communities, big business and banking interests, labor unions, professional syndicates,
foreign embassies, etc.) are consulted and must be taken into
account when the president is building support. In extreme crises
there have been a number of cases when, in face of an impotent
Parliament, national congresses or advisory bodies have come
into being outside Parliament. They have attempted to settle
problems *in camera* because it has traditionally been impossible
to discuss fundamental social cleavages on the floor of the Chamber.[33]

The Political Role of Parliament

With all of the factors that limit the power of the Parliament, it
is nonetheless true that although the "legislature" may not be
very strong, the "Chamber of Deputies" has considerable
strength. Primarily, the Chamber's strength derives from the
president's concern for the balancing and managing of support
for his regime. In so doing, he must give constant attention to the
Chamber, the members of which are there because they have
demonstrated their strength. The president needs to satisfy at
least their minimal demands or he will be faced with a stalemate.

33. For a discussion of this tendency see Pierre Rondot, "L'Experience du
College Unique dans le Systeme Representatif Libanais," *Revue Française de
Science Politique*, VII (1957), 67–87.

In this fashion support is marshaled for the government of the day, and legitimacy, however tenuous, is maintained. For a long time, and to a considerable extent even today, the Lebanese have agreed to live together by living alone, i.e., through maintaining the primacy of religious communities whose interests have to be reconciled (not merged) at the national level. The system has not been built on consensus but on accommodation.[34]

The Chamber of Deputies is the main "transmission box" where the executive's need for political support and the society's demands are brought together, meshed, and harmonized. Of course, inexperienced or inept drivers (political leaders) clash the gears occasionally, but if there is enough oil and grease this usually can be avoided. From time to time it is necessary to change gears, to constitute a new combination—a new ratio—to enable the system to move ahead at a faster or slower rate. To push the analogy further, the Speaker of the Chamber is the "clutch" of the system. In the Lebanese case the critics maintain that although the Parliament (and the system as a whole) may well serve this harmonizing function, it only moves in the lowest gears.

The question arises whether this system of limiting conflict and maintaining the system is adequate to meet the demands of modernization and development. Heretofore in Lebanon this has been left to the private sector, which has made considerable progress. But two criticisms are directed at the progress made thus far. First, it has been uneven, in the sense that some have shared much more than others in the increasing social product. This has led to demands for broadening the public sector and responsibility. Second, this progress and the political system have been maintained at the expense of considerable inefficiency in the public service, not to mention the liberal amount of financial irregularity in government. If the government is to increase its activities and responsibilities, it will have to rationalize its procedures and operations to a much greater degree than has been the case in the past—a prospect that may well threaten the system-maintenance qualities of the political process.

34. For a brief but frank statement of this point of view see Nabil Noujaim, "Qu'attendre de la nouvelle assemblée?" *Le Jour*, February 28, 1968.

"Shihabism" (the effort of President Shihab to improve the administration and spread the social product more evenly) can be seen as a response to these demands. The establishment of a Ministry of Planning and a Civil Service Commission, the tightening of administrative controls, and the expansion of the public sector (development projects) are some of the ways in which this has expressed itself. Criticisms now center more and more on the Parliament as the redoubt of the traditional past. To strengthen the "legislative" and "control" functions (in the absence of large political parties, without a stronger commitment to the legitimacy of the Lebanese state, and with the continued attachment to religious communities) without stripping the gears of the transmission, will require the best of long-demonstrated Lebanese political skills and a minimum of stress from outside the system.

Chapter 8

The National Assembly in the Politics of Kenya

Newell M. Stultz

Introduction

The purpose of this paper is to assess the role of the national legislature, the National Assembly, in the politics of Kenya.[1] More precisely, I have tried to see what contributions the National Assembly may have made to political development in that country.

Kenya was selected as the site of this research for two reasons of theoretical interest. First, it was possible to study the impact upon the Kenyan Parliament of two decisions which have also been made in a number of the new African states, for in Kenya both decisions were made after the country had been independent for nearly one year. These were (1) the transformation of Kenya from a constitutional-monarchy on the Westminster model into a republic of presidential form, and (2) the abolition of the existing two-party system in favor of a single-party system. The second reason was that since independence in 1963, Kenya may be said to have been a "tutelary democracy," one of the several classes of political systems first identified as such by Edward Shils that have been common among the states of the so-called developing areas.[2] Thus while the conclusions of this research

1. Evidence for this paper was gathered during a visit to Kenya in 1966 made possible through the generosity of the Summer Stipend Committee of Brown University. Some of this material appears also in my article, "Parliament in a Tutelary Democracy: A Recent Case in Kenya," *Journal of Politics* (forthcoming).
2. Edward Shils, "Political Development in the New States," *Comparative Studies in Society and History*, II (1959–1960), 389 ff.

apply with reasonable certainty only to Kenya, it was hoped that
they might suggest the character of legislatures in other polities
with similar general features. Subsequent research on parliaments
in other new states of former British black Africa has, in fact,
justified this hope.[3]

The decision to study the national legislature in an African
tutelary democracy was, however, motivated primarily by curios-
ity. There has been a tendency to dismiss legislatures in such
political systems as relatively unimportant, and, indeed, they
have received little attention.[4] Shils, for example, writes that
parliamentary institutions in tutelary democracies are "weak" and
commonly dominated or discouraged by the executive, whereas
James Coleman suggests that they will be "relatively non-func-
tioning in the rule-making process."[5] David Apter, who prefers to
term such systems "neo-mercantilist," has written that the legislature in a neo-mercantilist system will act "largely in a consultative capacity."[6] But these references (to quote Coleman) are to
the "governmental" functions of legislatures; is it not possible that
they have value in other terms? Superficially, it would seem that
they do, since everywhere in Africa where constitutional government has survived a national legislature has been maintained,
even at considerable expense. In Kenya, for example, the cost of
the National Assembly in 1965–1966, although less than 1 per
cent of the annual budget, was greater than the cost of maintaining any one of six ministries. Even in those African countries
where parliament has been abolished following a military take-

3. See my "Parliaments in Former British Black Africa," *Journal of Developing Areas* (forthcoming).

4. Treatments in depth of African legislatures have been limited to single country studies, and on the whole these have made little attempt to relate the legislature to the larger political process. In addition to studies cited elsewhere in this study, the reader may wish to see J. M. Lee, "Parliament in Republican Ghana," *Parliamentary Affairs*, XVI, No. 4 (Autumn, 1963), 376–395; G. F. Engholm, "The Westminster Model in Uganda," *International Journal*, XVIII, No. 4 (Autumn, 1963), 468–487; William Tordoff, "Parliament in Tanzania," *Journal of Commonwealth Political Studies*, III, No. 2 (July, 1965), 85–103; and John P. Mackintosh, "The Nigerian Federal Parliament," *Public Law*, Autumn, 1963, pp. 333–361.

5. Shils, "Political Development in the New States," p. 389; and James S. Coleman, "Conclusions: The Political Systems of the Developing Areas," in *The Politics of Developing Areas*, ed. Gabriel A. Almond and James S. Coleman (Princeton, N.J., 1960), p. 568.

6. David E. Apter, *The Politics of Modernization* (Chicago, 1965), p. 414.

over, the military governors have construed this as but a temporary suspension. In Africa, as elsewhere, a national political life
without a parliament would appear unthinkable. Why should this
be?

There are, however, certain dangers in asserting at this point
the fact of a particular role for the National Assembly in Kenya
politics that needs to be mentioned. First, from the standpoint of
the present African government and the incumbent members of
Parliament, the institution is very new, and if only for this reason,
there can be little doubt that such a continuing role as the
National Assembly will, in time, assume is still in the process of
being worked out. The precursor in the colonial period of the
present National Assembly was the Legislative Council. It was
first established in 1906, but it was not until 1944 that an African,
E. W. Mathu, sat on the Council for the first time.[7] Mathu was an
appointed member; the first election of Africans to the Council
did not occur until 1957, although Whites in Kenya had, voting
communally, elected their own representatives as early as 1919.
At the beginning of 1960, less than four years before Kenya's
independence, there were only eighteen Africans on the Council
of forty-eight members. A *de facto* African majority was agreed
upon later in that year, at which time the size of the Council was
increased to sixty-five members. Still, non-Africans—Whites,
Asians, and Arabs—were guaranteed as many as thirty seats.
Parliament, as it was constituted at independence on December
12, 1963, came into being only six months earlier. At this time
three important changes were introduced: the legislature was
made bicameral; reserved seats for Kenya's racial minorities were
abolished; and the number of all representatives (including senators) elected directly by the people was nearly tripled. As a
result, only one-sixth of the members of both houses at independence had served in earlier Legislative Councils.[8] Kenya thus
gained independence with a Parliament substantially lacking in
established customs and traditions, or experience.

7. Two Asians had been appointed to the council in 1919, together with one
Arab.
8. Cherry Gertzel, "Parliament in Independent Kenya," *Parliamentary Affairs*,
XIX, No. 4 (Autumn, 1966), 488.

A second, though similar reason for caution relates to the political climate in Kenya. As in many African countries, politics in Kenya since independence has been changeable, and this condition has created uncertainty in Parliament. As we shall see, changing partisan alignments among M.P.'s have been reflected in variations in the character of parliamentary proceedings, but it is by no means clear how future political developments in Kenya will affect those patterns of parliamentary performance that can now be identified.

Politically, Kenya was divided at its independence in 1963 between two parties. The dominant party then as now was the Kenya African National Union (KANU), which as a result of the general election of June, 1963, held 80 per cent of the 129 seats in the House of Representatives and 64 per cent of the 41 seats in the Senate. KANU provided the government at independence and its leader, Jomo Kenyatta, African hero of Kenya's struggle for independence, became the first prime minister. When Kenya became a republic in December, 1964, Kenyatta became the country's first president.

Opposition to KANU in 1963 was from the Kenya African Democratic Union (KADU), which held the remaining seats in both chambers. The major purpose of KADU's opposition was the protection of Kenya's smaller, more rural, and less modern tribes against the feared intrusions of the larger tribes, particularly the Kikuyu and the Luo. In November, 1964, however, in the face of an impending reduction in the autonomous powers of Kenya's regional governments, the leadership of KADU determined that the interests of its followers would be better served from within the ruling party than from outside it. Accordingly, on November 10, KADU announced its own dissolution, and KADU supporters in both houses of Parliament joined KANU. Kenya thus became a "voluntary" one-party state.

KANU's absorption of KADU did not eliminate opposition to the ruling party, it "internalized" it.[9] The result was confusion

9. G. F. Engholm and Ali A. Mazrui, "Crossing the Floor and the Tensions of Representation in East Africa," *Parliamentary Affairs*, XXI, No. 2 (Spring, 1968), 146.

and disharmony within KANU which, as we shall see, was reflected on the floor of Parliament. In major part, this confusion and disharmony was the product of a power struggle between ex-KADU moderates in KANU and so-called radicals in the party. In the end the moderates proved victorious. Ronald Ngala, former Leader of the KADU Opposition, is now one of eight KANU vice-presidents and has entered the cabinet as Minister for Cooperatives and Social Services. Meanwhile, the radicals, including former Vice-President Oginga Odinga, have been driven out of the party. In April, 1966, these radicals organized themselves into a new party, the Kenya People's Union (KPU), and in the so-called little general election of June, 1966, KPU returned to Parliament seven M.P.'s and two senators.[10] Kenya is thus a rare example in Africa of a country that renounced a two-party system in favor of a single-party system only to return to it. The impact of these developments upon the functioning of Parliament, if not profound, has, at least, been unsettling.

In this decade the literature of political science and, in particular, the sub-field of political science known as comparative politics has been rich in elaborations of the concept of political development, however defined. As yet, however, the discipline lacks consensus on the meanings these words should carry; they stand more as a signal of topical interest than as a rigorous empirical tool.[11] It is not my purpose to contribute here to this ongoing debate, but rather merely to assert a definition of political development that governs the organization and interpretation of the data that follows. I understand political development to be exhibited by a political system that, without resorting to increasing levels of coercion, maintains support for its authoritative allocation of values within a context, or environment, of what Karl Deutsch has termed "social mobilization."[12] The reader will

10. David Koff, "Kenya's Little General Election," *Africa Report*, XI, No. 7 (October, 1966), 57–60.
11. For a summary of different approaches, see Robert A. Packenham, "Approaches to the Study of Political Development," *World Politics*, XVII, No. 1 (October, 1964), 108–120.
12. Karl Deutsch, "Social Mobilization and Political Development," *American Political Science Review*, IV, No. 3 (September, 1961), 493–514. It would seem unnecessary to defend the proposition which is assumed in this paper that contemporary Kenya does present a context of "social mobilization."

already have noted my borrowing from the works of David Easton on the analysis of "political systems."[13]

More concretely, I take it that the level of political development of a political system is a product of the capacity of that system in three areas, and it is in this light that the National Assembly in Kenya will be examined. The first is the capacity of the political system to reduce political cleavage in society, that is, to forestall the emergence of political demands. We shall consider how the legal competence, parliamentary norms, structure, and party organization of the National Assembly contribute to such reduction, or fail to do so. In particular, we shall examine the impact on the legislative process of the voluntary creation of a one-party state in Kenya in 1964. That decision was clearly intended to reduce the level of political demands articulated in Parliament through a union of political structures. We shall gauge the consequences of that decision in terms of this objective.

Second, there is the capacity of the political system to produce outputs that are responsive to demands that are made upon the system. Such outputs generate what Easton terms "specific support" for the system, that is, practical reasons for acceptance of the system by citizens. This process, to be successful, requires the transmission of information: to the "producers" of outputs on conditions in the country, and to the "consumers" of outputs on the nature of the outputs themselves. The outputs are decisions. We shall ask how successful is the National Assembly in Kenya in providing the executive and the public with the information necessary for effective decision-making, and what role does Parliament play in deciding what outputs will be produced?

Finally, there is the capacity of the political system to develop "diffuse support" for itself and to promote the legitimacy of the rulers and the political process independent of specific decisions in response to demands. How does the National Assembly in Kenya contribute to the development of this "diffuse support"? Indeed, does it? Answers to these and the foregoing questions

13. See particularly *A Systems Analysis of Political Life* (New York, 1965).

will, it is hoped, identify the place and the importance of the National Assembly in Kenya's political development.

Reduction of Cleavage

When using the word *cleavage* I mean simply political differences in such matters as attitudes, opinions, and preferences. Clearly, then, efforts at the reduction of cleavage among members of a population cannot be separated analytically from the generation of either specific or diffuse support. Cleavage burdens the production of outputs and limits their public acceptability once they are produced. However, the reduction of cleavage not only enhances the capacity of a political system to produce effective outputs, it also concurrently decreases its need to do so, for cleavage produces political demands. It is in the sense of cleavage as an "input" variable, rather than as a factor bearing on system "output," that it is considered separately here.

Depoliticizing Norms

One method of reducing stresses that are the product of cleavage in a political system is to place issues that are likely to generate basic divisions outside the normal framework of political dispute. Such issues may be said to be "depoliticized," and in many countries this is attempted in part through constitutional restraints upon the legislative process. Kenya is such a country.

None of the provisions of the Kenyan Constitution may be altered by ordinary legislation, and it should be noted that these provisions cover many topics that in other countries are not usually matters of fundamental law, such as parliamentary procedure, financial regulations, police, and land tenure.[14] Indeed, the Kenyan Constitution, consisting of 247 articles and 11 schedules, is among the world's longest. Two methods of constitutional amendment were initially provided. The more difficult applied to so-called specially entrenched provisions. These covered such

14. The basic document is *The Kenya Independence Order in Council, 1963,* Schedule 2, *The Constitution of Kenya.*

questions as citizenship, individual rights, and the judiciary, among others. A bill amending any of these provisions required a three-fourths vote in the lower house, but a nine-tenths majority in the Senate. The second method applied to all other provisions. Here an amending bill required the support of three-fourths of the members of both chambers, or, alternately, a simple majority in each house and a two-thirds majority at a public referendum. The amending process was changed in 1965, and in late 1966 the Senate itself was abolished. An amendment to any part of the Constitution now requires only a 65 per cent vote in the single chamber National Assembly. However, it must be noted that, although one party has dominated Kenyan politics, constitutional restraints on the legislative process have not limited political controversy. Indeed, the lessening of these restraints since 1963 would seem to indicate that the Kenyan government is not fully convinced of the need to contain the competence of the ordinary political process by legal means.

Issues may also be depoliticized by tacit agreement, and it is apparent that the government has sought by such agreement to eliminate open discussion of tribal differences from the National Assembly. At the opening of the first session of Parliament in 1963, a number of M.P.'s appeared in tribal dress, but they were criticized openly for doing so,[15] and since then non-Western dress has been all but eliminated from the National Assembly. Indeed, there is little direct discussion of tribal matters in Parliament, and when it is suspected, disapproving cries of "tribalism" can be heard from among the members. Still, one can scarcely discount the importance of tribal identifications in Kenyan politics.

Elimination of Expressive Structures

A major way of reducing cleavages resulting from intense social diversity, at least in principle, is a policy of deliberate social "homogenization" of the population. Easton rightly notes, however, that the record of such attempts "suggests that deliberate efforts to draw members of a system more closely together

15. Government of Kenya, House of Representatives, *Official Report*, I (Part I), July 18, 1963, col. 1140.

through measures of assimilation may be the least effective way of achieving an integrated system."[16] In fact, a more effective means of avoiding stress resulting from, in particular, cultural diversity likely lies in some form of institutional pluralism allowing a considerable measure of autonomy to self-contained cultural, linguistic, and/or religious subgroups.

This latter approach was adopted in Kenya at its independence with respect to the more important tribal divisions in that country. When it had become clear that Africans were to rule in Kenya, after the 1960 Lancaster House constitutional conference in London, the most pressing political issue became whether Kenya was to be a unitary or a federal state. It was at this time that the Kenya African Democratic Union was organized which, it will be recalled, appealed to minority tribes that feared Kikuyu-Luo dominance of the country. KADU favored what was termed (in Swahili) *majimbo*, or *regionalism*, a point of view that substantially carried at the next to last constitutional talks in London in 1962.

Kenya thus gained independence under a constitution that created, in addition to the organs of the central government, several regional governments, each enjoying a high degree of autonomy with respect to such matters as land rights, tribal questions, and the maintenance of local law and order. The guarantor of this autonomy was the Senate, the upper house of the Kenyan Parliament for, as we have seen, under the Constitution a bill altering the powers of the regions could not be passed unless it was supported by three-fourths of the members of both houses of Parliament, or by a simple majority in both houses, with the approval of a two-thirds majority at a public referendum. In the absence of a public referendum, therefore, eleven senators were sufficient to veto a bill encroaching upon the autonomy of the regions. The same proportion of all members in the lower house could also veto such a bill, but the composition of the Senate made a legislative veto there more likely than in the House of Representatives on any proposal limiting the powers of the regions. The Constitution provided that all forty-one senators be

16. Easton, *op. cit.*, p. 250.

elected directly from single-member constituencies, or districts. As drawn in 1963, the boundaries of these districts tended to create tribally homogeneous constituencies and, unlike the constituencies for the lower house, operated, as J. H. Proctor has pointed out, "to the advantage of the smaller and less advanced tribes, giving them more seats in the Senate than they could expect to receive on the basis of numbers alone."[17]

Despite the protection of the Senate, the autonomy of the regional governments was short-lived. In October, 1964, the government published a bill to amend the Constitution. Its most dramatic provision was that the country be transformed into a republic, but a considerable reduction in the independent powers of the regions was concurrently proposed. Failure of the Senate to pass the bill by the necessary three-fourths majority (a simple majority was assured) would have forced a public referendum— a contest the government felt confident it could win by the required margin. Thus faced with the inevitability of the bill's enactment and the erosion of KADU's political base which would surely follow, the opposition voluntarily dissolved itself. The constitutional amendment then passed the Senate, forty-one votes to zero. Efforts at constitutional unity in Kenya had seemed to precipitate partisan unity as well.

The passing of "regionalism" in Kenya eliminated the foremost justification for the existence of the Senate, and immediately pressure commenced for its abolition.[18] Although it was true that the upper house retained a unique constitutional role as the primary guardian of the "especially entrenched" clauses of the Constitution, it was not supposed that these were likely to be threatened. Nor, for that matter, was it widely accepted that the Senate was more qualified for that role than the House of Representatives, or, indeed, even as well qualified. As regards other possible contributions of the Senate, e.g., checking legislation, educating the public, or promoting the interests of the regions, the record of the Senate had cast doubt upon its utility.[19] More-

17. J. H. Proctor, "The Role of the Senate in the Kenya Political System," *Parliamentary Affairs*, XVIII, No. 4 (Autumn, 1965), 394.
18. The constitutional powers of the regions were further reduced in 1965.
19. Proctor, *op. cit.*, pp. 397 ff.

over, from the standpoint of President Kenyatta, the division of Parliament into a House and a Senate was an artificial and unnecessary source of cleavage in Kenyan politics.[20] It was thus not surprising that at the end of 1966 the Senate was permanently dissolved and its members absorbed into an enlarged House of Representatives, now renamed the National Assembly. (Concurrently, the parliamentary elections due in 1968 were postponed until 1970.)

Union of Political Structures

The dissolution of the parliamentary opposition in November, 1964, is, of course, an obvious and dramatic example of an attempt to reduce political cleavage in Kenya through a union of political structures. Unlike the Opposition United Party in Ghana which was outlawed at a public referendum in 1964, the dissolution of KADU was voluntary. Still, although the government had given grudging recognition to the rights of KADU as the parliamentary opposition, considerable pressure had been brought on individual members of KADU to join KANU, and Kenyatta himself had taken few pains to disguise his predilection for a one-party state in the interests of national unity.

Analytically, the dissolution of KADU in late 1964 is particularly interesting, for through an examination of the proceedings of the National Assembly it may be possible to calculate the extent to which this event resulted in (or coincided with, if we are to avoid the suggestion of causality) greater consensus in Parliament. For convenience, we shall limit our concern to recorded roll call votes in the House of Representatives, by far the more important of the two chambers. Between December 13, 1963, and December 1, 1964, the House divided seven times, excluding two divisions required under the Constitution. Over these divisions the average Rice Index of Cohesion for the whole House was 41.4.[21] In contrast, between December 14, 1964, and October 22, 1965, the House divided six times, excluding two

20. *East African Standard*, February 16, 1967.
21. For discussion of the Rice Index of Cohesion, see Lee F. Anderson, Meredith W. Watts, Jr., and Allen R. Wilcox, *Legislative Roll-Call Analysis* (Evanston, Ill., 1966), pp. 32–35.

required divisions. Over these divisions, the average Rice Index of Cohesion was 39.9. By this indicator, then, it would seem that there was not in 1965, in the absence of KADU, greater consensus in the House of Representatives than there had been in 1964 when KADU had constituted the official opposition.

In 1964, over the seven roll-call votes mentioned above, the average Rice Index of Cohesion for KANU was 71.2. Comparing this figure with the average Rice Index of Cohesion for the House as a whole in 1965, given above, it is obvious that the inception of one-party politics in Kenya in November, 1964, rather than elimi-nating opposition from the House, internalized it in the ruling party, as has been said. But greater disunity within KANU in 1965 was not, as one might suppose, simply a direct consequence of the new membership in KANU of former opposition M.P.'s. If we exclude from the calculations for 1965 all KADU M.P.'s at the time of the dissolution of that party, the average Rice Index of Cohesion for the remaining segment of KANU in 1965 is 29.1, even lower than that for the House as a whole. In fact, the over-all level of support for the Government manifested in 1965 roll-call votes was not significantly lower among ex-KADU M.P.'s than among those who were members of KANU in 1964.

Actually, 1965 roll-call votes in the House of Representatives understate the absence of political consensus in Parliament at that time, for many of the backbenchers who accepted the govern-ment whip at formal divisions of the House felt free to speak against programs of the government in House debates and, in-deed, voted against the Government in unrecorded voice votes. In fact, the political independence of KANU in Parliament dur-ing the time Kenya was a one-party state was one of the cardinal features of the National Assembly and frequently has been com-mented upon by observers.[22]

The reasons that account for this "undisciplined" behavior of backbenchers are several and varied. One has been the obvious frustration of backbenchers at what they have perceived to be their impotence in the decision-making process in Kenya. We

22. See, for example, John Spencer, "Kenyatta's Kenya," *Africa Report,* XI, No. 5 (May, 1966), 8.

shall return to this point later. A second reason has been the absence of rewards for faithfulness to the government or, more importantly, stringent penalties for opposition. In particular, nomination of KANU party candidates has usually been beyond the effective control or influence of the national organs of the party. Nor has the party been able to render much assistance to those who were nominated. Indeed, in January, 1966, John Keen, the organizing secretary of the party, conceded in an open letter to Kenyatta that the party was insolvent.[23] But if the KANU M.P. has not been able to rely upon support from the party center for his political security, neither have most been able to depend upon their personal control of the local party machinery for continuance in office. Cherry Gertzel has pointed out that the basic unit of KANU, the branch, has been organized at the district level rather than at the level of the individual House constituency.[24] As a result, the individual M.P. has had to compete with several other M.P.'s and one Senator for the leadership of his local KANU branch, and reports of the defeat of M.P.'s in branch elections have not been uncommon. Thus most M.P.'s, unable to control their constituency party machinery, have had to develop local reputations to ensure their political security, and in Kenya, as elsewhere, a local reputation is ordinarily more likely to be built attacking the government rather than defending it. Undoubtedly to remedy this situation, the government enacted legislation in 1968 requiring candidates for election to Parliament to have the endorsement of the leader of a registered party.

There are some obvious exceptions to the statement that the government has been unable to reward loyal backbenchers, and these need to be mentioned. The prospect of holding cabinet and sub-cabinet positions clearly has been an inducement to cooperate with the government, and an awareness of this was certainly a factor in the creation of nineteen new ministerial posts and assistant minister positions between June, 1963, and the middle of 1966. A study by Jay E. Hakes of the voting records of twenty-six ministers and assistant ministers appointed after June, 1963, con-

23. *Ibid.*, p. 6.
24. Gertzel, "Parliament in Independent Kenya," p. 499.

cluded that as backbenchers most had shown greater loyalty to the government than had their colleagues from among whom they were chosen.[25] The salaries attached to these positions are among their obvious attractions. Members of Parliament earn an annual salary of £1,200, whereas ministers earn £3,550 and an assistant minister is paid £2,260 per annum.

Less conspicuous but nonetheless real patronage has been that involved in the appointment by the government of M.P.'s to paid positions on various statutory bodies, such as the Export Promotion Council and the Kenya National Trading Corporation. And in 1966 it was revealed that in several instances the government had garanteed private loans made to M.P.'s for the purchase of automobiles.[26] In April, 1966, responding to the resignations from KANU of nine senators and twenty-two M.P.'s (including the vice-president and two ministers) and their subsequent formation of the Kenya People's Union, the government pushed through Parliament an amendment to the Constitution requiring legislators who resign their party affiliations to resign also their seats and fight by-elections if they wish to remain in the National Assembly. This measure is clearly an attempt at structural reduction of political cleavage; it will be recalled that no such action was required of KADU M.P.'s joining the government in November, 1964. Still, so long as a government backbencher has not resigned from his party, the principal penalty for his failure to support the national leadership in the past would appear to have been limited to the withholding from him of the positive rewards of political support indicated above.

A third reason for the independence of government backbenchers in 1965 was that with KADU dissolved, M.P.'s who criticized policies of the cabinet were no longer open to the charge that they were aiding the opposition. Gertzel has noted that with the re-establishment of a formal opposition in June,

25. Jay E. Hakes, "Recruitment of Ministers from the Kenya Parliament 1963–1966" (unpublished term paper, Department of Political Science, Duke University, 1968), p. 18.
26. *East African Standard*, May 12, 1966.

1966, there was, at least initially, a noticeable decline in attacks upon the government from KANU backbenchers.[27]

Finally, we note again that the dissolution of KADU in 1964 strengthened "moderate" elements in KANU and set off a power struggle between those elements and "radicals" for control of the party. This struggle, which lasted for a period of approximately eighteen months until the formation of KPU, has been treated at length elsewhere.[28] The point to be made here is that throughout this prolonged period of internal crisis in KANU, the effective organization of KANU backbenchers in Parliament was impossible. Members of Parliament report that communication at this time between the Cabinet and KANU backbenchers as a group virtually ceased, in part due to the uncertainty that existed as to the extent and source of any leader's political support. The function of the KANU party whip at this time was limited to ensuring that sufficient M.P.'s were on hand at the time of mandatory divisions on constitutional amendments, but little attention was paid to how an M.P. might vote once he had been "whipped" onto the floor.

Representation

As Easton has observed, representative structures can be an important mechanism for the reduction of cleavage. Not only does representation enable groups to obtain access to some of the authority roles, it also "provides those who are affiliated with groups an opportunity to meet each other in a common forum so as to undertake negotiations to discover . . . the extent to which reconciliation of points of view and demands is feasible."[29] How far representational structures do reduce cleavage would seem to be related to (a) the extent to which all relevant groups are represented, (b) how proportionate that representation is to the political importance of each group, and (c) the standing of

---

27. Cherry J. Gertzel, "Kenya's Constitutional Changes," *East African Journal,* III, No. 9 (December, 1966), 25.
28. See, for example, Spencer, *op. cit.,* and Special Correspondent, "The Changing Face of Kenya Politics," *Transition,* V, No. 25 (February, 1966), 44–50.
29. Easton, *op. cit.,* p. 252.

"representatives" among those with whom they are ostensibly linked. Until the general election of 1963, Africans in Kenya held that their representation in the Legislative Council (and the Executive Council) was deficient in one or more of these respects, and, far from helping to reduce cleavage, African representation was in fact a source of political discord. This issue was finally closed, however, with the adoption (though over the fervent opposition of some members of Kenya's racial minorities) of a "one man, one vote" franchise in the independence Constitution of 1963.

Africans have in the main equated the electoral principle of "one man, one vote" with the achievement of representative democracy, but the application of this principle in Kenya has not resulted in proportionate representation for all groups, nor even in electoral equality among citizens. This latter shortcoming has resulted from the manner in which constituencies were delimitated in 1963. Mention has been made of the fact that the drawing of Senate districts in 1963 favored the smaller tribes. A similar bias has been said to have characterized the delimitation of the 117 singlemember House constituencies. In an extreme instance, 749 registered voters in Baringo East had an electoral weight equal to 47,017 voters in Nakuru East. In general, however, variations among constituencies with respect to the number of registered voters were less great and did not result in 1963 in a marked distortion of the preferences of the African electorate in the National Assembly, as some had feared it might.[30]

The first "one man, one vote" election in 1963 did fail, however, to return any Whites to Parliament, and only two Asians were elected. On the basis of numbers alone, this is about what one might have expected. In 1963 there were some 65,000 Whites and 180,000 Asians in a total population nearing nine million persons. But clearly these racial minorities, due to their capital, skills, and connections, were politically relevant far beyond what their numbers would suggest. This appears to have been appreciated by the African government. After the general election of 1963, two

30. Clyde Sanger and John Nottingham, "The Kenya General Election of 1963," *Journal of Modern African Studies*, II, No. 1 (March, 1964), 35.

additional Asians and three Whites were brought into the House among the twelve "specially elected" members.

The institution of specially elected members is a carry-over from the last years of the colonial period. Specially elected seats on the Legislative Council (later termed *national seats*) were first created in 1958. There were twelve such seats, and they were filled by the other members of the Council—Africans, Whites, Asians, and Arabs—sitting as an electoral college. Of the persons so elected, four had to be African, four White, and four Asian. The intention was to encourage persons to develop political support outside their own racial groups, which could be seen as a step, however limited, toward a universal franchise.[31] By 1963 a universal franchise was in operation, but the specially elected members were kept in the lower house, although the requirement of racial parity was abolished and the number of such seats was made variable—up to one-eleventh of all seats. Among other purposes, the specially elected seats have allowed, as we have seen, for representation in Parliament of racial minorities that otherwise might not be represented. Such a mechanism, it should be noted, does not guarantee the status of specially elected Asian and White M.P.'s within their own racial communities, and, indeed, those Asians and Whites who have secured seats in Parliament in this manner appear to be regarded less as representatives by persons of their race than as mavericks. In 1968 the Constitution was amended so that in the future specially elected members will be the direct nominees of the president, another example of the desire of the Kenyan executive for firmer control over the legislature.

Analysis of the representational character of governmental structures need not be limited to those structures that are formally required to have such a character. Cabinets (as well as, for example, judiciaries and bureaucracies) can be examined for their representativeness and should be, for the representative quality of these institutions may also contribute to the reduction of cleavage. In his previously cited paper, Jay E. Hakes has

31. George Bennett and Carl Rosberg, *The Kenyatta Election: Kenya, 1960–1961* (London, 1961), p. 14.

considered the Kenyan cabinet as a representative body. Because
of the close organic and political relationship between cabinet
and Parliament in Kenya—a relationship typical of governments
patterned on the Westminster model—it is pertinent to review
Hakes's findings here.

Hakes wished to compare the distribution of tribal affiliations
within the total population of Kenya and among members of the
cabinet, tribes being assumed to be important social referents. It
was not possible, however, always to identify the tribal affiliations
of specific individuals. Hakes, therefore, took as his critical variable provincial identification. Some desired information was lost
thereby, for provincial boundaries do not coincide exactly with
tribal divisions. On the other hand, provincial identifications are
not irrelevant to tribal questions, for the boundaries of Kenya's
provinces were drawn so that major tribes would not be mixed
together in a single province.

Comparisons were made at three different times: June, 1963;
January, 1965; and May, 1966. These comparisons show that over
a period of three years the Kenyan cabinet became steadily more
representative of the provincial distribution of the population.
Indeed, after President Kenyatta expanded his cabinet in May,
1966, in response to the formation of the Kenya People's Union,
the cabinet reflected more accurately the provincial distribution
of the Kenyan population than did the House as a whole.[32] This
had not been the case previously; an apparent increase in political cleavage thus coincided with greater geographic and tribal
balance in the cabinet.

This greater balance was certainly deliberate, as the following
illustration that has been noted by Hakes attests.[33] Central and
Southern Nyanza are two districts in southwestern Kenya where
more than one million persons and the bulk of the important Luo
tribe live. In April, 1966, two ministers and three backbenchers
from these districts resigned from KANU and joined KPU, leaving three KANU ministers and six KANU backbenchers from
these sections. When President Kenyatta decided to respond to
the formation of KPU by enlarging his cabinet in May, it was

32. Hakes, *op. cit.,* p. 23.   33. *Ibid.,* pp. 24–25.

necessary for the president to recruit half of the remaining KANU backbenchers from these districts if geographical balance in the cabinet were to be maintained. This was done even though it brought into the cabinet individuals whose voting records showed less loyalty to the government than backbenchers generally. Party loyalty, usually an important factor in the recruitment of cabinet ministers was on this occasion seemingly less important than securing geographic and tribal balance in the government.

Generation of Specific Support

Despite efforts to reduce cleavage, political differences in society are never wholly eliminated. These differences result in political demands, and the manner in which a political system responds to demands made upon it offers possibly the best grounds for evaluating that system. Here we consider the production of satisfactions (in response to demands) that generate specific support for the system. In this, we have said, parliament can serve two functions: it can inform and it can decide. Parliament can inform the authorities of public demands and of reactions to earlier political outputs, and it can inform the public of the decisions of the authorities. Further, parliament can participate authoritatively in the making of these decisions. We shall consider both contributions as they have been made by the National Assembly in Kenya.

Provision of Information

On December 14, 1964, President Kenyatta offered the most precise definition then available of the role of the individual Kenyan legislator, as seen by the executive. Speaking before a joint meeting of both houses of Parliament, the president asserted that "Members of Parliament must serve as a bridge between Government and people," representing to the Government the views of their constituents and then interpreting to their people the policies and decisions of the Government.[34] But by then it was

34. Republic of Kenya, House of Representatives, *Official Report*, IV, col. 5.

already clear that not all M.P.'s entirely shared this conception of their role. As early as June, 1964, Tom Mboya, then Minister for Justice and Constitutional Affairs, expressed the fear that if the January, 1964, ban on all public meetings were lifted, government backbenchers and even KANU party officials might try to undermine the government.[35] After the dissolution of KADU in November, 1964, a few individual backbenchers openly disavowed any duty to promote government policies among their constituents. "Elected MPs owe their loyalty to the people who elected them" and should not, in a one-party state, "be made accountable for the achievements and failures of the Government," opined Luke Obok, M.P., in a speech to a meeting of the International Press Institute in Nairobi on March 21, 1965.[36] Informed observers report that, in fact, only a small minority of M.P.'s have been active among their constituents.

This inaction of M.P.'s is evident in the government's repeated appeals for assistance. On November 2, 1965, President Kenyatta, addressing Parliament, reiterated and strengthened his earlier statement of the responsibilities of M.P.'s. The following excerpts from this address underline the president's concern:

The Members of Parliament do not simply have a narrow responsibility to their constituents. They have an over-riding duty to the State. Each Member is a link, binding the Republic to the people. And in each direction there is an obligation both to guide and lead.

Each Member must understand the position of the Government, and strengthen the whole institution of Parliament in the eyes of the people.

Members of this Parliament have a most important duty in the rural areas, to urge their people to follow the advice of technicians. . . . We must all work together to capture their imagination, and to see that they are interested and trained.[37]

In January, 1966, the KANU Parliamentary Group called upon all M.P.'s to help mobilize public opinion behind the decisions of the

35. *East African Standard,* June 1, 1964.
36. *Daily Nation,* March 22, 1965.
37. Republic of Kenya, House of Representatives, *Official Report,* VII, cols. 7–8, 13–14.

government.[38] And in the following May, in the course of his written introduction to the government's new *Development Plan 1966–1970*, the president declared that "in order to mobilize the people for the long struggle against poverty, misery and disease, all organizations must take part. . . . In particular, Party servants, Members of Parliament and Government servants must work together and in harmony."[39] It appears, however, that far from supporting the government's programs, those M.P.'s who have been active among their constituents have often attacked the government. John Spencer points out that, early in 1965, the president sought to control such criticism by requiring that all M.P.'s obtain the permission of the administration before addressing any public meeting, even in their own constituencies.[40]

The proceedings of Parliament themselves present an opportunity to inform the country of the thinking and decisions of the government, and a close reading of parliamentary speeches makes clear that the president and his ministers do regard the National Assembly as a valuable public forum from which to announce and defend their policies and that they contrive to obtain parliamentary time with this in mind. One of several means available for securing parliamentary time is that of offering a motion for debate. According to figures compiled by Gertzel, 211 motions (excluding motions for adjournment) were debated in the House of Representatives between June, 1963, and the end of April, 1966. Of these, nearly half—ninety-eight—had been introduced on behalf of the government.[41]

The accuracy of the assumption that the Kenyan public is aware of parliamentary debates is difficult to assess, but on limited evidence the assumption seems valid. These proceedings are reported in considerable depth in local newspapers; and the State-owned radio, the Voice of Kenya, does broadcast in both English and Swahili daily summaries of debates in the National Assembly. A high quality Hansard is printed and sold by the government printer; however, its considerable price likely keeps

38. *East African Standard*, January 6, 1966.
39. Republic of Kenya, *Development Plan, 1966–1970* p. v.
40. John Spencer, *op. cit.*, p. 8.
41. Gertzel, "Parliament in Independent Kenya," p. 504.

circulation down. The daily rush for tickets to the public galleries would seem an indication of an attentive public. These galleries, which seat 600 to 700 persons, are regularly filled at 2:30 P.M., the customary time of commencement of meetings of Parliament on weekdays. In contrast, there was little public interest in attending meetings of the Senate before it was abolished.

Just as the Kenyan populace learns little about its government from the individual activities of ordinary M.P.'s, so, too, the government gets little information from M.P.'s about the feelings of the people or their reactions to government programs. For such information on conditions in the country, the government appears to rely primarily upon the civil service and the police. Despite lengthy sessions—90 to 100 days per year—and comparatively free and open debate, M.P.'s make little systematic attempt to represent public opinion in Parliament. Moreover, it seems necessary to note that Parliamentary debates generally are remarkably uninformative and evidence a lack of expertise among nearly all persons who are not in the cabinet. Members of Parliament appear content to speak from their own direct, but limited personal experience and often, it seems, spontaneously, in reaction to initiatives of the government. The absence of continuing communication between M.P.'s and their constituents, previously mentioned, is one explanation for this behavior. A second is that Kenya lacks, as Lucian Pye asserts most non-Western countries lack, lobbyists who, were they to exist, might serve to educate legislators on behalf of circumstances and conditions as well as interests external to Parliament.[42] A final point is that a considerable number of these demands that *are* articulated in Parliament pertain not to the direct interests of the public but to the interests of the legislators qua legislators; in Easton's terms these are "within-puts." We shall return to this point shortly.

Demands and what Easton terms "information feedback," i.e., the response of the public to earlier outputs, could, of course, be generated by persons within the National Assembly. The standing orders provide for the appointment of select committees to

42. Lucian W. Pye, "The Non-Western Political Process," *Journal of Politics,* XX, No. 3 (August, 1958), 485.

investigate and report on various matters, one possible means for generating new information. To 1966, however, a select committee had been appointed only once, in 1965, to investigate alleged instances of misconduct on the part of two M.P.'s. Nor have individual M.P.'s succeeded in generating new information on their own. This is not surprising; individual M.P.'s have no staffs, nor, indeed, do they have offices, and the research facilities of the small parliamentary library are meager. Members of Parliament have added to the fund of public political "intelligence," to use Harold Lasswell's term, in but one significant way. Through their numerous questions to the government (more than twenty per sitting-day in the House in 1965) and the introduction of private member's motions, backbenchers have compelled the government on frequent occasions to reveal facts of its administration and to discuss matters which, Gertzel states, "the Government would have preferred to have had less publicly debated."[43] Such pressure has not contributed to the net amount of information possessed by the government; it has, however, increased the amount of information available to the Kenyan citizenry.

Decision-making

Open criticism of the government by its own backbenchers is a feature of numerous African parliaments and has been justified as a modern manifestation of the traditional African mode of building consensus for public policy. President Julius Nyerere of Tanzania, for example, has written: " 'They talk till they agree.' That gives you the very essence of traditional African democracy. It is rather a clumsy way of conducting affairs, . . . but discussion is one essential factor of any democracy; and the African is expert at it."[44] On December 14, 1964, President Kenyatta spoke similarly while defining the role of the Kenya House of Representatives:

What this house must contribute to the Republic is something far more than just machinery which can give the plans or requirements of

43. Gertzel, "Parliament in Independent Kenya," p. 492.
44. Julius Nyerere, "The African and Democracy," *Independent Black Africa,* ed. William John Hanna (Chicago, 1964), p. 523.

the Government their lawful status. This must be our forum, for discussion and proposal, for question, objection or advice. It must give full modern expression to the traditional African custom, by serving as the place where the elders and the spokesmen of the people are expected and enabled to confer.[45]

There is, however, one difficulty in accepting this interpretation of the National Assembly in Kenya. Debates in Parliament have not always resulted in agreement and consensus, in a synthesis of opposing views. In particular, such demands as are articulated by M.P.'s in Parliament have not, as Gertzel points out, resulted in changes in the policies of the government, although they have occasionally led to minor modifications in proposed measures.[46]

Members of Parliament might be supposedly capable of influencing legislation privately, but this is not known to have occurred to a significant extent. The KANU parliamentary caucus under the party constitution is not a policy-making organ, and, in any case, its meetings have been infrequent. Nor have legislators been able to lobby cabinet ministers. Indeed, on February 8, 1966, a motion for adjournment of the House of Representatives raised the difficulties of M.P.'s in gaining access to ministers and others in high office and the disrespect M.P.'s had allegedly suffered from subordinate officers when they had sought such access.[47] Particularly revealing is a flow-diagram of "How a Bill becomes a Law in the Kenya Republic" which appears as Appendix VI of *A Guide to the Constitutional Development of Kenya,* a publication of the Kenya Institute of Administration, the official training center for Kenya civil servants. According to this diagram, M.P.'s have no role in the discussion of legislation prior to its drafting and official introduction in Parliament. Thus, in the absence of parliamentary legislative initiatives—between 1963 and 1968 no private member's bill was introduced in Parliament —the law-making role of the National Assembly has been limited to the ratification of decisions taken elsewhere. During this same period, Parliament did not fail to enact a measure that was desired by the government.

45. Republic of Kenya, House of Representatives, *Official Report,* IV, col. 4.
46. Gertzel, "Parliament in Independent Kenya," p. 499.
47. Republic of Kenya, House of Representatives, *Official Report,* VIII, col. 637.

Legislators in Kenya have thus been comparatively unimportant in the decision-making process, and this has been an obvious source of frustration among M.P.'s and yet another cause of the independence of government backbenchers, previously identified. The most dramatic example of this independence occurred on June 18, 1964. On that date, KANU backbenchers joined KADU M.P.'s in the House of Representatives in passing, over the strenuous opposition of the cabinet, a motion calling upon the government to submit "Instruments" for an East African federation for ratification by Parliament within two months.[48] Backbench opposition to the cabinet has been most general, however, on questions of the status of M.P.'s, rather than on national policy issues. Four of the nine divisions of the House of Representatives in 1965 had to do with matters directly related to the prerogatives of M.P.'s *vis-à-vis* the executive, and on March 4, 1966, backbenchers voted to adjourn the House of Representatives early in protest against the absence of any members of the cabinet in the chamber.[49] Indeed, legislative support for the policies of the Kenyan government has appeared dependent less upon the perceived merit of these policies than upon the respect accorded the dignity and function of ordinary M.P.'s by the executive in the process of decision-making.

In addition to their legislative powers, M.P.'s have conciliar control over the executive to the extent that they can turn out a Government. Although Gertzel has written that "the first amendment to the Constitution, which established the Republic, radically altered the position of the executive by providing for a President who is both Head of state and Head of Government,"[50] the actual relationship is not greatly different from that which existed previously between Parliament and the prime minister. The president must be elected to the National Assembly from a single constituency, and he remains an M.P. with a vote even after he becomes president. The Constitution prescribes that the

48. Government of Kenya, House of Representatives, *Official Report*, III (Part I), col. 352.
49. Republic of Kenya, House of Representatives, *Official Report*, VIII, cols. 1745–1746.
50. Gertzel, "Parliament in Independent Kenya," p. 486.

cabinet, including the president, shall be responsible, collectively, to the National Assembly, and in the event of a deadlock between the executive and the legislature, the president must resign or dissolve Parliament and call for new elections. Ministers are appointed by the president who acts unilaterally, although they must be M.P.'s themselves.

Although the president is dependent upon a majority of the National Assembly for continuation in office, his election is always significantly by the popular vote of the electorate. (In 1964 the law stipulated that the Kenya prime minister at the establishment of the Republic on December 12 automatically became the new president.) This election is governed by regulations that make it likely, although not inevitable, that a president elected at a general election will have the support of a majority in Parliament, at least at the outset of his tenure.[51] However, until June, 1968, if a president died, or resigned without having dissolved Parliament, the National Assembly had the right to sit as an electoral college for the purpose of electing his successor. Now that right has been taken away; in the event of the death or resignation of the president, the vice president (a presidential nominee) may serve as acting president for a period up to ninety days, until a presidential election can be held. This constitutional change is undoubtedly linked to the increasing age of President Kenyatta, (who is thought to have been born in 1893) and his desire that any successor not lose authority to the legislature in the process of his election to office.

Generation of Diffuse Support

Diffuse support for a political system is attachment to the objects of that system for their own sake. "Except in the long

51. At the time of a general election, every candidate for election to the National Assembly is obliged to declare his support for one of those who have been nominated for president. Presidential candidates must also seek election to Parliament. On election day every elector casts a single vote, but it is counted twice: once for M.P. and once for president. The victorious presidential candidate is that person who is both elected to the National Assembly and receives more votes for president than any other candidate also elected to the National Assembly. Presidential elections may be necessary at times other than general elections. When such an election occurs, all candidates must be sitting M.P.'s.

run," Easton writes, "diffuse support is independent of the effects of daily outputs. It consists of a reserve of support that enables a system to weather the many storms when 'outputs cannot be balanced off against inputs of demands."[52] Obviously, the generation of diffuse support is particularly critical for the so-called new nations whose capacities for the development of specific support are usually highly restricted.

The inculcation in citizens of a belief in the legitimacy of the decisions, personnel, and institutions of government is a common means of generating diffuse support for the political system. In this process the role of parliament is usually central. Parliament is able to convey legitimacy because parliament is widely seen as possessing legitimacy, but the sources of that legitimacy need not be the same in every case.

In general, there are three sources of legitimacy: structural, personal, and ideological.[53] The first of these has little importance in Kenya, for as was pointed out early in this paper, neither history nor tradition validate the existence of the National Assembly as a political agency. Looking at the outside of the Senate chamber, the old Legislative Council, in 1966, a young M.P. observed to the writer that the building was "a sacred place, for it was there that the old men won our independence." The reference was to the building, however, not to the processes that had gone on within it; most African nationalists in Kenya believe that independence was won in spite of the mechanisms of colonial rule, not through them. Few in Kenya would argue for political continuity for its own sake. Indeed, much of the legitimacy of the institutions of the Kenya government lies in their departure from what went before, and if a structure can be traced back unchanged to the colonial period, that continuity may be dysfunctional for the creation of legitimacy. It seems relevant to note that at independence in 1963 most of the relics of the colonial years in the National Assembly building were systematically removed.

The personal authority—charisma—of President Kenyatta is doubtless of inestimable value for the legitimization of Kenya politics, but its value for the legitimization of the National Assembly specifically would seem minor, although it is certainly pres-

52. Easton, *op. cit.*, p. 273.   53. *Ibid.*, p. 287.

ent. As prime minister in 1964, Kenyatta appeared irregularly in
the House of Representatives and made only five policy statements. As president, he has appeared in the National Assembly
even less frequently, and then always in his presidential role,
although, as we have said, he remains an ordinary elected member with the right to participate directly in its proceedings. It has
been asserted privately that the president is not a polished parliamentarian and feels awkward in the give-and-take of parliamentary debate. Moreover, a leader whose statue is immediately
outside the members' entry and proclaims him the "Father of the
Nation" can perhaps be expected to wish to avoid the necessity of
answering, immediately and publicly, criticism of his administration on matters which are both significant and trivial. The standing of the National Assembly among the public unquestionably is
enhanced somewhat by virtue of the occasional appearance and
participation by the president, but it is also likely true that the
president's own standing would be eroded were that participation more frequent.

Indeed, Gertzel notes that the absence of the president from
the National Assembly has had the result of establishing in the
minds of many M.P.'s a distinction between the Government,
represented by ordinary ministers, and the executive, represented
by the president.[54] This distinction, which is unfounded in the
Constitution and unreal in the actual process of decision-making,
has, nevertheless, helped to make it possible for M.P.'s to profess
complete loyalty to the president while objecting strenuously to
particular policies of the government. The behavior of the president in this respect has de-emphasized the principle of collective
responsibility of the cabinet and has encouraged criticism of his
ministers individually. Concurrently, however, this behavior has
worked to keep criticism specific in character rather than general,
i.e., of the government as a whole, and hence has contained it.

The single most important source of the legitimacy of the
National Assembly is ideological. By reason of its legal compe-
tence and the character of its membership and recruitment, the
National Assembly validates the realization in Kenya of two prin-

54. Gertzel, "Parliament in Independent Kenya," p. 501.

ciples that are regarded as moral absolutes: national independence ("Uhuru") and popular government. "This Parliament," said President Kenyatta on December 14, 1964, "gives form and expression to the heart and mind of Kenya's people."[55]

Interestingly, no attempt appears to have been made to employ the concept of "African Personality" in Kenya as a legitimizing doctrine, as has been done in other African countries, notably Tanzania and (formerly) Ghana. In part, this failure can be seen in the typically western dress of legislators, previously mentioned, and in the exclusive use of English as the language of the National Assembly. (The government is, however, committed to the eventual introduction of Swahili in Parliament.) Also, it seems noteworthy that the government and M.P.'s accepted a white settler, Mr. Humphrey Slade, as Speaker of the House of Representatives in 1963 and did not insist that an African be in this prominent position. Moreover, the Deputy-Speaker, Dr. F. R. S. DeSouza, is an Asian.

As ideas give legitimacy to the National Assembly, so, too, the National Assembly is used to give added legitimacy to ideas (as well as to more specific decisions). This is particularly evident regarding the government's plans for the development of Kenya. Three diverse illustrations may suffice: The most comprehensive statement of the Government's over-all development strategy is the document entitled "African Socialism and its Application to Planning in Kenya." It was published as (parliamentary) Sessional Paper No. 10 of 1963–1965 and submitted by the President to the National Assembly for debate and approval. Second, the extension of the National Assembly building in 1964–1965 provided a convenient opportunity for the incorporation of distinctive symbols into the physical structure of Parliament. On the exterior of the new addition, twelve very large figures in stone frieze now suggest the Kenya national motto, *Harambee,* meaning "pull together" in Swahili. Finally, one notes the concern of the president that M.P.'s individually set an example of sober and industrious living, with particular attention to the development of the land in their home constituencies. "If when your work in

55. Republic of Kenya, House of Representatives, *Official Report,* IV, col. 3.

Nairobi is finished," Kenyatta has told M.P.'s, "you want to sleep in Nairobi, you want to run around and see the sights, you will be a vagabond. Your membership in Parliament will have no value."[56] The value referred to is clearly that of an instrument cabable of legitimizing new social norms.

Conclusions

This analysis of the National Assembly in Kenya bears out the suggestions of Shils, Coleman, and Apter quoted at the beginning of this paper that its "governmental" functions would be relatively unimportant. Nevertheless, Parliament in Kenya has to some extent performed "political" functions, notably in the reduction of cleavage, the ventilation of grievances and, more especially, the legitimization of the political system. These functions have not been anticipated—although not excluded—in prior considerations of the general system type; they are, however, important in the process of political development.

But the contributions of the National Assembly to the political development of Kenya may not be entirely positive. Apter has written that every type of political system is a particular mixture of the two reciprocal "functional requisites of government," information and coercion, which vary so as to maintain the symbolic and sanctional aspects of authority, i.e., legitimacy. Change in the relationship between the "functional requisites," Apter states, will be reflected in the relationship between the two minimum "structural requisites of government," i.e., authoritative decision-making and accountability. The national legislature, Apter writes, is among the structures of accountability that reveal "the responsiveness of the system to various reference groups in the community."[57] Applying these concepts to Kenya, the following analysis may be suggested: There exists in contemporary Kenya a conflict between the National Assembly and the executive growing out of the desires of M.P.'s for greater accountability in Kenya politics. Lacking a sense of meaningful participation in decision-making,

56. *Ibid.*, cols. 8–9, December 14, 1964. Translated from Swahili.
57. Apter, *op. cit.*, pp. 237–246.

the ordinary M.P. appears to find it necessary to assert himself publicly in opposition to the government to justify his position to himself and his constituents. The result has been legislative behavior that fails to create the maximum possible legitimacy for the Kenya government and, indeed, undermines that legitimacy to some extent. Some would likely interpret this behavior as demonstrating the usefulness of Parliament as a "safety valve" for releasing political tensions, but these tensions are those of legislators as legislators; they have little to do, in the words of Pye, with "the relative distribution of attitudes and values throughout the society."[58]

Three courses would appear to be open. The government may do nothing to change the structural characteristics of executive-legislative relations in Kenya and continue to suffer some erosion in the symbolic and sanctional aspects of its authority. In this event, Kenya would continue to be a tutelary democracy, but with decreasing public support. Second, the government could effect structural changes to bring more information into the Kenya political system through a decentralization of decision-making and a widening of accountability. Such a decision (which Apter states is unlikely in a neo-mercantilist system) would move Kenya toward a form of politics which Shils terms "political democracy" and Apter calls a "reconciliation system." Otherwise, the Kenya government could increase coercion (and, concurrently, the rewards for political conformity) in order to reduce present pressures for accountability while maintaining the legitimacy of its decision-making. In this event, Kenya politics would come to resemble a form Shils terms "modernizing oligarchy" and Apter names a "mobilization system." Limited evidence, principally the Government's extra-parliamentary treatment of members of the opposition KPU but also including other matters mentioned in this paper, suggest that Kenya may now be moving in this latter direction. Growing coercion in Kenya politics may foster political stability, particularly in the short run; it could not, however, under the definition we have employed in this paper foster political development.

58. Pye, *op. cit.*, p. 482.

Chapter 9

Congress in the Philippine Political System*

Robert B. Stauffer

The Philippine political system after more than two decades of independence still has a striking resemblance to the political institutions found in the United States, the country that ruled the island nation for more than forty years. Newspaper stories about appeals being taken to the Supreme Court, reports of outspoken congressional critics of the administration, and accounts of what the president has to say in turn about these critics encourage the casual American visitor in Manila to assume he knows what the system is like and what is happening within it. Certainly the institutional similarities are striking. Not only are the three main branches of government there in the familiar American constitutional checks and balance form, but they are backed up by a two-party system, a variety of interest groups that appear to be doing what interest groups are supposed to do in politics, and a press that obviously—or so it would seem—is fiercely independent. If our hypothetical tourist happens to be in the Philippines during a period when anti-Americanism is quiescent, he will lack the external stimulus to remind him that the Philippines is a proudly independent nation and that although the institutional form of the Philippine system may closely resemble that in the United States, the uses of the institutions and political processes coursing through them are militantly Filipino.

Of course the more knowledgeable Americans know that the

* I would like to express my appreciation to Amefil Agbayani, Henry Kariel, and Norman Meller for comments made on an earlier version of this paper, and to the Social Science Research Institute of the University of Hawaii for research support.

Philippine political system is not quite the formal reproduction of American political institutions that this lay view would suggest. At the system level, for example, the Philippines is a unitary state, not a federal one. At subsystem levels one finds that the American model has been altered repeatedly to respond to the needs of the Philippines. In the legislative branch, to illustrate, members of the House of Representatives are elected for four-year terms, not two, whereas their colleagues in the Senate share the American six-year term, but run at large in the nation rather than in electoral districts. Although the Americans provided for Senate districts, Filipinos changed to the present arrangement late in the Commonwealth era. Comparable modifications run throughout the political system.

More important differences exist between the two polities than these institutional variations suggest, even though cumulatively they probably have considerable significance. The most important basis of the non-institutional differences is that the respective Philippine and American political cultures condition all forms of political activity. Although the Philippine cluster of ideas and behavior patterns associated with politics has come to include a full-bodied acceptance of competition and conflict as well as related values that can be considered part of a politically developed society, an older tradition that traces back to pre-Spanish times holds to the idea of communal consensus and continues to constitute a strand in the current value system. This older tradition, reinforced by a variety of powerful family ties, small group loyalties, and rather rigid norms guiding interpersonal relations, infuses all additions to Philippine political culture and provides a distinctive synthesis that makes what goes on in the institutional setting completely Filipino.

The Philippine political culture, then, with its strong family base, its acceptance of a high degree of competition and conflict while yearning for a warmer, closer solidarity, and its powerful constraints on individual freedom of action resulting from social values of personal obligation that permeate the system, represents a major dimension differentiating the Philippine political system from the American model. There are other equally compelling forces at work. One has simply to look at the economy to realize how starkly different the Philippine material ecology is from the American. Although considerable diversification has taken place in industry in the last decade, the economy remains heavily tied to subsistence agriculture and to the production of a few tropical agricultural crops for export along with the export of some minerals and timber. The economy cannot provide nearly sufficient food for the population nor jobs for a rapidly expanding population. Rural tenancy rates, especially in the rice producing heartland of central Luzon, remain among the highest in the world. Urban slums and squatter settlements threaten metropolitan centers, and marginally existing populations simply represent the urban equivalent of widespread rural depression. At the same time, however, the economy supports a highly affluent upper class and a relatively rapidly expanding middle class. But, because of the limited resource base and the increased demands on it from the rapidly growing population and from the ever larger, upwardly mobile sectors, the total political system operates with a life-and-death earnestness that differentiates it from what most Americans experience in their politics, unless they happen to belong to minorities who have not had a share of the national plenitude but who are now fighting to become part of the system.

Certainly, the economic parameters of Philippine politics and in a lesser sense the social cannot be considered as providing generous support for an open, developed political system. Indeed, the usual list of prerequisites for one type of modern polity —the democratic—would largely rule out the possibility of the Philippines supporting such a political form.[1] But, if the Philippine success in replacing one set of elected political leaders with another with rather consistent regularity, in generating a constant flow of new demands and issues for political resolution, and in sustaining an expanding proportion of the population in participatory roles viewed as legitimate by nearly everyone is an indica-

---

1. The most widely cited source for the point of view that a democratic political system is always found in a relatively affluent socio-economic setting is Seymour M. Lipset, "Some Social Requisites of Democracy: Economic Development and Political Legitimacy," *American Political Science Review*, LIII (March, 1959), 69–105.

tion of a relatively developed democratic system, then the Philippines must be accepted as a democracy. If this is so, then we have in the Philippines an example of a system worth pondering—a relatively developed political system interacting with a grossly undeveloped economic system and with a traditional social system.[2]

The larger questions of how and why the Philippine political system manages to continue to function in a relatively viable and democratic fashion, despite the absence of what many consider to be necessary underlying social and economic prerequisites, can only be answered indirectly. As has been pointed out, one might argue that the Philippines simply represents an "exception," a deviant case that will fall back into a less politically developed system type if the socio-economic base remains static, or that will maintain its present political level of development only if sufficient growth takes place in other sectors. At the other extreme, one could revert to a pre-scientific approach and reject the deterministic (with probabilistic reservations) prerequisite model completely. Recently an intermediate position has been advanced based on the observation that existing measuring instruments have been too crude to register important variations in political system types and as a result have led to questionable conclusions about underlying relationships between variables.[3] The proposed

2. In a comparison of predicted national political development scores with actual score values Phillips Cutright found that the Philippines out of a list of seventy-seven nations had the second highest positive error—nearly two standard deviations of the residuals—indicating that the Philippine political system was "over developed" on the basis of the variables used in the prediction calculations. Only four Asian nations had positive errors between predicted and actual scores: India (6.4), the Philippines (10.8), Burma (5.7), and Indonesia (5.8). Cutright points out (1963) that even by that date "Burma and Indonesia have turned away from complex political organization and have abandoned multi-party politics." He adds, "The pressures in India and the Philippines toward similar political 'backsliding' may also be strong and whether they will follow the same path taken by Burma and Indonesia is problematic. If rapid economic-social development can occur they may achieve political stability." Phillips Cutright, "National Political Development: Measurement and Analysis," *American Sociological Review*, XXVIII (April, 1963), 263. The Cutright data and analysis fully support the point that the Philippine political system is highly developed in comparison with its socio-economic base and that this represents something of an anomalous situation.

3. These conclusions are contained in Deane E. Neubauer, "Some Conditions of Democracy," *American Political Science Review*, LXI (December, 1967), 1002–1009. Just as Cutright argued that the Lipset explanatory model was based on too crude a scoring system that did not permit scaling of national political

model of interrelationships between socio-economic systems and
political development provides considerably more flexibility than
any existing variant of the "prerequisite" paradigm. It provides
that once a social system has successfully passed a minimum
"threshold" level on the socio-economic variables, a variety of
political systems might be sustained by the resulting national
infrastructure. Although my guess is that subsequent sharpening
of the measuring instruments as well as of the conceptual framework will narrow this indeterminate territory, the optimistic over-
tones contained in the conclusions are attractive to anyone depressed by the pessimism of earlier predictive models.

Despite the predictive problem arising from the overly developed Philippine political system relative to its socio-economic
base, our concern is more directly related to how the Philippine
Congress fits into the currently operating Philippine political
system, and how it contributed to creating the existing polity. My
general evaluation of the latter is that the existing incongruity
between the systems, i.e., the developed political and the underdeveloped economic, can best be explained by the particular

systems, Neubauer points out that Cutright's national political development index
is inadequate because it does not measure political development but "the existence
over time of liberal-democratic regimes." He offers a "democratic performance"
index in its place and then correlates it with Cutright's socio-economic measures
for a selected sample of democratic nations. He concludes that "political development, to the extent that it represents democratic political development, is a
threshold phenomenon. Certain levels of 'basic' socio-economic development appear to be necessary to elevate countries to a level at which they can begin to
support complex, nation-wide patterns of political interaction, one of which may
be democracy. Once above this threshold, however, the degree to which a country
will 'maximize' certain forms of democratic practice is no longer a function of
continued socio-economic development" (p. 1007, emphasis added). Attention
should be directed to a weakness in this interpretation, however. While Neubauer
bases his case on the weakness of one of Cutright's measuring instruments, he
seems not to recognize that his own model is handicapped by relying on the
equally crude socio-economic indexes adopted from Cutright. If equally sensitive
indicators of variation in socio-economic factors were used along with his democratic performance index, underlying patterns of covariance could be expected to
be tapped.
Although the Philippines is not included in Neubauer's *sample* of democratic
nations, two comparable nations from the Cutright list are included—Mexico and
India. The Philippines either greatly outranked each of these on the actual/pre-
dicted development scores or was above India and at the same level as Mexico on
Cutright's "Relationship of Communications Development to Development" scat-
tergram, the only other comparison he provides. Clearly the Philippines falls safely
past the "threshold" beyond which national political institutions of a complex type
can be supported, despite the low degree of economic development compared with
industrialized nations.

roles that have been played by individuals as candidates for election to Congress and by members of Congress performing their various political tasks. This is not to imply that supporting achievements in public administration have not been important to the development of Philippine politics, nor that the role of the president has been anything but major. But moderately "developed" executive offices and administrative agencies have been almost as common among the less developed nations of the world as has been the lack of acceptable political patterns for increased participation, for holding the political class somewhat accountable, and for providing access for new demands. Although legislatures have almost never been viewed as having played a creative role in nation-building, and have even been pictured as standing in the way of rational national development, even a limited acquaintance with Philippine politics is sufficient to make us realize that this dominant view of legislatures is in need of qualification. Although the Philippine case will not prove that legislators must exist as part of a political system if political development is to take place, it might suggest an alternative model not currently included in the general theoretical literature,[4] and call attention to new roles—or functions—that the Philippine Congress has performed in the larger system that may have general applicability.

Functions of Legislatures

A great deal of the speculation about the functions performed by legislatures began with nineteenth-century British political theorists, for example, John Stuart Mill and Walter Bagehot. Mill was convinced that parliament should be viewed as an assembly to control the government and to serve the nation as its "Committee of Grievances" and "Congress of Opinions"; Bagehot held to a somewhat more directive function for parliament *vis à vis* the

4. The more theoretical aspects of the legislative system's role in political development have been presented elsewhere; see my "A Legislative Model of Political Development," *Philippine Journal of Public Administration*, XI (January, 1967), 3–12.

population, while sharing many of the positions held by Mill. Although there is certainly the possibility of some slippage because of changing rhetorical styles between nineteenth-century Britain and twentieth-century United States, I doubt that anyone in the earlier era postulated "conflict management" or "integration" as significant functions that were or should be performed by a legislature. And yet two of the most creative American research teams working on legislative behavior arrive at these as the *only* central functions performed by legislative assemblies.[5] Interestingly, political scientists working with British data continue to define legislative functions largely in the earlier terms, whereas those who work with material from political communities with more blatant problems of integration and conflict management see these as the vital functions that legislatures either do or should perform.[6]

More recently, increased attention has been paid to the types of roles that legislatures have played in the lesser developed nations and in the processes of nation-building.[7] In addition to work reported elsewhere in this book, elite studies have thrown light on these legislative functions as has work done by my colleagues at the University of Hawaii.[8] There is no agreement as yet, how-

5. Slightly different terminology is used by each group. See John C. Wahlke *et al.*, *The Legislative System: Explorations in Legislative Behavior* (New York, 1962), and Malcolm E. Jewell and Samuel C. Patterson, *The Legislative Process in the United States* (New York, 1966).

6. Giovanni Sartori makes the point, based on Italian and British experience, that the legislature is the agency most central to conflict resolution. "Introductory Report," Round-Table Meeting on Parliamentary Government, Bellagio, July 7–12, 1963.

7. Henry C. Hart in a paper that explores constituency relations of a selected number of Indian legislators calls his study "MPs as Nation-Builders." Draft prepared at the East-West Center, Honolulu, Hawaii, 1966.

8. Frederick W. Frey, *The Turkish Political Elite* (Cambridge, Mass., 1965). Norman Meller has recently completed research on legislative development in Micronesia and other selected Pacific island areas. A report of this research (with James Anthony) on the impact of parliamentary elections on political development is contained in *Fiji Goes to the Polls* (Honolulu, 1968). Meller's "The Identification and Classification of Legislatures," *Philippine Journal of Public Administration*, X (October, 1966), 308–319, is also concerned with the subject. Fred W. Riggs, in a paper presented at the 1966 meeting of the American Political Science Association, developed a model in which he probed the types of political systems based on patterns of interaction between legislatures and their related party systems on the one hand and the executive-administrative complex on the other. See "Structure and Function: A Dialectical Approach." Amefil R. M. Agbayani used Parsonian pattern variables to devise a measure for detecting change in legislative behavior in "Indices of Change: The Philippine Senate," *Philippine*

ever, on which formerly unspecified legislative function should be added to extant lists—or if any should be added. My own preference would be to use "conflict management" and "integration" as the two central legislative functions at the highest level of abstraction, but to define the content of each rather flexibly during this period when we have a limited range of empirical data upon which to base our theorizing. The approach that will be taken in handling data from the Philippine Congress will be largely inductive while recognizing that most of the specific functions to be discussed can be accommodated within one or the other broad functional headings of "conflict management" and "integration."

The Role of the Philippine Congress in Conflict Management

Probably the greater portion of mankind has lived in political systems based on values and myths that deny the presence of conflict and affirm the contrary model of a community that functions successfully because of a mystical consensus that binds all together. Certainly, this anti-conflict view of the proper community dominated Philippine political values until late in the nineteenth-century, by which time successive demands for opening the colonial system to wider Filipino participation led to the revolutionary waves of the 1890's. It was at the height of the revolution against Spain after the republic had been proclaimed that Philippine political leaders were faced with the problem of whether to continue to organize the political community, now claiming independence, under the old community-consensus values or whether to opt for a view of politics that accepted conflict and sought to build institutional channels through which it could

Journal of Public Administration, XI (January, 1967), 13–23, while Susan K. Harvey constructed a different measure using House data in "Indices of Change in Health Legislation: The Philippine House of Representatives, 1947–1959" (unpublished master's thesis, University of Hawaii, 1967). Lastly, a monograph that I have just completed touches on similar themes: "A Developmental Profile of the Philippine Congress."

be resolved. Although the exigencies of the war with Spain and shortly with the United States placed severe limits on the nation's leaders, and although the revolution was guilty of destroying some of its original creators in the name of unity, decisions were made in 1898–1899, nonetheless, to create a nation that would accept conflict as a natural condition of politics and that would also have an institutional setting within which a variety of functions deriving from this point of view could be handled. Specifically, the Philippine revolutionists created, simultaneously with their revolution, a representative assembly. This body—the Malolos Congress—early was forced to deal with conditions of considerable stress deriving from conflicts over the best policies to adopt toward Spain and the United States, over how to define the future of the Philippine nation in a constitution, how to control the president and the emerging administrative agencies, and how to improvise mechanisms for assuring contending factions in Congress a continued safe existence. In every instance, choices were unequivocally made by Congress that favored a system which openly tolerated continuing conflict. The Republic of the Philippines thus began its life with an assembly that from the first sitting made clear that the proper function of a legislature is not to be a quiet, unobtrusive, and pliant advisory body, but rather to play an active role in helping resolve important differences of opinion and interest that come before it.[9]

During the long American occupation that followed the brief period of the revolutionary Philippine Republic, the ideas expressed in the Malolos Congress that politics—i.e., a clash of interests and opinions—is a normal condition of a political community and that a legislative assembly is properly involved in conflict management have gained widespread acceptance. American domestic ideas on both the nature of politics and on the role of a legislature in the total political system fit, coincidentally, with the earlier patterns that had emerged in the Philippines.

9. Teodoro A. Agoncillo, a respected Philippine historian, argues for a different interpretation of the role of the Malolos Congress. He contends that the legislature exceeded its stipulated powers and was instrumental in taking control of the revolution from the working-class-based group that had earlier started it. See his *Malolos: The Crisis of the Republic* (Quezon City, 1960).

The congruence promised continued development so long as the emerging system could be established in Filipino minds as legitimately theirs. The feeling of verisimilitude flowing from the existence of a strong legislature bound by close electoral ties to its people helped make the distinction possible for the Filipinos. On the American side, unanticipated consequences of a strong legislature seen in the form of more numerous demands based on an increasingly mobilized population produced a more rapid "Filipinization" of the civil service and the courts than had been originally planned. When escalating pressures in the 1920's collided with an American domestic shift to conservative policies, all attempts by the United States to stave off further concessions and to hold back political development simply produced a rapid heightening of the congressionally based demands for national independence. The dialogue between the United States and the leaders of the Philippine Congress amply demonstrated that the latter was a powerful Filipino political institution, that it was the locale where national demands were articulated, and that in it bargains were made relative to their resolution. Although the creation of a Philippine president in the last years of the American era (when the Commonwealth was established) altered this generalization somewhat, Congress remained a significant power center and began testing its position in relation to a national rather than a colonial chief executive.

The ideas that politics legitimately involves and even rests on the acceptance of conflict and that a representative legislative assembly is one institutional setting for assuring that conflicts are brought into the open and given some systematic consideration had become commonplace in the Philippines by the end of active American control. From the re-establishment of the Philippine Republic in 1946 to the present, these ideas have flourished. Challenges have and do exist, of course. For example, the breakdown of competitive politics into physical violence has at times threatened the viability of an open political system. Congress also had to face a partial eclipse after it ceased to be the only avenue open to political demands and when it had to face the enormous resources available to an elected national chief executive. But the

Congress has consistently behaved in a fashion to eschew violence and to demonstrate a politics of competition. Further, it
steadily has been regaining its position as the center within which
negotiations have to be carried on with respect to conflicts affecting the larger polity. If political development means the ability of a political community to "deal with the issues arising out of
its common problems," to use Herbert Spiro's phrase, to generate
new issues and provide mechanisms for their resolution, and to
encourage participation, then the Philippines is politically developed. There is uniform agreement among those working with
Philippine materials that the Philippine political system can be
characterized as one based on bargaining, on an acceptance of
electoral competition, on a constant struggle within the political
elite, and on an increasing accommodation to the flow of demands from participant sectors of the public that seem to be
expanding relative to the total population. The result is a political
culture that emphasizes the importance of politics. In producing
that culture Congress historically has played a central role, as the
following discussion will attempt to show.

The Role of Congress in Political Socialization

For nearly three decades Congress provided the only national
political roles in the emerging Philippine political system. During
that period, which ended when the first Filipino president was
inaugurated, congressmen defined an extensive list of acceptable
forms of political behavior for Filipinos, both ordinary citizens
and members of the political elite. They demonstrated avenues
through which individuals could join the power structure and,
equally as important, that continued membership among the decision-makers was not permanent but could be reversed by an
electorate not satisfied with their performance. In this period of
political monopoly Congress established itself as a prime avenue
of access to the executive and administrative agencies—as the
conduit through which requests for quite specific types of government action were transmitted. Many of these took the form of
appeals for "pork barrel" grants, or for some other quite narrow
response. Although an argument can be made that Congress

socialized the Filipino people into viewing the political process in too highly personalistic terms, the counter position needs recognition. In their day-to-day activities during legislative sessions (and at a greatly increased tempo during electoral campaigns) congressmen and candidates for congressional office consistently gave quite precise and relatively narrow limits to the types of goods and services that could be expected to be provided by government. Since the full establishment of independence in 1946 this list has been expanded and represents a bargainable package. What has remained constant throughout has been the role played by Congress in socializing the electorate to politics. Although this role has long been shared with an elected national president, congressmen, because of their more intimate continuing contacts with constituents, still perform the task of translating new ideas into manageable dimensions upon which to make commitments. In the process a certain "pragmatization" of politics takes place.

In addition to their function of politicizing the electorate,[10] the Philippine legislature has played and continues to play a major role in conditioning the behavior of the political elite. Every Philippine president except one has stepped directly from a legislative career into the position of chief executive. Most presidents have held the top position in the Senate before making their move. To the degree that the highest national elected executive positions are filled by individuals drawn from Congress and from among the most successful congressmen, to that degree the legislature continues to contribute creatively to defining national political roles and in socializing individuals to fit them.

Any lesser developed community (an occasional minuscule oil sheikdom aside) faces intractable problems deriving from a nonexistent or too slowly expanding resource base. As a consequence, open competitive politics usually dies, and is replaced by some more closed system that promises elite protection. The writer would not argue that the economic and political elites in the

---

10. Another important facet of political socialization is discussed under the heading "Creating a Political Public" in the section "The Integrative Role of Congress."

Philippines are any less elitist in their life style than elsewhere. But I would point out that having been politically socialized through exposure to competitive politics, they have fewer grounds for irrational fears of the masses than in many other systems and have been forced, as well, to maintain rather strong ties with local leaders throughout the nation. As a result there may well be less fear between the classes and more contacts than in the majority of developing nations. If this is true, politics can continue to be the approach used to resolve the disputes over how resources are to be allocated.

The continued success of the legislature in performing its politicizing role, both for the electorate and for the elite, depends on various related legislative functions and to internally institutionalized mechanisms for managing conflict and creating trust. Two of these will suffice for illustrative purposes.

The establishment of conditions under which the rights of minorities are protected, especially insofar as these minorities attempt to affect the policy-making process, involves much more than what takes place within legislative chambers, and even more than that which transpires between the legislature and its related electoral and political party systems.[11] There is substantial probability, however, that without some institutional setting where

11. The constitutional provisions of the electoral system require that a candidate for a seat in the House must have resided in the district in which he runs for at least one year prior to election. No such rule applies to senators since they run at large from the nation as a whole. The electoral system also requires that voters must be literate, a provision that is interpreted liberally and which has less importance as an ever larger proportion of the population becomes educated.

Possible influences of the electoral system on the Philippine party system have not yet been investigated in any systematic fashion. The existence of single-member House districts, and of other single-office races (for governorships and mayoralty positions) might be advanced as being associated with the emergence and maintenance of the Philippine two-party system and with the inability of third parties to gain a foothold. The weaknesses of the two political parties, on the other hand, in part might be related to the electoral provisions that encourage "split-ticket" voting, as for senators (eight elected each two years, with the voter having complete freedom to use his eight votes as he chooses among the total list of candidates), and for most municipal council-type offices.

Most observers of the Philippine political party system point to the great similarity of the two major parties and to the instability of party ties. Each party is an alliance of political machines cutting across class and regional lines. Each has many of the characteristics Duverger incorporated in his "cadre" party model. The best discussion of Philippine political parties is found in Carl H. Landè, *Leaders, Factions, and Parties: The Structure of Philippine Politics* (New Haven, Conn., 1965).

minority spokesmen are confident of their physical security, are free to continue striving to become the majority, and are allocated relatively fair shares of resources, the chances of a wider respect for non-consensus points of view in the political community will be slim. A legislature is not a sufficient cause for the emergence of conditions conducive to active minority participation in politics, but a legislature or some institutional body performing the same function is probably a necessary condition for this to occur.

Every Philippine legislative session, beginning with the very first at Malolos, has had one or more minority positions maintained by groups of congressmen. In the earlier sessions these groups frequently were factions within the same dominant political party and often shifted according to the issue. Since the re-establishment of the Republic in 1946, majority and minority positions have corresponded to divisions between political parties, although individual membership in a party remains moderately fluid. Legislators at times shift from one political party to another so that on more than one occasion a House that started a session with a majority in the hands of the anti-administration party ended with the president's party in control. What is important, however, is that actors in the legislative system and for that matter the politically active in the larger community, accept as a proper form of political life the concentration in the legislature of outspoken minority participation in decision-making, whether the minority takes the form of an opposition party or whether it arises from within the ranks of the majority.[12] In either case there are long established traditions in each house that assure those in minority positions continued access to some of the forms of internal and external communication through which to argue their causes. One has only to read the speeches made during the "privileged hour" each day or to hear the arguments made by minority members interpellating a sponsor of a legislative meas-

12. An earlier Spanish tradition provided for a "fiscalizer" from the courts who would expose venalities in colonial administration. This tradition has been broadened, and has been shifted in large part to the legislature. Individual congressmen build reputations as "fiscalizers" of the administration or of their own party, and Congress as a whole is expected to play that role in relation to the president and the bureaucracy. More will be said about this below.

ure to appreciate how fully this is true.[13] Further, legislative
leaders work out agreements between the majority and the minority on the distribution of committee positions, on the allocation of debate time on important measures, and on the general
flow of legislative work. They also hammer out agreements on
how resources available for funding the work of the legislature as
well as the important pork barrel are to be divided among the
members. Although members of the majority receive preferential
treatment in this process, especially in the allocation of financial
resources, still, the Philippine Congress provides a secure base for
minority points of view to gain a hearing. The Congress guarantees minority spokesmen a setting supportive of active politics
even if every minority is not physically represented in the legislature.

A second example of a specialized politicization function performed by Congress on the members themselves is that of defining limits within which conflict must be kept. The Philippines has
a high incidence of violence at least if judged by its homicide
rate;[14] armed guards are quite common throughout urban areas
and so many individuals carry weapons that the sign "Please
Check Your Firearms" can be seen in such disparate places as
nightclubs or on the reception desk at a major college. The
Filipino emphasis on always maintaining an outwardly pleasant
and harmonious demeanor when dealing with others—what one
cultural anthropologist calls the attempt to achieve "smooth interpersonal relations"[15]—is certainly related to this syndrome toward

13. In the most recent session of Congress from which data have been collected
relating background characteristics of legislators with types of participation, I
found that minority party members introduced nearly 40 per cent of the bills that
were subsequently passed and that a near exact division of "privileged hour" time
for the 246 House and 69 Senate privileged speeches was the case. Data are from
the 1962 session.
14. On the basis of statistics used by Aprodicio A. Laquian in a recent study of
Manila, the 1963 city homicide rate was 44.4 per 100,000. This compares, for
example, with *national* levels of 22.0 for Mexico, 16.7 for Burma, 0.1 for Spain,
1.5 for Japan, and 5.1 for the United States. The Philippines was reported to have
a national ratio of 2.3 per 100,000 for the same year. The Manila figures are
contained in Aprodicio A. Laquian, *The City in Nation-Building* (Manila, 1966),
p. 68; the others are from the *Demographic Yearbook, 1965* (New York, 1966),
Table 44, pp. 762 ff.
15. Frank Lynch, S. J., compiler, *Four Readings on Philippine Values* (Quezon
City, 1964), in his "Social Acceptance," pp. 8–15.

violence. Social demands for the repression of aggressive feelings are frequently paid for in untoward violent outbursts.

The elaborate rules and rituals common to most legislative bodies have as their chief object the creation of a milieu wherein conflicting interests can carry on a continuing struggle while at the same time decision-making of the issue-by-issue variety typical of legislatures is facilitated. Indirectly, these codes of legislative behavior are also defenses against the possibility that legislative conflict may degenerate into violence. There are enough examples, historical as well as contemporary (e.g., the continuing riots within the Japanese Diet) to support the observation that preventing legislators from slipping from vigorous partisanship into violent behavior is not a purely academic concern.

The Philippine Congress has seen the line crossed on a few occasions, especially in earlier sessions, and at least some member still threatens to use violence against a colleague each year. For example, when President Marcos was a member of the House of Representatives, he constantly was involved in bitter floor battles, largely because he was one of the key "fiscalizers" of the immensely popular Magsaysay administration. These debates frequently approached threats of direct violence, and at least once he was challenged to a duel, a challenge he deflected by observing that dueling "is punishable under the Revised Penal Code."

Although congressional leaders must certainly rely on such personal methods for handling threats of violence and more generally, on the internalized restraints that are part of any civilized person's behavior, considerable attention also is given to specialized congressional constraints upon violent behavior. The rules of each house, for example, circumscribe legislators' behavior by defining methods for resolving anticipated conflicts and by stipulating a number of positive norms that, taken together, further reduce the possibility that legislative conflict will become violent. These latter norms include the usual prescriptions calling for certain niceties of address and rhetorical style of debate on the floor.

Congress makes considerable use of the organized leaders of both majority and minority parties to manage tension levels. One can frequently see the presiding officer intervene in a situation of mounting tension to warn one or both members to adhere to the rules or to temper his remarks. Or at moments when an interpellator is pushing dangerously close to his adversary's breaking point, a third member will pick up the interpellation and so act as a moderating force. Similar controls over behavior are exercised through the frequent formal and informal caucuses held by both parties in each house.

In addition to these forms of intervention by the formal leaders, another is used, and with great frequency. At any point when tempers seem to be wearing thin, when resistance to a bill is building up a head of steam, or when two members have approached the point of doing verbal violence to one another, the majority floor leader or the Chair will call for a brief suspension of the session. During the break that follows informal person-to-person channels are employed to cool off those involved or to shelve the item of contention until a more propitious time. These suspensions may last only a moment or two—just long enough for a few words to be exchanged between a small cluster of men on the floor—or may extend for longer periods and involve a sizeable number of individuals. The practice seems to represent a creative use of Filipino social patterns such as the reliance on a go-between in situations of difficult interpersonal relations, or the preference for relying on personal loyalties to reinforce formal norms. This combination of what might be called the traditional approach to conflict management coupled with the full package of formal mechanisms does much to explain the success the Philippine Congress has had in sustaining a setting where men battle vigorously, but where conflict is kept from becoming violent.

Control of the Executive Branch

If the Philippine legislature began historically at Malolos with a series of confrontations between the representative assembly and the Republic's president, developments during the American occupation were to continue the pattern and to provide for their multiplication. This was partially a result of the fact that the Philippine independence movement was organized essentially through Congress rather than externally in a mass party as was the case in India. From this locus a running battle lasting nearly three decades was carried on against the colonial administration and for Philippine independence. The struggle clearly established the separate institutional identity of Congress, as well as the central role of the legislature in fighting for national rights. Although it is true the emergence of an elected national chief executive altered the exclusiveness of this earlier congressional monopoly of civic virtue and political power as did the somewhat compromising events of World War II, still, Congress remains today, after a period of extensive modifications in power relationships, probably the most independent and influential legislature in the world of developing nations.

Congress exercises its influence over the executive branch through a variety of methods, no one of which is exotic in the slightest. The most extensive controls over the administration arise from the bargaining that goes on constantly before and during a session of Congress between the president and the legislative leaders over what will be passed and what will have to be paid by the chief executive for congressional cooperation. Although a separation of powers system may tend to promote such interbranch bargaining, the lack of a strong party system in the Philippines does much to increase it. Further, because in the centralized Philippine system the president has the authority to release or hold back funds already appropriated, especially, funds for pork barrel projects, much of the interbranch bargaining operates on a *quid pro quo* level with the chief executive following through on past commitments in return for which Congress accedes to new proposals made by the president while simultaneously extracting new commitments for future allocations. The control that is imposed is, of course, mutual. But, in the process, Congress has imposed a recognized set of parameters on where and how public resources are to be allocated and an important voice in any changes in established patterns.

Congress has a second method for exercising influence on executive behavior. The Philippine constitution provides that a joint House-Senate Commission on Appointments must approve all presidential appointments to office. Since the Constitution—expanded somewhat by later legislative enactments—provides that the president has a rather extensive list of positions at his disposal and that the Commission is provided with ample opportunity to make demands on the chief executive. Certainly its members have not been hesitant in using their powers in recent sessions, even to the point of being accused of harassing the president.

Congressmen have a third approach for influencing the behavior of selected individuals in the executive branch—cabinet members, top administrators, and even the president, for example. The privileged hour at the opening of each day's session is a time when one or more members in each house deliver formal speeches on subjects of general interest as the standing rules define the right. *General interest* has long been interpreted to cover critical attacks on administration policy proposals, on individuals in the administration, and on the manner in which established agencies are carrying out their functions. There is energetic competition for the opportunity to give a privileged speech: hopeful fiscalizers present themselves not only from the ranks of the minority party but from what we can call "backbenchers" in the majority. Conventional rules require that time be allocated with equity among the many who request it. Since the privileged hour provides more often than not the most exciting moments of each day's sitting, the press provides coverage on a regular basis, and since this is assured a pattern has been established to use the privileged hour speech as a conduit to the press as a means for mobilizing public opinion. As a result of the generous use of legislative time for privileged speeches, of the fiscalizing tradition, and of the close press coverage, Congress has created one of its most effective instruments for influencing policy emanating from the executive branch and for controlling certain aspects of behavior of individuals in the Administration.

Congress employs a fourth method for exercising a degree of control over administrative agencies. The congressional committee system is based on functional specialization similar to that employed in the United States Congress. Although membership on a Philippine congressional standing committee is less a result of seniority than in the United States, sufficient continuity of membership exists to assure that in any committee there are individuals who are knowledgeable in the subject matter that comes before them from administrative departments. Furthermore, technical experts appended to each committee as staff assistants provide both an additional degree of continuity and professional competence to strengthen Congress in its role as an agent of influence and control over the executive.

In addition to the standing committees of Congress a number of special *ad hoc* and quasi-permanent investigating committees exist. Since the reason for creating a special committee can usually be traced back to some problem—smuggling or corruption, for example—that in turn has a strong administration dimension, these investigating committees of Congress can be viewed as continuing experiments in devising tools for controlling the executive branch.

Congressmen, more as individuals than in any corporate sense, have another technique for trying to alter the behavior of administrators. A number of existing case studies on Philippine politics contain examples of a congressman using whatever powers he might be able to call upon to force a change in some type of administrative behavior strongly objected to by a vocal sector of his constituents.[16] The Philippines, like all new nations, inherited an administrative system that had been built and utilized during colonial rule. Although the Philippines had the most developed level of institutionalized political influence on colonial decision-making processes during the final years of foreign domination, still, the need to bring the administration under more politically responsible control and to humanize it remains. Direct intervention by a congressman on behalf of one of his constituents constitutes one process by which this takes place.

Congress and the Struggle for Political Power

The protracted and highly competitive electoral campaigns that are so prominently a part of the Philippine political system

16. An excellent collection of case studies is Raul P. de Guzman, ed., *Patterns of Decision-Making* (Manila, 1963).

no sooner come to an end on election day than a new phase of the continuing struggle for political power begins. Just as candidates for congressional seats are an integral part of the electoral phase of the struggle so are congressmen in the longer time that falls between periodic appeals to the voters.

Because of the competitive bargaining nature of campaigns, elected congressmen are "under the gun" to deliver on the specific promises they made to local political leaders and voters. Under conditions of extremely limited resources, each congressman is forced to engage in a persistent battle to assure a flow of outputs approximating his commitments. To accomplish this, a member of Congress will on occasion abandon a minority political party and join that of the majority; he will certainly make alliances that give promise of advancing the combined interests of the groups; and he will make log-rolling agreements with various fellow congressmen to make sure that some of his pet projects are passed. In all this maneuvering for position and for rewards the centralized nature of the Philippine political system makes Congress a highly visible focal point where all political struggles ultimately touch.

Not only is Congress the site of constant struggles over resource allocations that trace back to previous or continuing commitments of elected congressmen, but it is the political center where many preliminary battles are fought prior to the next electoral campaign. Broad working alliances are consummated to improve the status of the allying factions, weaker individuals attach themselves to stronger leaders, and the strongest constantly test their strength against other contenders for leadership. The ultimate object of much of the bargaining is control of the formal leadership offices in each house. Not only is occupying one of these—the position as president of the Senate—almost a rite of passage to the nation's top elected position, but the office in each house assures the group controlling it the extra political advantages of nationwide publicity, patronage, and related resources that play a key role in elections. What emerges from this analysis is a picture of Congress intimately connected with the processes through which individuals and groups are rewarded or punished and by which they advance in status and influence or lose ground.

The Integrative Role of Congress

The condition just described is an indirect indicator that Congress might be playing a role in national integration, especially since the mechanics of House apportionment assure that representatives from all parts of the nation sit in the legislature to take part in its politics even if the nation's voters tend to return a Senate largely drawn from one island, Luzon. Congress has performed, however, a variety of functions more directly related to integration. Although there is overlapping in the list, two can be singled out for comment.

Creating a National Political Elite

In the terminal stages of colonial control the future of the emerging nation is mortgaged by the type of political elite that is created. In one case the politically dominant may be mainly associated with the military, in another with the civil service, in yet another with a mass political party. In many instances the new political class represents the nation only because it claims to do so, when, in fact, its members are drawn from a narrow sector of the total population and are viewed by the larger population with suspicion. In the Philippine case the existence of a "national" legislature long before the nation achieved independence and regular congressional elections throughout the nation greatly contributed to the creation of a political class that was national in geographic spread and integrated in political outlook. Although a single charismatic leader can give momentary cohesion to a coalition of lesser leaders drawn from different parts of a nation, the tendency for charismatic types to rely on old associates can skew the representative nature of the top elite heavily against one or more regions or groups in the nation. Furthermore, the highly personal quality of a charismatic leader makes the question of succession one that reopens the very basis of national existence when it is forced on the people by his death. In the Philippines, congressional elections and the continuing enlargement of congressional power in the political system created the conditions that escaped each of these dangers. Long before independence was achieved, the Philippines had a political elite that was fully national, integrated, and not reliant on charisma as the cohesive force.[17]

The integrative role of Congress rests on much more, however, than the thin veneer of individuals elected to sit in its chambers. Not only do congressmen represent a national political elite in the horizontal sense, but they also constitute key links vertically. Each legislator is intricately linked with a chain of local leaders, descending through the province to the cities, towns, and barrios. These vertical lines of linkage are in constant use but are given their greatest utilization at each election, whether national or local. Every four years when House members must stand for election they mobilize their full chain of leaders down to barrio captains; conversely, when local leaders must stand for election two years later they rely on support flowing down to them from their House allies. Except for a different electoral cycle—one third elected every two years—and a less focused constituency, the same patterns hold true for Senate members. The over-all result is a massive broadening of the political elite but one that is still integrated nationally through a multiplicity of ties centering in Congress.

Although a national political class would seem to constitute a prerequisite without which national politics could hardly develop, whether such a class once in existence proves flexible enough to create and sustain a system of politics is another matter. Partially, at least, the answer rests on the degree of openness maintained by the political elite. The continued recruitment of individuals into all levels of the Philippine political class is a fact. At the congressional level, for example, there has regu-

17. This is not to deny the great power of Manuel Quezon, who many believe gave the Philippines leadership of a charismatic type during the 1920's and 1930's. However, his position was nested in a network of power relationships of the kind discussed. Furthermore, the political class held together in his absence during World War II, and survived his death without trauma.

larly been a turnover of about one third each election.[18] Whether this degree of openness can be carried on and whether the avenues for upward political mobility provided will be sufficient to meet demands are questions that can only be answered by future system performance.

Creating a Political Public

The political process that centered for a long period of time in Congress and is now shared with the presidency, in addition to creating a national political class, also fostered the emergence of a citizenry that was integrated on at least some measurable dimensions. In contrast to a number of new nations that went from extremely narrow limits of participation to instant complete suffrage, the Philippines repeated in its political history a pattern analogous to European and North American polities where the right to vote was extended slowly to an expanding proportion of the male population and then to women. In the Philippines this process was completed by the late 1930's, but even today the suffrage is limited by a literacy test that, although applied with great leniency, excludes many who would otherwise enjoy this form of political participation if such a test were not present.

As a result of the gradual rate at which the number included in formal political participation through the act of voting was increased, the Philippines achieved a degree of national integration that might not have been possible otherwise. Although isolated minorities still exist who are far from equal members of the

18. See Landè, *op. cit.*, p. 53. The percentage of turnover has decreased in recent years from more than half each election to the figure mentioned. I have reported other indicators of continued mobility in "Philippine Legislators and Their Changing Universe," *Journal of Politics,* XXVIII (August, 1966), 556–597. Both the Senate and the House in 1962 contained more members not identifiable with the old elite than with it. House members coming from families classified as possessing "extensive wealth" constituted approximately 50 per cent; those with moderate wealth, 40 per cent; and only 8.6 per cent in the "very limited" category. The Senate distribution was: "extensive wealth," 71 per cent; "moderate wealth," 21 per cent; and "very limited wealth," 8 per cent. The family background breakdown had not changed significantly between independence and the early 1960's. On the other hand, the percentage in each house coming from families of "extensive" wealth had more than doubled for the House, and had increased from less than 50 per cent to the 71 per cent figure in the Senate.

The implications from these figures are that the turnover rates are lessening, and that wealth rather than old family status seems most associated with upward mobility via election to Congress.

political community, certainly, the potentially destructive regional, linguistic, and religious differences that exist in the Philippines have been successfully bridged, and a national political system based on mutually shared values between the political elite and its popular base has been achieved.[19] Congress has contributed significantly to the creation of this level of political integration and to its continued existence.

The methods employed by congressmen in performing this integrative function with the electorate are those common to all legislative systems, although with certain features given more and some less prominence in the Philippines than elsewhere. The dialogue that takes place during elections between congressional candidates, their local leaders, and the voters translates broad national myths into local terms and articulates local demands in terms meaningful to the national political elite. Specific bargaining on pork barrel promises takes place, and greater definition is given these commitments during home visits from congressmen between campaigns and when local leaders visit Manila to speed up the processing of earlier claims. Concomitant with the intricate weaving back and forth between levels that takes place on pork barrel matters is the broader integrative educational role played by Congress as major public policies are debated during legislative sessions. These debates as well as the fiscalizing speeches are well covered by the mass media, and frequently a single major issue will emerge to dominate public interest through a large part of a session—as, for example, did the debate in 1966 on whether or not to send troops to Vietnam. Even the extensive reporting of the complex power shifts within each house and between congressional leaders and the chief executive contributes to a widespread understanding of how the Philippine political system operates and to continued acceptance of the system's legitimacy.[20]

19. Probably nine out of ten Filipinos could be counted on as included. The political system so far has survived its only major challenge, that which has come from the Huks, a movement that grew out of a guerrilla organization in World War II. It continues to try to build an essentially peasant-based alliance capable of overthrowing the existing system.

20. I should point out that not all intellectuals and journalists share this interpretation. Many of them view legislators as corrupt politicians, the whole process of political bargaining as somewhat dirty and seem to hold to an idealized picture of a great leader who will come and put things right in the Philippines.

Data do not exist to weigh the relative importance of the different types of political messages and the communications networks through which they flow. I would anticipate that when research is conducted in this area in the Philippines the barrio-level base will be found to relate to Congress through a linkage system of local leaders who rely heavily on face-to-face contacts, who articulate local interests, and who mobilize local political resources.[21] The local voters may well be found to have no greater knowledge of issues being debated nationally than is the case, for example, in the United States, but because of the greater salience of politics in the Philippines, they will be more knowledgeable of the interconnections between local and national power. I would further hypothesize that in the larger provincial cities greater reliance on mass media channels would be found, with a corresponding increase in knowledge and interest in the larger national issues being debated in Congress. This, of course, in no way precludes the overlapping of mass media channels with the more personal lines of political communication. Certainly an intimate overlapping takes place. With the rapid expansion in old and new mass communication media that is taking place, subtle shifts in the balance can be expected.

Congress also provides ready access for individual complaints and requests and for groups old and new to make their views known. In addition to the highly personal requests for action, individual congressmen and congressional committees receive formal petitions from public and private groups, both at the local, provincial, and national levels. The latter shade over into the establishment of continuing relations with an ever-larger number of associations of an interest group variety and with this a growing acceptance of lobbying as a type of activity that may be properly conducted in legislatures. The inherent flexibility of legislatures in providing access to new groups is amply demonstrated in the Philippine experience and suggests another facet of the continuing role that Congress plays in national integration.

21. The most complete discussion in general terms of the connections between local and national levels of political leadership in the Philippines is to be found in Landè, *op. cit.*, pp. 9–13, 82–83. An empirical case study touching in part on the same subject is Remigio E. Agpalo, "The Political Elite and the People: A Study of Politics in Occidental Mindoro" (unpublished). A fine summary is *Pandanggo Sa Ilaw: The Politics of Occidental Mindoro* (Quezon City, 1965).

The Legislative Function

Much has already been said indirectly about the legislative tasks performed by Congress. A major share in the development of a politics of competition in the Philippines must be credited to the steady flow of bills emerging from the legislative process, most representing successful resolutions of conflict at one level or another. The very ease with which larger political problems can be broken down into smaller units or old problems can be approached anew year after year in the form of legislative proposals promotes the acceptance of conflict because resolving mechanisms are so integrally part of the system. Similarly, the integrative functions of Congress have rested, in part at least, on the enactment of legislation providing pork barrel support for all parts of the nation and local bills for all districts.

A brief overview of changes in the quantitative flow of bills into the Philippine legislature as well as of the numbers passed is one suggestive index of the importance of the legislative function. In the period before independence, the total number of bills increased from about 500 per session in the early 1920's to above 1,000 by the time of World War II. The input fell somewhat immediately following independence but rose steadily from that time on. By the early 1960's, some 3,500 bills were introduced each year, at a ratio of more than ten in the House of Representatives for every one entered in the Senate. Figures from the combined regular and special sessions in 1967 totaled approximately 12,000,[22] a rather startling increase over earlier years. Although the great majority of these bills are of only local interest—changing the name of a school, providing for the creation of a new

22. The 1967 figure is an estimate based on a total of 11,244 bills introduced into the House that year. Secretary I. B. Pareja of the Philippines Congress, House of Representatives, supplied data for the 1967 work load. The great majority of these bills come from individual congressmen and especially from House members servicing local interests. Many senators propose measures of a more general nature that are addressed to broad national problems. Similarly the president always accounts for a cluster of important bills constituting his legislative program. In addition, less vital administrative proposals arrive in Congress from the various departments and agencies of government. Finally, the growing number of well organized interest groups provides a steadily increasing volume of requests to Congress. A case study of one such interest group is my *The Development of an Interest Group: The Philippine Medical Association* (Quezon City, 1966).

barrio, or granting a franchise—the sustained high quantitative level of legislative proposals as well as the marked upward trend points to the acceptance of Congress as an avenue through which to press requests.

In contrast with the numbers of bills introduced, measures passed each session have consistently totaled only a few hundred and have, because of the steady increase in the number introduced, constituted a diminishing proportion of proposals submitted. By the time of the Commonwealth era Congress was passing somewhat over 100 bills a year, up from half that level in the 1920's. By the mid-1950's more than 200 measures were approved by the legislature each year, and in the 1967 combined sessions, a total of 231 bills passed both houses.[23] A House of Representatives figure for the same year of 722 measures passed is, however, lower than several earlier sessions. In 1954, for example, the House passed 1,553 bills, 1,014 in 1946, but only 621 in 1962—a year of low legislative productivity because of an extended battle over leadership.

One conclusion that can be drawn from these figures is that Congress faces what can only be described as an avalanche of legislative proposals each session from which it must decide the quite limited number that will be debated and the even smaller number that will gain approval in both houses. The difficult task of determining priorities to govern the flood of legislation is largely decided in the caucuses that play a vital role in the decision-making process within each house.[24] The broad agree-

23. The fact that in 1967 only 2 per cent of all bills introduced in Congress ever passed both houses may be an indicator that the Philippine legislature has reached the point where it can no longer effectively process demands placed on it. While, undoubtedly, a small percentage of bills can provide mutual satisfaction to both legislators and constituents by the mere fact of being introduced to Congress, the great majority represent wants that can be met only by gaining congressional approval and subsequent administrative implementation. Although no quantitative data are available on the point, one might assume that a great number of bills that were considered of significant importance by their sponsors died among the 98 per cent that failed passage in 1967.

24. In keeping with the rather flexible political party ties that exist in the Philippines for both voters and elected officials, the majority and minority caucuses that control the flow of legislation in each house are not always built on party lines. Coalitions cutting across parties have frequently been the basis for effective internal organization within Congress. Once a majority has been hammered together in either house, however, firm control normally follows.

ments reached in these caucuses are, in turn, interpreted and applied in the standing committees after further consultations among members. Proposals that survive—and in 1967, 9,623 House bills died in committee out of 11,244 introduced—go through various stages beginning with public hearings at the committee level that are quite analogous to the process used in the United States Congress. Over-all coordination and control are supplied in each house by a Committee on Rules, each chaired by the majority floor leader and each in charge of making sure that caucus decisions are carried out. These political mechanisms seem to assure that ample opportunities are maintained for public access to the legislative process while providing the means for sifting through mountains of proposals for those that have political relevance, which is to say, have significant support behind them.

These important political decisions could not be made, however, without a great deal of assistance inside the houses of Congress for answering the kinds of technical questions raised by legislative proposals, as well as for coping with the sheer mechanics of keeping track of 12,000 bills in a short 100-day session. As early as 1930 Congress began to provide members with a modest amount of assistance for bill drafting, research, and secretarial support and to provide the houses with general services in the form of libraries and facilities for publishing some of the records resulting from congressional activities. These legislative services have been expanded through the years and today are organized, in the House, for example, in thirty different divisions, offices, and services. This House organization provides that the four top leadership positions are each provided with staff aides and that the four most important standing committees each has an administrative office and a technical staff assigned to it. Except for the coordinating activities over the whole legislative services staff centralized in the office of the House Secretary, all other units are organized on the basis of providing staff services to all members of the House. The list includes the Legislative Reference Division, the Library Service, the Bills and Index Division, and the Medical Clinic to mention a few of the fifteen included.

Although only four of the some thirty standing committees in the House are provided with parallel legislative service units of a permanent variety, each of the other committees receives full professional support from the various staff agencies and a more or less permanent relationship with those individuals who have specialized in the subject-matter area of the committee. This is especially true of individuals formally attached to the Office of Committee Consultants and Technical Staff who develop expertise in certain fields through long association with one of the standing committees.

There are some 600 career civil servants in the legislative services staff of the House of Representatives today. These are the people along with their Senate counterparts who provide much of the infrastructure support that makes possible the successful functioning of Congress. They do not make up the only professional support, however. Individual congressmen have their own staff assistants, of course, and in the House their number totals some 1,200 currently.[25] Although many of these perform routine non-professional tasks and others are employed because of their political skills, a large number possess professional credentials. These latter are the ones most frequently selected to fill positions open in the standing committees. And since many of these individuals continue from session to session, Congress is provided with an additional body of experts upon which it can draw to handle the proposals and other requests that pour in. The combination of career personnel and political appointees gives the congressmen a nice balance in his staff to meet the needs of professional competence as well as political obligation, and in each case with considerable generosity.

Conclusions

Although Congress performs functions in addition to the ones that have been made the subject of analysis,[26] these others are

25. These estimates were provided by Secretary Pareja.
26. Congress has performed a constituent function in the past and did so again in the 1967 session when both houses passed a joint resolution setting 1970 as the date for the election of a constitutional convention to rewrite the Philippine Constitution, the convention to meet June 1, 1971. Congress, in the same session,

certainly marginal by comparison. The most important overriding role that Congress has played in the Philippines has been to provide the institutional milieu within which a system of open, competitive politics could develop and to exert a variety of institutional pressures that both encouraged politics to break out but also gave it direction and patterning. Although this role has long been shared by an elected president and by locally elected officials, the original creation of a national political class, the working out of a pragmatic but flexible package of issues that constitute the "normal" dimensions of Philippine politics, the development of a Filipino style of electoral politics, and even the forging of a national political identity[27]—these were first fashioned by men intimately identified with Congress.

In doing these things Congress has performed creatively to build a political system that relies heavily on a politics component and that seems to have a built-in capacity to adjust to new situations. This relative success in turn traces back to the types of conflict management and integrative mechanisms that are centralized in Congress. The Philippine legislature was deeply involved in the political socialization process through which the electorate and the political class underwent a widespread value shift in the direction of accepting political conflict as a proper condition and through which they began to construct constraints to control violence. Similarly Congress contributed heavily to national integration by facilitating the emergence of a national political elite that was intimately connected with sub-national political leaders, the creation of a national electorate that was conditioned to a politics that knit local needs with national, and the blending of elite and mass in a manner that contains some

also proposed two immediate constitutional changes (one to increase the permissible number of House members from 120 to 180 and a second to allow members of Congress to become constitutional delegates, if elected, without forfeiting their legislative seats) that were submitted to the voters in a plebiscite held at the same time as elections that year. Congress can also perform certain judicial functions, as in impeachment cases and when judging contested elections.

27. Throughout the years the locale where the strongest nationalistic voices are raised has been in the houses of Congress. No chief executive, for example, has dared to do more than voice mild criticisms of minor aspects of American policies in the Philippines. A continuing number of distinguished congressional critics, in contrast, have done their best to alert their citizens to the areas that are still under American control and to the dangers that American power poses.

elements of dialogue and the promise of more. In the process Congress contributed a vital part of the creative energies that built the Philippine political community and continues to play a central role in keeping democratic politics alive. In the face of contemporary examples elsewhere of apolitical nation-building, and of internal voices demanding an end to politics, this is no small role.

Chapter 10

Staffing the Legislature

James A. Robinson

Introduction

Among the foremost criticisms in any appraisal of contemporary legislatures, inadequate, underpaid, and poorly trained staffs surely rank high. Whether one describes the Congress of the United States or the legislative branch in virtually any of the fifty states of the Union, the generalization applies that legislators enjoy little staff assistance in gathering information, in formulating and promoting alternatives, and in appraising the effectiveness of their decisions. What is true of American legislative staffs applies with even greater force to the British Parliament, and the assistance available to legislators in the "new states" of the underdeveloped nations is trivial and embarrassing when compared with that available in established parliaments. Even the American Congress, without doubt the legislature having the largest number of assistants, the most advanced professionalization of staffs, the most expansive quarters, and the best library facilities readily available, owns the reputation of being disadvantaged in its infrastructure relative to other governmental institutions, especially the executive branch.

Evidence of legislative deprivation comes from all quarters—from legislators themselves, from their overburdened staffs, from advocates of public policy hoping to reach and influence them, and from journalistic and scientific observers of legislatures in nearly every political system. Ambassadors have been known to reduce the size of their embassy staffs; occasional bureaucratic chiefs have been heard to say they could do with fewer personnel; "management experts" have reported "information overload" in executive agencies; and chief executives have abolished committees or reduced the number responsible to them. But no participant in, or observer of, any legislative forum testifies in favor of less, rather than more, parliamentary assistance.

The hearings of the Joint Committee on the Organization of Congress, Eighty-ninth Congress, document this for the United States, as does a contemporary survey of members of the House of Representatives.[1] Commissions and assemblies in individual states typically add their voices to the call for increased professional staff, secretarial assistance, and interns, as did the Illinois Commission on the Organization of the General Assembly in 1967 and as have recent national and regional sessions of the American Assembly and of the Citizens Conference on State Legislatures.[2] The current movement to enlarge the space available to members of the British Parliament responds to backbenchers' demands for greater assistance. Allan Kornberg's chapter (*supra*) includes information on the relative deprivation of staff in the Canadian House of Commons. L. M. Singhvi's description of the Indian L. K. Sabha (*supra*) and Ralph E. Crow's account of the Lebanese Chamber of Deputies (*supra*) contain similar reports of sparse office space, little assistance, and barely minimal reference books or services. And so it goes from parliament to parliament with rare exceptions, such as that of the Philippines to which Robert B. Stauffer briefly alludes in his essay (*supra*).

Universal as the demand is for more and better legislative staffing, it nevertheless remains appropriate to consider (1) the rationale for technical staffing in parliamentary bodies; (2) the particular forms of assistance that might be available; and (3) the present state of legislative staffing compared with what, by some criteria, seems necessary.

1. (Washington, 1966), and Roger H. Davidson, David M. Kovenock, and Michael K. O'Leary, *Congress in Crisis: Politics and Congressional Reform* (Belmont, Calif., 1966).

2. *Improving the State Legislature* (Urbana, Ill., 1967); *State Legislatures in American Politics*, ed. Alexander Heard (Englewood Cliffs, N.J., 1966), pp. 133–136; and *Compilation of Recommendations Pertaining to Legislative Improvement in the Fifty States* (Kansas City, Mo., 1967), *passim*.

Rationale for Staffing

Legislatures own many functions in addition to their original purpose, which in England was to help administer laws or rules governing the political system. Legislatures represent electorates; but, besides articulating or mirroring constituents' preferences, they also integrate, or aggregate or compromise, the variety of views that they reflect. These same institutions sometimes check and balance other governmental institutions within the same polity. Any theorist justifiably may assign any function to a legislature and appraise it according to its performance of that assignment. I join those who affirm that legislative assemblies ought to participate in *initiating* policies pertinent to the contemporary problems of any epoch. The expectation that parliamentary bodies should be innovative implies that they be active in a wide variety of policy-making roles or functions. Much of this section will be familiar to readers of my *Congress and Foreign Policy-Making* and of my contribution to the de Grazia symposium.[3] I venture to restate, slightly modify, and somewhat expand the main lines of previous arguments in order to generalize the doctrine of legislative initiative to all kinds of parliaments, without respect to the domestic or foreign content of policy.

If we begin by recognizing some universal characteristics, or functions, of any policy-making system, we are likely to enumerate such activities as gathering intelligence, formulating and promoting alternatives, selecting among alternatives, implementing and executing selected alternatives, appraising the effectiveness of the policy adopted, and terminating, renewing, or revising past policy. This conception of the stages involved in any decision obviously owes much to Harold D. Lasswell's famous essay, *The Decision Process: Seven Categories of Functional Analysis.*[4] And these stages resemble descriptions of problem-solving offered by John Dewey, Herbert Simon, and others. Their merit as a "con-

3. Rev. ed. (Homewood, Ill., 1967), and *Congress: The First Branch of Government*, ed. Alfred de Grazia (Garden City, N.Y., 1967), pp. 244–280.
4. (College Park, Md., 1956).

struct" lies in avoiding the simple constitutional distinctions—
legislative, executive, judicial—and in specifying a reasonably
wide but still manageable range of discrete activities that one
may observe.

I propose not to add anything to this "model" of decision-making, but rather to use it in two ways: first, to consider the role of
legislatures in modern political systems in the performance of
these functions; and second, to consider the performance of these
functions within the legislature itself. The first consideration
raises questions about the relative influence of the legislature and
the executive in the intelligence, recommendation, prescription,
and appraisal functions of the total system. The second asks
questions about who (or what position) performs such functions
within the legislature considered separately (similar inquiries
could be made concerning the executive branch, parties, courts,
and other arenas). In using this "model" to describe the role of
legislatures and to describe some of the internal workings of
legislatures, I take an historical, or developmental, perspective
and offer my reconstruction of the twentieth-century trends with
respect to legislative influence. Adopting the long view helps one
to see more clearly the relevance of staffing to the demands of
modern parliaments.

Twentieth-century policy-making differs from that of the nineteenth century in two ways: more problems or issues now reach
the agenda of governments, and information about public questions is at once more extensive and more complex. That governments now involve themselves in and with more issues than
formerly is the consequence of many factors—greater social complexity, influential philosophies of welfare, and the "information
revolution," which, among other effects, has helped increase the
visibility and articulation of deprived interests. The information
revolution, a "sub-set" or by-product of the Industrial Revolution,
not only has called to the focus of attention of decision-makers
the deprivations of certain people, but it has also accumulated
descriptions and analyses of their plight in sufficient detail that
policy-makers must grapple with information about the problems
every bit as much as with the problems themselves.

To appreciate the altered character of policy-making, especially the contribution of information to decisions, contrast the legislative experiences of the Calhouns, the Websters, and the Clays with those of the Tafts, the Johnsons, and the Kennedys. In the pre-Civil War era, legislators confronted more or less the same agenda of public issues for a half a century. Slavery, tariffs, and internal improvements very nearly dominated the attention of Congress from the founding of the new government in 1789 until the eve of the Civil War in 1860. The compact number of issues on which a legislator had to inform himself scarcely changed during his career, and the information relevant to them remained essentially the same for long periods. Indeed, it was an era in which debate revolved around broad normative issues of purpose rather than around empirical questions of the effectiveness of alternative avenues to agreed-upon goals.

By the end of the nineteenth century, however, a larger variety of problems and issues occupied the attention of Congress and the president. The Industrial Revolution promoted changes in the number and sources of immigrants; centralized population in urban centers; spawned new forms of corporate activities; reduced death rates and raised birth rates; and invented new modes of transportation and communication. Each change in established patterns upset someone's interests or temporarily disturbed another's, and those who were deprived articulated their complaints and supported them with facts and figures gathered in surveys and reports. The "Brandeis Brief" marked a revolution in judicial proceedings that already had occurred in legislative hearings, thanks to the muckraking investigations of Ida Tarbell, Lincoln Steffens, Jacob Riis, and other effective journalists.

It should be stressed that not only were public problems more numerous—i.e., demands on government to respond to value deprivations or to promote value indulgence—but that greater factual information was available on each problem. And the Industrial Revolution eventually generated such a plethora of data that the varying ways in which institutions processed new inputs of information affected their influence relative to that of other institutions.

I like to date the beginning of the Information Revolution at about 1885. By that year, the Bureau of the Census had fallen so far behind schedule in analyzing data collected from the swollen census of 1880 (the first time in which the decennial growth in population exceeded 10 million) that officials despaired of finishing that census before taking the next constitutionally required enumeration in 1890. It was then that Dr. Herman Hollerith, a Bureau official, developed procedures for transferring data to punched cards and processing them mechanically.[5]

The response of this executive agency was typical of the executive's response in general. That is, the executive branch specialized, bureaucratized, and mechanized. In 1887, when Woodrow Wilson published "The Study of Public Administration," in which he borrowed from Germanic theory and practice, he imported and reinforced the identification of bureaucracy with executive branches of government.[6] It seems to have occurred to few theorists or practitioners that legislatures also might augment their scanning and retrieval capabilities by bureaucratizing. Moreover, to study, teach, or prepare for public administration was to anticipate executive activities, not legislative. To this day, college and university curricula in public administration emphasize executive functions. Few programs specialize in preparing students to assume legislative staff positions, though the fifty states and the twenty-five urban areas with populations exceeding a half-million have legislative bodies whose longer agendas are filled with new and unprecedented challenges. Further, neither in space, staff, nor technical facilities did Congress augment its resources at a rate comparable to the executive's expansion. Congress passed the Pendleton Act in 1883, creating the Civil Service Commission and introducing professional criteria among executive branch

5. Dating the Information Revolution around 1880 is not so arbitrary as the example of the Hollerith card may make it seem. Other technical innovations that assisted the proliferation of recorded information also appeared about the same time. The first marketed typewriters were available in 1874, and John Robert Gregg introduced his method of shorthand in 1888, which system soon virtually replaced Pitman's and other previously developed forms of stenography, tachygraphy, and brachygraphy. See also Leon E. Truesdell, *The Development of Punch Card Tabulation in the Bureau of the Census, 1890–1940* (Washington, 1965).
6. *Political Science Quarterly*, II (1887), 197–222.

personnel. But it did nothing comparable for its own branch until the Legislative Reorganization Act of 1946.[7]

Within a generation we witnessed a substantial alteration in the roles and influence of Congress and the presidency. In the last quarter of the nineteenth century, legislative leadership was every bit as influential as the executive in identifying public problems, setting governmental agendas, and recommending new public policies. Congressional leaders enjoyed national reputations and found their prominent positions likely stepping stones to nomination to the White House, as the careers of James A. Garfield of Ohio, James G. Blaine of Maine, and William McKinley of Ohio indicate. And some who did not achieve the presidency were recognized as powerful commanders of Congress, such as Speakers Thomas B. Reed of Maine and Joseph G. Cannon of Illinois. After McKinley made his reputation in Congress (though he was finally defeated and had to get himself elected Governor of Ohio before winning the presidency), no powerful legislative leader attained the presidency until Lyndon B. Johnson's accession by accident. Warren G. Harding, Harry S Truman, and John F. Kennedy, senators before their election, were not congressional leaders, and Johnson, for all his parliamentary skills, could initiate very little independent senatorial, much less congressional action.

What displaced legislative predominance was, of course, as Lawrence Chamberlain's survey has shown, presidential initiative.[8] When Admiral George Dewey sought the presidency after the Spanish-American War, he offered himself as experienced in executing the orders of his superiors and, thus, qualified to implement congressional imperatives. Such a conception of the presidency, however, was not received with favor by an important segment of the political elites. Rather, Theodore Roosevelt made the White House a "bully pulpit" from which he dramatized attention to issues, proposed alternatives, and campaigned vigorously for his "world view." Roosevelt was explicit and conscious

7. Charles L. Clapp, *The Congressman: His Work as He Sees It* (Washington, 1963), pp. 254–258.
8. *The President, Congress, and Legislation* (New York, 1946).

about his "stewardship theory" of the office, as his autobiographical contrast of the Buchanan-Taft (passive) and Johnson-Lincoln (active) "types" subsequently revealed.[9] Wilson continued to conceive of the presidency as the center of innovation, upstaging Roosevelt ("Dammit, why didn't I think of that?") by restoring the precedent that had lapsed with Jefferson of addressing Congress in person.

Among the factors that made possible Roosevelt's and Wilson's new domination of Congress was the executive's advantage in information resources. Because the executive had its sources of data about public problems, it began to press measures on Congress's agenda, to draft bills that its allies introduced in the House or Senate, and to advocate its point of view in the news and editorial media and with party organizations in the states. When Warren Harding and Calvin Coolidge installed their "weak" administrations at 1600 Pennsylvania Avenue, Congress did not try to fill the vacuum with its versions of new programs. Instead, it waited for Hoover and then F. D. Roosevelt to initiate them. And with the second Roosevelt dates the never ceasing expectation that the President proposes and Congress disposes. That these are institutional or role expectations, not matters of party philosophy or individual predisposition, was confirmed during the administration of the next Republican president. Dwight D. Eisenhower was not a "weak" President by the standards of William Howard Taft or Rutherford B. Hayes. He too assumed the initiative, and when Democrats in Congress thought him derelict, they did not enact their own initiatives to deal with public needs, but criticized Eisenhower's "lack of leadership" in failing to press upon them a bold legislative program.

As a result of the developments of the last half century, the initiating and vetoing roles of Congress and the presidency have been exchanged. Congress once initiated; the president vetoed or signed legislation. Now, with rare exceptions, the president initiates, and Congress ratifies, delays, amends, or vetoes. The executive identifies problems, canvasses alternatives, dominates Congress's agenda with its preferred alternative, and appraises the

9. *The Autobiography of Theodore Roosevelt* (New York, 1958), pp. 197–200.

performance and effectiveness of selected policies. It does so partly because the problems and the information about them are so great as to exceed Congress's capacity to identify, characterize, and respond to them.

What is true of Congress also applies to state legislatures. The colonial distrust of governors and the preferred status of assemblies are remnants of the bygone past. State legislatures, as we shall detail later, are more handicapped than Congress, in space, staff, time, and almost every other pertinent resource. Harvey Walker has shown, for two different periods, that the executive's power of initiative exceeds that of the legislature in Ohio,[10] and I have little doubt that similar studies at different times and in different states would reveal similar patterns. Indeed, Alan J. Wyner's recent study of fourteen governors' offices indicates something of the executive domination of legislatures.[11] So too does Thomas Anton's portrayal of budget-making in Illinois.[12]

A similar trend would, I hypothesize, be observed for Britain, if the equivalent research were undertaken. My impressions are that the shift of initiative and influence from the House of Commons to the government antedates the American alteration in legislative-executive relations. In the latter half of the nineteenth century, John Stuart Mill and Walter Bagehot advocated and described Parliament's appraisal role, reviewing, acceding, delaying, questioning, or even defeating a bill and bringing down a Government, but not initiating or prescribing details of legislation and of policy.[13] Particularly important in Britain was the government's mastery of the parliamentary timetable in order to cope with what one writer has referred to as "the rising flood of national business."[14] The need to expand government control of

10. "Where Does Legislation Originate?" and "Well Springs of Our Laws," *National Municipal Review*, September, 1929, pp. 565–567, and October, 1939, pp. 689–693.
11. "The American Governors and Their Offices" (unpublished doctoral dissertation, Ohio State University, 1967).
12. *The Politics of State Expenditure in Illinois* (Urbana, Ill., 1966), pp. 147–177.
13. Mill, *Considerations on Representative Government* [1861] (Chicago, 1962), chap. v; Bagehot, *The English Constitution* [1865–1867] (New York, 1933).
14. Ronald Butt, *The Power of Parliament* (London, 1967), p. 89.

the scheduling of House of Commons affairs was accentuated by the obstructive efforts of Irish members to bring all business to a halt in the 1880's. This challenge to the very life of Parliament ended in virtually exclusive executive dominance of the legislative agenda and thus resolved a conflict that had raged between the two branches throughout most of the nineteenth century.[15]

In emerging nations, parliaments are uniformly dependent on the executive branch or on the one party that typically dominates new nations. The British parliamentary model, rather than the American congressional model, has most often been adopted in the former colonial areas; hence in such states, the role of the legislature applies even less to the intelligence and recommendation stages of policy-making. And when political instability occurs in the new nations, the fall of governments and the sources of strife are rarely dependent on parliament.[16] Party disputes may be acted out or ratified in parliament, but the legislature makes little independent contribution to changing governments.

In short, modern legislatures have lost influence to executives in several important stages of policy-making that they formerly dominated. Executives constitute the principal sources of information that reveal problems, that generate the core of alternative possibilities leading to legislative recommendations, and that monitor the subsequent effectiveness of a selected alternative. The explanation for this altered status of the two branches resides partly in the new requirements of and for information and in the different ways in which each branch has responded to the new requirements. The executive bureaucratized; and parliaments remained rather as before, relying on the resources of new members and slowly adding staff and acquiring more useful facilities.

If information has altered the institutional arrangements in the principal stages of national policy-making, it has also had an impact on policy-making within the legislature. Its main effects have been to involve executive officials more intimately in the internal procedures of legislatures, in providing intelligence, set-

15. *Ibid.*, pp. 85–89.
16. Data to support this generalization appear in Bruce M. Russett *et al.*, *World Handbook of Political and Social Indicators* (New Haven, Conn., 1964), pp. 103–104.

ting the agenda, determining the form of the bill that will first be considered, and stipulating to party leaders the "rock bottom" that will be acceptable in individual cases. In some state legislatures, the governor designates his party leaders. Although the president remains aloof from, though not uninvolved with, leadership selection in Congress, the prime minister and his government, of course, have some hand in filling a vacant speakership in Commons as well as in designating the leader of the House.

Consider Congress and the contribution of the executive to its intelligence, recommendation, and prescription functions. The intimate ways in which the executive branch influences legislative procedures can be illustrated by gathering together some familiar textbook observations.

The Intelligence Function

First, members desiring information relevant to a prospective bill are as likely to consult an executive agency as a legislative committee staff, or the Legislative Reference Service of the Library of Congress. Second, upon the introduction of any bill, the committee chairman ordinarily solicits the reaction of appropriate executive departments as a matter of routine. Third, if hearings are scheduled, a witness from the executive branch is likely to be the first to testify, so that to the extent newspapers, radio, and television inform congressmen who cannot attend hearings, the advantages of being first and making the news usually go to the executive.[17] The longer the hearings continue, the smaller the attendance of both members and journalists and the less the exposure in the mass media.

The Recommendation Function

First, it is well established that the executive agencies draft legislation for members to introduce. Second, the president, through a series of constitutionally and conventionally required messages, sends recommendations and specific legislative requests to the speaker, vice president, or committee chairmen. So too do departmental secretaries. These proposals occupy the foci

17. Bernard Cohen, *The Press and Foreign Policy* (Princeton, N.J., 1963).

of congressional attention and constitute the issues to be voted up or down or amended. To the extent that advantage flows to him who structures the conflict or sets the terms of debate by presenting the first alternative,[18] the executive is advantaged in influencing the recommendation stage of congressional procedures. Third, Congress often awaits the executive's recommendations rather than anticipating them and giving the issue prior formal consideration. Most congressmen, I believe, conceive their role as reacting to executive initiative rather than taking congressional initiative.

The Prescription Function

Executive influence extends to the timing of votes and to the strategies and tactics of bargaining about amendments and order of procedure during debate and deliberation. Under Presidents Kennedy and Johnson, Lawrence F. O'Brien developed a well-honed staff of liaison officials and procedures for coordinating their work.[19] Randall B. Ripley and Lewis A. Froman, Jr., have described the close ties between White House officials and the Democratic Party's whip system in the House of Representatives.[20] The effectiveness of the majority whip, although he has been elected by his party's caucus in the House, is closely related to his cooperation with the White House's antennae about members' positions.

In brief, executive influence permeates the internal workings of Congress as a decision arena, and the strength of the executive derives in part from its superior intelligence about problems and alternatives.

I have stressed interbranch relations, competition, and dependencies. Others would give less emphasis to executive-legislative relations so broadly conceived and would prefer to concentrate

18. E. E. Schattschneider, *The Semi-Sovereign People* (New York, 1961), p. 68.

19. O'Brien's strategies and resources are described in many of the books on the Kennedy and Johnson administrations. For example, see Patrick Anderson, *The Presidents' Men* (Garden City, N.Y., 1968), pp. 245–260.

20. Ripley, "The Party Whip Organizations in the United States House of Representatives," and Froman and Ripley, "Conditions for Party Leadership: The Case of the House Democrats," *American Political Science Review,* LVIII (1964), 561–576, and LIX (1965), 52–63.

on "policy systems" or "issue areas." The latter conceptions underline the existence of sets of participants from Congress, the executive, and private interests cooperating together and competing with other sets of participants, also from Congress, the executive, and private sectors. Such approaches to policy-making analysis recognize that neither the executive nor the legislature is ordinarily monolithic; both are usually pluralistic. Nevertheless, I believe one cannot escape the observation that the executive participants in such "policy systems" possess extraordinary information advantages over the other participants, including those among their allies in Congress. Consequently, whatever "model" one takes in studying national policy-making as a whole, or congressional policy-making in particular, he will come upon the primacy of the executive.

Inasmuch as this primacy finds some considerable part of its roots in the superior information resources of the executive, we may well consider particular forms of countervailing intelligence that legislatures might acquire. We need now to inquire into appropriate staffing possibilities and to move beyond a vague, naive homily that implies simply more information and bigger and better staffs.

Particular Requirements

I have indicated my desire to specify some appropriate information needs, recognizing that absolutely no merit attaches to the oversimplified propositions, "the more information, the better" and "the more alternatives, the better." Suitable practices for obtaining and processing information depend on certain other features of the legislature, which may vary greatly with time and place. What is appropriate for one legislature may not warrant adoption by another.

The developmental status of a legislature seems to me to affect the suitability for it of differing information systems. In this instance, status refers to a legislature's current relative prominence when compared with that of other governmental institutions, the presence or absence of opposition parties, and the affluence of the society. The "model" of American legislatures is obviously of limited applicability to emerging or transitional political systems. To propose that the trappings of Congress be exported indiscriminately to other systems would be as naive as the now discredited but once fashionable preoccupation of political scientists with grafting features of Britain's responsible parties onto American practices. To be specific, political systems that cannot afford a two-party system because they lack the talent to man an opposition party can surely be forgiven if they regard extensive parliamentary staffs as a luxury to be postponed until they pass the "take-off" stage of political development.

Opposition parties "waste" political talent. That the existence of a viable second party, most of whose members are temporarily disqualified from governing, is a luxury is dramatized by the opposition bench in legislatures patterned after the British model. To the left of the speaker sits a row of able men, of whom some reflect on former days of glory, when they conducted the affairs of government, and others contemplate the next election, following which they hope to be part of the new majority and entitled to a ministry of their own. In a presidential system one does not line up and display so publicly the "government in exile." Both parliamentary and presidential systems effectively use only about half the political talent available. Bicameral legislatures presumably offer more leadership opportunities than unicameral legislatures, and thus further tax the political resources of a nation. A country must be very "rich" indeed to value opposition parties for their own sake and to avoid national coalitions, all-party governments, or one-party regimes.

Just as legislatures vary in their information needs, legislators differ in the character of their demands for information, and, in well-developed legislatures, it may seem pertinent to allow individual members to select from several mechanisms those that they find most congenial. It goes without saying that legislators define their roles differently,[21] with the consequence that high levels of independent information may be more relevant to some roles (e.g., "trustee") than to others (e.g., "broker"), to an opposition leader than to an administration stalwart. We may take as one criterion for designing information systems for parliaments that they include a wide array of alternative forms of support to assist varying individual needs.

Among American congressmen, despite the "felt need" for more assistance, it is obvious that some use any additional staff resources for quite diverse purposes. In any legislature, we may count on certain members' assigning the additional staff employee to constituency work, party organization, or campaign public relations rather than to "problem-solving" in the capital city. However understandable and admirable the decision to make such arrangements from new resources, such purposes fall outside the rationale of the argument for more extensive staff assistance. Yet those who want legislatures to augment their intelligence function will probably be advised to accept the cost of occasional secondary or "corrupt" uses of the mechanisms that are primarily intended for other purposes. Otherwise, advocates of greater staff facilities may obtain less new aid than they seek.

It is undoubtedly worthwhile to conceive of staffing broadly and not to restrict its use to individuals full-time on the office payroll, on committee staffs, or in the Library of Congress or its equivalent. In Washington, why should not congressmen be able to requisition, up to a certain annual amount, funds for books, consultants, small conferences, personal travel, even occasional research contracts? The same applies to American state legislators, if they be disposed to use such channels of information. Whether similar practices fit the British system seems doubtful. One can, however, imagine that political systems such as Norway and Sweden, in which empiricism enjoys greater respect than in England where philosophic and humanistic traditions hold sway

---

21. Several scholars have clarified our collective understanding of role-taking in selected legislatures, including Lewis A. Dexter in Congress, John Wahlke, Heinz Eulau, William Buchanan, and LeRoy Ferguson in the American states, and Allan Kornberg in Canada.

in preparliamentary education, might find some personal information allowance suitable for their parliamentarians.

Obviously, information systems ought to be designed to complement or supplement rather than to duplicate the skills that legislators themselves bring to office. The recruitment patterns that segregate those who will serve from those who will not serve in legislative assemblies furnish an abundant supply of lawyers and businessmen but a relative handful of individuals versed in the problems of the welfare state, acquainted with developments in modern military strategy, familiar with the economics of developing areas, and on speaking terms with the relevance of science and the consequences of the "knowledge explosion" in national and global politics. This is the familiar recruitment pattern not only in the United States, both in Congress and in state assemblies,[22] but in many other countries also. Other papers in this volume summarize pertinent data for Canada, Britain, Lebanon, India, and other nations. Legislatures vary, of course, in their composition of occupations, backgrounds, and relative cosmopolitanism. In general, however, they are likely to recruit individuals interested in and talented for acquiring and handling power and making decisions. But their "content" specialties of law and commerce may be increasingly irrelevant to the substance of their decisions, just as former service in the armed forces or active reserves bears declining relevance for appraising alternative policies of weapons procurement or competing doctrines of deterrence strategies.

Engineers, physicians, and scientists, to name certain professions with apparent relevance to the substance of modern politics, find political careers less compatible with their private vocations, for the reasons that Max Weber and others have identified, than do lawyers and financiers. Yet American legislators show a preference for employing lawyers, when they want specialists, or journalists, when they want generalists. Dean Acheson has remarked that lawyers are admirably equipped by training and

22. For illustrative quantitative data, see Donald R. Matthews, *The Social Backgrounds of Political Decision-Makers* (New York, 1954), p. 30, and Committee for Economic Development, *Modernizing State Government* (New York, 1967), p. 33.

experience for solving problems brought to them by clients but
not so ably prepared for finding and selecting "problems," one of
the chief occupations of the political system.[23] It may be comfortable and congenial for legislators to hire assistants whose occupational experiences and skills duplicate or converge with their
own; it may be less conducive, however, to diversity and, hence,
to innovation.

To multiple forms of staffing and various procedures of information storing and retrieving, I think one should add space as a
legislative requirement. Beyond the symbolic importance of a
separate and imposing building to distinguish the independence
of one "branch" from another[24] is the vital expansion of a variety
of legislative services that adequate space permits. At present, in
the House of Commons and many state legislatures, it is difficult
to imagine that certain new services could be introduced or
present ones expanded without constructing new quarters. Private offices, personal correspondence secretaries, interns, and
other emoluments are often prohibited by the lack of appropriate
accommodations for housing them.

Even the United States Congress, despite two new buildings in
the last ten years, is cramped for quarters, as the most casual
inspection of hallways, basements, and even bathrooms will reveal. Congress, the most luxuriously equipped legislature, has by
no means kept pace with the expansion of executive office facilities, which have proliferated throughout Washington and the
surrounding countryside. One measure of the crowded conditions
of congressional quarters is the square footage available per each
office worker. The General Services Administration (GSA) rec-
ommends seventy-five to eighty-five square feet for each executive branch employee. House and senatorial employees often, if
not normally, have sixty square feet or less, considerably below
the GSA norm. One junior senator reported that after filing cabi-

23. Dean Acheson, *Morning and Noon* (Boston, 1965). See also David Gold,
"Lawyers in Politics," *Pacific Sociological Review*, IV (1961), 84; Heinz Eulau
and John Sprague, *Lawyers in Politics* (Indianapolis, 1964); and Herbert A.
Simon in *Varieties of Political Theory*, ed. David Easton (Englewood Cliffs, N.J.,
1966).
24. The early American experience is instructive in this regard. See James
Sterling Young, *The Washington Community, 1800–1828* (New York, 1967).

nets and other office equipment were accounted for, several of his assistants could enjoy an average of eighteen square feet each, or "less than a desk top."[25]

One other extra-legislative, indeed extra-governmental, alternative is available both for strengthening legislatures and for "checking" their exercise of power. I refer to organized practices of appraisal of particular governmental institutions and policies. The American Bar Association and some state bar associations, through their committees, maintain standing observation teams to monitor and report on the conduct of various programs. In the United States, political scientists have begun to emulate lawyers in their contributions to the continuing appraisal of institutions and policies. This is especially noticeable with respect to Congress. First, the Congressional Fellowship Program was established in 1953, and as one result, a number of political scientists and journalists adopted Congress as their object of continuing research. Second, the diffusion of internships to the states, most notably to California, increased the number of competent local observers in many jurisdictions. Third, the gradual improvements in political science techniques were applied to foreign as well as domestic legislatures, until a small cadre of specialists in legislative processes now exists. Fourth, these researchers are capable of providing legislative branches with independent and competent studies, as individual testimony before the Monroney-Madden Committee revealed. Indeed, a comparison of the hearings of the LaFollette-Monroney Committee in 1946 with those of the Monroney-Madden Committee in 1966 provides an object lesson in the advancement of political scientists' appraisals of Congress. Similar changes, I expect, can be observed in the coverage of Congress by journalists during the past twenty years.[26]

Only relatively affluent societies, however, can afford these extra-governmental practices. Political systems that lack talent and experience to maintain an opposition party and parliamen-

25. *Washington Post*, August 4, 1967.
26. For example, through the entrepreneurship of the distinguished publishers, Nelson and Henrietta Poynter, and the joint cooperation of journalists and political scientists, *Congressional Quarterly* was founded in January, 1945, and developed as a weekly, systematic, detailed review of the legislative branch, theretofore an often poorly covered institution among reporters.

tary staffs are not likely to be overrun with interns, journalists, and scholars with the expertise to appraise regularly and comprehensively their legislative institutions. Is it, therefore, appropriate to consider exporting political science as a form of foreign aid? Is it feasible for advanced countries with reputations for parliamentary stability to contribute, through an international organization, both money and rotating personnel to help encourage and perfect the development of legislative practices in underdeveloped countries? The Inter-Parliamentary Union (IPU), which recently produced a multi-nation survey of legislative institutions,[27] might be such an organization. Or the American Political Science Association's Asian Fellows program might be imitated or expanded, so that future legislative staff in other parliaments might intern in the staffs of American congressmen.

Such an appraisal component of multi-lateral foreign aid should meet some obvious criteria, including independence of particular national governments, invitation by host governments, and explicit development of alternative models of parliamentary processes to offer choice to client-institutions. In organizing any such effort, the experience of individual constitution-makers and rule-givers ought to be accumulated from the United States (James K. Pollock on Germany, Charles Zinn on Pakistan, among others, not to mention Commonwealth specialists who have participated in the adaptation of British institutions to overseas dominions and new nations).

I have omitted any reference to or recommendation of applications of automated data processing or other forms of electronic assistance to legislative institutions and individual legislators. Robert L. Chartrand of the Legislative Reference Service of the Library of Congress and Kenneth Janda of Northwestern University have written thoughtfully on "hardware" that might facilitate legislative work.[28] Others, including certain management consult-

27. *Parliaments: A Comparative Study on the Structure and Functioning of Representative Institutions in Fifty-Five Countries,* ed. Michael Ameller (London, 1966).
28. Chartrand's papers are usually inserted in the *Congressional Record.* Janda's arguments and expositions are collected in his *Information Retrieval: Applications to Political Science* (Indianapolis, 1968), esp. pp. 176–220. See also Charteand, Janda, and Michael Hugo, *Information Support, Program Budgeting, and the Congress* (New York, 1968).

ing firms and a major national broadcasting network, have advocated what amounts, in my view, to indiscriminate and inappropriate use of gadgetry in Congress and other legislatures. Technical facilities surely must be accepted or rejected according to political values and functions, not merely because they are available (e.g., electronic voting machines). They must serve, not master, politicians.

My rather conservative view presently is that legislators in underdeveloped nations need politically mature institutions first —gadgets, later. Undoubtedly, computer and electronics-trained personnel are available to manage automated data processing installations in many developing nations. But these skills are probably easier to come by than those we regard as political skills. Until the latter are in a reasonably abundant supply, I believe the application of hardware to legislative institutions deserves low ranking on a scale of priorities.

The Gap Between Current and Desirable Resources

My recommendations are indicated in the previous section—an array of supporting facilities; resources that are available to individual legislators as well as to committees or houses; recruitment programs and practices that complement rather than duplicate skills of legislators themselves; space; and an organized appraisal system outside the formal organs of government. Each of these deserves greater inventory and evaluation than presently is available, which is to say that the standard recommendation for more research is appropriate. In addition to the IPU report, already referred to, I have encountered only one stab at an inclusive comparison of the fifty state legislatures and their services, one produced by former Kansas Governor John Anderson's Citizens Conference on State Legislatures.[29] I know of nothing comparable to Donald G. Tacheron and Morris K. Udall's encyclopedia of

29. Calvin Clark, *A Survey of Legislative Services in the Fifty States* (Kansas City, Mo., 1967). Also see appendixes in the Eagleton Institute's *The New Jersey State Legislature* (Trenton, N.J., 1963).

services available to members of the House of Representatives for the Senate, for the states, or for foreign legislatures.[30] Case studies of particular innovations (e.g., effects of reapportionment) in the American states are now being conducted by the National Municipal League and the Eagleton Institute of Politics (Rutgers University). These should considerably enlarge our collective understanding of the relation of particular practices and procedures to other legislative processes and to policy outcome.

Meanwhile, the gap between available and desirable services remains. The Clark survey documents the inadequacy of staffing facilities in the American states. Consider the following:

1. Research services agency expenditures average less than $125,000 annually; the number of full-time staff members averages 10.5; the number of part-time staff members averages four (p. 12).

2. Bill-drafting services are available in forty-nine states; their staffs average six attorneys and eleven clerks (pp. 28–29).

3. Statutory and code revision services average three attorneys and 7.5 clerks, with an average expenditure of $57,000.

4. Forty-three states provide legislative fiscal services; forty-one, budget review and analysis; forty, a continuous review of revenue and expenditures; thirty-two, legislative post-audit (p. 39).

5. Fiscal services in twenty-one states in which data are available average $80,000 (p. 39); post-audit services in twenty-five states average $345,000 (p. 45).

6. One-third of the states do not assign clerical staff to the majority of standing committees (p. 50).

7. Eleven senates and five houses furnish a private secretary or clerical assistant to individual members. A stenographic pool serves twenty-eight senates and thirty houses. No clerical assistance is available in eleven senates and ten houses (p. 52).

8. Thirteen states provide technical or administrative assistance to the legislative leaders, and twenty-seven furnish additional clerical staff. In these states, the average number of leader-

30. *The Job of the Congressman* (Indianapolis, 1966).

ship staff is one assistant and two clerks in the house and one-half assistant and two clerks in the senate (p. 52).

These data indicate something of the differences between existing and desirable resources in the American states. Legal and fiscal services are emphasized more than social analysis; auditing and accounting are emphasized more than either planning or policy impact analysis; party and house leaders and standing committees do not have enough staff to maintain independence from the executive; and individual members have few legislative sources on which to rely for assistance.

The notable exception to the understaffed state legislature is, of course, California. The effects of the whole package of Unruh innovations have not been studied, although considerable description of the changes is in print and much information has been circulated by the grapevine of national legislative conferences and consultations. Since 1959, the permanent staff of the California Assembly has increased from five to sixty members, who are assigned to committees, to the legislative reference service, to the minority party, and to the Speaker. Each of the eighty legislators is authorized to appoint a field representative or administrative assistant in his district. Recruitment, except for field men, is on the basis of education and experience. Salaries are as high as $21,000. Training programs and promotional opportunities are integral to the whole staff operation. Political scientists and economists, as well as lawyers, fill the positions.[31]

Although the IPU survey of parliamentary "administrative services" is less comprehensive for national legislatures than is the Clark Report for American states, a similar gap exists in many foreign settings.

31. Lee Nichols, "The California Experience: Recruitment, Training and Promotion of State Legislative Staff," May, 1966 (mimeographed). Three speeches by Unruh are reprinted in "Organization of Congress," *Hearings, Joint Committee on the Organization of the Congress,* 89th Cong., 2nd Sess., Part 15, pp. 2296–2308. Also see George S. Blair and Houston I. Flourney, *Legislative Bodies in California* (Belmont, Calif., 1967), pp. 50–54.

Professor Alan J. Wyner of the University of California at Santa Barbara has undertaken to describe the array of legislative innovations introduced by Unruh and to assess their impact on the Assembly's initiative and influence. His study will appear among the Eagleton Institute's cases in legislative innovation. Since this was written, Lou Cannon has published his *Ronnie and Jesse: a Political Odyssey* (Garden City, 1969), which is devoted partly to Unruh as speakee.

1. In some countries, the secretary-general, or legislative services chief, is appointed by the executive, not by parliament (p. 85).

2. Staffs are sometimes drawn from among civil servants from branches of public administration not attached to parliament (p. 86).

3. Recommendation and initiation of legislation is now principally an executive function; parliaments confine themselves largely to deliberating and assenting to executive proposals (pp. 140–151).

These two reports illustrate the limits on varied services, individual resources, and complementary staff skills. Proposals to enlarge the House of Commons space to provide more services are currently under discussion.[32] If adopted, research on the changes or "differences" they induce ought to be carried out. Likewise, one ought to inquire into the impact of the separate office buildings in New Mexico, North Carolina, Arizona, and soon in Michigan on the role of the legislature.[33] Unless these dramatic innovations are studied concurrently with their adoption, we shall have about as much reliable knowledge about them as we have about the unicameral legislature in Nebraska, now thirty years old, or about the nonpartisan legislature in Minnesota, which is scant knowledge indeed.

Filling this gap depends first, however, on recognizing its existence and assuming a normative theory that assigns the legislature active, initiating, full-scale policy-making roles. The British tradition of parliamentary government, with increasing diminution of legislative influence, is widely diffused and is reinforced by certain philosophies of "the Administrative State," by limited resources, and by lack of emphasis on process itself as a policy issue. Hence, reopening and redefining classical questions of po-

32. The relative paucity of Parliament's sources of information may be seen in Peter G. Richards, *Parliament and Foreign Affairs* (Toronto, 1967), pp. 48–66.

33. Professor Preston Edsall of North Carolina State University is preparing such an appraisal, concentrating on the effects of the new North Carolina Legislative building on resources, status, time spent in Raleigh, relations with the governor, and comparisons with other states that have also erected separate legislative edifices. His essay also is part of the Eagleton series on legislative innovation.

litical power and responsibilities may well be in order. To this task, virtually every culture brings a relevant tradition of political theory.

Conclusion: Expectations about the Effects of Staffing

My recommendation for expanded staff assistance in all legislatures is founded on the premise that the legislature constitutes a viable and valuable check among a system of checks and balances. Yet, in candor, my personal expectations for renewing legislative influence in established polities and for creating it in new ones are not sanguine. Similar legislative pessimism is shared by others who have contemplated future power relations within national governments.[34] Some of the very causes of legislative decline in the late nineteenth and early twentieth centuries continue and thus maintain executive dominance in developed nations and favor executive power in new nations.

Thus, the prospect is not hopeful that legislative reforms, including increased staffing resources, will alter major patterns of governmental relations. They may decelerate the drift toward greater executive influence, but they give many appearances of "too little, too late." These words of caution are not meant to argue against staffing parliaments more effectively but rather are intended to qualify one's estimates of the impact of such innovations.[35]

If the legislature cannot occupy a strong position in competition with the executive for policy initiative, we must look beyond

34. Among others, see James MacGregor Burns, *Presidential Government: The Crucible of Leadership* (Boston, 1965), chap. ix; Samuel P. Huntington, "Congressional Responses to the Twentieth Century," *The Congress and America's Future*, ed. David B. Truman (Englewood Cliffs, N.J., 1965); Benjamin Akzin, "Legislation: Nature and Functions," *International Encyclopedia of the Social Sciences* (New York, 1968), IX, 226–228; and Ralph K. Huitt, "Legislation: Legislatures," *ibid.*, p. 236.

35. In his essay in this volume, John Grumm demonstrates that among American state legislatures, those with greater "legislative professionalism" are more likely to be responsive to social and policy demands than those with less professional assistance. This is remarkable evidence that, in one vital respect, staffing makes a difference.

narrow considerations of staffing potentialities. Other essays in this volume help to establish such a contextual analysis, into which our reflections on staffing may be cast. A contextual view suggests at least two other possibilities for maintaining the check and balance functions through legislative assemblies, for both of which possibilities staffing is relevant.

First, legislatures may accentuate their performance of the appraisal function in contrast to a diminution of participation in the recommendation and intelligence functions of national decision-making. By monitoring, reviewing, and evaluating past performance, legislatures could correct systematic injustices, discover effective strategies, and act as gadfly and examiner of executive conduct. The House of Lords may be a model for the performance of this function.

Second, political parties, either through competitive systems of parties or intra-party competition, may be the active check on executives, yet operate through the formalities of parliamentary settings. This is, of course, the doctrine of party responsibility, popular among political scientists impressed by the British system.

Whether the effective locus of countervailing power lies in an appraisal-oriented parliament or in parties cloaked in a parliamentary fiction, demands for information will increase. To meet this need, various forms of experience with staff along the lines we have indicated are available from which policy-makers may choose.

Chapter 11

Congressional Committee Professional Staffing: Capabilities and Constraints*

Samuel C. Patterson

The United States is a highly developed political system. It is a cosmopolitan urban society with a highly industrialized economy. Its political institutions are highly differentiated, very complex, and extremely stable. These are commonplaces and almost go without saying. We have nearly become accustomed to confining discussion about political development to the Third World, and the development of the highly modernized systems of the West are in danger of being ignored. One of the interesting properties of the highly developed political system is that knowledge tends to become power, that policy-making tends to be determined increasingly by knowledge rationally used, by scientific information, and decreasingly by purely political calculations of power, influence, or electoral advantage.

Political Development and the Intelligence Function

In addition to economic and political development, the United States has experienced considerable epistemological development. The enhanced role of knowledge in policy-making is indi-

* This study is a part of The Study of Congress project of the American Political Science Association, supported by a grant to the Association by the Carnegie Corporation. I am indebted to The Study of Congress, and particularly to Ralph K. Huitt, for the help which made my research on congressional committee staffing possible.

cated in the American case by the substantial evidence that the political leader has become increasingly autonomous, increasingly independent of the political demands of pressure groups, economic notables, or the mass electorate. Policy-making has become much more dependent than even a quarter of a century ago on scientific information, the advice of scientists, subject-matter expertise, and research. The American legislature now invariably requires professional staff personnel to provide at least an important segment of the domain of knowledge upon which policy decisions can be made. The "knowledgeable society" is a developmental construct with very great implications for the development of legislatures as organizations.[1]

As a political system becomes more highly developed, it comes to allocate its resources for defining and utilizing knowledge differently. Organizational intelligence in the highly developed system tends to involve supplying technical or scientific intelligence, research results, and "facts-and-figures." In the knowledgeable society a heavy investment is likely to be made in the intelligence function, and the stability or predictability of highly developed systems tends to lead to the use of intelligence resources for the supply of professional expertise. Specialists in technical knowledge supply information to political leaders, and they help to mobilize support for policy decisions. In political decision-making, professional staff experts "introduce a 'rational-responsible' bias—a more conscious examination of alternatives, of relevant factors beyond power, even of 'long-range' consequences."[2] They help to mobilize or maintain support by lending prestige to decision-makers, and by providing the kinds of factual justifications for policy alternatives peculiarly acceptable—even demanded—in a society heavily oriented to knowledge.

Purely political decision-making is still a significant phenomenon for the American political system. Policy arenas differ in the extent to which there is closure among experts about the facts,

1. Robert E. Lane, "The Decline of Politics and Ideology in a Knowledgeable Society," *American Sociological Review*, XXXI (October, 1966), 649–662.
2. Harold L. Wilensky, *Organizational Intelligence: Knowledge and Policy in Government and Industry* (New York, 1967), pp. 8–19; quotation at p. 15. Also, see Wilensky's *Intellectuals in Labor Unions* (New York, 1956), esp. pp. 39–60.

and political conflicts continue to occur because knowledge may be used by contending political forces to defend different policy alternatives. This paper focuses upon the professional staffs of committees of the United States Congress, where there is an increasing investment in the function of organizational intelligence, and where political decisions increasingly depend upon expert knowledge. A congressman's own office staff is largely political—mainly oriented to the re-election of the member, and thus pre-eminently involved in making contacts for constituents and maintaining communications with them. The committee staffs, more intimately involved in the making of public policy, are largely technical information specialists—facts-and-figures men.

The Development of Congress

Congress is a very highly institutionalized political structure. It has been extraordinarily adaptable, it is organizationally complex, it is autonomous, and it is coherent.[3] The institution underwent significant adjustments in the nineteenth century, and probably has adapted to the twentieth-century executive centered policy-initiation structure better than other Western parliamentary institutions. Over the nineteenth century, Congress grew increasingly complex internally, developing an established leadership structure and a highly refined and specialized decisional structure in its increasing numbers of committees and subcommittees. At the same time, it became more differentiated politically in the sense that it came to provide independent patterns of career mobility. Finally, first by partisan majoritarianism and then by consensus in the status structures of its committees, Congress has developed a high degree of coherence. Its coherence is now reflected in the high incidence of policy issues which are defined as non-partisan, in the well-developed normative patterns in the institution, and in its climate of high morale.

3. Samuel P. Huntington, "Political Development and Political Decay," *World Politics,* XVII (April, 1965), 386–430.

Congressional committee staffing has developed from the increasing complexity of Congress as an institution, from the accelerating specialization of members of Congress, and from the increasingly complex nature of policy issues with which Congress has dealt. The number of congressional committees was increased sporadically until some reductions were made in the 1920's. Further consolidations were made by the Legislative Reorganization Act of 1946. Since 1946, subcommittees have grown fairly steadily in number. Increases in the numbers of committees and subcommittees, in turn, have produced increases in the numbers of professional staff employees.

In the early days of the Republic congressional committees had, and probably needed, no staff. The first congressional committee staff man appears to have been employed by a secret committee of the Continental Congress.[4] But this was a temporary and unusual assignment. Congressional committees were a half century in becoming well established, and it was not until the House Ways and Means Committee hired a full-time clerk in 1856 that some kind of committee staffing became anything like a regular affair. Other major congressional committees acquired clerical help over the latter half of the nineteenth century.[5] The use of professional staff, as opposed to strictly clerical assistance, cannot date much before the mid-1920's, marked by the passage in 1924 of the first comprehensive legislative pay act authorizing appropriations for all committee employees.[6] Professional staffing

4. Early in 1776 the secret committee of correspondence and the "secret committee," later to be the committees on foreign affairs and commerce, employed Silas Deane, a former member of Congress, to engage in some dealings with French agents. See Edmund C. Burnett, *The Continental Congress* (New York, 1964), pp. 118–119.

5. The Appropriations Act of 1856 provided for hiring clerks for the Ways and Means Committee and the Senate Finance Committee. Other committees began to have full-time clerks as follows: House—Foreign Affairs, Judiciary, Military Affairs, and Naval Affairs in 1858; Appropriations in 1865; Banking and Currency in 1866; Agriculture and Pensions in 1872; Rivers and Harbors in 1884; Merchant Marine and Fisheries in 1888; and Rules in 1890; Senate—Commerce, Foreign Relations, Judiciary, Military Affairs, Naval Affairs, Pensions, and Post Office and Post Roads in 1861; Agriculture and Public Buildings and Grounds in 1864; Appropriations in 1867; Education and Labor in 1870; and Rules in 1876. Lindsay Rogers, "The Staffing of Congress," *Political Science Quarterly*, LVI (March, 1941), 1–22. See also Charles L. Clapp, *The Congressman: His Work as He Sees It* (Washington, 1963), pp. 254–255; George B. Galloway, *The Legislative Process in Congress* (New York, 1953), pp. 410–414; and Lauros G. McConachie, *Congressional Committees* (New York, 1898), pp. 65–66, 170–171, 293–294.

6. Rogers, *op. cit.*, p. 3.

for all committees became fully established with the passage of the Legislative Reorganization Act of 1946, which authorized each committee to hire four professional staff aids and six clerks.[7]

Until the end of World War II, committee staff personnel were, in the main, chosen on a patronage basis and served only while their patron, usually the committee chairman, was in office. There were a few exceptions to this: The Appropriations Committees had clerks who, though recruited on a patronage basis, became expert and served under several chairmen; and, the House Foreign Affairs Committee has had the same staff administrator since 1939.[8] However, the conditions of congressional committee staffing as of the immediate post-War years were succinctly summarized by former Congressman Jerry Voorhis:

> As for the regular committees, which constitute the very heart of the work of Congress, their entire staff consisted of one or two clerks and a "messenger." These people were always appointed by the chairman and they were almost always people from his own district who had been politically active on his behalf. But they were not even supposed to be trained for the work of advising a congressional committee regarding its legislative work. The most minor bureau in the Department of Agriculture had on its staff a dozen people far more highly trained, far better informed, and considerably better paid than anyone on the staff of the Committee on Agriculture of the House or Senate.[9]

Since 1946, committee staffs have become much more professionalized. Though political considerations sometimes are involved in staff appointments, most are appointed because of their competence. Tenure in staff positions is now secure in most committees, and salaries are competitive with those of executive agencies.[10]

Committee staffs have grown fairly steadily in size since the

7. These limitations did not apply to the Appropriations Committees. See Gladys M. Kammerer, "The Record of Congress in Committee Staffing," *American Political Science Review*, LV (December, 1951), 1126–1136; and Max M. Kampelman, "The Legislative Bureaucracy: Its Response to Political Change, 1953," *Journal of Politics*, XVI (August, 1954), 539–550.

8. Joseph P. Harris, *Congressional Control of Administration* (Washington, 1964), pp. 72–73; and Holbert N. Carroll, *The House of Representatives and Foreign Affairs* (Pittsburgh, 1958), pp. 102–109.

9. Jerry Voorhis, *Confessions of a Congressman* (Garden City, N.Y., 1947), p. 296.

10. See Legislative Reference Service, Library of Congress, *Senate Committee Staffing*, 88th Cong., 1st Sess., April 23, 1963; and, Joint Committee on the Organization of the Congress, *Organization of Congress: Final Report*, 89th Cong., 2nd Sess., July 28, 1966, pp. 21–23.

Reorganization Act was passed (see Figure 1). In 1947 House committees employed about 222 persons; staff size reached 770 employees in 1967. Senate committee staffs have grown from about 340 persons in 1952 to more than 620 in 1967. Of course, many of the employees of congressional committees are secretarial or clerical personnel. But the professional staffs have grown very markedly since 1946. Table 1 shows the sizes of the professional staffs of the House and Senate for the years 1948, 1952, and 1967. The Reorganization Act authorized sixty professional staff appointees for Senate standing committees and seventy-six for

Table 1. *Sizes of Congressional Committee Professional Staffs, 1948, 1952, and 1967*

Years	House	Senate
1948	51	42
1952	126	137
1967	269	319

Sources: Gladys M. Kammerer, "The Record of Congress in Committee Staffing," *American Political Science Review*, LV (December, 1951), 1130; George B. Galloway, *The Legislative Process in Congress* (New York, 1953), pp. 412–413; *Congressional Record* (Daily), CXIII, 90th Cong., 1st Sess., pp. H1488–H1498, S2313.

House committees. Additional permanent and temporary employees have been added for the Appropriations Committees, which were exempted from the Act, and by special authorizing resolutions which the committees have brought to their respective houses for approval.

Increases in staff activity are reflected very directly in steady increases in committee expenditures for inquiries and investigations (see Figure 2). The Eighty-fourth Congress authorized the expenditure of nearly $7 million for this purpose, though less than $4.8 million was actually expended. By the Eighty-ninth Con-

Figure 1. *House Committee Staff Personnel, 1947–1967*

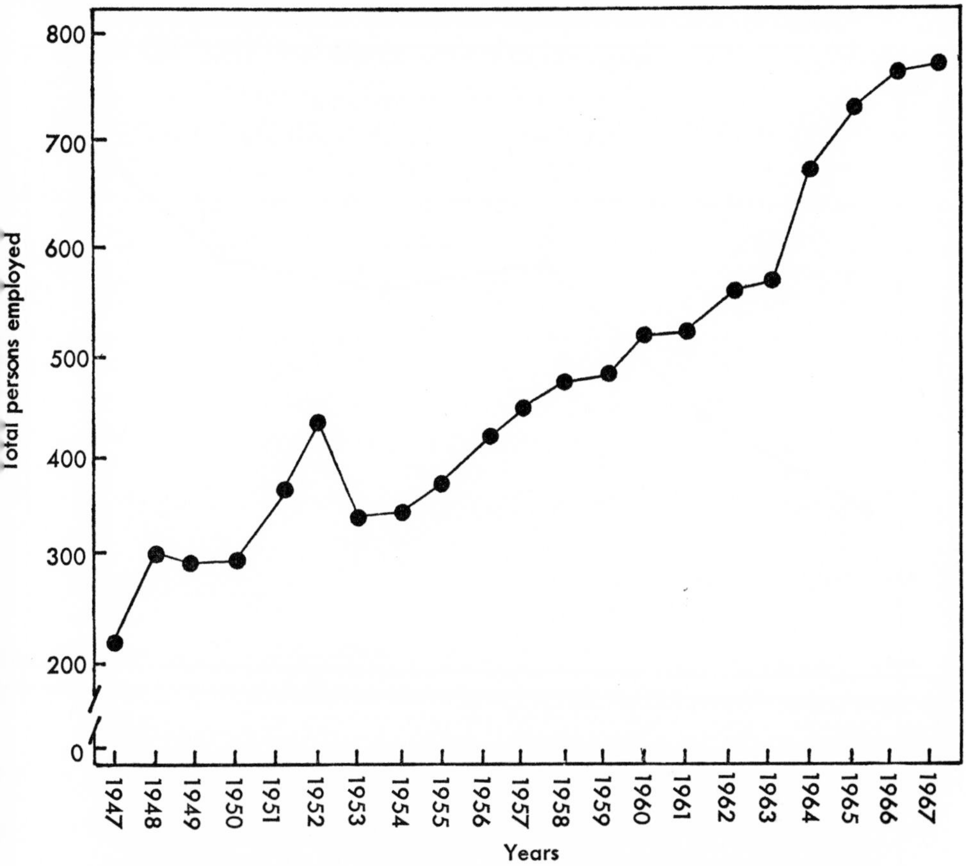

Sources: Margaret Fennell, Susan S. Koppel, and John S. Gosnell, *Statistical Study on the Staffing of Committees of the House of Representatives* (Washington, 1963); *Congressional Record*, CX, Pt. 1, 88th Cong., 2nd Sess., pp. 1179–1188; *Congressional Record* (Daily), CXI, 89th Cong., 1st Sess., pp. 1619–1628; *Congressional Record* (Daily), CXII, 89th Cong., 2nd Sess., pp. 830–839; *Congressional Record* (Daily), CXIII, 90th Cong., 1st Sess., pp. H1488–H1498.

The unusual increase in the size of committee staffs during the Second Session of the Eighty-second Congress occurred because of extraordinary subcommittee investigations of the Justice Department (Judiciary) and the administration of the internal revenue laws (Ways and Means), as well as an unusually large but temporary staff increase in the Public Works Committee.

Figure 2. *Committee Expenditures for Staff Inquiries and Investi-gations, 1955–1966*

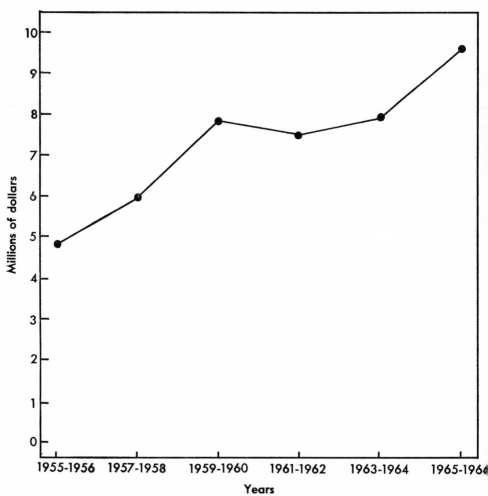

Source: Congressional Record (Daily), CXIII, 90th Cong., 1st Sess., p. S2166.

gress, more than $12 million was authorized, and nearly $9.6 million was spent for investigations and inquiries.

Congress has become an increasingly complex institution. Though the number of standing committees was reduced in 1946 from 81 to 34, this "streamlining" has been followed by a rather remarkable increase in the number of subcommittees—from 180 in 1945, to 253 in 1961, and to 376 in 1964. The tendency has been to staff these subcommittees, either separately or from increased full committee staffs, by special authorizations beyond those provided in the 1946 legislation. Thus, increased committee staffing, both in terms of men and money, follows the increased complexity of Congress as an institution, and the increasing workload which the institution processes.[11]

Utilization of Committee Staffs

Congressional committee staffs as they are now constituted are heavily utilized by committee and subcommittee chairmen and ranking minority members. The relationships between staff personnel and committee leaders generally are persistent, regular, and close. However, committee staff time is utilized also by the general congressional membership, by lobbyists, and by officials in executive agencies. Brief comments about each of these users of committee staffs will indicate the kinds of outside constraints on staffs which are operating in the congressional system.

Committee staffs are utilized by members of the Congress in general, although the evidence is mounting that such utilization is not of highest rank or of major significance. The best available data indicate that, on the average, only about 12 per cent of congressional effort for legislative research involved committee staffs, that about 21 per cent of the effort invested in preparation for committee meetings and hearings was committee staff related, and that less than 9 per cent of effort directed to the preparation for floor debate and voting involved committee staffs.

The data in Table 2 are based upon an analysis of interview responses from a reasonably adequate sample of 160 members of the House of Representatives. They suggest that, for the House as a whole, committee staff effort ranks third in importance of the

11. Joint Committee on the Organization of the Congress, *Organization of Congress: Final Report*, 89th Cong., 2nd Sess., July 28, 1966, pp. 59–74.

work agencies analyzed for members' legislative research and preparation for floor debate, and second for preparation for committee sessions.[12] Republicans and Democrats do not differ significantly in committee staff utilization, but members with high committee rank make much heavier use of committee staffs than do those with low seniority. In addition, committee chairmen and ranking minority members exhibit about the same extent of committee staff utilization.[13]

Table 2. *Sources of Legislative Effort by Congressmen*

Work done by:	Legislative research	Legislative activity Preparation for committee meetings and hearings	Preparation for floor debate
The member himself	30.2%	61.3%	59.6%
Members' office staffs	45.6	15.4	28.2
Committee staffs	11.7	20.9	8.7
Legislative reference service	9.0	1.4	2.8
Executive agency staffs	3.3	—	—
Other	0.2	1.0	0.7
Total	100.0	100.0	100.0

Source: John S. Saloma, "The Job of a Congressman: Some Perspectives on Time and Information" (unpublished paper, 1967), p. 34; preliminary analyses of these data appear in Donald G. Tacheron and Morris K. Udall, *The Job of the Congressman* (Indianapolis, 1966), pp. 280–288, and in *We Propose: A Modern Congress*, ed. Mary McInnis (New York, 1966), pp. 290–291.

Our evidence for the utilization of congressional committee staffs by executive agencies is much more tenuous than is the evidence for utilization by congressmen. It is clear that, especially with the increasing development of stable, professional committee staffs since 1946, executive agencies have come to pay a great deal of attention to some committee staffs, and to rely

12. Saloma asked each member to estimate the proportions of their total effort in legislative research, committee preparation, and floor preparation that could be attributed to themselves, their own staffs, the committee staffs, the LRS, executive agency staffs, and others. The proportions in Table 2 are averages of these proportions for the sample of 160 members. See also Lowell H. Hattery and Susan Hotheimer, "The Legislator's Source of Expert Information," *Public Opinion Quarterly*, XVIII (Fall, 1954), 300–303.

13. John S. Saloma, "The Job of a Congressman: Some Perspectives of Time and Information" (unpublished paper, 1967), pp. 36–39.

upon them heavily for help. Agency officials maintain very close contact with committee staff personnel, and much of the field, or network, of legislative-executive relations is filled with daily interactions between committee and agency staffs. Agency staffs maintain contact with committee staffs, for their own purposes, largely out of needs for anticipatory intelligence. The agency's success in congressional hearings may depend crucially upon effective anticipation of committee staff interests and concerns, since committee staff concerns tend to be, or to become, committee member concerns. Thus, it has been pointed out that

> continuity in legislative staffing has brought about a close relationship between committee staffs and career executives. Sometimes the career staffs of the two branches maintain contacts without specific participation by members of committees or by the politically appointed executives in the agencies. These relations gradually develop into meaningful bonds; they provide a line of communication that often has a marked bearing on the environment of the executive.[14]

Fenno has observed first-hand the closeness of these relationships for interactions between the Appropriations Committees and agency budget personnel. He has shown that "the subcommittee clerk on the one hand and the departmental budget officer or bureau officer on the other hand constitute the day-to-day linkage between the legislative and executive branches in appropriations matters."[15] Two executive agency budget officers described their relationships with Appropriations Committee staffs to Fenno in the following terms:

> [Departmental budget officer] I'm on close personal relationships with the members of the Committee's staff. During the working season (prior to the hearings) we're in constant contact, daily and on weekends, here or at home . . . we want to be sure they talk about important things and don't go running off into unimportant areas. Or, if there are going to be certain questions coming up, we want to know what they are. The Committee staff will tell us. And that's good. It's

---

14. Marver H. Bernstein, *The Job of the Federal Executive* (Washington, 1958), p. 109.
15. Richard F. Fenno, *The Power of the Purse: Appropriations Politics in Congress* (Boston, 1966), p. 304. See also Harold P. Green and Alan Rosenthal, *Government of the Atom* (New York, 1963), pp. 65–114, for a relevant analysis of the staff of the Joint Committee on Atomic Energy.

much better to be prepared than to say, "I don't know, I'll look it up."[16]

[Bureau budget officer] We have very friendly relations with the clerk . . . (he) will call us and tell us that Congressman X is worried about this or that program so we can be ready for it in the hearing. They help us to have a more fruitful hearing in that way. Or, they may ask us for additional data on something . . . that will help them out in understanding our program. Then they may be able to explain it to the congressman better than we can. The congressmen don't read our justifications very thoroughly—and I sympathize with them—but the clerks do. If we can help them in answering their questions, they may sell our program for us. They will sit in the hearings handing questions to the congressmen, and if we have given them information their questions will be more understandable.[17]

A great deal of committee staff time is involved in information exchange and negotiations with agency staff personnel. These interactions require a major part of the time of some congressional staff personnel, and it is also clear that staff-to-staff relations involve reciprocal staff utilization.

Lobbyists consume some committee staff time, although probably less than is suggested by the conventional wisdom about pressure politics. The extent of actual lobbyist-committee staff contact has not been measured carefully, but we do know that Washington lobbyists tend to prefer committee staff contacts to contacts with congressmen, their personal staffs, or executive agency staffs. Data gathered by Milbrath for 114 Washington lobbyists are shown in Table 3. He reports that "committee staff persons were selected as important (first or second choice) contacts by 61 per cent of the respondents . . . ," whereas "executive agency staff persons were selected by 49 per cent, and members of Congress by 42 per cent."[18] Furthermore, lobbyists prefer congressional staff personnel over other agencies as sources of inside information. Milbrath suggests that lobbyists prefer committee staff contacts because staff personnel are more accessible, because they are more expert in a subject-matter, and because information is more likely to be forthcoming from them.

16. *Ibid.*, pp. 304–305.   17. *Ibid.*, p. 305.
18. Lester W. Milbrath, *The Washington Lobbyists* (Chicago, 1963), pp. 267–270.

Our major concern is with committee utilization of committee professional staffs. The preponderant loyalties of committee staff personnel are to their committees and their leaders. They work in the committee rooms. Their work is, for most, hard and demanding. And, they work in a very special kind of institution. What are the capabilities of congressional staffs in this institution? What

Table 3. *Lobbyist Contacts and Preferred Information Sources*

Contacts and sources	Best contact or source	Second best contact or source
Locus for contacts		
Members of Congress	22.8%	14.9%
Staff assistant to members	6.1	9.6
Congressional committee staffs	24.6	28.9
Executive agency staffs	23.7	19.3
Other	10.5	.9
No response	12.3	26.3
Total	100.0	99.9
Sources of inside information		
Members of Congress	20.2%	14.9%
Congressional staffs	28.9	24.6
Executive agency staffs	14.0	15.8
Journalists	3.5	2.6
Other lobbyists	6.1	5.3
Other	14.0	13.2
No response	13.2	23.7
Total	99.9	100.1

Source: Lester W. Milbrath, *The Washington Lobbyists* (Chicago, 1963), pp. 266–268.

constraints impinge upon their roles and behavior? We turn now to analyzing these questions.

Capabilities of Committee Staffs

The professional staffs of congressional committees are, on the whole, sufficiently large and complex that they may be assessed in terms of their actual or potential *capabilities* on a rather wide canvas.[19] These personnel are engaged in a wide variety of activities, the general level of competence is high, and varied expertise is available. The major capabilities of committee staffs are intelligence, integration, innovation, and influence.

Intelligence

Clearly the most visible capability of committee staffs involves the intelligence function of the Congress. Staff men are "facts-and-figures" men, and for a great deal of their working time they are engaged in processing information and supplying it to committee members. As one staff man said, "The main job of the staff is to feed members relevant information."[20] Another said, "Here your job is a technician's job, providing the facts and details." Providing information is probably the central characteristic of the staff man's role definition. Not only do committee staffs process and supply information, but many committees have distinctive investigative staffs to acquire new information. Information resources are enormous, and the staff man is the information jobber for these great resources to the congressman. Furthermore, the staff is largely responsible for setting the agenda on the basis of which information is gathered, processed, and communicated to congressmen—and by and large these activities focus around the committee hearing. An astute staff member of the House Appropriations Committee summed up the job of the staff man:

We are finders of facts. We are assemblers and analyzers of facts. We do a certain amount of design engineering—sketching lines of pursuit to expose the composition of budget items to full view and trying to bring focus by relating them to alternatives. We are mechanical engineers—day-to-day disposition or arranging of the mechanics of the business. We are available for assistance on a wide-ranging

19. For an interesting discussion of political capability as the concept may be applied to whole political systems, see Gabriel A. Almond, "A Developmental Approach to Political Systems," *World Politics*, XVII (January, 1965), 195–205.

20. Unless it is indicated otherwise, comments about committee staffs and quotations from staff personnel are based upon intensive interviews with forty professional committee staff people employed by fifteen House and seven Senate committees. The interviews were conducted during the Summer, 1965, and Spring, 1966. They were focused interviews using some standard questions, averaging seventy-five minutes in length. Field notes were written in complete form from detailed notes subsequent to the interviews.

assortment of budget-related questions. We are draftsmen—assisting the committee in getting its business formalized for submission to the House.[21]

Integration

Committee staffs contribute to the integration of committees and subcommittees, they contribute to inter-cameral integration, and they contribute to legislative-executive integration. Fenno has commented on the importance of the committee staff for intra-committee integration.[22] Most committee staffs, and especially the most professionalized ones, are tightly knit groups, working closely together, often interchangeable, and frequently close socially. Highly integrated staffs eliminate a possible source of committee disintegration.

Again, committee staffs contribute to inter-cameral integration. Within each house, committees (and often subcommittees) work in isolation from other committees of that house. In general, committee staffs have more contact with staff members of the parallel committee in the other legislative body than they do with staff members of other committees in their own house. Some inter-cameral jealousies inhibit staff-to-staff collaboration between the House and Senate, but there is a great deal of coordination between houses at the staff level—and more than between members![23] This collaboration is most clearly manifested at the conference committee stage, which often involves staff negotiations prior to conference committee meetings to identify areas of real agreement and disagreement between House and Senate members. Sometimes conference committees do not actually meet, but rather conference reports are worked out by the rele-

21. From a speech by Paul M. Wilson, staff member of the House Committee on Appropriations, to the annual meeting of the National Association of State Budget Officers in Atlantic City, New Jersey, on August 11, 1964 (mimeographed text, p. 5).

22. Fenno, *op. cit.*, pp. 149–155, 182–188, 206–207.

23. Interviews with House and Senate Appropriations Committee and subcommittee staffs indicated some tension between House and Senate committees, especially in information sharing. The House staff is reluctant to share investigative reports with the Senate staff. The House and Senate staffs, like their members, have different conceptions of their goal orientation. Also, staff relations between House and Senate Committees on Government Operations have not been particularly friendly, but this seems to be due more to deteriorated personal relations than to institutional differences.

vant House and Senate committee staff personnel. A staff member
of the Senate Foreign Relations Committee described an episode
of this kind in discussing his relations with his House Foreign
Affairs Committee staff counterpart:

[House staff member] and I have worked out some tough problems
at the conference stage. One time in conference Senator Fulbright got
into an argument with Congressman Wayne Hays, and Hays walked
out in a huff. [House staff member] got Hays to come back, and then
Fulbright walked out mad. Then, I suggested some changes in language for the bill to [House staff member], and the two of us worked
it out together. [House staff member] took the language to Hays, who
finally said he'd approve but he knew Fulbright wouldn't. I took the
language to Fulbright, who said O. K., but he knew Hays would never
go along. Finally, [House staff member] and I got our respective
members to sign the conference report, although the full conference
never met physically.

Finally, committee staffs facilitate legislative-executive integration. Committee staff people have very close relations with
agency and department personnel—with cabinet officers, agency
heads, bureau chiefs, general counsels, and budget and fiscal
officers rather than with congressional liaison personnel.[24] Some
committee staffs are so close to agency staffs that the latter must
tend to work, in effect, as adjuncts to the committee staffs. House
committees like Veterans' Affairs, Public Works, Armed Services,
Interstate and Foreign Commerce, and Education and Labor,
and Senate committees like Armed Services and Labor and
Public Welfare, have particularly close relations with related
executive departments and agencies. In these cases contact is
very close; bill-drafting is likely to be done by agency staff personnel and not by the committee staff; committee reports on bills
are likely to be written by agency personnel, at least as a first
draft; and in general, agency information resources are the major
resources utilized by the committee staff. Agency and committee
staff personnel work closely together in preparation for commit-

24. For a good discussion of the work of congressional liaison offices, see
G. Russell Pipe, "Congressional Liaison: The Executive Branch Consolidates Its
Relations with Congress," *Public Administration Review*, XXVI (March, 1966),
14–24.

tee hearings, and agency success is frequently thought to be heavily dependent upon good relations with committee staffs.

Committee staffs are widely recruited from among executive branch employees, and sometimes committee staff people are appointed to major administrative positions. Such an intertwining of people is very marked between the Departments of Labor and Health, Education and Welfare, and the House Committee on Education and Labor and the Senate Committee on Labor and Public Welfare. Similar interchanges of staff have occurred between the Joint Committee on Atomic Energy and the Atomic Energy Commission, and between the Joint Committee on Internal Revenue Taxation and the Treasury Department.

Close working relations between executive agency staffs and committee staffs help establish indirect lines of communication to committee members. There are cases which are exceptional; that is, where executives may seek to cement lines of direct communication with committee members in order to offset difficulties with an unfriendly committee staff. Bernstein describes an executive who found that:

> Our experience has been that we have had to develop a direct relationship with committee members as an offset to some of the pet objectives of the professional staff. We were working on a rather technical problem, and there was some tendency for committee members to defer on technical points to the professional judgment of the staff.[25]

In general, however, close working staff-to-staff relationships pertain, and these relationships provide much of the cement that binds legislative and executive branches together. Commentators who make sweeping assertions about the alleged chaotic relations between Congress and the executive branch disregard the tight network of staff interaction, of informal staff-to-staff negotiation and collaboration, which, to adopt a phrase, "creeps in like green blades upon stony streets, gently though silently filling up the chinks between the laws."[26]

25. Bernstein, *op. cit.*, p. 109.
26. McConachie, *op. cit.*, pp. 328–329. McConachie used this felicitous expression in a somewhat different connection.

Innovation

Committee staffs have innovative capabilities. One of the reasons why committee staff people like their work is the opportunity to innovate, to initiate public policy, or see it initiated. Some committee staffs are more innovative than others, partly because of the nature of the staffs and committee leadership, and partly because of the nature of the legislation with which the committee deals. Thus, the House Committee on Science and Astronautics has an innovative orientation. The Committee on Education and Labor staff is not very innovative; most of its legislation comes prepackaged from the Departments of Labor or Health, Education and Welfare.

Eidenberg has attempted to show quantitatively the relationship between staff bureaucratization and committee innovation.[27] Based upon data from committee staff interviews, he ranked House committees on bureaucratization based on indices of specialization, hierarchy, coordination, impartiality, and merit employment. He also ranked committees in terms of the extent to which members initiated bills independent of the executive branch. He found that staff bureaucratization and committee innovation were significantly correlated ($r = .55$), with staff specialization contributing most to innovation.[28] Eidenberg suggests that "perhaps the bureaucratic staff allows members to initiate more, by doing the routine non-innovative things which otherwise the member must do for himself."[29] It may be added that staff members, especially those with long tenure in key staff positions, are about as likely to initiate legislation as are committee members themselves.[30]

27. See Eugene Eidenberg, "The Congressional Bureaucracy" (unpublished doctoral dissertation, Northwestern University, 1966), pp. 70–117.
28. *Ibid.*, p. 112.   29. *Ibid.*, p. 124.
30. Initiation and innovation are somewhat slippery conceptions, to be sure, but a number of staff people described to me projects which the staff was undertaking at their own initiative, and legislation they themselves were working on. A veteran of thirty-six years on the Hill pridefully described to me a series of enactments which he had authored. These things can be done, of course, only within the framework of what committee members will accept, and in terms of how adequately the staff man can anticipate that.

Influence

The case for the influence capability of committee staffs was realistically put by Freeman in the following way:

> . . . larger and more qualified staffs furnish committee leaders with information apart from the reports of the bureaucracy. They are also agents whose loyalties are more likely to lie in the direction of committee leaders. Yet, in another sense, increased committee staffing does not eliminate the dependency of committee members upon others for information, but only transfers it from bureaucrats to committee staff experts. The sources of a congressman's dependency upon some kinds of specialists lie considerably beyond the need for committee staff help; they lie in the many competing demands upon legislators' time and in the complex variety of issues which they must attempt to resolve. Consequently, well-entrenched, well-trained, and astute committee staff members are often in quite favorable positions to be "powers behind the scenes" insofar as committee members transfer their dependency to them.[31]

Committee staff personnel certainly do have a great deal of influence on public policy. They gather and analyze much of the information upon which policy is based, they plan and, to a very large extent, execute public hearings and investigations, and they draft legislation and the committee reports which not only justify committee recommendations of bills but contain sanctionable policy in themselves. Staff members are well-aware of their influence and the conditions under which it may be exercised. They know that their major influence is delegated, and that they must work within the general guidance of committee or subcommittee chairmen. They know that staff is more influential if committee members are ignorant or if they do not do their "homework." They know they are often "on the carpet" in executive sessions, and must make policy recommendations. And, they know their policy influence depends considerably upon their conformity to the unwritten rules of the game and their ability to persuade.

31. J. Leiper Freeman, *The Political Process: Executive Bureau–Legislative Committee Relations* (New York, 1965), pp. 111–112.

These aspects of staff influence capability are suggested in the following comments by staff members:

[House Armed Services Committee Staff Man] I feel that the staff has an enormous impact on the policy output of the committee. It works under the general guidance of the chairman, but has a pretty wide berth. Further, the advice or opinions of the staff is very often sought by agency staff people, and given regularly without consulting the members of the Committee; and, it usually is taken.

[House Appropriations Committee Staff Man] The policy influence of the staff depends upon the capabilities of members. When a sub-committee chairman doesn't do his homework, the handiwork of the staff man may be regularly seen. If that same staff man is transferred to work for a member who works hard, his handiwork is not seen.

Another staff member, from the House Veterans' Affairs Committee, emphasized the importance of trust in staff influence:

I feel the influence of the staff can't be over-emphasized. Our members are not too well-informed about veterans' affairs. The junior members are just learning, and the senior members are busy. They must rely on competent and trusted staff. In executive session, the staff always develops its policy position.

House committee staffs tend to have more direct contact with chairmen and committee members than do Senate committee staffs. The latter are more likely to communicate with their chairman through memoranda or through the administrative assistant in the senator's office. For this reason, Senate staff people tend to feel that they have more influence than their House brethren. In fact, this may be a delusion, and may only mean Senate staff people are further away from power than members of House staffs. One Senate staff man from the Labor and Public Welfare Committee said:

Senator Hill is a very busy man. He doesn't know what the staff is doing. The staff pretty much runs itself, and it seems to succeed in anticipating Hill's views. The Senator expects me to work things out, and I know it. He probably wouldn't recognize most of the subcommittee staff people if he saw them in the hall."

Another Senate Labor and Public Welfare Subcommittee staff man stressed the need for persuasiveness:

I like being close to the levers of power. My ideas have influence only to the extent that I can persuade the Senators that they are in the public interest. The staff man can have a lot of influence in these terms. If you know you can't persuade a member to your own policy position, you lay out the alternatives, and you've got to be as objective as you possibly can.

Staff influence varies among congressional committees as a result of differences in staff availability and competence, committee workload, and structural factors in committee organization. At the same time, the potential influence of committee staffs is considerable indeed.

A number of conditions in the congressional environment tend to provide substantial support for staff performance capability. The pay is good, and the "feast or famine" flow of work provides both for periods of very intense activity and periods of quiet and vacation. Most staff members like their work, so that morale is high. Professionalism, at least in word if not always in deed, is highly valued, and staff members regard themselves as professionals; they tend to be regarded that way by congressmen as well. There are important exceptions, but on the whole congressional committee work is relatively nonpartisan. The more nonpartisan the committee, the greater support for staff performance capability. Loyalty to committee and subcommittee chairmen is very strong, and the trust and confidence engendered in this relationship promotes staff capability. Staff personnel are very much anonymous, and they can work in an atmosphere largely free from the electoral insecurities and constituency demands faced by committee members. The personnel of most committees has, among the professional staffs, been very stable, political firings have been exceptional, and twice as many staff members have survived changes in the political majorities of the Congress.[32] Stability of top personnel has led to the development in most committees of reasonably effective staff organization

32. The first staff appointees after the passage of the Legislative Reorganization Act of 1946 were appointed by Republican chairmen. A large proportion were retained in 1949 when Democrats regained control of Congress. See Kammerer, *op. cit.*, pp. 1128–1129. When the Republicans regained control in the Eighty-third Congress, there were some staff changes and shifts of staff positions. See Kampelman, *op. cit.*, 546–550.

(though they differ widely in detail). Finally, a considerable proportion of the professional staff people have had wide experience in the areas in which they work, so that the structure of expertise is well-established; this specialization facilitates performance capability.

Congress is a very hoary institution in many ways. As an institution, by definition, behavior by participants is *constrained*.[33] Having explored some of the important facets of staff capability, we now turn to a consideration of the significant constraints on staff performance.

Constraints on Committee Staffs

A variety of biases in the congressional institution affect the behavior of committee professional staffs. These biases, or constraints, may be seen as limitations on staff capabilities, real or potential, brought about by the institutional environment. Here we can deal with constraints associated with group norms, committee leadership, staff organization, partisanship, isolation, and specialization. Focusing upon these sources of constraint will indicate in some important ways the manner in which Congress as an institution molds and shapes the behavior of the staff personnel who work within it.

Legislative Norms

Committee staff members tend to adopt the goal orientations dominant among members of the committees for which they work. Thus, staff members of the House Appropriations Committee tend to accept the budget cutting and treasury guarding orientation of the Committee, and members of the Senate Committee staff tend to accept its appellate orientation. The normative integration of committees varies fairly widely, and thus accepted goal orientations vary on the part of committee staffs.

33. For an interesting approach to organizational constraints, see Vernon E. Buck, "A Model for Viewing an Organization as a System of Constraints," in *Approaches to Organizational Design*, ed. James D. Thompson (Pittsburgh, 1966), pp. 103–172.

However, across committees it is possible to generalize about widely-shared normative standards generally reflected by staff personnel. The most salient of these norms are limited advocacy, chairman loyalty, deference, anonymity, specialization, and limited partisanship.

The staff norm of limited advocacy implies that the staff man will not press his own policy position too far; that he should be sensitive to limitations on the presentation of his own conclusions and proposals. A number of comments from staff professionals reflected this; one House Science and Astronautics staff man said:

> The Chairmen and subcommittee chairmen do their homework well, but they do ask for the opinion of the staff on policy matters. And, the staff does make recommendations without being asked to do so. But if a staff man makes a proposal or objects to a Committee decision, and the Committee disagrees, the staff man is expected to forget it.

The game of anticipating committee member antagonism or rejection, and limiting advocacy accordingly, is a delicate one. On the Senate side, a staff member from the Senate Aeronautical and Space Sciences Committee discussed this problem:

> In hearings, I do most of the questioning; in executive sessions, the Senators do most of the talking and I do most of the explaining. I sometimes feel between the devil and the deep blue sea. I try to stay out of serious disagreements between senators, and just provide information. But, on a number of occasions, I've argued for something that none of the Senators were prepared to accept. I remember once Senator Anderson admonished me jokingly that I didn't have to argue so vehemently for the agency.

A Senate Education Subcommittee staff member pointed out that "if you can't persuade a member to your own policy position, you lay out the alternatives and you've got to be as objective as you possibly can." And, a very highly regarded staff member of the Senate Armed Services Committee observed that "the job of the staff is to be objective, restrained, and not doctrinaire. The staff is expected to play down individual policy preferences. The more restrained the staff is, the more likely it is to be influential."

The norm of chairman loyalty is very crucial to the structure of congressional committee staffs, and here the sanctions for failure are likely to be immediate and terminal. Most committees delegate staff appointment to the chairman alone, and he is clearly the major figure in the staff man's employment relationship. In a variety of ways, staff members interviewed reflected their loyalty to the chairman. A Senate staff man said "it's hard to draw the line between what the Senator thinks and what I think." The prototypical manifestation of the norm of chairman loyalty is the so-called chairman's man who is appointed by, and obediently serves, the chairman first and foremost. This trusted chairman's man serves on the Veterans' Affairs Committee staff:

My basic job is to enhance the prestige of the Chairman. My job is that of ensuring that Congressman Teague is the No. 1 man in the country on veterans' affairs; that the final decisions on veterans' affairs are made by the staff and the Chairman, and not by the White House or by private groups . . . In executive sessions, it sometimes boils down to the staff and the Chairman against the rest of the Committee . . . When the Chairman of the Committee on Science and Astronautics retires, I hope to become a member of that staff, and to help make Mr. Teague No. 1 in space!

The norm of deference to congressmen is very strong, and is often reflected by staff comments about how staff members must "be on tap, and not on top," that they must not "try to run the show," or that "you must remember that staff is staff, and members are members." A staff member of the House Education and Labor Committee, a committee particularly sensitive to staff deference, accounted for the high staff turnover on the Committee in terms of successive violations of this norm:

One person brought in by Mr. Powell as education counsel began to think she was too important. She referred to bills as her own bills, rather than the members', and she antagonized members; so Powell had me fire her . . . One of the three labor chiefs lasted only two weeks. He committed the crime of going around to committee members announcing he was the new labor chief ready to take charge; their response to Powell was, "Who the hell is this?" Powell ordered me to fire him.

The norm of anonymity is equally powerful, and probably more difficult than others for staff members to live with. This norm is strongly reflected in the House Appropriations Committee, as Fenno has shown.[34] Anonymity is fiercely protected by members of this staff, but it is an important part of the expectations of other committee staffs as well. One staff member of an Appropriations subcommittee remarked about anonymity: "You have to be anonymous to be effective. Congressman Passman is Mr. Foreign Aid; you can't have me being Mr. Foreign Aid." Another Appropriations subcommittee staff member said: "A staff man has to be anonymous. He can't have any axe to grind. He can't have any politics. I try to be objective. I could staff anything." Some staff members are reluctant to take a prominent place in public committee activities, for fear of violating the anonymity norm:

[House Agriculture Committee Staff Man] The members increasingly ask my opinion on policy, since I've been around here so long. I was reluctant at first, but when they asked for my judgment I had to give it. At full Committee hearings, I try to keep out of asking questions. I suggest questions to the Chairman, and sometimes ask some myself, but I like not to. In executive sessions I talk more than I like, and it's a close line in give and take there.

[House Appropriations Subcommittee Staff Man] The staff man should stay in the background, and not become identified with particular policies, but this is not always easy to do. For instance, if the staff man asks a lot of questions in hearings it tends to take the glow off members, and you tend to become identified with particular policies.

[House Armed Services Staff Man] The acting Chairman asks me or one of the other staff men to ask questions in hearings. I don't like this very much. To me it makes the staff too prominent. In the role of the questionner, the staff man has to be very careful not to get any publicity, or to overstep his place.

One Senate committee, the Committee on Foreign Relations, has clearly stated written rules against staff publicity:

Members of the staff must not accept public speaking engagements or write for publication in the field of foreign relations without specific advance permission from the chief of staff or, in this case, from the Chairman. In any event, such public statements should avoid

34. As Fenno points out, only one member of the large Appropriations Committee staff lists his biography in the *Congressional Staff Directory*. See Fenno, *op. cit.*, p. 184; and Charles B. Brownson, compiler, *1967 Congressional Staff Directory* (Washington, 1967).

the expression of personal views and should not contain predictions of future, or interpretations of past, Committee action.[35]

Anonymity is not easy, nor is it always comfortable. Staff members who come to have great expertise naturally desire recognition. Often they are praised by committee members, and sometimes this occurs on the floor of the House or Senate.[36] But expertise encourages expression, and the rules prohibit public staff prominence. This can sometimes lead to frustration. One Senate staff man in an interview painfully but pridefully recounted his authorship of several law review articles published under the names of senators. At bar association meetings he has been asked why he has not published his ideas in the law reviews. He has, but none of his peers in the legal profession know it. Another Senate staff member, from the Labor and Public Welfare Subcommittee, said: "I practiced law for ten years before coming to work for the Committee, and I feel that in my practice I was better able to deal with people directly, to do direct service for people, whereas on the Committee this is impersonal. The impersonality and anonymity of the work is disturbing to me." And, a staff member from the House Appropriations Subcommittee said:

A staff man has to be a eunuch politically, and totally anonymous. If he can't do that, he won't last. The most frustrating part of the job is that a lot of work comes to nothing. You build a case, and do a lot of writing about something that is not politically feasible. A lot of good ideas go down the drain.

We shall discuss specialization and partisanship as structural biases in the congressional environment in a few paragraphs. In

35. From a Senate Committee on Foreign Relations memorandum entitled "Report of the Subcommittee on Staff Problems on General Staff Problems, of February 10, 1958, as Adopted by the Committee on March 4, 1958," dated March 4, 1958, p. 3.

36. See Fenno, *op. cit.*, p. 206. An example of praise of a staff man on the House floor is *Congressional Record* (Daily), CXI, 88th Cong., 1st Sess., p. 19120. On the occasion of presentation of the Military Construction Appropriation Bill, Congressman Sikes said, "We are privileged to have with us Frank Sanders, one of the most capable staff members on Capitol Hill. His great source of information plus his constant and dedicated efforts are invaluable. We have a new staff member, Robert Nicholas, with whom I am very highly pleased. He has been willing, cooperative and helpful."

this context, specialization and limited partisanship operate as normative expectations for committee staff members. In general, committee staff people are expected to specialize and develop a subject-matter expertise. The confidence which committee members have in the staff is dependent upon their demonstrated expertness. As one House Veterans' Affairs Committee staff man put it: "One unwritten rule of the game has to do with competence. Members have a lot at stake, and must be able to trust the staff. In this relation, the staff man gets only about one major mistake. This tends to make the staff fairly conservative."

Although clearly some committees are more partisan in the manner in which the decision-making process operates than others, a very wide range of committee activity is nonpartisan. Further, there does exist the general expectation of limited partisanship, even though there is considerable slippage in the implementation of this expectation. The most widely respected staff men are the most nonpartisan ones, and the performance capability of the staff is highly associated with nonpartisan decision-making climates. A large number of professional staff people report working for members of both parties; some have served both under Republican and Democratic chairmen; and many report writing both majority and minority views for committee reports on bills. Fenno has pointed to the very nonpartisan character of the staff of the House Appropriations Committee, and much the same is the case for a number of other congressional committees, including Ways and Means, Science and Astronautics, Armed Services, Foreign Affairs, Interior and Insular Affairs, and Un-American Activities on the House side, Senate Appropriations and Foreign Relations on the Senate side, the Joint Committees on Atomic Energy and Internal Revenue Taxation, and the Joint Economic Committee.[37]

37. Fenno, *op. cit.*, pp. 184–185. See also John F. Manley, "The House Committee on Ways and Means: Conflict Management in a Congressional Committee," *American Political Science Review*, LIX (December, 1965), 927–939; and, for a sharp contrast, see Fenno's comments on the House Committee Education and Labor in Frank J. Munger and Richard F. Fenno, Jr., *National Politics and Federal Aid to Education* (Syracuse, N.Y., 1962), pp. 106–136. On the Joint Committee on Atomic Energy, see Green and Rosenthal, *op. cit.*, pp. 65–66.

Committee Leadership

The performance of a congressional committee staff is very much dependent upon the committee or subcommittee chairman, and to some extent upon the ranking minority leaders. In addition to loyalty to the chairman, the staff must learn to anticipate the reactions of the chairman and behave accordingly. In the words of a House subcommittee staff member, "you have to be able to anticipate what the Chairman and members want, and you can't check with them too often to cover yourself because then they get annoyed at being bothered all the time. You have to develop a feel for the members, and this takes time." The chairman is the key figure in the world of the staff man, and sensing what he wants is a major part of the game.

On the whole, House staff people are in greater proximity to the chairman than are Senate staff people, and thus Senate staffs are more likely to have to get their cues for behavior from the chairman indirectly—through the senator's office staff, from memoranda, or on the telephone. This more distant relationship between senators and Senate staffs seems to lend itself to indecision and inactivity in staffs where the chairman is very busy, and perhaps concentrating his energies on the work of other committees or subcommittees.

When a hiatus develops between a committee or subcommittee staff director or major staff assistant and the chairman, the consequences are disastrous for staff performance. Three situations of this sort existed in House Committees during the Eighty-ninth Congress. The glaring case is that of the Committee on Education and Labor under the aegis of Chairman Powell. The staff was in a chaotic condition as a result of the lack of trust between Mr. Powell and the professional staff. A similarly anomic condition could be found on the Select Labor Subcommittee, where the staff man realized he didn't have the confidence of the acting chairman and could not figure out why, where no real use was made of the staff man, and where he hardly saw the chairman over a period of several months. Finally, lack of mutual confidence between Chairman Bonner and the staff of the Committee on Merchant Marine and Fisheries weakened the effectiveness of that staff, and made life miserable for some staff members.

On most committees of the House and Senate, staff appointments either are made outright by the full committee chairman or the subcommittee chairmen, or, when staff directors are involved in the appointment process, the chairmen clear appointments. The House and Senate committees on foreign affairs and the Joint Committee on Atomic Energy utilize personnel subcommittees for staff appointments. There are three comments which can be made quickly about staff appointment. First, most committees have not experienced much turnover among professional staff personnel, so the appointment process is not frequently invoked. Second, most professional staff appointments are made on the basis of competence, and not primarily on the basis of partisan considerations. The House Appropriations Committee is an excellent example of merit recruitment. During the Eighty-fifth Congress, Chairman Cannon made a rare statement on the House floor about Appropriations Committee staff appointments:

Of the 50 members of the staff accredited to the Committee on Appropriations, I have appointed all but 6. I have not known at the time of appointment—and I do not know today—to what political party, to what church or to what fraternal organizations a single one of the 50 belong, and may I say further, Mr. Chairman, that none of them are from my congressional district, or from my own State. I have never exercised personal political preference in the appointment of any of them.[38]

Finally, some staff are appointed on a patronage basis, but these appointees have a very marked tendency to "go professional." Where committees have both positions of staff director and chief clerk, the latter is most likely to be a political appointment; and, it is common on Senate committee staffs for there to be a "chairman's man" appointed on a political basis. But it should be reiterated that the biases of the system tend to press even political appointees in the direction of professionalism.

38. *Congressional Record* (Daily), CVIII, 85th Cong., 1st Sess., p. 6319.

Staff Organization

Staff organization varies widely in detail.[39] In general, three patterns of staff organization can be found in congressional committees. With relevant examples, these three patterns are depicted in Figure 3. The patterns in Figure 3 do not reflect some

Figure 3. *Patterns of Staff Organization*

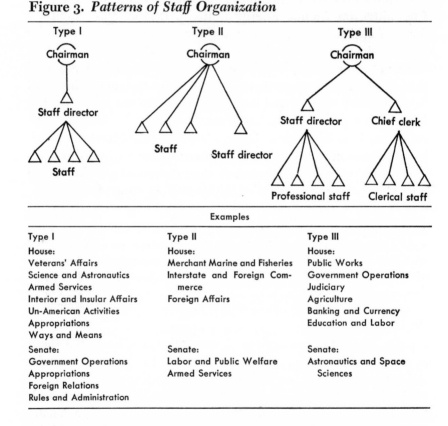

Examples

Type I	Type II	Type III
House:	House:	House:
Veterans' Affairs	Merchant Marine and Fisheries	Public Works
Science and Astronautics	Interstate and Foreign Com-	Government Operations
Armed Services	merce	Judiciary
Interior and Insular Affairs	Foreign Affairs	Agriculture
Un-American Activities		Banking and Currency
Appropriations		Education and Labor
Ways and Means		
Senate:	Senate:	Senate:
Government Operations	Labor and Public Welfare	Astronautics and Space
Appropriations	Armed Services	Sciences
Foreign Relations		
Rules and Administration		

important variants: some committees have independent subcommittee staffs appointed by subcommittee chairmen (House: Public Works, Merchant Marine and Fisheries, Government Op-

39. For further organizational details, see Kenneth Kofmehl, *Professional Staffs of Congress* (West Lafayette, Ind., 1962), pp. 37–51.

erations, Education and Labor; Senate: Labor and Public Welfare, Government Operations, Appropriations). Type I Senate committees frequently have as an adjunct to the chairman, and independent of the rest of the staff, a chairman's man. Still, the three types in Figure 3 portray the main parameters of staff organization. The hierarchical Type I staff is one in which the chairman's staff contacts go mainly through the staff director, who commands both clerical and professional staff personnel. These staffs are easier to explain in terms of organizational relationships, and staff members of these committees were better able to describe the organizational structure. These Type I staff arrangements probably promote staff performance. The staff director of the Senate Government Operations Committee described his organization in a way which suggests this. He related that under Senator Aiken's chairmanship the responsibilities of staff director and chief clerk were separate, but when Senator McClellan became chairman Aiken recommended that this not be continued—not "to create positions for two prima donnas who argue all the time over what is who's job"—and staff supervision was given to one staff director.

The Type II staff is one in which the committee or subcommittee chairman deals with all of the professional staff on pretty much an equal footing, with the staff director or chief clerk (use of titles varies) directing the clerical staff. This arrangement is more demanding for the committee or subcommittee chairman, and tends to be utilized where the professional staff is small.

The Type III staff involves dual leadership, with a staff director supervising the professional staff and a chief clerk directing the clerical staff. This kind of organizational structure works reasonably well in some committees, but seems excessively prone to tension between the two staff leaders. This arises especially when the staff director is a professional and the chief clerk is a political appointee. Staff performance tends to suffer when staff director and chief clerk are at loggerheads.

Even where committees regularly do business through standing subcommittees, there is a tendency, especially on the House side, to maintain full committee control over the staff. Staff may then be temporarily assigned to subcommittees. This organizational strategy helps the full committee chairman to maintain control of subcommittees and their chairmen, and it serves to facilitate staff integration and coordination as well.

Partisanship

The partisan aspect of congressional committee staffing has received more attention inside and outside Congress than any other aspect of staffing. Although the Legislative Reorganization Act of 1946 did not contemplate it, a number of committees and subcommittees have designated certain staff positions as belonging to the minority members, in some cases these members of the staff are officed separately, and in most of these cases the minority staff is appointed by the ranking minority member of the committee or subcommittee.[40] In recent years, some Republican congressmen have vigorously advocated increases in minority staffing, and some increases have been effected.[41] These members regard the inadequacy of minority staff as a constraint on their performance as members of the loyal opposition. This is not the place for a full-blown discussion of the issue of minority staffing.[42] Some of the arguments are fully weather-worn. To the degree committee staffs are structured in partisan terms, such structures are relevant to consideration of congressional constraints on staffing.

We have already pointed to the strength of the committee staff norm of limited partisanship. Staff assistance for members of the minority party goes far beyond the numbers explicitly designated as minority staff. The problem is really not one of availability. For instance, the House Committee on Armed Services has no staff members designated as minority staff; but, the Chief Counsel,

40. The Joint Committee on the Organization of Congress recommended allocating two professional and one clerical position to each committee, and "fair representation" on subcommittee staffs. See *Organization of Congress: Final Report*, 89th Cong., 2nd Sess., July 28, 1966, pp. 21–22.

41. The case has been most recently argued by Congressman James C. Cleveland in "The Need for Increased Minority Staffing," in Mary McInnis, *op. cit.*, pp. 5–19. Also, see Clapp, *op. cit.*, pp. 258–261.

42. See James D. Cochrane, "Partisan Aspects of Congressional Committee Staffing," *Western Political Quarterly*, XVII (June, 1964), 338–348; and Kofmehl, *op. cit.*, pp. 52–69.

who directs the staff, was appointed to the staff by a Republican chairman. A long-time general counsel of the House Agriculture Committee was appointed in 1947 by a Republican chairman. The executive director of the House Science and Astronautics Committee staff was first a Republican appointee of the Armed Services committee staff. And, the chief clerk and staff director of the Senate Committee on Government Operations got his appointment on the recommendation of the ranking Republican Senator. On the House District Committee, the ranking Republican picks the minority clerk, but this designation is entirely nominal, and this staff member works as a regular member of the staff; the Committee counsel is a nominal Republican, and the clerk, though a registered Democrat, regularly votes Republican. The ranking Republican on the House Merchant Marine and Fisheries Committee wanted a staff man assigned to the minority, and selected for this position a man already on the staff who was known to be a Democrat. Other examples abound.

Some committees, like House and Senate Armed Services, House Science and Astronautics, Interior and Insular Affairs, Ways and Means, and Senate Foreign Relations, have no minority staff and are entirely nonpartisan. The staff serves all members of the committee. Other committees—like those of House Merchant Marine and Fisheries, Foreign Affairs, and Agriculture; and, Senate Astronautics and Space Sciences, Government Operations, Appropriations, and Rules and Administration—have staffs directed to serve all committee members, but minority staffs are designated as special contacts for Republicans. Still other committees have very separate minority staffs. The separate minority staff may work more or less closely with the majority staff; they may be closed out of the majority staff operations completely. A House Public Works Committee staff member said, "They participate in the work of the staff, but perhaps are somewhat slighted in the sense that they are often kept informed rather than participating from the beginning." The staff of House Interstate and Foreign Commerce is very nonpartisan, but there is a staff man for the minority who works entirely apart from the regular staff—"he works exclusively with the minority, although minority members do not work exclusively with him." Arrangements are essentially the same in the House Government Operations, Judiciary, and Appropriations staffs. In the case of Appropriations, the minority staff is housed in a different building, and, because it is virtually the private staff of the ranking minority member, it is not considered a part of the Committee's professional staff. House Education and Labor, Senate Labor and Public Welfare, and House Banking and Currency exemplify committees where the staff is not really available to the minority committee members. For instance, the Chief Clerk and Staff Director of one of these staffs said, "The minority staff is completely segregated, and only minimally kept informed. . . . Minority members of the Committee deal exclusively with the minority staff; they don't ask for help from the majority staff. . . . I have no dealings with minority congressmen."

Most staff members attribute nonpartisanship in staff operations to nonpartisan decision-making behavior on the part of committees themselves. The House and Senate committees dealing with education, labor, and welfare legislation, which is obviously very controversial, have difficulty developing nonpartisan professional staffs. Staff operations clearly are impaired. Where committees handling relatively nonpartisan legislation are concerned, minority staffs may be a hindrance to staff operations. For instance, one Senate Appropriations Subcommittee staff man pointed out:

> There is a minority man assigned to this subcommittee. We don't work at cross-purposes, but he doesn't help me much. Actually, he is some trouble, because when Republicans ask him questions he usually has to ask me. It takes up my time, and the members had just as well ask me directly. The subcommittee almost never divides along party lines; we've had minority views once in thirteen years.

On the whole, Republicans tend to use the regular staff of committees on which they serve, and minority staffs (where they are designated) on committees of which they are not members. When 149 House Republicans were asked in 1965 by the staff of the Republican Task Force on Congressional Reform and Minority Staffing whether "At any time this year, have you requested additional staff for yourself or on behalf of other minority members of the committee and been turned down?" 71.8 per cent said no, and it was clear that some of those reporting yes had actually been turned down by the ranking minority member of the committee.

Isolation

Congressional committees are independent and autonomous little legislatures. In each house, committee staffs tend to be very much isolated from one another, and where committees have independent subcommittees their staffs often are isolated too. Though degrees of contact and coordination vary, on the whole each House committee staff has little to do with other committees' staffs, and the same is true in the Senate. Committee staff isolation probably is less consequential for collaboration and coordination in the Senate because of the high incidence of overlapping committee leadership. For example, Senator Russell is chairman of the Armed Services Committee, and also chairman of the Appropriations Subcommittee on Department of Defense. He chairs one committee to authorize defense funds and another to approve appropriations. The two staffs work closely together, and the two committees frequently hold joint hearings.[43]

Most staff members report very little contact with staff people on other committees or subcommittees. More inter-cameral contact is reported than intra-cameral contact, though across the board there is not much of either. The most isolated committees are Veterans' Affairs and Un-American Activities. Neither has a counterpart committee in the Senate.

Staff isolation is a result of the balkanization of Congress into highly institutionalized committees. It is reinforced by the structure of committee prestige, institutional jealousies, and inter-cameral hostilities. Staff loyalties and identifications are committee-specific. At the same time, committee structures are divisions

43. I also have the strong impression that the staffs of House Foreign Affairs and Senate Foreign Relations work in close harmony. Both chiefs of staff reported constant contact, embellished with impressive examples. But Holbert Carroll argues otherwise. See Carroll, *op. cit.*, pp. 230–231.

of labor which encourage subject-matter expertise, and specialization itself seems to support and reinforce committee staff isolation. Of course, staff isolation tends to produce duplication and ignorance in intelligence effort; it works against House and congressional integration but tends to facilitate committee integration, and it probably increases staff influence. Policy innovation in a narrow sense may be facilitated by staff isolation, but one suspects that innovation of far-reaching consequence is made rather unlikely.

Specialization

Committee staffing is very highly specialized, and as has been pointed out specialization is a part of the normative mandate of the committee structure. Specialization encourages staff isolation, but it is strongly associated with staff influence, integration, and innovation. Staff members invariably describe their jobs in specialist terms, and even staff directors tend to stress their subject-matter expertise more than their general management activities in describing their jobs. Of course, specialization varies, and there is some generalist-specialist tension in the staff system. The structural problem of specialization can best be illustrated by looking at the staff of the House Appropriations Committee. In this staff, attempts have been made to develop generality and interchangeability of specialist competence. Although the Committee has standing subcommittees with fixed subject-matter jurisdictions and a permanent staff assigned to them, the staff director has sought to rotate the staff. Also, he has attempted to assign two different subcommittee staff men to a bill, one with major responsibility and the other as "back up" man. This has not been very successful. In practice, subcommittee staff men seldom have time to work as "back up" men on the parts of the appropriations legislation being processed by other subcommittees. Rotation of staff has not worked well either. As the Staff Director said, "I would like to rotate the subcommittee people more, but the subcommittee chairmen get too attached to them. When this was tried a few years ago, the subcommittee chairmen went up in smoke."

Conclusion

This analysis of congressional committee professional staffs is impressionistic in many respects, and raises a variety of questions which call for more systematic answers. The analysis touches upon, but does not really resolve, the over-arching question, "Are congressional commmittee staffs adequate for a modern legislative institution?" The question involves many imponderables. Among them is that of staff size. Some have said that committee staffs are, on the whole, properly nonpartisan, competent, and effective, but that the staffs of committees are too small to support congressional needs. The question of adequate staff size is an extraordinarily difficult question to answer. Most present staff personnel regard the staffs as about adequate in size, though some recommended small increases. The Joint Committee on the Organization of Congress, after some study, recommended small increases in the minimum personnel authorizations, but most committees are now well above the newly-recommended minimum. Under present arrangements, congressional committees (and notably the Appropriations Committees) can have about whatever number of professional staff employees they think they need. Most committees have opted for fairly small professional staffs. These small staffs draw upon the staff resources of departments and agencies, the Legislative Reference Service, the General Accounting Office, the Office of Legislative Counsel, hired temporary consultants, and independent investigative staffs. Staffs cannot be so large that the congressmen on committees and subcommittees cannot manage them or cannot meaningfully consume what the staffs do.

Another vexing problem is that of partisanship. It is one thing to observe that staff performance capability is facilitated by nonpartisan staffing, and quite another to suggest taking all of the partisanship out of congressional politics. Partisan differences do matter, and the committee structure of Congress already siphons off a great deal of the potential partisanship of public issues. The institutional dampers on partisan conflict are very desirable up to some point, but it is possible that congressional sub-structures are already excessively de-partisanized. To the extent that nonpartisan professional staffs, competent and well entrenched in congressional committees and subcommittees, support and tend to enlarge nonpartisan committee decision-making, there will remain some danger of bureaucratizing both information processing and policy-making in Congress.

Chapter 12

Structural Determinants of Legislative Output

John G. Grumm

Predicting the consequences of changes in political institutions, particularly in regard to the performance of these institutions, should certainly be one of the major purposes of political science. But one observes rather little research directed explicitly to this end. The behavioralists, who are undoubtedly the best equipped methodologically to investigate this subject, have generally tended to avoid investigations of political institutions or formal structures. Presumably, this is because they regard them as relatively insignificant in the shaping of political behavior. Admittedly, the effects of institutions or structures on behavior are not as direct and obvious as they were once considered to be, and often institutional or structural "reforms" have not produced the results intended by the reformers, but the behavioral influence of institutions and the consequences of changes in them should be regarded as an open empirical question. Purposeful as well as accidental structural changes will continue to be made, and it behooves us to understand something about the linkages between institutional characteristics and the behavior of the political system.

The state legislatures in the United States are undergoing at present some of the most profound changes in their histories. Baker vs. Carr probably signaled the beginning of the era of change, but the era has developed into something more than a reapportionment revolution. Reapportionment has, in turn, served to focus more attention on other aspects of the state

legislatures and in some cases has altered the political environment to the extent that other changes in these institutions could
be more readily accomplished. A reform movement has been
building up during the last few years which may bring about
some far reaching structural alterations in these state legislative
bodies.[1] At this stage we need to have a better understanding of
how these changes might affect the performance of the legislature
and its final product or output.

The Process Model

Studies dealing with the interaction of structural factors with
legislative performance or output have, either explicitly or implicitly, incorporated a model of the policy process that looks something like the following.[2]

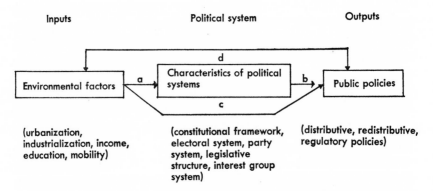

This model is highly simplified, of course, but such simplifica-
tion is probably appropriate considering the rather rudimentary
development of the empirical basis for this research. In this

1. Grants of close to a million dollars each have been made in the last four
years to the National Municipal League and the Citizens Conference on State
Legislatures for research on the promotion of legislative "improvement." Other
substantial grants for various programs to improve state legislatures have been
made to the Eagleton Institute of Politics and the American Political Science
Association. The Ford Foundation and the Carnegie Corporation have been the
major donors.
2. This adapted from Thomas Dye, *Politics, Economics, and the Public* (New
York, 1966), p. 4.

model the environmental factors are conceived as creating or stimulating the demands that are the actual inputs to the legislative system. Both the formal, or legal, as well as the informal aspects of the political system are regarded as variables. The outputs are public policies in the form of appropriations or substantive legislation. The policies may be distributive in nature, which means that they would sanction the payment of public funds to individuals directly or indirectly. Welfare programs are the most notable example of these. They may be redistributive, in which case the flow of money would be in the other direction from the individual to the government through taxation, fees, or fines. Or they may be regulatory policies, which involve the control and regulation of organizations or individuals by the government or a governmental agency.

The linkages shown in this model (a, b, c, and d) should serve, however, to point up some of the possible explanations of policy outcomes as well as to the possibility of a reciprocal effect of policy on inputs (feedback loop, d). The model suggests also that the relations between the environment and the system's output may be affected by specified characteristics of the political system. If route c is the main causal path, this indicates that the response of the system to a given environmental stimulus is uniform across political systems with varying structural characteristics or, conversely, that environment variations produce variations in output that are independent of structural characteristics of the system. On the other hand, a route following paths a and b signifies that the response of the political system varies according to variations in certain structural characteristics of the system and that these characteristics are determined to a degree by some aspect of the environment. In such a case, the environmental factor being analyzed does not directly provide the stimulus for the output response but, in psychological terms, alters the response mechanism in such a way that the output is affected.

A mixed condition would exist if paths a, b, and c were all involved to roughly the same extent. This would indicate that the particular environmental influence was generating inputs which tended to bring about a pattern of responses or outputs of a

particular nature, and that the manner in which the system responded to these was determined by a set of system characteristics which themselves were affected by the same environmental
influence. If all relationships were in the same direction (all
positive or all negative), the influence of the environment on the
structural characteristics of the system would produce an additive effect on output; that is, the environmental factor would not
only be producing pressures and demands for a particular output,
but would also be helping to create the system conditions which
would make it easier to obtain the designated output. A hypothetical example might involve urbanization as the environmental
factor and the system of apportionment of legislative districts as
the structural factor. A high degree of urbanization in a state
might generate demands for increased state financial aid to large
cities, and it might also create pressures that would lead to a
more equitable apportionment of the state legislature, which, in
turn, might make it easier to pass the desired legislation.

The mixed condition described above, or any condition in
which at least paths *b* and *c* were activated, should be able to
provide us with the basis for an operational definition of system
"responsiveness." If path *c* exists, we can by analysis determine
what responses are associated with variations in the environmental factor under examination, and we might also operationally
define these responses as "appropriate" to the demands generated
by the particular environmental factor. If path *b* also exists, we
can conclude that the tendency of the system to make the appropriate response is at least partially dependent upon the system
characteristics being examined, and we can readily determine by
analysis what conditions facilitate the appropriate response. Recognizing that systems might respond in a variety of ways to the
same stimulus, and that we would not want to consider a system
responsive merely because it made any sort of a response, we
might then define "responsiveness" as the ability of a system to
make an "appropriate" response in the sense defined above. This
we would deem to be the most significant aspect of legislative
performance and the major criterion on which it should be evaluated.

Based on this definition, I have examined a number of legislative system characteristics hypothetically related to the responsiveness of the system. These characteristics include the system of apportionment of legislative districts, the "professional" status of the legislature, and some general representational factors. For the sake of comprehensiveness, I have used the findings of my own research as well as that of others.

Apportionment

Almost all systematic, comparative studies which have sought to determine effects of apportionment on legislative performance or output have yielded negative or inconclusive results. It was often assumed that important policy differences existed between urban and rural constituencies and that the overrepresentation of rural interests in the malapportioned legislatures gave those interests a substantial advantage in the making of public policy. But the findings of Jacob, Hofferbert, Derge, Flinn, Brady and Edmonds, and Grumm appear to raise some doubts that variations in malapportionment account for any significant variations in policy.

Jacob studied the effects of malapportionment on party competition, highway funds distribution, and some welfare expenditures and found that conditions in the states with the most malapportioned legislatures were not noticeably different from conditions in well-apportioned states.[3] Hofferbert hypothesized that the amount of state aid received by large cities would be sensitive to the degree of malapportionment of state legislatures. He ranked states according to the percentage of the state's general revenue that went to its two largest cities in 1962 and also according to how well apportioned they were. On this basis the data yielded a rank-order correlation coefficient on only .22, and he concluded that this did not indicate a significant relation. In addition, he correlated his apportionment ranking with a "wel-

3. Herbert Jacob, "The Consequences of Malapportionments: A Note of Caution," *Social Forces*, XLIII (December, 1964), 256–261.

fare orientation" ranking, and this produced a coefficient of only .03, which caused him to reject the hypothesis that the greater the "imbalance in the state's apportionment, the less likely the legislature is to pass 'liberal' or welfare-oriented policies beneficial to urban groups."[4]

Brady and Edmonds examined four policy areas in relation to two indexes of malapportionment. The areas were Kerr-Mills plan adoptions, "right-to-work" laws, state liquor monopolies, and state income tax programs. They found no significant relationships with one of the malapportionment measures (Schubert-Press Index) but did find a significant association between the other measure (David-Eisenberg Index) and Kerr-Mills adoptions and "right-to-work" laws. Nevertheless, they were not able to attribute to malapportionment any substantial influence over policy output. At least, they concluded, it "is not as significant a factor as has been posited."[5]

Derge's findings support these others, although his study was not a systematic, comparative examination of policy output as a dependent variable. In his examination of over 19,000 roll-call votes in Missouri and Illinois over a ten-year period, he concluded that, at the voting stage, there was no evidence of rural-urban antagonism.[6] Flinn's study of urban-rural factionalism in Ohio produced results that coincide with Derge's.[7] My analysis of approximately 1,600 roll-call votes in two sessions of the Kansas legislature revealed only two bills on which there was a significant division between legislators from rural constituencies as compared with those from urban districts.[8]

4. Hofferbert's "welfare orientation" index is a combination of mean per-recipient expenditures for aid to the blind, old age assistance, unemployment compensation, and aid to dependent children, and expenditures for elementary and secondary education. Averages for the bienniums in the period 1952–1961 were used. Richard Hofferbert, "The Relation between Public Policy and Some Structural and Environmental Variables in the American States," *American Political Science Review*, LX (March, 1966), 74, 75.

5. David Brady and Douglas Edmonds, *The Effects of Malapportionment on Policy Output in the American States* (Iowa City, Iowa, 1966).

6. David Derge, "Metropolitan and Outstate Alignments in Illinois and Missouri Legislative Delegations," *American Political Science Review*, LII (December, 1958), 1065.

7. Thomas A. Flinn, "The Outline of Ohio Politics," *Western Political Quarterly*, XIII (September, 1960), 702–721.

8. John G. Grumm, "The Means of Measuring Conflict and Cohesion in the Legislature," *Southwestern Social Science Quarterly*, XLIV (March, 1964), 377–388.

Perhaps the most rigorous analysis of the independent effects of malapportionment on policy output has been conducted by Thomas Dye. He examined five policy areas as measured by fifty-four indicator variables and correlated these data with three separate indexes of malapportionment.[9] But his most important improvement over previous analyses was the use of "economic development" as a control variable.[10] Although he found significant correlations between some of the policy variables and some of the indexes of malapportionment, when economic development was held constant most of these vanished. Consequently, he concludes that the correlations between policy and malapportionment were spurious and a result of the joint effect of economic development and both factors. If we were to put this in terms of our model previously shown, we would designate route c as the major causal path and conclude that this particular political system characteristic had little or no independent modifying effect on legislative performance, at least as indicated by legislative policy outcomes.

This would appear to be Dye's conclusion, but a demurrer needs to be entered at this point. There is not always a perfect correspondence between Dye's conclusions and his data. There are, for example, significant partial correlations between one of his apportionment measures (the "Index of Urban Underrepresentation") and two of his education policy variables—percentage of total school revenue from the state ($-.43$) and pupil-teacher ratio ($-.41$). Since both of these are negative and are

9. The three apportionment measures used by Dye were (1) an "index of representativeness," which was devised by Manning Dauer and Robert Kelsay ("Unrepresentative States," *National Municipal Review*, XLIV, 1955, 551–575) and was based on the theoretical minimum percentage of a state's population that can elect a majority in each house; (2) an "index of urban representation" devised by Paul David and Ralph Eisenberg (*Devaluation of the Urban and Suburban Vote*, Charlottesville, 1961) based on the value of a vote cast in the individual districts as represented by the ratio of each constituency to the average constituency in the state; and (3) an "apportionment score" based on a measure proposed by Glendon Schubert and Charles Press, which combines inverted coefficients of variation for each state with statistical measures of skewness and kurtosis in the distribution of the districts by size of populations ("Measuring Malapportionment," *American Political Science Review*, LVII, June, 1964, 968–970).

10. Dye used four measures of economic development: industrialization (one minus the percentage of the work force engaged in agriculture), urbanization (percentage of the population living in incorporated places of 2,500 or more or in urban fringes of cities of 50,000 or more), median family income, and median school years completed. *Op. cit.*, pp. 28–34.

partial coefficients, we can conclude that, regardless of the level
of the state's economic development, the better apportioned legislatures tend to emit policy outputs that result in lower pupil-
teacher ratios in the schools and a lower degree of state participation in public school finance. A number of the other educational
policy variables also came close to having significant partial correlations with malapportionment. Some of the legislative roll-call
studies also suggest that public school policy may be the one area
that is sensitive to the manner in which the legislature is apportioned. Of the very small number of bills that evoked urban-rural
conflict in the Kansas legislative sessions of 1957, 1959, and 1965,
one dealt with school district consolidation and another with the
apportionment of state aid to public schools.[11] Malcolm Jewell
also reports this to be one of the few areas in which urban and
rural legislators may differ.[12]

Admittedly, the evidence for accepting the hypothesis of a
causal relationship between malapportionment and educational
policy is not very strong, but it is, however, too strong to permit
us to reject it. Certainly it is not possible on the basis of this
evidence to predict with any precision what the differences will
be in policies that emanate from well-apportioned legislatures as
compared to malapportioned ones. Unfortunately, most of the
indicator variables used are only very rough measures of these
underlying policy dimensions. We can, however, put some of the
various pieces of evidence together and suggest a tentative conclusion. This would state that the more malapportioned a legislature, the more its educational policy decisions will tend toward
the allocation of a high level of state aid to local school districts,
with a minimum amount of state control in the distribution of
this aid; and the more equitably apportioned the legislature, the
greater will be the tendency toward placing limits and controls
on the allocation of state school aid, which will also tend to be at
a somewhat lower level. This would need to be tested more sys-

11. Grumm, *loc. cit.;* and "The Kansas Legislature: Republican Coalition," in
Midwestern Legislative Politics (Iowa City, Iowa, 1966), pp. 57–96.
12. Malcolm Jewell, *The State Legislature: Politics and Practice* (New York,
1962), p. 65.

tematically, but the data from a number of the studies mentioned above do fit reasonably well into that interpretation.

We have by no means tested all of the possible hypotheses relating malapportionment to public policies. So far, researchers have had to rely principally on financial indicators of latent policies. This has left the whole field of regulatory policies virtually unexamined[13] and has even restricted the scope of investigation in fields where financial indicators are only one of the dimensions of policy decisions. It is certainly probable that an as yet unexamined aspect of legislative policy output will be shown to be highly sensitive to different degrees of malapportionment.

The system of apportionment is one element involved in the "representativeness" of the political system. Other elements would include the party system, particularly the degree of party competition, and the electoral system. A number of studies, taking policy output as the dependent variable, have analyzed the hypothetical effects of party competition as an independent variable. Probably the most notable of these, at least from the standpoint of analytical sophistication, is that of Dawson and Robinson.[14] They were concerned only with welfare policy, which they measured by means of nine variables that included four revenue items and five expenditure items. They ranked the states according to each of the nine and then ranked them according to the degree of party competition using the averages of three percentages for a twenty-year period (1938–1958). These three were the percentages of seats held by the majority party in each house of the legislature and the percentage of the popular vote for the winning candidate for governor. They found some moderately high correlations between interparty competition and several welfare outputs, including benefit payments per recipient and per capital welfare expenditures. But these coefficients were substan-

13. Dye does deal with a domain that he regards as "public regulation," but his indicator variables seem to be only vaguely or very generally related to specific regulatory policies. This category includes such variables as "public employees' salaries," "number of bills enacted," and the "crime rate." The latter might be considered to be more appropriate to the input side than the output. Dye, *op. cit.,* pp. 210–235.

14. Richard Dawson and James Robinson, "Inter-Party Competition, Economic Variables, and Welfare Policies in American States," *Journal of Politics,* XXV (May, 1963), 265–289.

tially reduced when the states were divided into three per capita income levels and the correlations were recomputed for each of these. Their conclusion was that party competition was not as important in determining welfare policy as socio-economic factors, especially personal income. It appeared that the more politically competitive states also tended to be the more economically developed states; and, being better able to afford it, they tended to be more liberal in their welfare allotments.

Dye came to about the same conclusion after investigating the hypothetical effects of seventeen health and welfare policy measures on the degree of party competition in the upper and lower houses of the state legislatures. His measure of competition was based on the average of the percentage of seats held by the minority party in each house over a ten-year period from 1954 to 1964. As did Dawson and Robinson, he found correlations he regarded as significant with most of the measures based on size of payments to recipients in the various welfare categories. Again all of these were reduced below his designated level of significance when economic development variables were held constant. His conclusion was that the degree of competitiveness within the legislature has, by itself, no liberalizing effect on welfare policies.[15]

A cross-national study by Phillips Cutright provides some seemingly contradictory evidence to that of Dye and Dawson and Robinson. He constructed an index to measure the degree of social security coverage of a nation's population and related this to another index of "political representativeness." The latter was purportedly a measure of the amount of accessibility that the people have to the ruling elite in the parliament and executive bureaucracy. As in the other two studies, economic development (as measured by energy consumption, urbanization, and literacy) was held constant, in this case by analyzing the relationship between representativeness and level of social security coverage at five different levels of development. He found that, even with economic development controlled, the more representative gov-

15. Dye, *op. cit.*, p. 258.

ernments generally introduced programs earlier than the less representative ones. Within the lowest levels of development, however, there was little relationship between representativeness and the social security index, presumably because these nations did not have the resources for such social programs; thus, regardless of how potentially responsive their governments might be, there was realistically little possibility of responding to demand for welfare legislation. At the highest levels of development, on the other hand, the social security index was quite closely and positively related to political representativeness.[16]

Can we reconcile Cutright's results with those mentioned previously? Of course, one should not expect very close correspondence with these others since Cutright's social security index is quite different from the welfare policy measures used in the comparative state studies. Furthermore, his representativeness index was composed not only of inter-party competition measures but measures relating to the electoral system and other aspects of the party system. And, finally, he conducted his analysis across nations instead of states in a federal system that imposes a certain degree of uniformity on state welfare policies. But, a closer look at the Dawson and Robinson data opens up the possibility of reconciling it with Cutright's. Although the former divided the states into three groups to partial out the effects of economic development (as measured by per capita income in this case), the latter divided his nations into five groups. Roughly speaking, the Dawson-Robinson middle and lowest groups correspond in terms of averages to about the highest and second highest Cutright groups. In both studies it was these groups that showed some correlation between welfare policy and party competition in the one case and representativeness in the other. In Cutright's lowest economic groups and in Dawson and Robinson's highest, there was virtually no correlation.

In an attempt to approach a higher degree of comparability between the two sets of data, I re-analyzed the state data on

16. Phillips Cutright, "Political Structure, Economic Development, and National Social Security Programs," *American Journal of Sociology*, LXX (1965), 537–550.

party competition and welfare policies by following Cutright in employing a single index of welfare orientation and using Dawson and Robinson's three economic groupings. The index of welfare orientation constructed by Hofferbert for his study of the relationship between welfare policy and apportionment was used rather than Cutright's own index which was somewhat inappropriate for American states. I also used Hofferbert's index of interparty competition instead of Dawson and Robinson's, since his was based on the votes for a larger number of offices and appeared to gauge better the underlying political competition within the electorate. My analysis showed a moderately high rank-order correlation between welfare policy and party competition (.68) for the states with the lowest per capita incomes and only a slightly smaller coefficient (.59) for the middle group of states. For the group with the highest incomes it was only .15. These were all higher coefficients in the respective economic categories than those reported by Dawson and Robinson for any of their measures of welfare orientation.

Again, a reassessment must be made regarding the relationship of this responsiveness factor with legislative output. And, again, one should be cautioned that any revised conclusions cannot be held with a high degree of confidence due to the sketchy nature of the evidence. But the following seems to be a reasonable interpretation of the findings so far: The level of economic development of a nation or a state in a federal system has a high degree of influence on the "representativeness" of the political institutions in the former and on the level of political competition, at least, in the latter. Economic development also creates the conditions under which "liberal" or extensive welfare programs are made possible. In the very poor nations of the world—and presumably no American states would fall in this group—these conditions have not reached the threshold level where any sort of social security program can be adequately financed. Thus, regardless of how responsive the nation's political institutions may be themselves, little is done to relieve the pressures for welfare legislation since the financial resources for it do not exist. Among the richest American states, the reverse conditions exist. Their fiscal resources are so abundant that the most liberal welfare programs can be adopted without much strain on the state budget. With the encouragement and financial participation of the federal government, not even the most unresponsive of these states' governments will generally fail to legislate relatively generous provisions in their welfare laws. This, then, is a possible explanation for the lack of correlation between welfare policy and representativeness in the poorest nation and the richest states.

The middle group, on the other hand—that is, the wealthier 40 per cent of the nations and the remaining two-thirds of the American states—generally find themselves in a financial condition that will permit them to support social security programs of moderate magnitudes, but such programs will not be forthcoming or be very generous where the legislature and executive are not responsive to popular demands. Where the public has poor access to the legislative and executive elite, the latter will hold out longer before instituting welfare programs and will be more parsimonious with the provisions of these programs. Presumably, access is better and responsiveness greater where there is a high degree of competition in the party system. One-party states and one-party nations, on the whole, respond less readily to the welfare demands of the publics. This analysis, then, should provide a reasonable explanation for the relatively high correlation between party competition and welfare liberalism among Cutright's richer nations and Dawson and Robinson's middle and lower economic groups of states.

Legislative Professionalism

The institutional factors mentioned above are only partially within the control of the legislature (apportionment) or not directly within its control at all (party competition). The legislature itself, however, has comparatively direct control over its supporting services and the expenditures made in the operation of the legislative branch, including salaries of members.[17] Some legislatures may be characterized as highly "professional." By this I mean that their members and their committees are well staffed; good informational services are available to them; a variety of services and aids such as bill drafting and statutory revision are maintained and well supported; and the legislators themselves are well paid, tend to think of their legislative jobs as full-time or close to it, and regard their legislative role as something of a professional one. Other legislatures are poorly staffed, with little or nothing in the way of legislative services, and the members are poorly paid and regard their legislative work as encompassing a very insignificant part of their life. It happens that most of these factors go together in a sort of syndrome of professionalism or amateurism. This is a dimension that varies widely among state legislatures in the United States, and is one that is currently changing very rapidly in many states, generally toward the professional end of this continuum.

One might hypothesize that the legislatures that fell close to the professional end of this continuum (where the members devoted a great deal of their time to their legislative jobs, where they had good access to a wide variety of informational sources, and where they were better able to gauge popular demands) would tend to be more responsive to at least some kinds of demands than would be the case with legislatures that fell at the opposite end of the continuum. This is the hypothesis underlying the analysis presented below. It will be tested by analyzing the interrelationships between legislative professionalism as a structural variable, a comprehensive set of environmental factors, and a number of legislative output measures to see if these relationships conform to a pattern consistent with the proposed operational definition of "responsiveness."

Such an analysis would be rather incomplete if one merely selected one or two environmental factors and one or two policy output areas. So, in order to be as comprehensive as possible, I

17. In fourteen states the salaries are actually set by the state constitution, and in five additional states a maximum is put on legislative salaries by the constitution. In the other thirty-one, however, salaries are legally controlled by the legislature itself.

put together as many measures of environmental influence and policy outputs as were available and appeared relevant. The problem of handling all of these measures in an orderly or systematic manner was solved through the use of factor analysis.[18] This technique provides a reasonably objective means of establishing the categories among a vast array of data, of selecting measures relating to these categories, and of combining or weighting these measures into a single index for each class. A basic proposition of factor analysis is that the relationships between a complex system of variables can be represented simply and economically by a small number of factors. Factors common to a number of variables can be thought of as either causing the relationships between the variables or as embodying the concept that represents these interrelations. For this paper, factor analysis is used in the latter sense. Thus, a large number of measures of legislative output, environmental influence, or professionalism can be combined and reduced to a small number of factors.

When factor analysis is used in this manner—that is, as a method of index construction—the factors can be considered as composite indexes measuring the various dimensions of the domain being investigated. The factor loadings, therefore, provide the system of weights by which the relevant variables are combined in the construction of each index. The factor scores computed from these loadings provide an index score for each of the states or its legislature on each of the dimensions.[19]

Policy Output Factors

Thirty-one quantitative measures of policy output for the fifty states were factor analyzed into five factors. These can most

18. For those interested in a basic understanding of this technique, see Benjamin Fruchter, *Introduction to Factor Analysis* (Princeton, N.J., 1954); or for a more thorough understanding, see H. H. Harmon, *Modern Factor Analysis* (Chicago, 1960). The technique employed here is the "Alpha" method, the most distinguishing feature of which is the use of communality estimates based on coefficients of multiple determination of each variable with every other variable. The original factor loadings are rotated orthoganally according to the "varimax" criteria. The sets of ecological and output factors selected for rotation each accounted for about two-thirds of the variance in the original correlation matrix of variables. The single factor used for the professionalism index accounted for 57 per cent of the original variance.

19. See Henry F. Kaiser, "Formulas for Component Scores," *Psychometrika,* XXVII (March, 1962), 83–87.

readily be identified by the variables that are highly loaded on them, as shown in Table 1.

According to those variables loaded on Factor I, it may be labeled the *welfare-liberalism* factor. Almost all of the measures

---

Table 1. *Output Factor Loadings* (Variables with loadings $> \pm .500$)

Variables	Factor loadings
Factor I—Welfare liberalism	
Old age assistance, average monthly payment per recipient (December, 1964)	.852
Aid to dependent children, average monthly payment per recipient (December, 1964)	.819
Aid to the blind, average monthly payment per recipient (December, 1964)	.785
Unemployment compensation, average weekly payment per recipient (1963)	.727
Average teachers' salaries (1964)	.695
Expenditures on police protection per capita (1963)	.661
Public school expenditures per capita (1963)	.642
Aid to permanently and totally disabled, average monthly payment per recipient (December, 1964)	.571
Average weekly earnings of full-time state employees (1964)	.565
Factor II—Governmental size	
State expenditures for higher education per capita (1964)	.895
Total state expenditures per $1,000 personal income (1964)	.835
Full-time state government employees per 10,000 population (1964)	.754
General revenue of state government per capita (1964)	.677
Total state expenditures per capita (1964)	.646
Average weekly earnings of full-time state employees (1964)	.554
Public school expenditures per capita (1963)	.551
Factor III—Financial centralization	
State taxes per $1,000 personal income	.833
Percentage of state and local revenue coming from the state (1963)	.772
Percentage of local school revenue from the state (1964–1965)	.713
State intergovernmental expenditures per capita (1964)	.697
General sales and gross receipts tax per $1,000 personal income (1964)	.649
Factor IV—Progressive taxation	
Individual income tax as a percentage of total state taxes (1964)	.657
Individual income tax collections per $1,000 personal income (1964)	.650
Individual income tax rate range (highest rate minus lowest) (1964)	.618
Sales and gross receipt tax as a percentage of total state taxes (1964)	.583
Factor V—Governmental expansion	
Expenditures for police protection per capita (1963)	.614
Increase in general expenditures per capita (1953–1963)	.604
State debt outstanding per capita (1963)	.549
Average teachers' salaries (1964)	.518
Public school expenditures per $1,000 personal income (1963)	−.506

of welfare policy were highly related to this dimension. A couple of variables connected with educational policy were also involved, which suggests that the two are closely connected, but this factor appears to be more concerned with the liberality or parsimony of the states' welfare programs. Table 2, which presents the scores for the output factors, shows that the more affluent states of the North had the highest degrees of welfare liberalism, whereas the poorer states, primarily in the South, tended to be quite conservative in this respect.

Table 2. *Factor Scores for Five Output Factors* (States with scores $> \pm$ 1.000)

Factor I		Factor II		Factor III		Factor IV		Factor V	
Calif.	2.563	Alaska	4.304	N.M.	2.036	Del.	3.102	Nev.	2.298
Wis.	1.894	Utah	1.740	Wis.	1.944	Mass.	1.866	Del.	2.203
Mass.	1.773	R.I.	1.487	La.	1.637	Alaska	1.641	Alaska	1.022
N.Y.	1.671	N.M.	1.255	S.C.	1.525	N.D.	1.531	Conn.	1.816
Mich.	1.142	N.D.	1.162	N.C.	1.462	Idaho	1.245	Va.	1.282
Ill.	1.096	Colo.	1.066	Del.	1.453	W.Va.	1.226	Fla.	1.230
Ind.	1.051			Miss.	1.301	Ore.	1.211	Mo.	1.185
Kans.	1.051			Wash.	1.264	N.C.	1.119	Ky.	1.161
N.J.	1.013			R.I.	1.197			R.I.	1.002
				Mich.	1.158				
Tex.	−1.073	S.C.	−1.093	S.D.	−1.147	Ind.	−1.085	Ala.	−1.017
Maine	−1.084	Md.	−1.148	Mont.	−1.273	Mich.	−1.218	Ia.	−1.106
Tenn.	−1.170	Ohio	−1.195	N.J.	−1.540	Tex.	−1.225	Mont.	−1.260
S.C.	−1.287	Pa.	−1.309	Va.	−1.593	Utah	−1.339	Ind.	−1.351
W.Va.	−1.403	Mass.	−1.979	N.H.	−2.211	Ill.	−1.600	Okla.	−1.374
Ga.	−1.492			Nebr.	−2.758	Nev.	−1.940	Minn.	−1.463
Ark.	−1.613							S.D.	−1.667
Miss.	−1.798							N.D.	−1.719
Ky.	−1.887							Ark.	−1.745
Va.	−1.889							Kans.	−1.802

The second output factor represents the magnitude of the state government's operations adjusted for the size of its population. The label *governmental size* may be somewhat misleading unless it is kept in mind that the variables loaded on this factor are essentially expressed in per capita amounts. The states that scored highest here were by no means the largest or the ones that spent the most money. In fact, some of the biggest total spenders were on the negative end of this scale. The ones with the highest scores appeared rather to be the smallest states that were probably unable to realize the "economies of scale" enjoyed by the larger states.

Factor III is related to revenue collection and distribution. It is labeled *financial centralization* because most of the variables loaded on it are measures of the relative magnitude of the state tax bite and of the degree to which state-collected revenues predominate in the total state-local revenue system.

Factor IV is essentially a measure of the progressiveness of the state's tax structure. One of the highly loaded variables on this factor is the income tax-rate range, which is a reasonably direct measure of the progressiveness of this tax. Two other variables with high loadings on the factor are indicators of the degrees to which the state relies on the income tax as its major source of revenue. Since the income tax is the only important tax that tends to be progressive in its operation, this has been called the *progressive taxation* factor. The sales tax is also loaded on this factor, though not very highly, due to the fact that there is a tendency for states to impose both taxes or neither.

The fifth major dimension was labeled *governmental expansion* although this was not very clearly delineated. The basis for this labeling was the loadings on the factor of two variables signifying expansion of the state budget, these two being "increase in general expenditures per capita, (1953–63)" and "state debt outstanding per capita." The factor might also have been called a *police protection* or *public safety* factor, since per capita expenditures for police protection had the highest loadings. For the purposes of the present analysis, however, it does not make a great deal of difference how it is labeled. Often in factor analysis there are one or two factors that are difficult to identify simply and clearly.

Ecological Factors

On the "input" side of the legislative system forty-five ecological variables were factor analyzed with the result that four factors were extracted. The variables with high loadings on these factors are shown in Table 3.

The first factor clearly relates to economic affluence, although the educational level of the population is inextricably involved in it. The variable with the highest loading (though negative) is "per cent failures in draft board mental test." This is closely related to the level of education of the population, probably even more so than median number of school years completed. But, again, the label is not terribly important; it might be regarded as a combined economic and educational factor.

Table 4 shows the states with the highest scores on each of the ecological factors. What clearly stands out in regard to Factor I is its North-South orientation. States with the high positive scores are all among the northernmost in the country. Those with the highest negative scores are all in the South with the exception of the border-state of Kentucky.

Factor II clearly represents population expansion. If the first factor has a North-South orientation, this one is aligned on an East-West basis. All of the states with high positive scores are in the West, with the exception of Florida, which is, after all, very similar demographically to a western state.

Factor III is the "urbanization" factor. The urban percentage of the population has the highest loading on this, and most of the other highly loaded variables are related to urbanism. This can be distinguished from Factor II in that the states with high scores on the latter are expanding rapidly in population and are probably becoming more urban as a result, but those with high scores on Factor III are already highly urbanized and have generally more stable populations.

Factor IV is another that presents some difficulties in defining. Since it includes a number of measures of the amounts of federal money entering the state, it was decided to label it the *federal support* factor.

Professionalism Index

In constructing a "Professionalism Index" the first step was to define a small number of variables that were most obviously connected with this quality. Four were designated: (1) compen-

Table 3. *Ecological Factor Loadings*
(Variables with loadings $< \pm .500$)

Variables	Factor loadings
Factor I—Economic affluence	
Retail sales per capita (1963)	.830
Median school years completed of persons over twenty-five (1960)	.782
Sound housing, percentage of total (1960)	.668
Increase in percentage of Negro population (1950–1963)	.655
Estimated market value of all property in state, per capita (1961)	.623
Foreign and mixed parentage as a percentage of total population (1960)	.616
Telephones per 1,000 population (1963)	.615
Income per capita (1963)	.586
College enrollment per 10,000 population (1964)	.531
Percentage failures in draft board mental test (1963)	−.943
Negro percentage of population (1960)	−.867
Increase in per capita income (1950–1960)	−.579
Population per lawyer (1963)	−.540
Factor II—Population expansion	
Increase in urban percentage of population (1950–1960)	.761
Percentage population increase (1960–1963)	.743
Average value per farm (1959)	.722
Construction expenditures per capita (1963)	.716
Net migration, 1960–1963, as a percentage of 1960 population	.685
Increase in value added by agriculture (1950–1960)	.682
Increase in value added by manufacturing (1954–1963)	.677
Average acreage per farm (1959)	.640
Percentage of 1960 population residing in different county than in 1955	.637
Crime rate: offense per 100,000 population (1965)	.573
Percentage of land in state owned by federal government (1963)	.522
Value added by manufacturing per capita (1963)	−.540

sation of legislators,[20] (2) total length of sessions during the 1963–1964 biennium,[21] (3) expenditures for legislative services and operations during the same biennium,[22] and (4) a "legislative services" score. The latter was based on a study by the Citizens

20. This is the computed realized compensation of the average legislator in each of the states for the 1964–1965 biennium from data in the *Book of the States, 1966–67* (Chicago, 1966), pp. 43–49. Where pay was based wholly or partially on per diem amounts, these were multiplied by the number of days in session to produce total realized compensation.

21. *Ibid.*, pp. 62–63.

22. These are the figures reported under "Expenditures on the Legislative Branch," in U.S. Bureau of Census, *Compendium of State Government Finance in 1964* (Washington, 1964), less the total amount paid for legislative compensation. They include therefore all expenditures for the operation and maintenance of the legislature and its facilities and services, but do not include pay to legislators.

Factor III—Urbanization	
Urban percentage of population (1960)	.856
Physicians per 100,000 population (1962)	.740
Telephones per 1,000 population (1963)	.698
Federal income and employment tax collections per capita (1963)	.693
Income per capita (1963)	.665
Crime rate: offenses per 100,000 population (1965)	.664
Sound housing, percentage of total (1960)	.656
Value added by manufacturing, per capita (1963)	.639
Percentage of urban population in state's largest S.M.A. (1963)	.628
Total population of state (1963)	.596
Newspaper circulation per 1,000 population (1964)	.583
Median age (1960)	.521
Population per square mile (1963)	.502
Workers who walked to work, percentage of total population (1960)	—.656
Percentage of state and local revenue from federal government (1963)	—.628
Per capita federal grants to state and local governments (1963)	—.507
Factor IV—Federal support	
Increase in college enrollments (1950–1960)	.888
Total federal expenditures per capita (1963)	.857
Federal defense expenditures per capita (1963)	.793
Increase in expenditures for new plant and equipment (1954–1963)	.707
Per capita federal grants to state and local governments (1963)	.676
Percentage of 1960 population residing in different county than in 1955	.655
Percentage of land in state owned by federal government (1963)	.589
Percentage of state and local revenue from federal government (1963)	.504
Percentage increase in per capita federal grants to state and local governments (1953–1960)	—.522
Percentage owner-occupancy of all housing (1960)	—.518

Conference on State Legislatures of the legislative services provided by each of the fifty states.[23] The score was constructed by means of a point system by which state legislatures were graded according to such considerations as the extent of the services actually provided, the size of the staff involved, and the degree to which the services were used by the legislators.

The next step was to examine other variables relating to the legislative process and select those that were correlated with the other four. Twelve such were scrutinized, but only one was deemed to have a sufficiently high average correlation with the

23. Calvin W. Clark, *A Survey of Legislative Services in the Fifty States* (Kansas City, Mo., 1967).

four original variables to be considered as an additional measure of this dimension. This was the number of bills introduced in both houses during the biennium.[24]

The next step was to factor analyze the five variables. The unrotated first factor loadings were then used to compute factors

Table 4. *Factor Scores for Four Ecological Factors* (States with scores $> \pm$ 1.000)

Factor I		Factor II		Factor III		Factor IV	
Iowa	1.676	Nev.	3.558	N.Y.	2.477	Alaska	6.061
Wyo.	1.494	Ariz.	2.986	Conn.	2.455	Hawaii	1.714
Wash.	1.326	Fla.	2.129	Calif.	1.851	Ky.	1.572
Mont.	1.201	Colo.	1.586	Mass.	1.795	Conn.	1.370
Wis.	1.123	Calif.	1.631	Ind.	1.744	Wyo.	1.234
N.D.	1.111	N.M.	1.609	R.I.	1.402	R.I.	1.100
Ill.	1.090			N.J.	1.253	Ind.	1.004
Minn.	1.059			Fla.	1.183		
				Pa.	1.142		
				Ky.	1.092		
				Nev.	1.007		
N.C.	−1.017	Pa.	−1.063	Miss.	−1.027	Minn.	−1.091
Ala.	−1.548	N.H.	−1.065	N.H.	−1.028	N.J.	−1.091
Va.	−1.577	Wis.	−1.077	N.C.	−1.066	Iowa	−1.114
Ky.	−1.624	Conn.	−1.084	Maine	−1.085	Ill.	−1.120
La.	−1.655	Maine	−1.094	Mont.	−1.243	Tenn.	−1.277
Ga.	−1.809	Mass.	−1.231	Nebr.	−1.251	Okla.	−1.407
Miss.	−2.227			Alaska	−1.261	Nebr.	−1.464
Ark.	−2.293			Minn.	−1.416	Ala.	−1.578
S.C.	−2.941			Idaho	−1.424	W.Va.	−1.848
				Wyo.	−1.716		
				Okla.	−1.944		
				N.D.	−1.970		
				W.Va.	−2.013		

scores for each of the states, and it was these scores that constituted the Professionalism Index. This unrotated first factor can be regarded as essentially representing the "common denominator" of all the variables. The index for each of the states is listed in Table 5 in order of the most "professional" to the least. The factor loadings for the five variables were as follows:

1. Biennial compensation of legislators (1964–65)   .814
2. Expenditures for legislative staff, services, operations, and printing (1963–64)   .787

24. *Book of States*, 1966–67, pp. 62–63.

3. Number of bills introduced in 1963–64 sessions   .787
4. Length of regular plus extra sessions, in calendar days
   (1963–64)   .730
5. Legislative services score   .661

Since there was not much variation among the loadings, there
was not much difference in the weighting of the variables in the
construction of the index. "Compensation of legislators" was

Table 5. *Professionalism Index*

Calif.	2.294	Ariz.	−0.100
Mass.	2.185	Okla.	−0.101
N.Y.	2.145	Nebr.	−0.107
Pa.	1.715	Maine	−0.114
Mich.	1.538	Miss.	−0.122
N.J.	1.455	Ind.	−0.150
Ill.	1.043	Colo.	−0.173
Hawaii	1.010	Alaska	−0.188
Wis.	0.837	Ky.	−0.218
Tex.	0.795	Kans.	−0.260
Ohio	0.599	W.Va.	−0.366
Ore.	0.396	Iowa	−0.382
S.C.	0.325	Va.	−0.613
Del.	0.317	Nev.	−0.697
Fla.	0.279	Ark.	−0.765
La.	0.273	S.D.	−0.821
Ga.	0.248	N.M.	−1.006
Conn.	0.226	Tenn.	−1.190
Md.	0.219	Vt.	−1.203
Minn.	0.203	N.H.	−1.357
Mo.	0.202	N.D.	−1.364
Wash.	0.142	Utah	−1.366
Ala.	0.104	Idaho	−1.545
R.I.	−0.065	Mont.	−1.827
N.C.	−0.096	Wyo.	−2.355

weighted highest, but it was only somewhat more important than
the other four, all of which contributed significantly to the index
values.

Causal Relationships

Table 6 presents the intercorrelations of the factor scores for
the ecological with the output factors and each of these with the
Professionalism Index. It appears from this that there may be

some connection between professionalism and the first two outputs and possibly also with the fifth. But it is also apparent that there are some interconnections between the Professionalism Index and the third ecological factor, and between the latter and these three outputs. To sort out the significant relationships among the many possible combinations, the techniques of causal modeling as developed by Simon and Blalock[25] were employed, and the results of this process are to be seen in Figures 1 through 4. The numbers above each of the paths are beta coefficients and

Table 6. *Correlation Matrix: Ecological Factors, Professionalism Index, and Output Factors*

	Economic affluence	Population expansion	Urbanization	Federal support	Profes- sionalism index
Professionalism index	−.090	−.159	.650	.003	—
Welfare-liberalism	.630	−.016	.402	.048	.431
Governmental size	.293	.268	−.342	.514	−.369
Financial centralization	−.260	.224	.098	.040	.206
Progressive taxation	.066	−.395	−.123	.175	.031
Governmental expansion	−.026	.026	.509	.422	.311

indicate the relative strength of the paths. Only those that are significant at $p \leq .01$ are shown. There is no figure to represent the forces acting on the third output factor, "financial centralization," since neither the Professionalism Index nor any of the ecological factors were significantly related to it. Coefficients of multiple determination with the output factor as the dependant variable are shown below the corresponding output.

The analysis behind Figure 1 signifies that legislative professionalism has an independent effect on legislative output, in this case on welfare policy. The effect is positive which means: the more professional the legislature, the more liberal the policy. Professionalism itself is strongly affected by urbanization—about 45 per cent of the variation in professionalism can be accounted for by urbanization. But the influence of urbanization on policy,

25. See Herbert A. Simon, *Models of Man* (New York, 1957), chaps. i-iii; and Hubert M. Blalock, Jr., *Causal Inference in Non-experimental Research* (Chapel Hill, N.C., 1964), chaps. i-iii.

Figure 1. *Determinants of Welfare Liberalism*

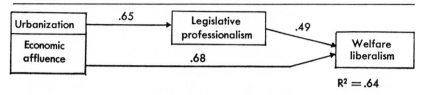

Figure 2. *Determinants of Governmental Size*

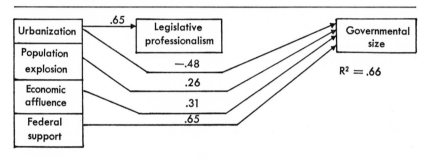

Figure 3. *Determinants of Progressive Taxation*

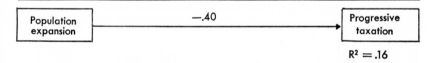

Figure 4. *Determinants of Governmental Expansion*

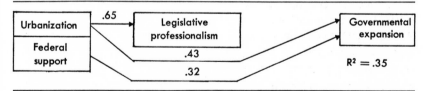

in terms of the variables considered here, is not direct and is only
made effective through legislative professionalism. This is to say
that any ultimate effect that urbanization may have on welfare
liberalism is due essentially to the impact of urbanization on

legislative professionalism, which sequentially has the more direct effect on welfare policies.

Does this analysis confirm the hypothesis that professional legislatures are more responsive than others? I would suggest that it does, although the evidence is not completely convincing. Both urbanization and economic affluence seem to be providing inputs that eventuate in outputs that can be assigned a position on the welfare-liberalism dimension. In regard to the former, it would be reasonable to assume that great pressures and demands would be built up in the more urbanized states for liberalization of welfare policies. The effect of the economic factor though would not be that of creating demands but of providing the conditions for liberal welfare policies. In both instances, welfare liberalism would appear to be the "appropriate" response to the demands or the conditions produced by these ecological factors in respect to their positive polarity.

There is one slight problem, however, with the above reasoning: the partial coefficient is a little too weak to confirm the appropriateness of the response to urbanization. No "path c" is shown in Figure 1 between urbanization and the output side. Curiously, legislative professionalism accounts for almost all of the correlation between urbanization and welfare liberalism. The partial correlation between these two is very small (.20) when professionalism is held constant, but it still might be argued that there is a tendency for the pressures for liberal welfare policies to be greater in the more urbanized states. Although it may not be totally convincing by itself, this evidence does seem to conform with less systematic observations; few observers would cast doubt on the conclusion that a greater degree of liberalism in welfare policies is an appropriate output to increased urbanization. Since all of the relationships between the two ecological factors and the Professionalism Index with this output factor are positive, we can conclude that a high degree of professionalism in the state legislature will tend to make it more responsive to inputs generated by a high level of urbanization and economic affluence.

One final observation with respect to the first model is the indication that economic affluence has no effect at all on legislative professionalism. Apparently, a state does not have to be rich in order to provide adequate support for its legislature!

The first model is the most interesting one from the standpoint of the hypothesis under investigation, since the results are more positive in this respect than in the other models. But the others reveal some interesting interrelationships among the ecological factors and policy outputs. Figure 2 presents these relationships in respect to the second output factor, governmental size. Although there was a moderately high simple correlation between professionalism and this policy output, it turned out to be entirely spurious, primarily due to the effect of urbanization on both of these.

It can be observed that the relationship between urbanization and governmental size is negative, which indicates that the most urbanized states tend to have smaller governmental operations in relation to their total population than the least urbanized ones. Undoubtedly, the explanation for this is that the highly urbanized states are also the largest ones, and they apparently find it possible to enjoy some of the economics of size. Regardless of the size of the state, there are certain minimum requirements in the way of governmental structure, facilities, and services that must be provided; thus, the less urbanized states, which also tend to have smaller populations, find they must spend more money, on a per capita basis, than the big states.

Economic affluence is also an important ecological factor contributing to governmental size, which certainly conforms with expectations. Population expansion is related to this output factor undoubtedly because of the necessity to spend extraordinary amounts of money on capital construction in those states with rapidly growing populations. Federal support is related to the size of the state government operations probably because of the need for the state to match federal money in many of the federally initiated programs, and because of increased state overhead costs resulting from federal projects and installations located within the state. It is rather comforting to note that the factors contained in the second model account for two-thirds of the variations in this policy output. This indicates that very little has been left out of the analysis as far as this output is concerned.

Figure 3 indicates the population expansion is the only ecological factor having any influence on the progressiveness of a state's system of taxation. Since the coefficient is negative, this means that rapidly expanding states tend to have less progressive tax policies than the more stable ones. Probably the explanation for this is that the expanding states are frequently faced with the need for rather large incremental increases in their budgets from year to year. In view of these pressures the progressiveness of the tax structure may easily suffer. Rates are raised inordinately on the middle- and lower-income groups because these make up the vast majority of taxpayers, and they can produce more revenue for the government than the comparatively small number of high income taxpayers. When further hikes in the income tax become politically impossible there will be a resort to an increase in the sales tax or other regressive taxes. In the more stable states a modicum of progressiveness presumably can be maintained by the legislature. Since there is less pressure for revenue increases, the tax system can still function in such a way as to contribute to the goal of economic justice as well as to raise revenue.

Figure 4 represents another example of spurious correlation in the relationship between the Professionalism Index and the output factor. The simple correlation between professionalism and governmental expansion was .31, but this was reduced effectively to zero when urbanization was held constant. Accordingly, if the more professional legislatures have a tendency to increase state budgets faster than the less professional ones, it is only because the pressures for budget increases are greater in the more urbanized states, and these states, as we have seen previously, tend to have more professional legislatures. One cannot assert in this case that professionalism tends to make a legislature more responsive to these types of demands, since there is no "path *b*" from this structural characteristic to the output. The increased professionalism produced by increased urbanization does not necessarily facilitate a general increase in the budget, although we have seen it does facilitate the selective increase in welfare expenditures.

Conclusions

The major question this paper has addressed itself to is whether the more representative legislatures or the better staffed and supported legislatures performed any better than the less representative or understaffed and poorly supported ones. The author has proposed that performance be evaluated on the basis of a "responsiveness" criterion and that this be determined, in turn, by an analysis of how the structural characteristics of the legislatures relate to legislative output in the context of the demands and conditions generated by the socio-economic environment in which the legislative system resides.

Except on the subject of reapportionment, the evidence turned out to be rather sparse on the effects of a "representativeness" dimension on output. Even in regard to reapportionment the findings were mainly negative. It appeared that reapportionment, in itself, is not likely to make any dramatic change in legislative output or responsiveness, although it may set the stage for later changes that will have greater consequences on the legislative product. One should be cautioned, however, that the results are not all in by any means on this matter. Close analysis showed that apportionment may have some important effects on educational policy and that there may be other policy areas, so far left unexamined, where apportionment may have an impact.

The hypothesis advanced by V. O. Key that differences in party competition affect the representativeness of the legislature and make them more responsive to popular demands has not been conclusively denied or confirmed. The argument advanced in this paper, however, is that the bulk of the evidence so far tends to support the hypothesis rather than refute it. Scholars working in this area have possibly been overly impressed by the discovery that socio-economic factors are important determinants of legislative policy, more powerful, it appears, than some of the political factors. Although this may be true, the impression should not be left that the structure and character of the political system have no effect on policy. Even after the influence of economic factors has been partialled out, differences in party competition in the state legislatures still account for some differences in policy.

Considerably more positive, however, were the findings relating to the dimension labeled *legislative professionalism.* It appeared quite certain that professionalism was closely related to liberalism, at least in the welfare area. The explanation offered for this was that professionalism tended to facilitate the legislatures' response to the demands generated by urbanization and the conditions provided by an advanced level of economic development. Although this structural feature had little or no relation to the other four areas of policy, the welfare area, which also encompassed educational policy in this formulation, was undoubtedly the most significant single area analyzed.

It is hoped that this analysis might be helpful to those contemplating changes in the state legislative institution. Often reform groups have gone about their "tinkering" with the system without any scientific notion as to the ultimate consequences for the system as a whole. There are many examples of this (the direct primary, initiative referendum, women's suffrage) which ultimately produced consequences that were unintended (or did not produce those intended). Now that the reformers are beginning to focus on the state legislatures, it would be well to understand to what their proposed "improvements" will lead. Obviously, we cannot predict all of the consequences, but even to be able to shed a dim light in the darkness seems worthwhile.

If reform groups should be able by their own efforts, to increase the professional status of some state legislatures, could we then expect any change in the legislative output? The evidence presented here suggests we could, at least with respect to the welfare-liberalism dimension and under certain economic conditions. The relationships between legislative professionalism and welfare-liberalism seem to be similar to those involving party competition and welfare policy. Since we would expect to find the demands for liberal welfare policies had already been satisfied in most of the affluent states, whereas many of the poor states would not be able to afford more liberal policies regardless of demands, the effects of legislative improvement would most probably be confined to a middle group of states where changes in policy were being demanded and where they were economically feasible.

Extrapolation of our evidence regarding legislative professionalism to the cross-national arena would suggest that altering the legislature to give it a more professional posture might prove generally effective in liberalizing welfare provisions in the moderately- and well-developed countries, but would not likely be effective in the underdeveloped nations. It is clear from all of the studies treating policy output as a dependent variable that economic conditions are extremely important determinants. Although I have presented some evidence that structural and political factors are also important, we have to recognize their effectiveness tends to vary with differing ecological conditions, particularly with economic development.

As a final consideration we should return to the point that almost all of the forementioned studies have been concerned with policy outputs that could readily be quantified, and that almost all of this quantification has been based on financial indicators. It is not terribly surprising to discover that financial indicators of policy are sensitive to economic variables. In view of the nature of the data, the correlations of structural and political variables with these policy indicators, although possibly weaker, seem less trivial than those of economic variables with policy. Still, we might well expect to find stronger correlations between structural-political factors and policy if we were able to measure regulatory policy quantitatively. It is reasonable to assume, also, that economic determinants are relatively less important in this area. There is great need now to develop valid measures of regulatory output, so that we will have the data base on which to produce a more comprehensive picture of the intricate interrelationships between ecology, structure, and policy.

Chapter 13

Attitudinal Determinants of Legislative Behavior: The Utility of Role Analysis[*]

Malcolm E. Jewell

In recent years students of American state and national legislatures have devoted considerable attention to the analysis of roles.
This research has been inspired by the study of four state legislatures conducted in the 1950's by Wahlke, Eulau, Ferguson, and
Buchanan and reported most fully in *The Legislative System.*[1]
Wahlke and his associates demonstrated that there are differences in the way state legislators view their responsibilities and
the demands made on them by other political actors. They used
the concept of role to delineate these legislative attitudes, and
defined a number of role orientations that were most common
among state legislators. They did not, with few exceptions, try to
explore the reasons why legislators held particular role orientations, although they recognized the large number of variables
that might be pertinent to such a causal analysis.[2] Moreover, they
did not attempt to demonstrate what impact role concepts have
on the behavior of legislators. Subsequent research has shown
that members of other legislative bodies differ in their role concepts and that certain patterns of roles are commonly found. This
research has explored a number of variables that may help to
explain the role concepts of various types of legislators, but it has

* I am indebted to the National Municipal League, which made funds available for some of the research reported in this paper, and the following persons who
read an earlier draft and offered many helpful suggestions: Allan Kornberg,
Samuel C. Patterson, John W. Soule, Ronald D. Hedlund, Roger H. Davidson,
Kenneth Janda, Kenneth Prewitt, and Charles G. Bell.
1. John C. Wahlke *et. al., The Legislative System* (New York, 1962).
2. *Ibid.*, pp. 21–24.

added little to our knowledge about the effects of roles on behavior of legislators.

The fact that a number of scholars have succeeded in using the concept of role to delineate and compare the attitudes of legislators does not necessarily mean that role analysis is a valuable technique for legislative studies. What do we hope to learn from role analysis? In the introductory chapter of *The Legislative System*, Wahlke *et al.*, explain why they chose role as the focal point of that study. They were trying to relate the study of individual behavior "to problems of legislative structure and function which are the traditional concern of students in this field," and they decided that role provided the best possible vehicle for that purpose. "The chief utility of the role-theory model of the legislative actor is that, unlike other models, it pinpoints those aspects of legislators' behavior which make the legislature an institution."[3] The authors used role as a conceptual tool for examining how legislators behave in order to provide a better understanding of the legislative process. Although they asserted that "role theory helps us predict certain general types of response by legislators, given certain types of stimuli,"[4] the authors did not try to prove that legislators holding different role orientations will respond differently to the demands made on them.

Role analysis may be useful for conceptual clarification, but legislative scholars need tools of analysis that will also contribute to explanation and prediction of legislative behavior. They may agree that logically there must be a link between role concepts and behavior of legislators. But they want to know how that link can be measured empirically, how strong it is, and whether knowledge concerning that linkage can add significantly to what we already know about the causes of legislative behavior. Moreover, it is important to explore the sources of roles. Unless we can explain why legislators differ in their role concepts, role analysis may strengthen our predictive powers without increasing our ability to explain the legislative process. If our investigation should show that some role orientations are simply surrogates for

3. *Ibid.*, pp. 8–9.   4. *Ibid.*, p. 20.

some other variable—education, personality, and legislative ten-ure—that perhaps could be measured more precisely, then role would appear to be less useful as a technique of analysis.

This paper has two purposes. The first is to assess the contribu-tion of role analysis and explore its potential in the study of American legislative systems. I will summarize the progress that has been made in explaining the causes of legislative role con-cepts and will discuss the problems that are involved in trying to measure the effects of role concepts on behavior. The second purpose is to outline some thoughts about the utility of role analysis in cross-national studies of legislative systems. Theoreti-cally, if role analysis is productive in American legislative studies, it ought to be useful in cross-national studies as well. Some of the specific roles that have assumed greatest importance in American studies may have less significance in other countries. There may be consensus among legislators in another country concerning a particular role about which American legislators disagree. On the other hand, if legislative institutions and norms are weaker, as is often true in developing countries, there may be less consensus on roles.

The Concept of Role in a Legislative System

Because the term *role* has been given various shades of mean-ing by social scientists, it is important to be precise about its use in legislative analysis. Role refers to the pattern of expectations or norms of behavior that are associated with a position in a social structure. The role of a legislator consists of the rights, duties, and obligations that are expected of anyone holding that position. According to Wahlke *et al.*,

An important characteristic of role is that it always relates to an actor's confrontations with other actors in a role relationship. It is a concept which assumes the existence of interpersonal relations. . . . Any role, therefore, can analytically be divided into role sectors, each sector comprising those norms appropriate to some particular 'coun-ter-role,' i.e., to encounters with persons occupying some particular counterposition or status.[5]

5. *Ibid.*, pp. 10–11.

Many of the legislator's interactions are with his fellow legislators, including those holding such positions as floor leader or committee chairman; the roles pertaining to these relationships are sometimes called the core-roles sector. Another important sector is the client roles, referring to relations with constituents, lobbyists, executive officials, and others who make demands on the legislator.

A person occupying almost any position in an organization will discover that other persons have expectations and make demands on him that are diverse and may even be contradictory. The position of a legislator is different only because it is the focal point for demands from so many actors in the legislative system, and because the essence of the legislator's job is the reconciliation of these demands. In the process of reconciling these demands, the legislator must resolve role conflicts, the incompatible expectations of various persons and groups that claim his support. In order to resolve role conflicts the legislator must determine what his posture will be with respect to other actors in the system. For example, if two lobbyists each claim that the legislator has a special responsibility to the group each represents, he may decide to accept the claim of one or the other or deny the claims of both.

We would expect to find a considerable measure of consensus about roles among legislators, and even among other actors in the legislative system. This should result from the norms of the national or state political culture and more specifically the norms of the legislative institution. "Unless there is some minimal level of agreement about what constitutes the legislative role and its various component sectors the role could not be said to exist. Without some minimum of consensus the legislature would cease to be an institutionalized group."[6] Yet research has shown that, within certain limits, legislators differ in their interpretation of some role sectors. The term *role orientation* refers to a distinct "pattern of norms making up a particular role" or "systematic differences in legislators' conceptions of a particular component of the role of legislator."[7] We might find that a particular role orientation, such as trustee, delegate, or politico, is predominant

6. *Ibid.*, p. 15. 7. *Ibid.*, p. 16.

in one legislature, whereas in another all three orientations are common. If more than one orientation for a particular role sector is found in a legislature, we want to discover the orientation held by each member and if possible the reason why he conceives of his role in this way. This does not mean that the legislator deliberately and consciously adopts a particular role orientation, nor does it mean that he consistently follows a particular orientation. If he articulates a definable role orientation it may result from internalizing certain norms of the legislative system, accepting as legitimate the demands of others, or deliberately choosing among well recognized alternatives.

Research has shown that a person is more likely to be responsive to the expectations and demands of others if he believes that these are legitimate and/or are supported by sanctions.[8] Role analysis of a legislative system makes it possible to identify who may legitimately make demands on legislators and what is the range of demands that they may legitimately make. If the norms of the legislative system are specific and widely accepted, all of the participants may recognize what are the bounds of legitimacy. For example, if one of the legislative norms is a high degree of party loyalty, it might be unthinkable for an outside group to ask a legislator to vote against his party; such a demand would be widely regarded as an illegitimate one. If the system is not so well integrated and norms are less pervasive, legislators might have different viewpoints about what was legitimate. Research in American states has shown that some (but not most) legislators would exclude lobbyists, or certain categories of lobbyists, from the ranks of those who can legitimately make demands on them. We know less about how legislators calculate potential sanctions in evaluating the claims of others. We do know that the persons and groups to which a legislator is most attentive are usually either those who can enhance (or undermine) his influence in the legislature or those who can affect his chances for re-election. There are many examples of legislators who appear very responsive to the demands of a person or group command-

8. Neal Gross, Ward S. Mason, and Alexander W. McEachern, *Explorations in Role Analysis* (New York, 1958).

ing powerful sanctions, inside or outside the legislature. But the legislator's perception of a group's legitimacy is probably more important than the sanctions that he thinks it possesses.

Sources of Role Concepts

System Norms and Structures

In the broadest sense the roles of legislators, and of other participants in the legislative system, are defined by the norms of the political culture that prevails in any society. In the process of political socialization, these norms will be internalized not only by political actors but by ordinary citizens. The structure of party systems and governmental organs will also have an effect on legislative roles. Because political cultural norms and political structures do not vary greatly among the states of this country, the impact of such norms has received little attention in role analysis at the state legislative level.

A few examples will illustrate the importance of cultural norms and political structures. In a nation like Britain the tradition and practice of strong, cohesive parties not only makes a legislator more responsive to the demands of his party than to other groups but it minimizes the claims that other groups make on the legislator. In all Western democracies there is a powerful norm of legitimacy for political opposition that has an obvious effect on the roles of legislators. By contrast, in an Asian or African country where the political culture prescribes a one-party state, the role of opposition and criticism may be prohibited or seriously restricted for legislators. It is equally important to point out that if the norms of the political culture are vague or ambivalent regarding an issue there may be greater variation in the role concepts of legislators. Since the days of Burke, democratic theory has been ambiguous about the representative role of legislator, and as a consequence members of state legislatures disagree about whether they should be trustees or delegates.

The norms of a legislative body are, of course, affected by those of the political culture, but there may be more specific legislative norms that have a direct bearing on role concepts. If the legislative body has strong traditions and substantial continuity of membership, these norms are likely to be better understood and more widely accepted by legislators. These norms may affect legislators in various ways. The veteran member may have internalized the norms and conformed to them unconsciously, whereas the freshman may be more conscious of the confining effect of the norms. We know also that there are sometimes mavericks who refuse to conform to some of these norms, perhaps at the cost of reducing their effectiveness in the legislature.[9] The norms of a legislature prescribe a member's relationships with his colleagues. They may require deference to seniority, courtesy in debate, reciprocity on private bills and minor favors, and respect for committee prerogatives, for example.[10] In addition there may be legislative norms regarding a member's relationships with those outside the legislature, though these are not likely to be so strict. The norms might prohibit a legislator from soliciting favors from a lobbyist, might permit or encourage him to bargain with the governor for patronage, or might tolerate sensitivity to constituent pressures even on party issues if these pressures jeopardized his re-election.[11]

The more pervasive the legislative and political cultural norms, the more uniform will be the role concepts of legislators. We can assume that in any polity and in any legislature there are some norms that have an impact on roles, and we will be better able to measure that impact when more cross-state and cross-national research has been done on roles. The four-state study revealed a number of differences in role patterns among the four legislatures, most of which appeared to be related to differences in political party systems, gubernatorial influence, and the level of legislative professionalization.[12] Because most studies of roles

9. Ralph K. Huitt, "The Outsider in the Senate: An Alternative Role," *American Political Science Review*, LV (1961), 566–575.
10. Donald R. Matthews, *U.S. Senators and Their World* (Chapel Hill, N.C., 1960), chap. v.
11. See, for example, Samuel C. Patterson, "The Role of the Deviant in the State Legislative System: The Wisconsin Assembly," *Western Political Quarterly*, XIV (1961), 460–472.
12. Wahlke *et al.*, *op. cit.*, chaps. xvi, xvii.

have been limited to a single legislature, more attention has been devoted to differences in role concepts among individual legislators. These differences have proved to be considerable, and thus we can conclude that the political cultural and legislative norms in this country are vague or inconsistent on questions pertinent to roles. What are the sources of these variations in individual role concepts?

Personal Characteristics

We can reasonably assume that each legislator has certain attitudes and preferences that are fundamental to his role concepts. Wahlke *et al.* describe the sources of these attitudes:

Legislators do not begin to acquire and form their legislative role concepts and orientations only at the official dawn of their legislative careers. Before that moment they have probably heard and thought about legislative work more than has the average citizen and, in many cases, even before it occurred to them that they might some day hold such office. . . . We can, therefore, conceive that each legislator-to-be possesses some sort of "role potential," according to the attitudes, roles, and other personal characteristics shaped by such "demographic variables" as age, sex, ethnicity, religion, education, and socioeconomic status. . . .[13]

These characteristics may, for example, produce a legislator who relies heavily on others for advice and has a delegate role orientation or one who has great confidence in his own judgment and has a trustee orientation. In theory a legislator's role concepts might be shaped by nearly every aspect of his personality, education, socio-economic status, political socialization, ideological beliefs, career goals, and political experience. In practice it may be difficult to isolate those variables having an impact that is strong and direct enough to be measured. Some of the efforts to measure such relationships are summarized later in the paper.

Perceived Expectations of Others

Despite the importance of norms and the legislator's own attitude, his roles with respect to other actors and groups are likely

13. *Ibid.,* p. 23.

to be affected by his perception of what these others expect of him. The legislator who is a strong trustee may pay less attention than a delegate would, but even the most self-reliant legislator can not be oblivious to the attitudes that others have concerning his responsibilities. These others include colleagues in the legislature, individuals and groups within the constituency, and those outside the constituency—such as the chief executive, governmental agencies, and many lobbyists.

The legislator may have inaccurate perceptions; he may fail to understand what others expect or fail to gauge correctly the intensity of these expectations. He may misjudge the sanctions supporting demands. The more experienced and the more sophisticated legislators ought to be more accurate in their perceptions. It seems likely that legislators will perceive more accurately the expectations of persons or groups in close proximity. The legislator probably knows quite well what his floor leader or committee chairman expects of him, for example. The gap between perception and reality may be greater in constituency relationships because constituents are less articulate or consistent in their expectations, and it is relatively easy for a legislator to deceive himself about what constituents expect him to do.

The role concepts of a legislator and other political actors may change over time because each adjusts to the expectations of others. For example, a freshman legislator and an inexperienced lobbyist would have expectations regarding each other that were based on certain shared norms and the personal characteristics of each, but neither would understand much about what the other expected. As they came to know each other better, they would not only gain more accurate perceptions of each other's expectations but they might become more willing to recognize these expectations as legitimate. The lobbyist, as he became aware of other pressures on the legislator, might begin to expect less of him; the legislator, as he recognized the validity of some of the lobbyist's demands, might become more responsive to them. This process of adjustment, what might be considered as partially internalizing the expectations of others, is one of the ways in which experienced legislators reduce role conflict.

The variables that might affect a legislator's role with respect to an interest group are illustrated in Figure 1. The diagram shows that the attitudes of all the actors involved are shaped by the norms of the political culture and of the legislature. The expectations and sanctions of the group affect a legislator's role only to the extent that he perceives them and regards the expectations as legitimate. The legislator may also be influenced by the opinions of others about his proper relationship to the interest group; these might include not only legislators but the governor, a newspaper, other interest groups, or his constituents.

If the members of a legislature differ in their concepts of representational and client roles, one reason for this may be

Figure 1. *Variables Affecting a Legislator's Role With Respect to an Interest Group*

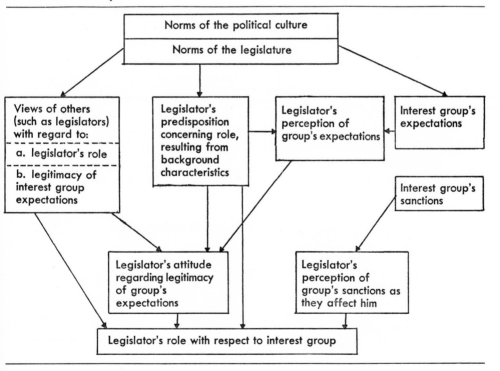

differences in the perceptions of their districts. Not only do the characteristics of districts differ, but constituent opinion is likely to be vague and inconsistent enough so that perception of it may be distorted. Several factors may affect the legislator's perspective of his district. How great are the demands made on him by constituents? Are these demands generally compatible or contradictory, largely organized or unorganized? How much do constituents know about the major issues? How well organized is the local party, and what are its demands on him? How great is the prospect of defeat in the primary or general election if he fails to pay sufficient attention to constituent demands? The legislator's perceptions may be inaccurate. To varying degrees legislators hear what they want to from their districts. The trustee may persuade himself that his constituents want him to use his own judgment. The conservative may exaggerate the conservative nature of constituency viewpoints.[14] But the legislator's perceptions are also based, however imperfectly, on the demands articulated by constituents, and these, in turn, are affected by the character of the constituency.[15] Several specific characteristics of a district appear most likely to determine how a legislator perceives and evaluates the expectations of his constituents and the sanctions at their disposal. These include the size of the district and the diversity of interests found within it, its socio-economic level and urban-rural nature, the balance of party strength and the nature of party and interest group organizations in the district, and its structure as a single- or multi-member district. Most of these variables may be measured easily in quantitative terms.

Research on Variables Affecting Roles

To identify precisely those variables that have the greatest effect on role concepts and determine the relative weight of each

14. Lewis A. Dexter, "The Representative and His District," *Human Organization,* XVI (1957), 2–13.

15. The Survey Research Center's study of constituent-congressional relationships includes data on correlations between constituency attitudes on issues and congressmen's perceptions of these attitudes. See Warren E. Miller and Donald E. Stokes, "Constituency Influence in Congress," *American Political Science Review,* LVII (1963), 45–56.

would require some form of multivariate analysis. Sophisticated multivariate techniques require more precise quantitative measurement of variables than is possible in some cases; the most serious obstacle is the difficulty of quantifying the dependent variables—the role orientations. The control of more than a very few variables through cross-tabulation requires a larger number of subjects than can usually be found in a legislative study. If there are a number of variables that contribute to the differences in role concepts among members of a legislature, as the data below suggest, then role is not simply a surrogate for one or a few variables. It may be a useful technique for summarizing these variables and establishing linkages between them and legislative behavior. If the number of pertinent variables is large, studies that emphasize only a few may ignore more important variables, but a replication of role studies may serve to identify any variables that have a particularly close and consistent association with specific role sectors and appear to explain differences in role concepts.

Several scholars in recent years have explored the sources of roles in legislatures at the national, state, or local level.[16] A summary of their findings will show how many different variables are associated with differences in roles and how much these variables differ in importance from one legislature to another (Tables 1

16. The studies cited in Tables 1 and 3 and in the text are drawn from the following sources. *Iowa:* Ronald D. Hedlund, "Legislative Socialization and Role Orientations" (mimeographed, Laboratory for Political Research, University of Iowa, 1967). *Michigan, 1967:* John W. Soule, "The Influence of Political Socialization, Interpersonal Values, and Differential Recruitment Patterns on Legislative Adaptation: The Michigan House of Representatives" (unpublished doctoral dissertation, University of Kentucky, 1967). *Michigan, 1961:* Robert S. Friedman and Sybil L. Stokes, "The Role of Constitution-Maker as Representative," *Midwest Journal of Political Science,* IX (1965), 148–166. *Four States:* Wahlke *et al., op. cit. Pennsylvania:* Frank J. Sorauf, *Party and Representation* (New York, 1963), chap. vi. *California:* Charles G. Bell and Charles Price, "Pre-Legislative Sources of Representational Roles," *Midwest Journal of Political Science,* XIII (1969). *Canada:* Allan Kornberg, *Canadian Legislative Behavior* (New York, 1967). *Congress:* Roger H. Davidson, "Representational Roles of Congressmen" (paper prepared for the September, 1968, meeting of the American Political Science Association). *San Francisco Area City Councils:* Kenneth Prewitt, Heinz Eulau, and Betty H. Zisk, "Political Socialization and Political Roles," *Public Opinion Quarterly,* XXX (Winter, 1966–1967), 569–582. *Indiana:* Kenneth Janda, "Some Theory and Data on Representational Roles and Legislative Behavior" (unpublished manuscript). Professors Hedlund, Kornberg, and Davidson also made available unpublished data.

and 3). Because the representational role has been most often studied, this will be the focus of attention. In addition to summarizing findings from other studies, I will include (in Table 2) findings from a study of legislators in nine metropolitan counties in seven states, conducted in the spring and summer of 1967. A total of 141 legislators were interviewed, most in person but some through mailed questionnaires. The purpose of this study was to determine how changes in the method of districting (a shift from multi-member to single-member) affected the behavior of legislators, and in the course of the interview legislators were asked questions designed to determine their representational and areal roles.[17]

Because political parties are important sources of norms and voting cues in many legislative bodies, we might expect that Democrats and Republicans would have different role orientations. Studies of congressmen and of legislators in Iowa and in the four-state study have shown that Republicans are slightly more likely to be delegates and Democrats to be trustees. My study of metropolitan legislators, however, showed the reverse to be true, and surveys of Michigan and Indiana legislators found that there was little difference between members of the two parties. Because the results have been contradictory and the relationships have not usually been statistically significant, we may speculate that whatever partisan differences occur with respect to the representational roles of state legislators result from factors that are pertinent to specific states. There is probably nothing inherent in Republican or Democratic membership that is conducive to a particular role. Kornberg found that in the Canadian Parliament members of the right-wing parties were much more likely to assume a delegate role (gamma $= .47$) and more likely to have a local focus (gamma $= .34$) than were members of left-wing parties. He speculates that this might be

---

17. I contacted 119 legislators (over 70 per cent of the total) in Cuyahoga and Hamilton counties in Ohio, Shelby and Davidson counties in Tennessee, Denver County in Colorado, Harris County in Texas, Marion County in Indiana, and Jefferson County in Kentucky: I was also able to use data collected by Professor Brett Hawkins of the University of Georgia for 22 legislators (40 per cent) in three counties of the Atlanta, Georgia, metropolitan area.

related in some way to the majority position held by the right-wing parties.

Background Characteristics of Legislators

Because representational role depends so closely on a legislator's confidence in his own judgment, we would expect it to be related in some way to his psychological characteristics. Political scientists studying roles have seldom explored this area, probably not only because of their reluctance to plunge into the deep waters of psychology but also because it is difficult to identify and measure those psychological variables that might have the greatest effect on roles. A study of legislators in Iowa included such attitudinal variables as alienation, faith in people, social distance, authoritarianism, and toleration; a Michigan study included such interpersonal values as support, conformity, recognition, independence, benevolence, and leadership. Each study found a single variable that was significantly related to representational role (Table 1). Psychological variables are likely to remain important but elusive sources of roles.

Despite recent interest in political socialization, there have been few attempts to link differences in the time or manner of socialization to legislative roles. It might be hypothesized that a legislator whose interest in politics dates back to an early age would place more confidence in his own judgment and adopt a trustee role, but the few studies on the topic show contradictory results (Table 1).

Both education and occupation seem to be logical sources for representational roles. The better educated member and the one whose profession has enhanced his experience and knowledge about government and public affairs ought to be confident of his own judgment and might be scornful of constituents who are less well informed about legislation. In several studies there is strong and consistent evidence of a positive relationship between higher education and a trustee orientation but in other studies the level of education appears to make no difference. In most studies the clearest contrast was between those who had, and those who had not, graduated from college. Among metropolitan legislators the average education level was higher, but the roles of those with graduate or professional training differed from those without. Several studies have also shown that better educated legislators are likely to have an areal focus larger than just their district. The effect of occupation on representational role does not appear to be quite so great (Table 1). Among metropolitan legislators professional men were more inclined to the trustee role than were businessmen, but the small number of white-collar and blue-collar workers also included a high proportion of trustees. Canadian

Table 1. *Relationships between Representational Role and Various Personal Background Characteristics of Legislators: Findings of Several Legislative Studies*

Findings concerning representational role	Study[a]	Correlation[b]	Level of significance
Psychological factors			
1. Legislators with a low faith in people are more likely to be trustees.	Iowa	.083 (tau b)	.01
2. Legislators who place a high value on exercising leadership are more likely to be trustees.	Michigan, 1967	.340 (G)	.01
Political socialization			
1. Legislators who were introduced to politics after adolescence and before entering politics are more likely to be delegates.	Iowa	.061 (tau b)	.05
2. Legislators who were socialized before becoming adults are more likely to be trustees.	San Francisco City Councils	.170 (G)	n.s.
3. Legislators who were socialized as adults are more likely to be trustees.	Four states	.170 (G)	
Education			
1. Legislators with a higher level of education are more likely to be trustees.	Michigan, 1967	.360 (G)	.01
	Canada	.390 (G)	.05
	California	.370 (biserial)	.05
	Metropolitan	.450 (G)	.01
2. There is little relationship between education and representational role.	Iowa	.040 (G)	n.s.
	Congress		n.s.
	Indiana		n.s.
Occupation			
1. Legislators having a higher status occupation are more likely to be trustees.	Iowa	.170 (G)	n.s.
	Canada	.250 (G)	n.s.
	Metropolitan	.190 (G)	n.s.

professionals and businessmen were more likely to be trustees than those in other occupations.

Several hypotheses are possible about the way in which roles might be affected by a legislator's career goals. One who aspires to an office higher than his present legislative position might not dare to be a trustee because so many interests must be satisfied if his ambition is to be fulfilled. On the other hand, such a legislator may incline toward a trustee role because he sees less need of responding to demands within his present district. The latter

2. There is little relationship between occupational status and representational role.	Congress		n.s.
	Indiana		n.s.
Career goals			
1. Legislators with higher career aspirations are more likely to be trustees.	Michigan, 1967	.250 (G)	.05
2. There is little relationship between career goals and representational role.	Iowa	.070 (G)	n.s.
Ideology			
1. Legislators with stronger ideological views are more likely to be trustees.	Metropolitan	.120 (G)	n.s.
2. More conservative legislators are more likely to be trustees.	Metropolitan	.130 (G)	n.s.
3. There is little relationship between ideology and representational role.	Indiana		n.s.
Legislative seniority			
1. Legislators with longer legislative tenure are more likely to be trustees.	Congress	.390 (G)	.01
	Canada	.220 (G)	n.s.
2. There is little relationship between seniority and representational role.	Iowa	.060 (G)	n.s.
	Michigan, 1967		n.s.
	Pennsylvania		
	Metropolitan	.020 (G)	n.s.
Party and campaign experience			
1. Legislators with more service in party organizations are more likely to be delegates.	Pennsylvania		
2. Legislators who have been active in party organizations are more likely to be trustees.	California	.350 (biserial)	.05
3. Legislators who have been more active in campaigns are more likely to be trustees.	California	.600 (biserial)	.05

a. The sources of these findings are identified fully in footnote 16.
b. Correlations used are: gamma (G), tau b, and biserial r.

argument is supported by the Michigan study (Table 1), but other studies show little or no relationship.

In studying metropolitan legislators, I hypothesized that those who were most strongly identified with an ideological position would be trustees. To measure ideology, I asked legislators to rank themselves on a five-point scale from strong liberal to strong conservative. The results (Table 2) suggest that both the strength and direction of ideological commitment may be related to representational role. It is the moderate liberals who are least inclined to the trustee role, and the middle-of-the-road group that has the most delegates, but the relationships are not strong enough to be more than suggestive.

I have talked to some members who asserted that they entered the legislature expecting to rely heavily on constituent advice, but soon learned that it was poorly informed and unrepresentative. We might expect legislators to develop stronger trustee orientations as they accumulate experience in their job. The study of congressmen showed that seniority is strongly related to a trustee orientation. (Congressmen were divided into: freshmen, those with two to five terms, and those over five terms.) Seniority is also related to a trustee role in Canada. Studies of legislators in several states, however, have shown little or no relationship between seniority and representational role (Table 1). I found that there were differences in roles according to seniority, but these were not in any consistent direction, and the highest proportion of trustees were third-term legislators (Table 2).

A study by Bell and Price has shown that some legislators change their role orientation during their first year of service. They interviewed thirty-one freshman legislators in California before (or shortly after) their election, and interviewed them again after a year of service. Almost half of these changed their role orientation sufficiently after one year to be reclassified from one category to another among the three (trustee, politico, and delegate), but only one changed from delegate to trustee and no one took the opposite route. The largest shifts were from politico to trustee and from delegate to politico, and eleven of the fourteen who shifted moved in that direction (toward trustee and

Table 2. *Relationships between Representational Role and Various Partisan, Personal, and District Characteristics of Legislators in Nine Metropolitan Counties*

Characteristics	Representational role			Correlation	Level of significance
	Trustee	Politico	Delegate		
Party					
Republican (55)	58%	26%	16%	.13	n.s.
Democratic (78)	46	37	17	cont. coef.	
Education					
Graduate or professional					
training (76)	59	34	7	.45	.01
College graduate (27)	44	30	26	gamma	
High school or some college (21)	29	29	43		
Occupation					
Professional (72)	57	32	11	.19	n.s.
Business (43)	42	30	28	gamma	
White collar and blue collar (9)	66	22	11		
Ideology					
Strong conservative (8)	63	25	13	.13	n.s.
Moderate conservative (35)	54	34	11	gamma	
Middle-of-road (21)	57	14	29		
Moderate liberal (27)	30	52	19		
Strong liberal (10)	60	40	0		
Legislative seniority					
4 + terms (22)	36	41	23	.02	n.s.
3 terms (18)	72	28	0	gamma	
2 terms (29)	45	41	14		
1st term (64)	53	27	20		
Margin in general election					
50–59% (73)	53	29	18	.07	n.s.
60–69% (30)	57	27	17	gamma	
70–99% (9)	33	56	11		
Unopposed (21)	43	43	14		
Districting method					
County-wide multi-member (17)	59	24	18	.31	n.s.
Smaller multi-member (22)	55	27	18	cont. coef.	
Multi- and single-member					
district alternation (23)	61	30	9		
Single-member recently (58)	48	40	12		
Single-member over long					
period (12)	33	17	50		

away from delegate). These changes may result simply from greater self confidence after a year of experience or from the influence of fellow legislators. Another possibility is that legislators may begin to abandon the delegate role when they begin to recognize how little informed advice they get from constituents.[18]

18. Bell and Price, *op. cit.*, pp. 261–264.

A Pennsylvania study showed that legislators with experience in party work were more likely to be delegates, perhaps because in that state they were more likely to have been selected by party organizations and consequently were sensitive to the demands of such organizations. In California, however, newly elected legislators were more likely to be trustees if they had been active in party organizations and in previous political campaigns.

It is evident that no single background variable adequately explains role selection, and that variables which appear particularly important in one legislative body often prove to be of little importance in another. There is some evidence that personality factors may have more effect on legislative role than has usually been realized. Education and occupation, of course, are closely related, and data from the study of metropolitan legislators indicate that both have an effect on representational role. Legislators engaged in professions, such as law and teaching, were most inclined to be trustees; nearly all, of course, had graduate or professional training. Among businessmen, whatever their educational level, there was a lower proportion of trustees, but businessmen without any graduate or professional training were more inclined to be delegates than those who had such training. Similarly, a cross-tabulation of party and education shows that both influence the role orientations of metropolitan legislators. Republicans were more likely to be trustees at any given level of education; education was related to a trustee role for both Democrats and Republicans; and the levels of education were approximately the same for members of both parties.

Characteristics of Districts

A legislator who is strongly inclined to rely on his own judgment might not be influenced by the nature of his district, but we might expect most other legislators to take account of district characteristics in selecting roles. Political scientists have hypothesized that legislators from closely competitive two-party districts would be less likely to vote with their party than those from safe districts, although the data from several studies are inconclusive.[19] Similar logic would lead us to hypothesize that close competition in a district would force a legislator to be a delegate and to pay close attention to constituency demands. A strong relationship, in the predicted direction, has been found between representational role and the level of competition in congressional districts (Table 3). This relationship is true for members of both parties, although it is stronger for Democrats (gamma = .62). The congressional study also demonstrated that members from marginal districts were more likely than those from safe districts to define their areal role in district rather than national terms (gamma = .30), and this held true for members of both parties.

Most state legislatures also include districts that vary widely in levels of competition, but studies at the state level concerning the effect of competition have led to conflicting conclusions. Michigan legislators from more competitive districts were more likely to be delegates, but the relationship was not significant. Metropolitan legislators who won by less than 70 per cent, however, were more likely to be trustees than those who had very large majorities or were unopposed, but the differences were not significant (Table 2). There was no consistent relationship between roles of metropolitan legislators and their margin in primary elections. In the four-state legislative study, legislators from the more competitive districts were more likely to define their areal role in district terms (gamma = .25).

Kornberg found that Canadian legislators who came from more competitive districts were only slightly less inclined to a trustee role than those from safe districts (gamma = .09), but he found a stronger relationship in the same direction between representational role and the member's perception of competition in his district (gamma = .24). There were considerable differences between objective and subjective measurements of district competition (gamma = .56).[20] It is logical that the perceived level of

19. See the data summarized in Malcolm E. Jewell and Samuel C. Patterson, *The Legislative Process in the United States* (New York, 1966), pp. 438–444.
20. Kornberg, *op. cit.*, p. 111, and also "Perception and Constituency Influence on Legislative Behavior," *Western Political Quarterly*, XIX (1966), 285–292.

competition should be more closely related to role, and this finding suggests that studies of other legislatures might show that competition has a greater impact if it were measured in terms of perceived competition.

The familiar, though unproven, hypothesis about the effect of district competition on roles ought to be recognized as only one aspect of a more general hypothesis, which might be stated as follows: Any characteristic of a district that makes more direct, visible, or compelling the demands of constituents will make a legislator more inclined to adopt a delegate rather than a trustee role. There are a variety of district characteristics that might have such an effect, and few of them (other than competition) have attracted much attention in research on legislative roles.

One might hypothesize that a legislator would be exposed more directly to constituency demands in a small, rural district than in a metropolitan district; alternatively one could argue that constituents would be better organized and thus more compelling in their demands in the metropolis. Data from several studies show either no relationship or a weak correlation between metropolitanism and a trustee orientation (Table 3). There is a higher correlation in Canada, but it declines if education and party affiliation are held constant.

Several different methods of districting are used for the election of state legislators in metropolitan counties. Some metropolitan counties constitute at-large, multi-member districts; some are divided into several multi-member districts; and some are divided into single-member districts. Several states have recently shifted to single-member districts.

We might expect the legislators in a smaller district to be more visible and more accessible to their constituents and to be more conscious of demands made by these constituents. On the other hand, a member of a county-wide delegation may be better able to escape the pressures of a single group or may believe that groups making conflicting demands on him have roughly equal amounts of popular support in a county. A number of metropolitan legislators whom I interviewed expressed the opinion that there was more pressure from constituents in single-member dis-

Table 3. *Relationships between Representational Role and Various District Characteristics of Legislators: Findings of Several Legislative Studies*

Findings concerning representational role	Study[a]	Correlations[b]	Level of significance
Level of party competition			
1. Legislators from competitive districts are more likely to be delegates.	Congress	.51 (G)	.01
	Michigan, 1967	.15 (G)	n.s.
	Canada	.09 (G)	n.s.
2. Legislators who perceive their district as competitive are more likely to be delegates.	Canada	.24 (G)	.05
3. There is little relationship between competition and representational role.	Metropolitan	.07 (G)	n.s.
4. There is little relationship between perceived competition and representational role.	Indiana		n.s.
Metropolitan versus rural districts			
1. Metropolitan legislators are more likely to be trustees.	Michigan, 1961	.22 (G)	n.s.
	Canada	.30 (G)	.05
2. There is little relationship between metropolitan status of district and representational role.	Iowa	.00 (G)	n.s.
	Congress	.00 (lam.)	n.s.
	Indiana		n.s.
Form of districting			
1. In metropolitan counties, legislators elected at large, rather than by district, are more likely to be trustees.	Metropolitan	.17 (G)	n.s.
Homogeneity of district			
1. Legislators who perceive their district as having many kinds of people are more likely to be trustees.	Iowa	.54 (G)	.05

a. The sources of these findings are identified fully in footnote 16.
b. Correlations used are: gamma (G) and lambda (lam.).

tricts than they had previously experienced when they represented the entire county. If the choice of representational role may be affected by district characteristics, the adoption of single-member districting in a metropolitan county might lead some members to change their role orientations. A few legislators explicitly recognized such a change and argued that a legislator representing a small district would have to assume a delegate role if he hoped to be re-elected.

The data in Table 2 show that there is a weak relationship (not significant) between representational role and the method of districting. The largest proportion of trustees are in counties that still have at-large elections or are divided into a few multi-member districts and in a county (Denver, Colorado) that has alternated between districting plans but was using a county-wide district plan at the time of the interview. The largest proportion of delegates are in a county that has long used single-member districts. In the counties that have recently shifted from county-wide to single-member districts we find the largest proportion of politicos, possibly because the recent shift has complicated the process of role selection. (In the counties that have recently adopted districting, newly elected members are more likely to be delegates and less likely to be trustees than those members previously elected county-wide, but the differences are small).

The kind of districting method that is used has a strong effect on the areal role of metropolitan legislators. They were asked how they perceived their constituency in geographic terms. Did it include the whole county or only some portion of the county? (They were not asked to choose between district and state orientations.) Most, but not all, legislators described the constituency in terms of the district that elected them. The proportion who said they tried to represent the whole county ranged from three-fourths for those elected from the whole county to one-third for those elected in a single-member district. The proportion who tried to represent a district or particular geographic area ranged from about 60 per cent of those elected in a single-member district to less than 10 per cent of those elected county-wide. Some legislators said that this role varied considerably from issue to issue. We might expect such a role to be perfectly related to the type of district; the fact that it is not suggests that in this case personal and district characteristics both have an effect.

One final example of the effect of district characteristics on representational role is found in the Iowa study. Those legislators who perceived their district as including so many different kinds of people that it was hard to know what they wanted were more likely to be trustees (Table 3). The high correlation between perceived district homogeneity and a trustee orientation in one state suggests not only that this relationship should be pursued in other studies but that, in dealing with characteristics of a district that are not obvious, the legislator's perception is more pertinent to role than is the characteristic itself.

There is evidence from the metropolitan study that both personal background and constituency characteristics are independently related to constituency role. The proportions of legislators having different educational and occupational levels are roughly the same in counties with various types of districts. The legislators with more education and with professional occupation are more likely to be trustees, whatever type of district they are elected from. Moreover, legislators with equivalent educational and occupational levels are more likely to be delegates or politicos if they are elected in single-member districts. (The low proportion of trustees in the single-member districts of Kentucky, however, may result from a low proportion of legislators with graduate or professional training.) Members of the two parties are not so evenly distributed among the counties, but in the counties that have recently adopted single-member districts there are members of both parties, and Republicans have a slightly greater preference for a trustee role.

The evidence concerning possible sources of legislative roles is fragmentary and sometimes contradictory. For these reasons it would be hazardous to draw any firm conclusions about the sources of roles. The evidence does suggest that no single variable offers an adequate causal explanation and that characteristics of districts as well as personal qualities and experience of legislators are associated with differences in roles. The fact that so many variables appear to have some effect on roles enhances the value of role as an analytical concept. It is doubtful that we could ever measure with great accuracy the impact that a combination of personal and district variables has on the attitudes and perceptions of an entire legislative body. Role provides a shortcut, a way of summarizing the total effect that these various forces have on legislators. An examination of the sources of role is useful because it can make us aware of the complexity of causal factors and point out those which are most likely to be important.

The Problem of Relating Roles to Behavior

An analysis of the sources of roles is not an end in itself, nor is it enough to describe the patterns of roles that are found in a legislature. The value of role analysis for most political scientists lies in its potential for improving explanation and prediction of legislative behavior. As yet, this is a potential that remains largely unrealized in practice. The problems of relating roles to behavior need to be understood in order to define both the limitations and potential of role analysis. Because roll-call voting is the form of legislative behavior that has been most carefully scrutinized by political scientists, it is useful to start with that topic.

Research on Roll-Call Voting

We might ask first how successful political scientists have been in predicting or explaining roll-call voting without the use of role analysis. Studies of Congress and state legislatures have demonstrated the importance of party membership and membership in such legislative subgroups as committees and state and local delegations in predicting votes.[21] The characteristics of constituencies (particularly their socio-economic makeup and voting records) have also proved to be important.[22] Sometimes the pressure of the governor, administrative agencies, or interest groups clearly contributes to the outcome.[23] The personal viewpoint of a legislator, though often difficult to measure in isolation, obviously has an effect on his vote. As the subject matter of roll-calls varies, the importance of these variables changes. Rarely is a single variable adequate for predicting the votes of members on all

21. See Jewell and Patterson, *op. cit.*, pp. 416–426, for a summary of evidence concerning the importance of party. See also Hugh LeBlanc, "Voting in State Senates: Party and Constituency Influences," *Midwest Journal of Political Science*, XIII (1969), 33–57. For evidence of committee unity in voting on the floor, see Matthews, *op. cit.*, pp. 166–175. The unity of state delegations is discussed in David B. Truman, "The State Delegations and the Structure of Party Voting in the U.S. House of Representatives," *American Political Science Review*, L (1956), 1023–1045.
22. The effect of district characteristics is discussed in Jewell and Patterson, *op. cit.*, pp. 435–444.
23. For an example of the governor's influence, see *ibid.*, p. 446.

roll-calls. Party affiliation, for example, may be a perfect predictor of voting on some issues and useless in predicting votes on others.

The best measure of our ability to predict roll-call behavior without using role analysis is Shapiro's recent computer simulation of roll-call voting in the U.S. House of Representatives. Shapiro made extensive use of the existing roll-call literature in determining which variables to choose and how much weight to assign to each. His model includes: the previous votes of a member on similar bills; his party, committee, and state delegation membership; his region and constituency; and certain information about each bill, such as whether it is a part of the president's program. These data were used to predict whether the member would be strongly disposed to take a stand on the bill and if not what were the prospects that he would be influenced by other members of the House (based on an estimate of probabilities and the use of random numbers). The model made it possible to predict the actual vote on bills with a reasonably high degree of accuracy and to predict the vote of individual members accurately 84 per cent of the time on a small group of roll-calls. It is noteworthy that each of the variables contributed something to successful prediction; when the simulation was run with one or another variable omitted, a lower level of prediction was obtained.[24]

Shapiro's simulation confirms the conclusions of other roll-call studies. It is possible to predict roll-call votes quite accurately by using a number of variables. Further use of simulation and other multivariate techniques should make it possible to determine more precisely the weight that should be assigned to each variable and to identify those variables that contribute relatively little to prediction. The importance of particular variables will vary from issue to issue, however, and these differences must be taken into account in any predictive model. It is obviously more difficult to predict votes when the relevant variables have contradictory effects; this is illustrated in the computer simulation by a

24. Michael J. Shapiro, "The House and the Federal Role: A Computer Simulation of Roll-Call Voting," *American Political Science Review*, LXII (1968), 494–517.

lower percentage of accurate predictions for southern congressmen.

Utility of Role Analysis in Studies of Voting

An analysis of roles might add to our predictive ability in those
cases where the relevant variables have contradictory effects on a
legislature. These are usually the cases in which a legislator is
cross-pressured, that is, subjected to conflicting demands. It is
useful to know a legislator's role concepts because they tell us
how much importance or priority he gives to various demands. In
other words, we can tell to what extent a legislator shares the
expectations that others have concerning the way he should perform his job. These expectations include not only the explicit and
overt demands of others but norms that the legislator has internalized, such as a strong sense of party loyalty. A specific role
orientation means a predisposition or inclination to act in a particular way; it indicates a probability, not a certainty, about
voting or any other action. If we know enough about a legislator's
role concepts, we should be able to predict more accurately how
he will respond to demands, how he will vote. In the case of
southern congressmen, for example, the computer simulation
might be more accurate if the member's sense of obligation or
responsibility to the congressional party could be measured and
inserted into the program.

Whether, in practice, a knowledge of roles adds much or little
to our predictive ability, it should enhance our ability to explain
how legislators act. When several relevant variables point in the
same direction, it may be possible to predict voting with a high
percentage of success and even measure the weights of each
variable without understanding much about how legislators make
voting decisions. Moreover, when a legislator's votes are predicted by a computer from variables such as constituency characteristics or affiliations within the legislature, we run the risk of
perceiving him as a mere robot, responding automatically to
stimuli. In fact, we know that the attitudes and perceptions of
legislators affect the way they respond to demands. The question

remains whether we can gain accurate enough information about roles to contribute to the study of roll-call voting.

Despite the interest shown by legislative scholars in both roles and roll-calls, there have been few attempts to demonstrate that particular role sectors are related to voting behavior of legislators. Ferguson and Klein, using data from the four-state study, found that in four legislative bodies members whose role orientation was one of party loyalty were more likely to support the party in roll-call voting; in two houses the opposite situation occurred; and in two houses party role seemed to have little effect on voting.[25] Sorauf found that in Pennsylvania the legislators who voted most consistently with the party were more likely to be trustees and were less likely to be delegates or to be district-oriented than those with a less loyal voting record, but the differences were not very large.[26]

A fundamental problem of relating roles to any kind of legislative behavior is that of accurately ascertaining role concepts through questioning legislators. Those engaged in role research have used a variety of questions, some open-ended and some more precise, in their efforts to measure the attitudes of legislators. The differences not only make it hard to compare the results of research but also suggest the difficulties of trying to probe deep-seated and perhaps complex attitudes by means of a few questions.

Another methodological problem in role analysis is the classification of legislators. When we refer to a legislator as a delegate, politico, or trustee, we are applying a stereotype to him. Francis believes that it is more useful to think of such a typology as a continuum or dimension.[27] In theory, if our measuring techniques were precise enough, legislators could be located at any number of points along the dimension. Actually several scholars have classified legislators by scoring their degree of agreement with

25. LeRoy C. Ferguson and Bernard W. Klein, "An Attempt to Correlate the Voting Records of Legislators with Attitudes toward Party," *Public Opinion Quarterly*, XXXI (1967), pp. 422–426.

26. Sorauf, *op. cit.*, p. 140.

27. Wayne Francis, "The Role Concept in Legislatures: A Probability Model and a Note on Cognitive Structure," *Journal of Politics*, XXVII (1965), 567–585.

several questions and then have defined those with a particular range of scores as trustee or delegate, for example.[28] If role is viewed as a continuum, when we specify a legislator's position on the continuum, we are not making a firm prediction that he will always act a certain way, but are asserting a probability of his acting that way. To view roles in terms of probabilities is to recognize that legislators will not always act in accord with a particular role orientation, if contradictory pressures become too intense. Francis argues that this approach is preferable because it avoids the problem of "inconsistent role playing" and views "a legislator as a truly multi-dimensional person whose behavior is determined by the relevance of different roles to a particular situation and the degree to which he is oriented to those roles."[29]

Other scholars believe it is more useful to conceive of role orientations as discrete categories. Logically this means that legislators should be placed in such a category only if they have a clear and strong belief that a legislator ought to act in the specified way; this also suggests that some legislators with ambiguous or ambivalent viewpoints should not be classified at all. If this approach is followed the researcher may use open-ended questions and exclude from classification those whose answers do not pertain to a particular role (as the authors of the four-state study did), or he may use more precise questions but exclude from classification those whose answers place them in a middle position. Janda, for example, believes that such transitional concepts as "politico" should not be used because the meaning of such concepts is unclear and because they may be regarded "as indicating the *absence* of any role orientation."[30] If one is trying to use roles to predict voting or other legislative behavior, such an approach has the disadvantage of excluding a number of legislators from the analysis. It may have, however, the advantage of strengthening the predictive power of roles in the case of those legislators who are included.

Even if we can devise ways of delineating the legislator's role orientations more accurately, it may be difficult to determine

28. Bell and Price, *op. cit.;* Janda, *op. cit.,* pp. 259–261.
29. Francis, *op. cit.,* p. 570.   30. Janda, *op. cit.,* p. 9.

whether that role is pertinent to a specific situation or issue. Client roles describe the legislator's attitude toward the expectations or demands of others. To predict how he will vote on a bill we need to know not only the legislator's attitude toward these demands, but whether he perceives that such demands are being made regarding the bill.

The problem can be illustrated by referring to several roles most often discussed in legislative research. A trustee, by definition, is a legislator who relies heavily on his own judgment regarding bills. But the legislature deals with a wide variety of bills during a session, and even the most ardent trustee does not have a point of view or adequate information about every one. When he does not, the trustee turns to others—inside or outside the legislature—for advice. In a broad sense, a delegate is defined as one who relies heavily for advice on others, but he is usually identified in research as one who gives particular attention to the advice of his constituents. Such a district-oriented delegate will presumably make a great effort to learn the views of constituents, and when he discovers that there is a strong and consistent demand in the district he will usually vote in accordance with it. Interviews with state legislators, including delegates, make it clear, however, that relatively few bills produce such strong demands within their districts. The state legislature attracts relatively little attention from constituents, and a large proportion of its agenda is concerned with issues of interest to very few groups or localities. Congressmen, most of whom have greater experience and who are dealing with a larger proportion of important and controversial issues, probably are more often able to perceive and evaluate constituent opinion. But the state legislator who is a delegate, who is sensitive to constituent opinion, is likely to find such opinion—and follow it—on only a few issues during a session. For the most part, he must look elsewhere for advice.

In order for a particular role to be useful as a predictor of voting behavior, it must be relevant to a substantial number of bills, and it must be possible for the analyst to identify such bills without such elaborate efforts as interviewing legislators on each bill. Representational and areal roles can rarely be used to predict votes because: (1) constituent opinion is so often vague and unidentifiable from the legislator's perspective; and (2) because it is difficult to determine on which bills the legislator does perceive strong constituent opinions.

By contrast, a partisan role should be useful as a predictor of voting if it is possible to determine accurately the member's attitude toward the expectations of his party. It is usually clear, to both the outside observer and the legislator, what bills the party leadership has designated as party bills, though the amount of pressure and persuasion applied in support of such a measure may not be obvious. In some legislatures where there is a strong norm of party unity, however, there may be relatively little variation in the party roles articulated by most legislators. Similarly, in legislatures where such a partisan norm is lacking, most members may enunciate a very low level of party loyalty. Whether or not partisan norms are in evidence, the governor is likely to initiate and support bills which are clearly identified as part of his program. A knowledge of the legislator's role with respect to the governor's expectations should be valuable in predicting his vote on such bills.

The demands of interest groups are often well known to both the legislator and the outside observer, and consequently we might expect the legislator's general role with respect to interest groups to be a valuable predictor of behavior. On most controversial issues, however, different groups will make conflicting demands. We would need to know something specific about the legislator's role orientations toward each group to make a prediction about his vote, and such detailed information is not easily compiled.

In order to fully understand and to predict the impact of roles on voting behavior we must know not only what the legislator's attitude is toward the expectations of many groups, but how frequently and forcefully he perceives these groups as expressing these expectations. The closer these groups are to him, the less difficulty he has in recognizing what they want. Party leaders, the governor, lobbyists, and colleagues on a committee or in a local delegation are usually explicit and unmistakable in making their desires known. The expectations of constituents are usually less clear, and more likely to be distorted because of faulty perception. It is well recognized by political scientists and legislators alike that the letters and phone calls may be unrepresentative though they may measure the intensity of constituent concern over an issue. Experienced legislators who know their district well may believe that they can judge what constituent opinion is without having to rely on the mail and telephone contacts, and on major issues they may be right. But on most issues, particularly in the state legislature, even the most experienced member with a district-delegate orientation must turn for advice to those who are in, or closer to, the legislature.

Can roles be useful in predicting legislative voting behavior? There is no simple answer. Some roles can serve that purpose in particular circumstances. If it is feasible to determine on what issues demands are being made by a specific actor in the legislative system, a knowledge of the legislator's attitude toward the expectations of that actor should help to predict his voting behavior. Some roles, such as the trustee-delegate orientation, seldom meet this criterion. Even when a role has little predictive value, it may remain a valuable tool of analysis and understanding. Legislators must make decisions about their fundamental attitude toward the many groups that tell them what they ought to do, and the concept of role seems ideally suited to describe this process.

Role Analysis and General Legislative Behavior

The utility of role analysis for explaining other forms of legislative behavior has seldom been explored, perhaps because political scientists have focused so much of their attention on the dependent variable of voting. At an earlier stage in the passage of legislation, in committee, the decisions of legislators are sometimes veiled in secrecy and more difficult to study. We know from Fenno's study that committee norms may be pervasive enough so that there is little difference among congressmen in their roles as committee members.[31] Jones's study of the Agriculture Commit-

31. Richard F. Fenno, Jr., "The House Appropriations Committee as a Political System: The Problem of Integration," *American Political Science Review*, LVI (1962), 310–324.

tee shows that in some committees partisan and interest group demands undermine the effectiveness of committee norms and lead members to assume a variety of roles.[32] What we lack are studies showing how the behavior of committee members is influenced by their roles.

Legislative outputs include more than the passage of bills, and consequently, we need to explain the behavior of legislators in other areas of decision-making. Legislative outputs include, among other things, the oversight of executive agencies and the satisfaction of constituent requests, sometimes described as errand-running. How a legislator deals with any "client," whether executive agency, lobbyist, or constituent, presumably depends on his client role concepts. In some cases, legislative norms may be so clear and widely accepted that there is little room for differences in legislative roles. For example, congressional norms (and appropriations for staffing) clearly require members to service the needs of constituents, whether this means sending them a booklet on baby care or finding out why a veteran has not received his pension.

In other cases legislative norms may be less explicit, and variations in roles may provide some clues to behavior. A number of years ago Huitt used the concept of role to describe various patterns of behavior by members of congressional committees reviewing the policies and actions of executive agencies.[33] Congressmen use committee hearings to prosecute or defend an agency, to promote the cause of an interest group seeking policy changes, or to force an agency to deal more favorably with a constituent. There has been relatively little attention to congressional oversight of the executive, and Huitt's illustration of the utility of role analysis in this area has not been followed up.

We know that there are differences in the specific steps legislators take to keep in touch with their constituents. A small but increasing minority (particularly at the congressional level) conduct polls. Some pay more attention than others to mail on

32. Charles O. Jones, "Representation in Congress: The Case of the House Agriculture Committee," *American Political Science Review*, LV (1961), 358–367.
33. Ralph K. Huitt, "The Congressional Committee: A Case Study," *American Political Science Review*, XLVIII (1954), pp. 340–365.

legislative issues; some make greater efforts to attend meetings in their district; and some use election campaigns as an opportunity to determine constituent attitudes. Some legislators make a great effort, through speeches, newsletters, and radio or television appearances, to influence the thinking of constituents. It is very possible that the extent and nature of legislative efforts to maintain contacts with constituents have a significant impact on the level of public support for the legislature. Consequently, it is important to understand what motivates legislators to devote more or less attention to constituency contacts, and we would expect to find that role analysis would provide some clues to the answer. We might expect, for example, that delegates would take more steps to determine the views of constituents on issues and that trustees would be more interested in making constituents understand and accept their views.

Legislators differ in their day-to-day relationships with lobbyists. Some are relatively accessible, some are hard to see, and others appear to be suspicious and even hostile. When a legislator shares some common interest with a lobbyist, he must decide how closely to cooperate with him in a legislative campaign, whether to accept the lobbyist's advice on tactical questions, and whether to serve as a spokesman for the interest group on the floor. The legislator may, of course, be influenced by factors such as personal friendship for the lobbyist, but his choices are likely to be shaped by his underlying attitudes about the legitimacy of the group's claims and the propriety of a legislator's working so closely with a lobbyist.

Legislative analysts have sometimes used the role concept to describe a member's own expectations regarding his career and his purpose in the legislature. If we understand why he came to the legislature, what he hopes to achieve, what he perceives as his duty—all of which might be called purposive roles—we can better explain his decisions about seeking to play a more active and influential part in the legislature, and seeking re-election or election to some other office. Barber has shown that the motivations for entering the legislature and the intention of serving several terms help to explain the types and extent of activities in the legislature.[34] It may be argued that career motivations and plans for legislative service are not properly described as roles, because they are not primarily shaped by either norms of the legislative system or the expectations of others in the system. Career motivations and plans result principally from a legislator's own choices, but they may be of fundamental importance in his definition of the responsibilities of his job.

Utility of Role Analysis in Cross-National Research

Role analysis should be a useful technique for studying legislative systems in other countries and for making cross-national comparisons of legislative systems. The studies done in the United States ought to be of value in showing how role analysis may be used and what some of its limitations are, but it would be a mistake to assume that the specific roles delineated in American studies will prove to be the most pertinent ones for study in other countries. Role analysis in this country has been focused on the specific differences among legislators in role concepts and the factors that may cause these differences. In cross-national research we are likely to be more interested in determining how much consensus there is on roles, among legislators and among other actors in the legislative system of a particular nation, and how much legislative role concepts differ from one nation to another. Role analysis has considerable potential because it should provide clues for answering several of those questions which are most important to the study of comparative legislative systems.

Scholars are often interested in the political culture of a nation. In a new or rapidly changing nation, it is important to determine how much consensus has been achieved on basic attitudes and values, particularly among elites. A measure of this would be the degree of consensus on role concepts among actors in the legislative system. One question of importance in many developing

34. James D. Barber, *The Lawmakers* (New Haven, Conn., 1965).

nations is the attitude of elites toward political opposition. Is there consensus that organized political opposition is legitimate, or is there consensus that there must be only a single party and that the nation can not afford an organized opposition? Is this question a source of fundamental disagreement among elites? One excellent test of such elite attitudes would be the perceptions of legislators concerning their job—whether they consider it legitimate to participate in organized opposition, such as parties or factions, within the legislature and how they regarded other legislators who might do so. For example, when the opposition party was dissolved in Kenya (as described in Newell Stultz's chapter in this volume) an examination of legislators' role concepts would have helped to determine to what extent political opposition was still regarded as legitimate by legislators. We would expect that in developing nations, particularly those that are fragmented along ethnic, religious, or tribal lines, there will be less consensus on norms among the participants in a legislative system, and that this might be reflected in diverse role orientations of legislators and other actors.

One purpose of cross-national legislative studies is to determine how legislatures become established and develop into strong, viable institutions. One measure of institutionalization is the development of widely accepted and clearly understood norms. An indication of the institutional weakness of many American state legislatures is a lower level of consensus on norms than is found in Congress, for example.[35] If there are well-developed legislative norms, there should be greater consensus concerning at least some of the roles of legislators. One measure of institutionalization achieved by the Philippine Congress, which is cited in Stauffer's chapter, is the existence of norms guaranteeing that minority groups can function effectively in Congress. A study of roles in the Philippine Congress might provide a fuller picture of how effective such norms are.

Another purpose of comparative legislative studies is to determine what functions legislatures serve in different political systems. One of the recurring themes in this volume is that these

35. Jewell and Patterson, *op. cit.*, pp. 375–380.

functions differ from one nation to another and that the legislative functions that are familiar in Western democracies are not likely to be duplicated in developing nations. One way of identifying these functions is by asking legislators broad questions about how they perceive their job. Though their answers may have to be translated into theoretically more meaningful concepts, they ought to be of considerable value. If decision-making on legislation is not a major function, this fact is likely to be recognized by the legislator in describing his role. If he emphasizes being the spokesman for interests and running errands for constituents, this would suggest that the representational function is of major importance. It would be interesting to know, for example, whether Philippine legislators recognize the function that Stauffer cites as being important in his chapter, and how they might articulate these in describing their job.

Whatever functions a legislature may serve, in order to evaluate its performance we need to know what demands are being made on it. A study of legislators' roles should tell us what groups the legislators perceive as making demands and which of these are recognized as legitimate. If the perceptions of members in a legislature differ in this respect, it becomes important to explore reasons for the differences. The next step would be to study those who are perceived as making demands and to find out what they expect from the legislature and how much congruence there is between their concepts of legislative roles and functions and those held by members of the legislature.

In any legislative body it is important to determine how members perceive the demands made on them by the executive and how much agreement there is between members of both branches about their roles. One criterion of legislative institutionalization is the legislature's ability to exercise some degree of independence from the executive. In those nations where the legislature is beginning to emerge as an important institution, we would expect to find conflicting views among various participants in the legislative system regarding this issue. Newell Stultz's study of Kenya provides an excellent example of conflict between President Kenyatta and some members of Parliament regarding the roles of members vis-à-vis the government. The president and his supporters in Parliament believe that members have an "over-riding duty to the State" and must defend and explain the government's policies to their constituents, whereas dissident members deny such a responsibility. This is a case where differences in role concepts are symptomatic of fundamental differences regarding the function of the legislature and the underlying philosophy of the political system.

A study of the various client roles articulated by legislators would provide insights into the ties between legislators and political groups outside the legislature. In those Western democracies where a local party organization controls nominations, role analysis would show how much loyalty legislators owe to these local parties. For example, are there any differences in the British Parliament between Labour and Conservative members in their roles with respect to both local and national party organizations outside of Parliament? Kornberg has touched on this problem in his study of the Canadian Parliament.[36] In a nation like West Germany, where many legislators have close ties to interest groups, it would be particularly valuable to collect data on roles that would show how much priority members gave to the claims of these groups, as compared with the demands of other groups such as party.[37]

The legislative bodies of some developing nations include special groups of elected or appointed members who are supposed to represent ethnic or religious minorities that might not otherwise be represented; examples include Kenya and Ceylon. Somewhat similar is the system Crow describes for dividing seats among religious communities in Lebanon. Where there are such institutional devices for representing particular ethnic or religious groups, role analysis would be valuable as a means of determining whether such legislators have an exclusive loyalty to such a group, and, if not, how they resolve the claims of these groups and others such as parties. When party organizations are super-

36. Kornberg, *Canadian Legislative Behavior*, pp. 126–129.
37. See Gerhard Loewenberg, *Parliament in the German Political System* (Ithaca, N.Y., 1967), pp. 75–84, 111–113, 121–128, 197–199.

imposed on ethnic or religious groupings, complex problems may result, as Crow describes in his chapter, and a knowledge of legislative role perceptions would be particularly useful.

The whole question of a legislator's relations with his constituents is an important one in any nation. In a less developed country, with low levels of education and communication, we might expect that constituents would be poorly informed about the legislature, be poorly organized, and make relatively few demands on legislators. We would expect legislators, both because they are part of a small elite in the country and because they probably perceive few demands from constituents, to play the role of trustees rather than delegates. A knowledge of a legislator's representational role concepts would not only give us insight into his attitudes but would provide clues to the organization of demands within his constituency.

Differences in districts, according to region or urban-rural categories, might be one cause of whatever differences in role cognitions may be found in a legislature. Some legislators, of course, are elected at large or represent non-geographical groupings. If we found large differences in role conceptions within a legislature, we would want to explore the personal background of legislators for an explanation. The more diverse the nation, with respect to race, religion, or other characteristics, and the weaker the impact of political cultural norms, the more important personal background might be in determining the role concepts of legislators. Although we have not found consistent differences in role concepts between Democrats and Republicans, party would be more likely to affect role in those nations where the differences between parties are greater.

Role analysis provides one method for explaining how the legislative process works. If the legislative functions include decision-making on substantive policy questions, role analysis should help to explain how such decisions are made, who exercises power within the legislature, and what forces outside the legislatures have the greatest impact on the process. The limited utility of role analysis for predicting behavior, discussed earlier in this paper, is of little importance because our initial efforts at cross-national research will, of necessity, be focused more on explanation and comparison than on prediction. Moreover, roll-call votes, the dependent variable in so many studies of United States legislatures, are less important as a measurement of legislative behavior in many foreign legislatures.

Although the concept of role may be very useful, some of the specific role orientations described in American studies may not be transferable or comparable to those in other legislative systems. If we could determine what proportion of members were

Table 4. Representational Roles of Members of State Legislatures, United States Congress, and Canadian Parliament

Legislature	N	Trustee	Politico	Delegate
California	49	55%	25%	20%
New Jersey	54	61	22	17
Ohio	114	56	29	15
Tennessee	78	81	13	6
Wisconsin	81	23	5	72
Pennsylvania	105	33	27	39
Indiana	233	20	61	19
Iowa	100	36	—	64
Michigan	95	37	31	33
United States Congress	84	29	46	23
Canada	165	15	36	49

trustees, or were party-oriented or district-oriented, in various legislatures, the comparative utility of the role concept would seem to be enhanced. Studies of representational roles in this country and Canada have suggested that the proportions of trustees, politicos, and delegates vary considerably among the states, as Table 4 shows.[38]

Various explanations have been offered for the different proportions of specific representational role orientations found in

38. The data for California, New Jersey, Ohio, Tennessee, Wisconsin, and Pennsylvania are summarized in Jewell and Patterson, *op. cit.*, p. 398. Sources of other data are: Indiana—Janda, *op. cit.*, p. 29; Iowa—Hedlund, *op. cit.*, p. 18; Michigan—Soule, *op. cit.*, p. 212; Congress—Davidson, *op. cit.*, p. 15; Canada—Kornberg, *Canadian Legislative Behavior*, p. 108. The data for Indiana include all legislative candidates.

these legislatures,[39] but it seems highly likely that some of these differences are the results of variations in methodology. As noted earlier, there have been differences in the form and substance of questions asked, in the methods of coding, and in the classification of legislators into groups. (The Iowa study used four groups, combined into two in Table 4, and the Indiana study used three groups but ignored the politicos—the largest group—in analysis of the results.) The number of legislators not classifiable (not included in the totals of Table 4) ranged from only 1 per cent in Pennsylvania to over one-third for the states in the four-state study (at the top of Table 4). Unless the same questions are used and there is agreement about how to classify legislators and how to handle those who are difficult to classify, it will not be meaningful to make comparisons among specific role orientations or speculate about reasons why differences are found among the legislatures.

There are additional difficulties involved in making comparisons among specific role orientations in cross-national research, even if methodological uniformity is attempted. For example, it will be difficult to devise questions, and translate them, so as to make the questions meaningful to legislators in different nations. In order to make the questions meaningful and pertinent to a variety of legislative situations, it may be necessary to vary the wording of questions. Once this is done, precise comparisons of the results become difficult.

The value of role analysis in cross-national legislative studies is not that it is likely to permit the precise comparison of various legislative types in neat tabular form. It is valuable because it provides a means for studying the legislature as an institution: its relationship to the political system and culture; its development as an institution; its relationship to other organs of government; and its impact on its own members. It is one means for exploring theoretically interesting questions about the functions of legislative bodies and the demands made on them in various political systems. It is a flexible technique, tested in previous research, and appropriate for comparative analysis.

39. See Wahlke *et al., op. cit.*, pp. 281–282, and Kornberg, *op. cit.*, pp. 107–109.

Chapter 14

Comparative Legislative Studies and Services: Notes for a Program[*]

Lloyd D. Musolf and Fred W. Riggs

Introduction

In those countries which have successfully achieved industrialization and economic growth while safeguarding free democratic institutions, one finds energetic and influential legislatures, parliaments, chambers of deputies, or other types of "elected assemblies." Put most strongly, one might argue that national develop-

[*] This study, in its original form, constituted a set of recommendations submitted to the Agency for International Development in May 1968 in fulfillment of a contract between that governmental agency and the American Society for Public Administration. The circumstances under which the contract originated are explained in Chapter I.

The statement of recommendations here does not imply any commitment by AID to finance the suggested program. Certain activities of the types recommended might be financed by foundations, universities, or other institutions, or under educational and cultural exchange programs of the State Department. At such time as Congress provides appropriations, the establishment of Comparative Legislative Studies Centers might also be considered under the provisions of the International Education Act of 1966.

Although the authors accept full responsibility for statements in the paper, they owe—because of the nature of the project—more than the usual debt of gratitude to others: to the Comparative Administration Group which, under ASPA, carried out the terms of the contract; to Larry Margolis, who was the first principal investigator under the contract and who largely organized the launching of the study; to the members of the advisory committee, whose experience as scholars, practitioners, or close observers of the legislative process proved invaluable in several lengthy meetings at which successive drafts of the recommendations were discussed; to an advisory panel of about seventy-five persons, many of whose members made creative suggestions in correspondence; to individuals who attended a planning conference at Planting Fields, New York, which elaborated ideas and pitfalls associated with such a program; to the New York State Senate, the Graduate School of Public Administration of the State University of New York, the Conference of University Bureaus of Governmental Research, and the American Society of Public Administration, all of whom gave research or logistical support.

ment—economic, social, political, and administrative—can occur in a democratic fashion (i.e., with a participative and responsive government) only if elected assemblies play an important role in the process. At the very least, one could contend that the emergence of relatively effective assemblies can accelerate national development and, further, increase the likelihood that such development will occur along democratic lines.

These, of course, are hypotheses which might be falsified by the emergence of a developed and democratic country without an influential elective assembly. Meanwhile, we can see that in some of the less developed countries which are relatively democratic and stable—such as India, the Philippines, Jamaica, and others—elected assemblies do play important lawmaking and political roles. Moreover, at least in the long run, they also clearly promote developmental purposes—by channeling conflict, giving representation to the basic social groups, developing a national identity, legitimizing major governmental policies, enhancing the rule of law, educating the public on major current issues, and strengthening responsive administration of governmental programs. Such important functions may, it is true, make economic development less orderly. The enactment of Title IX of the Foreign Assistance Act, however, is testimony that Congress is aware of the need to balance orderliness in economic development with values associated with democracy. It should also be noted that an elected assembly is only a part of a democratic structure which includes a system of elections and a competitive party system.

The example afforded by the Indian Parliament in setting up a major Administrative Reforms Commission is one that will be widely studied and probably emulated in other countries of Asia, and perhaps also in Africa and Latin America. The task forces of this Commission are seriously studying administrative obstacles to the success of development programs in many public policy fields ranging from agriculture and food supply to public health, education, family planning, and urbanization. Thus the Indian Parliament may—as history will determine—play an important role in facilitating Indian development. Moreover, if it is successful, the prospects seem good that this pattern of development will be democratic, as it has been in the past. Similar observations could be made in the Philippines.

A vigorous legislature is the best assurance that citizens can find an outlet for their legitimate grievances. The importance of encouraging the formation of interest groups and autonomous citizen groups in developing countries can not be overemphasized. These steps toward democratic development can, however, be nullified if such groups are coopted by the bureaucracy or a ruling party, an eventuality that a strong legislature probably would prevent.

In the light of these considerations it is argued that a Program of Legislative Studies and Services would be advantageous. Several important reservations need to be stated, however, which seriously qualify any efforts that may be made to this end.

First, what we now know in this field is so fragmentary and inconclusive, and so limited is the supply of experts, that we must recognize the provisional character of any undertaking and the priority need for institution building and research in order to generate new tested knowledge and the required human resources. At every step of the way, however, hypotheses must be tested against actual situations and their relevance checked through the close association of scholars and practitioners.

Second, the subject is one of unusual sensitivity and complexity. Basic decisions about the role which elected assemblies play in any country must be made by the leaders of these countries without external intervention. However, the fact that almost all the governments in the world today, even those under military one-party rule, have experimented with the establishment of elected assemblies shows the remarkable appeal of this fundamental institution of government. Moreover, there is ample evidence that legislators and parliamentarians, staff members, civil servants, and scholars in quite a few of the less developed countries would like to learn more about the experience with elected assemblies of Western countries. That this is so is demonstrated by the continuous stream of such people who have visited—and continue to visit—Congress and our state legislatures, as well as the Parliament of Great Britain, and the legislatures of some other countries.

Third, it should not be thought that to the limited extent that legislative services have been provided and studies pursued, these steps have taken place only in the United States. We should, rather, recognize the importance and relevance of parliamentary services and studies carried on in England and Continental Europe and, indeed, in countries such as India, where a new but vigorous Institute of Constitutional and Parliamentary Studies is working in this field. Any effective program of legislative studies and services ought, therefore, to be based on international cooperation rather than unilateral action.

Fourth, in addition to seeking international cooperation, a Program of Legislative Studies and Services must seek cooperation at home. The range of training needs and educational needs for an adequate Program is so great as to require full cooperation between selected universities and legislatures in this country. The organization of a Program must take this critical need for cooperation into account.

The recommendations which follow are designed to meet these conditions, while responding to the urgent need for action to enhance the prospects of national development in all program fields in accordance with shared democratic ideals. The recommendations envision legislative studies and services as coordinate elements in the Program.

Recommendations

Recommendation No. 1

Comparative Legislative Studies Centers should be established at five carefully-selected American universities. They should serve as international exchange centers for the strengthening of legislatures abroad through a better understanding of the development of legislatures here and abroad. Geographical specialization among the Centers should be encouraged.

In complex Western societies, legislatures have appeared to decline in influence and prestige in the twentieth century. Some regard the nineteenth century as the heyday of parliaments. In any event, the demands of a modern, industrialized society place a tremendous strain upon the policy-making resources of a nation.

In their drive to become economically more developed, the new nations should be given the opportunity to develop viable legislatures if they wish. The purpose of the Comparative Legislative Studies Centers (CLSC's) to be established under this Program is to build resources toward this end. It would be presumptuous to assume that such Centers would be founts of American wisdom for the new nations, but it is clear that they could serve as bases for a cooperative international effort involving not only this country and the developing nations but also European countries with experience in assisting legislative development.

Before describing the Comparative Legislative Studies Centers, we might suggest several ways in which their role as international exchange bodies could be implemented. Each Center should develop cooperative relationships with appropriate overseas bodies. These might include institutes experienced in dealing with problems of legislative development, such as the Institute of Constitutional and Parliamentary Studies in New Delhi and the Institute of Commonwealth Studies in London, or overseas groups less specifically concerned in the past with legislative matters than those just mentioned. Appropriate groups might be found in a university or a legislature, in a relatively developed country or in one just beginning development. The interest of the overseas groups in cooperating with a CLSC should be an important guideline. Conceivably, in some countries with a very weak elected assembly, the most fruitful cooperating body might be a university law school or political science department.

The international character of each CLSC should also be promoted through regularized faculty exchange, with one post in a Center filled annually on a rotating basis from overseas. To the extent feasible, a Center should annually recruit a faculty member from the university in which the Center is located to spend a year at one of the overseas bodies with which a relationship has been established. Both the American and foreign exchange faculty should engage in teaching and research that will contribute to a better understanding of the legislative process in a developmental context. Further suggestions for strengthening the international ties of CLSCs will appear under the discussion of Recommendation 2.

Comparative Legislative Studies Centers should represent an amalgam of the skills of a state university and a state legislature. A state university, especially when located near a state capital, tends to have a network of contacts with the state legislature. For the purposes of the Program, state legislatures are more appropriate than Congress. The level of operations and resources available to developing countries are more nearly equivalent to those of American states than to Washington. Also, the states, like the developing nations, are diverse in resource levels. The availability and resources of state universities, especially the strength of their link to a state legislature should be kept in mind. For economy of effort in establishing CLSC's, full advantage should be taken of existing university-legislature liaisons and, in particular, of the broker function often served by the university institutes and bureaus.

A rich variety of university-legislature relationships in the fifty states as well as a wide range of emphases in university programs is suggested by two surveys conducted in connection with this investigation.[1] The outstanding qualities of the first four universities surveyed were, respectively, excellent contact with developing countries, an expanding range of legislative study programs, an emphasis on public policy studies, and considerable experience with intern programs. These findings indicate that in the universities of this country resources to answer many needs can be found. One of the responding universities has even suggested that, were a Comparative Legislative Service Center to be located there, universities near state capitals in two adjoining states would like to join in a cooperative program.

Each Comparative Legislative Service Center should be

1. One canvassed leading possibilities for the location of CLSC's; the other surveyed relationships between state universities and state legislatures.

headed by a director with outstanding academic qualifications and, ideally, experience in dealing with legislatures here and overseas, as well as an interest in political and administrative development. There should be the equivalent of two additional full-time professional staffs. Supporting staff should include personnel to coordinate legislative fellowship programs, conferences, and visits of overseas legislators and staffs, to develop information and documentation facilities, and to undertake other tasks as described in Recommendation 2. At the time of the establishment of each CLSC, an advisory committee reflecting academic and legislative interests, both domestic and foreign, should be appointed.

External grants-in-aid would be necessary to facilitate the creation of each CLSC. Such grants should be provided through the proposed Program in order to facilitate coordination of effort in a national and international Program. A subcontracting mechanism would be used, with the host university assuming full responsibility for the administration of external funds.

It is anticipated that the local legislature and university would make a matching contribution to finance each CLSC. It is particularly important for the legislature close to the host university to make such a contribution, because it may pave the way for eventual assumption by the legislature and university of full responsibility for the cost of a continuing program in the field of legislative studies and services, after, let us say, an initial period of ten years during which external assistance would be provided, perhaps on a progressively diminishing scale.

Recommendation No. 2

Comparative Legislative Studies Centers should have as their goals the testing of hypotheses about legislatures and legislative development and the devising of programs of teaching and training. Both goals should be undertaken in the context of an international exchange of resources and knowledge.

It is admittedly ambitious to ask that CLSC's attempt to construct and test hypotheses related to legislatures and political development. Still, the goal is well worth stating. It would help to coordinate the efforts of the CLSC's and the Program Team (the subject of the next recommendation). It would prevent research from being skewed in the direction of abstract model building. It would provide a stimulating element in the activities of CLSC's and increase their zest for cooperative international activities.

Both the procedures for testing hypotheses and the substance of what is being tested would require careful consideration, of course. As to the latter, several topics and situations may be mentioned as perhaps deserving further exploration.[2] Some are suggested by the papers in this volume. The papers on Canada and Lebanon suggest an investigation into the allocation of legislative positions in terms of ethnicity. Under what circumstances does a nation employ this device and at what point is it likely to give it up? The paper dealing with "Structural Determinants of Legislative Output" might furnish the stimulus for testing the extent to which such environmental factors as urbanization and industrialization relate to the nature of policy outputs. It might be possible to posit the likely "mix" between distributive and redistributive policies under stated environmental conditions. The paper on "Staffing the Legislature" might spark investigation into optimal staffing combinations for specified types of elected assemblies. What mixture of such a basic service as bill drafting and of social science research, for example, might be sought?

To the extent feasible, a wide array of conditions in relatively developed countries might serve as kinds of laboratories. It is relevant to note that federalism may be more practical than the unitary principle for the unstable countries of Africa. Can American and Canadian experience be of assistance? Aside from federalism, do existing parliamentary systems furnish grist for hypotheses? What of relations between the legislature and the bureaucracy, between the cabinet and interest groups, between M.P.'s and constituency organizations? Granted that developing countries will develop their own versions of parliamentary systems, British and other experience is relevant for institution building. Can the states of the American South, for example, furnish guidelines for political development under conditions ap-

2. Particular thanks are due Allan Kornberg for suggestions.

proximating something less than a two-party system? Can a country like Canada, with its political subdivisions, serve as a model for the generation of economic and social development mainly through governmental initiative?

Obviously, Comparative Legislative Studies Centers need a strong international component even to begin the development of hypotheses. In beginning operations, the Centers should be supplied with adequate funds to permit on-the-spot visits to countries receptive to the idea of legislative assistance and to permit an adequate input of expertise from international affiliates and host-country experts and institutions.

The second important activity for a CLSC would consist of its teaching and training efforts. Such efforts should, where possible, recognize the probable staffing needs. Though American experience is not necessarily a guide, at least three kinds of legislative staff may be noted: service bureaus, which provide orderliness in legislative procedures; technical and research staff to conduct public policy research; and direct staff for leaders and committees, whose skill may be largely negotiational. If equivalent variety now exists in developing countries—or is implied by an insistence on the importance of legislatures to democratic development—then a CLSC must be ready to meet the challenge.

The amount of versatility demanded of Centers will be diminished by deliberate specialization among them. Geographical specialization is the most obvious, but functional specialization such as public policy studies, should not be ruled out. In the main, however, specialization is likely to be geographical. Among the universities surveyed, the University of Hawaii and the University of Puerto Rico have strong claims on this basis.

At each Center, the range of programs might include: master's and non-degree programs; on-campus courses and legislative "fellowships"; and library school courses and Legislative Reference Service training periods. Courses might be selected to emphasize the area of legislative and political processes or, alternatively, substantive areas with which a legislature might deal. The point is that considerable skill in tailoring individual programs for participants is required. This skill should include the ability to assess participants' previous educational qualifications, training, and on-the-job experience. Fellowships, rather than internships, are proposed; unlike interns, fellows would be observers—except to the extent that English language facility, acquaintance with American political institutions, or, possibly, previous experience on a legislative staff equipped them to undertake responsibilities, as interns usually do. To undertake a fellowship program, CLSC's would need one or more skilled liaison officers to work with the legislature.

Recruits for training programs would come from several kinds of sources. As the experience and capabilities of the CLSC's became known, AID Missions overseas and other agencies, public and private, would sponsor a growing number of participants. Such sponsorship would need the active and interested cooperation of legislatures in host countries; executive branch cooperation is also implied, for liaison with legislatures may be thought to require trained personnel. A shrewd assessment of the prospect of training existing staff members vs. recruiting outsiders for training would need to be made. In considering non-staff members as a source, the Program should not overlook students from developing countries who are already pursuing university studies in the United States. The Program should be publicized widely among these students and financial arrangements made sufficiently attractive to well-qualified individuals.

Each Comparative Legislative Studies Center should plan on an exchange program involving legislators from its state and from countries in the geographic area with which the Center deals. Typically such visits would be short-term, particularly in the case of the American legislators, and in the event foreign legislators wanted a more serious and extended learning experience, the CLSC could recommend a study program. Interest and support of the relevant state legislatures would be crucial to the success of the Centers. In arranging trips overseas for American legislators (and perhaps key staff), the Centers should be prepared to brief members of travel groups thoroughly prior to their departure and to arrange, preferably through an overseas associate member of the Program Team, for their reception by and introduction to their opposite numbers abroad.

Related to the legislator-exchange program is the task of dealing adequately with visitors. The CLSC's could perform a valuable service, one often not adequately handled at present, by skillfully ascertaining and answering the needs of foreign visitors who wish to learn more about American legislatures. This task should be accomplished in the context of the work of the Governmental Affairs Institute (GAI) in channeling foreign legislators, among others, into helpful programs. The CLSC's should constitute an invaluable resource for GAI. Similarly, the efforts of CLSC's should be carefully coordinated with the work of Meridian House and others in the exchange field; of the American Political Science Association in the domestic and foreign legislative fellowship field; of the Rand Corporation, the Midwest Research Institute, and others in the public policy field; and of such other enterprises as the National Conference of Legislative Leaders, the Council of State Governments, the Citizens Conference on State Legislatures, and the Eagleton Institute of Politics at Rutgers University.

At the time that the Comparative Legislative Studies Centers are established, a National Secretariat, which would also serve the Program Team, should be established at one of the CLSC's. The Secretariat would serve as the contact point for dealing with GAI and others on exchange programs. An even more critical task would be coordination of the informational, documentation, and archival activities of the Centers, thus providing national direction of the building of specialized collections. Presumably, the more permanent materials would go into the main library collections of the respective universities at which CLSC's were located, and the more transient materials into the CLSC's themselves. A master list of all materials, wherever located, would be kept by the Secretariat. If at all possible, the Secretariat's informational center duties should be carried out in the manner made famous by the Inter-University Consortium located at the University of Michigan. This would require a computerized data system, including information retrieval, that would involve other CLSC's and universities associated with the Program of Legislative Studies and Services.

Though located in the Center, the Secretariat would have its own budget and be directed by the Program Team through its Chairman. In addition to coordinating the data-collecting efforts of the CLSC's and acting as a national information center, the Secretariat's duties would include: publishing documents, bibliographic information, and other materials; arranging, when necessary, for *ad hoc* studies, surveys, reconnaisance work, and related projects; negotiating contracts with publishers, where appropriate; establishing liaison, including the exchange of information, publications, and resources, with American and foreign organizations interested in legislative services and studies; publishing a journal; and managing funds provided for the work of the Program Team.

As suggested under Recommendation 1, careful thought should be given to ways of making the CLSC's effective in overseas dealings. In part their effectiveness may depend on the strategy of financial support by AID. Perhaps AID assistance should in large measure concentrate on strengthening new and developing centers of expertise in the United States, and non-governmental organizations should support programs located in the developing countries. Such AID assistance as is given overseas might be channeled, not to elected assemblies, but to centers of expertise in legislative matters that could be established at local universities. In some instances, university law schools might provide the proper locale; alternatively, an institute of public administration or a political science department might do so.

Although the international character of the CLSC's has been stressed, this is no reason to overlook their value on the American scene. Aside from involving state legislators in the various ways noted previously, CLSC's could well serve as pre-entry and in-service training units for the staff of state legislatures. The availability of the Centers for this purpose should help to convince the appropriate legislatures of the utility of giving them partial financial support.

Recommendation No. 3

To provide direction for a national program and to assure adequate intellectual undergirding for the development of hypotheses for testing by Comparative Legislative Studies Centers, a Program Team consisting of eminent scholars of legislatures and legislative development should be appointed.

The Program Team, to which reference has already been made, would consist of ten members, one of whom would serve as chairman. Half the membership would be composed of the directors of the five Comparative Legislative Studies Centers. The other five members would be selected from among leading scholars at non-CLSC universities. This would permit an input from leading private universities, especially those with valuable pertinent resources. One obvious example is Duke University, with its Commonwealth Program. A National Secretariat, as noted above, would serve the Program Team.

At a minimum, the universities from which members of the Program Team are chosen should be able to offer a Ph.D. in political science and have an established capability in problems of international development, in comparative politics and administration, and in relevant foreign area studies. They should also agree that the Team member would conduct an advanced graduate seminar on the role of legislatures in national development, including the comparative study of American state legislatures and Congress, as well as elected assemblies in national and subnational governments abroad. Such a seminar would be offered by each Team member at least one semester (or quarter) a year for five years. Provision would be made for replacement of the Team member should circumstances require.

To the extent that the Program Team cannot reflect the variety of academic disciplines and specialties associated with legislative development, it should effect liaisons with the appropriate groups. Such liaisons are particularly important in view of the primitive state of research in the area of comparative legislative development, the urgent need to clarify concepts, and the basic work that needs to be done on the substance and procedure of hypothesis development and testing.

Just as the CLSC's would be jointly funded, so the efforts of Program Team members at non-CLSC universities might be financed both by AID and the individual universities. Items for AID funding would cover: (1) an outstanding scholar's salary for two years, including one full year on research leave, and the equivalent of a year's salary divided up to support summer research and part-time study during several academic years; and (2) funds about equal to two years' salary for the support of research assistantships, secretarial help, travel, and other expenses—a total amount roughly equivalent to the salary of the Team member for four years. The budget of the Program Team should include funds for such support to all of its members, including those directing CLSC's, thereby augmenting whatever other support the CLSC might secure. The host university would be expected to provide counterpart support in several ways, including funds for the expansion of its library holdings, support of the Team member's regular salary and his special seminar, salary support for faculty replacements for Team members on research leave, and other items recommended by the Project Team, and agreed to in advance. In the event that a Team member not in one of the CLSC's changes universities, it would be his responsibility to make equivalent arrangements with his new university. If the university had a CLSC, the contribution would remain with the university if its Team member changed positions, but only if the Project Team accepted the university's nominee as a new member.

Recommendation No. 4

For program enrichment and coordination, the Program Team should undertake to organize summer seminars, establish liaison with overseas scholars and institutions, encourage graduate training, expand curricula, and develop library resources.

As a unifying activity and in order to coordinate research nationally, the Program Team should organize a series of summer seminars. To a considerable degree, the model for these can be the summer seminars conducted by the Comparative Administration Group (CAG) of the American Society for Public Administration (ASPA). These seminars, from four to eight weeks in duration, consist of a small group of senior scholars and associated graduate students, who prepare, discuss, and revise papers for publication. As they have in several developmental fields, such seminars will stimulate interest in legislative studies as related to political development, generate research and teaching, and help bring promising younger scholars into a growing and lively subject.

The Program Team should use the first summer seminar to develop (1) the Program in greater detail and (2) a plan for relating research to hypothesis-testing procedures. A lament sometimes heard with respect to the CAG publication series, otherwise a veritable mine of information and speculation, is that propositions have not been extracted and tested. As the CAG seminars and publications have amply demonstrated their utility in the more abstract forms of model-building, the time has come to inaugurate an approach to research more closely related to operational needs. This emphasis need not foreclose, or even limit, research of the first type. Nevertheless, through the assistance of the Comparative Legislative Studies Centers, this approach should have the virtues of providing constant checks upon feasibility and opportunities to revise hypotheses under various field conditions.

At the first or second summer seminar, Team members should coordinate the design of the graduate seminars that they expect to conduct at their home universities. Subsequent summer seminars would be devoted to an analysis of plans for field research and comparative studies and to preliminary reporting on completed research.

As suggested under Recommendation 1, the sustained cooperation of interested scholars and institutions in European countries experienced in advising on legislatures, as well as of scholars and institutions in developing countries, is essential to the success of the Program. The foreign scholars who participate in the faculty exchange program in connection with CLSC's might be invited to become associate members of the Program Team. The same holds true for those who are asked to participate in summer seminars.

A plan for permitting properly qualified graduate students to conduct field research as part of their Ph.D. program in legislative studies is indispensable to the success of the Program. Thorough acquaintance with field conditions is essential for sound, hypothesis-oriented research. Production of adequately trained researchers is a vital institution building procedure in a relatively uncharted field. Fellowships are the key; American and foreign students who had taken the advanced graduate seminar taught by a member of the Program Team and interned in the nearby state legislature, or had equivalent experience, would be eligible to compete for national fellowships, each providing funds for two years. For the first three years of the Program, it is suggested that fifty fellowships be provided. A fellowship holder would spend the first year overseas, normally by arrangement with an overseas associate Team member as local sponsor. The student's second year should be spent writing his dissertation at his home university and reporting on his field research in the Team member's seminar. Overseas affiliates of the Team should be encouraged to recruit individuals for the graduate program whose activities after receiving the Ph.D. might focus upon establishment or enrichment of overseas Comparative Legislative Studies Centers. Such individuals might require funding for graduate study and American legislative internship experience prior to competing for a fellowship for field research.

Although the process of curriculum enrichment would chiefly involve the department of political science—either that department, or another established department or school, would grant the Ph.D.—a systematic attempt to involve representatives of other disciplines is advised. Their participation in graduate seminars and the summer seminars should further this goal. Topics amenable to such interdisciplinary treatment include: with law, the role of legislatures in the creation of positive law and problems of legislative drafting; with sociology, the relevance of organization theory to an understanding of legislatures; with anthropology, cultural factors affecting the behavior of legislators and their relations with constituents and public officials; with economics, national planning and the legislative function; with education, problems of education for citizenship and political participation, including membership in elective bodies at all levels of government.

Recommendation No. 5

The Program should be initiated through a contract between AID and ASPA/CAG for the establishment of the Program Team and the Comparative Legislative Studies Centers, with the possibility held open of direct contracts between AID and the universities in any situation where the latter make substantial contributions to the funding of CLSC's.

To get the Program off to a good start, it is desirable to have contractual arrangements for the Program Team and the Comparative Legislative Studies Centers made simultaneously, or virtually so. The existing ASPA/CAG machinery should be used to facilitate the completion of contract details. Thus, the CAG Advisory Committee for the Program of Legislative Studies and Services might be utilized for nominations for the Program Team. The contract itself could be made through ASPA, which has already proved its organizational capabilities for carrying on somewhat similar work through its administration of the Ford Foundation grants of a half-million dollars for the summer seminars and related activities of CAG.

The reason for permitting alternate contractual methods for the establishment of CLSC's revolves around the question of whether universities (and the legislatures of their states) would be willing and able to furnish matching funds. The benefits accruing to them from the establishment of a CLSC should motivate them to do so. If not, or if the process is drawn out, the Program Team could be authorized, by terms of the original contract between AID and ASPA, to negotiate subcontracts to establish CLSC's. When direct contracting between a university and AID is used, it is essential that the concurrence of the Program Team in the selection of the university site be obtained in order that the program be coordinated nationally.

As the Program develops, a growing number of trainees from abroad might be expected to participate. Initially, these might be financed chiefly through AID participant programs, but when the Program demonstrates its worth, individuals financed through other means should be attracted to it. Financing provisions should anticipate the substantial per-student cost of education and training that includes specialized courses, seminars, and internships.

The financing of research under the Program should reflect the fact that research output will be of several kinds. Because of AID's interest in supporting programs soundly grounded in research, it should be willing to finance expenses in connection with the formulation and testing of hypotheses in the legislative area. Designs calling for basic research might be submitted to private foundations and the National Science Foundation for support. For applied research on a direct-hire, in-house basis, AID and other agencies might want to consider individuals affiliated with the Program.

Since many of those participating in the Program would be foreign students and senior scholars, working through the affiliated members overseas, it scarcely need be pointed out that much of the research output which should be generated by this Program would be carried out abroad in the universities, institutes, and legislative reference services of the country most directly concerned. Appropriate assistance could be provided, as warranted, to these institutions, through contracts and grants. Moreover, cooperative relationships between American and foreign institutions taking part in the Program might lead to proposals for more informal projects in which, for example, new contractual relationships between an American CLSC and a cooperating institution overseas might be made to provide support for teaching, training, and related research as desired.

AID Funding Possibilities

In terms of AID funding for portions of the Program, the following possibilities appear to exist.

1. Participant training: The foreign trainees, both in CLSC courses of study and in the graduate seminars, could be financed under this Program. As participant training falls under "country money," it would be necessary to obtain the approval and support of the respective Missions and host countries.

2. Institution building: Overseas institutions relevant to the Program could be funded, at least in part, from grants of counterpart funds. Their effectiveness could also be increased indirectly through Section 211 (d) of the Foreign Assistance Act of 1961, as amended, which could be used to strengthen the capability of American institutions, such as universities, to assist overseas legislative institutes and other bodies. The use of 211 (d) funds to get CLSC's underway would be highly appropriate.

3. Research: Under Section 241 (a) of the Act it would be possible to fund research on the role of legislatures in the development process. Title IX, of course, sets forth a general theme of political development to which this Program, and research under it, could be related. Under Recommendation 5, a description of the way in which AID research support might relate to other sources is given.

4. Miscellaneous: Aside from the suggestions given above, any parts of the Program could be financed through the regional bureaus in AID. The American half of the exchange part of the Program (legislators, certain legislative staff members, professors) could be partly financed through the State Department's American Specialists Abroad Program, under the Mutual Educational and Cultural Exchange Act of 1961.

Program Levels and Stages

The assumption underlying the recommendations is that AID is interested in receiving the best judgment of the investigators concerning a Program of Legislative Studies and Services. Thus, what has been described is an optimal Program, irrespective of the sources of financing or the prospects for AID appropriations. It has not been thought particularly useful to assign costs to the various parts of the Program at this stage. Using the Comparative

Legislative Studies Centers as guides, under a medium-level Program, three Centers would be established, and under a minimum Program, one.

To begin the Program at the minimal level, AID could advise its Missions of the Program and of the opportunity to send carefully-selected participants to the Center. Before such action was approved, AID would, of course, wish to satisfy itself as to the adequacy of the level of operations at the Center.

The Comparative Administration Group can be considered a resource for AID in exploring the possibilities of the Program. As an indication of its interest and serious purpose, CAG established a Comparative Legislative Studies Committee and appropriated several thousand dollars in 1968, and again in 1969, to facilitate meetings of interested individuals. The meetings involved representatives of universities interested in the establishment of CLSC's and individuals interested in establishing the Program Team.

Chapter 15

Legislatures and Political Development[*]

Robert A. Packenham

Introduction

What Fenno[1] has written of studies of Congress applies also to the entire field of comparative legislative study: "these are the best of times, these are the worst of times." These are the best of times because there is greater interest in, and able attention to, some facets of legislative study than there has been in years, perhaps ever. These are the worst of times because these studies are disproportionately focused on American legislatures—especially the U.S. Congress—and because even in these studies some of the most crucial questions (notably, the consequences for the rest of the political system of legislative activity) are virtually ignored. Outside of the United States, and especially in the

* I wish to thank the Foreign Area Fellowship Program, which is administered by the Social Science Research Council and the American Council of Learned Societies under a grant from the Ford Foundation, for the fellowship which sent me to Brazil and thus initially enabled me to confront the issues treated in this paper. I am deeply grateful to the members and staff of the Brazilian Congress for their cooperation and hospitality during my stay in Brasília, and to other Brazilian friends and colleagues who tried to teach me something about politics in their country. I also want to express my appreciation to the American Society for Public Administration which, by sponsoring the Legislative Services Planning Conference at Planting Fields, Long Island (December 8–10, 1967), provided the occasion for writing the current essay; and to Professor John J. Johnson and the Committee on Latin American Studies of Stanford University for minor research expenses. I am especially indebted to Raymond E. Wolfinger, Victor Jones, Kenneth Prewitt, Thomas E. Skidmore, the members of the Planting Fields Conference, and colleagues and students at Stanford and elsewhere for their very helpful comments and criticisms, most of which I heeded and a few of which I ignored at my own peril. None of these organizations or individuals is responsible for any errors of fact or interpretation which may be present in the finished product.

1. Richard F. Fenno, Jr., book review, *American Political Science Review*, LVIII, No. 4 (December, 1964), 975.

so-called Third-World countries, knowledge of legislatures, and their relationship to other political institutions and processes, is extremely limited.

If one accepts for the moment the premise that existing knowledge is limited, what does this admittedly limited knowledge suggest about the consequences—which I call the functions—of legislative activity for the political system? It suggests that the principal function of most of the world's legislatures is not a decisional function. Most of them, that is to say, do not allocate values, or at least do not have this as their principal function. Other functions—i.e., legitimation and recruitment and socialization to other political roles—seem to be more important. Satisfactory concepts, methods, and data for determining with precision which functions are more and less important—and what important means—do not exist currently (or, if they exist, they are not used very much). But judgments, based on the best tools, data, and intelligent thinking available, can and must be made.

If one wants to "do something" about legislatures as a means to promote political development, then one must know something about the relationship between legislatures and political development. In particular, it would seem crucial to know the likely consequences of "strengthening" legislatures for other parts of the political system and for the capabilities of the political system as a whole. Yet it is precisely about these questions—the consequences of legislative activity—that existing knowledge is least impressive. Since knowledge of present and past consequences of legislative activity is, I believe, so imperfect, anyone seeking to change legislatures in any way has very little basis for predicting what the consequences of such changes will be for other parts of the political system and for total system performance. What little we do know suggests that strengthening legislatures in developing countries would, in most cases, probably impede the capacity for change which is often crucial for "modernization" and economic development.

Most of this paper seeks to document the themes set out in the first three paragraphs. In Sections II and III, I will indicate the functions of the legislatures of Brazil and some other developing countries. Section IV analyzes assumptions about the functions of legislatures in scholarly writings about legislatures. The concluding section offers some speculations about the relationship of legislatures to political development and the wisdom of a program of technical assistance for legislative services.

Now, let us turn to some cases. As noted, there seems to be no commonly accepted list of functions which legislatures perform, quite aside from the issue of how to rank their importance in different countries. Thus, my functions are *ad hoc*, but no more so than those utilized by other scholars. The foregoing comment recognizes, incidentally, that everyone who has written about legislatures is, explicitly or implicitly, a functionalist. That is to say, everyone writing about legislatures says or assumes that legislatures have consequences for the political system at large and provides some indication of what he thinks those consequences are. In short, in *this* sense, we are all functionalists.[2]

The Functions of the Brazilian National Congress

To begin with, I should like to specify in some greater detail than for the rest of the cases the functions of the Brazilian Congress from April, 1964, to July, 1965.[3] I must emphasize that what

2. "Function" has many meanings in the social sciences and even within political science. For example, Ernest Nagel cites six meanings of the term, only one of which is "consequence," the meaning used throughout this paper. *The Structure of Science* (New York, 1961), pp. 523–525. When I say, "we are all functionalists," I mean functions as consequences, *not* as "functional requisites," a concept and term I never employ in this paper.

3. The reason for this is that between September, 1964, and July, 1965, I lived in Brasília, studying the Brazilian national Congress, especially the lower house or Chamber of Deputies. This experience stimulated my interest in the questions treated in this paper, and led to the research about other legislatures and to the analysis and critique of paradigms in the broad field of comparative legislative study which are reported here.

A further personal word may be of interest to those interested in comparative legislative research. When I went to Brazil for the first time in June, 1964, I did not anticipate studying the Brazilian Congress. I did not choose to study it because of any earlier strong interest in legislatures. Briefly, I did so—like so many students of legislatures—because the Congress contained a sample of Brazilian politicians from all regions and parties of the country, who were relatively accessible; because, aside from some legalistic accounts, almost nothing had been written about it; and because, despite its apparently limited influence in Brazilian national policy-making, it seemed to be a not irrelevant political institution. In

follows is an interpretation based mostly on impressionistic evidence of these functions. No more than this is possible at this time. To put this functional analysis in perspective, it may be helpful to recall very briefly the context of legislative activity during this period.[4]

The Brazilian Congress has seldom been a "strong" legislature. Certainly this is true since 1930. During most of the period from 1930 to 1945, the personal apparatus of President Getúlio Vargas effectively contained the ability of the Congress to allocate values. From 1946 to 1964, Brazil was formally a democracy, with a constitutional political system largely patterned after that of the United States. But the Brazilian Congress was seldom if ever as powerful as the U.S. Congress, even though its influence varied during this period.

On April 2, 1964, the government of João Goulart was toppled in a coup dominated by the military. On April 9, an Institutional Act was promulgated by a three-man military Revolutionary Council. Besides calling for the election by the Congress of a new president for Brazil—who turned out to be, under military pressure, Army Chief of Staff Humberto Castello Branco—this (first) Institutional Act had two provisions which restricted the legislative function of the Congress. First, it enabled the president to require any bill sent by him to the Congress to be considered within thirty days by each house (thus allowing a maximum of sixty days), or at his discretion within thirty days for both houses in joint session. Any bill not considered and rejected within the period specified automatically became law. Second, it provided that only the president could initiate bills creating or increasing public expenditures. Nor could either house add amendments to

---

confronting a study of the Brazilian Congress, my first questions were: What should I study? What questions should I ask? What paradigms, concepts and methods in the scholarly literature might I adopt and adapt? The disappointing answers I got from this literature are what led me, in the first instance, to this essay.

The bulk of my research during those eight months was on the recruitment and adaptation to elite political roles of a sample of Brazilian deputies; the results of that research will, I hope, be published in due course.

4. For the most complete and well-documented treatment of Brazilian politics between 1930 and 1964, see Thomas E. Skidmore, *Politics in Brazil, 1930–1964: An Experiment in Democracy* (New York, 1967).

presidential bills which would increase expenditures.[5] These provisions substantially reduced the value-allocation function of Congress. Hitherto, the authority to take almost unlimited time to consider bills had given it a veto power of substantial weight; and the authority to raise public expenditures had enabled it to play a role, however limited, in the allocation of financial resources. With these two options closed, the Congress lost much of what genuine lawmaking function it had had. And it was to lose even more of this function after October 27, 1965.[6]

Some other features of the first Institutional Act deserve mention here. The proclamation which accompanied the text itself of the Act declared:

The victorious revolution invests itself with the exercise of the Constituent Power, which manifests itself either through popular election or revolution. Thus the victorious revolution, like the Constituent Power, legitimizes itself. It destroyed the former government and has the capacity to constitute the new government. In it is contained the normative strength inherent in the Constituent Power. The leaders of the victorious revolution, thanks to the action of the Armed Forces and the unequivocal support of the nation, represent the people and in their name exercise the Constituent Power, which only the people truly hold (*de que o Povo é o único titular*).

The present Institutional Act can only be issued by the victorious revolution, represented by the Commanders-in-Chief of the three armed services . . . Only they can appropriately state the norms and processes for constituting the new government and provide for it [the new government] the powers and juridical instruments which may assure the exercise of power in the exclusive interest of the country. In order to demonstrate that we do not intend to radicalize the revolutionary process, we have decided to maintain the Constitution of 1946, restricting ourselves to modifying it only regarding the powers of the President of the Republic . . . In order to reduce still further the complete [*plenos*] powers of the victorious revolution, we equally

5. Text of the *Ato Institucional*, Articles 3–5.
6. The second Institutional Act of October 27, 1965, and subsequent amendments to the Constitution, further restricted the powers of the Congress. See Institute for the Comparative Study of Political Systems, *Brazil: Election Factbook Number 2*, Supplement November, 1966 (Washington, 1966), pp. 3, 28. From that date to March, 1967, when a new Constitution took effect in Brazil, the Congress was even less powerful than it had been from April, 1964, to July, 1965. The Constitution of 1967 incorporated many of the main features of the Institutional Acts regarding presidential-congressional relations.

resolve to maintain the National Congress, except for the reservations with respect to its powers contained in this Institutional Act.

It is thus quite clear that the revolution does not seek to legitimate itself through the Congress. It is rather the Congress which receives from this Institutional Act, the consequence (resultante) *of the exercise of the Constituent Power inherent in all revolutions, its legitimacy.* (My translation, emphasis added)

Two points may be noted about this passage. First, there is the attempt to justify, in terms of a democratic ideal and "the people," what was obviously an unconstitutional seizure of power. Second, there is an explicit assertion, little emphasized in the subsequent rhetoric of the revolutionary government, that the revolution does not derive its legitimacy from the Congress, but rather vice versa. Both features warn both mass and elites alike that the revolutionary group in the military means to rule, constitutional traditions notwithstanding. But the references to popular sovereignty, and the fact that the substance of the final two sentences was seldom, if ever, publicly emphasized after the Institutional Act was issued, reveal that the revolutionary group did not want to push its point too far. For the maintenance of an active Congress, even if that action had little consequence for the allocation of values in Brazilian politics, was an important determinant of the legitimacy of the revolutionary government, despite what the proclamation declares.

Now I may proceed to offer some hypotheses about the functions of the Brazilian Congress from April, 1964, to July, 1965. I shall discuss these functions roughly in the order of their importance, i.e., starting with the ways in which the Congress—especially the Chamber of Deputies, the lower house—had the greatest consequences for the Brazilian political system, and proceeding to the ways in which it had the least consequences.

Consider three processes in the Brazilian political system: legitimation, or the production of acquiescence in, and/or support of, the moral right to rule of the government by the members of the political system (including the population at large as well as political elites); recruitment, socialization, and training to elite political roles; and political decision making or influence. My hypothesis is that the Brazilian legislature accounted for, or caused, a higher proportion of this totality of legitimation than it did of either of the other two processes, and that it accounted for a higher proportion of the totality of recruitment, socialization, and training to elite political roles than it did of the totality of political influence.

Indeed, whenever anyone speaks of the more and less important functions of legislatures, he usually if not always employs this kind of construct, although it is seldom made so explicit. Different functions may be more important in different political systems: for example, in the U.S. Congress, it may be that influence is a more important function than recruitment, socialization, and training to other elite political roles. Whenever functions are defined as consequences of legislative activity, however, characterizing any function as the most important one usually means that it is the process or set of processes—among all those processes for which the legislature has consequences—on which the legislature has its largest impact. That is, it causes a higher proportion of that total process than it causes of any other process. Note that this does not at all mean that the legislature produces or causes more of the process than any other institution or phenomenon. The comparisons are among the consequences of legislative activity, not between the consequences of legislative activity and the consequences of the activity of other institutions or phenomena.

The Legitimation Function

The legitimation function may be broken down into three types, all of which share the common characteristic of fostering acquiescence in, or support for, the moral right to rule of the government among the population at large as well as political elites.

Legitimation as a Latent Function. The Brazilian Congress during this period performed a latent legitimizing function insofar as its activities had the consequence of legitimizing the government in power at the time, even beyond what was intended or understood by the legislators. Simply by meeting regularly and uninterruptedly, the legislature produced, among the relevant populace and elites, a wider and deeper sense of the government's moral right to rule than would otherwise have obtained.

This was perhaps less well understood by legislators, journalists, and the populace at large, than by some elites in the military. It was in this sense an unintended consequence of the Congress's activity. For many legislators, the regular meetings of the legislature were perceived as a check upon the government in power. There was some small truth in this perception; but more important, and also more striking, was the tacit and dimly perceived sanctioning of the government which their very activity symbolized and nurtured. In short, the legislators, including and perhaps especially those in opposition, thought that their vigorous debates and the widely reported accounts of their activities in the press constituted a sharing of power with the military and the president. The fact, however, was that they were, even where their debate and activities had little or no consequence for elite decision-making, enhancing the power of the president insofar as congressional activity legitimized his role and thus provided him with a less costly means for exercising his power.

It is important to stress that this function was performed without many legislators and other elites being aware of it, no matter what decisions were taken by the legislature, and no matter how little or how much power was exerted by it. For the executive, backed by the military, there was always a way around a negative decision by the legislature in response to one of the executive's proposals. In fact, such negative responses seldom came, but even when they did, they were circumvented relatively easily. It seems fair to say that during this period the executive branch did not once fail to achieve its will on any crucial issue because of constraints imposed upon it by the legislative branch. This was true even though the legislators always had at least a minimal chance to reject the proposals of the Executive and on some minor issues managed to do so. In light of this, it appears that the most important function of the Brazilian Congress during this period was to legitimize, both in this latent as well as in an overt or manifest sense, the actions of the government in power.

Whether the legislature made decisions which appeared to have a significant impact upon recommendations from the executive, or whether in fact it had a relatively minor impact upon such recommendations, this function was being performed.[7]

Legitimation as a Manifest Function. A second important function of the Brazilian legislature was the familiar one of putting the legislative stamp of approval on initiatives taken elsewhere. This legitimizing function is distinguished from the previous latent function by the overt, conscious, and widely understood character of this legitimation, and by the fact that the Congress had to approve presidential initiatives for it to take effect. It is the legitimation function of legislatures as conventionally understood.

Like the latent legitimizing function, this manifest legitimizing function was performed not only in the domestic but also in the international sphere. Many Brazilian elites, including congressional elites, were aware that the Castello Branco regime acquired legitimacy in the international political system, and perhaps especially with respect to the United States, by virtue of allowing the Congress to remain open and carry on its activities at least formalistically.

The "Safety-Valve" or "Tension-Release" Function. One of the most important functions of the Brazilian Congress was to provide "safety-valves" for those tensions generated by the political process. Once again, completely aside from the decision-making

7. So far as I can tell from reading and discussions with Brazilians, the only times since independence the Brazilian Congress has been totally and indefinitely closed down or dissolved—as opposed to temporarily suspended—were during the periods from 1823 to 1826; from 1891 to 1894; and from 1930 to 1934 and 1937 to 1945. The rest of the time the Congress has been open and active, even though sometimes limited by or under attack from presidential emergency powers under the Constitution, institutional acts, and other measures. It is noteworthy that these three periods are among the few in Brazilian history in which the federal government is regarded as having been controlled by a kind of dictator (Dom Pedro I, Floriano Peixoto, and Getúlio Vargas), the present period excepted for the moment. The foregoing paragraph was written in 1967. In December, 1968, the Brazilian government failed to gain legislative support for a measure to suspend the immunity of two critical legislators. It then suspended Congressional sessions indefinitely and entered into a period of harsh authoritarian rule in which all pretense of democracy was abandoned. The indefinite suspension of Congress was one of a series of actions for which the regime paid dearly in the coin of legitimacy. Legislative sessions were being resumed as this book went to press in January, 1970.

powers which the Congress had, its activities had significant consequences for the political system insofar as they reduced tension, provided reassurance, and generally enhanced satisfaction with or acquiescence in the policies and programs of the ruling government. In this sense, the Congress was a safety-valve or way of letting off steam in a political system where nobody got all he wanted and/or where the government was not willing to let everyone have what he wanted. This seems to be one important explanation for the strikingly large percentage of press space devoted to the activities of the Congress during a period when its decision-making power was extremely low. Plenary session debates, committee meetings, party and factional strategy sessions, individal legislators' statements—all these activities were widely reported in the press, even though they seemed to make little difference for the allocation of values in the Brazilian polity. But they were a device for the release of tensions among both the relatively impotent legislators (who debated, met, spoke) and various layers of the attentive public (who read about the activities and thus gained some symbolic reassurance that the government was "democratic" and "vital").[8]

The Recruitment, Socialization, and Training Functions

Another function of the Brazilian Congress, less important than the ones just discussed but significant nevertheless, is that the legislature recruits, socializes, and trains politicians to and for other roles in the political system in which they may wield more power than they do as national legislators. For example, some politicians gain experience in the legislature which enables them to go on to other posts like governorships, national ministries, state ministries, and the like. They learn the norms of the elites, they learn political skills, and they acquire visibility and prestige resources which are useful to them in acquiring, maintaining and utilizing these other roles. In this sense, the activities of the Brazilian Congress constitute a training ground for Brazilian poli-

8. For some interesting theorizing about these and other symbolic uses of politics and political institutions, see Murray Edelman, *The Symbolic Uses of Politics* (Urbana, Ill., 1964), esp. pp. 31–33.

ticians. This activity has consequences for the political system at large which are significant and which are quite independent of any decision-making or influence functions which it may or may not have.[9]

The Decisional or Influence Function

The Brazilian Congress sometimes makes decisons that "count"; it allocates values; it gets somebody to do something he otherwise would not do. In short, it sometimes has influence. What follows details some of the ways and some of the circumstances under which this takes place.

The Lawmaking Function. Occasionally, on some issues at some times, the legislature exerts power in the traditional sense of the term *legislation*. During the 1964–1965 period, the activities of the Brazilian Congress produced little lawmaking in this sense. The proportion of bills initiated by the Congress which became enforced law was infinitesimal. The proportion was higher before 1964, though still small. From 1945 to 1964, particularly during the governments of Getúlio Vargas (1951–1954) and João Goulart (1961–1964), the power of the Congress in terms of vetoing recommendations made by the executive branch was sometimes substantial. However, this power was drastically reduced after the 1964 coup.

In terms of modifications of recommendations from the executive branch, there have been some exceptions to the generalization above. Examples of these would be the congressional modifications of the Agrarian Reform Bill of 1964 and even of the new constitution which was instituted in 1967. In both of these instances, as in a few others, significant modifications were made through negotiations with the Congress. But it seems fair to say that the executive branch had the power to override even the restrictions thrust up by the Congress. It could have closed down the Congress, passed the laws as originally formulated, and the government would probably have continued. The costs would

9. For a discussion of the recruitment, socialization, and training functions of the Philippine Congress, which appear to be highly significant in the Philippine political system, see the essay in this volume by Robert B. Stauffer.

have mainly taken the form of legitimacy costs for the Castello Branco administration.

The "Exit" Function. Under certain specific, relatively infrequent, but recurring conditions in Brazilian politics, the National Congress performs what may be called an "exit" function. When the political system seems to have reached an impasse and the mechanisms for decision-making which normally characterize Brazilian politics seem incapable of providing a way out of the situation, the elites sometimes turn to the legislature for either the substance or the form, or both, of a decision which will take the system out of the impasse. This "exit" function is a special case of the decision-making function.

No such function was performed by the Brazilian Congress during 1964–1965, but there are examples in recent Brazilian political history. In November, 1955, the military and the nation were split over whether the President-Vice President ticket of Juscelino Kubitschek and João Goulart, which had won the election, should take office. There were rumors that Acting President Carlos Luz, together with some other political and military officials, planned a preventive coup and were already taking steps toward this end. At about the same time other groups, also both military and civilian, but led by War Minister Henrique Lott, initiated a countercoup to assure that Kubitschek and Goulart might take office. By November 11, it was clear that the latter group had won. Congress went into session the same day. By a strictly partisan vote, the Chamber of Deputies recognized Nereu Ramos, the Speaker of the Senate and next in line according to the Constitution, as the new president. But it did not vote to impeach Luz, the Acting President. Nor did it vote any sanctions against him or President Café Filho, who was then "on leave" due to illness. It is a reasonable view that the coup and the vote of the Chamber were both wholly unconstitutional; at best, they were highly debatable. There was no attempt in the Congress to prove that "either Luz or Café Filho or any of their ministers were guilty of the plot whose prevention was the justification of Lott's coup."[10] Thus, it seems that the Congress had gone outside the

10. Skidmore, *op. cit.,* p. 156.

constitution, under military pressure, to help legitimize the victorious coup in the name of constitutionality. The ploy was not fully successful: the incident left a legacy of bitterness among the losers; and on November 22, when Café Filho announced that his illness was over and he was ready to reassume his presidential office, the Chamber of Deputies responded again to military pressure by voting to disqualify him (Café Filho) from office and by confirming Nereu Ramos as president until the following January. The Chamber's action, nevertheless, probably gave the coup greater legitimacy than it otherwise might have had, and the Congress may have made some small contribution to the decision itself.[11]

Another example is the decision to change from a presidential to a semi-Parliamentary form of government in September, 1961. This decision, the idea for which apparently had its origins in the Congress, grew out of a conflict over whether João Goulart, the Vice-President, should be allowed to assume the presidency upon the sudden, unexpected resignation of President Jânio Quadros on August 25. The controversy over this issue brought the nation literally to the verge of civil war. Because the military was divided, a compromise solution, proposed first by a congressional commission and then adopted by the whole Congress, carried the day. This solution provided that Goulart could assume the presidency, as the Constitution indicated, but it included also a constitutional amendment providing for a cabinet of ministers nominated by the president but serving at the pleasure of the Chamber of Deputies. Thus, the powers of the president were severely limited: this was the price demanded by the opposition to Goulart. Once in office, Goulart spent fourteen months maneuvering himself into a position where he could reclaim the full powers of his office through a successful national plebiscite.[12]

The Interest-Articulation Function. Debate in Congress, and press attention to this debate, do receive some attention from powerful Brazilian elites in the executive branch and the military. Although attention by these elites to such reflections of "public" opinion is not nearly so great as the proportion of space devoted

11. See *ibid.*, pp. 146–158, for details.   12. See *ibid.*, pp. 200–223.

to them in the press would suggest, they do have consequences for the political system. By representing or articulating "public" interests in some sense, congressmen do exert a limited amount of influence. The linkages between congressmen and wider publics in Brazil are, in general, extremely imperfect. Nevertheless, this "interest-articulation" function is worth noting, even though it is less important than the ones mentioned so far.

The Conflict-Resolution Function. Classically, legislatures are often thought of, especially in normative terms, as an ideal place for political interests to be presented, negotiated, and resolved. Any institution that could negotiate and resolve conflicts would be exercising a form of influence. The study of interest groups has shown that in many political systems such activities and functions occur much more in the bureaucracy and elsewhere, and less in legislatures, than had long been assumed. Nevertheless, the literature on legislatures in the United States and elsewhere indicates that students of legislative behavior still consider this function to be one of the most important ones which legislatures perform.

Such is not the case with respect to the Brazilian Congress since 1964. Legislators, as legislators, are not significant brokers for political interests. Since the Congress has little decison-making power as an institution, it makes little sense for interest group representatives to present their demands to congressmen and to try to have political conflicts resolved in Congress. The Congress did play a role in this respect from 1945 through 1964, although it was a limited one. Even this role has been greatly reduced since 1964.

The Administrative-Oversight and Patronage Functions. The Brazilian Congress is not very effective as a check upon the bureaucracy. Its political and other resources for exercising this kind of influence are extremely limited. This situation has been intensified by the physical shift of the Congress to Brasília, because 90 per cent or more of the administrative apparatus of the federal government has remained in Rio de Janeiro. Moreover, dismayed as American congressmen may be by their inability to control cabinet secretaries and bureaucrats in the American political system, they would be appalled at the plight of their counterparts in Brazil. Brazilian ministers seldom testified before congressional committees, which are active but not in the sense of chastising cabinet ministers. On the few occasions when cabinet ministers presented themselves to Congress, they usually made formal appearances before plenary sessions. In these the ministers spoke from a rostrum ten feet above the floor of the Congress and delivered long initial speeches, which could not be interrupted by congressional questions, and which were subject to only a limited number of scheduled questions (resembling short speeches) after the formal address. Most important, the restrictions in the first Institutional Act of 1964 and the new Constitution of 1967 with respect to control of federal budgets virtually deprived the Congress of the most powerful tool, classically, for legislatures to control the executive branch.[13]

Legislators who have control over financial resources thus have an instrument—patronage—which can be used to exert influence. But since this control has been so severely restricted, the patronage function has not been very important either. Nor is "errand-running"—casework, as it is called in the United States—translated into very much political influence. Congressmen in Brazil vary in the degrees to which they run errands to the bureaucracy for their constituents, but, in general, there was little of this activity during the period from 1964 to the present. Many deputies are indifferent about it and do it only for personal friends. Others make an effort but are severely limited in their capacity to carry on such activities by lack of staff and the capacity for indifference (which the legislators have little power to permeate) of the bureaucrats. This activity was considerably more important, it should be noted, during previous administrations when, among other differences, the Congress had the option of increasing the total size of the budget. This option was foreclosed by the first Institutional Act and the Constitution of 1967.

The foregoing account of the functions of the Brazilian Congress is designed to indicate the variety and, more importantly,

13. For these provisions in the new Constitution of 1967, see Osny Duarte Pereira, *A Constituicão do Brasil* (1967): *Introducão, Cotejas, e Anotacões* (Rio de Janeiro, 1967), pp. 416–467.

the relative importance of the functions which the Congress seems to perform in the political system. These functions are derived inductively. They grow out of an examination of the Brazilian case. They are not "functional requisites" for any legislature, although they are probably found in most of them. No claim is made for the special and unique correctness of this set of functions as opposed to another set which others might advance. However, what is emphasized here is that however the functions of the Brazilian Congress are defined or divided up, the influence function (or something like it) in its various forms is less important—and what "important" means here was indicated above—than the other two functions (or something like them) in their various forms. Despite the fact that its power has been drastically reduced, in terms of decision-making, since 1964, it is too simple to characterize this Congress only as a "rubber stamp" or "notary public" to certify executive decisions, as journalistic and other accounts frequently do. In fact, even if it had no decision-making power whatsoever, the other functions which it performs would be significant. These other functions must, it seems to me, be taken into account in assessing the role of the legislature in political development in Brazil. They would also seem to be relevant to any assessment of technical assistance to legislatures as a means for promoting political development.

The Functions of Legislatures in Some Other Developing Countries

Is the Brazilian case between 1964 and 1965 unique? Is it one of only a minority of cases where the legislature does not allocate values but has other significant functions? Or is it more like most of the legislatures of the world than the U.S. Congress?

Specialists in legislative studies have not studied the functions of legislatures very much, but what knowledge we have suggests that the Brazilian case is much closer to the mode than the U.S. Congress. Moreover, the functions of most legislatures seem to be so different from those of the U.S. Congress that it seems most unrealistic to expect that they can be made to operate even reasonably similarly in the foreseeable future. Perhaps more importantly, most of the legislatures of the world seem to have functions which do not fit at all closely the assumptions about functions adopted by most studies of legislatures. Although most studies use the working assumption that the principal function of legislatures is to allocate values,[14] this seems not to be the case for the vast majority of the world's legislatures.

In this section I shall present some data about the functions of legislatures in various developing countries. They are almost without exception the same kind of data as were offered previously about the Brazilian Congress, that is, the impressionistic observations of observers who immersed themselves in political life in some developing country or countries. There is, so far as I know, no better data to be had.

These interpretations of the functions of the legislatures in various developing countries were found through a perusal of articles in some nine professional journals over about the last ten years. All items are reported which were found to contain some material about the functions of legislatures. This review is not, of course, comprehensive; rather, it represents what data I could, with the aid of a graduate student assistant, get together in a relatively brief period of time.[15] There are probably some legislatures in developing countries which have a bigger impact on the allocation of values than these.[16] Yet this admittedly imperfect evidence supports, even more strongly than I had originally anticipated, the hypothesis that legislatures do not usually allocate values but nonetheless perform other significant functions in the political system.

14. See below, "The Comparative Study of Legislatures: Paradigms and Hypotheses."

15. This survey of journals was done for me by a graduate student assistant, Mr. Horst Hutter, whose help I gratefully acknoweldge. The journals he examined were *Parliamentary Affairs, Political Studies, World Politics, American Political Science Review, American Journal of Sociology, Western Political Science Quarterly,* and *Journal of Commonwealth Studies.*

16. See, for example, the essay by Robert B. Stauffer in this volume.

Tanzania[17]

After discussing and empirically documenting the trend toward concentration of power in the hands of the Tanzanian chief
executive, Fordoff lists the functions still performed by members
of Parliament (though not explicitly in functional terms). The
main ones are a limited amount of interest-articulation, patronage
through errand-running, and the socialization, recruitment, and
training of politicians for leadership. Fordoff observes that the
"principal [formal] function of the National Assembly is to legislate. . . . However, most bills are pushed through parliament by
the government on a 'certificate of urgency,'" so that very little
time remains for M.P.'s to get acquainted with the bill. "It [the
certificate of urgency procedure] prevents members in effect
from discussing impending legislation with their constituencies or
other interested parties" (p. 91). In general, influence on legislation has shifted from Parliament to the leadership of the single
parliamentary party. Most decisions are accordingly made outside of parliament.

The Central African Republic, Chad, Congo-Brazzaville, and Gabon[18]

Ballard writes of The Central African Republic, Chad, Congo-
Brazzaville, and Gabon, that: "Since the National Assembly of
each state is the most . . . identifiable representative institution,
each ethnic group and each region demand representation in it
roughly proportional to their numerical importance. This remains
true despite the assemblies' *loss of real legislative power*" (p. 304,
emphasis added). These regional and ethnic "demands" appear
not to be really answered; the parliamentarians serve the government rather than their constituencies: ". . . the government has
used the deputies as local spokesman for its policies and programs and has given them some control over local patronage . . .
candidates [are] chosen more for their loyalty [to the ruling elite]

17. William Fordoff, "Parliament in Tanzania," *Journal of Commonwealth
Political Studies*, III, No. 2 (July, 1965), 85–103.
18. John A. Ballard, "Four Equatorial States," *National Unity and Regionalism
in Eight African States*, ed. Gwendolyn Carter (Ithaca, N.Y., 1966), pp. 231–335.

than for their position as spokesmen of ethnic and regional interests" (p. 304).

What Ballard seems to be saying is that these four legislatures perform few decision-making functions, as that term is usually understood in regard to legislatures. But they do appear to be instruments with which the party can penetrate and influence the regional and ethnic units of the nation. This is a function which the legislature does not perform in Brazil: it is a form of influence, but one in which influence flows down from elites to masses rather than up from the masses to elites. It might be called a mobilization function.[19] Ballard's succinct description of the chief function of the legislature indicates that the activities of these four legislatures have two principal consequences—legitimation and mobilization—for the four political systems of which they are a part. As he says:

> The chief function of the Assembly, then, is to provide an organized and recognized body of loyal supporters of the regime who can claim to represent a national synthesis of particular interests and who therefore provide both a semblance of parliamentary approval for the policy and program of the regime [legitimation function] and practical support as a team of local political agents [mobilization function]. (p. 305)

Liberia[20]

Liebenow describes the decision-making power of the Liberian legislature in words very similar to mine about the Brazilian Congress:

> "None . . . could point to one significant measure which had emerged from the legislature without presidential approval, nor could they point to any major legislation which failed despite concerted and sustained support from the Executive Mansion . . . However, consultation behind the scene and surveying the opposition in advance are required to spare the President public political defeat" (pp. 354–355).

The latter reservation may be important, insofar as it specifies real political power for the legislature.

19. See David Apter, *The Politics of Modernization* (Chicago, 1965), *passim.*
20. J. Gus Liebenow, "Liberia," *African One Party States*, ed. Gwendolyn Carter (Ithaca, N.Y., 1962), pp. 325–394.

The Liberian legislature also appears to have an "educative function": "Its debates are lively, even though highly rhetorical in character and help to educate the local leadership and the general public regarding the significance of a new policy decision" (p. 355).

The Liberian legislature also serves as a recruiting, training, and socializing institution:

Despite the lack of significant power . . . the post of Senator or Representative is one which is eagerly sought. Membership in the Legislature automatically gives one the title 'Honorable' as well as the perquisites which are due to the very few elective officials in Liberia . . . Moreover, the legislature is regarded as a very attractive forum for the establishment of a national reputation. With success a young man may go on to the Supreme Court, an ambassadorship, the cabinet, or even as high as the presidency. (p. 357)

The main functions of the Liberian legislature seem to be legitimation and education of the masses. Liebenow sums it up by saying: "Elections provide the Liberian masses with the facade of participation in the national political process and permit the national leaders to explain and popularize their programs." (p. 363)

Guinea[21]

The legislature in Guinea, according to L. Gray Cowan, has virtually no genuine decision-making function.

The first and most basic tenet of PDG (*Parti Democratique de Guinee*) philosophy is the supremacy of the party over every aspect of the life of the individual and the state. The party is regarded as the repository of the popular will; the real organ of decision-making is neither government nor parliament but the party . . . The source of political power is expressly kept outside the provisions of the constitution, and the subordination of all organs of government to the party organization renders virtually meaningless the constitutional relationships of these organs to one another. (pp. 188, 208)

But the legislature does seem to have more importance in terms of legitimizing functions:

21. L. Gray Cowan, "Guinea," in *ibid.*, pp. 149–236.

The tasks of the cabinet and the legislature are defined clearly: they are to 'apply the decisions and *mots d'ordre* of the party.' . . . The legislature, then, is the ratifying arm of the party and the cabinet and administration its executive arms.

The function of the legislature as a ratifying body for the decisions of the Political Bureau has tended more and more since independence to take on symbolic and ceremonial aspects. Debates in the legislature are purely perfunctory since the question has already been decided. (pp. 206–207)

Ghana[22]

J. M. Lee provides us with an "examination of the functions of the National Assembly under the Republican Constitution" in Ghana from 1960 to 1963. This article addresses itself directly to our question, and hence is worth citing in some detail.

Lee finds that the National Assembly has virtually no decision-making function. "The function of the National Assembly within the presidential system . . . in fact amounts to little more than one of the functions of the party, that which stands in the lime-light and receives the greatest publicity. Through the assembly, the party shows itself to the world" (p. 379). The article emphasizes throughout the degree to which the CPP (Convention People's Party) completely overshadows the National Assembly as a decision-making institution. "It is hardly surprising in these conditions that members of Parliament seem to be just another kind of party functionary" (p. 380).

The legislature does seem to serve as a mechanism through which politicians are recruited and socialized to other, more powerful political roles. Members of Parliament "are the only party functionaries who can claim certain privileges of speech which attract publicity and who can aspire to the rewards of ministerial office. A seat in the National Assembly opens up new opportunities for the most ordinary party official" (p. 380).

As in the four African equatorial states discussed by Ballard, but unlike Brazil, the Ghanaian Parliament seemed to be one of the mechanisms the single-party leadership used to mobilize the

22. J. M. Lee, "Parliament in Republican Ghana," *Parliamentary Affairs* XVI (1962–1963), 376–393.

masses. "The functions of a member of parliament outside the
National Assembly betray all the tribal, regional and family
groupings which the party tries to encompass. . . . Members of
Parliament are . . . primarily expected to represent the government in their constituencies, to encourage, to warn, and to explain" (pp. 385-386).

Legitimation also seems to be an important function.

It is one of the principal ironies of the transplantation of the Westminster model from Britain to Ghana that it has produced almost a
complete reversal of the 'decorative and efficient' institutions of government. . . . The National Assembly of Ghana . . . might well be
regarded as the 'decorative' part . . . Parliament provides a show-
ground of considerable 'decorative' value for any item which the
President wishes to bring to popular attention. (pp. 389-390)

Lee also identifies the "safety-valve" function: "It would be fair
to add that the existence of M.P.'s provides a useful 'safety-valve'
for party discontents, as well as focus for the 'decorative' aspects
of Ghanaian life" (p. 390). The Ghanaian Parliament also served
to articulate interests:

The back-bench M.P. retains some positive political functions in the
representation of his constituents wherever the machinery of the party
or the efficiency of the President's Office fails to give an adequate
satisfaction to local interests. He can become a one-man lobby for his
own district because meetings of Parliament, infrequent although they
now are, offer an opportunity for airing grievances in public (p. 390).

Under certain very special circumstances, the legislature in
Ghana seems to have consequences for the political system which
correspond very nicely to the "exit" function described for the
Brazilian Congress: ". . . the National Assembly of Ghana assumes a new importance if there is a 'succession crisis' for the
Presidency. The decorative parts of the Constitution are sometimes called upon to be 'efficient' " (p. 392).[23]

23. For an interpretation consistent with the present one, but less directly
relevant and detailed, see David Apter and Robert A. Lystad, "Bureaucracy, Party,
and Constitutional Democracy: An Examination of Political Role Systems in
Ghana," in *Transition in Africa, Studies in Political Adaptation,* ed. Gwendolyn
Carter and William O. Brown (Boston, 1958), pp. 16–43. Ruth Schacter denies
that the legislature performs a legitimizing function at all; she argues that the
party was the only legitimizing political institution. See her "Single Party Systems
in West Africa," *American Political Science Review,* LV, No. 1 (March, 1961),
294–307, esp. 299.

In sum, the Parliament in Ghana had no decision-making function, as the term is conventionally understood. It had limited importance as an interest articulator. Under rare circumstances it might perform the "exit" function. Its main functions, however, seemed to be legitimation; mobilization; and recruitment, socialization, and training of political elites.

Egypt[24]

J. Harris Proctor has briefly described the functions of the Egyptian National Assembly in 1957–1958. His account is based upon a systematic empirical analysis of the debates of all forty-six meetings of the Parliament during the period. He wanted to investigate the claim in the Egyptian press that the Parliament was not a "rubber stamp" but an institution with influence.

He concludes that the National Assembly has little if any decision-making capacity or influence. Rather, it served to provide representative approval (in our terms, legitimacy) for what the government (i.e., the president) wanted done. The government's approval was necessary for a candidate to be nominated for election to the legislature. Debates contained little criticism of the government's program; what little criticism occurred was on matters of form rather than substance. The press's assertion that the National Assembly had influence, despite Proctor's finding that it did not, seems to be part of an attempt to legitimize the regime through the legislature.

Turkey[25]

In observing the Turkish parliamentary election of 1954, Hanson was struck by the lack of issues in the campaign, and asked the question: ". . . was there any point in going to the trouble, expense, and possible danger of organizing an election that gave the people no real choice, except between personalities?" He concludes that there was, and indicates some functions performed by elections and the elected legislature.

24. J. Harris Proctor, "The Legislative Activity of the Egyptian National Assembly of 1957–1958," *Parliamentary Affairs*, XIII (1959–1960), 213–226.

25. A. H. Hanson, "Democracy Transplanted: Reflections on a Turkish Election," *Parliamentary Affairs*, IX (1955–1956), 65–74.

First, they integrated the polity. Elections and legislative activity both symbolized and enhanced consensus in the Turkish political system. Second, they served to educate the public to some notion of democracy. Third, they legitimated the regime both at home and abroad. Fourth, they performed a safety-valve function: "All the evidence goes to show that the people are proud of their right to vote and exercise it seriously" (p. 73). Presumably, denial of this right would produce tensions in the electorate; hence, even though elections have little if any effect on public policy, they do reduce tension by providing the people with a means for "letting off steam."

Latin America

Scott surveyed, in an essay published in 1958, the role of "legislatures and legislation" in Latin America. He concluded that "The present role of the legislature in Latin America is not what the constitutions say it is. In most countries congress does not participate in determining national policy in the independent manner and to the extent usually deemed necessary to the successful operation of democratic and responsible government."[26] Ten years later, the generalization almost certainly still holds. Among the larger countries (above 8 million in population), only in Chile, and possibly Venezuela, may it be said of the legislature that decision-making is an important function except on rare occasions.

Japan[27]

Japan is perhaps not appropriately considered a "developing" country; nevertheless, the Japanese case is especially relevant for our purposes because of the Allied Occupation effort to implant democratic institutions, including legislatures with decision-making functions, after World War II. Brett provides us with a description and analysis of one session of one prefectural legislature

---

26. Robert E. Scott, "Legislatures and Legislation," in *Government and Politics in Latin America*, ed. Harold Eugene Davis (New York, 1958), pp. 290–332, quotation at p. 329.
27. Cecil C. Brett, "The Japanese Prefectural Legislature: Western Models-Oriental Adaptations," *Parliamentary Affairs*, XI (1957–1958), 23–37.

which was set up by the Occupation. His account provides a clue as to the likely outcome of technical assistance to legislatures as part of a foreign aid strategy for political development.

Brett concludes that this prefectural legislature does not perform the functions attributed to legislatures in the West, which are the functions the occupation forces hoped it would perform. Mainly, he refers to decision-making functions and the kind of restraint on the executive performed by a legislature in checks-and-balances political systems. He rejects the conclusion, however, that this legislature is "no more than a rubber stamp" (p. 33). He lists, apparently in no special order of importance, at least four significant functions.

First, it meets informally with the provincial government after a bill is drafted but before formal submission to the legislature. In these meetings it sometimes exerts a limited amount of influence. Second, it performs the manifest legitimizing function. That is, votes in the legislature usually merely confirm or ratify decisions made elsewhere but give them more legitimacy than they would otherwise have. Third, legislative activity reinforces and symbolizes a feature of Japanese political culture: it "is in keeping with the principle of social harmony which permeates Japanese society" (p. 36). Thus the legislature seems to perform an integration function, which may be related to, but seems a bit different from, the legitimation and catharsis functions already mentioned. Fourth, legislative activity is an elaborate social ritual which serves an educative function vis-à-vis the public at large.

Thus the Japanese prefectural legislature—or at least the one Brett studied—performs some significant functions in the polity, even though they are not the ones envisaged by the political engineers who set it up. Would it be wise to try to change its functions? Should this legislature have a greater influence on decisions, i.e., should it take on more of the decision-making function in Japanese society? Any answer to this question would have to consider the feasibility of the strategy, its consequences for the other functions, and the costs as well as the benefits likely to flow from such a change. Until much more is known about all of these questions, no scholar (or policy-maker) has much basis for knowing whether the strategy would be "good" or "bad" for political development.

This review of the functions of legislatures in some developing countries suggests two main conclusions. First, these legislatures have significant functions, but the principal one is usually not allocating values. Second, the functional categories utilized for the analysis of the Brazilian Congress are more or less useful for the analysis of the functions of other legislatures, although the other cases suggest still other categories (e.g., mobilization in Africa, but not in Brazil).

Although this survey of legislatures is far from comprehensive, there is little evidence that more than a mere handful of national legislatures in the world have decision-making as their principal functions. Even in such European democracies as England, Germany, and France, decision-making is not the most important function of the legislatures.[28] Thus, although in some legislatures —e.g., the United States, the Philippines[29]—legislating may be the most important function, these cases definitely seem to constitute a minority of national legislatures. Most of the world's legislatures do not legislate very much; of only a very few of them may it be said that legislating is the principal function.

The Comparative Study of Legislatures: Paradigms and Hypotheses

In this section I turn to the main corpus of the literature in political science about legislatures. I shall attempt to document my earlier assertions about the scant attention to functional questions in this literature. I shall also try to show how the persistent refusal seriously and rigorously to confront such questions severely limits the utility of this literature for research on legislatures in developing countries, and indeed most of the world.

Consider the following outline of possible topics and types of

28. See *Lawmakers in a Changing World*, ed. Elke Frank (Englewood Cliffs, N.J., 1966), pp. 30–82. See also my discussion below.
29. See *ibid.*, pp. 9–29, and the essays by Roger H. Davidson and Robert B. Stauffer in this volume.

studies to be made of legislatures. The six topics noted here encompass the foci, paradigms, and conceptual frameworks actually used, insofar as I can determine, in most or all of the studies of legislatures that have been done.

 I. Setting
  A. Historical
  B. Legal-Formal
 II. Socio-economic Backgrounds, Recruitment Patterns, and Personality Attributes of Legislators
 III. Internal Functioning
 IV. External Functioning or Relations
 V. Legislative Self-Images and Roles
 VI. The Functions of Legislatures in the Political System

Traditionally, studies of legislatures have treated topics I-A and I-B in some depth. I-B still gets considerable attention, but I-A has been relatively neglected, although this may be changing with respect to legislative studies in the United States.

In the burgeoning literature on legislatures, especially in the United States, the major emphases have been on topics II, III, V, and part of IV. Regarding the "external relations" of Congress, substantial attention has been devoted to the impact of constituency, party, interest groups, and other external variables upon legislatures, but less attention, in terms of systematic, empirical research, has been devoted to the impact of the executive branch upon the legislature. Relatively little attention has been paid to the impact of Congress—or other national legislatures—upon these external variables. Item VI—the functions of legislatures in political systems—has been practically ignored in the "comparative legislative behavior" literature, and rather weakly treated in the traditional literature on legislatures. (The characteristics of these two bodies of literature will be spelled out as I analyze each of them, below.)

If one wants to know the relationship of legislatures to political development, it is crucial to know the consequences of legislative activity. Thus, the emphases of the "comparative legislative behavior" literature and the weaknesses of the "traditional" literature on legislatures sharply limit the utility of these two bodies of knowledge for students of legislatures and political development.

Although I am critical of many of the works to be discussed, I do not deny that they have importance and usefulness for many purposes. Indeed, these works have been selected because they excellently represent the genres from which they are drawn. For example, in terms of most of the objectives of their authors, the comparative legislative behavior studies (see below) are by and large of very high quality. Authors working in this field (e.g., Wahlke, Eulau, Fenno) have done creative and original theoretical, methodological, and empirical work that has enriched political science. None of my criticism is meant to detract from these significant accomplishments.

What I mean to emphasize is that, in the light of what has been argued about the functions of most legislatures in the world, these studies provide inadequate paradigms and knowledge for understanding the roles of legislatures in developing countries. I believe this is a crucial fact to be noted, whether one's interests are in "pure" scholarship or in strengthening legislatures toward the end of political development.

The Comparative Legislative Behavior Literature

The characteristics of what I call the comparative legislative behavior literature are: (1) a focus on the individual legislator—his attitudes and actions—as the main unit of analysis; (2) an attempt to avoid prescription and concentrate on description and explanation; (3) an effort to be truly comparative, using the same concepts to gather comparable data in different places, thus enabling the analyst to control variables relatively rigorously; (4) an emphasis on quantification; (5) a persistent refusal to ask seriously, or answer with relevant data, questions about the functions of legislatures in the political system.

Three works may be considered as representative, for our purposes, of the field of comparative legislative behavior. These are Wahlke and Eulau, eds., *Legislative Behavior: A Reader in Theory and Research* (1959); Wahlke *et al.*, *The Legislative System: Explorations in Legislative Behavior* (1962); and Eulau and

Hinckley, "Legislative Institutions and Processes" (1966).[30] *Legislative Behavior* is a reader, with an introduction and commentary by the editors, analyzing approaches to, and bringing together studies in the field of comparative legislative behavior. It uses the term *legislature* in a somewhat restricted sense, to refer only to those elected bodies in political systems of the Western culture that engage in the functions of proposing, deliberating, and deciding about public policy (p. 3). Thus, the selections presented in this volume come mostly from studies of the American Congress and state legislatures, and to a lesser extent from studies of the British House of Commons, the German Bundestag, the Legislative Assembly of New South Wales, Australia, the French Parliament, and other European legislatures, past and present, which presumably perform "the functions of proposing, deliberating, and deciding about public policy." *The Legislative System* is based upon a comparative study in four American state legislatures. "Legislative Institutions and Processes" is a critical review article about legislative studies in the United States published between 1961 and 1964.

All three works meet our five criteria for comparative legislative behavior studies. They share another characteristic: they deal only with legislatures in the United States and the European cultural area; no data on legislatures in the Third World is offered in any of them. Why then are they considered here?

There are four reasons why I feel it is legitimate and even necessary and important to do so. First, they all are presented not primarily as studies of the legislature in the United States or England or wherever, but first and foremost as studies in comparative legislative behavior. Their titles express this: none of them says anything about places.

Second, the paradigms used in these studies have been and continue to be applied to the study of legislatures outside of the

30. John C. Wahlke and Heinz Eulau, eds., *Legislative Behavior: A Reader in Theory and Research* (Glencoe, Ill., 1959); John C. Wahlke *et al.*, *The Legislative System: Explorations in Legislative Behavior* (New York, 1962); Heinz Eulau and Katherine Hinckley, "Legislative Institutions and Processes," in *Political Science Annual: An International Review*, ed. James A. Robinson (Indianapolis, 1966), I, 85–189.

European culture area. The ready availability of these paradigms, and the alluring quality of the precise data that are readily gathered with them, have induced (seduced?) some serious students of legislatures into using these studies as models in research sites where they may not be, and in my judgment probably are not, most appropriate.

Third, these studies are generally of much higher quality, in terms of their objectives, than the "traditional" studies in terms of their objectives. As such they constitute some of the "best" knowledge we have about legislatures. This is in large part why they are so attractive. Therefore, it is appropriate to examine them in this context, if only to know how helpful the "best" knowledge we have about legislatures is for understanding the relationship between legislatures and political development.

Finally, examining these studies enables us to look at the assumptions about functions embodied in them and to compare these assumptions with the best data available about the actual functions of legislatures even in the political systems to which they allegedly apply. Incidentally, we discover that the functions of legislatures even in the European culture area apparently do not fit these assumptions. (See below.)

Legislative Behavior: A Reader in Theory and Research (1959). When *Legislative Behavior* appeared in 1959, it was the most comprehensive collection of articles in the field of comparative legislative behavior; perhaps it still is. Both the organization and content of the articles and the commentary of the editors reflected the prevailing (even though varied) assumptions, paradigms, and research emphases of students of comparative legislative behavior.

The book is divided into four sections. The first section is on the historical and institutional context of legislative behavior; it corresponds to topic I in the six-item list of topics noted above. The second section is on the political bases of legislative behavior —party, pressure group, and constituency relations with legislatures. Most of the selections in this section are concerned with the impact of these "political bases" upon legislative behavior; they have much less to say about the impact of legislative activity on party, pressure group, or constituency. This section corresponds to topic IV in the list of topics.

The third section is about the social and psychological bases of legislative behavior. It deals with recruitment and socio-economic characteristics of legislators; concepts of office and role held by legislators; and with personal and interpersonal orientations of legislators. Thus, it treats topics II, III, and V in the list above. Section four is on research orientations and techniques. It is almost solely of methodological interest, and the selections in it do not much illuminate major substantive hypotheses. Most of the methodological techniques treated—roll-call analysis, game theory, scaling, and bloc-cohesion indices—are useful mainly with respect to substantive questions under topic III above, namely, the internal functioning of legislatures.

Thus, the only topic in my six-item list of topics which is not treated in the Wahlke-Eulau reader is topic VI, the functions of legislatures in the political system. This omission is intentional and the editors state it explicitly themselves:

Comparative analysis of the functions of the many types of collectivity sometimes connoted by the term 'legislature' is no doubt urgently needed by political science, and historical analysis of the evolution and development of modern legislatures from earlier crypto- or pseudo-legislatures would no doubt illuminate legislative study. But such analyses could not be included within the limits of this volume. (p. 3)

But the absence of sustained attention to this function question does not mean the contributors and editors of the volume do not make functional assumptions, nor does it mean they say nothing about the functions of legislatures. Their introduction begins: "Of all political institutions, none is more vital to the process of linking governors and governed in relationships of authority. Without some understanding of its character and functioning, one can have only very partial understanding of the process of government and its place in society" (p. 3). This is a working assumption in the volume; no evidence is presented to support it. Is it true? Even if Wahlke and Eulau mean, by the adjective "modern," to exclude African, Asian, and Latin American cases like those already discussed, one may still question whether in many "modern" political systems no other institution is more vital to the phenomena of authority and responsibility than the legislature. In Great Britain, for example, the administration and the cabinet both may be more vital for these processes than Parliament.[31] In any event, *Legislative Behavior* does not present any data that might enable us to answer such a question, nor does it provide conceptual apparatus for trying to answer it.

There is one other "principal assumption" of the Wahlke-Eulau volume that deserves mention. This is the idea that

behavioral analysis and institutional analysis are not mutually exclusive categories . . . but rather are mutually independent approaches to the central problems of political inquiry. Without questions about institutional functions and structures as a guide, behavioral analyses obtain no theoretical focus relevant to the study of politics. (p. 3)

I could not agree more with both of these statements, but it is precisely because the answers (which are mostly implicit in the volume) to "questions about institutional functions" seem to me to be so incomplete and imperfect that I have doubts, for present purposes, about the relevance of much of the behavioral approach to legislative behavior that has been used so far.

Again: the problem is that the answer given by Wahlke and Eulau—and most of the writings they ably compile and comment upon—is that the principal function of legislatures is to legislate, that is, to make decisions. The only way to know if this is true is to examine the consequences of their activity. That is, one must find out if their activity results in other actors in the political system behaving in ways they would otherwise not behave. In short, does the legislature have influence? Does it in fact "allocate values"?

Seen in this perspective—which seems to me the only way one can see it—the question of the functions of the legislature involves studying not only the behavior of the legislators themselves, but also—and more importantly—the behavior of those

31. See especially S. A. Walkland, *The Legislative Process in Great Britain* (New York, 1968). See also Samuel Beer's essay, discussed below.

whom they presumably affect or influence. To know the functions of legislatures—where function is defined as consequences—it is not sufficient to study the behavior of legislators or the impact of other individuals or groups upon legislators; one must also study those units—individual, group, or nation—upon which the legislature presumably has an impact. The latter part of the formula, in fact, is probably more crucial than the former. And it is precisely here where the comparative legislative behavior literature, and *Legislative Behavior* as it represents it, are weak.

Commenting on the selections in Part III of the reader—on the social and psychological bases of legislative behavior—the editors reveal their view about what is

the central problem of legislative study—the behavior of legislators. Insofar as they (i.e., the selections in this part) seek to discover and to set forth in explicit terms significant uniformities in the behavior of human beings, they represent a step forward toward fuller understanding of legislative behavior. Once these uniformities are described, it becomes clear that *the* central task of legislative study includes both explanation of when and why the given uniformities occur and explanation of what differences their existence makes in the functioning of the legislature as a political institution. (p. 242, emphasis added)

It is clear from this passage that Wahlke and Eulau take a very different position than I do about what are the central problems in the study of legislatures. They hold that the principal focus should be on the behavior of legislators; I hold that it should be, first, upon consequences of what legislators do for other actors in the political system. They are arguing that the behavior of legislators determines the functions of legislative bodies; I am arguing that the functions of legislatures are determined by many forces without the legislature itself, and that one can study individual legislative behavior in great detail and still not have a very good understanding of the functions of the legislature in the political system. They argue that the study of individual legislator behavior reveals the functions of legislatures as institutions; I hold that it is necessary to study other actors to learn legislative functions, and that this task is prior to the study of individual legislators if one is to ask interesting questions about individual legislator behavior.

Because Wahlke and Eulau have focused on individual legislator behavior, and have not in fact made "questions about institutional functions" a "guide" to their "behavioral analyses," their work is not, as they hoped, very "useful to others in helping them place the study of legislatures in the broader context of political inquiry . . . [such as] relating the study of legislative behavior to the study of legislatures as institutions . . . and in suggesting relationships among the various institutions and behaviors that ultimately make up the process of government" (pp. 3–4).

The Legislative System (1962). *The Legislative System: Explorations in Legislative Behavior,* by Wahlke, Eulau, Buchanan, and Ferguson, was published in 1962. It appears to have had a very good reception among scholars,[32] is widely cited, and has been frequently used as a model for comparative legislative behavior research. One of its main virtues is that it is based upon systematic and comparable data from four American state legislatures; it remains perhaps the most comprehensive and precise comparative study of the genre.

I have no quarrel to make, here, with the study so far as it goes. But it does not go far enough. It does not even go as far as the authors promise. And it surely provides an inadequate paradigm for studying the legislatures of most of the world, especially those of most developing countries.

I shall attempt to document these assertions by citing and commenting upon a few key passages of the work. On page 5 we are told, quite rightly:

The commonplace notion that "legislation" is the chief task of a legislature and that it involves decisions by the legislature about what shall and shall not be law tends to equate "legislation" with . . . a general decision-making function. But not all legislatures "legislate" in a clear decisional sense. The Supreme Soviet of the USSR, to take the most obvious example, certainly does not do so. Whether or not any

32. See, for example, Donald R. Matthews' laudatory review in the *American Political Science Review,* LVII, No. 1 (March, 1963), 163–165. Matthews goes so far as to say that the theoretical portion of *The Legislative System* "represents the closest approach to a systematic, empirical theory of legislatures now in existence" (p. 164).

particular legislature does perform genuine decisional functions in the larger political system is essentially a question for empirical investigation.

Thus the authors expose the naiveté of the "commonplace" notion that "legislatures legislate," and note that the functions of legislatures are matters for empirical inquiry. But do they provide us with any such data? Do they even address the question of how one might get and classify and use such data? The answer is no. Rather, they adopt (pp. 6–7, 24) the very assumption, which they have just characterized as "commonplace" but wrong and naive, that "the legislatures we are studying *have functions comprehensible above all as 'lawmaking'*. Most important legislative actions are best conceived as decisions by the legislative body . . ." (p. 24, emphasis added).

The key passage of the book, for our purposes, appears on pp. 6–7:

Although . . . the functions performed by [the legislative] institution in each case must ultimately be determined by empirical inquiry, we have proceeded on the assumption that our four legislatures (and those of other American states, the U.S. Congress, and many parliamentary bodies in other systems) do in fact perform decisional, legitimizing, representative, and other functions. We have assumed that examination of the behavior of legislators will yield insight about performance of these functions by legislators in the four states and by legislative institutions more generally. But just as institutional and behavioral political study are interdependent, so, too, are structural and functional approaches. One can investigate the same problems by asking what functions are performed by a given institution, and how, as by asking what agencies or institutions perform a given function, and how? In other words, the theoretical conceptions guiding this research are behavioral, institutional (structural), and functional— not any one or the other.

Let me consider a number of elements in this passage.

". . . the functions performed by [the legislative] institution in each case must *ultimately* be determined by empirical inquiry. . . ." Shouldn't this be a *first* step? Otherwise, how does one know that the questions one asks about individual legislators' behavior are worth asking? It may or may not be that in the

American context enough data exists so that one can proceed to other questions. But this is surely not the case with respect to legislatures in most of the world; what evidence we have suggests that most of them do not have a strong legislative function; hence there is little reason to believe that using *The Legislative System* approach for studying them would be appropriate.

". . . we have proceeded on the assumption that our four legislatures (and those of other American states, the U.S. Congress, and many parliamentary bodies in other systems) do in fact perform decisional, legitimizing, representative, and other functions."

It does seem reasonable to assume, with Wahlke *et al.*, that American state legislatures and the U.S. Congress do in fact perform the decisional function, even though scholars have devoted relatively little serious attention to this question. But how much? How important is the decisional as contrasted with the other functions? To lump together "decisional, legitimizing, representative, *and other* functions" is both to deny, from the point of view of this paper, the most important distinctions, and, by using the escape category "and other functions," to turn away from some important questions. What the phrase does, in effect, is affirm that legislatures have consequences which are important for the political system (else why study them?), which I do not dispute, although some might; beyond this, it says nothing.

So far as I can tell, students of American state legislatures vary greatly in their assessments of the functions of these legislatures. Wright's conclusions are the most supportive of those who assume that decision-making is the principal function. In a study based on mailed questionnaires to state administrative officials, he reports that the administrators felt that the legislature exercised greater (generalized) control over their agency's affairs, had a greater tendency to reduce budget requests, and was less sympathetic to the goals of their agency, than the governors.[33]

---

33. Deil S. Wright, "Executive Leadership in State Administration," *Midwest Journal of Political Science*, XI, No. 1 (February, 1967), 1–26, esp. 3–6. The questionnaire was mailed to 1,357 officials in all 50 states, and 933 usable replies were received for a respectable 69 per cent response rate.

Although perception of "subjective" control is not the same as "objective" control, these data are interesting.

In a perceptive essay, Dye reaches two main conclusions: first, that "most state legislatures function as 'arbiters' of public policy rather than as 'initiators.' Policy initiation is the function of the governor, the bureaucrat, and the interest group. . . . [L]egislatures are placed in the role of responding to the stimulus provided by these 'groups' "; and second, that state legislatures "function to inject into public decision-making a parochial influence. Legislatures function to represent locally-organized interests, interests which are manifested in local rather than statewide constituencies."[34] The roles of "arbiter" and "veto group" are power roles, even if not as powerful as "initiators."

But Jacob and Anton reach different conclusions. Jacob's systematic analysis leads to the conclusion that legislatures are substantially less important as decision-making institutions in American state political systems than a variety of other variables, including other political institutions and actors like governors, parties, and interest groups. But he adds that the relatively low ranking of legislatures as a decision-making variable "does not mean that legislatures are mechanical rubber stamps that could just as well be eliminated. On the contrary, they perform essential, *legitimizing* functions in the American scheme of government and politics."[35] This dichotomization is overly simple as a tool for understanding in any detail the relative importance of various functions of American state legislatures, as my earlier discussion indicates; but it serves to rank "legislation" as less important that "legitimation," at least according to Jacob.

Anton goes further than Jacob. He argues that, with respect to one important aspect of the allocation of values in state political systems—expenditures—neither governors nor legislators nor any other state actor has very much control. He asserts that the "states have lost effective control over their expenditures," espe-

34. Thomas R. Dye, "State Legislative Politics," in *Politics in the American States,* ed. Herbert Jacob and Kenneth N. Vines (Boston and Toronto, 1965), pp. 200–201.

35. Herbert Jacob, "Dimensions of State Politics," in *State Legislatures in American Politics,* ed. Alexander Heard (Englewood Cliffs, N.J., 1966), p. 36. emphasis added.

cially to the federal government.[36] He finds a large gap between what state officials—including both legislators and executives—actually do and what they say, and that the most important consequence of all state actors' actions in the sphere of expenditures is symbolic. As he says:

> To interpret state expenditures in symbolic terms is not to say that state actions are inconsequential. The consequences are real enough, but they are not the consequences we normally look for. . . . Lacking . . . control [i.e., influence or power], actors behave *as though* they are powerful by following a script written in terms of easily understood symbols . . . If the tangible outcome of such behavior seldom corresponds to the symbols by which it is justified, nothing is lost, for it is not at all clear that tangible outcomes can be significantly influenced by anything done, or not done, by state actors. In this context use of these symbols provides a net gain, for they reassure actors and their audiences that powerful figures are engaged in important activities, in a significant governmental context.[37]

Anton's interpretation strongly suggests that the chief functions of legislatures in the American states, at least with respect to expenditures, is something very much like the legitimation function discussed earlier.

What seems to be needed, if one is to use functional categories seriously—in research about American state political systems no less than about developing countries—are statements about the functions legislatures perform under what conditions and with respect to what kinds of issues. Such an approach would require something like an adequate typology of the functions of legislative activity, where criteria of adequacy would include parsimony, exhaustiveness, mutual-exclusivity of categories, operational reference, and research-feasibility. Not only the studies analyzed here, but indeed virtually all of the extant literature on legislatures, fail in varying degrees to take such an approach.

Wahlke *et al.* use the phrase "many parliamentary bodies in other systems." The data I have presented, plus many other

36. Thomas J. Anton, "Roles and Symbols in the Determination of State Expenditures," *Midwest Journal of Political Science,* XI, No. 1 (February, 1957), 27–43, quotation at 37.
37. *Ibid.,* p. 43, emphasis in original.

sources, on the relative importance of decisional and other functions of legislatures in most of the world's legislative bodies would seem to indicate that even if their assumptions are true with respect to "many" parliaments, they still are talking only about a minority of cases, and probably a rather small minority.

"We have assumed that examination of the behavior of legislators will yield insight about performance of these functions by legislators in the four states and by legislative institutions generally." The excellent review by Eulau and Hinckley of the scholarly literature on legislative behavior in the United States produced between 1961 and 1964 reveals that this literature, of which *The Legislative System* is a part, apparently did not yield such insights. (I will comment on this review and treat this point in more detail below.)

". . . the theoretical conceptions guiding this research are behavioral, institutional (structural), and functional—not any one or the other." All three kinds of concepts are present in this work, yes. But in *The Legislative System* there are data mainly on the behavior of individual legislators. There are no data and apparently no insights about the functions of legislators and legislative structures for the rest of the political system.

"Legislative Institutions and Processes" (1966). The third and final benchmark of studies in the field of comparative legislative behavior is a critical review article by Eulau and Hinckley, "Legislative Institutions and Processes." It appears in *Political Science Annual: An International Review.* Significantly, the subtitle of the *Annual* notwithstanding, the Eulau-Hinckley review is limited exclusively to "research on American legislative behavior and institutions" (85n), and a rough check of the bibliographies of the other essays in the volume indicates that around 85 to 90 per cent of the citations are to studies principally or exclusively about the United States.

"Legislative Institutions and Processes" is especially appropriate for present purposes because it is a detailed, careful, and comprehensive review and critique of the literature in the "legislative behavior" field. Thus it is possible to use it as a basis for making inferences about the utility of the "legislative behavior" approach in American political science generally for the study of legislatures in most of the world.

Eulau and Hinckley subsume the vast majority of research on "legislative behavior, structures, functions, processes, and policies" under two rubrics, the "inside" and the "outside" models.[38] As they say:

> It may be granted that studies of legislative behavior, structures, functions, processes, and policies cannot be readily sheltered under a single conceptual net. Nevertheless, it seems to us that research on legislatures split fairly early along the lines of two models. The first of these, which might be termed the "inside" model, concerns legislative behavior and action as revealed in the growth of formal and informal substructures, groups, authority relations, influence patterns, and so on, *within the legislature.* The "outside" model conceives the legislature's and the legislator's activities *as products of* forces or influences beyond the institutional boundaries of the legislature—the electoral constituencies, district parties, pressure groups, executive agencies, and those socioeconomic and predispositional attributes that legislators import from the "outside" . . . [W]ith only a few significant exceptions, the study of legislatures has continued to follow one or the other of these two models. (p. 87, emphasis added)

Their "inside" model is roughly equivalent to my topic III and parts of topics II and V; their "outside" model to my topic IV and parts of II and V. I agree with their judgment that most research can legitimately be subsumed under one of these two models. This means, of course, that other possible approaches to the study of legislative behavior are relatively neglected, especially topic VI, the functions of legislatures in the political system. Even the "outside" model is concerned mostly with "the legislator's activities as products of" outside forces or influences, rather than the influence legislative activity brings to bear on "outside" variables.

There is some attention to functions of legislative activity where function is defined as consequences. Most of it is in connection with their discussion of "inside" model studies: there they are concerned with the consequences within the legislature

---

38. For an earlier application of this "inside-outside" dichotomy, see Nelson W. Polsby, "Two Strategies of Influence: Choosing a Majority Leader, 1962," in *New Perspectives on the House of Representatives,* ed. Robert L. Peabody and Nelson W. Polsby (Chicago, 1963), pp. 237–270.

of formal and informal structures and processes. But what treatment there is of the functions of legislatures and legislators with respect to individual and group actors outside the legislature itself comes in a relatively short (nine pages in a ninety-seven page article) section at the end called "Legislative Outputs: Consequences." It is here that Eulau and Hinckley's review, which in general seems to me an accurate and perceptive one, reveals the gross neglect in the legislative behavior literature of the fundamental question of the consequences of legislative activity for the political system.

In this section they find only eleven studies to review. They rate them substantially inferior in quality to the other studies in other areas of legislative research. Among the faults they cite are methodological "innocence," premature or *ad hoc* evaluations, and primitive conceptualization. For example, concepts like *integration, system-maintenance* or even *inputs and outputs* vanish, and we are back with older and cruder concepts like *Congress vis-à-vis the presidency, the role and impact of legislative institutions in the total government process,* and congressional *effectiveness*. The only ray of sunshine they find in this generally gloomy picture ("The one single exception to the general run of these studies. . . .") is a book on Congress and foreign policy, which at least one other reviewer has subjected to a severe and telling critique on almost all counts.[39]

While one could differ with Eulau and Hinckley on minor details, I share their main conclusions about the quantity and quality of these studies as compared with the other studies reviewed. Moreover, one final point must be made. It will be recalled that Wahlke *et al.*, in *The Legislative System*, "assumed that examination of the behavior of legislators will yield insight about the performance of these functions [i.e., decisional, legitimizing, representative, and other] by legislators in the four states *and by legislative institutions more generally*." Thus they argued that their book was guided by not only "behavioral" but also

---

39. See Eulau and Hinckley, pp. 177–178; for the critical review, see Nelson W. Polsby, "Foreign Policy and Congressional Activity, or, Can Congress Survive the Solicitude of Its Friends?" *World Politics*, XV, No. 2 (January, 1963), 354–359.

"functional" concepts and questions. Yet in Eulau and Hinckley's review of the literature under the heading of "Legislative Outputs: Consequences," there is not a single mention of *The Legislative System!* Nor is there any reference to any other work in the same genre of (comparative) legislative behavior studies. The citations in this section are completely different from the studies cited which use the "inside" and "outside" models. Either Eulau and Hinckley have failed to record the "insights" about legislative functions which allegedly were derivable from the "inside" and "outside" studies, or such insights were not forthcoming. I am inclined to believe that Eulau and Hinckley did not overlook anything; there was simply little or nothing to be learned from the comparative legislative behavior literature about the consequences of individual legislative behavior for the rest of the political system. Thus, we must conclude that this assumption of *The Legislative System,* and the genre of research which it represents, is false. Since this genre is overwhelmingly the prevailing one in American political science, one must have serious doubts about how much this literature can tell us that is illuminating about the relationship between legislatures and political development.

The "Traditional" Literature on Legislatures

The characteristics of what I call the "traditional" literature on legislatures are, by contrast with the "comparative legislative behavior" literature: (1) a focus on the "compleat legislature" as the main unit of analysis; (2) more mixing of prescriptions with description and explanation; (3) a tendency to concentrate on single legislatures in their political systems, and/or comparing them only in a relatively *ad hoc* fashion; (4) impressionistic essays rather than work supported with systematic, quantitative material; and (5) a much greater likelihood of asking and answering functional questions. Certainly, insofar as these studies are less precise and more impressionistic than the comparative legislative behavior studies, they are inferior in quality. But they have the great merit, for our purposes, of raising and providing tentative answers to the crucial functional questions.

Starting with more recent studies, one may ask whether the great increase in interest in the politics of developing areas over the last twenty years or so, and especially the work of the Committee on Comparative Politics of the Social Science Research Council, has led to much new knowledge about legislatures and political development. The answer, I think, is that it has not. The seven-volume series of political development studies published by the Princeton University Press, for example, includes no book on legislatures.[40] In general, it seems fair to say that the most influential studies in the field of comparative politics have, in the last twenty years, tended to focus less on political institutions than upon socio-economic and political cultural variables. To the extent that such studies have focused on institutions, almost every other kind of political institution—the military, political interest groups, bureaucracies, political parties—has received more attention than legislatures.

What knowledge we have of legislatures in developing countries seems to be a by-product of these other kinds of studies—if they say anything about them at all; or legal-formal works of limited utility; or country studies of the kind and quality indicated in sections II and III of this paper. The last-named of these does seem to have the virtue of raising the important functional questions first. On the other hand, they are relatively few in number, and they are usually rather impressionistic.

In searching for knowledge about legislatures and political development, one also looks to some older works in the comparative politics field. They are useful insofar as they raise functional questions, but are in general still rather unsatisfying, for reasons to be indicated.

One of the more useful of these is the essay on "Legislative Assemblies" for the 1933 edition of the *Encyclopedia of the Social*

40. *Communications and Political Development,* ed. Lucian W. Pye (1963); *Bureaucracy and Political Development,* ed. Joseph LaPalombara (1963); *Political Modernization in Turkey and Japan,* ed. Robert Ward and Dankwart A. Rustow (1964); *Education and Political Development,* ed. James S. Coleman (1965); *Political Culture and Political Development,* ed. Lucian W. Pye and Sidney Verba (1965); *Political Parties and Political Development,* ed. Joseph LaPalombara and Myron Weiner (1966); and Leonard Binder *et al., Crises in Political Development* (forthcoming).

Sciences, written by W. J. Shephard. What is striking is how little understanding of the functions of legislatures, and of the relationship between legislatures and political development, has advanced over what little Shephard was able to say in 1933.[41]

He begins with a statement that sounds quite "modern"—right out of Almond and Coleman, in fact:

> The history of social institutions discloses a gradual evolution from the undifferentiated primitive type with its wide variety of functions toward the ever-increasing specialization which is characteristic of modern institutions. At first there was no distinction between the areas of government, economics and religion, and even with the appearance of definite political institutions the functions which they performed were so generalized that they cannot be described as legislative, executive or judicial. (p. 355)

Although this excerpt implies that Shephard is imputing a unilinear progression from undifferentiated, generalized institutions toward differentiated, specialized ones, careful examination of the whole essay reveals that he finds many evidences of "steps-backward" in the long-run evolution of legislatures. Moreover, he foresees the continuing evolution of new forms in many countries rather than inevitable change toward the English or American models.

There are several passages in which Shephard relates the strength of the legislature to systemic political development. I will cite only one:

> In the evolution of constitutional government the period of monarchical absolutism has been frequently misunderstood as an interruption in the history of the legislative assembly. It was, however, an essential stage in the development of modern constitutionalism. The great function of absolutism in England as upon the continent was to weld the various dissevered and discordant elements of feudal society into a national unity. During this period parliaments and estates general

41. W. J. Shephard, "Legislative Assemblies," in *Encyclopaedia of the Social Sciences,* ed. E. R. A. Seligman (New York, 1933, 1957), IX, 355–361. Cf. the essays by Benjamin Akzin, Ralph K. Huitt, and John C. Wahlke under the topic "Legislation," in *International Encyclopedia of the Social Sciences,* ed. David L. Sills (New York, 1968), IX, 221–243.

either disappeared or became subservient instruments of the royal will. (p. 357)

If Shephard is right about the positive consequences of absolutism for political development in England and the continent, then he raises certain questions about the utility of strengthening legislatures in developing countries. The main question raised is: would strengthening legislatures there obstruct some contemporary equivalents of absolutism in developing countries which are important for their political development? Some of the most backward developing countries face problems of nation-building not unlike those confronted in Europe in the sixteenth and seventeenth centuries. In addition, today the political systems of not only very backward but also the relatively advanced developing countries face even more demands than were experienced in those early days. Would strengthening their legislatures help these political systems meet these demands? If it is debatable whether it is wise to strengthen legislatures in England, Europe, and the United States, is it not even more debatable that the same step would be wise (i.e., have positive consequences for political development) in Brazil and other developing countries?

If they should be strengthened, what should they be strengthened for? For allocating values more? Should this be done even in England or the United States? How good is our knowledge for answering these questions?

Friedrich's *Constitutional Government and Democracy* is a perennial source for scholars looking to the "older" works for wisdom, and the current effort is no exception. Friedrich's book has the virtue of drawing upon a great variety of "traditional" sources, even though his interpretation determines what we get out of them.[42] He argues that legislatures have two functions— the "deliberative" and "representative" functions. Although these have the virtue of parsimony, they are probably too all-encompassing, vague, and overlapping. Moreover, Friedrich almost surely does not separate "is" and "ought" in his discussion.

42. Carl J. Friedrich, *Constitutional Government and Democracy: Theory and Practice in Europe and America*, rev. ed. (Boston, 1950), chaps. xvi, xvii, including the bibliographical remarks and footnotes.

Here is his statement of the functions of legislatures:

Modern parliaments not only represent the 'will' of the people; they also deliberate. Their political function is a double one; as representatives they integrate the community through periodic appeals, based on a continuous process of education and propaganda; as a deliberative body they endeavor to solve concrete problems of communal activity: to do or not to do, that is the question. (p. 324)

The "deliberative" and "representative" functions are, for Friedrich, the only two functions of legislatures; all others are subsumed under them.

As to "mutual exclusivity," the other requirement of an adequate typology, Friedrich says: "While these two functions are closely intertwined, they may, from the standpoint of political science, usefully be distinguished . . ." (p. 324).

The least satisfactory aspect of Friedrich's handling of legislative functions is his mixing-up, so far as I can see, of "is" and "ought." Put differently, he often attributes to a structure—the legislature—functions which he thinks it "ought" to perform rather than those which, in fact, it does perform. For example, consider the following passage purportedly showing why legislatures are peculiarly fitted for lawmaking:

. . . the making of a rule presupposes that there is a series of events which have certain aspects in common. In other words, there must be a "normal" situation. This means that time is available for deliberation to determine what had best be done regarding such a situation. Representative, deliberative bodies require time, obviously, and therefore legislation seems to be peculiarly fitted for such bodies. (p. 269)

But why must "time" be available to make general rules? Why cannot they be made "quickly" by institutions that are not "representative bodies"? Have we not seen that rule-making in most of the world's polities is carried on principally not by legislatures but by executives and bureaucracies?

The idea that legislatures have legitimation and "safety-valve" functions is disparaged:

Some writers on the Continent have . . . been led into linking parliamentary deliberation to the romantic passion for everlasting

conveisation, a generalization which is as glittering as it is uninformed. For parliamentary deliberation is entirely focused upon and
organized with a view toward action, the enactment of a general rule.
The history and practice of parliamentary procedure prove this beyond doubt. (p. 269)

But even if parliamentary deliberation is "focused upon and
organized *with a view toward* action," and even if parliamentary
procedure supports this interpretation, it surely does not follow
that these foci, organizational arrangements, and procedures necessarily produce the desired consequences. In fact, as has been
indicated, they usually do not.

The same kinds of problems are evident in the treatment of
legislatures in Finer's *The Theory and Practice of Modern Government.*[43] In two passages he identifies what are, to him, the
functions of legislatures: "Legislatures, assemblies . . . meet to
accomplish a variety of functions: to make laws, to control the
executive, and to carry out a few judicial functions. . . . The
function of legislatures is to apply the presumed will of the
people to the creation of laws and the superintendence of their
administration" (p. 369), and, "Lower chambers occupy themselves with three main functions—lawmaking, control of the executive, and the development of policy . . ." (p. 436). In both of
these passages, Finer clearly is defining function as a purpose.
Throughout his later discussion he assumes that legislative activity produces consequences equivalent to these purposes. Thus he
implicitly, like Friedrich explicitly, uses formal "rules of procedure" to "explain" why and how legislatures actually legislate (p.
436; Friedrich, *op. cit.*, pp. 268–269).

Another interesting study in this "traditional" vein is Wheare's
Legislatures.[44] It is offered not as a guide to the legislatures of all
countries; rather, it "confines itself to countries where the legislature plays some significant part in the system of government, and
has done so for a considerable period" (Preface). Wheare never
clearly identifies what "parts" are "significant." What he presumably means is that the legislature has some decision-making role.

43. Herman Finer, *Theory and Practice of Modern Government*, rev. ed. (New
York, 1949).
44. K. C. Wheare, *Legislatures* (London, 1963).

But his own analysis makes clear that he feels this role is not significant for most legislatures, including most of those he treats in his book. His two main exceptions are the U.S. Congress and the French Parliament under the Third and Fourth Republics. These, he says later, "may *properly* claim the title of legislatures" (p. 168, emphasis added). Thus, Wheare means to exclude from his analysis legislatures which do not play "significant" roles in the political process; this presumably means decision-making; but only a few legislatures play this "significant" role. Yet elsewhere he talks as if there were many cases, and excludes a lot of legislatures (e.g., those in the "Third World") which, so far as I can see, are not clearly distinguishable from those non-decision-making legislatures which he does include (e.g., the British Parliament, the Bundestag).

Wheare, like all writers on legislatures, is in some measure a functionalist:

Parliaments and congresses and other similar assemblies are commonly called "legislatures" . . . [But] a large part of the time of these bodies is not devoted to law-making at all. One of their most important functions is to criticize the executive. In some countries they make or unmake governments. They debate great issues of public concern. They constitute a "grand inquest of the nation." They act as what John Stuart Mill called "a committee of grievances," and "a congress of opinions." (p. 1)

His functions, then, are: lawmaking; criticism of the executive; making or unmaking governments; and debate. In the comparative perspective already offered, this is obviously a pretty imperfect and incomplete list. "Function" is used in several senses: purpose, activity, and consequence. Nothing is said about, say, legitimation or recruitment.

Wheare also mixes "is" and "ought." He argues that:

many of the other important functions [i.e., beside law-making] of a parliament or congress *are* connected with and *arise* from its function of law-making. The discussion of grievances and the criticism of the executive and the debating of great or small issues *are* naturally and necessarily linked with the process of amending or making the law. In particular it is proper that a representative assembly *should* seek redress of grievances before passing a law to authorize that spending of money by the executive or the raising of taxes upon the citizens. (pp. 3–4, emphasis added)

Further he argues that "the occasion of law-making provides the opportunities for that debate and discussion and criticism which occupy so large a part of the time of many assemblies" (p. 4). Nevertheless, as in the Brazilian case, we have seen that "debate and discussion and criticism" occur and have consequences for the political system even where the legislature has relatively little impact on the allocation of values.

Wheare not only distinguishes between legislatures that make decisions and those that do not but are still "significant"; he also specifies the conditions of each. The distinction is fairly valid; the conditions appear not to be. He says that assemblies that divide up their work into committees, and that have "managers" of the government's legislation as "a distinct institution of the legislature with a responsibility to it," are "very active" in lawmaking, and "may properly claim the title of legislatures." Examples are the U.S. Congress, the French National Assembly under the Third and Fourth Republics, and other "European countries" (pp. 167–171). "On the other side," he goes on, "are the assemblies we call parliaments—assemblies whose principal business is talk." In these, work is not divided up into committees, and power does not rest there or with parliamentary leaders; it rests in the cabinet. In such a system, he argues, again mixing "is" and "ought," it is appropriate that parliament should "do nothing but talk."

He cites, approvingly, John Stuart Mill: "There has seldom been more misplaced derision" than toward a legislature that only "talks." "For Mill," Wheare observes, "the proper function of a representative assembly was to be a congress of opinions, a grand inquest of the nation, a place for talking, not a place for doing. Laws should not be made without its consent, and the price which the government must pay for consent was to listen to the advice of the assembly. What Mill advocated a century ago is still substantially the doctrine of today." He means also that it is the practice of today: "Making laws in Britain is something for which the government is responsible" (p. 169).

Considering Wheare's hypothesis against the Brazilian case, we find that the Brazilian legislature very much divides its work up into committees, but that it is not "very active" in lawmaking. And even though the Brazilian Congress is a forum for "public" opinion, an institution that "just talks," laws can be made without its consent; the government does not always listen to its advice, and it is not correct to say that it has to listen.

In his final chapter, on the decline of legislatures, Wheare raises, and suggests a tentative answer to, this important question: Is it wise, from the point of view of promoting political development, to strengthen the legislature? He correctly sees the question of whether legislatures have "declined" as a complicated one. His main conclusion is that "Absolutely their powers have increased. Relatively to the executive government, however, they have, in almost all cases, declined" (p. 221).

Of the French National Assembly under the Third and Fourth Republics (again, along with the U.S. Congress, an exception to his generalization), he says:

> What is certain is that the French legislature maintained its position as the maker and destroyer of cabinets throughout the period, and in this respect it suffered no decline, absolute or relative. Its history raises the question: Is decline necessarily a bad thing? Might it not have been a better thing for France if there had been a decline in the power of the legislature? . . . *A judgement on this question involves an opinion upon what are the proper functions of a legislature.* If the function is to produce and support a government, the French legislature was inefficient, but its inefficiency did not arise from a decline in its power. (p. 224, emphasis added)

I can only assent to Wheare's statement. And before one can judge what are the proper functions of legislatures, one must know something about what its functions are, and what it is reasonable to expect they might become. His tentative conclusion —the final sentence of the book—seems worth considering: "To do less and, perhaps thereby, to do it better, may often prove to be the best safeguard against the decline of legislatures" (p. 234).

The final work I wish to consider is an interesting collection of essays called *Lawmakers in a Changing World*.[45] All of the essays except one tend to take the "traditional" approach. They deal with a great variety of legislatures: the U.S. Congress, the British House of Commons, the French Parliament, the German Parliament, the Soviets of the U.S.S.R., the European Parliament of the European Community, the General Assembly of the United Nations, and ninety city councils in the San Francisco Bay Area. It is significant that the decision to do this kind of comparative work on legislatures—described by the editor as "one [political] sub-system crucial to all government" (p. 1), although this point is never explicated or documented—led all but one of the essayists to be much more centrally concerned with functional questions than is usually the case in the comparative legislative behavior literature. Aside from this general concern with the consequences of legislative activity for the political system at large, there is little that makes most of the essays comparable except that they all deal, in some way or other, with a political structure that is called a "legislature." The editor tries to give unity to the essays: "Despite the variety of approaches and styles, the central concern of all contributors is the lawmaker as a political actor and the legislature, or lawmaking, as a concept" (p. 3). But there is not much unity in "central concern" with "political actor," "legislature," and "lawmaking."

One inference from this volume may not surprise everyone, but it should bother those who adopt as a central premise of their research strategy the idea that the principal function of legislatures is to legislate. For these essays suggest that among the legislatures studied this premise applies only to the Congress of the United States! (I do not know whether it applies with respect to the San Francisco Bay Area councils, because that essay is strictly a study of their internal operations and does not address the question.) On the basis of these essays, and I do not have reason to doubt them, one would have to conclude that the principal functions of not only the European Parliament, the General Assembly, and the Soviets, but also of the legislatures of the United Kingdom, France and Germany, are not lawmaking.

45. Elke Frank, *op. cit.*

The two essays which address the question of the functions of their legislatures most directly are those by Beer on the British Parliament and Lindberg on the European Parliament. Therefore, I shall confine the discussion to them.

Beer[46] argues that the political power of the British parliament has "declined" drastically. Specifically, he means that "the probability that a cabinet will be defeated in the House of Commons" has declined "to the vanishing point," and that this historical trend is "by far the most important change in the position of Parliament" (p. 32). He sees this change as rooted in historical forces *mostly without the legislature itself* (like party, war, economic and social policy, and "the increasing specificity of the essential governmental decision") which are endemic, in greater or lesser degree, in "all self-governing countries." These forces are so strong, he adds, that "that great, traditional source of general rules, the legislature, [will] *probably lose its central place in the governmental system*" (p. 35, emphasis added).

Taking this trend and projection as his starting point, Beer speculates on what function the legislature might perform in order to help Britain cope with its problems and, incidentally, preserve itself as an institution. This leads him into a policy-prescribing stance, but the steps he takes en route to this position are illuminating for our purposes.

Essentially, his analysis leads him to the empirical conclusions that the British Parliament does criticize, does control the executive, and does help make laws—but not very much, and its ability to perform these functions keeps declining and is likely to decline still further. What is to be done? He finds a clue from Professor Crick's *The Reform of Parliament*, which he quotes as follows: "'Governing has now become a prolonged election campaign. Parliament is still the agreed arena in which most of the continuous election campaign is fought,' and the principal device by which 'the Parties obtain something like equal access to the ear of the electorate in the long formative period between the official campaigns'" (p. 43).

46. Samuel Beer, "The British Legislature and the Problem of Mobilizing Consent," in *ibid.*, pp. 30–48.

The struggle in the legislative arena has two consequences. One is that it enables voters to press government leaders to follow their wishes. Another is that it enables government leaders to "mobilize consent" among the electorate. The latter interests Beer most. Elections also "mobilize consent"; but "modern government cannot and does not rely solely upon the legitimizing effects of periodic elections. It must make continuous efforts to create consent for new programs and to sustain consent for old ones. It must mobilize consent between as well as at elections" (p. 45). Parliament, Beer feels, already does this, but very weakly; he is mainly concerned with suggesting ways it might do it better.

"I do not know," Beer observes, "of a theoretical exploration of this function by a political scientist." But he cites U.S. Congressman John Brademas on the "mobilization of consent" function in the American Congress:

The Congressman or Senator, by organizing community conferences, mailing materials and in other ways, can supply important information, interpretation, justification and leadership to his constituency . . . These activities of explaining, justifying, interpreting, interceding, all help, normally, to build acceptance for government policy, an essential process in democratic government (pp. 45–46).

It may be that this passage offers some clues toward ways in which strengthening legislative services can promote political development, but one should bear in mind the distinction between strengthening the legislative function, and strengthening the "consent mobilization" function, of legislatures through such assistance. The former might be impossible, or, to the extent it is feasible, have negative consequences for political development; the latter could be useful.

I do not know if Beer is right about the "consent mobilization" function of the British Parliament. Certainly the questions he raises, and tries to answer, place him in a better position to describe and understand the role of the legislature in the political system (and thus to make useful policy suggestions) than those raised by students of comparative legislative behavior.

The other essay of greatest interest here is the one by Lindberg on the European Parliament.[47] Lindberg faces, in extreme form, the (by now, I hope, familiar) question of how to deal conceptually with an institution called a "legislature" which is clearly not principally a lawmaking body. Yet he feels it is, somehow, an important institution. He decides that: "Since the European Parliament is more similar to national legislatures than to international assemblies in its general operation and in the motivations of its members, it is most useful to compare it to the former" (p. 105).

It is, in short, "of the genus 'legislatures,' and . . . operates in a functioning political system [although one] of a unique nature . . . that is still incipient and precarious" (p. 107). The European Parliament is different from national legislatures in that one cannot take for granted "the continued existence of a more or less stable and legitimate political community" (p. 107).

How does Lindberg deal with his problem? He draws a distinction between "political theories of allocation and political theories of systems-persistence" (p. 108). This distinction is roughly parallel to the one I have drawn between decisional or lawmaking functions and legitimation functions. Lindberg's statement of the distinction echoes a major theme of the current paper:

Political theories of allocation have provided the dominant direction for political research in general as well as for research in legislative institutions and processes. Students of legislatures have typically asked questions about the lawmaking functions of the legislature and about the role of the legislature in controlling or influencing the executive in its formulation and administration of public policy. Relatively little attention has been paid to the role of legislative institutions in the building up and maintenance of the political system itself. Here we are interested in such questions such as: How is it that a political system as such is able to persist through time? What is the role of the legislature, of representative institutions, in increasing the capacity of a political system to cope with the stresses of economic, social and political change? (p. 108)

Lindberg's idea of "system-persistence" is drawn, of course, from the work of David Easton. There are at least two frequently

47. Leon Lindberg, "The Role of the European Parliament in an Emerging European Community," in *ibid.*, pp. 101–128.

cited problems with this notion: political systems seldom break down or are destroyed; and even if they do disintegrate, it is difficult, empirically, to know when this occurs. Perhaps Easton's notion is particularly applicable for Lindberg's purposes, since he is dealing with a highly tenuous political system; but it is still difficult to know empirically when it might be "destroyed." Be this as it may, I can still examine Lindberg's use of the two kinds of "theories" or functions in this context, translating into my own language and concepts where necessary.

Lindberg sees the two major "allocative roles" (functions) of legislatures to be "lawmaking" and "control of the executive" (p. 109). Formally, the European Parliament lacks such powers. The "crucial variable" explaining this "is the partial and incipient nature of the system of which it is a part" (p. 111). Informally, the Parliament does have an allocative role, through what Lindberg, borrowing from Beer and Bagehot on Great Britain, calls "the lyrical function." The "lyrical function" is "the exercise of indirect influence by forcing holders of actual power to pay attention to what it [the legislature] says." According to Lindberg, it is through this "lyrical function" that the European parliament "has made its greatest progress" with regard to allocation. This function is not too dissimilar from Beer's "consent mobilization" function. In both cases government leaders (United Kingdom: prime minister and cabinet; European Community: Commissions and Councils of Ministers) use the Parliament to "mobilize consent" from their electorates (United Kingdom: British voters; European Community: national governments and parliaments).

The European Parliament is able to perform this function much less effectively than the British Parliament; this is because the British political system is much more stable and legitimate than the European Community. In Britain most power resides in the government; in the Community, it resides in the electorate. The function itself is much the same, however.

Lindberg is necessarily very "tentative and speculative" (p. 121) about the "systems-persistence role" of the European Parliament. He suggests a number of hypotheses, derived from Easton, about "the role a representative institution might play in helping the system reduce stress due to social diversity." Matching these against fragmentary evidence, he finds that the European Parliament probably performs the function of helping the system to persist only to the slightest degree if at all. Although he is guardedly inexplicit, he seems to be suggesting that strengthening the "lyrical" and "systems-persistence" functions of the European Parliament would be ways to enhance the likelihood of achieving a "real 'community' of common purpose and identification" (p. 127).

Legislatures, Political Development, and Technical Assistance

If one speaks of political development, one thinks of change toward something that is better. Political development is thus a normative concept. I should like to make explicit a normative premise of this paper, namely, that with respect to Third-World countries it is unwise to equate political development exclusively or even principally with political democracy, especially political democracy modeled after the United States. In many—probably most—of these countries the odds are against democracy as a viable form of government.[48] In these nations, where economic and social development are such critical and pressing tasks, less ambitious and less desirable (from the American point of view) kinds of political systems are not only more feasible but probably more relevant and preferable for achieving these economic and social goals—and in the long run, perhaps, even the political goals of freedom and equality.

In underdeveloped countries, greater national integration and identity, more governmental capacity and authority, increased participation in national affairs (which may be "mobilized" participation as well as democratic participation in the Western

---

48. Rupert Emerson, *From Empire to Nation: This Rise to Self-Assertion of Asian and African Peoples* (Cambridge, Mass., 1960), chap. XV; Dankwart A. Rustow, *A World of Nations: Problems of Political Modernization* (Washington, 1967), pp. 227–236; Seymour Martin Lipset, *The First New Nation: The United States in Historical and Comparative Perspective* (New York, 1963), p. 11.

sense), more equitable distribution of economic and social values, and a minimal protection of basic individual liberties (e.g., privacy, the rule of law), tend to be more realistic and appropriate goals of political development than the institutional arrangements of American political democracy (like stronger and more representative legislatures).[49] Just as European states during the Age of Absolutism, Mexico after 1910, Russia after 1917, and Cuba after 1959 were developing politically but were not democratic, so also political development for most "Third-World" countries will not necessarily be democratic, if indeed it occurs at all and they do not "decay" politically instead of "develop."[50] It may well be, as S. M. Lipset has suggested, that "Instead of speaking generally about democracy, it may be advisable to focus on the conditions which protect personal liberty, that is, on due process and the rule of law."[51] Instead of focusing on features of democracy almost distinctive to the United States—a relatively strong, representative national legislature—it may well be that the more generic but still significant political goals of the rule of law, privacy, and protection of the individual are the most that we in the United States (as well as the peoples of underdeveloped countries) can realistically hope for as criteria of political development in the Third World.

In societies like these that need and want change, moreover, political development should be seen not only as an end in itself but also as a means to achieve those values—economic, social, or political—which progressive leaders and the mass of the people regard as most important. No one can say with certainty which values are the highest priorities, or answer the even more difficult and important question of what the costs and benefits of realizing one value are in terms of other values. It is a reasonable judg-

49. On the themes of integration, authority, and equality, see the excellent treatment by Rustow, *op. cit.*, esp. pp. 36, 126–132; see also Samuel P. Huntington, "Political Development and Political Decay," *World Politics*, XVII, No. 3 (April, 1965), 386–393; and Gabriel A. Almond and G. Bingham Powell, *Comparative Politics: A Developmental Approach* (Boston, 1966), pp. 35 ff. On "basic individual liberties," see Lipset, *loc. cit.*, and Robert A. Packenham, "Foreign Aid and Political Development," paper delivered at the Brookings Institution Symposium on "The Theory and Practice of Political Development," Airlie Farms, Virginia (September 12–16, 1966), pp. 5–15.

50. Huntington, *op. cit.*, pp. 386–430.

51. Lipset, *loc. cit.*

ment, however, that they would include economic development, personal freedom from fear and tyranny (though not necessarily Western democracy), equitable distribution of economic and social values, and the other political values (political integration, etc.) previously mentioned. It seems extremely unlikely that Western democracy in general, and strong legislatures in particular, would rank higher than these values. In this sense, political development may usefully be defined in many instances as the will and capacity to cope with, and to generate, continuing transformation toward whichever values seem appropriate in the particular context. Among these, we suggest that three values, especially—economic development, personal freedom, and socioeconomic justice—would usually rank higher than Western-type democracy or strong legislatures.[52] Legislatures tend to represent, all over the world, more conservative and parochial interests than executives, even in democratic polities. This seems especially to be the case in presidential, as contrasted with parliamentary, political systems.[53] In societies that need and want change, and where political development may be defined as the will and capacity to cope with and to generate continuing transformation, it may not make such sense to strengthen the decision-making function of an institution that is likely to resist change.

52. I have elaborated these points and provided relevant citations in: "Foreign Aid and Political Development," *loc. cit.;* "The Study of Political Development," in *Approaches to the Study of Political Science,* ed. Michael Haas and Henry S. Kariel (San Francisco, forthcoming); and "Political-Development Doctrines in the American Foreign Aid Program," *World Politics,* XVIII, No. 2 (January, 1966), 200–205.

53. The notion that legislatures, especially in presidential polities, tend to be more conservative and parochial than executives is only a hypothesis, but one that deserves systematic attention. It seems to fit the case of Brazil nicely. There, denial of the franchise to illiterates combined with congressional representation based on total population (illiterates and literates) works to overrepresent conservative, landed elites from the very underdeveloped, low-literacy but high-population states of the Northeast. Scott seems to generalize this point to Latin America: "It is indeed a question whether, in most countries [of Latin America], a reduction in executive power would really increase congressional responsibility to the general citizenry, since the presidency is on the whole a more popular institution." *Op. cit.,* p. 331. But compare the case of the Philippine Congress, which, according to Stauffer's essay in this volume, has often been more change-oriented than the president.

For abundant evidence of the conservative orientation of the Third-World legislatures on the issue of land reform, see Samuel P. Huntington, *Political Order in Changing Societies* (New Haven and London, 1968), pp. 388–396.

There is, of course, considerable variation in the degree to which the foregoing remarks apply to different Third-World countries. Nor do I deny that in some countries under some conditions strengthening legislative decision-making may be a contribution to political development. The Philippines may be one such instance. One task of those interested in the relationship between legislatures and political development would be to learn more about these conditions. Current knowledge suggests, however, that in the vast majority of cases the criteria of political development already mentioned are far more relevant and appropriate to underdeveloped countries than those deriving from the example of the United States.

Moreover, it is insufficient to examine only the decision-making function of legislatures in order to assess the likely consequences for the political system of "strengthening" it. "Strengthening" the legislature for decision-making is likely to have an effect on the other, less manifest, functions of the legislature as well. What would these effects be? Again, current knowledge does not provide ready answers; getting answers is another task of students of the relationship between legislatures and political development. In the meantime, Merton's caution is appropriate:

. . . Moral judgements based *entirely* on an appraisal of manifest functions of a social structure are "unrealistic" in the strict sense, i.e., they do not take into account other actual consequences of that structure . . . "social reforms" or "social engineering" which ignore latent functions do so on pain of suffering acute disappointments and boomerang effects.[54]

Given the state of our knowledge about legislatures and political development, and even of the paradigms we have for gaining greater understanding about this relationship, technical assistance to strengthen legislatures may not be a good idea. It is true, of course, that policy-makers always act—and must act—with imperfect knowledge about the consequences of their actions. But there are greater and lesser degrees of understanding. Knowledge of the relationship of legislatures to political develop-

54. Robert K. Merton, *Social Theory and Social Structure*, rev. ed. (Glencoe, Ill., 1957), p. 72, emphasis in original.

ment is very poor relative to what is known about other institutions—like the military, interest groups, and political parties—and about the relationship of political culture, economic development, social structures, and other variables to political development. Even in these areas too little is known, but it is more than we have about legislatures.[55] Moreover, to the limited extent we do have knowledge, it suggests, as I have already indicated, that strengthening legislatures is more likely to impede political development than help it.

Still further, a distinction between "strictly political questions," such as "the relation of political parties, electoral procedures, and ideology to legislative performance," and relatively "apolitical" legislative services[56] may be misleading. If improving legislative services means strengthening the legislature, this involves a change in the political system which has political consequences. The old distinction between politics and administration has been badly battered, and with good reason. One does not make technical assistance apolitical by fiat or by giving it an antiseptic title. If a policy proposal has political consequences, then it is a political action, whatever phraseology may be used.

There are other reasons why a policy of technical assistance for legislative services might be unwise: for example, the scarcity of able personnel to implement the program; and the importance of the American political context in which the program would be carried out (it makes a difference whether Lyndon Johnson or John Kennedy is president). But these are problems and uncertainties for any political development strategy. There are, I believe, legitimate strategies that might be experimented with in order to promote political development with the instruments of U.S. foreign policy.[57] What I have been trying to document in this

55. For some relevant discussion and citations to this literature, see Robert A. Packenham, "Approaches to the Study of Political Development," *World Politics,* XVII, No. 1 (October, 1964), 108–120; Harry Eckstein and David Apter, eds., *Comparative Politics: A Reader* (New York, 1963), esp. Parts V, VI, VIII, IX; and John J. Johnson, ed., *The Role of the Military in Developing Countries* (Princeton, N.J., 1962).

56. Comparative Administrative Group, American Society for Public Administration, "Announcement: A Project on the Administrative Problems of Legislatures," (mimeographed, April, 1967).

57. See Robert A. Packenham, "Foreign Aid and Political Development," pp. 19–47.

paper are some conditions which make it unwise to use technical assistance to legislative services as a means toward this end.

Is it not possible that the idea of technical assistance for legislative services as a means of promoting political development springs from a desire, not clearly articulated, to export rather uncritically our own political system into areas where it may not be, and probably is not, appropriate? Proponents of this proposal will doubtless deny that this is so, and their denials will usually be sincere. But our provincialism goes deeper than we know. A project proposal for administrative services begins with three questionable propositions:

The widespread ineffectiveness of legislatures in the less developed countries hampers both political and administrative development. The political consequences of legislative weakness are self-evident. . . . [Therefore] it is now timely to launch an A.I.D. program dealing with this problem area because of the new emphasis on political development under Title 9.[58]

For reasons indicated throughout this paper, I would call into question, in turn, each of these three propositions. We do not know enough to be confident that these propositions are true or false; what little we know suggests, to me at least, that they are usually false. Nor can these issues be entirely avoided merely by "recalling that only those countries desiring to make use of these services will do so. The objective of the program is to mobilize or create resources which are available under conditions which apply to any activity. In other words, if it is desirable to provide them, the project aims at making it possible to do so."[59]

Even if some countries are themselves eager to accept such assistance, the United States must satisfy itself that it wants to give it. This raises the question of the "conditions" under which it is "desirable" to provide such assistance. And it is precisely these conditions that we usually do not know; what little we do know suggests that in most cases it would be undesirable.

58. Comparative Administrative Group, American Society for Public Administration, "Administrative Resources of Legislatures: A Project Proposal with Special Reference to Legislative Reference Services," (mimeographed, November 28, 1966), p. 1.

59. Minutes of Meeting of advisory committee, Legislative Services Project, Washington, D.C., May 17, 1967, p. 2.

I have not written this paper to argue that under no circumstances should a program of technical assistance for legislative services be forthcoming. I have tried to suggest that these circumstances will rarely be found, and that no such program should be undertaken until the kinds of questions raised here have been confronted and more satisfactorily answered.

Index

DATE DUE

GAYLORD			PRINTED IN U.S.A